A HISTORY
of
WESTERN
EDUCATION

A HISTORY
of
WESTERN
EDUCATION

Harry G. Good
THE OHIO STATE UNIVERSITY

James D. Teller
UNIVERSITY OF DALLAS

THIRD EDITION

THE MACMILLAN COMPANY
COLLIER-MACMILLAN LIMITED, LONDON

© *Copyright, The Macmillan Company, 1969*

All rights reserved. No part of this book may be reproduced or transmitted in any form or by any means, electronic or mechanical, including photocopying, recording or by any information storage and retrieval system, without permission in writing from the Publisher.

First Printing

Earlier editions copyright 1947 and © 1960 by The Macmillan Company

MINISTRY OF EDUCATION, ONTARIO
LIBRARY/INFORMATION CENTRE,
13th FLOOR, MOWAT BLOCK
QUEEN'S PARK, TORONTO 182, ONTARIO

JUL 2 5 1972

Library of Congress catalog card number: 69–11181
The Macmillan Company
Collier-Macmillan Canada, Ltd., Toronto, Ontario
Printed in the United States of America

PREFACE

Engraved in stone at one of the entrances to the Archives of the United States of America there is the motto: "The Past Is Prologue." In this book we test the validity of this hypothesis when it is applied to the history of Western education as narrated in the following twenty-two chapters. Some say that history never repeats itself. But if our hypothesis has any validity, a more accurate statement would be that history does repeat itself, but never exactly. The basic problems of education are persistent and perennial, and they must be solved anew by each generation in each culture. However, the solutions differ from one generation to another and from one culture to another so that the accumulated solutions constitute a vast historical laboratory.

Such a laboratory can in several ways serve those who are concerned with the problems of education. In the first place, those who are concerned with the improvement of teaching can learn much from a study of the way in which effective and even great teachers have actually taught their pupils. One truly empirical method of solving educational problems, then, is to study the methods of effective teachers. In the second place, any real acquaintance with the human activity that Dewey calls reflective thinking and any true appreciation of the state of mind that we label "critical attitude" necessitate some knowledge of the lives of the pioneers to whom we are indebted for this method and attitude. In the third place, a study of the lives of these pioneers will be rewarding not only as a source of information but also as a source of inspiration. Their successes and their failures cannot but stir the emotions of those who are responsible for that great human undertaking we call education. And this includes all of us—parents, teachers, statesmen, and all citizens—who share, by voice or by vote, in the direction of our educational institutions.

When writing had evolved and the school was instituted only five or six thousand years ago, the results of trial and error with occasional success came to be recorded for the warning and guidance of the young. Thus the area of light and certainty gradually pushed back the walls of darkness; the young could begin their study and investigation of the unknown at the points where the older generation had stopped. The past became the prologue to the extension of knowledge and the understanding of man and the world.

The school and the cuneiform script of ancient Sumer were very important instruments in man's progress. Cuneiform writing served the peoples of the Fertile Crescent until about 800 B.C., when cuneiform reached the Mediterranean; and then a new form of script, a true alphabet, was developed by the people of South Canaan, Crete, and Greece. This new way of writing was used to preserve the thought of Amos, Isaiah,

Homer, and other great Hebrew and Greek writers. The Greek, but not the Hebrew, alphabet even introduced characters for the vowels; and this form has served the West and much of the world until the present day. The school has been the means of promoting it and the ideas and ideals it records.

The early nations of Europe in promoting schools and learning became prologue to the present, when the schools have been taken over by the great nations of the West. The nations have used the schools to promote the welfare of their peoples, to govern them, and, not least, to reinforce their own power. To what is this past and present the prologue? Considering the long journey from the beginning to the present, neither teacher nor student can fail to see that they have been witnessing a great evolution in which every past has been prologue to a new and living present, one that they will inevitably help to form.

In this new edition, all chapters have been revised, and in Chapter 22 higher education under nationalism is treated; this is a somewhat infrequent topic in general histories of education. Added attention has been given to the doctrines and philosophies of the great writers, including Vives, who was one of the most original among Western educators. He is unaccountably neglected in most textbooks.

As the Table of Contents shows, we are presenting our subject in four parts; these are not merely temporal units, for each period has an outlook and character of its own.

H. G. G.
J. D. T.

CONTENTS

PART I: EDUCATION IN ANTIQUITY

1. THE ANCIENT EAST — 3
Civilization – High Civilization – Invention of Writing – The Cities – Sumer and Beyond – Hebrew Education – Summary – Questions – Notes and Sources

2. ANCIENT GREECE: THE EARLY WEST — 17
The Dawn – Sparta – Athens – The Athenian Schools – Periclean Age – Isocrates – Socrates and Plato – Aristotle – Summary – Questions – Notes and Sources

3. ROMAN PRACTICE AND THEORY — 41
Pre-Roman Settlements – The Greek Factor – Early Roman Instruction – Greco-Roman Education – Cicero as Historian of Education – Quintilian – Tacitus – Summary – Questions – Notes and Sources

PART II: EDUCATION AND THE CHURCH

4. THE EARLY MIDDLE AGES — 61
Some Main Topics – Expansion and Erosion – The Church in the West – Church and Philosophy – Christian Home and Pagan School – The Fading Light – Monasteries and Learning – Monastic Schools – Revival Under Charlemagne – Summary – Questions – Notes and Sources

5. MEDIEVAL REVIVAL OF LEARNING — 81
Decline After Charlemagne – In Medieval England – The Crusades – Chivalric Education – Medieval Towns – The Guilds – Schools in the Cities – Age of Translation – Theories of Education – The Rise of Universities – Summary – Questions – Notes and Sources

6. THE RENAISSANCE IN ITALY — 112
Classical Humanism – The Latin Language – Why the Renaissance Began in Italy – The Spirit of the Renaissance – Francesco Petrarch – The Recovery of Greek Authors – Diffusion of the Sources – An Early Humanist Writer on Education – Other Humanist Writers – Two Great Teachers – Influence of the Revival on Education – The Classics Crossing the Alps – Summary – Questions – Notes and Sources

7. SCHOOL AND CHURCH AT THE NORTH — 139
Humanism at the North – Erasmus – Vives – Peter Ramus of France – Language and Religion – Wycliffe and Hus – Towns and Schools – The Lutheran Movement – Spread of the Reformation – The Reformation in England – The Jesuits – Other Catholic Societies – Summary – Questions – Notes and Sources

8. FROM HUMANISM TO REALISM — 165
The Meaning of Realism – A Humanist with Realist Leanings – Realist Utopias – The Academies – Modern Science and Philosophy – Education for Statesmen and Men of Affairs – The Language Question – The Master Key to Universal Education – Influence of Ratke and Co-

menius – Education of Girls – Summary – Questions – Notes and Sources

PART III: ADAPTING EDUCATION TO CHILDREN

9. ROUSSEAU: A NEW THEORY OF EDUCATION ... 199
The Youth of Rousseau – Rousseau as a Student – Tutor for a Year – Social Theory – Nature and Education – The Newborn Child – Three Kinds of Learning – Intellectual Education – The Language Arts – Morals and Religion – Summary – Questions – Notes and Sources

10. BASEDOW AND PHILANTHROPIC EDUCATION ... 223
New Times – Introducing Basedow – Basedow's Philanthropinum – Judgment of a Novice – Salzmann's Philanthropinum – Pupil's Self-government – Judgment of the Philosopher – Summary – Questions – Notes and Sources

11. PESTALOZZI AND THE NEW ELEMENTARY SCHOOL ... 240
His Childhood – Young Manhood – Getting Settled – Neuhof – Authorship – Other Early Works – Stanz Episode – The Method – New Studies – Influence – Summary – Questions – Notes and Sources

12. FROM PESTALOZZI TO PUBLIC EDUCATION ... 268
Early Disciples – British Pestalozzians – American Pestalozzians – Pestalozzi's Fame Today – Fichte – Herbart in Early Life – Herbart as Tutor – Herbart on Pestalozzi – Herbart's Psychology – Froebel – Creation of the Kindergarten – Spread of the Kindergarten – Summary – Questions – Notes and Sources

PART IV: ADAPTING EDUCATION TO NATIONAL AIMS

13. NATIONALISM, INTERNATIONALISM, AND EDUCATION ... 295
The Rise of Nationalism – National Systems of Education – Nationalism, War, and Education – Internationalism, Peace, and Education – Summary – Questions – Notes and Sources

14. NATIONAL EDUCATION IN FRANCE ... 319
La Chalotais on National Education – The Plan of Condorcet – French Education to 1830 – Under the July Monarchy – Under Napoleon III – National Education Comes of Age – The University of France – Secondary School Reforms – French Education Since 1947 – French Nationalism and Education – Summary – Questions – Notes and Sources

15. NATIONAL TRENDS IN GERMAN EDUCATION ... 348
In the Eighteenth Century – Birth of the Fatherland – Founders of Schools for the Common People – Revolution and Reaction – The Unification of Germany – Education Under the Empire – Education Under the Weimar Republic – German Education Under the Nazis and the Aftermath – German Influence on American Education – Summary – Questions – Notes and Sources

16. NATIONALISM AND SOVIET EDUCATION ... 382
Russian Education Before the Revolution – Formative Ideas of Soviet Education – The Soviet Ten-Year School – Soviet Education Since

1956 – Soviet and American Education – Summary – Questions – Notes and Sources

17. EDUCATION IN ENGLAND   401

Early Beginnings – Philanthropic Efforts – Toward a Planned Education – Influence from Abroad – Rise of the National System – Democratizing the System – Extending National Control over the System – The Spread of English Influence to America – Summary – Questions – Notes and Sources

18. EVOLUTION OF AMERICAN STATE SCHOOLS   430

The Early Settlements – Transplanting Educational Institutions – Inventing Educational Institutions – Education for a More Perfect Union – The Lancasterian Schools – Rise of State Systems – Summary – Questions – Notes and Sources

19. THE AMERICAN NATIONAL SYSTEM   469

The Civil War and Its Aftermath – Interest of National Government in Education – From Normal Schools to Teachers' Colleges – Compulsory Attendance – Forming a Ladder System – Summary – Questions – Notes and Sources

20. NEW SCHOOLS FOR A NEW WORLD   492

The Introduction of Elementary Science – The Kindergarten in the United States – Introducing New Methods of Teaching – Breaking the Lock Step – Progressive Education – From Graded Schools to High Schools – Expansion of the High School Curriculum – Standardizing the High School – Reorganizing the System – New Goals and Functions – Summary – Questions – Notes and Sources

21. AMERICAN EDUCATION TODAY   546

Population Changes and American Schools – Federal Aid for Education – Progressive Education in Retreat – National Citizens Commission for the Public Schools – Integration and States Rights – Opportunity for Talent – Adult Education – Audiovisual Aids in Education – Summary – Questions – Notes and Sources

22. HIGHER EDUCATION UNDER NATIONALISM   569

The Soviet Universities – Polytechnical Education – Politics in Soviet Education – Soviet Union and International Education – Shoe on the Other Foot – Three Countries Meet – English Public Schools – Scottish Universities – Modern English Universities – Red Brick University – The Robbins Report – The French Spirit – French Universities – In Conclusion

INDEX   609

Part I
EDUCATION IN ANTIQUITY

Chapter 1

THE ANCIENT EAST

Early man was ignorant, but his ability to learn, not his ignorance, was his most important characteristic. Man is pre-eminently a learning animal. However, in the beginning what he learned died with him unless and until he was able to communicate it, which was possible only through language or gesture in direct and friendly contact with others. When men came together in groups and, after centuries, in settlements, communication became easier; it became in fact a form of unsystematic self-instruction, the earliest example of adult education. The young were inquisitive and, we shall assume, convinced that they could improve on the ways of their elders.

CIVILIZATION

When more stable groups developed, traditions also began and became man's earliest effort to preserve his history. As long as this was an oral record repeated around the campfire, it was constantly subject to additions and distortions. What was needed was a written record, the funding of experience so that it could be recovered at will, drawn like money from a bank or apples from a bin. This need was met by the evolution of writing, and later by libraries, museums, galleries, and other collections.

Schools to teach writing and libraries to preserve what was written were the earliest efforts to fund knowledge; but we must not expect too much too soon. Writing has often been invented but it is more difficult to perfect it and to spread the art widely. We learn about the beginning of the writing art from the young science of archaeology, a study that began independently in France, England, Denmark, and elsewhere. Thomas Jefferson in 1784 excavated an Indian burial mound in Virginia and described its contents and their arrangement. He was, so far, an archaeologist.

We shall report the rise of archaeology in Denmark: Early in the nineteenth century a collection of "antiquities" in Copenhagen was turned over to a young businessman, Christian Thomsen, who was to arrange them for a newly founded museum. He had little knowledge of archaeology, which had hardly existed as a science, but he had an inquiring mind. He had before him a collection of contributed materials; and it seemed that they could be grouped into tools, weapons, ritual objects, and containers. After working with them for a year or more he conceived the idea that the objects of stone were older than the metal ones, which he considered "too expensive" for an early society. At last he arranged his materials into four species: objects of stone, copper, bronze, and iron and drew the remarkable conclusion that this was the time order of their introduction and use.

Thomsen, however, had no true notion of the time covered by his "ages." Only Darwin and the study of French excavations in the Somme Valley convinced geologists such as Charles Lyell of the time involved in man's evolution. Thus was formed a more adequate calendar of prehistory, a means of assigning dates to the rise and progress of civilization.

One of the first and greatest marks of the rising civilization was the change from food gathering to food producing by planting grains and other crops and domesticating animals for food, clothing, and transport. The planting especially marked an epoch because it required settlement and cooperation. In these communities there was relative peace and a certain amount of trading and, when the distances were short, there was trade between neighboring settlements. Gradually a full complement of institutions developed. Such were the family, community, and other subgroups, and various institutions, religious, legal, financial, and military.

HIGH CIVILIZATION

By a high civilization we mean first one that became relatively settled and permanent, in which villages developed and in time grew into towns and then cities. In cities and even in towns there were permanent buildings, some of them for public use. Officials were chosen to make regulations, to maintain order within, and to guard against attacks from without. In cities specialized trades arose, the literary and fine arts were cultivated, and education arose but did not for a long period become a public interest.

The main fact is that civilization reached an advanced stage not over wide areas or at an equal pace, but only in a few locations while all the rest of the world remained barbarous or savage. There were only a few early high civilizations and they arose in four places: in Egypt; in the river valley north of the Persian Gulf; in northern India on the Indus River; and in east-central China on the Yellow River. One might suppose that the people in these areas were more vigorous, skilful, and intelligent than any who lived in other regions, but natural conditions must be taken into account; and when they are, the supposition becomes very doubtful.

Among the natural conditions shared by all these progressive areas and not found to the same degree elsewhere, we must name first the river valleys, along the Nile in Egypt, in Sumer between the Tigris and Euphrates in Mesopotamia—this word means between the rivers—and, as we have indicated, along the Indus and Yellow Rivers. The river bottoms were composed of fertile, easily worked soil, mostly silt, and the rivers provided water for irrigation, a very important advantage. In the great days of Sumer a system of canals and ditches watered its fields and gardens. The rivers in all the locations also became highways, easy means of transit and transport.

The rivers of Sumer made the bottomland and then, ploughing new courses, swept much of the soil out into the great gulf—which at one time extended far up to the point where the great rivers almost came together. Smaller streams, the Karun and others, flowed into the gulf from east and west and their deposits made a breakwater across the gulf creating a lake. The Tigris and Euphrates filled the lake and made a plain composed of new soil eventually stretching from the region of Baghdad to that of Al Ubaid.

The great rivers of Mesopotamia were not gentle and periodic in their flow like the Nile. When great rains lasted for days in the northern mountains where they and their tributaries had their rise, they caused great floods that moved masses of clay and silt they deposited to a depth of several feet in the lower valley. A character named Ziusudra in a Sumerian account plays the part assigned to Noah in the similar story of the Deluge in the Bible (Gen. 6–9).

The four sites—the Delta of the Nile, Sumer, the lower Indus River, and the Yellow River—all lie near the middle belt of the North Temperate Zone, between thirty and forty degrees of latitude, and did not suffer unduly from torrid heat or arctic cold. Egypt and Mesopotamia were the two oldest highly civilized areas in the world, older by three thousand years than the classical Greek civilization.

Herodotus, visiting Egypt in the fifth pre-Christian century, called that country "the gift of the river," a remark so apt that it will not be forgotten. Plato, in his *Timaeus*, reported that the Egyptians considered the Greeks "mere children," without any old men to hand down ancient tradition. There is a measure of truth in this, but Greek intellectuals were interested in Egyptian mathematics, astronomy, medicine, and the arts and carried these studies far beyond the Egyptian level. Plato in his *Laws* referred to an Egyptian number game in which the children performed a problem in division by subtraction. Using only practical methods the Egyptians constructed a right angle and measured the circle. Their value of *pi* was three and one seventh. They did not develop demonstrative geometry. Aristotle in his *Politics* repeatedly refers to Egypt. At one point (Book V, xi), he explained that tyrants, any tyrants, maintained their oppressive rule by, for example, suppressing all chance for education and by keeping the entire population continuously at work so that it would have no time or opportunity to hatch conspiracies. He said the rulers of Egypt applied this harsh method in the construction of the pyramids.

Our chief subject will be the civilization developed in Mesopotamia because in that land a series of special writing schools were developed in the third millennium before our era. In ancient times, the land was called Sumer and the people, Sumerians; but today the region is called Babylonia. It lies at the eastern extremity of the Fertile Crescent, a broad strip that is green during part of the year and that stretches, like a giant bow bent toward the north, around the Arabian Desert from the Persian Gulf on the east to Egypt on the west. Both Egypt and Sumer developed high civilizations in the fourth millennium, B.C., and there was communication between them, a point to keep in mind.

INVENTION OF WRITING

The need for writing and records has an obvious relation to the rise of schools but it may not be sufficient cause. In Sumer the use of writing led to the formation of schools; in Egypt it, perhaps, did not. In Egypt the art was spread by apprenticeship. The writing materials in the two countries were also different: washed clay was used in Sumer and papyrus, a plant that grows in the Nile, in Egypt. From the pith or split stems of this plant, laid crosswise in two layers to form a square, glued together and rolled and pressed smooth, a paper-like surface was made; and, indeed, the word *paper* was derived from *papyros*. The edges of separate sheets were joined to make a strip that could be made into a roll. On papyrus they wrote with ink applied with a brush. In the dry climate of Egypt the rolls, and even single sheets lost in the sands, last indefinitely and the script remains distinct.

The Egyptian writing was beautiful, the Sumerian, practical, but not very handsome. The Egyptian writing was called hieroglyphic, two Greek words meaning "sacred carving." Writing in both countries began, as in many other places, as a series of pictures. In Egypt it was later greatly simplified and became formal, losing its earlier graceful lines, and was called demotic from *demos*, the people. Egyptian writing did not spread as widely as the Sumerian, which almost covered the Near East.

Sumer, without papyrus or other writing materials, used soft clay tablets of any moderate size. On these they wrote with a stylus, making marks in the clay but without using ink. Both sides of the tablets could be used and when they were sun dried or fire baked they were practically indestructible unless broken or crushed. Great numbers of such tablets have been dug up and are in the museums of many countries where they can be read, translated, and published—as many have been. They are the sources of nearly all that we know about Sumer.

The first writing was done by tracing lines with the point of the stylus; and, as in Egypt or among some North American Indians, they began by drawing pictures. The principle used was the one often found in children's books and in advertising, that of the rebus. An outline of a man's head could mean either *head* or *man*, and the context usually determined which was meant; but drawing with the point of the stylus on clay is not easy. It was easier to make patterns with the blunt end by stamping. This made wedge-shaped marks and gave the writing its name of cuneiform.

The Sumerian language was composed largely of one-syllable words and the syllables could be moved around to make parts of new words not related to the original. Two parallel wavy lines meant *water* and when added to the picture for head the word *headwater* or, if required, *origin* might be the meaning. There was one further step. The drawings became more and more formal so that the character for head no longer looked like the object; but a single pattern or character was used for each syllable.

By these methods, with five or six hundred characters, the Sumerian language could be put down on clay or other material. The writing was syllabic, not alphabetic, and it could be, and was, adapted to many languages. It was used in writing Akkadian, Babylonian, Assyrian, Hittite, and others. Thus, the cuneiform invented in Sumer was used all through the Fertile Crescent for a period of two thousand years.

It will be easy to see why learning to write was an arduous task, an intellectual activity needing and well deserving the services of trained teachers and a formal school. It took the Sumerians several hundred years, beginning about 3100 B.C., to make this much progress; and it may tend to moderate our own pride if we remember that English writing is far from perfect and our spelling is positively unintelligent.

THE CITIES

There were hamlets, villages, even towns in very early times but the first cities arose about 3500 B.C. in Sumer. This statement also implies the best definition of the word city: a settlement larger and more complex than a town. We have to operate with this because all other attempts to define the word come back to this one. The complexity is important for it was this increase in the number and variety of activities, vocations, and institutions of the cities that demanded the services of writers and of schools to prepare them. The first schools in the world were largely vocational, in purpose, more like a modern business college than any other school. Sumerian writing was difficult and demanded long and careful training for mastery, hence the need for a long period of teaching and practice.

Not only did the cities have the earliest schools but they alone had any schools until modern times. Country children had to wait until the Reformation or even until the rise of the modern public school systems. It is apparent today that the cities and the suburbs have grown until they cover whole counties and a great part of some states. The best schools are now in the suburbs and many of the worst are in the slums of the inner city.

We know little of the quality of the Sumerian schools. A sketch of the locale will be useful. Sumer had an area of about two thirds that of Rhode Island. The distance from Siffar to the Persian Gulf was about two hundred miles and at the widest point the two rivers are one hundred miles apart. There were a dozen cities; and Ur, one of the largest, was west of the Euphrates. Rhode Island has about twenty cities of ten thousand people or over and Providence has two hundred thousand. This is to show that a rich agricultural district like Sumer was clearly able to support a dozen cities and many villages. The historians disagree wildly in their estimates of the population.

The Sumerian cities were free city-states at first but were conquered by Sargon the Great, regained their freedom for a few centuries, and were again incorporated into an empire. The people were very industrious, working in the fields, conducting irrigation and drainage operations, sowing, reaping, transporting, buying, and selling. Many owned land and other private property; others were employees; not a few, both natives and captives, men and women, were slaves. There were wars between the cities and, therefore, generals and captains to lead the armies. Many trades and the finer arts were practiced. Business and government including the courts required detailed records.

The people, as the Apostle Paul said of the Athenians, were very religious. The temple, the central religious institution in each city, owned land and employed many workers. As in Greece, the gods were supposed to dwell in a lofty place, Mount Olympus at Athens, so in Sumer the gods and heaven were "up there"; but there were no high places. This is why they built step-pyramids, or ziggurats, with the temples on top of them. From one of these tall structures the Hebrew writer (Gen. II) doubtless obtained his idea of the Tower of Babel.

SUMER AND BEYOND

Schools to teach writing, including the writing of figures and some calculation, arose about 2500 B.C.; but writing itself, as indicated here, began five or six centuries earlier. Some schools were private and some were connected with the local temple. In either case the main purpose was practical, the cultivation of a practical skill and vocation. There was a practical reason for the temple schools: namely, that the temples owned property and carried on important businesses. Much of the wealth of a Sumerian city was the property of its temple, or palace.

The oldest known script was found in the ancient city of Erech and consists of a large number of tablets with business notations. Some tablets contain lists of words and some of these were, long after, used in schools for practice lessons. Before they had schools, writing was taught in a sort of apprenticeship. There was also another purpose in the lists of words, an encyclopedic purpose, that is, to list, by classes, the names of all kinds of things. The result, if completed, would have been a classified list of all nouns.

Sumer schooldays: Sumerian tablet inscribed with essay on school life. (Courtesy of Professor Samuel N. Kramer, University of Pennsylvania Museum.)

The Sumerian pupil began with signs for syllables such as ba, ta, za, nun, sin, tan, and so on; next he learned to write words made up of syllables already known; then common phrases, sentences, short compositions. If the present-day student has access to a collection of old schoolbooks he may find English spelling books that used this plan. The complete mastery of the writing of the language was a great part of the work of Sumerian pupils. As in modern times, so in ancient times, the student could not master the language without learning a great deal of what the language dealt with. Sumerians knew this as well as we do for they had a riddle asking: "He whose eyes are closed goes in and when he comes out his eyes are wide open; what is it?" The answer, of course, is "The School!"

All the writing was done on clay tablets and the school was called the tablet house. When archaeologists after their digging speak of the recovery of Sumerian textbooks they mean collections of tablets dealing with related subjects. Today's textbooks give the facts of a subject and the appropriate explanation of the facts, a theory, it may be, of the changes in animal forms or evolution. The Sumerian tablets give only the names of animals, insects, plants, precious stones, minerals, cities, stars, gods, and other objects and persons. Especially noteworthy to modern students is the absence of science and credible history. These are modern subjects.

There is evidence that the pupils came from an upper social class, not the highest perhaps but even kings boasted of their learning. We give an example subsequently. It is not strange that kings magnified their attainments, for the Sumerians tended to be a boastful people. This seems to be characteristic of the ancient peoples in general, and it may be a general human trait.

School discipline was harsh and corporal punishment was not excluded. Only a small proportion of the youth can have attended the schools; but the extensive array of Sumerian literature, quite unrelated to business or administration, suggests that some people who did not learn to write may have been able to read. It is also possible that there were public readings; and the hymns and other literary pieces were used in temple ceremonies.

The most surprising fact about the cuneiform writing is its spread from its place of origin in Sumer over the whole of the Fertile Crescent almost to the borders of Classical Greece, but no further. It spread first to the Semitic nation of Akkad, or Accad as the King James Bible (Gen. 10:10) has it. After long years and many military engagements all of Sumer was conquered but, also, as has repeatedly happened, the rude conqueror was in his turn taken captive intellectually by his more cultured victim. Akkad did not give up its language but, being illiterate, it learned to write its own Semitic tongue in Sumer's cuneiform script. Many tablets have been recovered that served as dictionaries and parallel translations in Sumerian-Akkadian form. The same process continued in Babylonia, Assyria, and other nations to the west. These and other countries, like Akkad, kept their own languages but, as we have said, used cuneiform characters in writing them.

The literature of Sumer is part of the process of education in the Ancient East, but we can give only a very little space to it. The land between the rivers sustained almost a dozen cities and many villages. From the mounds archaeologists have recovered and sent to the great museums quantities of vases, jewels, statues, and the implements and weapons of peace and war.

They have also dug up massive quantities of clay tablets, mostly business and legal records. Among these three was a legal code, the earliest in history that has been found. It was formed two centuries before the famous Babylonian Code of Hammurabi of about 1760 B.C.; but it was written on clay tablets rather than on a stone column and was, therefore, less conspicuous and less well preserved. Only sections of it have been found.

Nine tenths of the cuneiform tablets, it has been estimated, deal with practical matters such as commercial and administrative records; one tenth deal with literature in a broad sense of the word, including both religious and secular writing: hymns, proverbs, moral advice, and elegies as well as poems, narratives, and epics. Much of the literature deals with the gods, a vast pantheon of very human beings, human divinities as one might say. Kings also appear in these writings, but few private persons appear and even those who do are rarely given names.

The epic of Gilgamesh is far and away the best-known Sumerian literary work. It is not a long poem, only about fifty pages, and it has been pieced together from tablets found at different places. It has been translated into many modern languages. A prose version, *The Epic of Gilgamesh* by N. K. Sanders (Penguin Books, 1960), begins this way:

O Gilgamesh, lord of Kullah, great is thy praise. This was the man to whom all things were known; this was the king [of the City of Uruk which stood between Babylon and Ur] who knew the countries of the world. He was wise, he saw mysteries and knew secret things, he brought us a tale of days before the flood. He went on a long journey, was weary, worn-out with labor, and returning, engraved on a stone the whole story.

The story includes accounts of a great friendship; a long journey; a perilous adventure in which the hero killed Humbaba, the monster who guarded the Cedar Forest; the death of Enkidu, his great friend and companion; and the unsuccessful search by Gilgamesh for eternal life. This he thought he had attained but it was taken away from him, lost not through sin as in the Garden of Eden, but through a lapse of attention. The journey to the Cedar Forest and the killing of its guardian is, no doubt, symbolic of Sumer's great need for a supply of wood to which the hero is supposed to have opened the way.

The history of the text of the Gilgamesh epic is not clear. Separate incidents of the tale certainly go back to Sumerian times, but other sections may have been composed later in Babylonian times. Akkadian texts do not always give the stories in the same sequence as the Sumerian and may have added new incidents. The epic was apparently not written in finished form by a single original author but grew in the imagination and on the lips of people until a prehomeric Homer came along and welded the anecdotes into a great work. Perhaps it even, as has been said, influenced the real Homer in his composition of the *Odyssey*.

A number of Sumerian library catalogues have been found, although on broken tablets. Libraries were located in temples, and in Babylonia almost certainly in schools; but there, as in Sumer, the books (that is, tablets) were scattered, so that hardly any large literary works escaped intact; and scholars must patiently and persistently bring the separated tablets and fragments together in order to restore the originals as nearly as possible.

The largest cuneiform library was founded not in Sumer but in Nineveh many centuries after the freedom of the cities of ancient Sumer had been destroyed by a Semitic conqueror, Sargon the Great. He was a military genius who conquered all southern Mesopotamia and established an autocratic state that put an end to the freedom of the cities in which a high civilization had flowered. Sargon was hostile not to Sumerian culture but to political disorder. He intended to foster learning but he destroyed the free cities, learning's birthplace and home. Under his and his successors' autocracy, learning struggled and at last died. It was revived in the free Greek cities of Asia Minor and of the mainland, especially Athens.

Much of the learning was preserved in the great library, already mentioned, which was established by Ashurbanipal, the king who ruled Babylonia from 669–626 B.C. The latter date is uncertain and the birthdate is unknown. His Greek name was Sardanapolis.

Ashurbanipal claimed to have received a careful, extended, and varied education. He was taught to shoot with the bow, to ride horses and chariots, to watch the omens, and to explain the heavens. The knowledge of mathematics and astronomy was cultivated by the Babylonians. But Ashurbanipal also understood "the beautiful writings in Sumerian that are obscure, in Akkadian that are difficult to keep in mind"; all these it was his pleasure "to repeat." This self-eulogy was probably truthful and certainly boastful, and it sounds as though he respected these skills and arts because they were old and admired by others. This would be at least one reason why he wanted a library and why he sent emissaries to all parts of the once literary world to gather texts, not only to promote progress in the future but to honor the past and magnify himself. Certainly learning was in a decline in the seventh century and continued in the downward way.

Schools continued to teach but not to discover new knowledge. In Palestine, the Hebrews, and on the seacoast, the Phoenicians, thought new thoughts, and new writings were appearing. Also, new ways of writing appeared among those peoples; and the Greeks created the alphabet that we call ours. With that invention cuneiform disappeared from the books and the Sumerians from the memory of mankind, to be rediscovered only two centuries ago.

Westward the course of empire took its way; and it was accompanied or followed by learning and schools. The Greeks, in their free cities, the inventors of new stories and discoverers of new sciences, became the teachers of Europe.

We must not fail to insert a caution against misunderstanding the preceding information. The invention of writing did not make memory work unnecessary. People continued to learn and to hold in mind all that they could readily retain. So the story of Gilgamesh was committed to memory and told to companies, young and old, and told with variations clearly. Things that people delighted to tell were put into story form or set up as poetry. So the Hebrews learned the Ten Commandments and taught them to their children orally, even though they were written down in the sacred Book. So the poems of Homer were passed on from generation to new generation for centuries before the Greeks learned to write. The development of the art of writing among the Greeks was a slow process that required centuries before they were able to write fluently in regular, continuous language. Few of the children who attended school had a book. The Greek schoolboy had a tablet and every day wrote a few lines on it from dictation; and these lines he tried to commit to memory. The Sumerians, as we have seen, found writing useful; and most useful for the financial records that were hard to retain in mind. A record was useful also because copies could be given to each party concerned. We must try to realize how different practice and results in the ancient school were from those of the present. We now turn to the Hebrew schools.

HEBREW EDUCATION

The Bible preserves the history of the Hebrew people and nation. In Genesis we read that Abram, later renamed Abraham, who was to be the father of the Hebrews, came from Ur of the Chaldees, a city of Sumer. He was commanded to leave his home in order to seek a new home in a "promised Land." This he found at the far-western end of the Fertile Crescent in Canaan, also known as Palestine and as the Holy Land. This land, near the eastern shores of the Mediterranean Sea, lay in the path of the armies and traders passing between Egypt and the powers of Asia.

We shall see that the Hebrews made a contribution to the development of the Greek, the Western, alphabet. Indirectly, through their relations with the Christian Church, they made great contributions to education in the West. In origin and location, however, they were an Asian nation, and a short account of their early progress in the education of children belongs in this place.

Family and religious institutions instructed the young through the early centuries. Parents and religious leaders taught through the spoken word in those times, for the Hebrews did not develop the art of writing until perhaps 1000 B.C. Amos, Isaiah, and the other literate prophets lived in the late ninth, the eighth, and following pre-Christian centuries. Before these times the teaching was oral in mode, religious in content and purpose, and intended to change both faith and conduct, belief and action.

The elementary school must have come into Palestine and Judea without notice. It had become widespread by the early years of the Roman Empire. The statesman and moralist Seneca confessed that the Jews knew the reasons for their religious ceremonies whereas others, including the Romans without question, merely went through the motions, ignorantly. The reason, one reason certainly, was that Judea was a theocracy in which the law was the "law of God." Even the capture of Jerusalem and the destruction of the temple in A.D. 70 changed only the civil government and not the Jewish law.

All Jews were commanded to take part in the worship services and this required a knowledge of the language of the liturgy; and in literate times all the young were to learn to read. Thus religion became a force for general literateness. At a time when the young Greeks and Romans were restricted in their educational opportunity by differences in class and wealth the Jews came close to educational democracy. This does not mean that schooling was free but the fees were low and all the children were to attend. One of the factors in making education accessible was the synagogue, literally "meeting house." The word, curiously, is not Hebraic but Greek. The synagogue was a house of prayer, religious discussion, and interpretation of the Torah, the law; it was widely distributed.

Torah, the law, is also taken to mean teaching, and actually an authoritative teaching that commands all pupils. It is the divine wisdom. For the Hebrews, this attitude fixed the curriculum that could be adapted to the slight abilities of the young but could not be exhausted. Its study was to be continued into old age. Children were sent to school at the age of seven or when they could "safely cross a bridge" and certainly find their way. They continued to attend even in their teens. The instruction was largely individual even in a school of many children; the method was *memoriter*, the discipline apt to be physical and sometimes brutal. No schools are perfect, but the Hebrew schools had a great part in preserving the Hebrew people from extinction.

SUMMARY

At a certain stage in any civilization knowledge that cannot be accurately remembered in sufficient detail will begin to accumulate. Some examples would evidently be laws, court decisions, contracts, the calendar, religious formulas and festivals, scientific observations, and treasured stories. These and others must not only be preserved but they must be accessible when needed. At some point along this road, writing becomes so necessary that it will be invented. As more people are required to keep and to consult such records, schools will be organized. This point was reached in Sumer between 3100 and 2500 B.C.

After a glance at the rise of high civilizations arising in a few favored places, the invention of writing is considered because it was the need for religious, legal, literary, and especially practical writings that caused the rise of schools. Schools are the most important means for the spread of education and the central institution in a history of education. Schools are not the only such means. Learning occurs in many ordinary experiences and contacts, such as family living, vocations, crafts, arts, public service, and others, without writing. Apprenticeship, imitation, and cooperation can transmit to larger circles and to the young what has been learned; over the centuries great progress has taken place by such means.

Like the invention of the steam engine the invention of writing was a process, not an event but a process to which many people must have contributed over a long period of time. An early, if not the first, step was the drawing of a picture to represent an object or an idea. Other steps followed until a usable system had been formed, a system adequate for the time. At such a time a fatal human weakness set in to block further progress; the usable was accepted as "good enough" and improvement stopped. The Sumerians stopped with the syllabic system and none of those who borrowed the system, none of the successive generations of teachers, had the enterprise to attempt improvement.

Schools and cities were interrelated. In the cities there were many positions for those who were able to write and to conduct business; and there were numbers of boys within walking distance from any central point where a school could be located. The schools grew as the cities prospered.

The Sumerian schools left many difficulties to be resolved. The need for a simpler system of writing and a less cumbersome writing material were serious problems. Think of carrying a story the length of Gilgamesh home from the library.

Another nation, the Hebrews, developed family and school education in early times. Among that people the Christian Church developed and both Hebrew and Christian peoples and organizations were to have great influence in education in Western countries.

QUESTIONS

1. How, in one page, is education best defined? Civilization? School?
2. Compare the significance of the invention of writing with that of the wheel; the family.
3. Did the rivers or the climate have the greater influence in locating early civilizations?

4. Using the *Encyclopaedia Brittanica* and other sources, compare the early education of Sumer and Egypt.
5. Why do so few names of leaders occur in the account of Sumerian education?

NOTES AND SOURCES

Much work has been done in recent years in ancient history and prehistory, and older books should be used with caution. Although still useful, they may not be up-to-date on all topics. Pertinent articles in the latest edition of the *Encyclopaedia Brittanica* deal with such topics as Egypt, Sumer, Alphabet, and many others. The bibliographies in C. G. Starr (see below) will be helpful. There is an account of ancient Babylonia in Herodotus I, 189–200.

CHILDE, V. GORDON, *Man Makes Himself*, London, Watts & Co., 1939.

CHIERA, EDWARD, *They Wrote on Clay, the Babylonian Tablets Speak Today*, Phoenix Books, Chicago, The University of Chicago Press, 1938. Edited by George G. Cameron.

EBNER, ELIEZER, *Elementary Education in Ancient Israel*, New York, Bloch Publishing Company, 1956. Notes and bibliography much better than most books on its subject.

KRAMER, SAMUEL NOAH, *The Sumerians, Their History, Culture and Character*, Chicago, The University of Chicago Press [1939]. (This is the third revision of this book. Titles vary.)

RAPPORT, SAMUEL, and HELEN WRIGHT, *Archaeology*, New York, Washington Square Press, 1964. See articles by Geoffrey Bibby, Sir Leonard Woolley, James Baikie, and others.

SANDERS, N. K., *The Epic of Gilgamesh*, Baltimore, Penguin, L 100, 1960. This is a prose translation. There is an excellent introduction. Other translations, prose and verse, are available.

SJOBERG, GIDEON, "The Origin and Evolution of Cities," *Scientific American*, September, 1965, pp. 55–63.

STARR, CHESTER G., *A History of the Ancient World*, New York, Oxford University Press, 1965.

WOOLLEY, C. LEONARD, *Ur of the Chaldees*, Penguin, A 27, 1950. Sir Leonard Woolley excavated Ur and made remarkable discoveries.

Chapter 2

ANCIENT GREECE: THE EARLY WEST

Athenians under a master were thought by Herodotus to be no better than others, but when they were victorious through their own efforts, they realized that "freedom is best." The same historian reported that when Miletus, having driven out one tyrant, "tasted freedom" she refused to accept another. In hard lessons and by slow stages, many of the Greek states came to agree with the Theban Pindar, that "Law is king over all"— even over kings.

The geography of the country served as a school. An arrangement of narrow valleys, rough mountains, small plains, and numerous islands, the physical features of Greece created the small city-states in which the people were close to the government. None were far from the sea and they were within reach of Asia Minor, Phoenicia, Egypt, and even Italy and were exposed to the contrasting ideas, customs, and arts from which to choose and on which to make improvements.

Writing was such a custom and art. The Phoenicians had developed a kind of alphabet with characters obtained in Egypt and developed in south Canaan. It was written from right to left and used twenty-two signs, for consonants only. It was far simpler than the syllabic cuneiform with its several hundred characters. The Greeks added signs for the vowels and changed the direction of writing to go from left to right. Before 700 B.C. it was in use over much of the Greek world; in time it was borrowed by the entire West. Our alphabet is Greek in origin.

Note the significance of the achievement: the cuneiform, which had been in use for a few thousand years over large areas, could be written only by a "learned scribe," and one who had acquired an extended education through years of effort. The Greek alphabet could be learned in a few days or weeks by a child in an elementary school; and writing at once became an invaluable tool in one's own mental development. Its invention, therefore, was one of the great achievements in the history of education.

Education could have become universal at once but it did not. Slavery, labor needs, and social class were to prevent such an extension; but it did gradually become a social custom and a public concern. Athens and Sparta developed two contrasting systems. From these Plato and Aristotle and their followers formed two philosophies of education; and their principles are still available to us and will be considered subsequently.

With these Western ideas and tools, the Greeks formed and polished a Western language, Greek, which, as any dictionary will show, has had great influence on English and other modern languages. It is an Indo-European speech, kin to Latin and other tongues of the West. It is both a cause and a means in the development of Western civilization.

THE DAWN

During an extended prehistorical period the early Greeks, speaking different dialects, drifted southward from Macedonia, perhaps also from Albania, and even from the Danube basin. They gradually occupied the three sides of the Aegean Sea, its islands, including the largest, Crete, which may be regarded as the fourth side of a land-locked Aegean. Some of them entered Crete about 2000 B.C. and erected a city and a great palace at Knossos. Smaller palaces were built at other places on the island, and such structures also arose on the mainland at Mycenae. Developments in Crete are ascribed to King Minos, who developed a navy, and are part of what is called the Minoan civilization. The Minoans, we repeat, were Greeks; but Jews, Phoenicians, and others lived among them. They had learned to write and wrote in Greek.

The Greeks were a maritime people but this does not mean that all or any large proportion of them were sailors. They replenished their supply of slaves by piratical expeditions. As means of defense against pirates most Greek cities were located some distance inland. Knossos was three and a half miles from the coast. The palace, when uncovered in 1900, was found to consist of large halls, paved courts, and many connecting rooms. Beautiful fresco paintings adorned the walls; there was polished black pottery; there were many small sculptures; and the sacred symbols of dove, snake, and two-headed ox were repeated. The Minoans worshiped on the tops of mountains and at altars in their homes.

The great period of Minoan Crete extended from about 200 to 1400 B.C. In the latter year there was an eruption and explosion of a great volcano in an island of the southern Aegean. A part of the island sank beneath the waters; and eastern and central Crete, including Knossos, were covered with melted rock and ash and destroyed by fire. The survivors moved to the western parts of the island. For reasons that are not entirely clear, Greek lands, including the mainland, passed through a dark age that lasted for centuries.

SPARTA

The early Greeks were not as united and peaceful as one might assume. The historians Herodotus and Thucydides reported that their ancestors had been members of wandering tribes speaking different dialects. In their migrations they pushed others, including other Greeks, out of their settlements in order to gain richer lands and easier living for themselves. They could hardly be called farmers because, from fear of being themselves dispossessed, they did little planting. Calling all others barbarians, they were themselves barbarians. Piracy was not only a frequent but also an accepted vocation. When strangers appeared the natives would ask one another, "Are they pirates?" in the same tone in which they might have asked, "Are they sailors?"

Although war, migrations, and piracy continued, the leading Greek states had found permanent locations by the seventh century B.C. By 700 the Spartans had fastened their "iron sway" on Laconia and most of Lacedaemon. Sparta itself comprised a group of villages in a level plain with buildings so mean that now their exact location is in doubt. Athens, which sometimes claimed that it was the oldest permanent settlement, had its Acropolis on which it erected the great Parthenon. The contrast that this comparison suggests is perhaps not unfair to Sparta; but on the other hand, we must remember that Plato found much to commend in the simplicity, self-restraint, unity, and morality of Spartan life.

Sparta was composed of three classes of people: the Spartans who were citizens; the Perioeci who worked the land but who had no political rights; and the Helots who were slaves owned by the state. The two servile classes were many times as numerous as the Spartans whom they supported and served.

The ruling class did not engage in manual labor but devoted itself to military and civic activities and to the kind of education needed by those who had to order and restrain a large subject population always primed for revolution and sometimes engaging in it. Only the citizen-soldiers, the Spartans, received any education and this was mainly physical, military, and moral; however, they shared with other Greeks their religion, language, and literature. They aimed at physical vigor, determination, courage, military skill, obedience to law and regular authority.

Only healthy children were raised to become citizens; others were exposed to die but were sometimes adopted by the subject classes. Boys lived with their mothers until the age of seven when they were transferred to barracks under the control of a *paidonomos*, a leader, or ruler of boys. The whole number was organized in smaller groups each under the command of a young man who had completed his training.

The physical education was deliberately made hard in order to develop endurance and the willingness to do with a minimum of clothing, food, and rest. Winter and summer the boys went shoeless. They were taught to steal; were punished if detected; and were also whipped, not for crime but as a test of endurance. In some cases they died under the official lashing. Ball games were among the more civilized of their sports, which included also the pentathlon: running, jumping, throwing the discus and javelin, and boxing. Most severe was the pancratium, which included wrestling, boxing, gouging, and essentially fighting without rules.

Mental and moral training were involved in the dances and music. The youth were taught to play on the lyre and to sing both solo and in chorus. The Doric chant and dance both developed and expressed patriotic and religious feeling; and these were about the same sentiment, for their religion was largely patriotism.

Reading and writing were not included in the public education. When these were privately acquired they led the student to Homer and to Pindar, the poet of athletes and games. The Spartans had slight reputation for learning, but they were famous for a sharp wit that has been named for them, laconic. When one complained that their swords were too short, old King Agis replied that they were "long enough to reach the enemy." "Return with your shield or on it," was a mother's farewell to her son going into battle. One who proposed to make Sparta a democracy was told to "Try it in your family." This reply was particularly apt, for it was considered by other Greeks that the Spartan women had too much freedom and influence on public affairs.

Girls received a public athletic training in the sports of the pentathlon but not including boxing. They were organized into troops, like the boys, by ages; they danced, sang, marched, and took part in public religious rites; but they lived at home, not like boys in barracks. Spartan maidens were not so expert in spinning and weaving as their Athenian cousins but they were good housekeepers and managers, were famous as nurses, and were active in the discussion of public policy. This Spartan regard for the opinions of women seemed odd to the rest of the Greeks, but it seems to have influenced Plato. So, also, did the Spartan custom of public education and its especial stress on public, that is, military, civic, and moral goals. Plato and Aristotle, two of the greatest philosophers, came to endorse public education, and in recent centuries it has become the mode in the West. It began in Greek (Spartan) practice and Greek (Athenian) theory but has changed greatly in character and purpose.

Two ancient views on the Spartans will serve as a summary. A Greek exile, Demaratus, when urged to speak freely (Herodotus VII, 101–104) told King Xerxes, "The Spartans are the best of all men when fighting in a body; for, though free, yet they are not free in all things. Law is set over them as their master which they fear much more than your subjects fear you." Their master commanded them to die rather than to retreat; but, although not stated here, we should add that they were less valiant in single combat.

The second view of Sparta comes from Aristotle. He attacked the Spartan constitution and way of life because of their results—making war and conquest the purpose of the state and of life at the expense of civilization. Sparta aimed at empire and material prosperity. Aristotle concluded that the Spartans were not a happy people when they had both and in losing them, they lost the chance to become civilized, and all that makes life worth living (*Politics*, VII, Chap. 14).

ATHENS

The Greeks who lived in Attica were mistaken in believing that they were the original settlers and had always lived there. They were mistaken because they had absorbed those who were there before them and had completely Hellenized them. This reveals one great difference between the Athenians and the Dorians who, as we saw, enslaved those who had come into Lacedaemon before them; and it also helps to explain the nearly irresistible tendency of writers to contrast the Athenians with the Spartans —freedom with repression.

The Athenians were inventive rather than imitative. They were daring and frequently attempted tasks that they found too difficult. They welcomed foreign ideas and to satisfy their curiosity they traveled over the Aegean, Mediterranean, and other seas. St. Paul, at a much later time, discovered that the Athenians were, even in about A.D. 65, interested "only in hearing or telling some new idea"; but they did not neglect opportunities to pursue pleasure and found it in works of art, drama, and athletic spectacles. In these and other respects they differed from the Spartans; but it is worth remembering that most of what we know about Sparta has been transmitted by Athenians.

Athens was the larger of the two. By 700 B.C. the country was fully occupied but the population was still growing in several ways: by natural increase, by the immigration of foreign traders and manufacturers (called *metics*), by the acquisition of slaves in war, by raids, or by purchase. Many foreigners lived in Piraeus, the port city of Athens. Among its numerous businesses there was the shield factory of Cephalus and his sons. Their home became the scene of Plato's *Republic*, when one of their slaves was sent to detain Socrates, who was about to return to Athens. Many slaves were not the servants of cultivated families; some were used in the silver mines of Laurium, where the work was hard and life likely to be short.

There was no census but it has been estimated that Athens had a population of about 200,000 in the fifth century B.C., including 80,000 slaves and 20,000 metics. The population increased in later times. A part of that growth was caused by the crowding of the rural population of Attica into the city. To feed the people, Athens tried to keep the seas open through the Hellespont and to the wheat-growing districts of what is now the Ukraine.

The development of Athenian democracy was one of the great achievements of the ancient world. The influence of Sparta was always on the side of conservatism and oligarchy but in 508 B.C., against Spartan opposition, a popular Athenian leader, Cleisthenes (c. 510 B.C.), instituted a system that put the basic political power into the hands of small local units called demes. These units were collected into groups of three demes, one from Athens, one from the coast, and the third from the interior of Attica. This undercut the power of the aristocracy and of the rich and aimed at the principle, "one man, one vote."

By the opening of the fifth century B.C., Athens had laid the foundations of her democratic constitution and this was of the greatest importance to Western political freedom and Western public education. Next in significance to these two great interests was her philosophy. Even those thinkers who were born elsewhere often found their audience in Athens. Socrates and Plato were Athenians and Aristotle taught in the city for many years. We shall consider the doctrines of these three after we have reviewed the teaching of the elements in the capital city.

THE ATHENIAN SCHOOLS

The schools of Athens almost realized the ideal of individual instruction that some modern educators try to promote; and it is a fair speculation that there were two reasons for this condition: the small number of pupils and the lack of any theory or example of class instruction. Some have claimed that all or nearly all males in Athens were able to read, but the lack of manuscripts for a whole people and the pressure of work on the young of the poorer classes make such a conclusion doubtful. Under more favorable conditions, as when printing made books cheap, many may learn to read without benefits of schools.

In wealthy families, nurses who were usually slaves cared for the children but free Spartan women, because they were thought especially capable, were often preferred. That Athenian parents loved and indulged their children is shown in literature and inscriptions. There were cradle songs, children's stories, toys, and games. The manufacture of dolls was an Athenian industry. The games were such universal favorites as marbles, leap frog, hoops, ball games, and knuckle bones. Children's games are among the most conservative and persistent of customs.

Schooling began at the age of seven. The rich had a manservant, called a pedagogue, to escort the boys to and from school. He was to keep them from loitering and gadding about. Boys were expected to be modest and the pedagogue had the duty to train them and the right to punish them for disobedience. Girls did not attend school but were trained in the home.

There were three different schools: the letters school for reading and writing; the music school for lyric poetry and the lyre; and the gymnastic school, or palaestra. These were private schools and the parents paid fees

Greek school scene: Teacher of flute at left; of literature, center; pedagogue, or boy-leader, right. Instruction was mainly individual. (Courtesy of the Bettman Archive.)

to the masters. The boys, perhaps usually, attended the letters and music schools in the morning and the gymnastic school in the afternoon. There were few laws on schools and education and no public standards. There is no solid information about attendance but it seems that in the later classical period, in the fourth century and in later centuries, boys continued at school into their teens and enrolled in the ephebic (military) corps at eighteen where their training ended at the age of twenty. This can have been true only of the upper class.

The teaching was mechanical and *memoriter*. The teacher first taught the alphabet, then syllables, and then words. Reading was essentially word-calling; and these practices were continued by similarly untrained teachers until recent times, even into the nineteenth century. In the attention given to poetry, music, and gymnastics, however, the Athenian schools were far ahead of later European and American practice. Not until modern times did the schools of Western Europe or America again introduce such activities and studies. The illustrations sufficiently indicate the ancient school equipment, which did not include desks or blackboards; and they show that, in addition to the lyre, a flute or pipe was used. It was not favored in comparison with the lyre, which allowed poetry and an accompaniment to be combined; and there were other objections to its use. Playing the flute, in puffing out the cheeks, distorted the face. It was for these reasons that, according to Plutarch, Alcibiades in school refused to play this instrument. There was even a third objection: the flute was associated with Bacchic festivals and schools are universally charged with moral as well as mental training.

Writing was taught from a copy set by the teacher on a wax tablet with a stylus. The boy traced the copy, following the groove, his hand sometimes guided by the master's. When he was able to make a passable copy, the master dictated some lines from a poem, which the boy wrote down and then memorized. In this way in the absence of books, children gained a knowledge of Homer and the lyric poets. To be ignorant of literature was to be uneducated.

Arithmetic, if taught at all, was not extensively taught, and in business it was carried out mainly on the fingers or the abacus. Strangely, the great mathematicians, Euclid, Archimedes, and others who developed the measurement of the circle and "counted" the sand on the seashore were unable to invent an adequate way of writing numbers. Perhaps the prejudice against business was involved. In business, signs and gestures were used and they were effective with persons who were illiterate or who spoke different languages. In arithmetic the Hindu-Arabic notation can be compared to the alphabet in writing, but it developed about A.D. 800 and came into wide use by 1200.

Instruction in singing and playing the lyre was undertaken after some progress had been made in writing, and in early times all these lessons were given by the same teacher; but later there were separate music schools, each taught by a "citharist." The musical skills were social requisites, and the lyre was regarded as a national instrument and as favored by Apollo. Equally important was the belief that music was not mere recreation but was a means of forming character and disposition. In this ethical education the words were considered an essential element and the later tendency to emphasize instrumental music was lamented as a sign of decadence.

Gymnastics, the third form of education, was not less important than music; and in the dance, music was an element of physical education. The pentathlon provided the basic exercises. The Greeks aimed at health, strength, and endurance but also at skill, grace, and the shapely figure shown in the sculptures of the Greek artists. Gymnastics also had a moral aim, the development of courage, so that, as Plato said, the young man would not "play the coward in war or on any other occasion." The exercises were taught in a special school, the palacstra, by a special teacher and, in later life, were continued in the public gymnasium. In the latter part of the fourth century, the ephebic institution mentioned here was introduced; it may, with its horseback riding, marching, and military exercises, be regarded as a phase of physical education.

A class in ancient Greece with instructor playing lyre while reciting poetry. (Courtesy of the Bettman Archive.)

Girls received their education, mainly moral and domestic training, from their mothers in the home. There were no schools for girls. Women and girls lived in apartments separate from the men's and were neither hostesses nor guests at men's parties. They rarely appeared in public except at religious ceremonies. A marriage was sealed by a legal ceremony and did not imply a romantic attachment. If a marriage remained childless, the husband could return the wife with her dowry to her parents. She was not a spiritual or social companion to her husband; and by Pericles, it was considered a merit if men, neither approving nor disapproving, did not speak of her at all. Except for women's participation in religion, Athenian culture was a men's culture.

The schools did not teach religion because religion was deeply imbedded in literature and in domestic and political life. Greek religion was largely a matter of ritual and ceremony to be carried out by the individual or the priest at sacred shrines or on sacred days. The state watched over the public worship because the support of the gods was believed essential to the public welfare. To the ancient Greeks the modern separation of church and state was unthinkable.

As the Greek conception of man's relations to the divine became more spiritualized, the advanced thinkers became dissatisfied with the old views of the gods and their very imperfect morality. Thus Plato proposed to edit Homer to make him teach that the gods never do evil or cause evil to be done, never mislead anyone, and that they never change. But this was not the view of the average citizen. The religion of the people included a great deal of crude superstition; and religion was a means of foretelling the future, of placating the jealous gods, averting misfortune, and increasing one's own health and prosperity. This religion may have been lacking in theology but it aroused strong feelings. In 399 B.C., the "enlightened" Athenians condemned Socrates for introducing new gods and corrupting the youth. The schools did not teach religion but they clearly helped to transmit it.

The lack of sufficient knowledge makes it difficult to see Athenian formal schooling and education—two distinct entities—in clear perspective. There was no organized secondary school system; and even the primary schools can hardly be called a system. Learning to read was a much more difficult task than it is in modern times. All "books" were handwritten and the scripts varied. Although they had a good alphabet, they used upper-case letters only and did not leave any spaces between one word and the next. Often the teacher had the only manuscript and dictated daily portions to be written by the pupil on a wax tablet and memorized. Normally the pupil had no parchment or papyrus for a permanent and continuous text of a poem. When a boy had completed his schooling, he was able to carry away only what he remembered. Many, no doubt, soon lost the skill in reading they had attained.

People also considered the conduct and moral ideals of the boys of far more value and of greater social import than their reading, writing, and intellectual cleverness. The teaching of the home began soon after birth and the laws and politics of the state continued into adolescence this most important of all instruction. The Greek dramatists, orators, historians, and philosophers, having acquired the rudiments, carried on and completed their education without further schooling.

The best way to close this section will involve a short historical criticism of its contents. The account is limited in the time to which it applies. It deals with schools in the fifth and fourth centuries before Christ. This was the so-called Hellenic or classical age and it was followed by a Hellenistic and cosmopolitan era that offered a somewhat more varied, and often more superficial, schooling in the third century and after.

In 500 to 300 B.C., the number of pupils was small and was composed largely of upper-class boys. This was approved of by Plato with his pro-Spartan prejudices; and although Athens was a democracy, the people generally selected educated men for leadership, men who could read and write, men who were able speakers with courteous, affable manners, an aristocracy of culture if not of birth, but often of birth as well.

This information and much of the content of this section cannot be found directly stated in the ancient records. Herodotus and Thucydides, two of the greatest of the Greek historians, lived and wrote in the period treated earlier in this chapter, but they tell us nothing about the schools. Thucydides does, indeed, quote Pericles (d. 429 B.C.), as saying that Athens "is the school of Hellas." He meant that Athens was an example, or model; and his incisive statement is a figure of speech. In the speech he deprecates the painful discipline imposed on the Spartan youth from early childhood while "we" at Athens "live just as we please" and yet "we" are just as ready as they to encounter any danger from those who oppose us.

PERICLEAN AGE

The Athens of Pericles jealously guarded its constitutional democracy but the highest positions were usually filled, as already noted, from the upper classes. There was a strong prejudice against tradesmen, professionals, and even artists, who sold their great paintings and sculptures. The common people were proud of the social aristocracy and they wildly cheered Alcibiades when one of his drivers won a chariot race in the Olympic games.

With all their egotism and often serious misconduct, the aristocracy made up an important class among the population. By serving as the audience and the patrons of the higher teachers or Sophiste, they helped to develop higher education and prepared young Athenians for public life. The word, *Sophist*, at first meant wise man but it soon came to have a derogatory meaning, as in sophistry. The Sophists were foreigners who came to Athens, where the market and the money were, to sell their special knowledge and skill in argument. Because they were professionals and in some cases made excessive or wholly false claims, Plato and others turned against the entire class; but Socrates, Plato's great hero, was really an Athenian Sophist who sought truth and refused to accept fees.

Literary and grammatical instruction was developed in the age of Pericles and became a study for mature men. About 450 B.C. the Sophists Protagoras (481–411 B.C.) and Hippias of Elis, both learned men, founded the study of grammar as a science. They studied and classified speech sounds and grammatical forms, such as genders, tenses, and moods. By introducing system into the grammatical wilderness they created a powerful instrument for the study of their own language and a method for the investigation of other languages.

In the schools for children, poetry was studied or memorized but the Sophists undertook the study of prose; and this led to the invention of rhetoric as a science or art of public speaking. Gorgias, from Sicily, sometimes considered the founder of this study, and after whom Plato named one of his dialogues, was known for his ornate style, use of poetical words, balanced clauses, strongly accented rhythms, and parallelism of structure—

Classic Greek head, by Pheidias, Fifth Century B.C.

hardly a style for everyday. He had a great influence on the most famous teacher of rhetoric, Isocrates (436–338 B.C.), who will be more fully treated subsequently. Oratory had a remarkable growth in Athens and most of Greece. It was useful in the courts, in political assemblies and on the platform as a fine art. In court cases the principals had to plead their cases themselves, but the speeches were written for them by orators. Antiphon, in the fifth century, was the first distinguished Athenian orator; others were Lysias, Isaeus, and the most famous, Demosthenes (c. 385–322 B.C.).

Logic was a third art taught by the Sophists who came to Athens for employment. Zeno, of Elea in Southern Italy, who flourished about 460 B.C., is regarded as the founder of logic and Aristotle continued the development of the theory and developed the figures of the syllogism. These disciplines—grammar, rhetoric, and logic—were instruments in promoting and perfecting other subjects: geography, medicine, political theory, and others. Sophists laid the foundations of several new disciplines in the fourth century B.C. They charged fees for lessons and this was the "higher education" of that time; but with the exception of Plato's Academy and Aristotle's Lyceum and a few others there were no formal classes or organized schools. In the advancement of learning, the Periclean Age formed a brilliant period in the ancient world, the most brilliant in ancient history.

ISOCRATES

Isocrates (436–338 B.C.) was nine years older than Plato and, outliving him by an equal span, reached the extraordinary age of ninety-eight. Both became famous as writers of artistic prose and cultivated such subjects as politics, ethics, and education, but Isocrates did not have the stature of his contemporary in pure philosophy.

Both were teachers and fortune gave each of them a great advantage for the pursuit of a relatively unremunerative vocation—they were born wealthy. Plato belonged to the aristocracy, he inherited his wealth and was able to conserve it. Isocrates was the son of a rich flute manufacturer named Theodorus, who gave him a thorough education; but he apparently was not, as Plato seems to suggest, in the Socratic circle. In the *Phaedrus*, Plato has Socrates say of him:

I think that he has a genius which soars above the orations of Lysias, and he has a character of a finer mold. My impression is that he will marvelously improve as he grows older . . . [and will excel] all former rhetoricians . . . I believe . . . that some divine impulse will lead him to things higher still. For there is an element of philosophy in his nature.

If we may paraphrase, Plato is saying that Isocrates is greater than a speech writer such as Lysias, he is a rhetorician and will be a greater one. He may even become a philosopher. This is the beginning of a long war in education, a war between practical wisdom and eloquence against philosophy and science as the chief means of education. The struggle continued through Greek and Roman times. Under other names it has been waged for two thousand years.

There was, in fact, an element of philosophy in Isocrates; it was political philosophy, whereas that of Plato and Socrates was moral philosophy. The political philosophy of Isocrates asked, "What in the long run is desirable, expedient?" The ethical philosophy of Socrates and Plato asked, "What is right (just, virtuous), in order that we may follow it even though it should lead us to accept the cup of hemlock?" Many have believed that the world is essentially moral and that the right is also the expedient. It was the purpose of Plato and Aristotle by logical (scientific) methods to discover what the essential nature of the world is.

Education, as it developed in Greece and Rome, followed Isocrates, emphasizing practical and political goals and the cultivation of eloquent speech both as a means and a worthy attainment. The "Training of Children," ascribed to Plutarch, follows this path and so do Tacitus, in his "Dialogue on Oratory," and Quintilian. Even Plato made concessions in the Laws. Philosophy became a study for the selected few.

As we have noticed the family of Isocrates, we may approach him also from another side through the family of Lysias, whose period extended from about 450 to 370 B.C. He lived with his brother Polemarchus and their father Cephalus, the wealthy owner of a shield factory in Piraeus, the seaport of Athens. Their home is the scene of Plato's dramatic *Republic* and every reader will always remember the smiling conversation between Socrates and the aged Cephalus that opens the dialogue.

Both families were broken up in the disorders of the closing fourth century; that of Cephalus by the Thirty Tyrants and that of Theodorus in the Peloponesian War; and their resources were stolen or dissipated. Lysias and Isocrates turned to speech-writing for a living; and some of the speeches of each are in existence. The reader must know that in the courts, as has been said, litigants had to plead their own causes; no lawyer could plead for them; but they could employ a lawyer-orator to prepare cases and pleas for them. For this service the speech writer was paid, or received a gift.

Isocrates had a physical defect that kept him from the platform, but for about a decade he wrote speeches for others, an occupation that he despised. A few years after 400 B.C., he opened what became a highly successful school. Report said that he had one hundred students—not at any one time as some have supposed but in all—and some of them came to be persons of importance. Some of his students remained under his tuition for several years. His teaching was largely tutorial; this was true of Plato's Academy; it was even true of the elementary schools of ancient Athens and Rome. With time the Roman schools became larger, and Quintilian even argued that the young student of oratory needed an audience to give drive and fire to his speaking. Otherwise it would tend to be a mere recitation.

A few of the writings of Isocrates are political speeches such as the *Philippics* and *Areopagitica*, a title used also in modern times; but most, whatever the title, are essays, exhortations, encomia, or works on education and instructions to students of rhetoric and oratory. We shall deal briefly with the latter kind. One of these was called *Against the Sophists*. Evidently it was a matter of concern to Isocrates to dissociate himself from all irresponsible traveling teachers who claimed, for large fees, to perform much more than they were able to perform. Plato shows this same concern; and Aristophanes, in *The Clouds*, unjustly ridicules Socrates as a Sophist. They were a plague in early Greek education but also a stimulant.

Isocrates in his oration against the Sophists said they had become so impudent as to claim that they could make a youth rich and happy and they promised to do this for a moderate sum; but, he added, if they offered to sell other great possessions at prices far below their value, they would have to admit that they were insane. On the next page, he said, in the same vein, that it cannot be less than absurd that those who claim to teach virtue and temperance as an art afraid to trust their own disciples. He draws a line between what can and what cannot be taught to anyone of ordinary mind. Subjects such as rhetoric, grammar, or arithmetic can be acquired up to a certain level by all, but oratory and virtue only by those who have sufficient genius and originality.

The *Antidosis*, or *On the Exchange of Estates*, is a defence by Isocrates of his own claims and practice. It was written when he was eighty-two years old and shows, incidentally, that he had recouped his fortune. It also shows directly that be was classified with the Sophists and the writers of law speeches. He reports, correctly, that he was engaged in Pan-Hellenic politics; that is, in an effort to unite all the Greeks by inciting them to attack the Persian Empire. But the book ends as one should expect in a defence of rhetorical education as the glory of Athens. His pupils included some famous names, including the Greek historians Epirus and Theopompus, who are considered in J. B. Bury's *The Greek Historians*.

SOCRATES AND PLATO

Socrates (469–399 B.C.) was, according to Aristotle, the founder of ethics; but on those foundations Aristotle erected a solid and lofty building. Socrates was doubtless stimulated by the Sophists but differed from them in important ways. He was an Athenian; he did not travel or exhibit his virtuosity for pay; and he made a serious effort to improve himself and fellow Athenians. For his contributions to ethics and to education he might be treated with the creators of grammar, rhetoric, and logic; but his close association with Plato and Plato's with Aristotle make a triad of uniquely original and constructive thinkers.

Socrates, dissatisfied with the opinions of the Sophists, demanded truth. Using his razor-sharp dialectical method, he reduced them to silence and a desire to learn. This is the meaning of the Socratic Irony.

It was also the relativism of the Sophists that led him to the second step: definition. Morality, he saw, required knowledge that had to be accepted by all and he found it in the concept or idea of a generalized class defined in abstract and universal terms; the idea of man is a concept.

Socrates was himself eager to learn and in this set an example to the proud, who offered an uncertain doctrine at high prices. He was skilful in drawing out the ideas of his respondents and leading them to general ideas, concepts that helped to solve new problems. This drawing out of meanings and applications is the maieutic method. We should notice that the noun *concept* comes from the verb "to conceive," meaning "to become pregnant with." This makes the use of maieutic, or midwifery, appropriate for the third step. Socrates serves as the midwife; the pupil gives birth to new ideas.

The three steps were a contribution to educational theory. We do not know whether they were designed by Socrates or by Plato, but they are usually ascribed to the older man. In Socrates' latter years Athens was passing through a revolutionary period when the foundations of government were quaking. He was accused of impiety and of having a bad influence on the young. In 399 B.C. he was executed by the city he had served. His greatest pupil, Plato, continued his work.

Plato erected an imposing edifice of educational theory. His teachings are found in his famous dialogues, especially the *Laws, Protagoras, Symposium,* and *Phaedrus,* and in the *Republic,* from every standpoint his most important work. He was one of the most original and comprehensive thinkers of all time. His views on education were influenced by Socrates, by the Sophists, by Spartan practice, and by current political conditions in Athens.

We shall offer only a brief and simplified account of Plato's theory of education as found in the *Republic*. In that work Plato accepted some of the main outlines of the education and practice of Athens but offered criticism also. The poets, he said, had misrepresented the gods as quarreling among themselves, as changing their minds, and as often doing evil deeds. God must be represented, said Plato, as perfect, unchanging, and never doing evil. The heroes must be depicted as truly heroic and, therefore, as proper models for the youth. Homer must be expurgated before being used in the schools. Music and gymnastic, likewise, were to be simplified and purified in order that they might be fitted to lead the boy or girl to become temperate, courageous, healthy, and devoted to the state. Women were to have the same education and opportunities as men and to perform the same services to the state.

Plato proposed to extend the educational system to include a series of mathematical studies: arithmetic, geometry, astronomy, music, and finally logic, or the science of thinking and of final truth. He recognized the practical values of such studies, but his main purpose was to teach the meaning and the method of attaining truth as distinct from mere opinion.

In addition to its educational function the school had also a selective function. Pupils were to be sent to school only as long as they received real benefit from the instruction. Plato thought many pupils would be dismissed early in the course because they lacked the capacity for advanced study. He considered that only a few were able to profit from the study of logic or advanced mathematics. His scheme of selection was fairly complex and was applied in a series of stages that were intended to select gradually but more and more closely the most able from the less gifted. His criteria were such as the following: love of knowledge, ability to learn, strength and skill, self-control, devotion to the public good, aptness to resist evil and deceit, and capacity for abstract thinking. Those who passed the successive tests and reached the highest levels of wisdom and devotion to the state were to rule the state. The government was, therefore, to be based on knowledge of principles and truth. Not power or propaganda, but science and philosophy were to control. The philosopher was to be king.

The same scheme that selected the rulers also separated out, first, the working classes and, secondly, the soldiers or defenders of the state. Thus there were to be three classes of citizens: The lowest were the producers of food, clothing, and shelter—the merchants, the bankers, and all those who provided the economic resources of the state. These, he thought, were moved mainly by desires and appetites and they were to be controlled by those wiser than themselves. The middle class was composed of soldiers who were to be men of honor and courage. The thinkers or philosophers formed the highest and ruling class. This social scheme was paired with a psychological scheme to which it was parallel and on which it depended. Each person, said Plato, is composed of three kinds of elements: appetite, spirit, and reason; and these seek, in the same order, wealth, honor, and wisdom. One is a just or righteous person in whom reason rules the body and the appetites; and that is a just state in which the most completely rational, the wise, rule, the soldiers fight, and the workers labor. The state is an individual "writ large." The problem of the *Republic* is the problem of justice or righteousness. Plato's justice, therefore, is a harmony in which all qualities and all individuals are in their proper places performing their proper functions. To repeat it in more general form, that is a just state or society in which each individual is in the place for which his nature and capacity fit him, doing those things and only those that he can do best.

For Plato the state was "the Great Society," the highest ethical community, which alone made the good life of the individual possible. To the state, therefore, the individual owed a natural loyalty and obedience. Plato's educational scheme was throughout a social, not an individualistic, scheme. This is also true of Greek educational theory as a whole. His ideal state was to have power over the political, economic, domestic, and cultural life of its citizens; and he concerned himself a great deal with the upper classes in all those relations and not with the lower classes. The laboring and industrial groups were considered mainly as means.

Plato feared change because it seemed, and in his day tended to be, destructive, not constructively progressive. He feared ambition, individualism, and egoism, because they destroyed the needed unity of society. The state was to control and regulate property, children, and the family. All selfishness that might stem from family interests or the pursuit of wealth and power were to be suppressed by a firmly established communism. Loyalty to the state was to be the highest loyalty and education the state's highest function.

The educational system of the *Republic* is an intellectualist scheme based on knowledge and understanding. Virtue is the result of intelligence. This leaves little room for poetry and art, and in his more ascetic moods Plato would have suppressed both. The *Republic* is itself, however, a great work of art as well as of thought, and it has influenced many of the world's philosophers and its political and educational thinkers.

ARISTOTLE

Although Plato's pupil, and duly respectful of his master's views, Aristotle was a man of independent and original mind. He was devoted to a wide range of subjects including the natural and especially the life sciences. His views on education are expounded in an ethicopolitical work that has been divided into two dealing, respectively, with ethics and politics. In colleges, the *Ethics* is read in courses on philosophy and the *Politics* by students of government or political science. For Aristotle they dealt with one subject—namely, the good life for man as an individual who is a member of a society and a citizen of a state.

According to the *Ethics* the human end, the complete satisfaction of life for man, is happiness (not pleasure); for it is always chosen for itself alone and never on account of something else. By contrast, honor, pleasure, or intellect are given as examples of good things valued for themselves and also for something else. Happiness is an energy, not merely a passive state, and it presupposes virtue, prudence, wisdom, and other characteristics. Happiness is not wholly independent of more physical and worldly factors, such as health and wealth. Happiness is to be acquired through learning, habit, and exercise, and "if anything is a divine gift" we must believe that happiness is a gift of God.

Virtues, which are essential to happiness, are usually means between extremes. For example, courage is a mean between fear and rashness; liberality, between prodigality and stinginess, and so forth.

Aristotle emphasizes the importance of early education for the attainment of happiness. This account of the *Ethics* is a mere introduction. The student should study the book.

The views of Plato and Aristotle are adapted to an aristocratic society. Athens was a democracy, but it was ruled not by the many poor who had to work for a living but by the few who had the time and brains to devise plans and the eloquence to promote them. This should not seem strange to those who have seen a political boss use for his own purposes the laws passed to make him "honest."

The educational views of Plato and Aristotle are in harmony with this kind of political democracy and social aristocracy. To understand them we must rid ourselves of all notions of vocational education. It was Aristotle who applied *liberal* or "for free men" to the kind of education that interested him. To work for pay was considered demeaning; to accept a fee was degrading. Only those who had money or who, like Socrates, were able to live without it, were thought likely to be devoted to virtue or to be fit for education.

In the final chapter of his *Ethics* (Book X, Chap. IX), Aristotle provided a transition to the *Politics*. This chapter is given to education for, Aristotle said, it is not enough to know the theory of virtue but we must also endeavor to practice it. He did not believe that the masses could be led to practice virtue; only young men of liberal minds would make the effort to develop a generous character, truly fond of what is honorable and eager in pursuit of virtue. Only those of the better sort should be given the best education, an education that must be regulated by law and provided by the state. We turn now to his major treatment of public education.

In dealing directly with the subject of education, Aristotle in the *Politics* is much concerned with the use of schooling in support of the constitution. The *polis* or state, he says, is composed of many members; and education is the means of making it into a community, developing its unity. Elsewhere he wrote that education should be in the spirit of the constitution, producing a democratic spirit in a democracy and an oligarchic temper in an oligarchy. This emphasis on education as a method in support of the government is a reflection of the instability of the governments of the Greek states. In stable governments today, as in the United States, it is just assumed that that the educational system will support democratic government, but after the American Revolution, the Fathers were much concerned to have education support the new Constitution.

To assure the support of the constitution by education, and not for that reason only, Aristotle has the legislature to plan and regulate education. The education of the young is to be the legislature's chief concern, for moral as well as for political reasons. Men must be trained and must develop good habits if they are to develop character and become virtuous.

Sparta is to be praised for her education of citizens for the state, but Sparta's policy was too largely only a war policy. Recent writers, said Aristotle, have praised Sparta for this, but it is a view that can be easily refuted by argument and has now been refuted by the evidence of fact. Today the Spartans have lost their empire. They were not happy when they were powerful and now they lack the preparation to become a cultivated and rational people.

Before there was any science of eugenics, Aristotle offered some advice in matters of marriage and the procreation of children. He was able to give reasonable advice on the care of infants and children before they attained the age of seven. He wrote on their food, exercise, the toughening process by exposure to cold, games, and a careful watch over the tales and incidents presented. Very little of their time was to be passed in the company of slaves. They were to see and hear nothing vulgar, and this applied also to pictures and plays. These and comparable matters were fit subjects even for legislation. Aristotle was not wholly original in these observations and cautions; and Locke and others were less so because they read Aristotle.

Schoolwork began at seven and was to be regulated by law. There was to be a common system of state education: one system, not two as Plato proposed. All subjects were to be liberal, that is, suitable for free men, meaning men who did not need to work for their daily bread. He considered five subjects: reading, writing, drawing, music, and physical training. Both music and drawing were to be taught for use in the cultivation of leisurely arts. By leisure, Aristotle meant what moderns mean by liberal studies, those that cultivate the higher gifts in contrast with occupational or recreational activities.

The last and incomplete section of the eighth "book" of the *Politics* deals with the study of music—the study of the lyre and the voice. "Flute-playing has nothing to do with the mind"; this may reflect an old prejudice. Music is also valuable as a means of relieving the passions. This is the doctrine of katharsis, which has been overexploited by some moderns. The *Politics* ends in the middle of a paragraph.

The three philosophers beginning with Socrates regarded virtue as the great aim of life. Their theory of education is, therefore, based on a theory of life. Now virtue is a condition of the person or soul and the aim of life can be attained only through education. All of them considered the aims and means of education, but Aristotle most systematically. Modern thinkers and democrats, most of all, reject his division of people into upper and lower classes, an idea that he took from Plato and from Greek practice. Among moderns, Nietzsche is an important but not the only exception to the view that all can and should be educated.

Another comparison of the group will be necessary: Socrates wrote nothing; Plato, a series of artistic, semipoetic dialogues in which his idealist philosophy is suggested and evolved rather than stated; and Aristotle, a long row of specialized textbooks. These include several works on logic, a subject on which others had written but of which he was the true founder; on physics; on metaphysics; on the history of animals, a remarkable biological work based on observation; on psychology; on ethics and politics, which we have reviewed too briefly; on rhetoric; on poetry; and on other topics. The point is that Aristotle was the crowning head and end of a long line of Greek philosophers, beginning with Thales of Miletus in the sixth century

B.C. Henceforth knowledge was to become more and more highly specialized and knowledge rather than virtue tended to become the aim of education.

With Aristotle the Hellenic or classical age of Greece came to an end; it was followed by a diluted form of Hellenic culture called Hellenistic. Alexander the Great (356–323 B.C.), Aristotle's pupil, carried Greek power and ideas over the Near East and on to the borders of India. The city of Alexandria, on the Egyptian shores of the Mediterranean, founded by the great conqueror, with its library and museum, became the Hellenistic capital of the learned world. Greeks, Egyptians, Jews and Christians, Euclid, Ptolemy, the seventy translators of the Septuagint Old Testament (the Hebrew Bible), Eusebius and Origen, and others studied and taught there.

Euclid worked in Alexandria in about 290 B.C. His system of geometry became a schoolbook and remained for two thousand years the standard textbook in its field, and it is still the chief source of high school geometry; but newer methods are now in the process of superseding it. Archimedes worked in Alexandria for a time; and there Hero (c. 100 B.C.) showed that a reflected ray of light follows the shortest possible path. At Alexandria, Claudius Ptolemy, in the second century A.D., put Greek knowledge of geography and astronomy into the scientific form that served the world until Copernicus.

In a history of Western education we need not cover the Hellenistic period in the East. We shall return to the Greek influence on Roman education and learning. We shall see that the Romans were highly selective in their reception of Greek learning and culture and this raises an interesting question: Were the Romans and the Greeks different in nature or different by reason of different conditioning?

SUMMARY

The land and their neighbors had great influence on the development of the life and education of the Greeks. The borrowed alphabet that they improved and transmitted to the West was one of their most valuable gifts to the world.

Sparta and Athens with their contrasting systems became the leaders of the two types of education among the Greeks. Sparta was conservative and used a system of education, without schools, to prevent change. The economy, politics, and all customs were applied to the training of the young, so that education and war were the only public activities of the people. Education kept the three classes of the nation—the Spartans, the workers, and the slaves—intact and separate. The training that applied to boys and girls was physical, military, and moral. They succeeded in their desire to prevent change and incidentally gave Plato the central idea of his great educational romance, a story completely lacking in individual characters.

Athens also had three classes—the educated and wealthy, the workers, and the slaves. We should actually consider a fourth class, the noncitizens or foreigners who lived in Attica, especially in the busy seaport of Piraeus. Athens, or Attica, was a busy agricultural, industrial, commercial, and seafaring country, democratic and progressive. Her schools were literary, musical, and gymnastic. The democracy of Athens was a major reason for her development of literature, philosophy, art, architecture, and a freedom of spirit that are great by world standards today.

The Periclean Age, including the two centuries from 500 to 300 B.C., was one of the great periods of intellectual history. This was the period of Socrates, Isocrates, Plato, Aristotle, and many lesser but yet great thinkers. Basic educational studies—grammar, rhetoric, and logic—were organized. Plato saw the usefulness of mathematics to a conservative philosophy. Isocrates developed the theory and practice of public speaking; and the war between oratory and philosophy in education followed. It will not be necessary to repeat the summary of the *Republic*, which is given in the text. Aristotle's *Ethics* and *Politics* are contributions to educational theory that retain great value today.

QUESTIONS

1. Consider the following statement: We must necessarily fail in any attempt to explain Greek achievement on the basis of race, geography, or the influence of previous civilizations. True, partly true, or wholly false? Why do we consider the factors named and similar ones?
2. Do Spartan conditions help to explain Spartan education?
3. The ancient Spartan ideals and practices affected later education. Is the modern Spartanism in certain countries likely to affect education in other countries?
4. Distinguish between "formal education" in the sense in which this phrase is used on page 15, formalized education, and formative education.
5. Compare ancient Greek education with the educational provision of an American city or school district, considering the pupils and classes of people, the curriculum, the methods, the equipment, the purposes, and any other features.
6. Why did the Sophists lay great stress on argumentation and oratory?
7. Why did the Athenian schools give little attention to informational subjects?
8. Why is the Socratic method inappropriate in the teaching of botany?

9. If the goals of Isocrates and Plato can be harmonized, show how. If not, which do you accept and why?
10. Compare and distinguish between the politics and education of Plato's *Republic* and those of modern totalitarian states.

NOTES AND SOURCES

A book that must have done much to fulfil its announced purpose—namely, "to enlist recruits" for the study of its subject—is the following small volume: T. R. Glover, *The Ancient World, A Beginning*, Cambridge University Press, 1935, 388 pp. It provides a minimum of background for the history of education in the classical ages.

The Homeric poems and all later literature by Greek, and some Latin, writers are sources for Greek life and education. See the Loeb Classical Library, New York, G. P. Putnam. Paul Monroe's *Source Book of the History of Education for the Greek and Roman Period* (New York, The Macmillan Company, 1901) has useful selections from many important works.

New discoveries in early Greek history have been accumulating, especially in the present century. Some of the recent ones may be studied in *Archaeology* (paperback, W-851) edited by Samuel Rapport and Helen Wright (Washington Square Press, New York University, 1964). On the decipherment of the Minoan script, see the section on "The Aegean." On an early cataclysm in Greece, see Rhys Carpenter, *Discontinuity in Greek Civilization*, Cambridge University Press, 1966, 80 pp.; and John Lear, "The Volcano that Shaped the Western World," *Saturday Review*, November 5, 1966; and "Reply" by Elliott Roberts, same magazine for February 4, 1967.

A new history of education in ancient Greece and Rome is by Henri I. Marrou, Professor of Early Christian History at the Sorbonne, Paris. It appeared first in 1948. The third edition, translated into English by George Lamb under the title *A History of Education in Antiquity* (New York, The New American Library) is in paperback, Mentor 552. Antiquity here means classical antiquity, and Greece receives nearly three times as much space as Rome. Mesopotamia, Egypt, and the Hebrews are not treated. There are two chapters on early Christian and early medieval schools. The author has read the sources, the commentaries, and the histories of his chosen areas.

BLOCH, RAYMOND, "The Origins of the Olympic Games," *Scientific American*, 219:78–85 (August, 1968).

BURNET, JOHN, *Aristotle on Education*, fifth edition, Cambridge, Mass., Harvard University Press, 1928, 141 pp.

FORBES, CLARENCE A., *Greek Physical Education*, New York, Century Company, 1929, 300 pp.

GARDINER, E. NORMAN, *Athletics of the Ancient World*, London, Oxford University Press, 1930, 246 pp. A detailed treatment by the author of *Greek Athletic Sports and Festivals* (1910).

HATCH, EDWIN, *The Influence of Greek Ideas and Usages Upon the Christian Church*, London, William and Norgate, 1914, 359 pp.

Jaeger, Werner, *Paideia, The Ideals of Greek Culture*, New York, Oxford University Press, 1939–1944, 3 vols.

Kenyon, Frederic G., *Books and Readers in Ancient Greece and Rome*, New York, Oxford University Press, 1932, 136 pp. "Two Greek School Tablets," *Journal of Hellenic Studies*, 29:29–40 (1909).

Klein, Anita E., *Child Life in Greek Art*, New York, Columbia University Press, 1932, 62 pp.

Nettleship, Richard L., *Lectures on the Republic of Plato*, London, Macmillan Company, Ltd., 1936, 364 pp. A useful interpretation of Plato's *Republic*.

Sidgwick, Henry, "The Sophists," *Journal of Philosophy*, Cambridge, England, 4 (1872–1873): 288–307.

Van Hook, LaRue, *Greek Life and Thought*, New York, Columbia University Press, 1923, 329 pp.

Woody, Thomas, *Philostratus: Concerning Gymnastics*, Ann Arbor, Michigan, American Physical Education Association, 1936, 30 pp. The text of a Greek sophist's literary essay on athletic training and competition. And more valuable is the same gifted author's *Life and Education in Early Societies*, New York, The Macmillan Company, 1949, illustrated, 825 pp.

Chapter 3

ROMAN PRACTICE AND THEORY

Greece and Rome after long-continued hostility were united by the power of the Roman sword and sovereignty. We note the title of the union: The Roman Empire! The two peoples were so different that, except for geniuses like the Greek Polybius and the Roman Cicero, they rarely understood each other. And yet they supplemented each other to produce Western civilization. How this happened the present and following chapters will gradually, if imperfectly, reveal.

When history began to light up the Italian political landscape the Romans were confined to a village, a fortified hill, and some farming land. They had not progressed much above barbarism. There were no schools and for some centuries there would not be any. Children received their training in the family from the parents who strove for high quality in manners and morals, and without doubt often attained it; but their success in instilling knowledge, good taste, varied interests, and even skill in reading and writing may have been much less; and such attainments were perhaps hardly desired.

In the late pre-Christian centuries, by about 250 B.C., schools were established under Greek influence and often with a Greek slave as the teacher. A body of educational theory gradually developed and the way was prepared for the formation and spread of a high-order Greco-Roman culture. It spread, first, to the countries of western Europe and thence, eventually, to both Latin and English America. So, the American boy or girl who learns to read and write is indebted, first, to ancient Sumer and, then, to ancient Greece for a skill and an alphabet that were transmitted to him by ancient Rome. History tells about matters that have lasted as well as some that have not.

PRE-ROMAN SETTLEMENTS

We must progress slowly as the Romans did. Before they could spread their own culture they had to develop and perfect it. The small and rude villages, with thatch-roofed houses or huts, of early Rome resembled those of their neighbors, the Italic tribes of Latins, Oscans, and others. Far to the north in Italy, the Gauls, aggregations of Celtic tribes were settling in the valley of the Po River. Some had come from the southern parts of what later was France; others, from the Balkans, used the Brenner Pass or came across the Adriatic Sea or along its northern coasts. Thus the mountains and valleys of Italy were thinly peopled in such a way that the settlers did not rasp much against each other. They lived by hunting, fishing, and other ways of food-gathering, such as raising cattle and some primitive farming.

Other settlers were more immediately important to the Romans. Such were the Etruscans who lived directly across the Tiber from early Rome. Who they were is not really well-known. They must have come from the East for they had made contact with the Greeks and had Greek ideas in art and decoration. They introduced a form of the Greek alphabet into Italy and to the Romans. Their language was not Latin, however, nor Greek, nor any other Indo-European speech, but it has not been deciphered. They were more numerous than the Romans and for a time controlled Rome and most of the western shore down to Campania. They were eventually conquered, in about 500 B.C. and were absorbed into the Roman state. Some of the most important Roman families came from an Etruscan ancestry and were proud of it.

Of all the peoples with whom early Rome had to deal, the Greeks had the greatest significance for them and for us, in their cultural and educational influence. A Greek colony was established in 750 B.C. at Cumae, near the site of the recently established Rome, only three years after the traditional date (753 B.C.) for the founding of the city. The Greeks had come this far up the west coast for copper, which the Etruscans controlled.

The large Greek cities were located far to the south: Tarentum; Sybaris, whose wealth and luxury suggested the word sybarite; Croton; Rhegium; Locri; and others. These were on the heel and sole of the Italian boot. Syracuse, founded in 734 B.C. by Corinthians, was the largest of several large cities in Sicily. Sardina and smaller islands had Greek settlements. Marsilia near the mouth of the Rhone River became the present Marseilles. These settlers were generally far in advance of the Romans in civilization; and centuries were to pass before the Romans became able and willing to learn what the Greeks could teach them.

The Greeks had not come as teachers but for commercial and other practical reasons. The favorable location on the coasts of southern Italy and the islands—the soil, moisture, and climate—attracted impoverished farmers and ambitious traders from overpopulated areas. And the Greek states were in the business, one can almost say, of sending out colonies. The mother cities usually hoped for support from their daughters in war and trade and often obtained it. We should note the distribution of the Greek people: East of mainland Greece they populated the islands and Asia Minor; and on the west, they spread over Italy and the islands in reverse order.

On the African coast, only a short space across the sea from the southwestern tip of Sicily, a Semitic people had planted the important city of Carthage. They had colonies in Sicily and Spain and, being a commercial power, they maintained a navy. A far-seeing traveller in the western Mediterranean in the fourth century B.C. might have predicted the triangular conflict that would develop. He might have predicted that the independent citystate organization would not be able to withstand the concentrated force of power with continental Italy to support it. Carthage also lacked nearby allies. She did have great generals, one of the greatest being Hannibal, whom Cicero and other Romans continued to hate after they no longer feared him. He taught the Romans how to fight him and this was his undoing. But he was also denied reinforcements.

THE GREEK FACTOR

Because they spoke cognate languages, we may readily believe that the Greeks and the Romans stemmed from a common ancestry. Leaving their early home at different times, they may have chosen different directions, one trail leading successive waves of migrants to the lands and islands of the Aegean Sea. These came into contact with the more civilized people of the Fertile Crescent and Egypt. These new surroundings would stimulate the growth of new ideas, arts, and skills. All three—ideas, arts, and skills— were involved whenever they met strange races, and in the process the Greeks learned to write. Writings in an early form of Greek have been found in Crete and on the Greek mainland that may go back to 1400 B.C. and further. Civilization, coming from the ancient East and Egypt, made a long leap forward when it reached the impressionable people who came to be known as Hellenes or Greeks.

The ancient Indo-European nest, from which the future Greeks had departed, gave out, perhaps at a much later time, another swarm that chose a more westerly course leading them to the narrow plains and mountains of a still savage or barbarous Italy. These became the Romans. It is not necessary to suppose that the "original nature" of the two peoples was the same. Certainly from the earliest historical times the Romans were more grave, austere, resolute, and practical than the Greeks; they were organizers and administrators. One finds it difficult to believe that these traits were entirely acquired; they must have been part of that original nature of which psychologists speak.

Greek influence, it has been said, without proof or even evidence, must have been active in Rome from the first. It may be true. Greek cities in Italy were about as old as Rome; and Greek traders may have sailed up the Tiber with woolen stuffs to exchange for wheat or copper. We know that the Etruscans brought the Greek alphabet, but not when; and we should doubt that a great many Romans learned to write in Etruscan times. It was not until 450 B.C. that the laws of the Twelve Tables were set up in the capital; and this is evidence of, at least, a small literate public. Several examples of wax tablets survive, tablets that have Etruscan forms of the Greek alphabet across the top for boys to copy on the waxed space below.

In the third century B.C., the names of teachers who knew both languages began to appear. In 272 B.C., Livius Andronicus was brought as a slave from Tarentum to Rome. Obtaining his freedom, he became a teacher and translated the *Odyssey* into Latin. It became and long remained a schoolbook. Other Latin poems helped in supplementing the Twelve Tables. Other slaves were brought in as teachers. Even Cato, who was hostile to most Greek ways and ideas, brought a Greek slave, the poet Chilon, from Sardinia in 204 B.C. He would not let him teach his son but rented him out as a teacher to less wary families. A third bilingual teacher of the third centry was the Italian, Ennius, who had received a Greek education and wrote his *Annals* and also poems for the schools. By the time of his death in 178 B.C., the teaching of Greek in Rome had lost its novelty without gaining universal acceptance. We are speaking of the educated class, for there must have been large numbers with little schooling even in the native language. That there was formal opposition to the teaching of Greek is shown by the Senate's decree in 161 B.C. to expel all teachers of Greek and all philosophers. This and other decrees, in 173 and 154 B.C., were not effective; to stop the penetration by Greek thought and manners was beyond the power of the conservatives.

Only two years after the decree of 161 B.C., an accident kept a learned Greek in Rome while his broken leg was healing. This was Crates of Mallos who had come on political business with an embassy; but being detained, he gave a series of lectures on Greek literature. Crates, a distinguished scholar, was without doubt solicited by Romans to give the lectures. That there was an audience with sufficient interest in Greek literature and knowledge of the language to understand the lecturer proves that great intellectual changes were taking place in Rome.

EARLY ROMAN INSTRUCTION

We shall not spend time on Plutarch's report on the education of Romulus and Remus, which he told as gossip merely; or on the story of the abduction of Virginia, an adolescent girl, on the way home from school, as retold in Macaulay's verses. Young women did not attend school in early Rome and neither of those accounts is credible. If a child was formally taught anywhere in early Rome, it was in the home and usually by the father and mother. When public office, high rank, or wealth made this inconvenient, teachers were brought into the home; examples can be found to support this, but the literature is not rich in cases and particulars. The Romans did not think highly of elementary teachers or teaching.

The Roman father's autocratic power, the *patria potestas*, included power over the child's life and destiny. It must have led many times to intolerable abuses and conflicts; and it was no doubt a remnant of savagery that had not been left behind. Even Roman legal authorities were somewhat shocked by it. Gaius, the famous legal scholar, said, "The right of dominion which we have over our children is peculiar to the citizens of Rome, nor is there any race of men who have a dominion similar to ours." But this is only an opinion, for we do not know what customs may have been accepted and followed by all the savage peoples of the early world. Also, largely unknown is the extent to which civilized Romans used their "right of dominion." Most certain is the tendency of such absolute power to hinder any loosening of restrictions over the young, any sowing of the seed of freedom. To continue the exercise of absolute power over grown boys and young men must have had a hardening influence on the father. As we shall see subsequently in the case of Cato, some of these stubborn Romans would do everything for their sons except loosen the parental harness.

Education in ancient Rome was practical; and, as elsewhere among the early-culture peoples, it was carried on in the family. The people, or some of them, must have been able to read in the time of Appius Claudius (450 B.C.) because at that time the laws of the Twelve Tables were set up in the forum for their instruction. Boys were required to memorize the text of the Laws. This does not prove that there were no schools. It is a great mistake to suppose that all people must be illiterate where there are no schools, although doubtless many will be illiterate or only slightly literate under such conditions. And it would be a greater mistake to suppose that literacy was the only or the main objective of early education at Rome or elsewhere. Obedience to law and custom and the maintenance of religion and morals were the main objectives of early education. But when schools were established, and sometimes before, attention was directed to the teaching of reading and writing and of arithmetic, all of which were usually taught for practical use.

Whether education was conducted in the family, as in very early times, or in the family and the school, as in later times, what the Romans most cared about was that the children acquire and embody the moral and social virtues. Such virtues were piety, which meant love of country, and justice, truthfulness, and *gravitas*. The family in Rome had a much larger place in life, greater unity and purity, and greater influence than in Greece and the East. The mother, although she had no part in public affairs, was held in esteem, contributed to the family councils, and deeply affected the tone of society. Rome produced such high-minded matrons as Cornelia, the mother of Tiberius and Gaius Groechus, leaders in the struggle for social justice. Their failure and murder revealed large rifts in the constitution of the Republic. Their mother, who called them her "jewels" was only one of many notable Roman women. Quintilian names others. Their education may not have gone beyond the primary grades and certainly did not reach the advanced classes. In early times there was a prejudice against oratory as a study even for men.

Small boys were taught simple habits and family custom and manners by the mother. Other kinds of practical education were taken up by the father where the mother left off. The boy was present when the father conducted the family religious rites. He went with his father into the fields and gained skill with the hoe and reaping hook and in all the activities of the farm. Boys of different social classes learned different skills. An upper-class boy saw his father deal out justice among his clients and conduct business affairs; he learned about politics and parties in visits to the forum. The tradition of learning by observation and participation rather than in school from books was deeply rooted and continued for a long time. Cicero and Tacitus both insisted that both citizenship and public speaking must be learned by practice. Books and schools alone, they held, will not be effective but they did not neglect the books.

An example of family instruction is given in the biography of Marcus Cato (234–149 B.C.), a senator and consul, noted for his devotion to Roman laws and traditions. Plutarch reported that

> . . . as soon as his son was able to learn, Cato took him personally in charge and taught him his letters, although he had an accomplished slave named Chilon who was a schoolmaster and gave lessons to many boys. But Cato, to use his own words, would not have a slave abuse his son nor perhaps pull his ears for being slow at his lessons; nor would he have his boy owe a slave so precious a gift as learning. So he became himself the boy's guide in letters just as he taught him the laws of Rome and bodily exercises; not merely to throw the javelin, to fight in Armor or to ride but also to use his fists in boxing, to bear heat and cold and to swim against the currents and eddies of a river.

This means that Cato taught his boy to read Latin, for he knew no Greek and was opposed to its use. The exercises were obviously military, not athletic, exercises. The scene is laid in the second half of the third century, almost exactly two centuries after that tablet with the Twelve Tables of the Roman law was set up, according to tradition, by Appius Claudius. Schools to teach Latin may have been set up in that period. There were no legal requirements. Anyone could open a school, without permit, certificate, examination, or inspection, and without a building.

Before 300 B.C. the Romans lacked many useful things: coined money, timepieces, butter, and sugar; but they had honey, "Heaven's gift" as Virgil says, for the bees brought it "from the skies." And they had what was more important: roads to bind the Roman world together and the Roman law to make them one people, indissoluble for a thousand years.

GRECO-ROMAN EDUCATION

Greek and Roman school laws and public regulations were not numerous and were not always strictly enforced. Of the latter statement the decrees listed here are ready examples. Of the steps toward the Hellenization of Rome there is no precise record, but we are certain that they were not planned and outlined from the beginning but that they evolved without much notice. The Roman school was in part borrowed from the Greek system (which was several centuries older) and is, therefore, called Greco-Roman. As we have shown there was contact between the two civilizations almost from the beginning of Rome and the ultimate debt to Greece was quite large.

There was no strict system of education in either country but in time Rome developed clearer outlines and stages than the Greeks. Family education, with or without educated slaves or hired tutors to give the instruction, was one practice that tended to hinder the rise of a system. The problem continued so that Quintilian, at the end of the first century A.D., argued against it. There were no set ages when schooling was to begin and end, only vague custom, and there were no examinations and no graduation. The three stages or schools were the *ludus*, a word meaning play; the grammar school; and the rhetoric school. The stages were clearly marked at Rome but the course and years were not.

The *ludus* accepted the child at about the age of seven, but the ancients, Greek and Roman, were not agreed on this. Some would have had school begin as early as our Headstart, but they had no suitable program for young children. The teachers lacked the genius of Caesar or Cicero and began woodenly, as we think, to teach the names of the letters before showing the letters themselves; next the child had to recognize each letter and attach the name to it; then came syllables, words, and reading from manuscripts written in capital letters and without spaces between the words. Counting and the irregular notation in arithmetic presented other occasions for blows and tears. The discipline was physical and harsh. In both Rome and rural Italy there must have been many illiterate people and many places without schools. We must not in imagination transplant modern ideas and conditions to pre-Christian times.

The grammar school took the boy at about the age of twelve and kept him for three or four years on reading, writing, the poets, and arithmetic, sometimes including the study of rhetoric and public speaking. Quintilian, protesting, said this ". . . is eminently ridiculous, a youth seems unfit to

Roman school. Relief from tomb at Neumagen. (Courtesy of the Bettman Archive.)

be sent to the teacher of declamation until he already knows how to declaim" (*Institutes*, II, 1, 3). Of the rhetoric school there is a full account in Quintilian's *Institutes*. The rhetoric school required several years to teach the varied knowledge of history, literature, government, philosophy, science, and other subjects with which the orator was to be familiar and to give the needed practice in public speaking.

Both the Greeks and the Romans promoted the kind of education that modern Western nations call liberal as in the "liberal arts." They differed in their emphases. Greece stressed athletics and gymnastics; and Rome, military training, as Cato showed. The Greeks cultivated music, dancing, and the arts. Cicero said, "Nobody dances unless he is tipsy." Virgil lists the skills of the two peoples in the sixth book of his *Aeneid*. He said "others," that is the Greeks, would carve statues, win cases in the courts, and "with pointed wand" would trace the courses of the stars; but the Romans would "with sovereign sway rule the nations." These ideals fit together neatly. These are the fine and liberal arts and the political arts that remained the educational ideals of the West until the nineteenth century. But then agriculture, engineering, technology, the physical, biological, and now the behavioral sciences began to subordinate or crowd out the liberal arts.

CICERO AS HISTORIAN OF EDUCATION

Cicero's self-esteem led him to tell about his early studies, beginning many paragraphs with: "As a boy," "In my youth," or "When I was young." It may have been the same feeling that led him also to write the history of his profession in Rome, the profession of public speaking, which played a great part in politics and government. In one of his historical and biographical works, the *De Oratore*, he has a short history of higher or oratorical education; and in another, the *Brutus*, he calls the roll of the great orators and tells of his own education and career.

For a long period, Rome tried to keep out Greek ideas and customs just as every nation prefers its own laws and teaching to foreign substitutes; but after Greece had gradually made great inroads, especially among the higher classes, the foreign language and culture became a status symbol, that for certain purposes, was preferred to Latin.

Under these circumstances, young Cicero in a letter to a friend wrote about his youth to say, "When I was a boy, I remember that a certain Plotius [Gallus] was the first to teach rhetoric in Latin. Everybody was crowding into his school including the best students and I was disappointed that I was not permitted to attend; but on the advice of highly educated friends, I stayed away. They declared that declamation in the Greek language was much better training." The school by L. Plotius Gallus was opened in 93 B.C., when Cicero was thirteen years old. Later Cicero became a strong Grecian and even went to Greece in early manhood to complete his education.

The censors closed the Plotius school within a year, strangely declaring that it was against the established custom of the Roman people. One would think that it would be the most indigenous practice in the world for a Latin people to have Latin schools; but the censors had a reason for their action. They wanted to limit training in oratory to the aristocracy and they considered that by requiring the study of a foreign language, this longer course would become too expensive for the poor. The Latin rhetoric school soon returned in spite of the censors. Quintilian, as we shall see, although he favored the study of Greek, taught a Latin school.

In his boyhood instead of going to school—although according to Plutarch he also attended school for a time—Cicero practiced at home under private teachers, writing and declaiming his own speeches daily in both languages. Later in life as he looked back on his career, Cicero tended to undervalue these early studies. He said in *De Oratore* (III, xx),

> Having been educated in my boyhood with great care by my father and having brought into the forum such a portion of talent as I am conscious of possessing and not as much as others may think, I cannot say that I learned everything as it ought to be learned, for I engaged in public business most early of all men, and [he is speaking of the defence of Roscius] at one-and-twenty years brought to trial a man of the highest rank and the greatest eloquence, and the forum has been my school and practice with the laws and institutions of the Roman people, and the customs of our ancestors, my instructors.

He continued to speak of what he learned in his various offices and at Athens where he admitted he should have studied longer. We may incidentally correct Cicero, as Tacitus in his *Dialogue* shows Cicero did not engage in public business "most early of all men."

Many Romans, as we know, were very critical of the Greeks, not unlike the French attitude toward the Germans; but Cicero frequently acknowledged his debt to Hellas. When, in his youth, he came back from his study tour he was jubilant. His voice had been brought under control, his language moderated, and his health restored. Besides, he had learned a great deal. In his latter years he went to the Greeks for subjects and some ideas for his books on friendship, old age, and other topics. He remained a thorough Roman, but he acknowledged his debt to the older and more sensitive civilization. How fully Roman he was, how much he loved his homeland, is shown here in a further passage on the Twelve Tables in *De Oratore* (I, xliv).

He said,

> Though all the world exclaim against me, I will say what I think: that single little book of the Twelve Tables, if anyone look to the fountains and sources of laws, seems to me assuredly, to surpass the libraries of all the philosophers, both in weight of authority, and in plenitude of ability. And if our country has our love, as it ought to have in the highest degree,—our country, I say, of which the force and natural attraction is so strong, that one of the wisest of mankind (Odysseus) preferred his Ithaca, fixed, like a little nest, among the roughest of rocks, to immortality itself—with what affection ought we to be warmed towards such a country as ours which, preeminently above all other countries, is the seat of virtue, empire, and dignity?

Cicero was always a Roman.

As this passage shows, Cicero was a sincere lover of his country, as he should have been, for it had given him not only family and education but also opportunity to render service and to gain high position and influence.

He was, perhaps, partly because he was a "new man," one of the people, not the aristocracy, accustomed to estimate his services too highly. He liked to think of himself as the savior of his country. Rome was in need of a savior but his battles were only skirmishes. For more than a century the Republic had been in disorder and now it was breaking up. Caesar saw this but Cicero did not. Cicero was a great lawyer, a consummate defense attorney, but as a statesman, in the circumstances as they existed, he was inadequate.

He was a great orator, one of the world's great political speakers, and we have seen him as a historian of oratory and of oratorical education. He was a great personality. When Caesar was at the height of his power, he said, "How can I help becoming disliked when a man like Cicero has to wait my convenience for an interview?"

Years after the murder of Cicero demanded by Anthony, and consented to by Octavian, the latter, now emperor, came upon a boy in the palace reading a book that he tried to hide when he was discovered. Augustus asked to see it and stood a long while reading. When he returned it he remarked, "A great man and a lover of his country." The book was by Cicero but the title was not given in the story.

Seventy years ago when boys in the classical college, after toiling over Cicero's speeches, were, in senior year, allowed to read some of his humanistic and idealistic writings, they found him a friendly human being, a man of all times, ancient and modern.

QUINTILIAN

The greatest Roman writer on education was the Spaniard, Marcus Fabius Quintilian, who lived about A.D. 35 to 95. Both dates have been questioned; and other biographical statements, excepting his own, are likewise uncertain. We have the twelve books of his *Institutes of Oratory*, completed soon after A.D. 90. Almost lost to view in the Middle Ages, the recovery of a complete copy in A.D. 1406 at St. Gall in Switzerland was a great event in the revival of learning. The most interesting parts to us today are the early books, which treat the care and teaching of small children; the critical survey of Greek and Roman literature in Book Ten; and Book Twelve, which discusses the moral character of the orator.

The *Institutes* came out more than a century after oratory had ceased to exercise any great political influence; but the word, as key words tend to do, persisted. Schools also are highly conservative institutions and continue to teach what they have been teaching. Their graduates, as we say now, did not however become orators but lawyers, administrators, and political servants of the Empire.

The main body of the *Institutes* deals with rhetoric, the science and practical use of the Latin language. This would be useful in all public affairs. We note also Quintilian's admiration for Cicero, one of the great masters of Roman speech; but he was not trying to prepare boys to repeat Cicero's work. In teaching he kept as close to the old practice as the new time would permit.

After finishing his schooling in Rome, Quintilian seems to have returned to Spain to practice and teach law and oratory, a combination of callings that is by no means unusual in Spanish America today. In A.D. 68 he returned to Rome to follow the same occupations. In the course of time, Vespasian created an imperial chair of rhetoric and installed Quintilian in it at a high annual salary. Meanwhile he also taught children of the aristocracy and the palace. He retired from such labors eventually to write his book. It may seem a little ironical that Quintilian is hardly known as an orator, politician, or statesman until we recall that by Quintilian's time these professions had become practically extinct.

The *Institutes* begins with advice to parents to have high hopes and form favorable opinions concerning the capacities of their sons. The character and speech of all who attend them, all nurses, slaves, and pedagogues must be pure. The pedagogues should be men of learning, but if they are ignorant they must not pretend to know.

He began at the beginning: The boy should speak Greek before Latin but not too long before, else his Latin speech might be affected. The boy is to speak both languages as a native. He attacked the custom of teaching the names of the letters before the letters were shown; and he proposed the use of ivory letters, such as only wealthy parents could provide. After this bit of originality he drops into the groove of old custom. After the letters came syllables, words, and sentences.

The boy was to learn to write legibly, carefully; no scribbling was to be permitted. Doubtless the letters were to be written separately as in "manuscript writing," not cursively; and the words were to be joined with the spaces no wider than those between adjoining letters. Correct pronunciation was stressed and he recommended practice with tongue-twisters. He gave no examples but we suggest a couple of English illustrations: "she sells sea shells" and "around the rugged rocks the ragged rascal ran." He advised the "rapid rolling forth" of such sentences. Reading, writing, and speaking were the basic skills for the small boy. There have been people who held that the Romans had no ideas for the improvement of primary education, but they were mistaken.

Should the boy be taught at home or sent to school? Quintilian had a firm answer. Some considered home instruction better because the boy received the entire attention of the tutor, or preferred the home because it would safeguard his morals. One of Quintilian's strongest convictions is affirmed by his answer to the second issue. He wrote,

If it were certain that schools, though advantageous to studies, are pernicious to morals, a virtuous course of life would seem to me preferable to one even of the most distinguished eloquence. But in my opinion the two are combined and inseparable, for I am convinced that no one can be an orator who is not a good man; but even if anyone could, I am unwilling that he should be.

This view, further emphasized in Book Twelve, was the view of Cato who defined an orator this way: "An orator is a good man skilled in speaking."

In the argument, Quintilian charged that the Roman homes were both luxurious and impure. Children, he said, crawl on purple before they can walk. Fancy foods tickle their palates before they can talk. We are delighted when they utter anything immodest. They see our mistresses; every room rings with impure songs. It was true; Horace had announced it in his *Satires* a century earlier; it was one of the results of the conquest of Greece that Rome was filled with thousands of domestic slaves and that concubinage had become common. We see what Quintilian's answer was but he may have been mistaken. The boy continued to live at home and the school may have been a second source of infection.

Competition among boys was considered one of the school's great advantages over solitary instruction. Quintilian recalled an example from his own schooldays. The master divided the class according to the performance of each pupil, from top to bottom. Declamations were presented in that order. Judgments were pronounced on the performance of each, "and great was the strife among us for distinction." Each pupil was assigned to his place. The headship of the class conferred the highest honor, but the end of the month gave the losers another chance to become winners. Quintilian thought this method provided the strongest incitement to strive for victory.

A good memory, a teachable disposition, and an inquiring mind were traits in pupils that Quintilian desired; above all, a good memory was desirable. And memory is a two-fold faculty: the ability to receive with ease, and the capacity to retain with fidelity. In Book Eleven, Chapter eleven, there is another much longer passage on memory. That oratorical studies are so much a matter of memory is one of the great shortcomings of those studies as a basic means of education. Cicero, in a truer opinion, said that one will never learn well what he does not learn (grasp) quickly; that is, insight is what counts.

To the use of corporal punishment, very common in Rome, Quintilian was strictly opposed. He called it a disgrace, a punishment fit only for slaves; he said that if a boy is so base that reproof will be ineffective, stripes will only harden him. He asserted that if the boy is required to do his work regularly there will be no need for the rod. Punishment seems required only because the pedagogues are negligent and do not hold the boys to their work. This study-hall type of duty seems unusual and no solution is offered.

But Quintilian asked, "After you have coerced the boy with stripes, how will you treat him when he becomes a young man?" We shall not enter into the more technical treatment of rhetoric that begins in the latter half of Book Two. In the next section we shall see that others asked, if Quintilian did not, why so much effort should be devoted to an art and a profession that had become largely useless.

TACITUS

In the decadence of the ancient world, Rome followed Athens more closely than she had in her ascent. It is always easier to follow the leader in going down than in climbing up a steep slope. Upon the demand of Anthony, Cicero was proscribed and, in 43 B.C., assassinated.

In little more than a century the historian Tacitus, in his *Dialogue on Oratory*, considered the decline of the art and explained the causes. He ascribed them in general to "the indolence of the young, the carelessness of parents, the ignorance of the teacher, and the neglect of the ancient discipline." He was most severe in his remarks on the school, which even in Cicero's time had been called "the school of impudence." He continued, "But in these days we have our youths taken to the professor's theater, the rhetoricians, as we call them . . . to schools in which it is hard to tell whether the place itself, or their fellow-scholars, or the character of their studies, do their minds most harm."

"As for the place," he continued, "there is no such thing as reverence, for no one enters it who is not as ignorant as the rest. As for the scholars, there can be no improvement, when boys and striplings with equal assurance address, and are addressed by other boys and striplings. As for the mental exercises themselves, they are the reverse of beneficial [because] subjects remote from reality are actually used for declamation [and are] dwelt upon in grand language." What an appraisal, an attack! And this was the judgment of a somewhat younger contemporary of Quintilian, a teacher who wrote of the school as he wished it to be and as, under his direction, it probably was. But Quintilian also touched on some of the same evils.

There was a basic cause for the decline of oratory and the schools of oratory—namely, the failure and death of the Republic and the erection upon its ruins of the Empire by Caesar and Augustus. Tacitus knew, and in the end he said, that, in an autocracy, issues and causes are decided not by reason, not by argument, but by power; and this is the conclusion of the *Dialogue*. This is the reason why Quintilian, although still speaking of oratory chose to transform the school into a school of rhetoric, that is, a school of language and literature.

SUMMARY

Three centuries after the "founding of the city," the Twelve Tables of the Roman law were publicly posted. This indicated the existence of an orderly society with a certain but undefined extent of literacy. The law affirmed an extraordinary degree of power by the father over his family but said nothing about the education of his children.

In the early centuries of Roman history, education was carried on chiefly in the family; and although the people remained a nation of farmer-soldiers it was vocational and military, similar to that described in Plutarch's life of the elder Cato as late as 200 B.C. If the father were literate the boy might learn to read and perhaps to write. Those who learned to read were exercised on the Twelve Tables, a difficult book. Roman elementary schools may have existed by 300 B.C. or earlier, but there is no direct knowledge of them, only inferences from later conditions.

Some Greek influence entered Rome in early times but with the conquest of Greece in 146 B.C. it became a flood. Thousands of Greek slaves, many well-educated men, were brought into Italy, one of them being Polybius, the historian. Literary, philosophical, and aesthetic Greece and conservative, organizing, administrative Rome supplemented each other. Schools became more numerous in the second century. The advanced schools for the upper classes became bilingual, as the compound Greco-Roman indicates. The government's efforts to bar Greek influence failed.

Cicero practiced speaking in both languages but at times he claimed that the law court, not home or school, was his real training ground. He, however, acknowledged his debt to Greek studies, including those carried on in Greece itself. His admiration for the Twelve Tables shows how basically Roman he always remained, but his late humanistic writings based on Greek sources reveal the other side of his interests.

Under the conditions of the Empire, education, always conservative, changed little. And yet, Quintilian, although he was no innovator, began to emphasize friendly relations between teacher and pupils, high standards of conduct, humanistic literature, and skill in the use of language rather than political oratory. His book and Cicero's *De Oratore* and the *Brutus* have value not only as sources for the history of education but also for its philosophy. Finally, Tacitus showed that political change had made the old oratorical education obsolete.

QUESTIONS

1. When "The school is life" what is taught? Read Plutarch's life of Cato the Elder; but the question may be considered broadly and in reference to modern conditions.

2. Why did the early Romans oppose the intrusion of Greek learning and culture? Why did the Roman Senate oppose the study of Latin oratory? Were the two inconsistent?
3. How did Roman and Greek education differ in spirit, content, and organization?
4. Modern nations have had many great orators and debaters: Gladstone, Lloyd George, Lincoln, Douglas, and others. Why the intensive study of oratory in Rome? Why did they continue the study in the Empire?
5. Why did Rome fail to develop great scientists?
6. How do Quintilian and Tacitus agree in their views of Roman education?
7. How may the education of girls have been affected by the emphasis on the teaching of oratory?

NOTES AND SOURCES

The *Source Book* by Monroe and the *History* by Marrou, noticed in the second chapter will be useful here. The chief Latin as well as the Greek authors are included in the Loeb Classical Series; but two titles in Bohn's Classical Library are Cicero's *De Oratore* and his *Brutus*, together with some of his letters, and all in one volume; and Quintilian's *Institutes of Oratory*, in two volumes. Both works have been translated and annotated by J. S. Watson.

Aubrey Gwynn's *Roman Education from Cicero to Quintilian*, published in 1926 by the Clarendon Press of Oxford, is now also in paperback, No. 29 of the "Classics in Education" published at New York by the Teachers College Press of Columbia University. The original bibliography of sixty volumes has been included in the reprint of this excellent book.

A stimulating volume by Jerome Carcafino on *Dairly Life in Ancient Rome, The People and City at the Height of the Empire* (New Haven, Yale University Press, 1940, 342 pp.) was edited by Professor Henry T. Rowell of the Johns Hopkins University, and was translated from the French by E. O. Lorimer. There is a useful chapter, Number V, on "Education and Religion." Many of the other chapters have valuable background materials; and for this, see the topic: "Public Readings," p. 194 ff. There is an index.

CHASE, W. J., translator and editor, *The Distichs of Cato*, University of Wisconsin Studies in the Social Sciences and History, No. 7, 1922, 43 pp.; *The Ars Minor of Donatus*, same series, No. 11, 1926, 55 pp.

CLARK, DONALD, *Rhetoric in Greco-Roman Education*, New York, Columbia University Press, 1957, 285 pp.

FOWLER, W. WARDE, *Social Life at Rome in the Age of Cicero*, New York, The Macmillan Company, 1926, 362 pp.

FRIEDLANDER, LUDWIG, *Roman Life and Manners under the Early Empire*, London, George Routledge & Sons, Ltd., 1908–1913, 4 vols.

JULLIEN, EMILE, *Les professeurs de littérature dans l'ancienne Rome, et leur enseignement depuis l'origine jusqu'à la mort d'Auguste*, Paris, Ernest Lerous, 1885, 379 pp.

MOHLER, S. L. "The Iuvenes and Roman Education," *Transactions of the American Philological Association*, 68:442–479, 1937.

ODGERS, MERLE M., "Quintilian's Rhetorical Predecessors," *Transactions of the American Philological Association* 65:25–36 (1935); "Quintilian's Use of Earlier Literature," *Classical Philology*, 28:182–188 (July, 1933).

PETERSSON, TORSTEN, *Cicero, a Biography*, Berkeley, University of California Press, 1920, 699 pp. There are many accounts of Cicero but this is a very full one.

PHARR, CLYDE, "Roman Legal Education," *Classical Journal*, 34:257–70, February, 1939.

THOMPSON, JAMES WESTFALL, *Ancient Libraries*, Berkeley, University of California Press, 1940, 120 pp.

WILKINS, A. S., *Roman Education*, New York, The Macmillan Company, 1905, 100 pp.

Part II

EDUCATION AND THE CHURCH

Chapter 4

THE EARLY MIDDLE AGES

The ten or twelve centuries between the decline of Rome and the rise and growth of modern civilization cover what we call the Middle Ages; but there was no precise year or even century when the intervening period between ancient and modern times began or ended. Beginning and ending were both unnoticed at the time because the effects of many, even great, changes cannot be estimated until after the dust settles. Indeed historical periods are only a device to aid the memory. It has been customary to set A.D. 500 to 1500 as the limits of the Middle Ages; and to this custom there cannot be any serious objection if we understand that nothing of great importance happened in those two years; that is, the middle ages without capital letters, began and ended gradually, imperceptibly.

They ended and modern times began at different times in the several departments of life. Gunpowder and firearms, two tremendous inventions, brought on modern warfare in about 1400. Movable type and paper, perhaps equally significant discoveries, were joined to produce printed books about 1450. Luther's Theses of 1517 helped to increase the dissent that had long threatened the unity of the Church and to promote Protestantism. It can be argued that modern education began, not in the Renaissance, but about 1800 when European states established public school systems; but if we must have one year to mark the end of the Middle Ages the choice may well fall on 1500 or 1600. We shall return to this point.

We should particularly notice that history deals with men, with what they do and suffer, alone and in groups, as the generations pass. In the West, as the Middle Ages were becoming modern, men came to be recognized as individuals and as persons. This was in great part a result of the new spirit moving in Christianity. It is a movement still far from its completion.

SOME MAIN TOPICS

Our list is not a table of contents. It must include Rome and Constantinople, especially Rome. There were now two religions, a divided Christianity and Islam. The barbarian invasions had a great effect on the character of the new nations they helped to form. There was a great and growing array of inventions and discoveries including the invention of the compass and the discovery of America, the use of the sea route to the Far East, and the determination of the true shape of the earth. Not least among the changes were the new forms of schools.

Whether the barbarians or the Christian Church, in their joint take-over of the Roman Empire, had the greater influence in the Middle Ages is a question. The two eventually became one as the church converted the barbarians. The birth of Christ came about in the twenty-seventh year of Augustus. Within a generation after the crucifixion, many were converted to the new faith, especially those in the cities. In Rome at least a few of the early converts were members of "Caesar's household" and Paul, landing in Italy, met "brethren" before he reached Rome. To convert the masses took a long time. In later centuries the church became a political force and through the monasteries and other institutions an educational agency.

Islam, another powerful religion, was founded in the seventh century by Mohammed (570–632). The founder had been a trader and caravan leader in Arabia and his followers are often called Arabs or Moslems, the latter word conveying the idea of surrender. Islam is monotheistic, forbidding the worship of idols; and this tenet kept Moslems from the practice of sculpture and painting. Islam prohibits the use of alcoholic beverages and insists on bodily cleanliness. Daily prayers at set times are demanded. The religion allows polygamy and includes the belief in a physical resurrection.

Mohammed accepted Moses, Christ, and others as prophets but put himself forward as The Prophet. Like many Christians and others of the time, he expected the early end of the world. Even this short sketch shows that Mohammedanism and Christianity are both developments growing out of Judaism; but whereas the *Koran* is the sacred book of the Moslems, the Christian Bible contains the Old Testament as well as the New. The hostility of the two descendants toward the parent faith and toward each other is a sad commentary on human reasonableness, a commentary much amplified by the Israeli-Arab war of 1967, which was in part a religious war.

The Moslems in the beginning soon began a career of military conquest that carried them over the Near East, across North Africa, and into Spain and France. They were stopped in 732 at the battle of Tours but held part of Spain for a long time. They were not completely dislodged until 1492, another hint that the Middle Ages were ending. The results were quite different elsewhere. Much of Africa, not merely the Mediterranean strip, is Mohammedan today. They held the Near East and the Turkish Moslems took Constantinople, the capital of the eastern Roman Empire in 1453 and swept over southeastern Europe, to the gates of Vienna. It must be said that the nations they conquered were economically and militarily weak and unable to mount a vigorous resistance.

The Moslems in Spain were to have a great influence on scholarship in the West but mainly in the later Middle Ages. They brought knowledge of Aristotle's logic and philosophy and of Greek science. The medieval universities were indebted to knowledge and ideas recovered from the ancient world by the Moslems.

EXPANSION AND EROSION

We are dealing mainly with western Europe, a large and important part of the Roman Empire—and a part whose future was dependent on the fate of the entire Empire. We should notice the great areas and diverse peoples to be governed and the endless boundaries to be defended as the Empire grew. At its greatest extent it included a great part of Asia. That region known as the East had been conquered by Alexander the Great in a brief but masterful career (336–323 B.C.). He conquered the nations, erected cities, such as Alexandria, appointed Greek governors, located settlers, and spread ideas from Greece to the banks of the Indus River. He had control of Egypt, Assyria, the Fertile Crescent, and the Tigris-Euphrates basin where civilization had arisen sixty centuries earlier. Much of the Hellenistic culture that he planted continued to grow.

The Roman Empire was much more extensive than Alexander's, which extended only eastward from Greece and Egypt; Rome controlled also the area west to the Atlantic Ocean. Roman power on the east stopped at the Euphrates; on the north it was bounded by the Danube and the Rhine and included France and Spain. All of Africa north of the Sahara, Egypt and the islands of the Mediterranean, together with Greece, were Roman territory. The defense of so overextended a boundary line strained the resources of the government; and even when mass movement was halted, infiltration persisted. In the time of Caesar in 50 B.C., many barbarians in small groups found their way across the Rhine into Gaul.

For several centuries, Britain was a part of the Empire. Although Caesar's two invasions had no lasting effect, a firm foothold was gained a century later, about A.D. 50, and in a long generation, Agricola, the father-in-law of Tacitus, conquered and pretty well pacified the island. Cities arose, roads were built, and a thriving trade grew up; but when the Empire declined, the legions had to be withdrawn. In the fifth century, Jutes, Angles, and Saxons entered and, being themselves civilized, gradually transformed Britain into an England able to absorb the Danish invaders of the tenth century. In fact, the decline of Rome and the barbarian invasions were correlative and mutually dependent, each on the other.

We shall present a brief review. The Empire was established to overcome the defects of the Republic. Augustus desired to be known as the founder of a new and lasting republic and the designer of its ideal constitution; but no institutions are perfect and, therefore, none are permanent. Augustus, however, had succeeded well and for two centuries after his service as Princeps or First Citizen, the nation enjoyed its longest period of peace. In the third century trouble began; and, although the difficulties were resolved, they were preceded and followed by a decline that was not until later recognized as the beginning of the Middle Ages. We could find an even earlier beginning. The philosopher-emperor Marcus Aurelius (r. A.D. 161–180) had to spend most of his reign in the field guarding the frontier along the Danube. Contemporaries, as noted here, do not usually understand the full meaning of passing events.

THE CHURCH IN THE WEST

The church arose three centuries before the medieval period began and its earliest history is written in the New Testament, particularly in the Acts of the Apostles. Christianity began with the teaching of Jesus. He taught that God is our Father; that we, His children, are brothers and should live brotherly lives, and that through His grace we may do so. He taught the infinite worth of every person. He was gentle. He looked upon children and people of all ages with kindly sympathy and a deep compassion and upon nature with the eyes of a poet. He did not attempt to prove his intuition by argument. His life was a living example of his teaching. Churches have tried, almost from the first, and largely in vain, to embody his example and teaching in rigid doctrinal statements, the Creeds.

Christianity, as noted, spread quickly to the large cities of the Roman Empire. By the middle of the first century (A.D. 50) there was a Christian group to whom St. Paul addressed his "Letter to the Romans." Antioch, Corinth, and Alexandria were other early centers of the Christian movement. For three centuries the Christians were often assailed by mobs and arrested by the government. They refused to worship at pagan shrines and this was construed as treason. Early in the fourth century Christianity was recognized as a legal religion and in 325 it was accepted by the emperor, Constantine, as the official religion of the state. A church council of the same year adopted the Nicene Creed, which defined the orthodox belief including that of the Roman Catholic Church.

The Catholic Church received her school curriculum through Rome and also copied the imperial pattern of organization in which the schools had a relatively small part. In the early Middle Ages the governmental unit of the church was the city with its congregations. This was a diocese, meaning district, or governmental unit. The bishop was the ruler and head of the clergy of the diocese. His throne, or *cathedra*, was in the cathedral church, which often had a school. Some cathedral schools, such as the one in Paris, became very important institutions in the later medieval period.

The dioceses or areas of bishoprics were grouped into sees under metropolitans, or patriarchs. In the entire East there were four patriarchates: Alexandria, Jerusalem, Antioch, and Constantinople, this last being the highest or ecumenical office. In the West there was only one comparable center, Rome. When East and West separated, Rome remained as the site of the papacy.

The church preserved and transmitted learning in the Middle Ages. Its organization remained intact through invasions, the decay of civilization, and the gradual breakup of the civil government. The Empire fell; but the church stood firm, spread, and grew in power. In 476, when the last Roman emperor was deposed, the Bishop of Rome remained, unchecked by any secular power, the patriarch of Italy, North Africa, France, and Spain. Ireland, where in about 416 St. Patrick ended his labors, was the last province before the fall of Rome to come under the rule of the church. The first to be added after that event was Scotland and then the country of the Salic Franks. In 496, Clovis, the Frankish chieftain, and three thousand of his warriors were baptized. To Clovis we owe the law or code of the Franks, or Germans, which is quite separate from the Greek-Roman-Christian tradition. One of the features of the Salic code is the limitation which it places on the inheritance of property by women.

Columba was the great missionary to Scotland. From Ireland and Scotland the religion was carried to England, where the monastery of Lindisfarme was founded in 624. Pope Gregory had meanwhile sent a party of missionaries to southern England. They established themselves at Canterbury and in fifty years completed the religion's conquest of most of the island. Next came Germany where neither the legions of Rome nor the missionaries of the church had been able to secure a permanent bridgehead until the time of Boniface (c. 680–754). He established Fulda, a monastery that gained great fame, and spread the faith in Hesse, Bavaria and Thuringia. Where the church prospered, its cathedrals, monasteries, and schools spread the ancient learning, or as much as the clergy retained and approved.

CHURCH AND PHILOSOPHY

The writers of the New Testament, although they were Hebrews, wrote in Greek, the international language and the language of philosophy, science, and literature. It became also the language of the developing religion. One example of its international use is furnished by the Greek version of the Hebrew Scriptures, called the Septuagint because, according to tradition, it was prepared by about seventy translators. The translation was made in Alexandria in the third century before Christ; and it shows that many dispersed Jews preferred a Greek to the original Hebrew text. The writers of the New Testament, in quoting from the Old, used the Septuagint instead of making their own translations. Faithful Jewish scholars such as Philo of Alexandria (c. 20 B.C.–A.D. 53) thought the Old Testament theology could be harmonized with the philosophy of Plato; and many Christians thought the same of the New Testament doctrines.

The new religion, as well as the old, was affected by the movement toward concord and harmony. In two centuries after the Christian religion and Greek philosophy met, the religion had itself become a philosophy for many. "We teach the same as the Greeks," said Justin Martyr (c. 100–165), "but we only are hated for our teachings." "Our books show," said Tertullian (c. 160–230) addressing the emperor, "that our doctrines are not new"; and even our opponents admit that Christianity is a philosophy, teaching the approved virtues of chastity, justice, and temperance. "Therefore," he declared, "you should not persecute us." We shall immediately see that there were other views, and Tertullian frequently spoke with a different voice.

Different tendencies within Christianity struggled from early times for mastery. One was the ascetic attitude that led men to renounce the world and to choose an austere otherworldliness that was to prove hostile to learning and the spirit of inquiry. Early monasticism showed this unfriendly attitude most; and later when libraries were established and some monks became scholars, the system did little more than to repair some of the harm done to learning earlier.

From the beginning the church showed a missionary spirit; witness the extensive travels of St. Paul to establish Christian groups and the letters to keep them loyal and to teach them. We have already mentioned some of those who spread the gospel to Great Britain and other lands. A third and the largest group of believers were laymen who followed secular occupations of all kinds. Many church leaders also had to follow more than one occupation serving as bishops, abbots, administrators, teachers, and others. Thus the church became involved in the affairs of the world and the world in those of the church. Perhaps that is as it should be; at least some of those who took an absolutistic position found themselves in difficulty. Absolutism sometimes encroached upon the scope of learning. Some Christians rigorously excluded all pagan learning from their lives. One of these was Tatian, born about A.D. 110 and liberally educated in Greek philosophy. He had a speculative mind and was won for Christianity by its monotheism, or, as he said, "by the government of all by one Being," a doctrine that, at one stroke, liberated him from "the tyranny of a thousand demons." In his "Address to the Greeks" he launched a violent attack on pagan thought. Another, already mentioned, was Tertullian, born in Carthage, deeply schooled in philosophy and rhetoric, and intended for the law. As a Christian he became an austere puritan who, in hostility to pagan learning, outstripped Tatian. Christianity was for him a mighty supernatural reality that could have no concern with the pale theories of the philosophers. In Greek thought, it seemed to him, lurked the sources of all future heresies, a view widely held in later times. But even Tertullian was unable to do without the secular learning he so vigorously assailed. This is a symbol of what happened in the church at large. Pagan learning could not be either accepted or rejected; a middle ground had to be found.

Late in the ancient world, that is, about the beginning of the medieval period, some Christian scholars and writers, the so-called church fathers, made a fairly satisfactory adjustment of the conflict between religion and learning. St. Jerome (c. 347–420) was one of these, but he was often unhappy with the result. His most important achievement was the preparation of the Latin translation of the Bible called the Vulgate. He was a facile writer and left many letters and pamphlets because he found it difficult to stay out of any current controversy. He was somewhat vague about the desired relations between religion and scholarship. One night when he was ill he had a dream that he regarded as a vision in which he was accused of being a Ciceronian and not a Christian. He was so shocked by this revelation that he temporarily gave up his classical studies. However, the effect of the experience wore off and years later he concluded that it was only a dream. He was, in fact, an industrious student of Greek and Hebrew and his translation of the Bible was improved by these studies. Even so it was still influenced by the older *Itala* version. He spent his last twenty-five years in a monastery that he had founded.

Augustine (354–430), the near contemporary of Jerome, although not as learned in Greek and Hebrew, was a greater genius and a more serene personality. He was born at Tagaste in Numidia and was educated at home, at Madaura, and finally at Carthage. His father, Patricius, a local judge, was a pagan but his mother, Monica, was a Christian. As soon as they became aware of his great gifts they planned for his complete education in the usual courses of grammar, literature, rhetoric, and philosophy. Greek was already being omitted in the African schools and Augustine's exposure to it led him only to hate it, a response that he later regretted.

Although he had been intended for the law, he began to teach rhetoric, a calling frequently, as we have seen, combined with legal work. He began teaching at Carthage but the students of the city were riotous and broke up schools; he moved to Rome where they were docile but failed to pay their bills. He soon received an official appointment at Milan where he came under the influence of a great preacher and bishop, Ambrose (340–397). At this time Augustine was a Manichean, believing the world ruled by two opposing principles, the light and good against the dark and evil powers. Under the preaching of Ambrose he was converted. He then returned home and was soon, against his desire, ordained to the priesthood and four years later was chosen bishop, the Bishop of Hippo. Most of this short sketch is taken from his wonderful autobiography to which he gave the more accurate title, *Confessions*. He was acknowledging God's dealings with him and confessing his sins. It became the pattern for more egotistic writers, such as Petrarch and Rousseau.

Although Augustine was constantly occupied in administration, promotion, and preaching—some hundreds of sermons remain as evidence of the latter—he unaccountably found time to write a great body of letters and many books. To be sure he did not write all this with his own hand but employed secretaries. He remained active to the last. His *Retractations* was published just before his death in 430. The best-known and the greatest of his writings was *The City of God*, which occupied him for thirteen years while he carried on his office and issued other books. Gibbon is said to have praised the book but he actually, after admitting that he was not very familiar with it, condemned it. The book was long popular but its outline is somewhat blurred from having been on the anvil too long.

The City of God was called out by the fall of Rome. In 410 Alaric and his barbarous Visigoths stunned the world by capturing "The Eternal City." Augustine said the catastrophe was not, as claimed, caused by Christianity but by the decline in civic loyalty, patriotism, and virtue among the pagans themselves; and on the other hand, he said the truly eternal and heavenly city is composed of those who do the will of God. These are they who accept the unity of Father, Son, and Spirit and live pure, holy lives. The answer was based on the Nicene Creed adopted in 325.

The height of power attained by the Christian Church over the affairs and the officers of the secular world is illustrated by an incident in which Ambrose was the key person. The Emperor Theodosius the Great (c. 346–395) sent soldiers to massacre a rioting mob in Thessalonica, now called Salonika. It was an unjustifiable misuse of power. Ambrose made the proud and powerful ruler do penance before he would admit him to the sacraments.

CHRISTIAN HOME AND PAGAN SCHOOL

In pre-Christian times, the schools, literature, the theater, entertainment and society in general were naturally pagan. Life among the Hebrews would be the only exception. Some of the books studied were those that Plato had condemned for their low morals. Quintilian also had said, "The Greeks are licentious in many of their writings and I should be loath to interpret Horace in certain passages." We should not be surprised that Christians condemned books that had offended the moral sense of Plato and Quintilian. The ideas of the Christian home and the pagan school were conflicting. What to do in this situation was a problem in every family with children. Tertullian, in a passage, "on the difficulties of schoolmasters" attempted to deal with the problem, but only Christian schools could provide a solution satisfactory to the Christian family.

The earliest such schools may have left no record but in the second century there were schools, or at least classes, called catechumenal, for new converts; and others more advanced, the catechetical, to deal with mature inquirers. The more elementary instruction was given to prepare catechumens for church membership. Classes meeting only once or twice a week cannot be compared with the regular schools of literature and rhetoric.

The catechetical school was a means of harmonizing and integrating philosophy and Christian doctrine. Each such school was a private lectureship. Perhaps the first was the one opened in Alexandria in about the year 125. Valentinus, a student in this early one, opened a similar school at Rome. A second such school at Alexandria was founded in 179. Two of its famous teachers were Clement (c. 150–220) and Origen (c. 185–254). Other catechetical schools were located at Antioch, Edessa, Caesarea, Carthage, and other places. The purpose of these schools was to defend Christianity against outside attacks; and in this, Origen was the mastermind of the age; but ironically, he was himself accused of heresy. His method was one of personal consultation and argument; but he also lectured and directed the reading of inquirers and opponents. He did a vast amount of literary work.

That there were Christian teachers in some of the ordinary schools in the early centuries is shown by Tertullian's writings and by the decree of Julian the Apostate against Christian teaching in the literary schools. Incidentally, Julian never professed Christianity and was a normal pagan not an apostate at all. Many homes no doubt gave Christian instruction to counteract the pagan influence of the schools. The problem was not solved at any given time but the desired result was attained gradually in the course of centuries. The edict by Justinian (529) closing all pagan schools was hardly needed; most of them had already disappeared.

THE FADING LIGHT

In the difficult transition from the Empire to the church, much knowledge and many books were lost; much also was saved by the copyists, the schools, and textbook writers, and by the great churchmen. Among the last-named we have already spoken of the learned Jerome and the colorful and stimulating Augustine. The Vulgate translation of the Bible of one and the *Confessions* and the *City of God* of the other, together with the numerous letters of both, kept the lamp of learning lighted but the supply of fuel was growing small. Augustine, for example, read Cicero's Hortensius but it later disappeared. Greek sources were in less demand than the Latin. The church emphasized the reading of devotional and, in general, religious books to the neglect of pagan literature.

In the next century, Boethius (480–524) wrote his *Consolation of Philosophy* and many who read it did not perceive that it was not a Christian book. Christians and Platonists sometimes traveled the same road for great distances. Boethius also wrote schoolbooks in arithmetic, geometry, and music. He had an extensive plan for a Latin translation of Plato and Aristotle but he was able to complete only a small part of the logic of Aristotle. This book was, however, to play an important part in learning in the time of Abelard. Boethius could do no more, for his life was cut short at the age of forty-four. Accused by the Ostrogothic King Theodoric the Great of plotting against his rule, Boethius was committed to prison and later executed. He wrote the *Consolations* without access to any books.

Another medieval scholar, Martianus Capella wrote *The Marriage of Philology and Mercury*, a title that may be paraphrased as the union of learning and practical wisdom. The substance of the book is a treatment of the seven liberal arts—namely, grammar, rhetoric, dialectic, arithmetic, geometry, astronomy, and music. The first three were known as the trivium, or three ways to knowledge; and the last four made up the quadrivium, the four ways. Perhaps the division into the trivium and quadrivium was not made until the later medieval age.

The subjects of the liberal arts go back to Plato and Aristotle and Greek educational custom. Grammar, rhetoric, and logic are necessarily included in any literary course; and the Athenian schools emphasized music, as Plato and Aristotle also did. Arithmetic, geometry, and astronomy are demanded in the seventh book of the *Republic*. After some vacillation in the early middle period, when the number of arts was reduced to six, and in a later period, when eight and even nine were demanded, the seven were chosen and became standard; but not all students studied all of them. Many confined themselves to the trivium; and also, the teaching varied in thoroughness. The medieval standard curriculum was after all, in practice, not uniform.

This last point can be illustrated from the first art, grammar. For aid in mastering the first difficulties in Latin, the pupil was directed to Donatus, Aelius Donatus was one of the teachers of Jerome, who was, without a doubt, his most proficient pupil. The small Latin grammar, the *Ars minor* of Donatus, was intended for beginners. It came into such general use that any elementary grammar was called a Donatus or Donat, in the same way early Americans asked for a Webster when they wanted a dictionary. Donatus also wrote a more advanced *Ars major*, the greater art, and a book on Terence. Another larger Latin grammar was written by Priscian in the sixth century. At a time when Greek had almost disappeared from the schools, Priscian's grammar had a special use because it contained many Greek quotations.

A small booklet that may have been nearly universal in the schools was called the *Distichs of Cato*. It was by an unknown author, or compiler, probably a teacher. In form, it was a collection of couplets in Latin verse, quite abstract in content but easy to read and easy to memorize. Before paper became abundant what was not committed to the memory was not effectively taught or learned. Before recent times, only in ancient Sumer did the schools have enough writing material. It is not generally realized that paper transformed schools not only by way of printing but also by supplying cheap writing material.

Cassiodorus followed Boethius as secretary and minister to King Theodoric and succeeding rulers. He founded the monastery of Vivarium, or Fishpond, usually named Viviers, in the south of Italy. This afforded him a learned retirement near the sea after his public life ended. He became a great collector of manuscripts at the beginning of the Dark Ages, when they would have been lost without his care. One of his practices is not to be approved: He advised scribes to correct mistakes in old writings so carefully that the correction would seem to be part of the original composition. His teaching of sacred and profane letters is on the seven liberal arts and, considering the time, it is not surprising that he dealt mainly with the trivium. He dealt also with one of the humbler arts not among the honored seven: the art of spelling. His collection included an ancient illustrated herbal that like other such works was more artistic than scientific. The practice of dating events from the Christian era is said to have originated in his monastery.

The *Etymologies* by Isidore of Seville purported to be a compendium of all knowledge; but Isidore had neither the philosophic interests of Boethius nor the learning of Cassiodorus. His work was a compilation in twenty books or chapters dealing with forty or more subjects extending from agriculture to medicine and public athletic games. Such encyclopedias, filled with disjointed information, were not unusual in the Dark Ages and this one by Isidore was one of the most popular.

The decline of learning began in Roman times; and this tendency was accelerated in the dark sixth and seventh centuries through the invasions of barbarians, the decrease of wealth and population, and the growing distaste of the churchmen for secular learning. The investigative spirit had never been as strong in Rome as in Greece, and it was further weakened in the Middle Ages because it was accompanied by a loss in critical judgment and historical sense. We must note that history was not one of the liberal arts and the period produced no great historians.

The habit of taking a knowledge of words for the understanding of things and ideas, the practice of summarizing large fields of learning in meager outlines, and of compiling from previous compilations became almost universal. The lamps of learning were growing dim but some learning that might have been lost was saved. Either of two possible titles would be appropriate for this section. We call it "The Fading Light," but we might call it "The Preservation of Learning"—that is, of a little learning in danger of extinction.

MONASTERIES AND LEARNING

Austerity and asceticism as elements of religion were sometimes practiced in ancient societies, but in Judaism by only a few small groups and apparently not at all by Christians before about A.D. 200. Early Christian ascetics in Egypt lived as hermits in caves, on top of pillars, and in other isolated and uncomfortable places. The word *monk*, from the Greek *monos*, meaning "alone," was correctly applied to one who lived as a hermit. To people of the West this seemed harsh and self-serving and in Europe, companies of monks formed monasteries in which each had his own cell but all also took part in common work, meals, and worship.

Monasticism was up to a certain level a civilizing agency in a partly barbarous Europe. In a period when cities were declining, transportation breaking down, piracy common, and food supply uncertain, a self-supporting institution in the country was useful; it was able to provide a subsistence, companionship with retirement, and guidance in religious devotions. On the material side, even though each monk took a vow of poverty and was in fact penniless, the monastery might be wealthy, with lands, buildings, including a large church, a guest house, shops and industrial equipment, and much movable property. There might be associate and daughter institutions conducted under the same rule as the original monastery.

The Benedictine monasteries were such a group with many members in different parts of western Europe. Saint Benedict, for whom the group or order was named, was born at Nursia in central Italy in about 480 and died in 543 or later. His family sent him to school in Rome but he left, without completing his course, to live in an isolated spot for meditation and worship —in fact, as a monk. There were many others of a similar mind. All descriptions and explanations of the actual conditions are mere speculations. Either originally or later he served as the leader of a group of more than a hundred, which moved to Monte Cassino, between Naples and Rome. In about the year 526, published the famous rule named for him.

By *rule* (in Latin, *regula*) we are to understand a scheme of life and government for monks who are, therefore, called regular clergy, whereas priests who were not connected with a monastery but served people of their time in the "world" were secular clergy. The Benedictine rule shows that the author was a practical administrator able to strike a balance between severity and laxity. At the head of his monastery was the abbot, elected by the members and empowered to compel obedience but required to consult all members on important decisions. Novices after their period of probation took vows of chastity, poverty, and obedience. The whole day and night was parceled out between work, worship, and reading for Benedict called idleness "the enemy of the soul." The rule and the practice of the monasteries dignified manual labor as an activity fit for free men not merely for slaves as in the ancient world. Each week one member was selected to read while the rest ate their dinner. Silence was a monastic virtue and reading at table reduced the urge to gossip or to nudge your neighbor. Copying manuscripts, often borrowed ones, increased the library and unfortunately too often increased the errors in valuable texts. It was said that "a monastery without a library is like a castle without an armory." Manuscripts written on parchment, beautifully illuminated and bound in decorative covers, were and are costly. Much of the ancient learning and literature was lost in the Dark Ages; but much that was saved was preserved in monasteries. The wide dissemination of learning had to wait for cheaper books and more numerous schools.

The buildings of a large monastery were sometimes built around an open space or square called a garth. On the inner or garth side of the buildings there often was an open arcade or colonnade called the cloister. This word and its adjective, *cloistral*, are often applied to monastic arts, practices, and institutions; hence the term *cloistral school*. Novices, entering as children, continued their education in the monastery. We cannot give details, but if it is remembered that there were in later years thousands of monasteries for men and others for women in western Europe, we can gain an idea of their educational accomplishment. The schools were often small, however, and for a full assessment on the debit side, routine; the failure to invent and experiment must also be taken into the account.

MONASTIC SCHOOLS

Schools were a necessity because boys and especially orphans were dedicated at early ages. Children not intended for monastic life were sometimes taught. Benedict admitted children of wealthy Romans into his school. In some places in the Dark Ages, a monastery offered the only schooling that was available. In some cases the children intended for the monastery, called *oblati*, or those "offered," and the others, the *externi*, were taught in separate schools. Books for the schools, and other books also, some of them original works, were produced in the scriptorium. The library served not only the school but the whole institution. Early monastic libraries were small. Alcuin in the eighth century reported about forty authors who were represented in the library at York; Church Fathers, Latin classicists, grammarians, and medieval writers. The collection is used to show what was available to Alcuin, but one is more impressed by what was wanting. Later medieval libraries were sometimes much larger, even containing a few thousand books. Monasteries sometimes manufactured books for sale. And, a special case, the first English printer, John Caxton, set up a press in the abbey at Westminster and its abbot was one of his most munificent patrons.

The discipline in the schools, although generally strict, varied widely; the course was uniform beginning with the words, forms, and practice of spoken Latin and continuing with the seven liberal arts. Pupils in the schools, like the monks, had to speak Latin. Otherwise, it would not have been education, perhaps not religion. The first task of the school, therefore, was the teaching of a language foreign to northern Europe. The vernacular was used in teaching the first words and phrases but this practice was discontinued early in the course.

Of the formal subjects, Latin ranked highest. When the boy had mastered the rudiments he was set to read Aesop, as arranged about A.D. 400, and the moral sentences in the *Distichs of Cato*, already noted here. Both of these were used as first reading books for centuries. One of the main tasks was that of building up a vocabulary. Verse helped in locating the "longs" and "shorts" in Latin words. Music was taught to the small boys along with reading and grammar because it was needed to take part in the church services.

For further reading matter the master might turn to Virgil or one of the Christian poets such as Prudentius (c. 400) and to the psalms. The costliness and, therefore, the scarcity of books was one of the persistent school problems. A monastery might have a considerable library without being able to supply the necessary schoolbooks. No more than three boys to one book was the rule in one cloister. Another equally serious and persistent problem, already noticed, was the lack of enough writing material. This was unfortunate because it helped to make memorizing the chief exercise and attainment of the school and thereby to pervert the entire educative process. Parchment was expensive and the manufacture of paper was delayed almost to the end of the medieval period. Then, except for the fact that fixed customs tend to persist, these two educational problems, the lack of books and paper, were solved at a stroke. Memorizing persisted; and, indeed, some of it is necessary.

Rhetoric followed grammar; but it was no longer the ancient study. As we have seen, it was deteriorating in the time of Quintilian; and this process continued until it came to mean letter-writing, keeping records, and drawing up legal papers, a subject called *dictamen*. *Ars Dictaminis* is the title of some medieval schoolbooks. Dialectic or logic, the third study of the trivium, was based on what was left of Aristotle's work, some of it provided by Boethius. The complete logical works of Aristotle, the founder of the subject, were recovered in the twelfth and thirteenth centuries. In that period logic was the chief subject in advanced schools.

The studies of the quadrivium declined to a level that must be called trivial. The mathematical and astronomical studies were chiefly applied in calculating the date of Easter and other movable festivals. Geometry was adulterated with geography, taking it back to the original meaning of earth-measurement. All the elementary studies were taught as preparation for theology, "the queen of the sciences." The lowest depth of the depression of learning came in the sixth century; but conditions varied in different regions, and the sixth century was a time of great activity in Ireland. Another revival is linked with the Carolingian rulers of Frankland; it began under the ancestors of Charlemagne and reached its height while he was ruler early in the ninth century. Afterward military conditions and the invasions of the Northmen led to further loss of learning.

REVIVAL UNDER CHARLEMAGNE

Charlemagne (742-814) was one of the great men of history and his time, one of the great moments of medieval Europe. In 732, his grandfather Charles Martel (the Hammer) turned back the Mohammedans at the decisive battle of Tours and before long they were pushed back across the Pyrenees. About the same time dissension among the Mohammedans and the vigorous defense of the emperor at Constantinople prevented any advance into eastern Europe. Although the pressure was to be renewed about the time of the Reformation, at the moment it was clear that Europe, except Spain, was to be Christian and not Moslem. When Charles came to the throne in 768 the current of progress was already in motion.

Charles was a great man and also an attractive figure. His biographer, Einhard, speaks of his merry eyes; he was tall, robust, and well proportioned. Whether in action or repose he impressed everyone with a sense of dignity and authority. He was great as a commander, as a ruler, as a builder, and as a faithful son of the church. It might be too much to expect that all of his conduct met the church's ideals. As a statesman he recognized the power of public opinion, education, and religion but he did not merely follow these forces; he molded them to support his own purposes. Third in a succession of great princes and rulers, and a man of ideas, he never learned to write. Education in the three parts of Gaul was a specialty, not a universal need; and kings could hire secretaries.

To his court at Aachen, Charles invited many kinds of talent. His educational counselors included three from Italy, still the most cultivated part of his empire and most closely connected with the Roman See. The three selected were Peter of Pisa, Paulinus of Aquileia, and Paul the Deacon. The last wrote a *History of the Lombards,* which won praise from Gibbon. Another was Theodulf of France, or perhaps of Spain. Charles, who appointed his own bishops, made Theodulf bishop of Orleans, where he, as surely seems right, became one of the king's staunchest supporters. He was also a poet and wrote the hymn "All Glory, Laud, and Honor." Best known of Charlemagne's educational advisors was Alcuin (735-804) from the cathedral school at York where he had been educated in the Roman Church. This was a requirement for Charles who, as early as 769, had declared his whole-hearted "allegiance to the apostolic See in all things." Alcuin was not a great scholar but a skilful teacher, and he was influential as an advisor on educational policy. He had first met Charles in 781, and was invited to become head of the palace school. After fifteen years he was allowed, at his own request, to retire to the famous monastery of St. Martin's of Tours as abbot.

Soon after Alcuin had been brought to serve as head of Charlemagne's palace school, the king took occasion to instruct the clergy on the conduct of education. The Englishman probably had a share in preparing the famous capitulary of 786, "on the cultivation of letters." It said that the errors in the writings of churchmen suggest that their understanding of the Bible may also be faulty. It urged them to study literature and rhetoric for the Scriptures contain many figures of speech. Men who are willing and able to teach should set up schools; and to see to this is the solemn duty of all bishops and abbots.

An effort was made to prepare a correct text of all the books of the Old and New Testaments—a difficult task—and when it was completed, the emperor ordered that all copies of the Bible should be corrected to correspond with Alcuin's model. We may doubt that either the king or his adviser understood what this command involved; but some mistakes were eliminated. A second stage in the king's educational program was reached in 789 when he directed the Council of Aachen to review the problems of education in the Empire. The Council passed a decree requiring all monasteries and cathedrals to maintain schools to teach the book of psalms, singing, grammar, and the *computus*—namely, the calculation of the dates of the movable festivals of the church. Illiterate priests were to be dismissed and appointments were to be made from only those who had passed a literary examination. Such examinations are not infallible and the rule was perhaps soon relaxed. It is known, at all events, that there were illiterate priests after Charlemagne, and even in the time of the Lutheran Reformation.

Even the children of the masses came within the scope of Charlemagne's endeavor. The monastery gates were opened, perhaps somewhat reluctantly, to children who would not become monks but were to be taught as *externi*. This result was promoted by the rescripts of about 801. Finally the emperor caught a fleeting vision of universal education and compulsory attendance at school. It was only a glimpse and came about in this way: Charles discovered and revived the decree of the Synod of Vaison, held in 529, almost three centuries earlier. That decree ordered that all pastors, "as is the very salutary custom all over Italy," should receive young persons into their parish houses to teach them singing and reading and the commands of God. Charles ordered that all priests were, without charge, to maintain schools in villages and parish houses and were not to refuse any who came to them for instruction in letters. "No one should, henceforth, dare to administer baptism to anyone who was unable to repeat the Creed and the Lord's Prayer," and severe penalties were prescribed for those who would not learn these formularies in the Latin tongue. It will not be necessary to say that these orders were not carried out; but it is worthwhile to reflect on the historical fact that it was in 1873, more than a thousand years after Charlemagne before the state established compulsory attendance at school in France. There was no thought of state education in the mind of Charlemagne.

The new system of education wherein the church performed great services was to a large degree the achievement of Charlemagne and Alcuin. Charles, as we know, ruled by his personal influence and after his death the Empire rapidly disintegrated; but his influence did not wholly disappear.

SUMMARY

Historical periods are set up as aids to memory and they abound in vast generalizations that are useful only if we remember they are only more or less true. The changes they designate can be likened to a river, the water rising and falling, the flow increasing and slowing down. In the field of letters and learning, the Middle Ages formed the period A.D. 500–1500, or perhaps A.D. 300–1600.

By conquering and colonizing, Alexander the Great had spread the language and learning of Greece so widely in the Eastern world that he has been called the Apostle of the Greeks. Alexandria became a second Athens. In the early Christian centuries, Greek philosophy deeply influenced Christian thought. The catechumenal and catechetical schools were established to teach Christian doctrine and to erect a defense against philosophical attack. In defending itself, Christian theology absorbed much of neo-Platonic thought.

A similar union was formed in the school curriculum of the West. This curriculum was composed of the remains of Greek, Hebrew, and Roman ideas and learning. It was the first task of the Middle Ages to make this synthesis; and this was accomplished under the auspices of the church and her schools. In the period of political decline, barbarian invasion, and civil disorder, the church preserved what it could use. Much of ancient culture had already disappeared from the West; and of what remained, much was neglected. The spirit of investigation and criticism, the sense of history, and the hope of progress were almost entirely absent. Learning, embodied in outlines, summaries, and selections, was merely preserved.

The monastic and cathedral schools taught the seven liberal arts, philosophy, and theology. In the scriptoria, books were copied and new ones written. Libraries, although never large, gradually increased in size. Charlemagne drew to his court learned men from several parts of his empire and attempted to stimulate the clergy to increased scholastic activity. He even hoped to spread some slight degree of learning among the laity. This example of state interest in education was not to be followed until much later. In the next century the great English king Alfred exhibited a similar concern for education, although on a smaller stage. But the period of educational quiescence was now over, and in the next period the Middle Ages became much more active and progressive.

QUESTIONS

1. Was the medieval period in its educational development a coherent historical unit or did it include divergent trends?
2. Show that the Middle Ages attempted a synthesis of Greek, Roman, and Judean-Christian knowledge and ideas. Was this union inevitable or might it have been avoided; and if so, with what results?
3. Why did the Christian teachers in spite of their opposition to pagan literature after all use it in their schools? And how did they justify its use?
4. How did the Roman civil organization affect the organization of the Christian Church? How did this affect the schools?
5. Why did the schoolbooks of the Middle Ages tend to become formal and abstract summaries?
6. Why did Western monasticism develop only after the great persecutions came to an end?
7. Why did the monasteries carry on a great variety of economic activities; and why did they also foster reading, schools, the manufacture of books, singing, and other arts?
8. Why were books expensive in the Middle Ages?
9. From the account of Eginhard or Einhard (see bibliography), write a paper on the character and personality of Charlemagne.
10. Why did Charlemagne draw his educational advisers from Italy and England rather than from his own Frankland?
11. In what respects do Charlemagne's efforts mark an advance from the education of preceding centuries? How did his efforts differ from those of the Roman emperors? Was this an example of genuine state activity in education?
12. From J. M. Clark's history of *The Abbey of St. Gall*, write an account of the intellectual and musical activities of that monastery. Were all or most monasteries as enlightened as St. Gall?

NOTES AND SOURCES

An excellent account of the general curriculum in medieval times has been prepared by Dr. Paul Abelson. The sixty or more sources used by him deal largely with the teaching of the Latin language. Knowledge of Latin gave access to other knowledge including the knowledge of logic, the quadrivium, and religion.

Sixty pages are devoted to Latin, to grammar, and to rhetoric, including authors, methods, textbooks, vocabularies, and "dictionaries." There is a section on *Dictamen*, or the writing of legal documents. Logic and the subjects of the quadrivium are treated with attention to the extent to which they were taught in schools and universities.

The complete title is Paul Abelson, *The Seven Liberal Arts. A Study in Medieval Culture*, New York, Teachers College, Columbia University, 1906, 150 pp.

Instead of writing about monasticism or about monasteries, in general, J. M. Clark of Glasgow University has prepared an interesting book about the history and cultural activities of one such institution, the Abbey of Saint Gall, one of the most famous institutions of its class. Saint Gall had a school, at times two schools, an inner school for *ablati*, and an outer for *externi*, usually sons of the nobility; and also a library, scriptorium, and other literary and cultural facilities. St. Gall was located near Lake Constance in a rough terrain and began its work two centuries before Charlemagne, who was both friend and patron. Its history extended to the time of Napoleon who ordered its dissolution in 1805.

The history of the Abbey shows that the cultural work of such institutions sometimes extended far beyond the seven liberal arts. St. Gall became noted for work in the arts, especially in illuminated manuscripts but also in painting and stained glass, in music, the drama, and other literature, and perhaps most of all for its library.

In the ninth century there were four hundred manuscripts. In spite of fire, theft, and other calamities, the collection became much larger. Unfortunately, the Council of Constance met nearby (1414–1418) and, needing records of earlier conciliar and papal decrees, they borrowed these manuscripts and failed to return them. At this time also, Poggio Bracciolini came and found a complete text of Quintilian. He copied it in fifty-four days and returned it.

This book should be used much more by students than it has been in the past. The title is James Midgeley Clark, *The Abbey of St. Gall as a Center of Literature and Art*, Cambridge University Press, 1926, 322 pp.

EGINHARD (EINHARD), *Life of Charlemagne*, Translated by Samuel Epes Turner, Cincinnati, American Book Company, 1883, 83 pp. Also translated into many other languages: into German by Groszen in Meyers Volksbücher, Leipzig, n.d.

GASQUET, F. A., CARDINAL, *English Monastic Life*, London, Methuen & Company, Ltd., 1919, fifth edition, 326 pp.

GLOVER, TERROT R., *Life and Letters in the Fourth Century*, New York, G. E. Stechert & Company, 1924, 398 pp.

LABRIOLLE, PIERRE DE, *History and Literature of Latin Christianity from Tertullian to Boethius*, Translated by Herbert Wilson, London, Kegan Paul, Trench & Company, 1929, 555 pp.

MULLINGER, G. B., *The Schools of Charles the Great and the Restoration of Education in the Ninth Century*, London, Longmans, Green and Company, 1877, 193 pp.

RAND, EDWARD K., *Founders of the Middle Ages*, Cambridge, Harvard University Press, 1928, 365 pp.

SANFORD, EVA M., Translator, *On the Government of God, by Salvian*, New York, Columbia University Press, 1930, 241 pp. Fifth-century document giving views of taxation, games, manners, and morals of Romans and barbarians.

SINGER, CHARLES, *From Magic to Science. Essays on the Scientific Twilight*, New York, Boni and Liveright, 1928, 253 pp.

SPECHT, FRANZ ANTON, *Geschichte des Unterrichtswesens in Deutschland . . . bis zur Mitte des dreizehnten Jahrhunderts*, Stuttgart, J. B. Cotta, 1885, 441 pp.

TAYLOR, HENRY OSBORN, *The Medieval Mind: A History of Thought and Emotion in the Middle Ages*, New York, The Macmillan Company, 1927, 2 vols.

WORKMAN, HERBERT B., *The Evolution of the Monastic Ideal*, London, Charles H. Kelly, 1913, 368 pp.

Chapter 5

MEDIEVAL REVIVAL OF LEARNING

Under the successors of Charlemagne the Empire, weakened by the rise of feudalism and attacked from without by the Northmen, or vikings, began to disintegrate. A strong government would have repelled or at least lessened these evils but the rising nations of western Europe were everywhere still weak. The decline was not uniform. England suffered much from invasions, because the island was so accessible to the Danes and Norwegians, but her civilization began to grow by the ninth century. We shall deal with feudalism and the vikings first and later with England under Alfred the Great, for the reason that these set the problems for king and kingdom.

In the ninth century the Moslems still ruled Spain, North Africa, Sicily, and part of Italy. From these bases they were able to cut the lines of commerce by which Europe obtained supplies from the East. The appearance in the Middle East of a new and aggressive breed of Mohammedans, the Seljuk Turks, stirred up the West to organize the Crusades, beginning in 1096.

The eleventh century can be considered as the turning point for medieval conditions. The earlier losses, the long accumulated deficits on the balance sheet of knowledge, culture, and welfare were overcome between the eleventh century and the end of the Middle Ages. In that time there were positive gains sufficient to make the period a time of great progress. If we extend the period to 1600, it will include the Italian or classical revival. And even though this is to be treated in a separate chapter, it is easy to show connections between the medieval and classical studies. One may well consider whether there were two separate revivals or only one continuous forward movement.

We shall not press the question here but we may, for a moment, look ahead over the late Middle Ages. They were marked by an increase in population, growing cities, and the extension of commerce. Great cathedrals attest the genius of that time in architecture. Charlemagne had built at Aachen, or Aix-la-Chapelle, a beautiful basilica that Einhard praised, but it could not compare with the soaring and vaulted cathedrals at Amiens, Rheims, and scores of other cities throughout western Europe. There was a renaissance in the major arts of sculpture and painting and in many minor ones. Scholastic logic, philosophy, and theology aroused the interest of Abelard in the twelfth century and of others then and later. Schools increased in number and in the variety of their studies, which now extended from the simple skills of writing and arithmetic to the learned professions taught in the new universities. The revival in classical education raised to a higher level the earlier revival from which it had sprung.

DECLINE AFTER CHARLEMAGNE

Two centuries of growing feudalism, invasions, and disorder followed the close of Charlemagne's reign. His successors were not exceptionally weak rulers but they were not able to lead and dominate as he had done. The first and great mistake was made when the Empire was divided into three parts to accommodate each of Charlemagne's three sons; this bad beginning was continued until the areas of the present France and Germany each consisted of about twenty independent countries with the chances for conflict greatly increased.

The division was carried even further, for fragmentation lay at the base of the feudal system that spread over western Europe. In the feudal system, the land controlled by lord, count, king, or emperor was divided into separate areas called benefices or fiefs. A fief is a tract of land given to a vassal for the support of his dependents and himself in return for services or a part of the produce of the land given to him. There was an infinite variety in these arrangements but one very frequent kind of service was military.

The system arose in Europe when the Roman Empire, having become unable to maintain armies and administrative services, paid for these necessities with the only goods remaining, land. In a barbarous world this system spread far and developed many variations and problems. To gain a fairly complete understanding of the system and its variations would require a mass of data and extended study. Historians have done some of this work for us and they point out that the system prevented the free movement of people. Vassals had to stay on their acres to cultivate and defend them. Also, in a condition of rural uniformity, such as feudalism imposed, the role of learning and the arts was reduced if not suppressed.

Monasticism and the monastic school fitted well into the feudal system. The school provided the kind and degree of education demanded by the church and often no more. Monastic lands provided food, the wool for clothing, and the skins for parchment, but the monks were confined to the land like the vassals they were. The monastery was like a fief, an oasis, self-sufficient and independent of its surroundings. But this condition came to an end when the raids by the heathen vikings began, for they did not spare even the monasteries. Their attacks are not well recorded, but from the *Anglo-Saxon Chronicle,* said to be the earliest historical work in a modern tongue (Old English), we have what appears to be a factual account of an invasion of England in 787. The story says that three ships appeared in Wessex and the king's officer, not knowing who they were, went to arrest them and was killed. The part of the account that claims these to have been the first Danish ships to anchor in England may be erroneous. It is certain that many followed.

In the ninth and tenth centuries, the Northmen raided many Scottish and English monasteries including the old and famous houses of Iona and Lindisfarne. Most of England, including the city of London, was ravaged with fire and sword. Wales escaped. Many of the famous cities on the continent—Paris, Utrecht, Seville, and others—were taken and burned. Europe was not prepared to resist them effectively. They appeared suddenly, moved fast, struck, and if the odds were against them, disappeared in their swift boats. Later they sometimes settled in a captured city and lived off the neighboring country. In time they brought their families and made the settlement permanent, absorbing and being absorbed by the earlier population. This was how a section of France became Normandy, the region of the Normans whose ancestors had been Northmen or heathen vikings. In 1066, we all know, William of Normandy became the conqueror of England.

The vikings sailed many seas: They settled on the Mediterranean coasts of France and Italy; they visited the Black Sea region; they made a settlement in Russia at what was later Novgorod. Before the discovery of the mariner's compass they skirted the coast of Greenland and eventually settled there. Others landed on the coast of North America apparently at several places from Labrador to New England. They called the country Vinland.

As this story indicates, the Scandinavian peoples adjust themselves readily to the conditions in which they find themselves, acquiring the language, religion, and customs of their neighbors. In Gaul they adopted the Roman Catholic faith and developed a Norman-French speech. In the United States they blend more readily with the mass of the people in Minnesota than the Germans do in Wisconsin. Indeed, in Pennsylvania, many Germans whose ancestors arrived before the American Revolution still prefer to speak the language of Luther rather than that of William Penn.

During those feudal times of which we are speaking, the Moslems maintained control of Spain and of the western Mediterranean Sea, including the islands of Sicily, Corsica, and Sardinia. They raided and settled on the coasts of Italy and France. They plundered the shipping of the cities and controlled leading ports. They burned the church of St. Peter's at Rome and sacked the mother monastery of the Benedictines at Monte Cassino. It was not until 1095 that Genoa and Pisa, combining their forces and fleets, recovered control of their sea routes; and this had the most direct effect on the prosperity of those cities and on the support they were able to give to the Crusades.

IN MEDIEVAL ENGLAND

Before we come to the Crusades we shall go back to England, which had its own educational history. The English king, Alfred the Great (849–899), was born a generation after the death of Charlemagne and on his smaller stage performed a comparable service as ruler and promoter of culture. He was also, in contrast with the great Frank, a scholar under difficult conditions; but to form a firm judgment on this we need to know more than we do of the rise and decline of learning in Britain. We provide only an outline but we shall return to Alfred before long.

The Roman general Agricola, completed the investment of Britain before the end of the first Christian century; and the army remained on guard until the early fifth century. Agricola, according to his biographer, Tacitus, "provided a liberal education for the sons of British chieftains." We do not know how long or widely this policy was practiced, but it was a bitter kind of generosity. Its purpose was to make prospective enemies too luxurious and soft to fight, so Tacitus reported.

During the Roman occupation and its peace, the Latin language and learning were brought in not only by soldiers but also by active churchmen. The tradition that Christianity had been introduced by A.D. 200 has no external support, but it is not in itself unlikely. The presence of three English bishops at the Council of Arles (A.D. 314) in southern France is evidence of an active religious movement. It could not remain unhindered. In the fifth century after the Roman evacuation, the heathen Jutes, Angles, and Saxons came from Denmark and Germany to destroy the Latin and Celtic cultures except in Wales. The Latin came back just before A.D. 600 when Pope Gregory the Great sent Augustine (another Augustine, not the Bishop of Hippo), and forty other monks from Rome to promote the conversion of Britain where there were seven or more kingdoms, all resolutely heathen. The mission established itself at Canterbury in Kent where the church of St. Martin from Roman times was still standing. We must not lose ourselves in the struggles between Irish and Roman Christianity over the date of Easter and matters of ritual.

The names and books of a few authors will tell us much about the state of learning and letters in the seventh and following centuries. Sometimes we do not know the name as in the case of the author of the *Twelve*

Abuses of the Age. This is a small book in excellent Latin by one whose reading had been extensive and varied, religious and secular. He omitted the preface and began in this manner: "Twelve are the abuses of the age, that is: the scholar without works, the old man without religion, the young man without obedience, the rich man who giveth not alms, the woman without modesty, the master without virtue, the contentious Christian, the proud poor man, the unjust king, the negligent bishop, the common folk without discipline, the people without law." Only the first deals with scholarship; the rest deal with moral and religious "abuses." Each of these is the subject or text for an exposition.

The great writers of the age, in addition to their scholarly and religious works also produced schoolbooks. A West Saxon, Aldhelm (639–711) was a lifelong student—"I who thought myself a scholar, am beginning again to be a pupil"—a sentence from Jerome, expressed his condition. He knew many of the Latin writers, classical and Christian. Benedict Biscop, who lived until 690, founded the monasteries of Wearmouth (674) and Jarrow (682) in Northumbria and was a great collector of manuscripts and founder of libraries. As if those monasteries and their books had been prepared for him, Bede (672–735) was given as an oblate to Biscop at an early age and spent his life in Wearmouth and Jarrow. The Venerable Bede, as he is often called, was the author of the *Ecclesiastical History of the English Nation,* and of other books. Many of these men also wrote schoolbooks on spelling, arithmetic, grammar, and chronology. So Bede wrote a little book on chronology proposing to date events from the birth of Christ, not from the Creation. He was not the first to express this idea.

When Alfred, in 871, became king of Wessex, the country of the West Saxons, England was still suffering from the last of three great invasions: Roman, Anglo-Saxon, and Danish. This last one began about 787 and was an exercise of plunder, pillage, and murder; but when the invaders had made room for themselves they established peaceful settlements. In 886, Alfred became king of England but he controlled only the area lying south of the line from London to Liverpool. The rest was still the region of the Danelaw. As king he organized, ruled, and defended his kingdom; as a scholar he wrote and translated books, as we have indicated.

One of his chief works was a translation, from Latin into Anglo-Saxon, of the *Pastoral Rule* or *Charge* of Pope Gregory the Great, which Alfred also called the *Sheperd's Book,* referring to any "shepherd of souls." In the introduction to his translation, he wrote,

> King Alfred bids greet Bishop Waerferth with loving words and with friendship; and I let it be known to thee that it has very often come into my mind what wise men there formerly were throughout England, both of sacred and secular orders. . . .
> I remembered also how I saw the country before it had been all ravaged and burned; how the churches throughout the whole of England stood filled with

treasures and books. There was also a great multitude of God's servants, but they could not understand anything of the books because they were not written in their own language.

Remembering that the "law" given in Hebrew was translated into Greek and then into Latin, it seemed good to Alfred to translate other good books into Anglo-Saxon and he began with the *Pastoral Care* by Gregory. He told Bishop Waerferth that he was having a copy sent to every bishopric in his kingdom and that from these copies others might be made. He added,

Therefore it seems better to me, if you agree, for us also to translate some of the books which are most needful for all men to know into the language which we can all understand; and for you to see to it as can easily be done if we have tranquility enough, that all the free-born youth now in England who are rich enough to be able to devote themselves to it, be set to learn as long as they are not fit for any other occupation, until they are well able to read English writing; and let those afterwards be taught more in the Latin language who are to continue learning, and be promoted to a higher rank.

His biographer reported that Alfred established a school for his own children, for the sons of nobles, and even for some of the common people's children. He translated other books besides the *Pastoral Care*, especially Boethius's *Consolation of Philosophy*, which he loved, and which stimulated him to include his own thoughts in a free translation.

THE CRUSADES

The first Crusade (1096) was preached by a monk of Cluny who had become Pope Urban II. The monastery of Cluny had started a reform of the entire Benedictine Order. The church had long wished to check the constant civil war brought about by feudal conditions. The feudal system regulated the conduct of vassals in relation to their overlord, but there was no system or regulation controlling the conduct of a vassal with or against other vassals. This was a great defect in feudal law. The monks of Cluny, with the support of powerful laymen, had moved for the restoration of peace and order, the Peace of God as it was called. All who committed outrages, attacked the peace-loving, or violated sacred places were solemnly excommunicated. The Peace of God was gradually supplemented by the Truce of God, which banned all fighting each week from Wednesday evening to the following Monday morning. This may look like a way to promote peace but no leader of an army would stop at nightfall on a day of victory to permit his opponent to regroup his forces and to seek new recruits. Pope Urban was in Clermont seeking a renewal of the Truce of God when in November, 1095, by an eloquent address, he launched the first Crusade: "God Wills It," the people shouted—or so the legend said.

The Crusades were made possible by the increasing unity of the West under papal leadership. People were overcoming some of the former localisms and tribalism, becoming willing to carry out a large project together. And because the Crusades were military pilgrimages to the holiest of Christian shrines, they were taken as an expression of self-denial and asceticism. In the Middle Ages, pilgrimages were an accepted form of penance; and in preaching the first Crusade, Pope Urban felt justified in promising immediate entrance into paradise to any crusader who died repenting of his sins.

We have a contemporary estimate of the effect of the pope's program and promise. It was written by the historian Ekkehard, who had gone to Jerusalem in 1101. He reported that nearly a hundred thousand, an estimate only, undertook the service of God from countries including what is at present France, Britain, Ireland, Belgium, and Galicia in northern Spain "and perhaps others." Germany was hardly represented or not at all. Ekkehard said the crusaders carried the sign of the cross, hoping that they might triumph as had earlier invaders under Constantine who had in a vision seen a cross with the words *in hoc signo vinces,* meaning: "By this sign you shall conquer." That was early in the fourth century and this the end of the eleventh century.

The time was favorable, for the invasion from the North had ended and Europe was comparatively peaceful. National and commercial interests and rivalries were not yet strong. There were few competing demands on the barons, dukes, and kings. The blessing of the church had been given to the lesser crusaders against the Moslems of Spain and North Africa. Under these circumstances one can understand the enthusiasm for the great adventure of 1096.

The first Crusade was followed by others. There were eight major and many smaller Crusades during the next two centuries. We shall deal only with their influence upon civilization and education. They were not entirely holy wars and the crusaders were not all chivalrous men risking their lives in a noble cause. Economic interests were involved and a popular writer has held that because cotton is an Arabic word this product was introduced into the West through the Crusades; but this is making history, not writing it. The luxurious life of the East impressed the crusaders. Descriptions of great cities were sent home by leaders unable to write, who employed a monk or secretary. In an illiterate age the letters could not be generally read when they arrived at their destination in the West.

The battles of the crusaders were often unnecessarily brutal. They cut off the heads of the slain victims and carried them back to camp to prove their prowess. When Jerusalem fell (1099), they engaged in a regular pogrom, against Jews and Moslems alike. In Europe, also, the Crusades caused anti-Jewish riots. We must, however, reckon with the likelihood that some of these stories are exaggerated. There is, indeed, a difficulty involved in the idea of a holy war to be carried on in the name of the Christ of the New Testament.

The crusaders suffered from a lack of knowledge about health and the great difficulty in applying what they knew. They are said to have been responsible for the outbreak of leprosy in Europe. It has been asserted that the Crusades had a direct influence on the improvement of surgery and the increase in the number of hospitals. Many of the lords who went on crusade did not return to claim their fiefs. Their serfs and vassals escaped to neighboring towns to swell the growing middle class. The removal of barons strengthened the power of the kings. The crusaders who came back returned with a wider knowledge of the world.

Only the first Crusade went wholly by land. More and more the later crusaders traveled over the Mediterranean on routes that had long been used for trade. This was safer and easier on the feet than the long trek overland. The travelers depended on the Italian and other ports to furnish transport, supplies, ships, and sailors. Italy became the purveyor to the crusading armies, and a great impulse to her developing commerce ensued. The Crusades were a great factor in preparing Italy for the Renaissance and revival of learning. This was their greatest educational influence. Chivalry also developed from the crusading movement and this led to a form of showy aristocratic education.

CHIVALRIC EDUCATION

The institution of chivalry grew up in a feudal society and received its greatest impetus during the period of the Crusades. It continued in full vigor for centuries and continued to influence education even in modern times. The word is derived from the French for horse, *cheval*, whence chevalier, which as a military term meant cavalryman or knight. For the origin of much of the elaborate etiquette and many of the terms of chivalry, one must also go to the French; but the institution as a whole was not purely French. Some of its customs arose in Germany; many of its moral ideas such as loyalty, truthfulness, respect for womanhood, and knightly honor were developed under the influence of Christianity. But, although chivalry may have softened the customs and manners of a rude age, it can hardly be held that the institution was ever truly Christian. It was too aristocratic and recognized no obligation to the common man. It set a moral and social gulf between the nobleman who lived in the castle and those who labored in the manor, the artisans in the city, and even the priest who ministered in the church. Chivalry was based on a caste system.

In the early feudal age, the young nobleman was not expected to have a literary education. His profession was that of a mounted warrior. At seven the boy became a page and learned to serve at table, to carve, and also to hunt. Heraldry and chess were included. At fourteen he became a squire and served as a valet to his knight in putting on his armor and caring for his horse. Fourteen years of service as page and squire prepared the young man for knighthood at the age of twenty-one. After a night of vigil in the church, communion was administered. The candidate was invested with his arms and armor, he knelt at the altar, the sword was laid across his shoulders, and he rose a full-fledged knight.

Chivalric education was not a uniform and static system but one that was adaptable and able to survive under changing conditions. In later times it included many refinements that would have been scorned in a ruder time: music both vocal and instrumental, dancing, the art of love as well as of war, and even some of the sciences, especially the mathematical and military ones. Chaucer's squire is an illustration. He could ride the war horse but he was equally adept at singing and composing songs, playing on the flute, and dancing. In Chaucer's description, drawing gets as much emphasis as the ability to unhorse an opponent. Chivalric tendencies did not die out with chivalry. Schemes for the education of the prince and later of the gentleman and the lady showed traces of chivalric influences. Writers, including Castiglione and Sir Thomas Elyot, favored chivalric ideals. The French academies and the German "knightly academies," the works of Montaigne, Locke, and others, down to the eighteenth century, were influenced by chivalric ideas. Basedow's scheme of 1774 for physical education was prepared for a knightly academy in which he was teaching. As feudalism was at war with commerce, the knight with the burgher, so chivalric education was opposed by the practical and civil education of modern life; but it survived long after it became out-of-date.

MEDIEVAL TOWNS

In Western history, industry, commerce, and urban prosperity have promoted education. There are many more illustrations than exceptions. The earliest schools were opened in the cities of Sumer and these were followed by others in towns of the Fertile Crescent and of the Greeks, Romans, and Moslems. We may notice some cases of the reversed trend. In the Middle Ages the decay of cities turned education over to the comparatively ineffective monastery schools; and in the present United States the children of the "inner city" are at a greater disadvantage than those of the open country: Slum schools have deteriorated and country schools have improved.

We return to conditions in the Middle Ages. The growth of cathedral towns affected educational opportunity. The decline of commerce and of population increased the influence of the bishops. The clerical population of a large city included not only those employed at the cathedral and not only priests but also numerous officials, legal counsels, secretaries, teachers and students in the cathedral school, and even the students and scholars studying in the cathedral library. Towns had market days during the week and, during part of the year, fairs, where not only cloth and food but also books in manuscript were sold. In a cathedral town and in the area that made up the diocese, the bishop was both the civil and the religious head. He administered the law, repaired the streets and walls, and organized the defense.

Other towns grew up around fortified sites. This is the meaning of the word borough or burgh, an Anglo-Saxon word, used in place-names as in Edinburgh, or Strasburg. As a fortified place the borough had no commercial purpose; but in some cases, commercial quarters developed outside the walls. These were then enclosed by outer walls and in such a community a future city often arose. To become a real city the cathedral town or fortified borough had to develop a middle class of workers and merchants and to acquire corporate privileges with officials to carry them into effect.

The industry and trade of the city are closely linked together. Industry must have workers, materials, and markets; commerce finds the markets, brings the raw materials, and supplies the physical needs of the workers. Both industry and commerce are aided by compact population, political stability, just laws, and easy transportation. Money, credit, weights and measures, correct methods of calculation, adequate bookkeeping, and means of communication were other essentials; and these at once suggest the necessity for education. In general, education, broadly speaking, is necessary to an advanced economic system.

The cities of Italy were prepared to take advantage of the new knowledge and new markets that developed in the twelfth century, partly through the Crusades. Venice and Genoa developed their shipping and became great carriers from and to the East. Venice, especially, became a strong link between East and West. She kept up her connection with Constantinople and prospered in trade with that city.

By more than one path goods were transported between the North and these ports. An eastern route used the Danube to Vienna; a western route crossed Switzerland to the Rhine and followed the Seine to Paris; but the Brenner Pass gave the most direct access from Italy to Germany. This third track led to Innsbruck, where it began to fan out in different directions: to the Flemish Coast, to Scandinavia, and to all parts of Germany. Trade routes often led through mountain passes, down river valleys, and employed boats when possible. At points of loading, cities arose. Transportation was laborious and, therefore, expensive.

Venice in later times catered to the German trade, and as early as 1228 a German chamber of commerce was established in the Rialto. Young German businessmen were sent to Italy to study business methods in that advanced society. There was a movement in the other direction also. Italian business and banking houses were located at the North, but only after that region had attained economic maturity. The North furnished raw materials and its people were engaged in hard labor and were exposed to greater risks from industrial accidents. Southern German cities, such as Nuremberg and Augsburg, were in the middle belt between North and South and were reached earlier by Italian art and learning. The great Albrecht Dürer, painter and wood-engraver, flourished about 1500.

In the later medieval times, Italy began to strike back at the Mohammedans who had invested the cities on the islands and the mainland. Genoa and Pisa were rivals in trade but, as already noted, they joined forces against the Moslems; and they played necessary parts in the Crusades. Pisa, also, became the port for the trade of Florence, the capital of the Italian Renaissance. Before the Renaissance, Florence had become wealthy through the wool and silk manufacturers and the work of its goldsmiths, artists, and collectors.

In Florence, the Medici were rich and powerful. They were bankers for much of Europe, from the fourteenth to the sixteenth century. Cosimi de Medici (1384–1464), known as "the elder," was a banker, ruler, and patron of all the fine arts. In form, Florence was a democracy; but in fact, it was an oligarchy under a succession of great families. It is not surprising that it was turbulent nor that the workers' guilds helped to make it so.

Commerce not only followed the natural trade routes but it also demanded their improvement. To understand the situation we must rid ourselves of all ideas of modern transportation. Where water transport was not available, goods were carried on the backs of men or animals. Roads had to be kept in repair and bridges were preferred to fords. To protect their packs and cargoes, merchants traveled in armed bands. Church and state each tried to do its share in making roads and seas safe. The church excommunicated pirates and highwaymen and invoked the Truce of God for the protection of travelers, pilgrims, and merchants. Treaties between nations began to include safe-conduct clauses for traders. The English Magna Carta guaranteed them legal protection; and many cities, eager for the success of their annual fairs or their regular trade, granted them privileges and legal safeguards. In the twelfth century, Italian towns set up a commercial postal system and they also carried private letters. This was an improvement over the ancient Roman post, which carried only official messages.

With the increasing volume and variety of commercial relations, better records became necessary, and so it came about that the Italians invented double-entry bookkeeping sometime in the twelfth century. As late as the eighteenth century, American schoolmasters, conducting private schools in cities, advertised in the newspapers the fact that they were teaching bookkeeping after "the Italian method of double entry." At about the same time, it was in 1202, a great invention from abroad was introduced into Italy—the Hindu-Arabic system of writing numbers with the zero in all empty spaces. This is really a great matter but now that it is commonplace it is almost impossible to interest a child, or even an educated adult, in it. It was difficult, also, to secure the adoption of the new notation. From Italy it was carried north along the trade routes, but four centuries were to elapse before it came into universal use.

THE GUILDS

The merchants and craftsmen of a town were organized into guilds or associations with statutes, officers, and economic, as well as political, rights. They were established for the mutual protection of the members, and the advancement of their interests. Some guilds were of the nature of labor unions and cooperative societies combined, whereas the greater guilds more nearly resembled associations of manufacturers and chambers of commerce. The guilds are of importance in social and educational history because they carried on a system of vocational education that helped to develop a lower middle class of free, independent workingmen. These were an antidote to serfdom.

Guilds varied in scope. Some were simple, comprising only those engaged in one craft or trade; others included several, usually related, occupations. The form of organization of some was democratic and of others it may have been oligarchic or capitalistic. In some guilds the power was seized by a special group who exploited the rest. Some guilds, like certain labor unions, excluded particular minorities or races from practicing a trade; or they restricted the numbers of those admitted. The word *guild*, therefore, stands for diverse social phenomena. Most students think of the small-industry and local guilds with friendly personal relations between an apprentice and the teacher-employer and with plenty of room at the top for every apprentice to become a master-workman. This condition was not universal.

In crafts as in chivalry there were three stages: the apprentice, journeyman, and master-workman. In the guild the series could be interrupted and the third stage especially was not opened to every journeyman. The number of apprentices allowed to any master could be limited by a guild. The most frequent number in the small guilds was two, but sons of the master were not counted and new apprentices might be taken on before the terms of those about to be finished had been completed. This was done to avoid the difficulty of a shop being left without experienced workers. Some apprentices were not allowed to become master-workmen, whereas the son of the master might be promoted without the usual training.

Children were apprenticed early. The period of apprenticeship in different trades ranged from two to ten years, but the most frequent term seems to have been seven years. Both the age at entrance and the length of the training varied from trade to trade and in relation to other circumstances. Only masters of good character were allowed to take apprentices. At the beginning there was usually a short period of probation for the young worker. This was followed by a contract, called an indenture, between the master and the boy's father. The master agreed to teach his trade, to supply food, clothes, and lodging, and to stand *in loco parentis* to the apprentice. In the usual small crafts, the boy became a member of the master's household and ate at the family table. The apprentice on his part agreed to be obedient and dutiful, not to marry while in training, to keep the secrets of the craft, to work faithfully, and to conduct himself honorably. The indenture was executed by a notary before witnesses and sealed with the proper oaths. Abuses such as running away or excessive cruelty to the boy were to be laid before the guild officers. When the young man had completed his training he received a certificate to the fact and was free to seek employment wherever it might be found.

The guilds were the channels of vocational education; and apprenticeship was the means of providing an adequate succession of skilled workers. The workshop was the technical school of the Middle Ages. At a time when all the common articles of daily use were made by hand, skill in a craft gave the journeyman the means to earn an adequate living, establish a family, perform his civic duties, and live a satisfying life among his equals. Literary education was not included in apprenticeship, but late medieval and modern indentures provided that the boy must be given the opportunity to learn to read, write, and do common arithmetic. These skills could be acquired in evening schools or from tutors.

Guilds also established Latin schools for boys who wished to prepare for a learned profession. These were called medieval guild schools, which was unfortunate as will appear. They were numerous. Of thirty-three English guilds studied by A. F. Leach, twenty-eight at some time maintained guild schools of the usual Latin grammar variety. The primary purpose was philanthropic. We must repeat that they did not teach trades, for the use of the words *guild schools* constantly confuses students; they gave literary education of secondary grade to boys who later might go to a university to study law, medicine, or divinity. Thus, a guild of Worcester, England, "time out of mind" maintained a school that, at the Reformation, had "above the number of a hundred scholars." Famous London guild schools were the Stationers School, the Mercers School, and—one of the most distinguished of all—the Merchant Taylors School, whose first headmaster was the great educator, Richard Mulcaster.

Guilds, also, especially in Germany, maintained apprenticeship schools. Individual apprenticeship in the workshop was replaced by regular teaching in schools of different types. In the city of Munich, for instance, the associations of artisans maintained a variety of technical schools from early times until about 1900, when Georg Kerschensteiner incorporated them into the public school system. Later he was brought to the United States to urge Americans to vote for vocational education to be given to children before they had a good general and liberal education. Let us return to the German example: In Berlin the merchants' association maintained six continuation schools to teach commercial skills to children; so, for example, the tailors' association had a school taught by master tailors, cutters, and designers from the large tailoring establishments. No one questions the need for vocational education but the guild system may not have been the best. Nor has the problem been solved. New inventions, new tastes, new tariffs, population increases, and other factors preclude a set solution.

We noticed that the guild organizations gave members opportunities for political self-education. Especially in the free towns or communes, the guilds joined forces with all the discontented classes against the rich and powerful. Each guild was a corporation whose members, as in a small republic, deliberated and voted and thus gained a practical civic education. There were struggles between groups within a guild, between guilds, and between a guild and the town. There were problems of taxation, of military and police duty, and of the apportionment of privileges and obligations. In dealing with these problems, the members learned to gain their ends by finding a solution that was acceptable. This might not be easy considering the numbers involved. We must not leave the subject without giving an idea of the numbers that might be involved. The wool-working guild of Florence, already mentioned here, called the *Arte di Calimala*, had twenty thousand and later thirty thousand members. Such large proportions of the total population must have been influential in the politics of the city as labor unions are today. Guilds of such size were also very unusual.

SCHOOLS IN THE CITIES

City schools arose in Germany in the thirteenth century, if not before. Documents from Cologne on the Rhine show the existence of city Latin schools in 1234. Wroclaw, formerly Breslan, in Poland, located a hundred miles east of Dresden, in 1267, asked leave to build a city school so placed that the children would not need to cross unsafe bridges. The course of studies may also have been involved. Hamburg, on the Elbe River in northwest Germany, by appeal to the pope against the local clergy, gained permission to establish a city school—a proposal that the cathedral authorities had fought for eight years.

The struggle at Hamburg was not unusual. Local church authorities opposed the city schools as an invasion of their privileges. The cathedral might be willing to allow the city schools to teach writing and arithmetic and even the more advanced practical studies, but not Latin. When the clergy and the city courts could not adjust such disputes, the case was sometimes taken to the pope who frequently decided, as at Hamburg, in favor of the town and against the priests. Usually there was no difficulty over purely vernacular schools. The trouble arose when a vernacular school wished to teach Latin also. The lower clergy were not always well-trained and feared the loss of prestige if the general public scholars should become as highly educated as they were. Luther at the Reformation published some examples of priests who had hardly any of the literary qualifications expected of them.

The deeper issue may have been secularism. If the city, a guild, or a private society of teachers were to teach Latin, rhetoric, and perhaps logic, these functions of the church, or of churchmen, would become a business like any other. The church held that all life should be religious; but city and private schools were thought likely to place civic and business interests ahead of or in competition with religion.

The writing school was more specialized and less church-related than the usual vernacular school. The writing school also taught business arithmetic and bookkeeping to the sons, and sometimes to the daughters, of the middle classes. At a higher level these schools taught the *ars dictaminis* or *dictamen*, mentioned earlier. Such schools existed in Italian cities in the tenth century. Evidently those who learned this art prepared to use or to practice commercial law.

Business letters and records were still in Latin in the early centuries of this period; but it was not the Latin of Cicero or even the Latin of the ordinary Roman citizen. It was medieval Latin, not ignorant or stupid Latin, but only the speech of its day. Latin had been in use for a long time in the later medieval period and, of course, it had changed just as English has changed in the much shorter period since Chaucer. The frequent use of prepositions instead of word endings was one characteristic, but this and other changes did not make the language any less clear or less effective. It was "bad Latin" only when it was written or spoken by ignorant persons. Gradually, by the thirteenth and later centuries, it became Italian, Spanish, and so on; that is, it became the vernacular speech of modern times, and this change occurred in business practice and was taught in business schools. Business schools became practical and usually private but sometimes they became public schools. At first they used Latin but later the vernacular. The changes began in the tenth or eleventh centuries and were completed by the thirteenth or later.

The vernacular schools, although they multiplied rapidly, were often humble enough. They were often called reading and writing or writing and reckoning schools. That many of them existed in England, Scotland, Germany, and elsewhere long before the Reformation is clear. They grew rapidly about 1350 or 1400, which is about a century later than the beginnings of the city Latin schools. They became almost general by 1500;

a Mainz leaflet of 1498 asserted that "everybody now wants to read and write." It has been estimated that the city of Nuremberg in the sixteenth century had about fifty reckoning, that is, arithmetic, masters; and they formed a guild. This is an early example of a teachers' association.

Most of our information about these early vernacular schools comes from records of disputes and lawsuits. Lubeck had several German schools about 1400, and in 1418 a formal agreement was drawn up between the city and the scholasticus. The latter consented to the maintenance of four German writing schools on condition that one third of the fees received should be turned over to the cathedral. A similar solution was reached at Brunswick in 1420. It was agreed that the writing masters should confine themselves to the common language, teaching no Latin at all. That the contract had to be reaffirmed later in the century is evidence that it was not always observed.

On the other hand, Latin schools often gave elementary instruction. This was true of the burg schools of Scotland, which go back to the thirteenth or even the twelfth century, as in Stirling and Perth. In Amsterdam the city Latin schools had to fight against encroachment by the writing masters. Hamburg, in about 1400, limited the number and attendance of common schools to protect the interests of the Latin schools. But all this legislation was the effort to sweep out the ocean with a broom. At the end of another century (1500) the Hamburg scholasticus complained that "new schools are almost daily opened by old women and other persons." This was changing the words but not the spirit of the Mainz leaflet previously quoted. It also shows again that many unauthorized schools were being opened everywhere, in homes, tailors' shops, and other rooms where indoor occupations could be combined with elementary teaching. The poor were seeking education for their children. The closing Middle Ages saw vigorous competition in school-founding.

The writing and reckoning schools taught arithmetic and bookkeeping and were the chief agencies to introduce the Hindu-Arabic numerals and the new methods of computation into the West. The rise of commerce and cities both changed and increased the educational demands of the times. Bookkeeping, commercial arithmetic, the need for commercial and manorial records, and the recording of city and guild minutes and accounts all gave employment to a growing class of men who made their living as writers, accountants, and secretaries. Private correspondence also increased, and men made a business of writing letters for those who could not write their own. Setting up their desks in the open at a busy corner, they plied their trade. These were often teachers who earned an extra penny in this way. A vernacular literature was growing up rapidly and with it grew the general desire to learn to read. The wealthy and influential people of the towns desired a regular education in Latin and the seven liberal arts for their sons. The common people demanded vernacular schooling and a ready acquaintance with figures and the pen. With the growth of the cities, both classes of schools multiplied. Meanwhile knowledge also advanced rapidly. In the last three centuries of the Middle Ages the population of Europe may have doubled, but the available knowledge multiplied many times—knowledge of the sciences and medicine, of law, philosophy, and theology. It was this great increase in knowledge that led to the foundation of the universities. The schools, which had served the West as the main carriers of its rather meager learning, now became inadequate.

AGE OF TRANSLATION

We shall now briefly review the contributions to Western learning made by the Arabs in Spain, a topic to which we referred in the preceding chapter. The conquest of North Africa proved more difficult than that of the East, and Carthage was not captured until 698. A decade was consumed in providing a firm government for the region. Then, in 711, a Moslem general, Gebel Tarik, landed near the rock named for him, Gibraltar, conquered most of Spain, crossed the Pyrenees, and in 735 was stopped at the battle of Tours. But the Moslems held ground in France until 769, when they were driven back into Spain. In Spain they remained and built up a remarkable civilization but were finally dislodged in 1492, after seven hundred and fifty years.

Most of Spain had been quickly overrun but was difficult to pacify and govern. During periods of vigorous rule, Moslem Spain was prosperous and her cities rivaled in wealth, luxury, and pleasure the cities of the East. Cordova, the capital, competed with Bagdad and Constantinople in the arts of civilized life and far excelled Paris and every other city north of the Pyrenees. In the ninth and tenth centuries, Cordova had a half-million inhabitants for whom it provided well-lighted paved streets, public baths, and a bridge across the Guadalquiver to connect the city with its southern suburbs. Seville, Valencia, and Granada were other famous cities; but Toledo was the greatest center of scholarship and continued to be famous for its science and philosophy after it had again, in 1085, become Christian.

At Toledo, in the twelfth century, Archbishop Raymond was the founder and patron of a vigorous school of translators. Arabic continued in Toledo to be the official language of law and business for two hundred years. Many Christians whose faith and practice were assimilated to those of Islam lived in a separate quarter of the city and spoke two languages, Arabic and a form of low Latin on the way to becoming Spanish. They were called Mozarabs; that is, would-be or imitation Arabs. The Latin language was written with Arabic characters, which were used also on coins minted by

Spanish kings. Even the ritual of the Catholic Church showed Mozarabic influences. Similar assimilation in the direction of Islam was shown by Jews who adopted the language, dress, manners, and, in a very few cases, the faith of Islam.

The recovery of ancient, especially Greek, science and philosophy was a major factor in the medieval Renaissance; and the Arabs in Spain were the chief agents in making that learning available to the West. The religious principles of the Moslems, especially their monotheism, kept them from the cultivation of the arts of painting and sculpture and the study of Greek epic and dramatic literature. Perhaps for that reason they devoted themselves diligently to Greek science and the logic of Aristotle. If they had applied a similar industry to the writings of Homer, Euripides, Xenophon, and Thucydides, and of the Romans, Cicero, Virgil, and Horace, the literary Renaissance might have arisen in the twelfth century in Spain and France rather than in Italy two centuries later.

Next to Spain, the most convenient gate through which the ancient learning could be brought to Europe was Sicily. That central island had been in Moslem hands for two centuries before the Normans came, and a large Moslem population remained there. But the new eagerness of European scholars for a broader learning did more for the success of the movement than the place, the particular people, or the actual books that were available for translation. It was not the Arabs who translated books into Latin but the Latin scholars who translated from Arabic into the scholars' language of western Europe. Before the twelfth century the schools had only the books by Donatus, Capella, Cassiodorus, Isidore, Boethius, Pope Gregory, and others. The monastery and cathedral libraries had the works, including the letters of Jerome, of Augustine, Bede, and others; but for want of free access and for the fact of illiteracy they were not widely read. There was no general reading public.

With the dozen or more first-line translators from Arabic into Latin we can deal only briefly. Adelhard of Bath translated Euclid's *Elements* and the astronomical tables of Al-Khwarizmi. He also wrote original works on "natural questions"—a science miscellany that was popular in the Middle Ages—and books on astronomy and the astrolabe. Another mathematical translator was the Italian, Plato of Tivoli, who lived in Barcelona for a dozen years after 1124. Leonardo Fibonacci was not a translator but an original writer on mathematics and the first to explain the Hindu-Arabic numerals to Christian Europe. This he did in his *Liber Abaci*, the book of the abacus. He also wrote some more advanced books on mathematics. Robert of Chester translated the algebra of Al-Khwarizmi and revised Adelhard's version of the astronomical tables of the same author. In 1143, Robert of Chester finished a Latin version of the Koran.

How the scientific and mathematical minds of the twelfth century were affected by the discovery of Greek science in an Arabic dress may be seen in the *Philosophia* of Daniel of Morley. He found the scholastics of Paris filled with a "pretentious ignorance" and hastened to Toledo "to hear the world's great masters." There he became a pupil of Gerard of Cremona, one of the most prolific and learned translators of that time. Gerard had received a thorough Latin education in Italy and studied Arabic in Spain, where he found and translated Ptolemy's *Almagest*—a vast work combining geography and astronomy compiled by Claudius Ptolemy in the second Christian century. The work was the basis of the so-called Ptolemaic system that remained authoritative until Copernicus (1473–1543).

Meanwhile, in Sicily and northern Italy, scholars had again begun to translate directly from the Greek into Latin. Greek science and the Aristotelian philosophy were again made available in their entirety to the Christian schools and universities of Europe. Aristotle was to scholasticism, to theology, and to advanced studies in the liberal arts what Galen was to the study of medicine and the Digest of Justinian to the study of law. When we take into account the wide range of the subjects treated by Aristotle, and the persistence of his influence down to our own time, we see that he was the most important author in the medieval Renaissance. The material for that revival was available only when Aristotle's works became available.

The introduction of Aristotle into Western education took place in the two centuries between 1100 and 1300. Abelard (1079–1142) knew only parts of two of Aristotle's writings on logic. In about 1128 James of Venice translated from Greek into Latin Aristotle's *Topics, Prior and Posterior Analytics* and a book dealing with logical fallacies. This group was called the New Logic—new only in the sense that they were newly made available to western Europe. The work of Boethius was again brought into circulation and new translations of the logical works of Aristotle from Arabic into Latin were circulated. All this work of recovery occurred in the twelfth century; the acceptance of the works by the church and the schools took another century, as we shall see. And if we turn back a few paragraphs we see that the twelfth century was also the time when many mathematical works were translated from the Arabic. We should notice also that logic and mathematics are tools of learning, useful in securing quantitative results and irrefutable conclusions in other fields.

Several of the shorter works dealing with natural history were introduced before 1200. The other writings appeared a little later. Most of these like the logical works came either directly from the Greek or by way of the Arabic. The works dealing with social and ethical questions—the *Ethics, Politics, Economics, and Rhetoric*—were translated by 1275, making all of Aristotle's writings available and available to a larger public than ever before. His books became required reading and were treated in courses in the universities.

THEORIES OF EDUCATION

The Middle Ages had no writers on education of the quality of Plato, Aristotle, or Quintilian, and under the circumstances teachers doubtless tended to imitate their former masters or, in emergencies, to follow their own impulses. At least we do not hear that they studied the example of Socrates, read Plato's *Phaedrus*, or discussed the questions treated by the great Roman writers on education. There were no such schools for teachers and only a few writers are known to have dealt with education. We shall consider two.

At the beginning of the fourteenth century (in about 1306), Pierre Dubois, a French jurist and publicist, wrote *On the Recovery of the Holy Land* or, in Latin, *De Recuperatione Terre Sancta*. The idea of another Crusade is not to be taken seriously; the title is a mere device, a container for all sorts of ideas that were intended to interest King Edward I of England and, secondly, King Philip IV of France (the Fair). Although Dubois was a successful lawyer and twice a member of the Estates General of France, this and several other pamphlets seem to have had no great influence.

Very little is known about the life of Dubois. He left no letters or other personal papers. As a writer he was careless, quoting from memory, not always correctly, confusing Augustine of Hippo with Augustine of Canterbury, and attending too little to a proper organization of his manuscript—a man in a hurry. He heard the great Thomas Aquinas and the less great Siger de Brabant at the University of Paris. Siger was tinged with heresy and for that reason was dismissed from the university in 1276. Dubois was born about 1250 and heard these men sometime between 1266 when Siger joined the faculty and 1272 when Aquinas left it. This period covered the adolescence of Dubois, from the age of sixteen to twenty-two, when a youth's views become firmly settled. He may have been diverted from the study of theology by Siger de Brabant. At least he became a lawyer, not a priest. The University of Orléans, not far away, had a civil law faculty, which Paris lacked; and Dubois may have acquired his knowledge of law at Orléans.

In his *Recovery*, Dubois deals with many topics, but we shall deal only with two passages on education. We begin with Section XLV, which repeats and goes beyond an earlier section. He proposed to send boys and girls to school at the early age of four years, thus anticipating Headstart. Those who could not come so early could be admitted later. He also anticipated a rudimentary kind of phrenology, for he proposed to have boys chosen whose heads were "well shaped." The teachers were also to be selected: They were to be skilful and experienced, but we are not told where such persons were to be found or how they could be prepared.

Lessons were to begin with the Psalter or Book of Psalms and these selections were to be sung as well as read or perhaps orally committed to

Lecture by a scholar. Facsimile of a woodcut from the first half of the sixteenth century. ("Lecture" frequently meant dictation.)

memory. Much of the teaching consisted of the lessons being read over and over by the teacher or an assistant with repetition by the pupils—simple memory work. With the Psalms, Donatus was taken up. And then "when a boy is hearing the book of Cato's *Distichs* read and other minor authors he should have four long lessons a day, or as much as his natural capacity can stand; let him not go to sleep over these." In some cases, the master read first, then another, perhaps an assistant, read and the boy repeated after him. Almost certainly, a lack of books was one great difficulty. As soon as the boys had made a little progress they were to speak Latin only. The Bible was read to the boys who also memorized long passages.

Composition was to be reserved to the evening hours, but the scarcity of parchment must have restricted the writing that could be required. The Golden Legend of the Saints and stories of the poets were considered proper material for composition. In these early years, therefore, the pupils learned to read, speak, and write Latin—after a fashion—and this was to be accomplished in six to eight years, when secondary education was begun. This consisted of the three philosophies: mental or logic, moral or ethics, and natural or science, and one or more additional languages, Greek, Arabic, or Aramaic. Compendia and summaries were to be used. Reading by the master and repetition by the pupils continued to be the chief methods. We should remember that when Dubois was writing, the University of Paris was about as old as the American land-grant colleges are today, a full century.

A second medieval work on schools and teaching is called *Commendation of the Clerk*, that is, cleric. It was written by an unknown German, apparently himself a clergyman, and it appeared fifty or more years after the *Recovery of the Holy Land* by Dubois. It deals with some practical questions such as schoolhouses in relation to climate, pupils in relation to temperament, and teachers with or without licenses. We learn that schoolhouses were not provided with artificial heat and needed to be built of solid materials to conserve the internal warmth in winter and to keep out the heat of the sun in summer. We are advised that the nobility of learning is such that it should not be bestowed on those suffering from incurable disease or afflicted by noticeable physical defects. And, thirdly, the teacher's license is no certain guarantee of superior teaching ability.

Pupils were to begin school at the age of seven. When they had learned to write the letters correctly, to make syllables, and to combine syllables into words, the time would have come to teach them the "etymology" of the words they were using. But perhaps he meant the parts of speech and the word endings. It was the Latin language that was in question. Meanwhile texts teaching moral lessons, poems, and rhetoric and even the "other sciences" were introduced gradually. He approved what he called the custom of the time, namely, "combining the practice of music with the milk of grammar and . . . practical arithmetic." Later metaphysics and other advanced philosophy were studied and schooling was completed by the third period of seven years at the age of twenty-eight. Thus a master-teacher was prepared.

The question arose whether a Christian clergyman might be permitted to study the secular arts. "And it seems not. Reason convinces us that a Christian should not sweat over the books of the Gentiles because their arguments are contrary to the Catholic faith." For example, Aristotle held that the world is eternal, not created; and Averroes manifestly denied the possibility of eternal life. This line is continued, but we have presented enough to suggest the source of the crisis in Christian education that developed from the study of Aristotle and other pagan scholars. Our anonymous author was not satisfied with this conclusion; he had a last word. That word was that to study pagan learning to lead men to the worship of the true God was not only permissible, but highly desirable.

THE RISE OF UNIVERSITIES

The early history of the oldest universities is obscure. They were not planned and founded to satisfy a set scheme; they grew out of the work of scholars who drew around themselves large numbers of professional and other advanced students. Gradually associations of masters and comparable bodies of students were organized and customs, regulations, exercises, and degrees developed and the pope, king, or emperor set his seal upon the evolving institution and accorded it specific rights and privileges. At this point the university, one is tempted to say, was created; but we should rather say that the university had evolved and all that civil and religious powers did was to recognize and give approval to the fact.

We select two from many possible examples: Bologna and Paris. In each case a number of great teachers in a city able to supply the needs of students was the essential factor. In Bologna, at the crossroads of northern Italy, a famous student of Roman law, Irnerius, and other teachers supported the claims of Italian cities that were seeking freedom from control by the Holy Roman Empire. They based their arguments on the rights conferred on the cities by ancient Roman charters that were part of the ancient Roman law.

Roman law, in the form of the Twelve Tables revered by Cicero, was already old when Cicero wrote. Law must have been in force when Rome was a village and it is in use today in the Latin countries of Europe and America. The oldest books of the Bible are not much older. In republican Rome, laws were the acts of assemblies or the Senate; as the governments of the Empire became more and more autocratic, the edicts or "constitutions" of the emperors and the writings of jurists became law. When Justinian, in about A.D. 528, became emperor in Constantinople, he appointed a commission to collect and organize (a) the constitutions of the emperors and

(b) the doctrines of the jurists. The vast collection of the constitutions became the *Code* and that of the writings or doctrines of the jurists is the *Digest*. Irnerius and his contemporaries lectured on the *Digest* and referred to the *Code* when necessary.

The lecturing must receive attention. To lecture is to read and a lectern is a reading desk to hold the book or paper. In the medieval days of few books and no school library every student brought writing materials to take down the lecturer's words as he read from the *Digest,* for example, or from his comments, interpretation, and emendation of the author under discussion. When the student became a lecturer the process would be continued until the commentary became more voluminous than the text.

Why, at Bologna and other cities, there were many students where there had not been any before, it is easy to see. The cities themselves were a primary cause. The cities brought together large numbers with conflicting interests, buying and selling, making loans and wills, collecting debts, and committing crimes of violence. Courts were needed and lawyers to look after the interests of clients; lawyers who knew the law and its provisions, history, and philosophy obtained the larger numbers of clients and that is why they studied under Irnerius. The same reasoning applied to doctors and their patients. There was a very early center of medical instruction at Salerno in Italy, but because it did not develop into a university we shall not tell its story. Many universities, at Paris for example, had medical faculties; but at Paris the theological faculty was more famous. Usually there was a man as well as a city, a scholar and teacher, often a debator or controversialist, that drew students to a school. We know this was true in Bologna. In Paris the cathedral school of Nôtre Dame had become a leading center for the study of religious doctrines through the teaching and controversies of William of Champeaux (1070–1121), Abelard (1079–1142), and other theologians. Abelard has special claims on our interest: He was keen, eloquent, arrogant, personally attractive, and therefore, able to draw numbers of eager students. He and others were exploring and developing the power of logic as an instrument of learning just as in later periods mathematics, laboratories, field work, and archaeological excavation became tools for the increase of knowledge. So, Abelard invented a small instrument; he called it *Sic et Non*, or *Yes and No*. It was a book of one hundred fifty-eight questions such as, "Is God one or not?" and after each question he set down the opposing statements by leading thinkers, churchmen, and others without stating any conclusion.

Abelard was not a skeptic; but he was pursued, almost persecuted, by Bernard of Clairvaux, who succeeded in having some of Abelard's teaching condemned by a church council. While Abelard was on his way to Rome to seek vindication from the pope, death intervened. He was not a skeptic but, rather, an inquirer; and it was one of the important conditions of the Middle Ages that many earnest men could not distinguish between investigation

Disputation at the University of Paris about 1400. Notice the professor's text and the academic dress of all participants. (Courtesy of the Bettman Archive.)

and disbelief. Abelard declared that the purpose of the *Sic et Non* was to encourage thinking because "through doubt we are led to inquire and through inquiry we discover truth." That the method became immediately fruitful is shown by the appearance of works that imitated it. One of these was the *Sentences* of Peter Lombard, who attended Abelard's lectures. The *Sentences* reported what the great authorities had said on theological questions. Gratian, a monk of Bologna, prepared the *Decretum,* a "harmony of discordant canons"; that is, of the statements of the canon or church law as contrasted with the Roman law. These books, because the authors had less faith in the skill of students or less personal courage than Abelard, drew and stated the conclusions to which the materials led.

The universities of the Middle Ages, like the so-called private universities of the present, were incorporated higher schools, equipped with a charter, seal, by-laws, and officers. Other schools were directly controlled by a church, city, guild, founder, or private owner; but the universities were legal persons, ordinarily free from external control. Being in the same world as other agents they were, naturally, not free from external influences. Both the church and the empire, as well as kings, bishops, and the Dominican and Franciscan Orders, found ways of shaping their policies and of using them for purposes other than the pursuit and promulgation of knowledge and truth.

The earliest universities, Bologna, Paris, and Oxford, developed late in the twelfth century. Early in the next century Cambridge and Montpellier were chartered; later several were founded in Italy, Spain, and southern France. Prague (1347) was the first German, partly Czech, foundation. Vienna was opened in 1365 and the Polish university of Cracow at about the same time. New institutions were opened in the fifteenth century in several countries including Scotland. About eighty universities were open in Europe by 1500; and if we extend our period to 1600 we must add a few Latin-American institutions. Other universities founded in the seventeenth century include Harvard in 1636. Gradually the movement encircled the globe.

The university charters gave grants of privileges, or rights, to the institutions, their faculties, and students. Thus the university could control its organization and policy and try to punish students for misdemeanors. Students from foreign lands appreciated this privilege because local courts were sometimes prejudiced against them. In the heated state of opinion that resulted from "town and gown" riots in a tempestuous age, this was a valuable safeguard, and one that could also be abused.

Universities had the right to suspend lectures and to go on strike when living conditions, food prices, or violence became intolerable. Because the institution brought money into the city, the university was able to exert a certain leverage against an unjust community. A university strike had a technical name; it was a *cessalio,* a stoppage of operations. The next step, if all efforts at reconciliation failed, was the migration, a removal to a more suitable place if one was found. The migration was easy in the Middle Ages when the institutions had no laboratories, or library, and used rented buildings. In the third place, the universities had the right to set student requirements; control the granting of degrees; to examine, license, employ, and dismiss professors; and to direct the inner economy of the institution. There was a period when the students of Bologna and other southern universities were in control, but this did not last. Universities have generally been controlled by professors, administrators, external agencies, or a combination of these, although in modern times, students are often given membership on various boards and committees.

The students at first lived in rented rooms and later in buildings entirely occupied by students and supervised by the university. When instructors were assigned to such a student hall, when an organization had been effected, and when some of the elementary instruction was given in the hall, this constituent part of a university came to be known as a college. The English universities at Oxford and Cambridge have retained this collegiate form and exhibit most fully the medieval arrangement. These English colleges bear something of the same relation to the controlling university as the states of the Union bear to the government of the United States. They have their own personnel, organization, and internal regulations; and the university has a general faculty, regulations, requirements, and confers degrees.

Students in medieval times were young, often arriving at the age of twelve or thirteen—hence the need for regulation and supervision. They were often foreigners in a strange land. Their rooms were unheated and the streets were dark and inadequately policed. There were few if any forms of legitimate amusement. One gathers that life in a medieval university was often irregular and sometimes incredibly violent.

Universities resulted from a general popular demand that they, in turn, stimulated. They were fostered by the papacy, emperor, and kings, partly because these rulers benefitted from their instruction—in law and theology especially—but also for the increase and spread of knowledge in general. They prospered because the leaders, if not the masses felt a need for them. They offered new opportunities and new vocations to the young men. The numbers of their students were not as large as the chroniclers reported. Perhaps no medieval university, not even Paris, had more than six thousand students at one time; and the smaller institutions counted their numbers in hundreds not thousands.

The instruction, as already stated, was bookish and authoritarian. We can hardly realize the submissiveness of the medieval mind to the authority of Aristotle, "the Philosopher," and Galen, and to the theological textbooks. Lectures were not contributions to knowledge or systematic treatments of a field but rather commentaries on a book or efforts to harmonize conflicting views. But after all—although orthodoxy in law, medicine, and theology was favored—heresy gradually increased as the arguments were sharpened and new knowledge was introduced until, in the sixteenth century, Peter Ramus of the University of Paris argued that *all* that Aristotle taught is false. This was an absurdity but it shows that modern times had arrived for him.

SUMMARY

The later Middle Ages is a time of recovery and also of progress, of new ideas and institutions. The medieval revival prepared the way for the classical revival in Italy, which is often taken as the beginning of the modern era. Cities, commerce, architecture, schools and universities pointed the way to the future and led the way.

In the ninth and tenth centures feudalism spread over Europe. Feudalism was the opposite of central rule, of urbanism, commerce, architecture,—in a word it was ruralism. This gave an opportunity to the vikings and they spread destruction over much of Europe; but they became civilized and of this change the work of Alfred the Great is an early example. He was an example and promoter of Christian education. One of the features of learning in England to which he contributed was the use of a modern language, Old English, for scholarly purposes.

The Crusades served to unite the West, increase its knowledge of the world, develop means of transport, and make Europe aware of a civilization that was more advanced than its own. When barons were long absent or failed to return, their serfs and villains often escaped to the towns and joined the growing class of urban freemen. The Crusades, therefore, contributed to the growth of chivalry and the arts of the man on horseback and also to the growth of cities and urban education.

Chivalric education developed ideals of knightly honor, service, military skills, and courtesy; and out of this grew the education of the prince, diplomat, and gentleman. Upper-class education was long influenced by chivalric ideas, aims, and practice.

In northern Europe, villages became towns and some towns grew to become cities. This urban trend was of the highest importance in three types of education: vocational education through apprenticeship fostered by the guilds; elementary education including reading, writing, arithmetic, bookkeeping, and the drawing up of legal papers; and classical education in Latin schools and universities. In all history, the city, from Sumer to Paris to San Francisco, has been the mother of learning.

The twelfth and later centuries brought to the West a knowledge of the ancient Greek classics including those of Aristotle. This knowledge came by way of the Arabs in Spain and also directly through Constantinople. We have called this the age of translation, but the recovery of Homer and Thucycides and the classical revival will be treated in the following chapter. The Middles Ages were weak in educational theories, but we have summarized the ideas of two writers, Pierre Dubois and a German whose name has been lost.

Universities began to form themselves in the twelfth century. They were independent corporations of students and professors devoted to higher learning. Their most important privileges were the rights of self-government and of granting their degrees and selecting their teachers without outside interference. They educated new classes of professional servants of state and church, increased learning, multiplied books, and served as arbiters in disputed matters of government and religion. Their inability to free themselves from a dependence on authors, who were regarded as authorities, was their chief intellectual defect. Before the end of the Middle Ages, authors other than the literary masters of Greece and Rome were again recovered in the Italian Renaissance. Gradually the full complement of ancient culture was restored; but this was both an age of restoration and a creative period.

QUESTIONS

1. How can the division of the Middle Ages into an early and a late period be justified?
2. The fief is the central feature of feudalism. What would you take to be the central feature of the strong state? Of the great city?
3. Can you argue, against the view of this textbook, that education produces the strong state and the great city?
4. Chivalric education has fared rather badly in literature. Find examples and consider why it has had "a bad press."
5. In considering the probable reasons why guilds established Latin schools and scholarships in universities, consider and compare the Rockefeller family's support of universities, research, and Colonial Williamsburg.
6. The probability is great that in medieval schools the treatment of the pupils was strict, harsh, even brutal. Why is this question ignored in the literature?
7. Why did Christian scholars learn Arabic to acquire a knowledge of Greek writings instead of learning Greek?
8. Consider the statement: The medieval universities were vocational schools.
9. How do modern teaching methods in mathematics and the exact sciences differ from those used in the medieval universities? Why?

NOTES AND SOURCES

The university was the most important educational institution to develop in the Middle Ages. After some preliminary steps at Bologna, the real form of the institution developed in the twelfth century. The instruction was always in Latin and so were the books. Some acquaintance with that language was the unstated entrance requirement. This knowledge could be acquired in monastic, cathedral, and other schools. These schools and the universities may be thought of as a natural system, one not overtly established to form a system. We list three famous works in different languages dealing with the rise of universities. The German work by Dereifle appeared first, the French book by d'Irsay is readable, and the revised Rashdall is the fullest and best. The internal development of university organization has been treated by Pearl Kibre.

Other books in the following list deal with nonliterary education—namely, chivalric education for princes, soldiers, and gentlemen and apprenticeship for craftsmen. All of these institutions including the universities prepared the learners for practice. Some would claim that this was the main difference between medieval and the humanistic education of the Renaissance.

We call attention to two one-volume textbooks on medieval history. Students will profit by using them.

ADAMSON, JOHN WILLIAM, "*The Illiterate Anglo-Saxon*" *and Other Essays*, Cambridge University Press, 1944, 167 pp. On Pierre Dubois *see* Walther Brandt; and Carl Stephenson's *Medieval History*, p. 169.

BRANDT, WALTER, *Pierre Dubois's "The Recovery of the Holy Land,"* New York, Columbia University Press, 1956, 251 pp. With introduction and notes.

COMPAYRÉ, GABRIEL, *Abelard and the Origin and Early History of Universities*, New York, Charles Scribner's Sons, 1893, 315 pp.

CORNISH, F. W., *Chivalry*, New York, The Macmillan Company, 1901, 369 pp.

DENIFLE, H. HEINRICH, *Die Entstchung der Universitäten des Mittelalters bis 1400*, Graz, Akademische Druck-und Verlagsanstalt, 1956, 814 pp. Reproduction of a famous book first published in 1885.

GABRIEL, ASTRIK L., *The Educational Ideas of Vincent of Beauvais*, Notre Dame, Ind., The Medieval Institute, University of Notre Dame, 1960, 62 pp. This is Volume IV of a series edited by Gabriel and J. N. Garvin and issued by the Institute.

GAUTIER, LEON, *Chivalry*, London, Routledge & Sons, 1891, 499 pp.

HASKINS, CHARLES HOMER, *The Renaissance of the Twelfth Century*, Cambridge, Harvard University Press, 1933, 437 pp.; *The Rise of Universities*, New York, Henry Holt and Company, 1923, 134 pp.

HITTI, PHILIP K., *History of the Arabs*, London, The Macmillan Company, 1937, 767 pp.

IRSAY, STEPHEN D', *Histoire des universitaires françaises et étrangères*, Paris, A. Picard, 1935, 2 vols.

KIBRE, PEARL, *The Nations in the Medieval Universities*, Cambridge, Mass., Medieval Academy of America, 1948, 240 pp.; *Scholarship Privileges in the Middle Ages . . . at Bologna, Padua, Paris, Oxford*, Cambridge, Mass., Medieval Academy of America, 1962, 455 pp.

KREY, AUGUST A., *The First Crusade, The Accounts of Eye-Witnesses and Participants*, Princeton, N.J., Princeton University Press, 1921, 209 pp.

LEACH, ARTHUR FRANCIS, *Educational Charters and Documents, 598 1909*, Cambridge University Press, 1911, 582 pp.; *The Schools of Medieval England*, New York, The Macmillan Company, 1915, 349 pp.

LIEBESCHUTZ, HANS, *Medieval Humanism in the Life and Writings of John of Salisbury*, London, The Wartburg Institute, University of London, 1950, 126 pp.

LUCHAIRE, ACHILLE, *Social France in the Time of Philip Augustus.* Translated by E. B. Krehbiel, New York, Peter Smith, 1929, 441 pp. Intimate social history including school and university life.

MACCABE, JOSEPH, *Peter Abelard*, New York, G. P. Putnam's Sons, 1901, 402 pp.

PAINTER, SIDNEY, *French Chivalry, Chivalric Ideas and Practices in Medieval France*, Baltimore, Johns Hopkins Press, 1940, 179 pp.

PIRENNE, HENRI, *Medieval Cities: Their Origins and the Revival of Trade*, Princeton, N.J., Princeton University Press, 1925, 249 pp.; *A History of Europe . . . to the Sixteenth Century*, New York, W. W. Norton and Co., 1939, 624 pp.

RASHDALL, HASTINGS, *The Universities of Europe in the Middle Ages*, Revised by F. M. Powicke and A. B. Embden, Oxford, Clarendon Press, 1936, 3 vols.

RENARD, GEORGES, *Guilds in the Middle Ages*, London, George Bell and Sons, 1919, 139 pp.

ROBSON, J. A., *Wyclif and the Oxford Schools*, Cambridge University Press, 1961, 268 pp.

STEPHENSON, CARL, *Medieval History*, New York, Harper & Brothers, 1935, 707 pp.

THALLON, IDA C., "A Medieval Humanist, Michael Akonunatis," in *Vassar Medieval Studies*, New Haven, Conn., Yale University Press, 1923, pp. 273-313.

THOMPSON, JAMES W., *The Literacy of the Laity in the Middle Ages*, New York, Burt Franklin, 1960, 198 pp.

THORNDIKE, LYNN, *The History of Medieval Europe*, Boston, Houghton Mifflin Company, 1917, 682 pp.; *A History of Magic and Experimental Science in the First Thirteen Centuries of Our Era*, New York, The Macmillan Company, 1923-1941, 6 vols.

Chapter 6

THE RENAISSANCE IN ITALY

We shall begin with the meaning of the word *renaissance*. Every age that, through the revival of an earlier culture, develops new life and creative activity forms a renaissance. The medical and physical sciences are today the centers of a great scientific renaissance; the entire western world after the American and French Revolutions experienced a renaissance of liberalism, humanitarianism, and democracy; but, with those who wish to emphasize the continuity of human evolution, the word is out of favor. These students point out that the Middle Ages were not as dark, the transitions of history not as abrupt, and the Renaissance not as glorious as they have been painted. Yet the word has its uses; it is not to be too lightly given up. The desired continuity of history may be secured by recognizing the large number of renaissance periods, noting their interconnections, and tracing their causes. We shall, therefore, with C. H. Haskins, speak of the rapid progress after 1100 as "the twelfth-century Renaissance," which continued through the thirteenth century. We shall consider, furthermore, the development of northern Europe after 1500 as the northern Renaissance. Between these two occurred the Italian Renaissance of the fourteenth and fifteenth centuries with its recovery of classical Humanism, which is our present topic.

The Italian Renaissance was more than the revival of ancient learning and the recovery of the ideal of liberal education. Intimately related to the revival of learning was the artistic revival and a great development of civil and political life. Indeed it was more than a revival for, like every true renaissance, it was a creative period. The artistic achievements between Giotto and Tintoretto were accomplished by many painters, sculptors, and architects, each great enough to mark an epoch. Their age was dominated by the ideals of the fine arts quite as much as our time is controlled by scientific concepts. Furniture and costume, war and religion, and morality, and politics were all judged by artistic standards. Symonds said, "From the Pope upon St. Peter's chair to the clerks in the Florentine counting-house, every Italian was a judge of art, and estimated all things in terms of their artistic qualities." But the wonder of their age is not their ability to judge and criticize, but to produce. They solved difficult technical problems of perspective, coloring, and composition; but more than that, they had something of importance to say together with the genius to create an art language capable of saying it effectively.

We owe to Italy also the fuller recovery of the two ancient literatures of Greece and Rome that is called the revival of learning. That service to civilization was rendered in the fourteenth century, at the last possible moment because Constantinople, which had preserved important Greek manuscripts, was captured by the Turks in 1453. The Moslems of the Middle Ages had paid little attention to the literary and artistic work of Greece; and now, in the fourteenth century, the Italians were the only people immediately capable of understanding Greek poetry and philosophy. It was Italy in turn that roused the sleeping North. We shall see that the recovery itself was a creative act. It was no mere physical discovery of dead books, but a taking to heart and into the understanding of the thought and feelings of the ancients. The great writers, Homer, Herodotus, Xenophon, and others were available in the West in libraries, but there were not many readers of Greek. Latin authors were read more widely, but here also there was need for an awakening, a renewed appreciation.

The period was marked not only by the recovery of old literatures but also by the rise of a new one, the modern Italian. The first great modern classic was the epic of Dante. The prose and verse of Petrarch and Boccaccio, as well as the development of the sonnet as a literary art form, were further Italian contributions to the earliest great literature in a modern tongue.

The development of Italian literature was closely related to the growth of Italian political institutions. The unit was the city-state, recalling the similar organizations of ancient Greece. Each of these political entities was composed of several classes: the nobility, merchants, mercenary soldiers, and workingmen organized into powerful guilds. The population was torn with the strife and dissension of the classes; and between the several cities there existed competition and even hatred rather than cooperation. Each of these states, with their concentration of wealth, extensive public works, and oligarchical or democratic government, was able to reward its abler citizens with positions of honor, power, or wealth; and the intense civic development of the times is merely the other side of an equally intense individualism. The Italian city-state was a cause of the decline of these medieval institutions: the universal church, the empire, and feudalism; and a money economy was becoming general. One evidence of this latter change was the coinage of the states, the gold florin of the great financial center, Florence, being a prime example. Meanwhile the use of gunpowder, the mariner's compass, paper and printing and the march of geographical discovery were other features of the Italian Renaissance. If the age must have a set beginning and ending we may take the birth of Petrarch in 1304 and the sack of Rome in 1527 as these dates. At the birth of Petrarch, Dante still had seventeen years to live; and in any case most of the period falls within the conventional period of the Middle Ages. When Charles V secured control of the peninsula (1527), the Renaissance in Italy was over, the Reformation in Germany was in full career, and Catholicism was preparing the Counter-Reformation.

CLASSICAL HUMANISM

The recovery of classical literature and the Humanistic movement, which together make up the revival of learning, are, for the student of education, the most important phases of the Renaissance. Humanism combined the aims of self-realization and self-expression with the older ideal of a liberal education. Aristotle's concept of a liberal education as the culture of citizens—free men in a free state—again acquired the secular connotation that it had in Greek times; but also it was often given an individualistic, even an egoistic turn. As a reaction against medieval feeling, Humanism stressed the interests of a worldly, civilized life in an earthly city in contrast with preparation for a world to come. On the other hand, Humanism generally accepted Greek and even Christian ethics and was, therefore, opposed to all radical naturalism. But actually the philosophies of the Italian Humanists were so divergent that no simple classification will do justice to all their views.

In education, Humanism was the study of great human achievement and thought as these are preserved in the greatest writers. Such study is necessarily historical, for we can no longer interview Pericles or Plato and we can speak of them with assurance only if we know them as characters in their times. The works of man are of the most various kinds, but most of them are anonymous and can be studied only as they have affected the material world, tradition, or the written record. The Humanists studied the record chiefly, although the beginnings of classical archaeology fall within the Italian Renaissance. Books, however, contain more than information; they offer inspiration and guidance also. As De Quincey taught, there is a literature of knowledge but there is also the literature of power. It was the latter, the drama, epic, oratory, and philosophy—in general the great authors who are notable for form and expression as well as content—that formed the Humanistic curriculum. The matters treated by these writers are chiefly human life and values; hence, the term *Humanism* is appropriate to such studies.

The values that were stressed most in the Italian Renaissance were aesthetic, ethical, and political: the interest in beauty and the aesthetic experience, and the interest in conduct and political life. In both respects the Italians of the fourteenth century believed that they could learn from the ancients, and there were at that time no other literatures so rich in beauty, so freighted with meaning, and so competent to give guidance as the Greek and Roman. In addition, the Roman literature was the product of their own ancestors on their own soil, and it therefore appealed powerfully to their patriotic feeling. They gradually discovered, also, that the Roman writers had been inspired and taught by the Greeks and that they could be fully understood only by those who were acquainted with the Greek models.

Those studies are humanistic that present, analyze, and criticize human thought, feelings, and conduct. History, literature, philosophy, and social anthropology are leading humanistic studies. The writings of the Greeks and Romans in these and cognate fields are sometimes called the ancient or classical humanities; and comparable writings, in modern tongues, may be called modern humanities. Whether ancient or modern, humanism emphasizes man, not God or nature but man, as a politically, ethically, and aesthetically free being. Human freedom is one of the postulates of humanism; and the Renaissance demand for individual freedom is of the essence of the new education. The Humanist education of that age was not professional like that of the medieval universities. The Humanists contrasted their own general, liberal, and preprofessional culture with all that was technical, narrowly practical, and vocational. This contrast is still accepted by many who urge that a balanced education must give due attention both to the purposes of life and the means of living, both to the humanistic and the technical needs of the student.

THE LATIN LANGUAGE

At the Renaissance, Latin was still a living language, in constant use by the church, in the professions, and in the schools. Just because it had been in continuous use for many centuries it was no longer the Latin of the Romans. Quintilian, who lived until about A.D. 100, is sometimes called the last of the classical writers. In this long stretch of time the Christian Church had introduced new ideas and a new vocabulary, and great changes had taken place even in the structure and the idioms of the language. Medieval Latin in itself may have been no worse than classical Latin, but it was different. In one respect, the history of medieval Latin had been unfortunate; it frequently had to grow in a foreign soil. It developed largely among a non-Latin and a barbarous people who spoke Teutonic or Slavic dialects and who learned Latin only at school. Because they frequently did not really know what the accepted Latin forms were the language was corrupted through the ignorance of its users.

The Italian Humanists, having fallen in love with the works of the great Roman authors, especially Cicero, readily discovered the difference between contemporary and classical Latin. They hastily jumped to the conclusion that Ciceronian speech should be made the standard for their own day, and like schoolboys went about trying to find mistakes in the letters and books of the dignitaries of their time; and they found them. "Ignoramus! Blockhead!" they shouted, just as though Europe had not changed since the time of Cicero. They set up an inappropriate language standard for literature and the schools; and it was, in part, their pedantic imitation that killed the Latin language. But its demise was hastened by the growth of the modern tongues, which had been reduced to writing and gradually displaced the ancient even in books for scholars. Yet the Latin lived on for a long time. Secondary schools and universities were conducted in classical Latin, and Latin textbooks were used until about 1700, or even later. The Catholic Church, for some purposes, uses it today, but now the vernacular may be used even in celebrating the mass. Schools and universities, of course, still teach Latin and Greek, but they no longer generally use either as the language of instruction.

WHY THE RENAISSANCE BEGAN IN ITALY

The earlier view that the Italian Renaissance was a sudden upheaval and revolt against the Middle Ages is now discredited. It occurred in the later Middle Ages because the earlier period had prepared the way for it. The Renaissance is a good example of historical continuity, although the people who lived at that time thought they were creating a fundamental break with tradition. Even in the Middle Ages the idea of a revival or renaissance was common; but what men looked for was a religious revival. The monastic reformers, especially Francis of Assisi, are examples. With the religious hopes arose also visions of the rise of Italy and the reestablishment of the Roman Empire. Dante, in his *de Monarchia*, following the argument of Thomas Aquinas, proposed a world empire. In 1347, Rienzi (1313–1354), the orator and tribune, believed himself to have reopened a new and glorious period of Roman supremacy. The papacy had deserted Rome for Avignon on the banks of the Rhone. Rienzi restored the republic, revived the self-government of the city, and invited all Italy to aid in establishing a united nation. This political scheme was based on archaeology and the traditions and laws of antiquity. Rienzi failed tragically, but his ideas lived on and were adopted by Petrarch, the greatest writer then living. Ideas of a revival and rebirth were, therefore, not new; and certain features of the Renaissance can certainly be traced from the twelfth century onward. Italy was the focal point. Because of her location, Italy had long been the bridge between the East and the West over which trade and travel passed in either direction. It was her location that had enabled Italy to control the whole Mediterranean area during imperial times. Because of this, and because Italy had been the seat of the Roman Empire, it was practically inevitable that the revival of the ancient civilization should first take place there. There were the ancient sites and monuments, the names, the traditions of past grandeur; there the Italian language furnished access by easy stages to the Latin from which it was derived; and there the Roman law was still a living institution. The Humanists were the first classical archaeologists. The popes and princes of Italy were the first collectors of ancient sculptures. And the artists studied the antique for inspiration for their own creations. Insofar as the Renaissance was a Latin revival, it was clearly inevitable that it should begin in Italy. And until 1396 the revival was almost entirely Latin. Neither Petrarch nor Boccaccio knew much Greek, and Petrarch at least, just because he was one of the most highly cultivated men of his time, felt this as a serious defect. Again the revival took place in Italy because of her centers of wealth and taste and her active public and patriotic spirit. The private and public means for gratifying taste in art and learning were at hand. Wealthy individuals, cities, despots, and the church established libraries, galleries, and schools and maintained collectors, copyists, scholars, and teachers.

THE SPIRIT OF THE RENAISSANCE

The first modern man, a new psychological phenomenon, is often said to have appeared in the Renaissance. Instead of the humble and penitent member of a class or an order, we see a self-conscious and self-sufficient individual seeking power and fame through art, learning, war, and even crime. George Eliot in *Romola* depicts such a one in the head of the Bardi family, who demands an eternity of fame as a scholar and collector of books.

The Humanists frequently lived by the patronage of the great, and they often reflected the egotism and arrogance that they caught from their sponsors. From their pedestals they looked down on the vulgar, who knew not Cicero and who spoke only the lowly vernacular. Thus Petrarch said, "Who indeed could excite envy in me, who do not envy even Virgil?" and as for Dante, "our poet," who writes in the common tongue of tavern keepers, weavers, and butchers, we must realize "how little the plaudits of the unschooled multitude weigh with scholars." It is for us today to realize how far such men were from any concept of popular education.

The man of the Renaissance was the all-sided man, *l'uomo universale*, showing often the most extraordinary versatility. Dante was a publicist, theologian, philosopher, and poet. Leonardo da Vinci and Raphael had the widest interests and were skilled in the most various arts. Or consider Leon Battista Alberti (c. 1404–1472): He was the author of a famous work on education, *The Care of the Family*, was a noted gymnast, a scholar, author, musician, and an important art critic; but his *forte* was architecture in which he achieved real greatness. Only a little less variously gifted was Cellini (1500–1571), the author of a well-known autobiography that presents a picture, not only of himself, but of his times.

These, and the other great men of the time, were strongly individualistic; but this applied only to the great and those of the upper classes. The peasants and the workingmen were not yet free. The lower guilds were held in subjection. It was the rulers, courtiers, condottiere, and the scholars and artists who freed themselves from tradition and exhibited *virtu*—that is, self-assertion and personal independence. Good examples of this radical individualism are found in Machiavelli, the author of *The Prince*; in Cellini, who was so extreme that he was not typical; and, at the other end of the scale, the sensitive and refined Botticelli. As another caution against broad generalization on the men of the Renaissance, we may recall that the Middle Ages also were not without their individuals, for they produced Abelard. Yet we do not mean to withdraw the statement that individualism is a basic characteristic of the greater men of the fourteenth century. Further evidence is contributed by literature with its abundance of personal writing, autobiographies, memoirs, and letters.

The men of the Renaissance were notable letter writers. This was a type of literature little cultivated in the Middle Ages. Petrarch and Erasmus are among the great letter writers of all time, and that is the reason why we know their characters so well. One has to keep in mind that many letters were written for publication; but, carefully handled, the personal correspondence of the period is a good measure of the new individualism. In letters and autobiographies the souls of these men are opened to the gaze of all who read.

Almost from the first, in the revival of learning, men feared the return of paganism, a renewal of the old struggle between the ancient gods and Christianity; and the famous historian Jacob Burkhardt even declared that it had arrived. These fears were in some measure realized. Increasing attention was paid to Stoicism and especially to Seneca's *Morals*; but under cover of Stoicism, practice was often Epicurean. Bembo, who was an officer of the papal household, advised Sadoleto to omit from his studies the letters of St. Paul lest the barbarous Latin of the Vulgate should spoil his style. Even for the titles of the officers of the church, the classical style was employed: Thus the pope was designated *Pontifex Maximus* and the college of cardinals *Senatus Sacer*. These were not the diversions of outsiders; churchmen themselves became Humanists. Chaucer, contemporary with Wycliffe, in his "Prologue" ridicules the clerics. One of the great events that assured the success of the new learning was the election, in 1447, of

Pope Nicholas V (1397–1455). "On that day the new learning took possession of the Holy See, and Rome began to be considered the capital of the Renaissance." The most skeptical Humanists and artists did not launch an open attack against a church that gave them employment or that might turn on them and chain them to the stake; but veiled sarcasm and oblique attacks on the Christian faith and institutions were common. Poggio, Filelfo, and Valla used such tactics. Although indifferent or hostile to religion and the church, in all ceremonial matters they conformed. Macaulay has brilliantly vindicated Machiavelli's cynical and amoral political theory on the ground that in the *Prince* the virtues of a great mind shine through the corruptions of a degenerate age. This is to say that the virtues are those of the author and the vices those of his time! This picture again is not true of all Humanists and not of many of the teachers. Vittorino was much concerned for the moral and religious education of his pupils as were Vergerius, Sadoleto, and others.

FRANCESCO PETRARCH

Petrarch was one of the first and greatest of the Humanists. In his life and work he exemplified the eager search for manuscripts, the early interest in Greek, the passionate love of Cicero, and the literary temperament that led him and his contemporaries to lay too much emphasis on words and mere eloquence. This is a matter of importance for education. The exaggerated attention to style and the constant effort to imitate the sounding periods of Cicero were defects, not only of Petrarch, but of the whole revival and its education. The schools came to put eloquence on a par with intellect and good character and, in fact, it was too often accepted as a substitute for them.

Petrarch, a Florentine by nationality, was born at Arezzo in 1304 where his parents, "poor but honorable folk," were living in exile. His childhood was spent near Florence, at Pisa, and, from his ninth year, at Avignon where the pope had "long held the Church of Christ in shameful exile." In these words Petrarch revealed his loyalty to Rome. He regarded the Romans as his ancestors and the ancient empire as his country. In his brief autobiography, he told the story of his life to the age of forty-seven. He studied law at Montpellier and Bologna. What impressed him most in this study was the frequent reference to Roman antiquity. He described the transfer of his allegiance from the law to the classics. He returned home at the age of twenty-two, not as a lawyer but as a Humanist. The Colonna family became his patrons and bestowed benefices on him. He traveled in the north to collect manuscripts. On a journey to Paris and the Netherlands, he discovered some lost orations of Cicero. In Italy, he found the manuscript of some of Cicero's letters to Atticus, to his brother Quintus, and to Brutus.

"Whenever I took a journey," he said, "I always turned aside to any old monasteries that I chanced to see in the distance, saying to myself, 'who knows whether some scrap of the writings that I covet may not lie there?' " He recovered some of these writings, but he was more successful in stimulating others than in making great finds himself.

Upon his return from his northern journey, Petrarch settled near Avignon in a beautiful, secluded spot called Vaucluse. There he lived the life he praised in his *De Vita Solitaria*, or "On the Secluded Life." Many of the books that were to make him famous were written at Vaucluse, where he enjoyed a retired but epicurean life. There he received, on the same day, letters from the Senate at Rome and from the University of Paris offering him the crown of laurel for his poetry. The coincidence does not seem so remarkable to us, for we know it was contrived by Petrarch himself. Most of his books are conscious or unconscious autobiography, and the *De Vita Solitaria* belongs to this class. It is dedicated to a clerical friend. The title itself should call to mind the fact that monasticism was still a very active force in the world. Petrarch's only brother was a monk, and Petrarch admits that the brother had made the better choice. Nor was this merely a formal concession. Petrarch himself wished to be a sincere follower of the faith as well as a Humanist, and there was a lifelong conflict in his soul.

Three historical trends met in him to be resolved as they might be. From ancient times came the ideal of a liberal education, literally an education appropriate for freemen, not for slaves or the working class. This was the view expressed by Plato in the *Theatetus*, that only the man of leisure has the opportunity to pursue truth for its own sake. All other men are driven by circumstances to sacrifice truth to expediency. The lawyer must serve his client; the merchant, the politician, and every practical man must seek a practical and never the ideal result. From the Middle Ages, in the second place, the monastic and in general the religious life called to Petrarch and his contemporaries to renounce the world and to accept truth from the hand of revelation. And recently, men had come to see again the greatness of ancient Rome and Roman literature. The way to truth and beauty seemed to Petrarch to lie in the study of the thoughts of the ancients; Cicero, Virgil, and Seneca. Each of these three traditions had a part in forming the mind of Petrarch.

In form, the *De Vita Solitaria* is an extended letter. The friend to whom it was addressed was never long absent from his thought as he penned its three hundred pages. And friendly converse was to be one of the chief pleasures of this epicurean hermitage, for "no solitude is so profound, no house so small, no door so narrow, but it may open to a friend." In substance, he is writing about himself as one does in a letter, he is writing a vindication, an *apologia pro vita sua*. The book was written, as we have seen, at beautiful Vaucluse to extol the simple life. Occasionally we almost seem to catch the accents of Rousseau praising the life according to nature and leading an attack upon that sink of wickedness that is the city; but not for long. Almost immediately Petrarch turns on himself to say that only a learned solitude is tolerable, one well stocked with books and applied to study and writing, in words like these "to read what our forerunners have written and to write what later generations may wish to read, to pay to posterity the debt which we cannot pay to the dead for the gift of their writings, and yet not remain altogether ungrateful to the dead, but to make their names more popular if they are unknown, to restore them if they have been forgotten, to dig them out if they have been buried in the ruins of time and to hand them down to our grandchildren as objects of veneration, to carry them in the heart, and by cherishing, remembering and celebrating their fame in every way, to pay them a homage that is due to their genius even though it is not commensurate with their genius"—this is his ideal of the solitary life.

To what books did this fourteenth-century man of letters have access? His library of about two hundred volumes contained the great Roman historians, with the exception of Tacitus, and the great Roman poets, with the exception of Lucretius. He had the greater part of Quintilian and often quoted him. His Seneca and Cicero were not complete, but he had most of them, and he had several of the great Latin Fathers: Ambrose, Jerome, and Augustine and used them. Petrarch was not able to read Greek but he had Latin translations of the *Timaeus* of Plato, the *Ethics* and *Politics* of Aristotle, and a crude version of Homer that Leontius Pilatus made for him and for Boccaccio.

Some remarkable Latin finds were not made until after Petrarch's time. Niccolo Niccoli discovered a complete copy of Cicero's *De Oratore*, which contains the orator's theory of education and his criticism of ancient educational practice. Poggio, in 1416, found at St. Gall a complete copy of Quintilian, a discovery that created remarkable enthusiasm among scholars. He also discovered a number of other rare works in the same monastery, including six of Cicero's orations.

THE RECOVERY OF GREEK AUTHORS

Most Greek literary manuscripts that remained had been transcribed within the bounds of the Byzantine empire. Even before the dispersion of the manuscripts, which followed the fall of the capital to the Turks in 1453, Greeks had found their way to Italy and had taught their language there. The first of importance was Manuel Chrysoloras (c. 1350–1415), who came as an ambassador from the emperor and was persuaded by the city of Florence to stay to teach the Greek language. This engagement, said Symonds, assured the future of Greek in Europe. Beginning in 1396 he taught for three years at Florence and had among his pupils Guarino,

Filelfo, Poggio, Leonardo Bruni, and Traversari. Chrysoloras seems to have left Florence for Pavia to escape the jealousy and spite of Niccolo Niccoli, Lorenzo de Medici's literary adviser. Chrysoloras taught in Pavia until about 1400. His work was of the utmost importance to the study of Greek, and therefore to the proper understanding of the Latin authors and to the whole development of learning in the West.

Other Greeks came early in the fifteenth century. G. G. Plethon (c. 1355–1450), who was born at Constantinople, lectured in Florence and inspired the founding there of a Platonic academy, which affected the thought not of Italy alone but also of Germany. Bessarion (1403–1472), who had been a pupil of Plethon, attended the Council of Florence in 1439, joined the Church of Rome, became a cardinal, and in 1471 was almost elected pope. His large collection of Greek manuscripts became the nucleus of the famous library of St. Mark's in Venice. Theodore Gaza (c. 1400–1475), another Greek, came to Italy in 1438. He became a teacher of Greek, and, at the same time, a pupil of Latin in the school of Vittorino. Cardinal Bessarion became his patron and Pope Nicholas V invited him to Rome, in 1451, to aid in an ambitious program for the translation of the Greek classics into Latin. The death of the pope interfered with these plans, but Bessarion translated parts of Theophrastus and Aristotle into Latin and Cicero *On Old Age* and *On Friendship* into Greek. He prepared the first fairly complete Greek grammar to be written in Italy. It was used long and widely as a textbook. Before this, Greek could be learned only by word of mouth, and competent teachers were scarce in the West before the time of Erasmus.

Not only did Greek teachers come to Italy in the first half of the fifteenth century, but a movement in the opposite direction also took place. Italian scholars went to Constantinople and resided there for long periods to learn the language and to gather manuscripts. Among these was Guarino da Verona (c. 1370–1460). For five years he lived at Constantinople, in the family of Chrysoloras, whose daughter he married. Returning to Italy he taught in Venice, where Vittorino was his pupil, and later at Florence and Verona. Finally he became head of the famous Italian court school at Ferrara. Guarino was active as an editor and commentator and served as translator to the Council of Ferrara (1438). He had a son, Battista, who succeeded him in the court school of Ferrara. Battista wrote an account of his father's methods of teaching. It shows that a knowledge of Greek was by that time considered essential to the understanding of the Latin language and literature. The recovery of Greek had changed the Renaissance perspective of the history of culture and civilization.

Fifteen years later than Guarino, Aurispa (c. 1370–1459), a scholar from Sicily, visited Constantinople and returned in 1423 with more than two hundred manuscripts. Filelfo (1398–1481) served in a diplomatic post in the city on the Bosphorus and worked for seven years in its great libraries, returning with another large collection of Greek authors. Later he became a wandering scholar and lectured on the classics in the leading Italian cities. This illustrates the fact that there were few permanent positions for Humanists in the Italian universities until the middle of the fifteenth century. The universities expended their energies on the professional studies of law, medicine, and theology and made no provision for liberal studies. Only very gradually did they establish chairs of rhetoric and poetry. The Humanists, meanwhile, served as free-lance letcurers, took private pupils, found positions as secretaries or librarians, or enlisted under the banner of a wealthy patron.

DIFFUSION OF THE SOURCES

The next step to be taken, when many of the famous authors had been recovered, was the multiplication of copies in manuscript and printed form and the founding of libraries. The fifteenth century saw the formation of many remarkable collections; and their story was told by the shrewd but gossipy bookseller Vespasiano da Bisticci in his *Memoirs* of the illustrious men of his time. Libraries were built up by rulers like the Medici of Florence and the Sforza of Milan; by the higher clergy, including the popes who developed the Vatican library; by wealthy merchants and bankers; and by scholars. Vespasiano, who had every reason to be interested in the movement because he was the agent for many buyers, described the assembling of almost a score of great libraries. Books were obtained by purchase when possible, but more frequently by having skilful writers make manuscript copies.

Classical libraries flourished for a half-century before the development of printing. A new class of professional writers distinguished both for their learning and their beautiful handwriting produced the finest manuscripts. Those who had mastered Greek received the honorable title of *scrittori* and were well paid, because they were few. The less highly educated and less skilful writers had to work for a moderate wage. Frequently scholars made their own copies, either because they were poor or because *scrittori* were not to be had. Petrarch thus copied with his own hand a work of Cicero, because he would not put up with the "vile sloth" of the available copyists. Not only the *scrittori* but some of the great scholars wrote the beautiful Italian hand that had come into use in the fourteenth century. Parchment was always used for the books that were intended for the great collections. The writing in these manuscripts is artistic and regular yet individual; and they are so appropriately ornamented with scrolls, miniatures, and borders that they are a delight to the eye. Every such book had a character of its own and was usually decked out with a sumptuous binding, often of velvet with silver clasps.

To provide some illustrative details we now turn to Vespasiano da Bisticci's *Lives of Illustrious Men of the Fifteenth Century*, usually called the Vespasiano *Memoirs*. The author lived from 1421 to 1498 and, through his business, came into intimate contact with many of the leading Humanists, princes, and popes of that century. But he was more than a mere trader in manuscripts. He read widely and was a keen observer and a good judge of what would prove interesting about the life and character of the famous men whom he met. He was not a stylist; but his greatest weakness as a writer is the result of his amiability; he presents his characters in a favorable light only.

From Vespasiano we learn that Nicholas V, before he became pope, wished for money to do two things: to build great edifices and to buy books. He did the latter even in his days of poverty, and during his pontificate he did both. His personal library included the complete works of St. Augustine in twelve fine volumes; he annotated the works of the ancients with his own hand; he was himself one of the finest of calligraphers; he was familiar with the whole of Latin and Greek literature; and he was more skilled in classifying books than any other of his time. Hence, when Cosimo de Medici was furnishing a great library, he sent to Nicholas V for directions to guide him in organizing the collection. The pope gave similar aid to other library founders. All men of letters, said Vespasiano, owed much of the high regard in which their craft was held to the good offices of Pope Nicholas. It was the purpose of this first Humanist pope to found a great library at St. Peter's for the general use of the Roman court, and Vespasiano gave a list of the works that Pope Nicholas collected and the writers whom he employed.

Vespasiano presented even more elaborate accounts of the libraries of Federigo, Duke of Urbino, and of Cosimo de Medici. Duke Federigo's collection cost thirty thousand ducats, about seventy thousand dollars, worth several times that sum today. He spared neither cost nor labor and when he heard of a fine book, whether in Italy or elsewhere, he sent for it. After gathering all the notable titles in Latin, Greek, Hebrew, and Italian, he determined to dress every author worthily by binding him in scarlet and silver. "In his library," this dealer in fine manuscripts tells us, "all the books are superlatively good, and written with the pen, and had there been one printed volume it would have been ashamed in such company." From the account we learn that Vespasiano had before him complete catalogues of all the principal Italian libraries and even one of the library of Oxford University. We likewise have descriptions of the libraries established by Cosimo de Medici in Florence. When he did not have books enough to furnish the library of St. Mark's as it deserved, the executors of Niccolo Niccoli agreed to transfer all the books left by that scholar to St. Mark's, "letting the books be at the general service of all those who might like to use them." This contains the germ of the public library idea. In each book, there was a note indicating that it had belonged to the collection of Niccoli. When Cosimo wished to furnish the library of San Lorenzo he applied to Vespasiano, who told him that such a collection could not be purchased but that the books would have to be transcribed. And Vespasiano was commissioned to have the books copied. "He was anxious that I should use all possible despatch, and, after the library was begun, as there was no lack of money, I engaged forty-five scribes and completed two hundred volumes in twenty-two months, taking as a model the library of Pope Nicholas and following directions written by his own hand, which Pope Nicholas had given to Cosimo." According to this, it took one scribe about five months to complete a volume. The libraries of Bessarion, Alessandro Sforza, and others are also described by the genial bookseller of Florence. When the life of Vespasiano closed, in 1498, the day of the printed book was already far advanced. And, although the printing press was necessary for the wide dispersion of learning, the beginnings of Humanism were made with manuscript sources. Petrarch and all the early scholars knew no other.

The use of movable type for printing on paper first came in about 1438. It had a very great influence in the spread of the classical authors and in providing books for schools. Now for the first time books became cheap and uniform. Copies of the same edition were as like as two peas, paging and all. This was a great convenience for pupils and teachers. Grammars, dictionaries, phrase and conversation books, and other aids to learning came from the press. By and by even scholars and the wealthy purchased printed books; and printing in its turn became a fine art. Among the Renaissance printers who took a scholarly and an artistic interest in their products were Aldus of Venice, Froben of Basel, and the Estiennes of Paris and Geneva. The Aldine classics, in handy pocket form, were and are famous. Although the editions were small according to modern standards, running about three hundred copies each on the average, the printing press made possible a far wider distribution of good literature than the world had ever known.

The discovery and distribution of classical books led to critical work. Two forms of criticism are the textual and the historical. The autographs of the classics had all long since disappeared, and by repeated copyings the text had become corrupt. However, the printers desired to issue the most accurate or authentic text that scholarship could produce. The textual critic, by collating the available manuscripts, attempted to settle from the various readings what was the true or original reading. Historical criticism aimed to determine the authorship, time of writing, the purpose of the author, and similar matters that were in doubt. Laurentius Valla worked along such lines in proving that the so-called *Donation of Constantine* was a forgery, produced not in the fourth century, as had been claimed, but in the seventh or some later time.

AN EARLY HUMANIST WRITER ON EDUCATION

The first great writer on education to recommend the new learning and to propose a liberal education as his aim was Pier Paolo Vergerio, or Vergerius. Vergerius was born in 1349 and became a professor at Padua and Florence. He lived too early to find a place in Vespasiano's gallery of famous Humanists. When Chrysoloras came to Florence to introduce the study of Greek, Vergerius was already forty-seven years old, but so great was his enthusiasm for the new study that he took his place at school among the boys who were learning their declensions. His treatise, "On Character and Liberal Studies," was written eight years later, in 1404; and it is such a book as ought to be expected of a man of noble character who has devoted his days and nights to liberal studies. It is wise in its practical demands, elevated in tone, and charmingly written. For two centuries the little book was used as a guide by Humanist educators; and today it provides an excellent introduction to the greatest of those teachers, Vittorino da Feltre. Before we take up Vittorino's school and the other Humanist schools we shall review the writings that served as guidebooks to the teachers of that time.

Vergerius wrote his little book for a particular boy of his acquaintance, one of the noble Carrara family. "Your distinguished ancestor," he said to the lad, "used to say that a parent owes his child three advantages: a good name, a country to be proud of, and a sound education. The last of these is the most important and failure in it is beyond remedy. You bear an honored name, you are of a house long eminent in 'our ancient and most learned city of Padua.' The most important aim, now, is that you should secure a good education."

Until boys come to the age of understanding, rivalry is a necessary spur to learning. Talents differ, and those with only modest capacities have the most need of education that their defects may be made good. Evil conduct and sin must be rigorously repressed. Language must be carefully guarded. An unsocial temper must be mellowed and friendliness developed. Idleness and intemperance in food and drink are to be shunned. Children must not be too much indulged and therefore family education should be avoided.

Vergerius, like Vittorino, aimed to combine Christian faith and conduct with ancient learning. His definition of a liberal education has become classic and we quote it:

We call those studies liberal which are worthy of a free man; those studies by which we attain and practice virtue and wisdom; that education which calls forth, trains, and develops those highest gifts of body and mind which ennoble men and which are rightly judged to rank next in dignity to virtue only, for to a vulgar temper gain and pleasure are the one aim of existence, to a lofty nature, moral worth and fame.

Such an education must be begun early for we shall not attain wisdom in our later years unless in our earliest we enter sincerely into the search. To be able to speak and write with elegance is of the utmost advantage for both public and private life. And a knowledge of literature enables us to use our leisure pleasantly and profitably. Think, by contrast, of Domitian, who, although he was the son of an emperor, could find nothing more amusing for his leisure hours than killing flies. Literature we must remember consists not of facts alone but of thoughts and style also. I do not think that thoughts without style and certainly not facts alone will be likely o attract much notice or secure a sure survival. What greater charm can life offer than this power of making the past, the present, and even the future our own by means of literature? We may say, with Cicero, how bright a household is the family of books.

Thus, Vergerius had already begun to debate that common Renaissance topic, namely, which subjects of study are to be considered essential in a liberal education. The first and foremost is literature. An important part of literature is history, which is both attractive and useful. Moral philosophy and eloquence follow close after. By philosophy we learn what is true; eloquence teaches us to say it convincingly; and history carries the light of experience. Poetry, music, logic, arithmetic, and geometry should be added and, if necessary, a professional study such as medicine or law.

How shall we teach and how learn? Vergerius warns against attempting too much at once or passing too rapidly from one subject to another. Only if we are systematic and put our heart into one subject at a time can we hope to succeed. Again, we must remember that mental endowments differ. Tasks and guidance must be adapted to the child's powers. Given good ability, three methods will be found useful: a systematic review every evening of what was done during the day; the practice of discussing each lesson with another student or with several; and the teaching to a younger student of what we have recently learned. Perseverance is essential. To give a set period to study every day, to work vigorously, and to permit no interruption are practices to be recommended strongly.

Education is to call forth and develop the highest gifts of body and mind. We have been speaking of the mind but you, he said to the boy, have wisely chosen to excel in both. And for physical and military fitness, courage and endurance are required. Here the Spartans and the Romans have set us the prime examples. "The Lacedaemonian discipline was indeed severe. The boys were so trained that in their contests they could not yield nor confess themselves vanquished; the severest tests produced no cry of pain, though blood might flow and consciousness itself give way.

The result was that all antiquity rehearses the deathless courage of the Spartans in the field; their arms were to them part of their very selves, to be cast away, or laid down, only with their lives."

Training in arms should begin early, as soon as the boy is able to use his limbs. Those exercises should be chosen that will strengthen the body and maintain its health. Physical education, as the mental, must be adapted to the child's nature and capacities. The Greek pentathlon: swimming, horsemanship, use of shield, spear, sword, and club all are necessary in the training of the soldier. The chariot of the Homeric Greeks and the legion of the Romans have both disappeared. We must adapt our training to our own day in which cavalry is the chief arm; and it is desirable to include the wider aspects of the art of war, such as strategy and tactics, discipline, supplies, and the management of encampments and winter quarters. Both war and peace will demand recreation, such as ball games, hunting, hawking, and fishing; and, indoors, games of skill, not chance, music and song, and especially good books. Lastly we must not be neglectful of our personal habits. Our dress should be suitable to time, place, and circumstance; we should learn to be gracious in manner and of a cheerful spirit. This was an admirable program for a boy's development; and it was as eloquent in statement as it was wise.

OTHER HUMANIST WRITERS

Some of the Humanists favored the education of upper-class girls in the new learning. Vittorino and his contemporaries acted on this principle, admitting girls to their classes. Within a year after Vergerius issued his treatise on the education of boys, Leonardo Bruni addressed an educational tract to Baptista Malatesta, daughter of the famous ducal house of Urbino. The tract covers only a few pages, and he used this space chiefly to select the subjects Baptista was to study. He recommended a full course of literature, history, and poetry. Like most Humanists he condemned astrology; and for girls, mathematics was considered unsuitable. Rhetoric and oratory, too, were thought to lie outside a woman's sphere of activity. Religion and ethics were, however, considered to be very important. Morals had been treated by the noblest minds of Greece and Rome. The Greek, Roman, and Christian ethical writers demanded the serious study of a cultivated Christian lady. This, and all other studies, depended on a sound foundation without which nothing can be accomplished; and that foundation consisted in a thorough knowledge of the Latin language.

More elaborate was the treatise written for young King Ladislas of Bohemia by Aeneas Sylvius Piccolomini, who afterward became Pope Pius II. His contemporary, the famous architect L. B. Alberti, wrote a work on the management of a family that contains important sections on educational aims and the curriculum. One of the most systematic treatises of the whole Renaissance, arranged in six books, is by Maffeo Vegio. And Battista, the son and successor of Guarino da Verona, wrote an interesting and discriminating account of his father's views and practice.

Altogether we owe to the Italian Humanists of the fourteenth and fifteenth centuries many works that deal entirely or in part with education. There was among these writers a singular unanimity in philosophy, curriculum, and method. This agreement was due to their limited materials, to the similarity of the conditions, and in particular to their dependence on the same authorities: namely, Plato, Aristotle, Cicero, and especially Quintilian, whose *Institutes of Oratory* formed the great guidebook of the educators of the Renaissance.

The tract "Upon the Method of Teaching and of Reading the Classical Authors" by Battista Guarino (1459) is the first to give a prominent place to Greek studies. It, therefore, shows that the fifteenth century began a new phase in Humanistic education. This is also shown by its narrower scope and its greater emphasis on scholarship.

The sections on methods of private study contain much good advice, some of which had already been given by Vergerius. Let the young student think of himself as preparing to teach what he is studying, advice that Quintilian gave us long ago. Let him read not only the text but every commentary. The precise meaning and force of every word is to be determined. He must write out his notes as if for publication. The practice of making extracts is to be commended, as is that of providing parallel passages from several authors. Like the Pythagoreans, he must review each evening what he learned by day, each month the whole reading of the preceding four weeks. Translation and the comparison of translations by others are useful exercises. Reading aloud is valuable to mind and body. Definite hours must be devoted to study, and the plan decided on must be followed without interruption. We must recognize the crucial importance of a regular system in study; it is as important as "harmony of time and note" in a chorus. In conclusion, Battista Guarino quotes Cicero on literature as the inspiration of youth, the joy of old age, the ornament of success, and the solace of adversity. Books do not offend or rebuke; they call up no empty hopes or fears. Through books alone will our converse be with the best and greatest minds among all the mighty men of the past. No leisure could be more nobly occupied than one spent among books.

Such were the views on education of writers in the Italian revival during the fourteenth and fifteenth centuries. Education had come to mean the cultivation of mind and body, the coordination of Greek and Christian morals, and the development of man as a citizen. Letters were not to be an excuse for withdrawal from active life. Aesthetic cultivation, good conduct, polite manners, and patriotism were all supposed to grow out of the liberal education that all the Humanists sought and praised. Letters and philosophy were regarded as the ideal preparation for professional study. Ancient writers were studied for aid in war, politics, agriculture, and other practical concerns. Yet some even then began to sense a danger in the compromises involved in the union of the new learning and the old, compromises between Greek and Christian ethics, between the new thirst for fame and the old humility, between the pagan classics and the Christian gospel. Individualism was becoming rampant and in extreme spirits overstepped all bounds in the later Renaissance. The old struggle between antiquity and Christian faith and morals was again breaking out. Among the teachers who were able to effect a working compromise were Guarino da Verona and Vittorino da Feltre.

TWO GREAT TEACHERS

Guarino we have already noticed as a scholar in Greek and a collector of Greek manuscripts. His school at Ferrara attained a European reputation, and pupils came from distant countries—from Germany, France, and even England. He made available in a Latin translation the educational essay attributed to Plutarch that came to stand beside Quintilian on the Humanist teacher's shelf of professional books. His moral character and his influence on his students were greatly praised, and he read the Christian Scriptures and the Church Fathers with his pupils. He was a thoroughgoing Humanist scholar and a particular admirer of Cicero and Virgil. In a letter to a pupil he outlined a method of study that he ascribed to his father-in-law, Chrysoloras. This concerns reading and interpretation. By reading aloud comprehension is aided. This is to be followed by grammatical analysis and a careful study of the exact sense, by repetition, and by a careful summary. Translation is not to be slavish, but faithful. Beautiful passages are to be copied into a book of selections and to be memorized. The books that are read are to be discussed with other students and with friends. The educational doctrines given to the world by his son Battista, which have already been mentioned, were confessedly those of the father also.

Vittorino was more exclusively a teacher than Guarino. He wrote nothing, collected no manuscripts, and took no part in public affairs; yet his fame was equally widespread and has proved just as lasting. Vittorino Rambaldoni of Feltre was born in a mountain village of the eastern Alps in 1378. The father, although poor, had some education and the town, although remote and lacking in cultural resources, yet gave Vittorino the opportunity to acquire the rudiments of Latin. At the age of eighteen he entered the University of Padua, with which Petrarch had been associated. He even studied under one of Petrarch's disciples; and he may have met Vergerius, who was a Paduan professor. Being very poor, he earned his way by tutoring pupils in Latin. He studied mathematics, which was still a rare accomplishment, for Euclid was just being revived. He studied Greek with Guarino who, on his return from Constantinople, set up a school in Venice.

He was a spare, active man, simple in his habits, dress, and tastes, and beloved in the best social circles of the city and the university. For twenty years he had been a student and a private and public teacher at Padua and at Venice. His schools had drawn to him the sons of the great families of the two cities. But he taught not only the rich. Remembering his own youthful struggles, he received some poor boys free while the rich paid the usual fees. In 1423, the Marquis of Mantua, Gianfrancesco Gonzaga, invited him to become head of the Mantuan court school. He had to be persuaded; concessions were offered. Vittorino might fix his own salary, have complete control of the school and pupils, continue his custom of giving free education to some talented poor boys; and it was urged as a great opportunity for a great teacher to have the chance to educate the future Marquis of Mantua. Although somewhat unwillingly, Vittorino consented and spent the remaining twenty-three years of his life as head of the court school of Mantua.

The children of the prince formed the nucleus of the school. There were three boys and a girl when the master arrived. Another daughter, Cecilia, and a son were born later. The sons of the nobility and of rich merchants, together with poor boys of ability and many foreigners, swelled the numbers until there was, for that time, a large boarding school. Learned Greeks from the East came to study Latin with Vittorino. The ages of the pupils varied: Some were as young as six or eight years and several stayed on until they were in their middle twenties and beyond. Valla, who was one of Vittorino's most famous pupils, remained until he was twenty-three but apparently served as an assistant. Sassuolo was twenty-one when he entered but he had charge of the music instruction and was, therefore, a teacher as well as a pupil. Other famous pupils were John Andrea, later a bishop, Corraro, Perotti, who became a professor of rhetoric and an official in the Roman Curia, and Ognibene, who was to be Vittorino's successor as head of the school.

The school was housed in a large casino or clubhouse, which had been called the House of Pleasure but which Vittorino renamed the Pleasant House and redecorated with murals of children at play. Surrounding this schoolhouse, which was flanked by other buildings used for sleeping and dining quarters, were large grounds with trees and gardens. Through the plain below, the Mincio River flowed. The great teacher was the father and companion of his school family. He took care of their health, took part in their games, and accompanied them to the foothills or the lakeshore in the hot summer. No luxuries were allowed even to princes. Strict discipline of the body by games and exercises, good manners and good conduct, and serious study were demanded of all. But the dominating influence in the school was the Christian spirit and the personality of Vittorino.

The youngest pupils began with letter games, spelling, and reading. Speaking and reading aloud with careful attention to articulation, tone, accent, and every quality of good speech were practiced daily. Declamation was taught as a means to eloquence. Composition and rhetoric were subjects of the greatest value to the future leader in public affairs or in the church. The Latin language was the language of instruction and the main subject of study. Greek was taught but not Italian, and this is what would be expected of a Humanist. Few doubted and everyone hoped that classical Latin was henceforth to be the universal language of scholars and leaders. The common people might have to be content with the common tongue. Vittorino laid great emphasis on the parallel study of Greek and Latin, each reinforcing the other; the study of the languages implied the deep and broad study of their literatures. The school gave a complete education in both ancient languages, in literature, poetry, rhetoric, history, and mathematics. This was also one of the first Renaissance schools to include games and physical activities. The historians came in for particular attention, especially Livy. It was no accident that a pupil of Vittorino prepared the first printed edition of Livy. Arithmetic was taught for practical use and for training in accuracy. In its early stages it was taught in games as Plato had advised. Geometry was one of the studies that Vittorino loved and in which he had acquired fame as a teacher. Astronomy and the elements of physics or natural philosophy were also included. Among the school activities there were choral singing, instrumental music, and dancing. Famous schools in the Renaissance were numerous, but none embodied more fully its educational ideals—the complete training of man for leisure and action, and especially for service to state and church—by means of the ancient literatures.

INFLUENCE OF THE REVIVAL ON EDUCATION

The most obvious educational influence from the revival, if not the most important, came in the transformation and expansion of the curriculum. The classical Roman authors and some Greek writers, together with the necessary language studies, displaced the medieval trivium of grammar, rhetoric, and dialectic. Many more authors and greater ones were read in the Humanist than in the medieval schools, and the curriculum was thereby greatly enriched. The new aims were the understanding of literature and of life through literature, rather than skill in logic and the scholastic philosophy or the professional study of law or medicine. The Humanists intended to offer a liberal, not a professional, education.

Of the authors, Cicero held the largest place. Not only his orations but also his letters, his *De Oratore* and *Brutus*, and his essays on friendship and old age were read. In this connection, the imitation of Cicero's prose became far too much an aim of the schools. This degenerate stylism was known as Ciceronianism, a word that designates the formalism of the late Renaissance education. This was one of the decadent tendencies against which Erasmus broke a lance. As education became more formal, grammatical, and stylistic, the great literary works received less attention.

Besides Cicero, other prose writers—Quintilian, and the historians, Sallust, Curtius, Caesar, and Livy—were read. Virgil was the great poet of the schools, but others were introduced, especially Horace, Ovid, and Lucan. In the Greek, Homer, the dramatists, the historians and biographers Xenophon, Herodotus, Plutarch, and the orators Demosthenes and Socrates were studied. Greek always received less emphasis than Latin. When the pupil could read and speak Latin he began rhetoric, composition, and oratory. Oratory again became one of the fine arts and held a much larger place in the Renaissance schools than it had in the Middle Ages. Latin composition and Latin verse-making were taught and usually Greek prose also. History as a science, the effort to learn what actually happened, was hardly understood in the Renaissance. On the contrary, it was more nearly a branch of ethics. Both history and ethics were studied for the same purpose, to improve public and private conduct.

Among the nonliterary studies, although the revival and its schools were primarily literary, there were music and physical education, including skill in the use of weapons. The new emphasis on the body in the Renaissance was one of the most striking contrasts with the Middle Ages. This remarkable change of interest and values is exhibited even more clearly in painting and sculpture, but it is also evident in education. The medieval schools did not engage in sports and games and the use of arms. Then the body was to be mortified, but now it was to be developed, admired, and used for civic and personal success and glory. Music also came into the schools. Vittorino had a special teacher of music, Sassuolo. Alberti was one of the noted organists of the time and included music in his proposed curriculum. For their theory of education in music both Vittorino and Alberti went back to Aristotle, who held that music had several functions: It was considered good for diversion, recreation, moral and civic education, and purification or catharsis. Castiglione assigned an important place to music in the education of the courtier and the high-born lady. Many of the Renaissance writers distinguished between elevating and debasing music and insisted on a careful selection of the compositions that were to be used. Some were also critical of the general run of music masters, who seem to have had a bad name. Dancing was not generally approved by the Renaissance educators, although Vittorino taught it. Drawing was not usually included. The natural sciences aroused little interest and were only gradually and grudgingly admitted even in the nineteenth century into the (classical) public schools of England.

One of the greatest defects of the Renaissance curriculum was the complete omission of the vernacular; and this suggests the even more basic fact that the Humanists had no conception of universal education and no message for the common people. The new studies appealed, however, to groups of people who might not have attended the medieval schools, such as the nobles, ruling classes, merchants, and bankers. When the poor were admitted into the new schools, they were drawn into the upper social strata. But the Humanists, with few exceptions, did nothing to provide an appropriate education for the poor. The education of girls made some progress among the upper classes.

Important improvements were made in the equipment of the schools: The printing press provided uniform texts, which made class discussion and the interpretation of the text feasible. It was no longer necessary to dictate the texts or to correct the numerous errors of manuscript copies. Aids to language study, grammars, lexicons, phrase books, and colloquies became numerous. Vastly more reading material became available. Themes, notebooks, and many new kinds of exercises were made possible through the use of paper.

New schools were founded: court schools in Italy, *collèges* and lycées in France, the gymnasium in Germany, and the reformed grammar school in England. Schools were much less likely to be controlled by the church. Their physical equipment was improved, playing fields were sometimes added, and there was a new attention to the health of the pupils. Friendlier relations were developed between teachers and pupils in the early Renaissance. Some of these gains were lost as the schools again became formal and standardized in the sixteenth century. And then a new, a realist, revival occurred.

THE CLASSICS CROSSING THE ALPS

The great Latin classics were not widely studied in the North until about a century after their revival in Italy; and then, as in Italy, the Greek revival followed the Latin at a distance of about fifty years.

One of the earliest Humanist circles in the North formed itself around Duke Humphrey of England in about 1425. He was the first English patron of Humanists, a collector of classical manuscripts and a contributor to the classical collections of his own university, Oxford, where he had been a student in Balliol College. Among the Italian translators whom he employed was Antonio Beccaria who had been a pupil of Vittorino. Not long after, young Englishmen began to go to Italy to study the classics just as, during the Middle Ages, they had gone to study law.

Holland and the Rhine country were not earlier in the field but were more important than England as centers of the rising northern Humanism. In Holland the voluntary religious society called the Brethren of the Common Life was founded in the fourteenth century. The members, mostly ordinary middle-class people, devoted themselves to pious works: the physical and spiritual care of students, copying manuscripts, teaching, and the establishment of schools. They were a loosely knit body, the members took no formal vows, and it is often difficult to distinguish the brothers from others who were only associated with them. Their early schools were not Humanistic, but by 1500 a change in this respect was noticeable. Hegius, the rector of the Brethren's school at Deventer, for example, placed that institution in the front rank of their schools; and, at his death in 1498, it was fairly classical in the content and spirit of its teaching.

Humanism developed slowly in France, where the University of Paris long opposed its introduction. The support of classical studies, in that country as in Italy, came more from the court and the princes than from the universities. When Francis I became king in 1515, the Humanists rejoiced in the prospect of support for their studies and they were not disappointed. William Budé, a distinguished scholar, was made royal librarian and the *Collège de France*, a Humanist institution, was founded. A royal printing press also was established, with Robert Estienne as printer. The city of Bordeaux, in 1534, founded the *Collège de Guyenne*, where Elie Vinet and Mathurin Cordier later became teachers.

In Germany, John Sturm organized the classical gymnasium of Strassburg in about 1538. Rudolph Agricola was, however, the greatest of the early German classicists. But since the Reformation was, at first, a German revolution, we shall deal with the German Humanists in the next chapter.

SUMMARY

The transition from medieval to modern times is called the Renaissance. Many phases of life were affected, including the fine arts, politics, exploration, and scholarship. The scholarly phase, or revival of learning, was a return to ancient literature. Roman law, never entirely lost, was revived in the Middle Ages. Science, medicine, mathematics, and the works of Aristotle were brought by the Moslems. The humane letters of Greece and Rome had not yet been revived. The appreciative and critical study of these classical authors formed the revival of learning. This study implied the use of classical instead of medieval Latin.

The Renaissance was hardly less creative in education than it was in the fine arts. The Greek ideal of liberal education was revived and it marks a radical change from medieval humility and submission. The Renaissance man tended to be proud, aggressive, and self-sufficient. These new attitudes influenced education in the direction of freedom for the individual; but the great teachers occupied an intermediate position on the question of freedom versus authority. The Humanist schools thus repeated history by again attempting to combine classical and Christian ideals. They aimed to cultivate both mind and body; they tried to prepare their pupils for active work in the world; and they developed intelligent methods of study and teaching and introduced a new curriculum. The curriculum still was, as in the Middle Ages, a collection of authors; but these were the great writers of Greece and Rome, not mere summarizers; they were read in their own language; and they were read critically and with historical perspective, not as final authorities. The Humanists favored the education of girls of the upper classes. They wrote industriously, but with limited originality, on educational theory. They created a new type of secondary school which still retains its prestige in large parts of the world, although it has everywhere come under heavy attack.

Humanism early developed a decadent tendency. It lost contact with science and with national and economic development; and the Humanists were not interested in the education of the common people or in the common life, language, or literature. Humanist education acquired the faults of the ancient Roman schools: It became formal, stylistic, and declamatory; and it came to be, itself, in need of reform. Education was in transition, but it did not in the Renaissance become fully modern.

QUESTIONS

1. How did the Italian Renaissance differ from the "Renaissance of the Twelfth Century?"
2. Consider chivalric education as a form of Humanism.
3. If mathematics were to be regarded as a Humanistic study, how should it be taught?
4. Were the great Greek and Roman writers Humanists? Could Humanism in the fourteenth century have developed without the ancient classics?
5. Did the Italian scholars become Humanists because they studied the classics or did they study the classics because they were Humanists?
6. What were the main characteristics of the Renaissance scholars? Which of these characteristics were exhibited in the life of Petrarch? Was Petrarch an entirely modern man?
7. Criticize, pro and con, the educational theory of Vergerius.
8. Discuss the judgment that the chief educational contribution of the Italian Renaissance was its emphasis on individual liberty of thought and expression.
9. Does Vittorino deserve his fame as a great teacher? Why, or why not?

10. Compare the curricula of the Renaissance schools and the medieval schools.
11. What improvements in the equipment and the methods of the schools occurred during the Renaissance?

NOTES AND SOURCES

Scholars have not always agreed on the significance of the Italian Renaissance. Petrarch, "the first modern man," was not wholly modern; Abelard was not entirely medieval; and it would not be wholly facetious to ask, "How about Caesar?" Although Petrarch may not have been the first modern man he was modern and a Humanist. He may have been among those who "early in the Renaissance," according to Dupuis, "rejected asceticism." Now, asceticism was greatly emphasized in the Middle Ages by the monastic orders, and Petrarch sometimes contemplated taking the vows. Could a Humanist be an ascetic?

Humanism tended to be secular and to some scholars seemed to be even pagan and anti-Christian. This whole question was reopened in the nineteenth century by Jakob Burckhardt (1818–97), a famous Swiss historian. The debate aroused by Burckhardt is continuing. See Tinsley Helton, editor, *The Renaissance, a Reconsideration*, Madison, University of Wisconsin Press, 1961, 160 pp., especially the paper on Burckhardt by Paul Kristeller.

BURCKHARDT, JAKOB, *The Civilization of the Renaissance in Italy*. Translated by S. G. C. Middlemore, New York, Harper & Brothers, 1929, 526 pp.

DUPUIS, ADRIAN M., *Philosophy of Education in Historical Perspective*, Chicago, Rand, McNally & Co., 1916, 308 pp.

FERGUSON, WALLACE K., *The Renaissance*, New York, Henry Holt and Company, Inc., 1940, 148 pp.

FIELD, LILIAN F., *An Introduction to the Study of the Renaissance*, London, Smith, Elder and Company, 1898, 304 pp.

FUNCK-BRENTANO, FRANTZ, *The Renaissance*, London, Geoffrey Bles, Ltd., 1936, 320 pp.

GEE, JOHN A., *The Life and Works of Thomas Lupset . . .*, New Haven, Conn., Yale University Press, 1928, 357 pp.

GEORGE, WILLIAM, AND EMILY WATERS, Translators, *The Vespasiano Memoirs, Lives of Illustrious Men of the XV Century*, New York, Lincoln MacVeigh, Dial Press, Inc., 1926, 475 pp.

HULME, EDWARD M., *The Renaissance, The Protestant Revolution, and the Catholic Reformation*, New York, Century Company, 1914, 589 pp.

LANCIANI, RODOLFO A., *The Golden Days of the Renaissance in Rome*, Boston, Houghton Mifflin Company, 1906, 340 pp.

LUCAS, HENRY STEPHEN, *The Renaissance and the Reformation*, New York, Harper & Brothers, 1934, 767 pp.

MITCHELL, R. J., *John Tiptoft, 1427–1470*, New York, Longmans, Green and Company, 1938, 263 pp.; *John Free, From Bristol to Rome in the Fifteenth Century*, Longmans, Green and Company, 1955, 157 pp.

NELSON, BROTHER JOEL STANISLAUS, *Aeneae Silvii De Liberorum Educatione*,

A Translation with an Introduction, Washington, D.C., The Catholic University of America Press, 1940, 241 pp.

ROBINSON, JAMES HARVEY, AND H. W. ROLFE, *Petrarch, the First Modern Scholar and Man of Letters*, New York, G. P. Putnam's Sons, 1914, 477 pp.

SANDYS, JOHN EDWIN, *Harvard Lectures on the Revival of Learning*, Cambridge University Press, 1905, 212 pp.

SYMONDS, JOHN ADDINGTON, *Renaissance in Italy*, New York, Charles Scribner's Sons, 1914–1915, 7 volumes. Of this there is also a two-volume Modern Library edition, New York, 1935. Volume two of the complete edition is entitled *The Revival of Learning*. Symonds has written and translated many works dealing with the Renaissance.

WOODWARD, WILLIAM HARRISON, *Vittorino da Feltre and Other Humanist Educators*, Cambridge University Press, 1912, 261 pp.

ZEITLIN, JACOB, *The Life of Solitude by Francis Petrarch*, Urbana, Ill., University of Illinois Press, 1924, 316 pp. A translation with introduction and notes. This work by Petrarch shows that he was not wholly "modern."

Chapter 7

SCHOOL AND CHURCH AT THE NORTH

This chapter might be called "The Reformation Era" or by those on the other side of the fence, "The Protestant Revolt"; but out on the open prairie, people would say, "Humanism at the North." Each of these titles indicates only one quality of a complex period; and we have chosen a phrase that includes all without naming any. In Italy school and church were separated and even hostile to each other, but in the North, schools became servants of the churches. The period was a composite one with many trends and discoveries not mentioned in any of our titles. These include the printing press, vernacular schools, biblical studies, scientific progress, and free speech.

HUMANISM AT THE NORTH

Humanism in Germany, Holland, England, and countries north of the Alps was linked with the Reformation. The great Humanist leaders Erasmus and Vives became prominent in the early decades of the sixteenth century. Erasmus studied in the schools of the Brethren of the Common Life, a famous Netherlands teaching society that did not become fully Humanistic until the latter part of that century. Vives, born in 1492 in Spain and entering the University of Paris in his middle youth, was warned that his Humanistic tendencies would hamper his promotion in the church. Greek was not much studied at the North before 1500. Most of the famous classical schools, including those established or reformed by John Colet in London, John Sturm in Strassburg, and Elie Vinet in Bordeaux, were products of the sixteenth century and models for those that followed. The great system of classical schools created by the Jesuits hardly began before 1550, at mid-century.

All this shows the error of supposing that the northern revival of learning had run its course before the Reformation. The two movements were not only contemporary; they were causally connected, developed together, and modified each other. The study of the Greek and Roman classics led to the study of the Christian classics: the Bible, St. Augustine, and many others. Martin Luther (1483-1546) made his decisive move in 1517 and the Reformation was in full career by 1520, when Erasmus and Vives were most active.

The founders of Humanist learning and schools at the North gained inspiration in Italy. Two examples will illustrate this: John Wessel of Groningen (1420-1489) studied with the Brethren of the Common Life at Zwolle, where he met and was deeply influenced by Thomas à Kempis, the reputed author of a famous book, the *Imitation of Christ*. When he reached the highest class, he did some teaching in the lower classes, for that was the practice in the school. He was a baker's son but his ability won him generous patrons, including Pope Sixtus IV. When he had finished his studies in Italy, the pope said to the young scholar, "Ask what you please as a parting gift." "Give me," was the request, "books from your library, Greek and Hebrew." One of the books given him was a copy of the Gospels in Greek, which is thought to have reached Erasmus when he was working on his New Testament in Greek. Wessel taught at the University of Heidelberg and was also a reformer of schools. In his views on indulgences he held a position similar to that of Luther.

Rudolph Agricola (1444-1485), like other Humanists, studied at many places: the elements at Erfurt, more advanced studies at Cologne, and at Louvain where he received the master's degree in law. Then, like Wessel, he went to Italy to study rhetoric at Pavia and the classics at Ferrara where "humane letters seemed to be in the very air." He was a pupil of the younger Guarino and of Theodore Gaza. Unlike most other Humanists he paid attention to the modern languages including German, which he already knew, French, and Italian. He taught at Heidelberg but died early. He did, however, leave a stimulating example to German literary students.

ERASMUS

Two of the greatest northern Humanists, Erasmus and Vives, were active in promoting not only classical but also biblical studies; and this was one of the primary differences between Humanism at the North and in Italy, where many of the leading scholars were hostile to the church and to religion itself. Both Erasmus and Vives remained in the church; but their studies and the vernacular translations of the Bible that grew out of their work aided the cause of the Reformation. Both believed, as Erasmus said, that there was no gulf between classical learning and the treasury of the gospels. He believed that the two could be joined and that the results would be sound learning, peace, and moral conduct. His influence extended throughout civilized Europe.

Erasmus wrote many books and we shall deal with his schoolbooks mainly. His first was the *Adages,* or *Familiar Quotations from the Classics.* He used each quotation as the subject or text for his comments or interpretation. Each commentary may include many further quotations. The book was reissued many times in enlarged forms with new quotations. This was a device used by authors in precopyright times to prevent the pirating of their books by other printers. A second book was his *Colloquies,* literally sample conversations between boys or boys and the teacher. Other writers, including Vives, wrote such books for use in schools in teaching easy Latin. Erasmus wrote two books on methods of teaching, and two of a general nature: one against war, the *Complaint of Peace,* and a famous satire, the *Praise of Folly,* which is still read by the general public.

His work on books written by others should also be noted. He aided William Lily to prepare a Latin grammar for St. Paul's School in London while he was teaching in English universities. He prepared a new edition of the well-known old *Distichs of Cato,* long used in medieval schools. This must have been a pot-boiler, a contribution to a phase or need of life not overlooked by Erasmus. He prepared new editions of ancient classics for the schools. We shall show at once that Erasmus was not only a superior kind of schoolmaster, as the foregoing must suggest.

Of all the books prepared by him, his edition of the New Testament in the original Greek had the widest influence and showed best his central purpose. The revival of learning had directed attention to the classics of the church as well as to those of Greece and Rome. Scholars in many lands saw that it was necessary to correct the text of the central book of the church, the New Testament. Spanish scholars were already revising the text for a new edition of the entire Bible. Erasmus had meanwhile prepared his Greek New Testament and it was published in 1516, several years before the Spanish version of the original text was ready. A revised second edition by Erasmus came out in 1519 and a third in 1522. Luther made a German translation of the Erasmian text in 1519. A French translation was published in 1520; and Tyndale's English rendering of the Greek was printed in 1525 on the continent. It was secretly introduced into England where the Wycliffe version from the Latin Vulgate had already made the New Testament familiar to English readers.

The new textual scholarship was aided by the printing press. Before printing, an author could not be sure that his book would remain as he wrote it. Every copyist was likely to introduce errors small or large, unimportant or vital. Thus students using copies of the same book could never be sure that they had exactly the same text before them. They had to expect omissions, interpolations, and other inaccuracies. Uniform texts hardly existed; and a text once corrected would in new copies accumulate new errors. Printing changed all of this. The one hundredth printed copy was exactly the same as the first. This made the gradual improvement of a text possible as better, usually older, manuscripts were found. The manuscripts available to Erasmus were not particularly good and more accurate versions were provided by later scholars.

VIVES

Juan Luis Vives was introduced in the preceding section as a Humanist and a younger contemporary of Erasmus, but he was much more than that. He wrote a short history of civilization as a process of inquiry and discovery that anticipated Francis Bacon. Civilization, he claimed, develops because men ask basic questions and find the answers. Contrary to Bacon he favored the use and development of the vernacular languages. He contributed to the growing study of psychology and of the natural sciences. He was, therefore, a Humanist with a realistic bent. He was also a social reformer. In a letter to Erasmus in October, 1528, he wrote, "I set the public good as my goal. I would eagerly promote that good in any way possible. In my opinion those are fortunate people who are serviceable in this matter."

From 1512 Vives lived in the Flemish city of Bruges earning his living by teaching and writing. In editing a new edition of the *City of God* by St. Augustine he pointed out that the early church baptized only adults, not infants, and did not require the celibacy of the clergy. His independence of mind was not approved by all. In England, in 1523 and later he lectured at Oxford, making that conservative university Humanistic according to Wolsey. For the Spanish-born Queen Catherine he wrote books on the education of women and girls. Another schoolbook by Vives was a Latin conversation book that was later equipped with a Spanish translation and called *Dialogos*. It has been reprinted in the twentieth century; and Foster Watson translated it into English with the title, *Tudor School-Boy Life*.

The great work on education by Vives is on educational philosophy, psychology, and methods of teaching. It has been too much neglected and can be read today for its contribution to present thought and practice. The book is the *De Disciplinis*, which is the larger half of a work "on the debasement of the liberal arts and the methods of transmitting learning." There is also a third part, which treats of the quality of educated men. The book was published at Antwerp, in 1531, and later in Germany, Holland, France, Italy, and elsewhere. The book on psychology, *De Anima et Vita*, "Of Mind and Life," was published in 1539. At the request of the burgomaster of his home city, Bruges, he wrote an influential little work on poor relief. A theological work came out after his death in 1540.

Vives, although he was a Humanist, had a strong interest in the study of nature and the principles of utility and their practical application as criteria for judging education and life. He assigned a place to modern languages in teaching the ancient. He proposed two devices: the use of notebooks for lists of words, idioms, eloquent passages; and the method of double translation from the foreign tongue into the native speech; and, laying it aside for a time, its retranslation into the original tongue. Roger Ascham recommended these two devices as if they were his own. The use of notebooks very probably came in with the free use of paper, but the method of double translation seems to have been an invention made by Vives.

Vives was one of the few great Humanists who knew several modern tongues. He knew Spanish and French and was acquainted with Flemish and English, but he was indebted to his early home for this interest in the vernaculars. One of his early teachers, Antonio de Lebrija, had prepared the first Spanish grammar and dictionary in 1492, the year when Vives was born. When children first go to school, Vives declared, they are to speak in their own tongue, using it in acquiring the elements of Latin. It is the duty of mother and teacher to preserve a pure native speech. This is quite contrary to the attitude of Erasmus, who was almost hostile to the common speech, and of Bacon, who had his works translated into Latin because he feared the modern tongues might disappear from the life of men and the face of the earth.

History and geography were to be taught as means of developing practical understanding and knowledge of public affairs. Vives held that school histories should not emphasize war but rather the arts and achievements of civilization. Modern history should be taught, not only the history of the great states, but also that of the smaller progressive nations. He joined Erasmus in the hope of achieving international peace.

In his psychology also Vives struck out along new lines. The senses, he said, are our first teachers and sight is the chief of the senses. He should have said that hearing is the chief sense in teaching; perhaps he did. Children vary widely in capacity, in ability to observe and to distinguish, in intelligence, and in judgment; but they vary also in persistence and power to pay attention and in mental vigor and energy. Some children are notable for skill with the hands, as in painting and weaving. He said, with Quintilian, that we can learn a great deal about individual children by watching them at play. He dealt extensively with the principles of association and gave many illustrations: The teacher should help the children recall what has been learned, by teaching the connections between ideas, by the use of surprise and wonder, by means of rhymes, and by serial arrangements. In Vives we have the elements of an educational psychology. He touched also on the borders of animal or comparative psychology; and he discovered a new sense, the muscular sense, as it is called, the sense of pressure, weight, or resistance. Once again in his emphasis on the inductive method of investigation he anticipated Francis Bacon; but it was Bacon, not Vives, who wrote *The Advancement of Learning*. His ideal school was to be an "academy"—a public school for boys and girls, and also for older people who needed vocational training or retraining. It was to be a day, not a boarding, school. We have not exhausted the thought of Vives, who was next to Quintilian, the greatest Spanish writer on education; but we can allow him no more space in a book on the broad subject of *Western Education*.

PETER RAMUS OF FRANCE

In his life and work, Peter Ramus carried out two of the great social changes that prepared the way for Rousseau. Ramus began as an Aristotelian and a Catholic and he became a Humanist and a Huguenot, a Protestant. He achieved and occupied the positions described in the preceding sections. He even approached Realism but did not actually become a Realist. Led by a very conservative institution, the University of Paris, French education resisted the pressures that affected Ramus, illustrating the principle stated earlier that new movements do not usually sweep away old conditions everywhere and at once.

We should study Ramus in his era. He lived in the middle of the sixteenth century (1515–1572), the century of Erasmus and Luther. When Ramus was born, Erasmus was almost fifty years old and Luther was past thirty, whereas Loyola, Vives, and Rabelais were in their early twenties. The Greek text of the New Testament, prepared by Erasmus, was translated into the vernacular languages of Europe. It was published in 1516 when Ramus was one year old; and he was two when Luther took the action that was to split Europe into warring religious camps.

Humanism anticipated and accompanied Protestantism and helped to produce it; but Ramus began as a poor boy and a Catholic. Having outgrown the lessons of the local schoolmaster he became a servant to a rich student in Paris and studied at night. In a few years he completed the secondary school studies and took up dialectic which he enjoyed until he came to see that as it was taught it had no applications to practical life. "When I came to Paris," he wrote, "I fell into the subtleties of the Sophists, and they taught me the liberal arts through questions and disputes, without ever showing me a single thing of profit or practical value."

It was his discovery of Plato and his picture of Socrates that pulled Ramus from the Aristotelian treadmill. It is also evident that he did not really know Aristotle. His courses in dialectic had limited him to the tricks and technics of logic, dry fodder without nourishment. By nature impulsive and extreme in his responses, one is hardly surprised that in his final examination he defended the thesis that "All that Aristotle taught is false." This was clever for it compelled the examiners to go outside of Aristotle for materials. He survived the examination and became a doctor of philosophy and teacher at the age of twenty-one. Later, Ramus moderated his distaste for Aristotle; but meanwhile he had discovered Plato and the skill of Socrates as depicted in the dialogues. Thus began his conversion to Humanism; but he had to fight against the extreme conservatism of the graduates of the University of Paris.

Peter Ramus

Three areas of study occupied much of his attention in his latter years. One was the study and teaching of eloquence and this he based largely on the teaching of the great Roman rhetoricians Cicero and Quintilian. His second area of interest and endeavor was in mathematics and physics and this work led him to the borders of realism. He wrote extensively on arithmetic and geometry and his books, although not highly original, were in use for many years. In physics he struck a new string by demanding that physics should be an observational science. Exactly one generation later, Francis Bacon (1561–1626) said the same thing; but neither acted on this insight. In the seventeenth century, Isaac Newton (1642–1727) far transcended those hints; and this may suggest a principle of history—namely, that from microscopic germs after long incubation, great events are sometimes born; but it is difficult to select the fertile germs, hence the difficulty of prediction.

The third great interest of Ramus in his latter years was the interpretation of Scripture. We cannot name the exact time when he became a Protestant. When the change became apparent, he at once lost the support of powerful friends in the government. In those troubled times he made a tour through Switzerland and Germany and it appears that he would have accepted an appointment at a foreign university, but none was offered. He came back by way of Geneva to France to be brutally murdered in the Saint Bartholomew's Day massacre in August, 1572. He had helped to set in motion ideas that were to grow for years and centuries.

LANGUAGE AND RELIGION

Early Christianity strongly opposed the pagan gods of Homer and Virgil, but by 1600 these divinities were dead. Some of the views of Plato, Aristotle, and the Stoics were absorbed by Christians and used by philosophers to broaden and support their Hebraic faith; but the essential facts and doctrines of Christianity were entirely independent of pagan learning. The Humanists read the classics as literature and history not as religion; but even though this is true, the separation was not absolute and the juxtaposition of the two developed a comparison—a study of comparative religion, as it was later called.

Language plays a major role in the transmission of both education and religion. The Christian religion was propagated through Greek, Latin, and Hebrew. The Greek New Testament of Erasmus was important to scholars, but its importance to the common people was the stimulus that it gave to translation into the languages they could read, if they read any. Erasmus worked for scholars.

The Bible was the favorite book among the common people. It circulated in England in a translation from the Vulgate made by John Wycliffe (c. 1320–1384), a century before Erasmus. An earlier version in French was made for the Waldenses of southern France, two centuries before Wycliffe; and there were still other versions made before the Reformation that contributed to the breach. Many churchmen forbade Bible-reading by laymen, but again it was tolerated; even bishops disagreed on the practice. When the translation by William Tyndale (c. 1492–1536) was smuggled into England, the archbishop of Canterbury burned all copies found; but the bishop of Norwich praised the translation. Sir Thomas More gave his unofficial opinion, saying, "I myself have seen and can show you Bibles fair and old, written in English, which have been known and seen by the bishop of the diocese, and left in the hands of laymen and women, whom he knew to be good Catholic people who used the books with devotion and soberness." Incidentally, More and Tyndale were executed, but only Tyndale for the Bible translation. Thomas More gave testimony on a related matter: He estimated that sixty per cent of the English in his time, the sixteenth century, were able to read; but qualifications suggest themselves. Did he include all levels of the people and exclude those who did not read well, only calling words? Erasmus also expressed the liberal Catholic position. He wrote with his customary eloquence,

I wish that even the weakest woman might read the gospels and the epistles of St. Paul. I wish they were translated into all the languages so as to be read and understood not only by Scots and Irishmen but even by Saracens and Turks. But the first step to their being read is to make them intelligible to the reader. I long for the day when the ploughman would sing a text of the Scripture at his ploughbeam; and that the weaver at his loom with this would drive away the tediousness of time, and the wayfaring man with this pastime would overcome the weariness of his journey. And to be short, I would that all the conversation of the Christian should be of the Scripture, for in a manner such are we as our daily tales are.

This is not only eloquent but also generous to modern languages, for poor folk! Erasmus, after all, did not work for scholars only.

Many bishops and other leaders feared the reading and discussion that Erasmus praised. They feared the new ideas and opinions and especially the indocility that would result; and from their standpoint they were right. The church had long been in great disarray; state and church were quarreling over taxation; and the people complained that the clergy were rich and lived at ease and in luxury, while beggars were seen everywhere.

Although he was a loyal son of the church, Vives joined in such complaints. He attacked the "pomp, pride, and luxury" of the clergy who "claim that they do not sell but yet compel the people to pay" for services. Antwerp was taking away the business of Bruges, which had great difficulty in taking care of its poor. Vives thought the church should help.

For over three fourths of the fourteenth century (1307–1377) the papacy was situated in Avignon where it was largely under the control of France. In the later fourteenth and early fifteenth centuries the headship of the church was claimed by two and even three "popes." The Council of Constance (1414–1418) resolved this difficulty and reestablished the papacy in Rome, but all these and many other local and general divisions and disputes left their mark and eventually led to the great division known as the Reformation.

The reading of the Bible in their own language by the common people was the subject of one of those disputes, as we have seen. This was a matter of educational as well as religious significance, a subject with which both education and religion were concerned. Latin, the language of the church, was in some degree a sacred language; and it is to be noted, and we have referred to it, that only in our day has the celebration of the mass in the vernacular been permitted.

WYCLIFFE AND HUS

John Wycliffe was educated at Oxford and became a successful and popular lecturer at the university. He seems to have begun as a conservative, but his reading and translation of the New Testament led him to become a liberal. He came to favor state confiscation of church funds that were misapplied, or excessively large, or unused. This policy, which was to appeal to Vives, gained support in England. The uncle of the king, and a great noble, John of Gaunt, came to support Wycliffe and his followers who were known as Lollards.

Wycliffe turned to theological and administrative questions. In the New Testament he found no mention of a pope or similar authoritative ruler. The rule seemed to be local and congregational. He had serious doubts about the Eucharist but he did not attack miracles in general. He followed the Waldenses in holding that salvation did not require the services of a priest. The pope condemned a large number of his propositions but as spread by his disciples they gained much attention and support in England. After the death of John of Gaunt, in 1399, and with the king's desire for rapproachement with the papacy, Lollardy was crushed.

Meanwhile, Wycliffe's doctrines had been carried by students to the Germans and Czechs of central Europe, where the University of Prague functioned somewhat as Oxford had done in England. At Prague, the Czech students did not get along well with the Germans and some transferred to Oxford. This was less difficult than it would be today because the Latin language was the universal language of instruction in the higher schools. Some returning Czech students, and especially Jerome of Prague, introduced Wycliffe's views into Bohemia where they were spread by John Hus. Meanwhile the Council of Constance (1414–1418) had met to end the Great Schism, when for a time there had been three "popes." The council summoned Hus to appear before this body, which had the power to make and unmake popes. Under a safe-conduct from the emperor, Hus came and was found guilty of heresy. Then all that was necessary was to convince the Emperor Sigismund that a promise to a heretic was not binding! Hus was burned at the stake. In 1579 all Bohemia burst into a violent rebellion that continued for many years. It was from this people that the great educator, Comenius, was to arise.

TOWNS AND SCHOOLS

Town life developed rapidly in England and on the continent including Germany during the last two of the medieval centuries; and a great need and desire for education spread in these growing centers. Prague had secured a university in 1348, the first such foundation in Germany; and as we have seen it was a leading point from which the ideas of Wycliffe were spread. Between 1348 and 1500, thirteen other German universities were established, including the famous ones of Heidelberg, Leipzig, and Tübingen. Wittenberg, where Luther taught, was founded in 1502.

Numerous schools also sprang into life and gained the support of wealthy citizens or of the municipalities themselves. Pupils came long distances, sometimes from foreign countries, to attend school or university. This was the era of the wandering scholars who secured food by begging or even by stealing it. The autobiography of Thomas Platter, a Swiss lad who spent several years with a band of students or *vagantes* traveling from school to school convinces the reader that many of these institutions were of little value. The city of Breslau had a variety of cathedral, guild, and vernacular schools. Thomas Platter, who attended one of its Latin schools, has left a graphic description of its arrangements and exercises. "In the school of St. Elizabeth," he wrote, "nine bachelors of arts read lectures at the same hour in the same room. [What confusion!] Greek had not yet penetrated into that part of the world. No one had any printed books in the school except the preceptor, who had a Terence. What was read had first to be dictated, then punctuated, then construed and at last explained." This was in the sixteenth century. No wonder he soon moved on in search of better instruction. He finally found it and became a learned man and a noted teacher. There were many good schools, but the bad ones made a deeper impression on those afflicted. Luther himself had been a begging student who sang for his bread in the streets of "the dear town of Eisenach," until Frau Cotta gave him a home. In later years he denounced the begging system as a waste of valuable time and a temptation to vagrancy and worse. Germany had many schools by 1500, but most were still medieval. In the sixteenth century they became classical and prepared the way to the new world of Erasmus, Vives, and Luther—and later of the great Jesuit scholars and teachers.

At the same time there was a renewed interest in the study of the Hebrew language. John Reuchlin, born in 1455, became a leading Hebraist and one of the first modern Gentiles to become skilled in the original language of the Old Testament. Spanish scholars in the following century, the sixteenth century, were to prepare a new version, as we have seen.

THE LUTHERAN MOVEMENT

The attack of Martin Luther (1483–1546) upon the papacy, like many historical movements, grew out of an incident. This incident arose in the campaign for the sale of indulgences in the vicinity of Wittenberg. The idea of indulgences for the reconciliation of sinners was not new, but it was not found in early Christianity. In the early days of the church the congregations themselves expelled flagrant offenders against the Christian code but readmitted them after their confession and penitence. In time these powers were taken over by the priests, then by the bishop, and at last by the pope. In the thirteenth century the doctrine of a treasury of good works was developed; and, accordingly, the sinner was to benefit from the good deeds of others—the saints and all pious people. Those merits were to be dispensed by the church to erring brethren as indulgences thus releasing their souls from penalties that the church had imposed on them. Scandal arose because the indulgences were sold for cash and the indulgence-sellers even accepted money payments instead of penitence. We have seen that, in the first Crusade, Pope Urban II (1095) promised any contrite Crusaders a remission of all penances as an inducement to participation in the Crusade. Money to rebuild St. Peter's at Rome was raised by selling indulgences; and Tetzel, the papal agent who directed the sale near Wittenberg seems to have used reprehensible methods to increase his sales. This aroused Luther who nailed his Ninety-five Theses on the door of the church on the first of November, All Saints' Day. The act had results that he had not anticipated. The effect was sudden and momentous. All Germany was aroused. Instead of a calm university debate, Luther had to lead a national revolution that was to split not only Germany but Europe into opposing religious parties.

Attacks on the Theses were answered by Luther in words that were read more widely than the original document. His colleagues at Wittenberg supported him and the students burned the countertheses of Tetzel. The sale of indulgences fell off rapidly. There was also a geographical phase of the dispute; it was a battle between the North and the South. Luther was summoned to Rome, but he refused to go. He appealed to his prince, the Elector Frederick, who supported him; the fate of Hus was avoided.

The young German Humanists, the citizens of the German towns, the people who desired a national church, and the princes who wanted to avoid the drain of money from their states generally supported the reforming party. Luther's pen was never at rest. He issued sermons, pamphlets, and books that were widely read. The titles of three of his books were *The*

Liberty of a Christian Man; To the Christian Nobility of the German Nation, which called for extensive educational reforms; and *On the Babylonian Captivity of the Church*. The printing press of Froben, the famous Swiss printer who also served Erasmus, was very active in spreading Luther's writings. This is incidental evidence that many thousands of Germans could read and that there must have been schools that have left no records: schools in homes and in the shops of tailors and other indoor workers. There were also those who read on street corners to those who could not read.

Luther's writings increased the numbers of his supporters; what had begun as a party threatened to become the entire German people. The church had to act and the pope excommunicated him, but many did not believe or pretended not to believe that the papal bull was genuine. Luther, however, received it and openly, solemnly, burned it outside the Elster Gate of Wittenberg. The separation from Rome was complete.

When ecclesiastical measures failed to crush Luther, the church turned to the empire; when he could not be reached as a heretic, they attempted to have him declared an outlaw. Luther was summoned by the Emperor Charles V, in 1521, to appear before the German Diet. This he did, but he firmly maintained his stand with the approval of the German princes. The imperial ban against him could not be executed. On his return from the Diet, fearing that he might be kidnapped, he was "captured" by friends and concealed in Castle Wartburg, where he translated the New Testament from the Greek of Erasmus. The Protestant religion, not entirely Lutheran, soon spread from Switzerland northward to include England and Scotland but not Ireland. There were, however, many Catholics within this great triangle and also Protestants outside.

Because Protestant Churches regarded teaching as one of their important functions they were interested in education perhaps even more than the Catholics; and the Catholic Church and laity had been active in education for many centuries. Protestants held that all children should be taught the Scriptures as the basis of faith, life, participation in public worship, and for service as an official of the church. The new churches were as much concerned for the education of leaders and more than the old church had been for the education of members, men and women, boys and girls. This last point is significant, for the Reformation gave the first widely applicable reason for the education of girls. Only a few nuns and a few wealthy or noble women were educated in earlier periods. Although Luther was not a Humanist, he favored the education both of the common people and of future leaders in church and state. He did not create vernacular education, which had been growing for several centuries, but he did what he could to further it. And in the vernacular schools, which developed after the Reformation, the children of the common people, boys and girls, received an elementary education.

The educational needs of the new period were greater and the resources were less than they had been. The Reformation, like all revolutions, was the cause of disorder and destruction, which tended to make the improvement and even the maintenance of schools more difficult. The monasteries and their schools and scriptoria were closed; foundations, scholarships, and endowments were embezzled by princes and nobles; many positions that had been filled by learned men were abolished; and much civil disorder and religious warfare resulted from the Reformation.

The large number of positions that were abolished can be seen from the fact that a city of fifty thousand people sometimes had as many as eight hundred priests, or one for every sixty-five of the population. To this we must add the persons connected with monasteries, chantries, and other institutions to get a full measure of the vast number of clergy in the medieval church. And, Luther said, because selfish parents see that they can no longer place their children on the bounty of monasteries and cathedrals, they refuse to educate them. "Why," they say, "should we educate our children if they are not to become priests, monks, and nuns, and thus earn a support?" The hollow piety and selfish aims of such persons, he adds, are sufficiently evident from their confession.

School and university attendance declined rapidly in the period. The universities of Erfurt and Rostock never recovered from the losses sustained; but the numbers at Cologne, Vienna, Leipzig, and Basel also were greatly reduced. Professorships were abandoned because there were no students to be taught. Only little Wittenberg, founded in 1502, said Luther, is doing its best; but even Wittenberg lost three fourths of its enrollment in the disastrous 1520s.

Luther attempted to stem the tide by his *Address to the Christian Nobility of Germany* (1520); by a *Letter to the Mayors and Aldermen in Behalf of Christian Schools* (1524); and by a *Sermon on the Duty of Sending Children to School* (1530). We should notice that these writings are addressed to rulers, civil officers, and parents, not to the clergy or the churches. One reason for this was that Luther realized the need of the state for educated public servants; and another that he needed the aid of the state to preserve the Reformation and to carry out his program for church and school. He was the first modern writer to urge compulsory attendance and proposed that the state should pass such legislation and enforce it. It was not until long after his death that any state followed his suggestion. Many of the larger nations did not enact compulsory attendance laws until the latter part of the nineteenth century; but the little state of Weimar, in 1619, demanded the compulsory education of all children in the vernacular. In all states, large and small, enforcement of such laws lagged considerably behind enactment.

Luther favored a broader curriculum for the vernacular school. Such schools at that time usually taught merely reading or reading with writing and arithmetic. There were also special schools of writing, arithmetic, and bookkeeping. He proposed to have music, poetry, and history, and "the whole course of mathematics" introduced. Luther was himself musical and would have both singing and instrumental music taught. He placed a high estimate on the work of the teacher and declared that this vocation was, next to that of the ministry, "the highest and best." Schools were to be cheerful and pleasant so that children might take delight in acquiring knowledge. In language typically vigorous and violent, he described the old school of the Middle Ages as "a hell or purgatory in which children were tortured and in which with much flogging and wretchedness they learned nothing." Unfortunately school discipline was not so easily reformed but remained harsh even until recent times. To show how readily an education might be acquired, he declared that he would be satisfied with a school that would be in session only two hours a day. With good methods and stimulating, friendly teachers that would be enough. The rest of the child's day could be devoted to play and to the learning of a trade. Luther did not propose any innovation in industrial education, as is sometimes claimed. Apprenticeship was common and effective and he was satisfied with its results. On secondary education, in which he was greatly interested, he had fewer suggestions to make. Along with all the other reformers, he supported the current classical program and emphasized the study of "the holy languages": Latin, Greek, and Hebrew. They were considered holy as well as "learned" because they were considered essential in the study of the Scriptures. Every "promising lad" was to be enabled and encouraged to attend a secondary school and, after that, the university.

In northern Germany, John Bugenhagen reorganized the churches, the Latin schools, and the parish schools in which German reading and writing were taught. Bugenhagen also worked in Denmark, and schools were developed for the common people in all the Scandinavian countries. Ability to read was made a requirement for confirmation and this, in turn, was a prerequisite to marriage. Thus an indirect form of compulsory schooling was developed. Melanchthon reformed the schools of Saxony, providing for elementary schools and especially Latin schools, in which he was most interested. John Sturm organized his Protestant Humanistic gymnasium at Strassburg in 1538. This school, with its nine-year course, was the first example of a type that became the dominant secondary school of Germany for centuries and remains to the present. One important fact about these and other German schools of the Reformation era is that state and church cooperated in their establishment and maintenance. The Reformation marks an important period in the transfer of the educational functions from the church to the state. From this time on, for several centuries, we see the increasing activity of the state in education until, in the eighteenth and early nineteenth centuries and after the democratic revolutions, the state took over these functions almost completely. As a result of this movement, elementary and secondary schools have become secular and civil rather than religious institutions.

SPREAD OF THE REFORMATION

The movement inaugurated by Luther spread far beyond Germany. The leader in Switzerland was a young Humanist who was so fond of music that he had contemplated entering a monastery to secure the leisure for developing his musical talents. His family did not wish him to become a monk and he became an eloquent and popular preacher instead. His name was Ulrich Zwingli. Coming to Zürich in 1519, he became the admired leader of a circle of young liberals. The reform movement began there almost immediately. Zwingli read one of the books of John Hus and was led to the conclusion that church tithes were or should be only voluntary offerings. From this he went on until Zürich, Basel, and Berne became fully Protestant. The mass was abolished by the citizens and council of Berne in 1528. The Swiss, in 1529, separated themselves from the Lutheran movement and developed an independent church, the German Reformed. The American branch of this Zwinglian church is now called the Reformed Church of the United States.

Geneva, in western Switzerland, became the capital of Calvinism. In the same year (1536), the city became politically independent and Protestant. Calvin's doctrinal position was accepted by the Huguenots of France, the Dutch Reformed communion of Holland, the Presbyterians of Scotland, and the Puritans of England and America.

John Calvin (1509–1564) grew up in Picardy, among a people known for their sympathy with Wycliffe and Hus. He was a brilliant student and was thoroughly educated in the classics, the law, and theology. Mathurin Cordier, already mentioned in connection with the *Collège de Guyenne*, was one of his teachers. At the University of Paris, Calvin belonged to the *Collège de Montaigu*, Erasmus's old school. About the same time another student, who was to become a world-famous leader, entered the same college. His name was Ignatius Loyola. Whether the future reformer and the founder of the Society of Jesus ever met is not known. Calvin was a Protestant as early as 1532, but he was not compelled to flee from France until three years later. After short periods at Strassburg and Basel he came to Geneva.

The secondary school of Geneva had seven classes. It was a Humanistic school with a thorough course in Latin, Greek, and rhetoric. Calvin drew several famous teachers to Geneva, including Cordier; Theodore Beza (1519–1605), who prepared a French translation of the New Testament; and Castellion (1515–1563), the author of a book of *Colloquies*. The Academy of Geneva (1559) was the nucleus of a university; but, at first, it gave instruction only in advanced Humanistic studies and theology. Medicine and theology were added later. The schools of the city attracted many foreign students who in their turn spread the educational influence of Geneva. And, in fact, Calvinism had an international aspect. Its interest in universal education, in the separation of church and state, and in a church government in which laymen participated influenced many countries. Two of these countries, Holland and Scotland, were particularly influential in promoting these principles in America.

THE REFORMATION IN ENGLAND

The Reformation in England was a political change rather than a religious movement among the people. Parliament in 1534 passed the Act of Supremacy, which separated England from Rome. The English Bible became common in the homes and the English language was used in the services of the church. An English catechism and the *Book of Common Prayer* were provided.

In England as in Germany the Reformation was educationally destructive. The monasteries and chantries were closed and their funds for the most part appropriated to political ends. Along with the monasteries, the monastic grammar schools were abolished and England was left poorer in educational opportunities than it had been before the Reformation. Although some schools were refounded, and some new schools were opened, the losses of the Reformation were not made good for a long time. Nothing was done by the government and little by the Anglican Church for elementary education. Private schools of the most diverse qualities grew up in villages and towns. Many of these were mere dame schools. Thus England developed a laissez-faire attitude in education that was to delay the development of an educational system and of universal opportunity for schooling until the latter nineteenth century, and of secondary education until the twentieth century. English individualism tended to restrict the functions and powers of government within narrow limits, and these limits did not permit the government to deal with schools. English religious toleration and the consequent growth of many dissenting sects, coupled with the desire to inculcate some form of religious belief in each school, further limited the educational activity of government. Churches and private individuals or groups, however, established schools. The dissenting academies of the seventeenth century were one such response.

THE JESUITS

The Society of Jesus, commonly known as the Jesuits, was founded in 1534, through the efforts of Ignatius Loyola (1491–1556), and was recognized by the Roman Church six years later. They immediately became active as preachers, missionaries, teachers, and school founders. They became a kind of flying squadron to recover for the Roman Church the territories lost through the Protestant revolution and to spread her influence to new countries. Active almost everywhere in Europe, the Jesuits soon came to America with the purpose of converting the Indians. As a result, they also became explorers in Canada and in the Mississippi and Ohio valleys. They went to Africa, to China, and to India as missionaries. All those who were sent out to distant lands, as well as those who worked in Europe, were given a thorough education in the schools they established.

Ignatius Loyola was chosen general of his Order and received the vows of his companions in 1541. The new Society became famous almost immediately, and numbers sought to join. A strict military discipline was employed from the first. There were four classes of associates: the novices, who were all carefully selected for zeal, devotion, and ability; the scholastics, who had been novices for at least two years and who had to spend at least five years in study and five more as teachers in junior classes; the coadjutors, who were preachers and teachers and from whom the heads of schools and houses were chosen; and the professed, who alone could share in the government of the Society. This long winnowing process assured that every Jesuit was a picked and a marked man. The constitution gave the general almost absolute power over the lives, the consciences, and the activities of the members; yet it also provided for a system of surveillance and an elaborate use of the confessional intended to keep everybody, even the general, in the line of duty and to prevent all illicit changes in the constitution. The government of the Society is autocratic and absolute and the general is a veritable czar. Historians, for example Ranke in his *History of the Papacy*, have not been slow to point out that, along with much that is good, this Society has done a great deal of evil through its secret and ruthless political machinations, its casuistry, and its blind obedience to the Catholic Church.

At the height of their power, the Jesuits were the most successful educators in Europe. Their schools were permanent, well supported, and well organized, and their teachers were selected and thoroughly educated in what they taught and in the methods of discipline and teaching. Everything was prescribed, not only the subjects and methods, but also the interpretations. The teachers had no freedom, and no innovations or experiments were allowed. They had a limited and attainable aim and used every available means to reach it. The fourth part of the Jesuit *Constitution* is the plan of studies, called the *Ratio Studiorum*. The *Ratio* was fully worked out and several times revised in the light of experience in teaching between the years 1584 and 1599, when it was adopted and issued to the schools. This work is a set of directions to teachers and school officers and it prescribes a system that leaves little to their judgment. It is an ironclad scheme. Once adopted, it became the law of Jesuit education until the suppression of the Society by the pope in 1773. After the Society was reestablished in 1814, the *Ratio* was revised again (1832) and some emphasis was placed on the vernacular language.

The Jesuit schools are almost exclusively secondary and higher institutions. At first, Loyola had devoted a portion of his efforts to social reform. He set up two orphanages in Rome, one for boys and one for girls. In these two hundred children were fed, clothed, and taught. The teaching included some handwork and vocational work. But this was soon given up, and thereafter the Society, except as an occasional work of charity, devoted all its educational efforts to the classical and theological education of boys and young men. There were no Jesuit schools for girls. The colleges were divided into junior and senior divisions. The former had a six-year course devoted to Latin grammar, literature, and rhetoric, and the latter a four-year course in literature, rhetoric, and logic. After completing the junior division, the future member of the Society was occupied for two years in the religious activities of his novitiate; and the senior division was followed by a period of several years in cadet or practice teaching under supervision. The whole program occupied the Jesuit up to the age of thirty or longer, when he became a full member of the Society and a professor. In the higher colleges, mathematics, logic, philosophy, and theology were taught in a course of from four to six years. The Greek and Hebrew languages were included but the emphasis throughout was on the Latin. It was the language of instruction and conversation, in and out of school, although even in the *Ratio* of 1599 the vernacular was permitted as an aid in teaching beginning pupils. Extraordinary emphasis was placed on skill in speaking and writing idiomatic Latin fluently. Equal emphasis was placed on skill in argument, on a knowledge of philosophy and theology, and on the development of character and complete devotion to the Society and the Roman Church. It may be as well to say that these ends do not seem to have been always compatible, each with the others.

The colleges were supported by endowments and donations; instruction was free. Externs, that is those who had not the intention of becoming Jesuits, were admitted, and contributions were often obtained from their parents. The Society became rich and has always catered to the wealthy, the aristocratic, and the powerful classes. But the success of the schools was due neither to money, which gave the means, nor to the curriculum, which was simply the formalized Humanism of the sixteenth century. Their success was due to their organization, methods, and men. The conduct of the pupils at their lessons and at play, and the methods of the teachers, were closely supervised. Supervision was exercised by the rector of each school and by his prefect of studies and prefect of discipline. The teachers were as carefully supervised as the pupils. A system of spying, or "manifestation," as it is called by Jesuits, was used in the schools and in the Society. Once a year each school was inspected by the provincial who had charge of the schools over a large area. The discipline, although firm, was mild and gentle, especially as compared with the brutality that ruled in the schools of the sixteenth century. Much use was made of rivalry and competition. Each boy had his opponent, each group of ten was pitted against another group of ten, and classes vied with classes.

One of the striking elements of Jesuit method was the assignment or prelection. We give here a greatly shortened example from the *Ratio*. It says, Let the teacher read the whole passage through. Let him explain the topic and its connection with what went before. After reading a single Latin sentence, let him explain the difficult words and phrases, not merely substituting one hard word for another. The vernacular may be used if necessary. Let him explain the allusions and make observations suitable to each class. Such was the prelection.

Another element in Jesuit method was the repetition. "At the end of the lectures some students, about ten at a time, will repeat during half an hour what they have heard, one of their fellow students of the Society, if possible, being put in charge of each group of ten." This passage illustrated another practice of the Jesuit schools, the use of monitors in teaching. Systematic daily, weekly, monthly, and yearly reviews were also carried out. Carefully organized written examinations were given. Add to this that the teachers were men selected for their ability and zeal; that they were prepared for their work by study and by teaching under the guidance of skilful teachers, and that they prepared to devote their lives to this profession and we shall understand why Francis Bacon, who was not a Jesuit, could say that the Jesuit schools were the best in Europe. He should have said, best for the purpose the Society followed.

OTHER CATHOLIC SOCIETIES

Other teaching societies, besides the Jesuits, developed Catholic schools. The Oratory of Divine Love grew up in Rome as a voluntary association, originally of fifty or more laymen and clergy, who were interested in church reform and devoted to Humanism, a pure life, and the theology of St. Augustine. Scattered by the sack of Rome in 1527, some of them found new homes in Venice, Genoa, and other cities where they formed groups of "Christian academies." Influenced by this Italian Oratory, the French Cardinal de Berulle in 1611 established the Oratory of France. De Berulle and his followers were devout Catholics who wished to improve the discipline and education of priests. The Oratory grew rapidly and established some famous schools such as the one at Juilly. They were influenced by the writing of Descartes; and the philosopher Malebranche was a member of the order. They aimed to cultivate close personal relations between teachers and pupils. Their schools were conducted in French and taught mathematics, physics, and the natural sciences. Polite accomplishments such as dancing and various games were taught. The Oratorians paid special attention to music and were known as *les pères au beau chant*. Palestrina had been an adherent of St. Philip Neri, one of the founders of the Italian Oratory, and had composed music for the congregation. The learned languages were not neglected, but their schools were realistic, a type that will be treated in the next chapter. The word *oratorio* seems to be derived from the name of these societies.

François Fénelon (1651–1715)

The Port Royalists, or Jansenists, which were founded by St. Cyran and Cornelius Jansen, established schools that resembled those of the Oratory. The theology of both groups was derived from St. Augustine; and their ascetic outlook led the Port Royalists to supervise their pupils very closely. For this reason, the schools and classes were kept small and the teachers lived with their pupils. The curriculum was, in general, similar to that of the Oratorians, although dancing was omitted. The Port Royalists, however, made an advance over the Oratorians by their excellent teaching of the French language and of logic. In logic, they used the inductive method. Their teachers wrote textbooks in grammar and logic that were widely used. The "Little Schools of Port Royal" lasted only from about 1646 to 1661 when, through the opposition of the Jesuits, the Society was dispersed. Their influence was far greater than their small numbers and short period of activity would suggest. Blaise Pascal was their greatest defender.

Catholic charity schools for the poor were established by several societies. One of these was the Brothers of the Christian Schools, founded by Jean Baptiste de la Salle in 1684. They were required to dedicate their lives to teaching and agreed not to become priests. They taught the vernacular language and religion. La Salle wrote a book of directions on organizing schools and teaching. It is called *The Conduct of Schools* and in general purpose, not in content, might be compared with the *Ratio Studiorum* of the Jesuits. The Christian Brothers developed a class system of teaching as compared with individual instruction. They classified their students into proficiency groups, used monitors to teach the younger pupils, and established a normal school for the preparation of teachers. Their schools increased rapidly in France and spread to foreign countries.

The Order of Ursulines was a society of nuns, devoted to the education of girls. France, in the seventeenth century, showed a strong interest in the best types of education for girls. The Abbé Fénelon wrote a widely influential book, *On the Education of Girls*. Fénelon believed that girls should be educated for homemaking and the care of a household as a career. This involved some training in law and business affairs and economic principles. An example of Fénelon's influence is seen in the fact that when the Philadelphia physician Benjamin Rush wrote on the education of American girls he followed the French abbé's outline. Fénelon had the direction of the education of some pupils of the royal family of France and prepared some historical and ethical books for them. These were read not only by schoolboys but by almost all readers of French literature. The most famous was *Télémaque*, a story that teaches that rulers should be the servants of their people.

The Reformation period greatly extended the educational opportunities of the common people, Catholic and Protestant, boys and girls. In secondary education, it continued the Humanistic tradition and used the old humanities for the service of the church. At the same time, it tended to overemphasize grammar and style and thus narrowed the meaning of Humanism until it became largely linguistic. The Reformation also gave an opening for the civil governments to participate more actively in education; and this trend toward state education continued to grow in the following centuries.

SUMMARY

The Reformation was a social evolution growing out of political, economic, moral, intellectual, and religious changes. Intellectually, the Reformation was connected with the Humanist movement. Both appealed to individual judgment, original sources, and the inspiration that was to be derived from a revered past. The Reformation directed its intellectual activity not so much toward aesthetic and political ends as to Bible study by means of the original tongues. Old Testament scholarship demanded a knowledge of Hebrew; and New Testament studies were aided by the revival of Greek and the more authentic Greek texts of Erasmus and others. The Reformation was, therefore, related to the revival of learning, but it was a broader movement.

The Reformation was a popular, not an aristocratic movement. Salvation by faith was an individualist principle. It applied to everyone of both sexes. It implied individual understanding. The Protestant religion became the religion of a book, the Bible; and personal faith presupposed knowledge and understanding of the Bible. On this path the reformers were led to support universal education. The Reformation was also a nationalist movement and resulted in the creation of national churches that used the national language in their services and their parish schools. The Reformation promoted, and was promoted by, the increasing use of the printing press. The vernacular school was adopted by the new churches with the favor and sometimes with the financial support of the government. This was the opening stage of the long progress toward national education, a result that the reformers neither foresaw nor desired.

Catholic education, which did not follow this trend, was led by the late Humanistic secondary schools of the Jesuits and the schools of the Christian Brothers, which provided an elementary vernacular education for poor children. The schools of the Christian Brothers taught reading, writing, arithmetic, morals, religion, and sometimes spinning or some other manual work. The curriculum of the elementary schools, both Protestant and Catholic, rarely extended these subjects. These were class schools and only much later were they superseded by the common, civil schools.

QUESTIONS

1. In what respects can the Renaissance in the North and the Reformation be linked as parts of a single movement? In what respects can they be distinguished from each other?
2. Which of the causes of the Reformation affected education and in what ways?
3. Was the extraordinary emotion generated by the Reformation due solely to piety and interest in religion? Explain.
4. Consider the invention of printing as a means in the democratization of knowledge. In what sense do you use the word *democratization?*
5. Consider the influence of the invention of printing on the Reformation movement.
6. Find some good books on the subject and trace the early history of the English Bible.
7. How did Humanism in the North differ from Humanism in Italy? How was it related to the Reformation?
8. Why did the Protestant Churches regard teaching as one of their chief functions? The Roman Catholic Church had conducted schools for a long time. Was the Protestant attitude on education different from the Catholic?
9. What were the names of the secondary schools of the Renaissance-Reformation period in the several countries? How similar or different were they?

NOTES AND SOURCES

The Reformation and the Society of Jesus are both highly controversial subjects, and although we have space for only a few titles, an attempt has been made to give representation to several interpretations. A few biographies of Erasmus and of Luther out of many are given.

ALLEN, PERCY S., *The Age of Erasmus,* New York, Oxford, Clarendon Press, 1934, 303 pp. *Erasmus: Lectures and Wayfaring Sketches,* Oxford, Clarendon Press, 1934, 216 pp. Mr. Allen edited *Sir Thomas More: Selections from His English Works,* and from *The Lives of Erasmus and Roper,* Oxford, Clarendon Press, 1924, 191 pp.; and an edition of Erasmus's *Letters,* in Latin, 10 vols.

BAILEY, NATHAN, Translator, and E. JOHNSON, Editor, *The Colloquies of Erasmus,* London, Reeves and Turner, 1878, 2 vols.

BAINTON, ROLAND H., *Here I Stand: A Life of Martin Luther,* New York, Abingdon-Cokesbury Press, 1950, 422 pp.; *Hunted Heretic; the Life and Death of Michael Servetus, 1511–1553,* Boston, Beacon Press, 1953, 270 pp.

BARRETT, EDWARD J. B., *The Jesuit Enigma,* New York, Boni and Liveright,

1927, 351 pp. An unfriendly and personal account by one who was dismissed from the Society.

BEARD, CHARLES, *The Reformation of the Sixteenth Century in Its Relation to Modern Thought and Knowledge*, London, William & Norgate, Ltd., 1907, 451 pp.

BORN, LESTER K., Editor, *The Education of a Christian Prince, By Desiderius Erasmus*, New York, Columbia University Press, 1936, 277 pp.

EBY, FREDERICK, *Early Protestant Educators*, New York, McGraw-Hill Book Company, Inc., 1931, 312 pp.

FARRELL, ALLAN P., *The Jesuit Code of Liberal Education; Development and Scope of the Ratio Studiorum*, Milwaukee, Wis., The Bruce Publishing Company, 1938, 478 pp.

FITZPATRICK, EDWARD A., *St. Ignatius and the Ratio Studiorum*, New York, McGraw-Hill Book Company, Inc., 1933, 275 pp.

FROUDE, JAMES A., *Life and Letters of Erasmus*, New York, Charles Scribner's Sons, 1894, 433 pp.

GRAVES, FRANK P., *Peter Ramus*, New York, The Macmillan Company, 1912, 226 pp.

GRISAR, HARTMANN, *Martin Luther, His Life and Work*. Adapted from the second German edition by Frank J. Eble, St. Louis, Mo., B. Herder Book Company, 1935, 609 pp. This is an impartial biography by a Catholic author and it has a bibliography.

HARNEY, MARTIN PATRICK, *The Jesuits in History, the Society of Jesus Through Four Centuries*, New York, The American Press, 1941, 513 pp.

LINDSAY, THOMAS M., *A History of the Reformation*, New York, Charles Scribner's Sons, 1906, 1907, 2 vols.

MCCABE, JOSEPH, *A Candid History of the Jesuits*, New York, G. P. Putnam's Sons, 1913, 451 pp.

MCGUCKEN, WILLIAM JOSEPH, *The Jesuits and Education; The Society's Principles and Practice, Especially in Secondary Education in the United States*, Milwaukee, Wis., The Bruce Publishing Company, 1932, 352 pp.

MANGAN, JOHN J., *Life, Character, and Influence of Desiderius Erasmus*, New York, The Macmillan Company, 1927, 2 vols.

MONROE, PAUL, *Thomas Platter and the Educational Renaissance of the Sixteenth Century*, New York, D. Appleton and Company, 1904, 227 pp.

MURRAY, ROBERT HENRY, *Erasmus and Luther: Their Attitude Toward Toleration*, London, Society for Promoting Christian Knowledge, 1920, 503 pp.

NICHOLS, FRANCIS M., *The Epistles of Erasmus*, New York, Longmans, Green and Company, 1901-1918, 3 vols. The selected letters, extending down to 1520, are in English and fully annotated.

PAINTER, F. V. N., *Luther on Education*, Philadelphia, Lutheran Publication Society, 1889, 282 pp. Luther's *Letter* (1524) and *Sermon* (1530) on education in English. The long introduction provided by the editor is uncritical.

SCHWICKERATH, ROBERT, *Jesuit Education, Its History and Principles*, St. Louis, Mo., B. Herder Book Company, 1904, 687 pp.

SMITH, PRESERVED, *Erasmus; a Study of His Life, Ideals, and Place in History*, New York, Harper & Brothers, 1923, 479 pp.; *The Age of the Reformation*, New York, Henry Holt and Company, Inc., 1920, 861 pp.

Stokes, Francis G., *Epistolae Abscurorum Virorum*, London, Chatto and Windus, 1925, 560 pp. The Latin text with an English translation and notes.

Watson, Foster, *Vives on Education;* a translation of the *De Tradendis Disciplinis*, Cambridge University Press, 1912, 261 pp.

Woodward, William H., *Desiderius Erasmus Concerning the Aim and Method of Education*, Cambridge, University Press, 1904, 244 pp.

Chapter 8

FROM HUMANISM TO REALISM

Not only the meaning but also the practical value of science was becoming clear in the seventeenth century as its application to military affairs and to surgery and medicine came to be recognized. New schools, called academies, began to provide a more practical education, including some of the sciences and mathematics. The French and German academies were intended for the noble and fashionable classes, but in England the academy was patronized by the mercantile and manufacturing classes, who were beginning to share in the leadership of society. The advances in natural science and education were paralleled by new doctrines of religious and political liberty, by the rise of international law, and by the foundation of modern philosophy. Both the national and cosmopolitan trends of the century helped to place the modern languages in a more favored position than they had ever occupied. The great writers of the time, Bacon, Locke, and Descartes, began to make more use of the mother tongue, and the Realist schools gave a place to modern foreign languages in their schedules.

Educational writers, such as Comenius and Locke, gave further emphasis to the need for modern curricula and improved methods, whereas Comenius and Mulcaster favored universal education. A deep and widespread optimism characterized the century, and utopians like Campanella and Andreae attempted to bring education into closer connection with society itself. One of the ways in which they attempted to do this was by supporting industrial and vocational education in schools. This was a new demand. Schools had always dealt with words and ideas but now they were asked to introduce materials and tools and to teach trades. Much progress was made in the century but more would have been possible had it not been for the religious wars that followed the Reformation: the Huguenot wars in France, the Puritan struggle in England, and the terrible and devastating Thirty Years War in Germany. The Utilitarian and Realist tendencies in education were also held back by the continued success of the Jesuit schools in Catholic countries. In the seventeenth century the Jesuits were still the greatest educators in Europe, and Realism could make little progress wherever their formal classicism was dominant. In spite of these deterrent influences, the seventeenth and eighteenth centuries, and not the Renaissance, can be taken to mark the real beginning of modern education.

THE MEANING OF REALISM

Realism in education may be compared with Realism in philosophy, or art, or literary criticism. It connotes concrete knowledge, practical and vocational skills, the learning of languages for commercial or diplomatic rather than for literary use, and the study of history, politics, law, and the sciences. It is, negatively, a reaction against the literary and artistic purposes of the Renaissance and against the classics. Among the Realists, the fine arts, music, dancing, and even literature were given very little place or none at all. Greek had always been a poor second to Latin in the schools of western Europe and the Realists wished to dispense with it altogether. In the seventeenth century, they still demanded instruction in Latin, not for the Humanistic reason that it is the key to a great literature, but because it continued to be widely used as the medium of communication in public affairs, in the sciences, by the universities, in international correspondence, and by the Catholic Church.

One of the catchwords of Realism was "things before words," and this was sometimes taken to mean "things and not words." But words themselves are "things" and will repay careful study. On the other hand, many real things can hardly be studied at all except by the extensive and careful use of words. Such "things" are the French Revolution, courage, loyalty, devotion to duty and country, and the doctrine of evolution. No one recommends mere verbalism, but neither should we attempt to teach a science, a craft, or even swimming, without the use of words. And yet the Realists emphasized an important element in all education—namely, the value of direct experience as a basis for teaching and learning.

A broad curriculum was one of the features of Realism. It is not unusual to find seventeenth-century Realists proposing the study of twenty-five or thirty subjects—including two or three languages such as Latin and French; and the vernacular, such as German or Spanish; two or three branches of mathematics; several social studies; a number of sciences—philosophical, military, and vocational branches—and a variety of polite accomplishments. The number, variety, and necessarily superficial treatment of the many studies was a general characteristic of early Realist education.

New methods came in with the new subjects. Languages were to be taught by direct methods, as by conversation and by composition. Travel, observation, demonstration, and the early beginnings of the laboratory facilitated new methods. Botanical gardens, cabinets of minerals, pictures, drawings, maps, globes, and instruments were introduced. Because better methods were used and the children actively engaged in doing things in school, the discipline became milder.

Realism was partly but not wholly an upper-class movement. The English academy was a middle-class school, Comenius and Mulcaster were concerned with the vernacular education of the common people, and the vocational education of mechanics was proposed by several Realists. The Reformation and Counter-Reformation had laid emphasis on the vernacular languages for the common people; and this emphasis was greatly increased by Realism. Thus the Realist movement of the seventeenth century gradually affected almost every phase of education, but the classical schools and the universities were still the dominant institutions. These long resisted the new influences.

A HUMANIST WITH REALIST LEANINGS

Early in the sixteenth century the Spanish scholar Juan Luis Vives (1492–1540) urged the study of nature and accepted the principles of utility and practical application as criteria for judging education and life. To modern languages, he assigned a place in the curriculum along with the ancient. He proposed two devices: the use of notebooks for lists of words, idioms, and eloquent passages; and, the method of double translation from the foreign tongue into the native speech and back again. The Englishman Roger Ascham, who recommended the same two devices, may have obtained these ideas from Vives.

Vives was one of the few great Humanists who was also versed in modern tongues. He knew Spanish and French and was acquainted with Flemish and English; and in this interest in the vernaculars he was not alone, for the famous Spaniard Antony de Lebrija had prepared the first Spanish grammar and dictionary in 1492, the year of Vives' birth. When children go to school, Vives declared, they are to speak in their own tongue, not in Latin. It is the duty of mother and teacher to preserve a pure native language.

History and geography were to be taught as means of developing practical understanding and knowledge of public affairs. The school histories, Vives held, should not emphasize war but rather the arts and achievements of civilization. Modern history should be emphasized, not only the history of the great states but also that of the smaller progressive nations. Like Erasmus, he was interested in the problem of international peace.

In his psychology, Vives struck out along new lines. The senses are our first teachers and sight is the chief of the senses. Children vary widely in capacity, in ability to observe and distinguish, in intelligence and judgment, but also in persistence and power to pay attention, and in mental vigor and energy. Some children are notable for skill with the hands as in painting or weaving. Some of these ideas he may have read in his favorite Quintilian and he certainly found there the thought that we can best discover the nature of children by watching them at play. The psychological principle for which Vives is best known is the Greek doctrine of association. He said: If two ideas occur together then at a later time the more important one will tend to call up the less important. He dealt also with forgetting and ascribed it to physical conditions, to imperfect understanding, and other features. The teacher should help the pupil recall what has been learned, by teaching the connections between ideas, by the use of surprise and wonder, by means of rhymes, and by serial arrangements. In Vives, we have some of the elements of an educational psychology, and he also anticipated Bacon and the inductive method of science. His ideal school or academy was to be a public institution, and education was to be extended to boys and girls. He prepared a highly successful book of school dialogues or colloquies somewhat like those of Erasmus, Cordier, and Castellion. In this little schoolbook, he incidentally threw much light upon the educational conditions of his time.

REALIST UTOPIAS

Utopia, taken literally, means "no place"; and taken figuratively, it can mean an imaginary or unreal place. The word was used (and perhaps coined) by Sir Thomas More for the subject and title of a book, *Utopia* (1516). On a diplomatic mission at the time, More was stationed in Bruges where he and Vives became friends. In the intervals of the slow-paced negotiations he wrote *Utopia*. It says little about education but in that little, it proposes to have men learn both a trade and the art of agriculture. The Utopians had all their knowledge in their own language and being placed out in "the wide sea" they had no occasion to learn any other. No doubt they sent out no diplomatic missions such as bored Sir Thomas More. Australia and nearby lands had not been discovered when he wrote. Industrial education and the use of the common language by scholars were proposals often made by Realists.

Utopias of the seventeenth rather than the sixteenth century frequently contain extended educational features. Among these were *Christianopolis* by John Valentine Andreae (1586–1654); the *Nova Solyma* of Samuel Gott; the *Commonwealth of Oceana* (1650) by James Harrington; and the *City of the Sun* by Thomas Campanella (1568–1639). Campanella was an Italian Dominican who had difficulties with the Spanish government and the Inquisition and wrote his book in prison. The political features of the *City of the Sun* were drawn from Plato, but in his educational views, Campanella was a Realist and an encyclopedist. His city was to be equipped with gardens and many kinds of collections. The walls of public gardens and many kinds of collections. The walls of public buildings were to be covered with pictures, maps, diagrams, and illustrations of the mechanical arts and of the various instruments and with portraits of the inventors and of other notable persons. He lived a century after Copernicus and, not surprisingly, anticipated the idea of the planetarium. Such devices, together with specimens of all created things and all human constructions, were to be used in the education of the young.

Education, in Campanella's city, began at birth; but children began to study the sciences at the age of six and this was followed by instruction in the practical arts. The utopian city was opposed to narrow specialization favoring instead an encyclopedic and more general knowledge and training. In regard to languages, however, the reverse of this policy was in force. The citizens held that, although languages must be studied, they need not be studied by all; rather, they might be assigned to a sufficient but small number of specialists. In this utopia, each citizen worked four hours each day, and the rest of the time was to be spent in "learning joyously," and in other recreations. Particular attention was given to industrial education, and even the officials and rulers had to be skilled in the physical sciences and practical arts.

England in the seventeenth century had a number of minor writers, such as Samuel Hartlib, John Dury, and William Petty, who gave expression to new ideas on vocational education. Hartlib was not English. He was a Polish merchant living in London and was bent on the establishment in his adopted city of an institute for physical investigation. This project made him the center of the group that invited Comenius to England. We should notice that this was some years before the Royal Society was started. The "Notes" at the end of this chapter refer to this episode.

Hartlib's *Description of Macaria* was a utopia in which all children, both boys and girls, were taught industrial occupations and agriculture. The constant pairing of these two occupations by utopians reflects the economic conditions in England at that time. Hartlib proposed a national bureau of vocational guidance and employment, an idea considered both in his time and ours. Inspired by Hartlib, John Dury wanted to have trades taught to the common people, also a present demand and need, especially of those in the "inner city." William Petty of the same circle proposed what amounted to a college of technology. He named a dozen skilled trades including that of manufacturing scientific instruments. Lenses were coming into use in the seventeenth century and that is why Galileo with a telescope of his own construction was first to see the moons of Jupiter and much else. That is also why Malpighi of Bologna, in 1661, was able to disprove the old notion that the blood spreads freely in the tissues of the body and showed instead that arteries and veins are connected by capillary tubes that carry the blood from one to the other.

A little book, *Of Education*, written by John Milton (1608–1674) presents another educational utopia. Its extravagent demand directed to the pupils and teachers is part of its utopianism. Milton admits that his program is not "a bow for everyman to shoot with that calls himself a teacher." And yet the English academies carried out most of Milton's demands. However, much must have been done rather superficially. He demanded the study of mathematics from arithmetic to geometry; "the easy grounds of religion" and Bible knowledge; and the technical professional studies of navigation, architecture, and fortification, for England was fighting a civil war. On the other hand he proposed the study of an improbable collection of languages: Latin, Greek, Hebrew, Chaldee, and Syriac; and of living tongues, Italian and, of course, English. Like Vives he was a Humanist and Realist and also like Vives he proposed a school that should offer a complete education to the age of twenty-one. Each called the school an academy and this name was used by Milton's fellow-Puritans.

THE ACADEMIES

At the Restoration, in 1660, when the Puritan clergy were dismissed from their livings and their youth were excluded from the universities, they established their own schools for secondary and theological education and named them academies. The first one was opened at Sheriffhales, in 1663, in a large manor house with close-clipped lawns and old trees. Not many of the academies could afford such fine homes, but otherwise the first one was typical of the seventy or eighty academies established later. They were generally small and, having no endowment, depended on fees for their support.

Sheriffhales may be taken as an example in a somewhat stately home. The founder, John Woodhouse, had studied at Cambridge and was a family chaplain when the Act of Uniformity silenced him in 1662. He conducted the academy for thirty-five years. The course of study occupied four years and included three ancient languages, English, and a wide range of subjects followed by professional studies in law, anatomy, and theology. There were practical exercises in surveying, dissecting, and debating. Excluded from Oxford and Cambridge, the academy students finished their academic studies at Scottish universities which were, of course, conducted by dissenters. In their use of English as the language of instruction, rather than Latin, there was a further resemblance between the northern universities and the English academies. Charles Morton, who later came to America and was vice-president of Harvard College, made this change to the use of English in teaching in his academy at Newington Green in 1680. This was several years before the German university of Jena took a similar step. These were pioneering efforts and it took more than fifty years to complete the transition to the vernacular as the language of instruction.

Newington Green under Morton was progressive in other ways. His academy had a form of self-government in which the pupils legislated for themselves. Others of the academies also became centers of democratic politics where future Whigs gained experience in public affairs. Many of the English dissenters were in sympathy with the Americans in their Revolution, and later with the French reform efforts. Among these dissenters was Joseph Priestley, who added new chapters to the science of chemistry and debatable views to the doctrines of religion, politics, and education. In education he definitely anticipated Herbert Spencer, who may have read him before writing "What knowledge is of most worth?"

Many manufacturers and businessmen of the north of England sent their sons to academies so that sometimes half the pupils were preparing for a business career. But the Puritans could not adequately support the schools. Some were closed, others became regular secondary schools with a classical curriculum, and a few were transformed into higher institutions. Manchester Academy, for example, became Manchester College of Oxford University. By 1820, when the somewhat similar academies in the United States were in their prime, the main era of the English dissenting academy was over.

A religious movement in Germany known as Pietism paralleled the English Puritanism and had a somewhat similar influence on education. August Hermann Francke (1663–1727) became a leading Pietist school founder. Late in the seventeenth century, he established at Halle a group of institutions, known as the Halle Foundation, including an elementary school for poor children, a Latin school, a scientific school for the ruling classes, and a school for teachers. In about the middle of the eighteenth century there were two thousand attending this group of schools. The distinguishing feature of this complex set of institutions was their Realist curriculum. They had cabinets of minerals and natural history, a chemistry laboratory, and a workshop for wood and glass. One of Francke's teachers, Christopher Semler, and a former pupil, the Reverend Julius Hecker, planned and established a *Realschule*, or Realist school, in Berlin in 1747. This was the first of a new kind of secondary school for Germany.

It had a Latin-scientific curriculum of six years that in the next century was extended to nine years and then prepared students for entrance to the university. This section has shown that the Realist movement was to some extent international; and it spread to America when, in the eighteenth century, conditions became favorable. Benjamin Franklin was the leader in founding such a school in Philadelphia in the middle of that century, and others followed.

MODERN SCIENCE AND PHILOSOPHY

Science became modern in the Renaissance, and after, when other great intellectual interests were progressing. The work of Columbus belongs to the fifteenth century, that of Copernicus to the sixteenth century, and that of Galileo to the seventeenth century. In those times the work of the world and its science and philosophy gradually became more modern. The same idea could be put in another way: Twenty-five years (1518–1543) will cover Magellan's circumnavigation of the globe, the new astronomy of Copernicus, and the new anatomy of Vesalius. Such achievements might lead one to assign the rise of modern science to the early decades of the Reformation period, but the real power of science was not understood until the following, the seventeenth, century.

In the seventeenth century, science came to be recognized as an international and cooperative enterprise when the first great scientific societies were founded in Italy, England, France, and other countries. The *Accademia dei Lincei* (that is, of the Lynxes) was founded in 1603 at Rome. Galileo was a member; and some of his pupils founded the *Accademia del Cimento* (experiment) in 1657 at Florence. The Royal Society of London began somewhat casually, but by 1660 it had become well organized and was chartered in 1662. The early history of the French Academy of Sciences also was little noticed but it became well organized by 1666. Under the leadership of Leibnitz, a royal academy was founded in Berlin in 1700; and only forty-three years later, Benjamin Franklin led in founding the American Philosophical Society in Philadelphia. In informing scientists of work already done or in progress and in calling attention to new problems, the publications of these societies were of the greatest value.

A deliberate effort to define the scientific method developed. Two of the pioneers in this field were Francis Bacon and René Descartes. In his definition of the inductive method, Bacon insisted on observation, experiment, and the industrious collecting of facts; but he did not sufficiently emphasize the importance of ideas, insights, and happy guesses as guides to investigation and to generalization. Mere labor alone, however unsparing, will not produce science. Genius is demanded and those investigators are most successful who are most adept in raising significant, answerable questions. Although Bacon did not see this clearly, yet by his literary power he did much to stimulate interest in discovery and in calling attention to the practical value of scientific knowledge.

While Bacon demanded experiment and new discoveries, Descartes called for incontrovertible proofs, which he sought by rational and mathematical methods. Descartes' *Discourse on Method* (1637), his *Rules for the Direction of the Mind,* and his *Search after Truth by the Light of Nature* are examples of a whole class of psychological and educational books. Locke wrote one that he called the *Conduct of the Understanding* (1706), and recent examples of the same class are sometimes entitled "How to Use Your Mind" and "How to Think." Descartes reduced his method to four rules somewhat as follows:

1. Accept as true nothing that it is possible to doubt.
2. Analyze every statement into its simplest elementary propositions.
3. Review each of these elementary propositions one by one.
4. Make your final enumeration so complete that nothing shall be omitted.

Descartes was impressed by the success of mathematics in finding indisputable proofs of its propositions and took the mathematical methods as his ideals in scientific investigation. But, although he was keenly aware that the senses may lead us into error, he did not neglect inductive and experimental work. He carried out dissections and was deeply interested in the work of Harvey and of Gilbert.

Scientific method is a compound of induction and deduction. Induction begins with some question and proceeds by observation and experiment. Deduction begins with an assumed or a demonstrated truth and draws its necessary implications. The proofs of elementary geometry are the handiest examples of deduction. Both induction and deduction are likely to involve unrecognized assumptions that may introduce errors into the conclusions. Every natural science seems to depend for its new matter on observation and induction, whereas necessary inference and deduction supply proofs of its general principles.

An example of scientific method that involved both the Baconian and the Cartesian elements together with a description of the progress of his thought had already been furnished by Copernicus, who published his *De Revolutionibus Orbium Celestium* in 1543. In the dedication of that work he explained how he had obtained his results. He said that (1) he became dissatisfied with the growing intricacy of the Ptolemaic theory; (2) he studied all previous views; (3) he proposed to himself a new and simpler theory; and (4) by observation and calculation he proved that his theory accounted for all known facts. A simplified account of his method might read about as follows:

When I had thought long on the traditional views concerning the paths of the heavenly bodies, it seemed to me lamentable that no better explanation had yet been proposed. Then I read the writings of the ancients and found that some of the Greeks had held that the earth moves about the sun and turns upon its axis. Gathering confidence from these suggestions, I conceived that I as well as they should have liberty to propose a more satisfactory theory of the motions in question. I then assumed the motions which I describe in the present work, and after careful investigation extending through years, I found that if the movements of the other planets were referred to the motion of the earth in its orbit about the sun all their observed phenomena can be satisfactorily explained and that a simple and harmonious system is the result. In accordance with this theory I have drawn up the plan of my work.

He had kept the manuscript of his book not for nine years as Horace recommends but for thirty-six years before he decided to publish it.

The invention of new instruments to aid observation, manipulation, and measurement was a third development in seventeenth-century science. Lenses were known to Archimedes, but spectacles seem to have been made in Italy in about 1289, and the telescope was developed in the Netherlands in about 1600. Anton Leeuwenhoek, with a simple microscope, discovered bacteria. Galileo, who made good use of the telescope, is said to have occasioned the invention of the compound microscope. Christian Huyghens (1629–1695) invented an improved eye-piece. He also invented the pendulum clock, although Galileo in 1582, at the age of eighteen, had used the pendulum, kept swinging by hand, to measure small intervals. The barometer, air pump, and thermometer are other instruments of the same period. Mathematical inventions of the same time were decimal fractions, logarithms, better symbols and notations, the analytic geometry of Descartes, and the calculus of Leibnitz and Newton. All these had much to do with the rapid development of science and its proper application.

For the history of science one must go to special books, and there are now many good ones; but a few names will provide a little orientation. We have already mentioned William Harvey, who discovered the circulation of the blood in 1616 but did not publish his complete results until 1628. Two famous microscopists, Malpighi and Leeuwenhoek, demonstrated the capillaries that Harvey had been unable to see; and Leeuwenhoek, with his keen sight and manipulative skill, observed the blood corpuscles and many forms of bacteria and protozoa. Harvey, with a simple lens, made contributions to embryology and developed the doctrine that each individual begins as a fertilized egg. Thomas Sydenham, who followed the principles of Hippocrates in tracing the natural history of diseases, had John Locke for an assistant and pupil. Sydenham is sometimes regarded as the founder of modern clinical medicine.

The contributions to physics and mechanics were equally notable.

William Gilbert in his *De Magnete* founded the new science of electricity. The genius of Galileo was shown, as Lagrange pointed out, not so much by his work in astronomy, which needed only a telescope and industry, but by his discoveries in mechanics. Near the end of his life, he published at Leyden a book, *Two New Sciences,* in which he announced the laws of falling bodies and the pendulum; determined the component motions of a projectile and its parabolic path; and described other experimental discoveries in dynamics, statics, and hydrostatics. The foundations of modern chemistry were laid by Robert Boyle who defined *element* as an irreducible substance, thus distinguishing between elements and compounds. Boyle also experimented on electricity and on the physiology of respiration. He is best known for his law that gas pressure and volume vary inversely. In the seventeenth century, the new mathematics, which was needed as a scientific tool, was supplied by Napier, who developed logarithms; by Descartes; Leibnitz; and Newton, whom we have already named; and by many lesser men. The work of Newton on light and gravitation was the crowning achievement of science in this period.

Although we shall be anticipating the developments of several centuries, it will be useful to indicate here some of the influences that the sciences gradually exerted on education. The first was that the sciences themselves were included in the curricula of schools. Many sciences were introduced into the Realist schools of the seventeenth century, although unfortunately they were usually taught from books. Secondly, the methods were gradually improved. Collections of minerals and of instruments such as the air pump, barometer, or prism were shown and demonstrated. Later on, laboratory demonstrations were given by the teacher, and still later the students were asked to carry on experiments. Observation and field excursions were used early, but the student laboratory was not common until the nineteenth century. The scientific method of discovery, somewhat after the manner described by Copernicus, was recommended by Rousseau as a method of teaching and was so employed by Pestalozzi and later teachers. Problems and projects were introduced not only in science but in other fields also. In the third place, science aided the improvement of the physical plant and the equipment of schools and provided the basis for the study and practice of hygiene, home economics, agriculture, and other practical arts and vocations. Fourthly, beginning with the inductive psychology of Vives and Locke, natural science furnished the model and some of the tools for a science of education, which began to develop in the present century. Finally, the greatest effect of science on education came from its influences on the spirit of the school. It made education more inductive, and investigative, and less authoritarian and memoriter. These changes, however, came slowly, and are not yet by any means complete or universal. We shall come across them again.

EDUCATION FOR STATESMEN AND MEN OF AFFAIRS

One result of the advancement of science was that a strong current of optimism was generated. This is felt in the views of the scientists and philosophers as well as in those of the educators whose task demands an optimism that, however, it does not always help to generate. Descartes and Bacon, Locke, Comenius, and the utopians were all optimists and prepared the way for the *theory of progress* in the following century. The sciences, said Descartes, should not be acquired singly like a skill or an art. All the sciences are merely applications of human wisdom or brains to the facts of nature; and they are so interconnected and so based on a common foundation that they can all be acquired together instead of attacking them one at a time. Reason, it seemed to Descartes, is evenly distributed among men, and by his method, which we have noted, anyone should be able to arrive at the scientific truths of nature. Bacon also thought that a good method would enable anyone to become a scientist and even a discoverer. Most of the great educators show the influence of the same current of optimism. This applied especially to Comenius but also to the most influential of all English writers on education, John Locke.

John Locke (1632–1704) was a man of the council table rather than the study, prudent and skillful rather than scintillating. Known for his genial friendliness, he was equally noted for self-restraint and the ability to hold his tongue. In that period of violent party strife, Locke was the confidential agent of Lord Shaftesbury. The same Dr. Fell of Oxford, whose unpopularity is still an unsolved mystery and is celebrated in the stanza,

> *I do not like you, Dr. Fell.*
> *The reason why I cannot tell;*
> *But this I know and know full well,*
> *I do not like you, Dr. Fell.*

was commissioned to spy upon him and set traps for him; but he was completely baffled by Locke's reserve and caution. In his *Some Thoughts Concerning Education*, Locke urged that children should early be taught to guard their speech.

Although Locke was not a man of the study, he wrote many books, and this in spite of the fact that he devoted much of his time for twenty years to a single one, the *Essay Concerning Human Understanding*. It is not an exaggeration to say that Locke applied only his spare time to composition and that most of his works are occasional writings, called out by the practical demands of the hour. Even the titles, the *Essay*, noted here, the *Letters on Toleration, Some Observations on Printed Money,* or *Some*

Thoughts Concerning Education show that many of his works were tracts for the times.

Born near Bristol, Locke was the son of a country lawyer, a Puritan who sent him to Westminster School and to Oxford. He became a lecturer in his college and his connection with the university lasted for thirty years, although much of this time he was not in residence. Like Milton, he had a highly unfavorable opinion of current education. What he thought of the English public schools is clear from his *Thoughts*. The scholastic course was still in vogue, and he sometimes wished that he had never gone to the university; but in that case we might never have heard of him. Oxford, with all its defects, was the making of him.

The bent of his mind is clearly shown by his early studies. In a fragment on the art of medicine, he wrote down this principle: "True knowledge grew first in the world by experience and rational observation; but proud man, not content with the knowledge that he was capable of, and which was useful to him, would needs penetrate into the hidden cause of things." He even presumed to lay down his own laws, which nature is to follow. In his Oxford period, Locke joined a chemistry club for which Boyle secured a lecturer from Germany. Anthony Wood, another member and later a political opponent, reported that Locke would not take notes quietly as the rest did but was "always prating and troublesome." This may simply mean that Locke's practical mind was "content with the knowledge that he was capable of and was against attempts to "penetrate into the hidden causes of things" as the alchemists tried to do. Locke was graduated a bachelor of medicine and sometimes prescribed for patients but, owing to difficulties with the university authorities, he never secured his final medical degree.

Returning from a diplomatic mission to Brandenburg in May, 1666, Locke resumed his work in Oxford. That summer, through some medical services, Locke made the acquaintance of the Earl of Shaftesbury. He was to serve for many years as secretary and as adviser in the education of the children and later the grandchildren of this patron. He was elected a Fellow of the Royal Society, which brought him into the circle of "the incomparable Mr. Newton." A mutual friend was Robert Boyle, who chose Locke as his literary executor. A question raised in a social group about this time started Locke on the composition of his *Essay Concerning the Human Understanding*. The question was, "What is the mind capable of knowing?" In developing his answer, Locke came to consider psychological and logical questions and earned the reputation of being one of the founders of modern psychology, as well as of a new species of philosophy, the critical philosophy that was carried forward by Berkeley, Hume, Kant, and later thinkers. The *Essay* occupied him intermittently for twenty years and appeared in the bookshops early in 1690. For the manuscript, on which he had worked so long, he received thirty pounds.

Two periods of foreign residence, first in France where he had charge of a pupil in about 1675 and later in Holland, broadened Locke's experience of life. In France he translated but did not publish the moral essays of the Jansenist, Pierre Nicole. This must have brought him close to the sphere of activity of the Abbé Fleury. Lord Shaftesbury wrote to Locke to inquire what books were used in the education of the dauphin, one of whose tutors was Fleury. We must mention this educator more particularly because of the likeness between his views and those of Locke. Claude Fleury (1640–1723) wrote a *Treatise on the Choice and Method of Studies*, which includes an early, perhaps the first, account of the history of education. It was, however, written to outline and defend a utilitarian course of study. Although it was finished in 1675, it was not immediately published. Locke was in France during these years, but there seems to be no evidence that the two authors met. Perhaps the explanation of the close similarity of their views is that both were influenced by Descartes, by Port Royal, and by the contemporary conditions in England and France. Be that as it may, Fleury's *Treatise* came out in 1686, shortly before Locke's *Thoughts Concerning Education*. Five editions of the *Thoughts* appeared in Locke's lifetime and a great many afterward. The first French translation, in 1695, by Pierre Coste, reached at least five editions. Besides the Dutch version, in 1698, mentioned by Locke in a preface, the book was also translated into Swedish, German, and Italian, and no doubt other languages.

Nor did the author dismiss the subject after the book had appeared but, as new editions came out, he added here a paragraph and there a page to the earlier text. This manner of composition explains the repetitions, digressions, and badly constructed sentences that one occasionally finds. There are also some deviations from Locke's usually good sense. But its merits were so great that we should not dwell on its imperfections. And it was influential. Much of the philanthropinist movement of the eighteenth century was in harmony with Locke's views, and he was read in the nineteenth century as well.

The educational optimism of the century was shown by Locke in the first paragraph of the *Thoughts*. He declared that men are, at least nine parts out of ten, formed by education rather than by heredity. This might mean that the school can make of a man what it will, just as a river at the source could easily be turned in a direction other than the one it has taken. As we have already noted, this view of Locke and others—that the nature of men can be changed by education—gave rise to an optimism in regard to society that was to lead in the succeeding age to a well-defined theory of progress.

Four principles form the foundation of Locke's educational doctrine. These can be named the principles of utility, of rationality, of practice or conditioning, and of direct experience; they will be discussed in this order.

Early in life, Locke prepared a short guide to conduct that would have delighted Benjamin Franklin: A man's proper business, he wrote, is to seek happiness and avoid misery. The most lasting pleasures come through health, reputation, knowledge, doing good, and the hope of eternal happiness. "In life," he added, "I must carefully look that it cross not any of those great and constant pleasures above mentioned." In again considering the aims of life and education, in the *Thoughts*, he included health, virtue, practical prudence, courtesy, industry, and knowledge. Virtue is here the greatest and controlling aim and in defining it Locke announces his principle of rationality. He wrote,

As the strength of the body lies chiefly in being able to endure hardship, so also does that of the mind. And the great principle and foundation of all virtue is placed in this, that a man is able to deny himself his own desires, cross his inclinations, and purely follow what reason directs as best, though appetite lean the other way.

This is the cornerstone of Locke's theory. He believed, with Descartes, that a man's reason can control his desires and stormy emotions and bring to a peaceful and rational end the conflict that otherwise rages between the good and evil forces of his inner life.

The ability to reason originates early in life and should be cultivated from the first, according to Locke; but, although it begins early, it develops slowly and therefore children must for a considerable time be directed by adults. Before the child can be permitted to make his own choices, at least in difficult cases and on weighty occasions, he must be conditioned, as the psychologists say, to make the right choices. And the right choices are those approved by reason. Conditioning or training in good habits is Locke's third principle. As Locke in one place put it, children are not in the right way until they take delight in laudable things. Claude Fleury, who held the same view, declared that he who can make pleasant what it is desired that children shall do will have discovered the great secret of education.

By example, by repetition and constant practice, through praise and blame, rewards and punishments, said Locke, good habits are to be formed and the moral law made clear, easy, and palatable. It is, therefore, necessary that children shall be brought up in a good society. This is the basis of Locke's attack on schools with their "herds of unruly boys"; and of his fear of the evil influence of vicious servants. "Children," he wrote, "are not to be taught by rules which will be always slipping out of their memories. What you think necessary for them to do, settle in them by an indispensable practice as often as the occasion returns," and even make occasions. Until children can reason and will follow reason, even though desire lean the other way, they must be habituated, trained, and conditioned to good and right conduct.

Both wisdom in practical affairs and good manners are best learned by experience. This is Locke's fourth principle, and he applied it chiefly in moral education. The world is full of cheats, follies, and faults, and to be forewarned is to be forearmed. This experience of the world must be carefully guarded so that the child can learn the true state of an evil world and can become a good judge of men without becoming corrupted. Knowledge of the world of men is to be given through this guarded experience; but Locke proposed to give knowledge of the physical world also through sensory experience, knowledge of countries and customs through travel, and skill in fencing and dancing and in the use of tools through practice and participation. This is an important principle, but Locke did not make as much use of it as did some other Realists. In geography and science he did not propose, as on his principles he should have done, to take children into the field.

Health is treated first in the *Thoughts*. His advice was mainly hygienic and was directed to the development of a strong constitution. He gave attention to diet, exercise, clothing, sleep, and good health habits. His main idea is the Spartan one of hardening and inuring the body to overcome any tendency to weakness and effeminacy. To the attainment of health and the moral and practical qualities, Locke devotes two thirds of his book. In one of the most important sections, the ninety-fourth, he said,

> The great work of a governor is to fashion the carriage and form the mind; to settle in his pupil good habits and the principles of virtue and wisdom; to give him little by little a view of mankind, and work him into a love of imitation of what is excellent and praiseworthy; and in the prosecution of it, to give him vigor, activity, and industry. The studies which he sets him upon are but as it were the exercises of his faculties, and employment of his time, to keep him from sauntering and idleness, to teach him application, and accustom him to take pains, and give him some little taste of what his own industry must perfect.

Information can be obtained as needed. "But of good breeding, knowledge of the world, virtue, industry, and love of reputation, he cannot have too much; and if he have these he will not long want information." And yet he devoted one third of his space to school subjects.

In the selection of these studies, he followed his utilitarian principle, keeping his eye on his main object, the education of a gentleman. The attaining of knowledge depends for a motive on curiosity, which is an "appetite" for knowledge and is to be carefully fostered in children, for it is "the great instrument of nature for overcoming the ignorance they were born with." We must encourage their questions and answer them truly and seriously. Children are travelers just landed in a new country and we who are old residents should be helpful to them.

When a child is able to talk it is time to teach him to read, and this can be done playfully with ivory letters and some easy, pleasant book. Writing should follow reading and should be begun soon afterward. He thought shorthand might be worth learning by young gentlemen. After English, French and then Latin were to be taken up. Languages should be learned by a conversational and nongrammatical method. Grammar should be taught only after a great deal of progress had been made in the languages; and Latin themes, verses, and the memorizing of long passages were to be omitted.

Arithmetic is recommended for early study because it offers the "easiest sort of abstract reasoning" but also because it is useful. Geography and astronomy are to be presented as mathematical subjects. The Copernican system is favored as the simplest and also the likeliest to be true. Geometry should follow, and the first six books of Euclid are enough for a gentleman. In every subject we should begin with what is simplest and plainest and should consider carefully what the child is capable of understanding. Many subjects were included in the scheme: history, rhetoric, logic, ethics, civil law, and Biblical history. Greek he thought unnecessary for a gentleman. Music he condemned because it wastes so much of a young man's time. Dancing, fencing, and a trade were to be taught. He named several suitable trades, but he favored gardening and carpentry. From such occupations were to be derived exercise, recreation, and a practical understanding of working conditions, as well as knowledge and experience that would be useful when the boy himself became an employer. The last period, when the boy was fairly mature, was to be spent in foreign travel with a tutor. Locke himself had served as the traveling tutor of a boy whom he directed through France.

Finally, he advised parents to consult their own reason in planning the education of their children rather than to follow old custom merely. In the *Thoughts* he did not deal with the education of the working class, but we know from other documents that he would have offered them only meager schooling. He dealt with a somewhat special subject, the education of an English gentleman, and he dealt with that subject, not exhaustively but comprehensively. The distinctive quality of Locke's educational doctrine is not only its common sense and cool Realism; it is that he saw men as the sculptor sees them, "in the round," as physical, intellectual, social, practical, moral, political, and religious beings. Education was to enable men to live well in all these dimensions.

THE LANGUAGE QUESTION

Educators in the seventeenth century were more conscious of language than ever before or since. The ancient Greeks studied only one language, their own. The Romans in the classical period added Greek to Latin, but by the fourth century Greek was again disappearing from the schools of the West. The schools of the earlier Middle Ages were conducted in Latin and taught no other language. With the Renaissance, we came into a new era. Classical Latin took the place of the medieval Latin and fifty years later Greek was reintroduced. With the development of Biblical investigation, Hebrew also was added, and trilingual colleges flourished at Salamanca, Paris, and Louvain. Meanwhile, the vernaculars were taught in the new elementary schools, and modern foreign tongues began to knock at the doors of academies and municipal schools. Obviously there was a language question. The languages tended to monopolize a curriculum that was at the same time hard pressed to admit more mathematics, history, science, and other subjects including several practical arts. The Realists offered various suggestions including the following: limiting the time for languages and devoting the rest of the school time to other subjects; teaching fewer languages; omitting Greek, and of course Hebrew, which was never widely taught; concentrating on languages as tools and omitting literature; using supposedly more effective methods of language teaching such as conversation, extensive, easy reading, careful selection of the vocabulary, and various crutches like interlinear translations or having the teacher translate instead of the pupils. The writers who dealt with the subject did not confine themselves to it, and to the greatest of them, Comenius, the language question is only a detail in a complete system of educational philosophy.

Vernacular schools had become far more numerous since their first appearance in the Midle Ages; and the church used the vernacular to teach the catechism and Bible, but usually only to the poor and to those who would receive no further schooling. In the seventeenth century the civil and practical advantages of vernacular education came to fuller recognition. Educators such as Ratke and Comenius; Peter Ramus of France, who wrote a grammar of the French language; a few Spaniards already mentioned; and several prominent English educators argued vigorously in favor of the vernacular.

Among the English reformers of language instruction was Richard Mulcaster (1530–1611), who was headmaster of Merchant Taylors' School for twenty-five years and of St. Paul's for twelve years and to whom we are indebted for a prophetic work on the teaching of English, *The First Part of the Elementarie Which Entreateth Chieflie of the Right Writing of the English Tung* (London, 1582). He demanded that all children should be taught to read, write, draw, sing, and play an instrument. With such a foundation, he declared that he could teach the boys in the grammar school more Latin in four years, between the ages of twelve and sixteen, than they could have learned without it in ten years. One of Mulcaster's chief interests was the improvement of the English language. He urged the preparation of an English dictionary and prepared a word list to aid in stabilizing English spelling. This was his list of the eight thousand most frequently used English words. He also proposed to reform the English universities and to establish in each a college of education.

Other English masters of the period who had the same concern were Brinsley and Hoole. John Brinsley (c. 1570–c. 1630) in his *Ludus Literarius or the Grammar Schoole* (London, 1612) expressed his conviction that boys should learn good English before undertaking Latin; and he insisted that the Latin school must take care to preserve and extend skill in the mother tongue. Too often, he declared, Latin was allowed to crowd out the English so that boys came up to the university unable to read and write their own language. And Charles Hoole (1610–1667), "Master of Arts and teacher of a private grammar school in Lothbury Garden, London," devoted a whole section of his *New Discovery of the Old Art of Teaching School* (London, 1660) to the teaching of English.

The most distinguished of the immediate predecessors of Comenius was Wolfgang Ratke (1571–1635), who was educated in the Johanneum in Hamburg, the school that Basedow later attended. Ratke's grandiose plans won the support of Prince Ludwig of Anhalt-Köthen who had founded the "Fruit-Bearing Society" for the purpose of improving the German language. Ratke favored the High German of Luther's Bible as the national speech and insisted that it must be taught first, before Latin. His plan for teaching the elements of Latin did not succeed, and Prince Ludwig withdrew his aid from the school. Ratke read the plays of Terence over and over with his class, both in Latin and in translation, but they still could not read Latin because they had been merely passive listeners. He proposed to develop a science of education that he intended to base on psychology and on an analysis of the subjects that were to be taught. He argued that the government should support the schools because of their great social and political importance. Of Ratke's influence we shall speak later. Comenius, who is one of the world's great educators, also dealt with the language question, but only as one element of his broad and profound conception of education.

THE MASTER KEY TO UNIVERSAL EDUCATION

John Amos Comenius (1592–1670), a Czech and a Moravian, was one of the great system builders in education. He came from the lower middle class—his father was a miller—and did not attend secondary school until he was sixteen. This late beginning is supposed to have forcibly directed his attention to the methods employed in teaching languages, about which he had a good deal to say. One of his teachers in the university of Herborn was the celebrated J. H. Alsted (1588–1638), from whom he acquired ideas on the scope and organization of the sciences. After a year at the University of Heidelberg, he became first a teacher, then pastor, and later bishop of the Moravian churches. The Thirty Years War began just when he became pastor at Fulneck, which was in the path of the invading armies. The little city was sacked, its people massacred, his wife killed, his library and manuscripts destroyed, and Comenius was driven into exile in Poland. There he taught in the gymnasium at Lissa. By that time his writings had already brought him a European reputation; and he was invited, in 1641, to come to England to serve as the head of a projected college of research. This scheme miscarried, and Comenius accepted from the Chancellor of Sweden a commission to prepare textbooks for the Latin schools of that country. During those years he lived in Elbing and also taught in the gymnasium of that town. In about 1650 he was called back to central Europe to reform the schools of Sáros-Patak, but after several years, when warfare again broke out in that region, he retired to Amsterdam where he continued to write to the end of his life.

Comenius produced about a hundred and seventy works, large and small, some in Czech and others in Latin. In the field of education, he wrote schoolbooks and works on theory. His most important theoretical work was *The Great Didactic* (1628) or "the art of teaching all things to all men"—that is, the master key with which to unlock all educational doors. Three years later he published the first of his language books, the Latin textbook, *Janua Linguarum Reserata* (1631), the open door to the languages. We shall consider the language texts first. The idea for the *Janua* came from Elias Boodin. A book of the same kind prepared by William Bateus, a Spanish Jesuit, was in wide use; but when Comenius issued his *Janua*, it swept all similar books off the boards. It was used in the schools of Europe for three centuries.

This famous textbook was based on eight thousand common Latin words arranged in sentences. The sentences are simple in the beginning and become progressively more difficult as we proceed through the book. Each page in a parallel column gave also the vernacular translation of the Latin. Connectives and other structural words were repeated, but each basic word was used only once. Verbal illustrations of the grammatical constructions were given. The book had a hundred chapters and told the story of the earth, man, and the divine government of the universe. The topics included the creation of the world; the heavens; the elements; the earth and its minerals, its plants, and its animals; man his body and his mind; the mechanic arts; social institutions; the various branches of knowledge; and the providence of God. The book, as we have said, became extremely popular, but it had two serious defects: It was as dry as a dictionary and like a dictionary it used each word only once. To acquire the complete vocabulary, it would have been necessary to commit it to memory.

The rest of Comenius's textbooks were built upon the same plan as the *Janua*. The *Vestibulum* was to precede the *Janua*, which had proved too difficult for beginners; and the *Atrium* and *Palatium* were to follow the

Janua. The *Thesaurus* was a reading book. The books were to be read and read again, the *Vestibulum* ten times over, until they were practically memorized.

The *Janua* and his other schoolbooks reveal another element in Comenius's educational philosophy. He believed that the correct way to build a curriculum was to follow the spiral plan, as it was later called. By this plan even the small child was to receive instruction about nature, man, and God, and all the topics named from the *Janua*. As the child grew and entered into a more advanced stage, the same round of topics was treated again but more fully and more penetratingly—and so on stage after stage. This plan of providing instruction in every department of knowledge at each period of growth was known as pansophism or encyclopedism.

On his visit to Sweden, Comenius had agreed to prepare the textbooks demanded by the chancellor for the schoolboys of that country. It was in November, 1642 that he settled down in Elbing for that purpose, but he found it difficult to devote his whole time to the work. He had a patron, de Geer, who provided assistants, and Elbing was a quiet town by the sea. But the difficulties of his exiled brethren and his propaganda for church union, the union of all Protestants, constantly diverted his thoughts from the schoolbooks. It was not until 1647 that the schoolbooks were about completed, together with the *Methodus Linguarum Novissima*, the newest language method. The best way to keep a language pure, he declared, is to found societies for this purpose.

The Hungarian Count Rakoczky invited him to organize a school at Sáros-Patak, where he arrived in May, 1650. The count agreed to build a schoolhouse with classrooms and boarding facilities and to furnish a printing press together with equipment and the staff to operate it. To arouse popular interest in the plan, Comenius delivered some public lectures on educational topics, and published his *Sketch of the Pan-Sophic School*. Owing to the death of his patron in 1652, the plan, which included a seven-year course, was not put into full operation; yet he carried on the school and the printing establishment and got out new editions of his schoolbooks. And, most important, he prepared for the beginners at Sáros-Patak the most celebrated of his works, the *Orbis Sensualium Pictus* (1657), the world of the senses in pictures. There were one hundred and fifty lessons on all subjects in the pansophic manner, and each lesson was illustrated. The text below the picture was in parallel columns, Latin in one and a translation in the other. Reference numbers helped the child to link the word with the pictured object.

The *Orbis Pictus* was immediately successful. The English version, for example, was made by a famous teacher, Charles Hoole, whose preface is dated, "From my school in Lothbury, London, January 25, 1658," less than a year after the first issue. The *Orbis Pictus* was neither altogether original with Comenius nor was it the first illustrated schoolbook; and its pictures were rather rough woodcuts. But it had so many good qualities that it was introduced into schools in most of Europe and remained in use for a long time. One hundred years after its first introduction Goethe, telling the story of his childhood, wrote,

No libraries for children had at that time been established. The old people themselves still had childish notions, and found it convenient to impart their own education to their successors. Except the *Orbis Pictus* of Amos Comenius, no book of the sort fell into our hands; but the large folio Bible, with copper plates by Merian, was diligently gone over leaf by leaf.

Another important means by which Comenius exerted influence was through *The Great Didactic* and other works on educational theory. To give a full account of the philosophy of Comenius would require many pages, but we must constantly remember that he was a Christian minister and a neo-Platonist and that, although no scientist, he was much influenced by the scientific activities of his time. He compares our whole life to a school; the world was created to serve as the training ground of the human race. Through man's failures, darkness and confusion have entered this school, but harmony and order can be restored through the cultivation of the understanding and the application of true knowledge. Mankind, he said, anticipating later theories of progress, has already passed through six stages and we are now entering into a seventh, that of panharmony in which the whole world will be enlightened. To accomplish this, there would be needed universal books, universal schools, a universal language, and an academy of science drawing its members from all the world. Education for Comenius was not a matter of learning this or that; it was the means to redeem mankind from the evils that made life worthless and unbearable.

There have been few works of educational theory as systematic and comprehensive as *The Great Didactic*, or that have claimed as much. Here is set forth "the whole art of teaching all things to all men," making them learned, virtuous, and pious. This claimed to be the master key to universal education. And this is not to introduce anything new into human nature. The "seeds" of learning, virtue, and piety are implanted in all men by nature. Let us first take learning or knowledge. Man is *naturally* capable of acquiring a knowledge of all things. His senses and his reason are given him for this purpose. Comenius stands in awe of "the marvelous wisdom of God" who was able to contrive the brain of man, which is able to receive and retain the impressions and images of a lifetime. Similarly, the seeds of virtue and piety are equally a part of the original nature of man.

A skeptic might be inclined to ask why, if it is "natural" for man to grow learned, virtuous, and pious, the world so often goes begging for those qualities. The answer of Comenius would not be different from the one Rousseau actually gave, that conditions, society, and the schools have been so bad that the seeds have had no chance to sprout and grow. Some of the defects of schools in the past have been that they have excluded the common people, have used poor methods, have taught words merely and not real knowledge, and have been cruel institutions for stuffing and flogging children rather than teaching them. We must build up good schools, "true forging-places of men." He gave no bad definition, Comenius said, who called man the teachable animal, but a man must be actually taught and taught well if he is to develop true manhood. All men need education, the clever and the stupid, the rich and the poor, that they may become men. There is in the doctrines of Comenius no ground for class education; to him education is an elemental human need, not a privilege. Schools must be universal and open to all. Girls as well as boys are to have a thorough education and one that shall be suitable to their duties in life.

Man can be most easily formed in youth while he is plastic and before the labor of adult life begins. Indeed, God has given man a long period of immaturity for this purpose. It is the long period of plasticity and growth that enables the child to become a man. This doctrine of Comenius is a surprising anticipation of a corollary to the doctrine of evolution that John Fiske developed under the term "the meaning of infancy."

All studies are to be taught to all children—for Comenius is an encylopedist—but not all can be fully mastered. Much can be done by applying to teaching the principles of which we find constant examples in nature. By applying these principles, Comenius believed that sure, easy, quick, and permanent learning can be attained. The principles were such as the following: Nature observes a suitable time; Nature prepares the material before she gives it form; in all operations of Nature, development is from within; Nature proceeds step by step without a break. These are four of the nine principles that deal with the certainty of learning; and there are similar groups dealing with ease or facility, permanence, and rapidity of learning. Altogether he considers thirty-seven principles of nature that are to guide our teaching. From them we are advised as follows: to teach what will be useful in life; to appeal to the senses and understanding rather than to the authority of books; that studies must not only be understood but must also be impressed on the memory; that studies must be carefully graded and organized; and that it is useful to have pupils teach other pupils for we learn nothing so well as what we teach to others.

Lest the student should think that these pages of *The Great Didactic* are devoted wholly to abstract discussion, we quote one of the finest passages, one that might have been written by Vittorino or Vives. Comenius wrote,

The school itself should be a pleasant place, and attractive to the eye both within and without. Within, the room should be bright and clean, its walls ornamented with pictures, portraits of celebrated men, geographical maps, historical plans, or other ornaments. Without, there should be an open place to walk and play in, for this is absolutely necessary for children, as we shall show later, and there should also be a garden attached, into which the scholars may be allowed to go from time to time, and where they may feast their eyes on trees, flowers, and plants. If this be done, boys will, in all probability, go to school with as much pleasure as to fairs, where they always hope to see and hear something new.

A golden rule for teachers is that everything should be presented to the senses, and to several of the senses, whenever possible. Sensation is the foundation of knowledge and there is nothing in the understanding that was not originally derived from the senses. The senses also are the most trusty servants of the memory and we always remember what we have first tasted, heard, or seen. The anatomy of the human body can be remembered better from a single dissection than from reading exhaustive volumes. If objects are not at hand, pictures or models can be used. The arts should be taught by practice! We learn to carve by carving, to dance by dancing, and to write, talk, and reason by carrying on these activities. In this way schools will become workshops, humming with activity. Rules and theory are essential, but they should follow and not precede observation and practice.

Languages are tools and only those languages that are necessary tools should be learned. But languages can be tools for different purposes because they can be used to arouse emotion, to stimulate speculation, to convey fact and information, or to lead us in the conduct of life itself. And yet, Comenius, in agreement with all the Realists, does not value language largely for its beauty of phrase or as a vehicle of noble emotion but chiefly as the carrier of information. For this function the mother tongue is most important, then the languages of neighboring nations, and then Latin. Only specialists will need other languages. Languages and concrete knowledge of fact should always be learned together. Some languages we must learn to speak, but of others a reading knowledge is sufficient. And we must not let the languages crowd more necessary subjects out of the course of study.

Knowledge, virtue, and piety are the three great ends of education. Virtue and piety should be taught by the practice of virtuous and religious acts but also through example and through reason. The Bible should rank above all other books in Christian schools; and Erasmus has shown, said Comenius, that it is suitable for children of all ages.

The plan of school organization that Comenius advised is one of the most striking features of his program, for he proposed to develop a one-class society; or rather he assumed that such a society already existed. He planned a complete system of education for all children of every rank and class. There were to be four periods of six years in this system and a school corresponding to each period; the school of infancy for the first six years, the vernacular school from six to twelve, the Latin school from twelve to eighteen, and the college of research for eighteen to twenty-four. Instead of this democratic plan, Erasmus accepted the dual system, with one school for the lower classes and another secondary-university sequence for the directing classes. Two hundred years after Comenius wrote his *Great Didactic*, the American democracy undertook to develop a single-track scheme in which all schools were to be open to all "the children of all the people."

A chapter in *The Great Didactic* is given to the school of infancy or, as the Germans translated the idea, the mother school. At about the same time Comenius wrote a separate book, which he called *The School for Little Children* (1633). This anticipated Pestalozzi's manual for mothers and also foreshadowed the kindergarten of Froebel. Everywhere, but here especially, Comenius revealed his kindly nature and his sympathetic observation of little children. He gives sensible advice on the care of their health and their safety. A healthy child is God's most precious gift to the home. Childhood should be joyous, and whatever promotes innocent joy should be given to children. Fables, stories, and songs are highly desirable; and children must play with other children. Natural objects, toys, tools, and a garden should be provided. Lessons and all learning must be made pleasant and the parents should prepare the child for school by showing him that school is a happy place. The encyclopedic curriculum appears in the plan of the school of infancy as well as in that of the more advanced schools.

INFLUENCE OF RATKE AND COMENIUS

Recently the democracy of Comenius has been out of fashion in several countries, especially in Germany where race and autocracy were in the saddle and rode mankind; but forty or fifty years ago the name of Comenius was honored the wide world over and especially in Germany where, in 1891, a Comenius-Gesellschaft was founded to study his work and to spread his views on popular education. Even in the seventeenth century both Comenius and Ratke had considerable influence in several German states. Ratke's influence was most evident in the Weimar ordinance of 1619; and that of Comenius in the school programs of Saxe-Gotha, Brunswick, Hesse, and other German states and cities.

Ratke's patroness was the Duchess Dorothea Maria of Weimar who provided for the introduction of his principles. The school instructions drawn up in 1619 instituted compulsory attendance the year around, except for four weeks in harvest, between the ages of six and twelve. This seems to be the earliest example of a compulsory attendance requirement by the civil authority. The school day was kept short, only four hours, and a long recess was allowed between classes. Corporal punishment was forbidden. Each pupil was to have his own book and each teacher his own classroom. The German language was to be thoroughly taught before the Latin was taken up. These were Ratkean ideas.

Duke Ernest (the Pious) of Saxe-Gotha (1601–1675) took another step toward a common school, in which the influence of both Ratke and Comenius can be seen. Duke Ernest was the son of Dorothea Maria of Weimar, and as advisers in the reform of the schools of his duchy he called first Sigismund Evenius, a moderate Ratkean, and then Andreas Reyher, a friend of Evenius and a disciple of Comenius. Others of his advisers show the same influence. Reyher was made rector of the gymnasium at Gotha. His instructions of 1641 began the reform and were in part copied in the ordinance of 1642, known as the Saxe-Gotha School Method.

Pietism was strong in Gotha, religious teaching was emphasized, and the clergy were appointed school visitors. Nor was this a mere form, for the local pastor was to visit the schools several times a week and to keep a list of all children between the compulsory attendance ages of five and twelve. In the year when Gotha adopted these requirements (1642), Massachusetts passed a law that was intended to achieve similar ends. By the age of twelve, the children in Gotha were expected to read German, repeat the catechism and Bible verses, report the main heads of a sermon, write legibly, calculate accurately, and sing, at least in chorus. A public examination of all children who were about to complete the course was held to determine whether they might be excused from further attendance. Two points are noteworthy: this was an example not of civil control but of state and church cooperation; and the objectives of the school were stated in terms of achievement and not formally in terms of years.

Next to Saxe-Gotha the old city and territories of Magdeburg showed most clearly the influence of Comenius. Its school code of 1658 established a four-level school system, each level comprising six years. The Comenian textbooks were used and Comenian aims were professed. Other states also introduced Comenian ideas, but almost everywhere the traditional Humanism was still too strong for the new Realism. Yet the doctrines of Comenius were here and there kept alive and his textbooks remained in use until Basedow and Salzmann developed a new Realism in the following century.

EDUCATION OF GIRLS

François Fénelon, a son of an impoverished noble family, was born in 1651 and, still poor but distinguished as a scholar and a high ecclesiastic, died in 1715. For many years he had served as Archbishop of Cambrai in ancient Flanders, surrounded by Huguenots. When a boy his health was delicate and he had a tutor who guided him while he developed lifelong skill and taste in the classics; but in his teens he after all attended a secondary school and entered the University of Paris. When he was seventeen, an uncle had him admitted to Saint Sulfice, a seminary for priests. His studies there made an impression that is reflected in his *Treatise on the Education of Girls*, which will be reviewed subsequently.

From two appointments he gained preparation for the composition of books on education. He was chosen as a guide in the education of the young sons of the royal family, a task in which the Abbé Fleury was associated with him; but more direct preparation for the writing of a work on the education of girls was gained in an earlier position. In 1678, when he was only twenty-seven years old, he was named as Superior and spiritual guide to a sisterhood of *Nouvelles Catholiques*, new Catholics, namely proselytes won from the Huguenots. Fénelon was led by a religious interest; but the drive against dissenters was political as well. The Huguenots were considered a threat to the state and a great hindrance to the king's policy and aim toward absolute power.

Fénelon took an active but certainly an assigned part in the effort to crush dissent. Ultimately he had second thoughts about this. Late in life he wrote to advise the Duke of Burgundy, "Above all never force your subjects to change their religion. No human power can penetrate the last defences of the human heart. Men can never be convinced by force; it only creates hypocrites."

The small book on the *Education of Girls* deals also with the education of boys: else why the attack on duelling? It actually begins to speak about "children" in the second chapter and for half of the treatise has boys as well as girls in mind. The church was adamant against coeducation and Fénelon does not propose it; but he believed that in childhood the same education was suitable for boys and girls. Not so Rousseau.

The teacher, Fénelon said, must be friendly, observant, and straightforward. There must be no deceit and no punishment. Recalcitrant boys must be punished by the father. Like Locke, Fénelon had difficulty in picturing the concrete processes in teaching and learning. The child's brain, we are repeatedly told, is warm, soft, and moist and our impressions on it should be appropriately light and delicate. Overstimulation is to be avoided. Children are apt to be too curious, too imitative, and emotional. They need guidance, not stimulation or excitement, and certainly they should not be overpressured. They must be shielded from other children with low manners and, perhaps, bad habits. True modesty is a precious result of good education.

At the proper, but not specified, time they must be taught to reason. He said, "In proportion as children's reason develops you should reason with them more and more about what is necessary for their own education." This was contrary to Rousseau's later opinion. Most of the seventh chapter deals with children's reasoning on religious topics; but it warns against errors caused by emotion and sentiment. Fénelon was doubtless influenced at this point by Descartes, and Locke agreed.

In instruction we should mingle the pleasant with the useful, a view held by Fleury and Locke and many others, no doubt. In teaching children we should have them write letters to friends or parents. History can be made to live by dramatizing it; for example, the story of Joseph from the Bible could be made into a play. To put such a piece on the stage would, however, involve a number of children; and Fénelon, like Rousseau, was wary about much company. Much of the book deals with religious education and there is a list of the common faults of children. Some are unresponsive, others artful and secretive, and some take sides and stir up disputes. There is no golden means in education to work wonders with all natures.

There are certain duties that usually fall to the care of women after marriage, and for such activities education is needed. Among their chief duties we must name the care and education of children, the direction of governnesses, the supervision of servants, and the management of household details and of financial income and outgo—a formidable list. A woman's learning should prepare her for her tasks; but such preparation, he claimed, was almost entirely lacking in France. The little book and its wise and kindly author are often praised, but the tense situation between the government, church, and the Huguenots affected Fénelon and his program.

SUMMARY

The definition of Realism, as of any other historical movement, depends on the standpoint occupied by the one who defines it. Realism may be regarded either as a broader Humanism or as a reaction against Humanism. Prominent Realists occupied each of these positions. It was the result of the early efforts to introduce science and practical arts into education, to rationalize methods of teaching, and to base education on direct experience. Realist education appealed especially to skilled workmen and to those who employed skilled workmen, the landlords and manufacturers. But there was also a fringe of aristocratic Realists who outlined the education of gentlemen, men of affairs, military leaders, and even princes. At the other extreme were Realists like Mulcaster and Comenius who urged universal vernacular schools. The Realists, therefore, proposed the transformation of the schools of all levels and for all classes.

Realist education was generally characterized by a broad curriculum, involving twenty or thirty subjects, including history and geography, the sciences, the modern languages and sometimes Latin; several polite accomplishments such as dancing or fencing; a trade; and a period of travel. Those with less money would have to omit some of these features. The

Realists developed new methods. They taught languages through translations, or other semidirect methods such as Ratke's. They introduced illustrative materials and tried to base their teaching on actual experience. Where possible they attempted to follow the method of science in the process of discovering new scientific laws. The Copernican method of discovery and the Cartesian method of proof began to influence instruction. In England the various inductive processes came to be known as the Baconian method.

Locke and Comenius were doubtless the most influential Realists. Locke employed the principles of utility, rationality, conditioning, and direct experience; and his aims were health, virtue, practical sense, courtesy, industry, and "learning"—that is, knowledge. Of these he considered learning both last and least; but he devoted more than half of his *Thoughts* to learning.

The master mind of Comenius attempted to fashion the master key of universal education, or to create the art of teaching all things to all men. Like all the Realists he was an optimist, and his *Great Didactic* was an unconscious Utopia, although an inspiring one. The noblest of his many noble conceptions was that of a one-class society and a ladder system of universal schools. The world of his day was not worthy of him; and, indeed, we still have to look forward to glimpse the Comenian goal.

QUESTIONS

1. Why did Realism appeal to pupils who were not reached by Humanism?
2. Illustrate the statement in the text that "words are things," and will repay careful study. Using the *Oxford English Dictionary*, trace the history of the word *academy*.
3. What relations can be made out between the new psychology and philosophy and the new methods of teaching?
4. Why were the seventeenth-century leaders optimists and authors of Utopias?
5. Why did both Puritans and Pietists lean toward Realism?
6. Why has modern science been more successful than Greek science? Name several ways in which the two movements and the conditions surrounding them differ.
7. What is meant by saying that Locke proposed an all-round education? How, in this respect, does Locke's scheme differ from medieval education? Compare it with the ancient Athenian plan.
8. Why, if the Realists had the whole truth, do the problems of language-teaching, language-learning, and the use of language occupy so large a place in educational discussion in all ages?

9. Compare the spiral plan of Comenius with the similar scheme of the Moslem schools. Can you find any similar plans today?
10. How can we, as Comenius proposed, "follow nature" in education? This topic is of special importance for we shall meet it again in connection with Rousseau and other educators.
11. How influential was Comenius and in what ways?

NOTES AND SOURCES

Comenius prepared four versions of his general theory, the second being the one translated by Keatinge. The fourth version was lost from about 1700 until 1935 when it was recovered from the remains of Francke's Institution at Halle. Edited by D. Tschizewskij and associates, it was published in 1960. See the following bibliography for the possible influence of Comenius on the movement that also led to the foundation of the Royal Society of London (the books by Young, Stimson, and Brown). Cited also is the work by Henry Hallam that contains a general estimate of Comenius. Hallam was no educator, but his view, except for one very broad statement, might have been accepted by Comenius.

Extracts from some of the minor writers, Hartlib, Petty, Dury, and Ratke, can be found in Barnard's *American Journal of Education*. There is an index published in a separate volume.

ADAMSON, JOHN WILLIAM, *The Educational Writings of John Locke*, New York, Longmans, Green and Co., 1912, 272 pp.; *Pioneers of Modern Education, 1600–1700*, Cambridge, University Press, 1921, 285 pp.

BARNARD, H. C., *The Little Schools of Port Royal*, Cambridge, University Press, 1913, 263 pp.; *The Port Royalists on Education*, Cambridge, University Press, 1918, 276 pp.; *The French Tradition in Education*, Cambridge, University Press, 1922, 319 pp. Fénelon on Education, A Translation of the *Traité de l'Éducation des Filles* . . . Cambridge, University Press, 1966, 152 pp.

BROWN, HARCOURT, *Scientific Organizations in Seventeenth Century France, 1620–1680*, Baltimore, 1930, 306 pp. A doctoral dissertation, Columbia University.

CAMPAGNAC, E. T., Editor, *A New Discovery of the Old Art of Teaching Schoole by Charles Hoole*, Liverpool, The University Press, 1913, 357 pp.; *Ludus Literarius; or the Grammar Schoole*, by John Brinsley, London, Constable & Company, Ltd., 1917, 363 pp.; *Mulcaster's Elementarie*, London, Clarendon Press, 1925, 292 pp.

COMENIUS, JOHN AMOS, *The Orbis Pictus*, Syracuse, N.Y., C. W. Bardeen, 1887. English and Latin in parallel columns. The English is that of Charles Hoole from the English edition of 1727. This reprint resembles the original but is not a facsimile.

FLEURY, CLAUDE, *Traité du Choix et de la Méthode des Études*, Paris, Louis Janet, 1822, 466 pp. This work, several times printed, which contains a short history of education, the first ever composed it is said, was written in 1675, but not published until 1686. There is an English edition, issued in London in 1695, with the title *The History, Choice, and Method of Studies by Monsieur Fleury.*

Fox Bourne, H. R., *The Life of John Locke,* New York, Harper & Brothers, 1876, 2 volumes.

Graves, Frank Pierrepont, *Great Educators of Three Centuries,* New York, The Macmillan Company, 1912, 289 pp. *Peter Ramus and the Educational Reformation of the Sixteenth Century,* New York, The Macmillan Company, 1912, 226 pp.

Held, Felix Emil, *Christianapolis . . . by John Valentin Andreae,* New York, Oxford University Press, 1916, 287 pp.

Keatinge, M. W., *The Great Didactic by John Amos Comenius,* London, A. & C. Black, Ltd., 1910, 2 vol. First edition, 1896.

McLachlan, H., *English Education Under the Test Acts, being the History of the Non-Conformist Academies, 1662–1820,* Manchester, Manchester University Press, 1931, 341 pp.

Monroe, Will S., *Comenius' School of Infancy,* Boston, D. C. Heath and Company, 1893, 99 pp.; *Comenius and the Beginnings of Educational Reform,* New York, Charles Scribner's Sons, 1900, 184 pp.

Morley, Henry, Editor, *Ideal Commonwealths,* London, George Routledge & Sons, Ltd., 1893, 284 pp.

Oliphant, James, *The Educational Writings of Richard Mulcaster,* Glasgow, J. Maclehose and Sons, 1903, 245 pp.

Painter, F. V. N., *Great Pedagogical Essays. Plato to Spencer,* New York, American Book Company, 1905, 426 pp.

Quick, Robert Hebert, Editor, *Mulcaster's Positions,* New York, Longmans, Green and Company, 1888, 309 pp.; *Some Thoughts Concerning Education by John Locke,* Cambridge University Press, 1895, 240 pp.; *Essays on Educational Reformers,* New York, D. Appleton & Company, 1907, 568 pp. The *Essays* went through several editions. Chapters V to XIII deal with sixteenth- and seventeenth-century subjects.

Spinka, Matthew, *John Amos Comenius: That Incomparable Moravian,* Chicago, University of Chicago Press, 1943, 117 pp.

Stimson, Dorethy, "Comenius and the Invisible College," *Isis,* September, 1935, pp. 373–388.

Tschizewskij, Dmitrij, and others, *Pampaedia of John Amos Comenius* (with Latin text and German translation), Heidelberg, 1960, 515 pp. Contains material on the influence of Comenius on the Royal Society period.

Turnbull, George Henry, *Samuel Hartlib, A Sketch of His Life and His Relation to J. A. Comenius,* Oxford University Press, 1920, 79 pp.

Young, Robert Fitzgibbon, *Comenius in England,* Oxford University Press, 1932, 99 pp.

Part III
ADAPTING EDUCATION TO CHILDREN

Chapter 9

ROUSSEAU: A NEW THEORY OF EDUCATION

Today, in the third century after the publication of Rousseau's *Émile*, the educational world is not yet in agreement about his goals and means. In the attack on the classical tradition he had been anticipated by Comenius, Locke, and others; but no one had suggested that the school should be abolished, that the child, with only the disguised ministration of an older comrade should educate himself. On the other hand, we must place in the list of educators who have followed him—at a distance in most cases—the names of Pestalozzi, Froebel, and other Germans; a few British; fewer French teachers; and John Dewey and his disciples in America. Those less obviously but yet materially influenced by Rousseau would form an army including nearly all who carefully review educational doctrines.

The new period in educational theory created by Rousseau was the fourth such era since the later Middle Ages. Those four were (1) scholasticism, with logic as its foremost instrument; (2) Humanism, which used the classical languages and literatures; (3) Realism based on modern languages and the natural sciences; and (4) the era introduced by Rousseau who proposed to adapt his methods to the growth of the child, the nature of the mind (psychology), and the nature of society in promoting growth and self-development as the aims of a new education. Now it appears that a conflict arose between the nature of the mind and the nature of society. We shall return to this point.

THE YOUTH OF ROUSSEAU

Beside the mind and society there was a third factor—his experience as a student and his success with his studies, or the lack of it—that helped to determine his views on education. We shall consider his early years.

Rousseau's mother died in giving him life and this he claimed as the first of his misfortunes. The mother, like her son, suffered from extreme sensibility. Whether she would have been able to draw him out of his dream world into the sober, rational one may be doubted. She had gathered and read a collection of tender romances. These the boy and his father consumed in readings that sometimes lasted all night. When the swallows began to twitter in the first faint light of the morning, the father, packing the lad off to bed, confessed, "I am more of a child than you are." He seems to have learned to read at an early age. He claims to have read Plutarch's *Lives*, strong fare for so small a boy. About the same time he was shut up in a garret, for several days, the story says, for having mutilated his Latin primer.

When he was ten years old, his father became involved in a brawl and to avoid a possible jail sentence he escaped from Geneva. Father and son saw little of each other thereafter. The son was taken by an aunt but he never had a real home, certainly a misfortune. For a few months, in 1724, when he was twelve, he and a cousin were the pupils of a minister. They were to learn, as he claimed, "Latin and all the sorry trash of an education," such, no doubt, as spelling, letter-writing, arithmetic, and religion.

Life was not always calm in the minister's family. The minister's wife sometimes punished the mischievous boys, but this did not seem to destroy their happiness. On one fatal day, however, Jean Jacques was accused, unjustly he avers, of breaking one of the lady's combs. A court was called into session and an explanation demanded. He maintained his innocence against convincing circumstantial evidence. The cousin and playmate was caught in an equally bad scrape. Uncle Gabriel was called; he came, made further inquiry and, accepting the evidence, gave the boys an almighty whaling. This was the end of peace for Jean Jacques and of his trust in the justice of men, even the best of them. The pain was bearable; but the sense of injustice was overpowering. All they could do was to shout, times without number, "Butcher! Hangman!" Rousseau spent much of his life in collecting proofs of the injustice and corruption of society and he concluded that a good education could be made possible only by the exclusion of such evils.

Society had other faults beside crude injustice. The routine of work was not to his liking. His egotism and pride set him against the master-servant relation as it applied to himself. Steady tasks interfered with his freedom. Much against his will he was, at the age of thirteen, apprenticed to a notary. He had long been an avid reader and gatherer of information. His uncle was impressed with his intelligence and gave him a good recommendation. But he had not been used to work and was unwilling to learn. He was soon dismissed with ridicule.

The next master was violent and mistreated him. He was to learn the engraver's trade, which he enjoyed and half-way mastered. If the master had been kind and patient with his inexpert beginnings, had overlooked his pilferings and other weaknesses, he might never have been heard of. But fate and he decided otherwise; he ran away. Before he left the vicinity of Geneva he made a discovery. The peasants in the country roundabout with whom he associated received him with greater kindness than the city people. They took him in, gave him bed and board in the most artless and friendliest manner. It was not charity, for they treated him as a fellow human being not as an inferior. The simple rural people were of a nobler kind than the highly civilized, artificial people of the city—a discovery, and an important lesson for life.

Rousseau also was discovered at the beginning of his wanderings. Roaming about without plan or destination, he came to a curé, M. de Pontverre. Rousseau reported, saying, "He received me kindly, talked about the heresy of Geneva, the authority of the Holy Mother Church, and invited me to dinner." Even when Rousseau had acquired experience it appears that he did not realize that he had been discovered by a skilled proselytizer of Rome. "I found little to reply to arguments which ended in this manner and I formed the opinion that curés who dined so well were at least as good as our minister." He was sent to a way-station for those who were about to abjure their Protestant faith. This he did at Turin where he was baptized and received into the Roman Catholic Church. Thereby he also surrendered his Genevan citizenship for which his ancestors had left France.

ROUSSEAU AS A STUDENT

In his brief apprenticeship he half-learned the engraver's trade, began to draw, and in writing developed a beautiful hand. Several years later, more Latin was to play a part. While he was a servant for a titled family in Turin, a younger son of the house discovered, so he wrote, that "my education, which had been commenced in so many things, was complete in none. Finding especially that I knew very little Latin, he undertook to teach me more. Arrangements for daily lessons were made but he put me into Virgil, of which I understood hardly anything. It was my fate . . . often to begin Latin afresh and never to learn it."

There are some difficulties in this story, as in others of his reminiscences. He should have loved Virgil, for he loved romance such as we have in the story of Dido and much else in the Aeneid. He finally claimed that he learned to read Latin, but this is ambiguous. Again he said that he was able to pick out bits of Virgil, Horace, and Tacitus, but this is not to read in the usual sense. After Turin he took up Latin twice again, the last time when he was twenty-six years old.

Leaving Turin he strolled through the beautiful countryside toward

France and continued to make progress in the language of the people. Skill with words was to be his greatest achievement and he seems to have been far more successful with incidental learning, picking up ideas, than with set lessons. He rebelled against regulation and constraint.

At Turin and later he met two priests who were to play a major role in the religious drama of the Savoyard vicar of *Émile*. First he met a Turin friend, the Abbé Gaimé, and then the Abbé Gatier, whom he met after he was settled with Madame de Warens of Annecy. She was the woman who had sent him to Italy in the first place. While there he took lessons in Latin from the Abbé Gatier, not for very long of course, only for part of a year in 1729. He was then seventeen. Each of the two priests had treated him kindly and in repayment he gave them important parts in the vicar of Savoy story already mentioned. It is not necessary to assume that

Jean Jacques Rousseau (1712–1778)

they held the views assigned to them in *Émile*. Madame de Warens was a more likely source. While staying with her, without cost for thirteen years, from age seventeen to thirty, he followed disconnected studies as his mood led him.

There were clear reasons why he became a social educational philosopher. He, finally, after a long period of mental blindness, discovered the state of France and the character of the Enlightenment. Rousseau was a great walker; but he said he had to walk at his ease and stop at his leisure. He loved both the grand mountains, at a distance usually, and the charming valleys. He liked to stop to talk to the peasants. On one of his tours he walked from Switzerland through Solothurn into France and, stopping at a cabin, offered to buy a meal. The peasants gave him some barley bread and milk as the best they could provide. When, in conversation, they became convinced that he was not a government official—not a tax collector—they went through a hidden trap door to the basement and returned with white bread, eggs, meat, and wine. They refused the offered payment and explained that they had to hide even provisions for otherwise they would suffer even more exorbitant taxation. Rousseau wrote, "What the good man said to me . . . made an impression on my mind that can never be effaced, serving as the seeds of an inextinguishable hatred which has grown up in my heart against the vexations these unhappy people bear, and against their oppressors." This was a first discovery of the evils that were ruining France. This was only a step; a full understanding took years.

His young teacher at Turin had taught him to read with care and to think about construction and style. He began to distinguish provincialisms from pure French and to practice reading aloud as a means of savoring the language—a practice that he was to continue with his own books as he wrote them. The artist was breaking from its chrysalis. Composition in his native tongue was the art in which he became most distinguished. He also had some success in music and he remarked that, although ignorant of music, if one begins to teach it, he will always learn a great deal more. It is strange that he did not make use of this well-known truth in his educational program.

TUTOR FOR A YEAR

Madame de Warens, who repeatedly tried to start Jean Jacques on an independent career, secured a place for him as a family tutor in a de Mably family. It was the only time in which he tried to dispense a general education. He surveyed his own attainments and concluded that he had "almost sufficient knowledge" and other qualifications for the task. It appears, however, that he trimmed his program somewhat to bring it within the scope of his knowledge. His greatest defeat, he felt, was not intellectual but temperamental, a "naturally gentle disposition" that flared up into a "violent temper" when things did not go well. He had a pervading feeling of inferiority; he lacked experiences in "high society"; he feared the exposure of his lack of detailed knowledge; he very much wanted to succeed at last after many starts and failures; and in accepting the appointment he referred to his desire to be treated as a social equal. These were all reasons for his nervous tension.

His pupils were sons of the Provost of Lyons, Jean Bonnot de Mably. The older boy, named Sainte-Marie, was bright but spoiled, the younger, dull, according to their new teacher. The family was distinguished. One brother of Jean Bonnot was the Abbé de Mably and another was the famous Condillac, an educator who reduced Locke's psychology to sensation. Rousseau also was a student of Locke, who is mentioned in *Émile*. Rousseau had no reason to complain of his treatment in the family and he did not; but after one year he resigned, convinced that he had not succeeded.

After this result, some teachers would have ceased to bother with education and would certainly not have thought of writing a book about it. Not Rousseau. He was convinced that the fault was not in him but in the system; this was the reason for his failure. He was partly right.

The report on his tutorial efforts, which he wrote for M. de Mably, but perhaps did not hand over, shows the influence of his reading. It is called, "Fragment of a Memorandum on the Education of Sainte-Marie." This, the first of his writings on education, may have led him to go on with the subject in whole books that oppose its standpoint, for the "Memorandum" is purely Lockian. He had not, when he wrote it in 1740, discovered the new standpoint of *Émile*. He said his first task as tutor was to gain an understanding of his pupils. This idea came from Locke, but Rousseau gave it a new and highly effective interpretation in the preface to *Émile*. The second point was the need for cooperation between parents and tutor. He proposed a secret code by which the tutor was to report on the boys' conduct, thus deceiving the children for their own good. Why not a private conference, or one including the boys; why this devious course?

As Locke also said, virtue is the most important result of a good education. It is, according to Rousseau, the basis of accuracy in thinking and good judgment; for a virtuous man would not let present pleasures sway his decision. The boy must learn to understand men so that he can make use of them through their virtues or even their vices. "You sir," he wrote to de Mably, "can help to develop his knowledge of men by consulting him about some invented situations. This will flatter his vanity." This section of the report is full of such sophistry, which did not come from

Locke but is pure Rousseau. Even in *Émile,* Rousseau frequently uses stratagems and tricks to deceive his pupil, a practice that shows the author in a bad light.

The order of studies was to be very simple. He proposed to teach his pupils to read Latin, not to speak or write it, in which he was not skilled. He admitted that he was able to read only snatches of Virgil or Tacitus. It is not clear that he realized the difference in difficulty of the two authors. The reason for the proposed slight training in Latin was that it was not necessary for a military career. He proposed to teach an "easy smattering" in history and geography, omitting all that savored of dryness and study. Some logic and a year of mathematics he considered necessary for officers who would be required to study fortification. Natural history— the most interesting of all branches of knowledge—literature, and, if time permitted, a study of morals and the law of nations were to complete the intellectual part of the scheme. He awaits the plan of studies that the Abbé de Mably has promised and he will follow it to the letter. A few months later he left the tutorship and he never again accepted a teaching position.

The "Memorandum" showed that Rousseau had not yet reached an independent position. There is no hint of delayed maturing, learning by inquiry and discovery, physical education, or of the evils of civilization.

SOCIAL THEORY

Émile is the chief but not the only source of Rousseau's views on education. Even *Émile* can be better understood by using his other works. A thinker does not usually develop his entire system in a regular manner and deliver it in finished form in one comprehensive statement. This applies to Kant, a younger contemporary, who did not hesitate to acknowledge his debt to Rousseau. The writings of Rousseau drew from many sources and experiences: his childhood punishment; his many failures in study, especially in Latin, and in teaching; the peasants who had to hide their meat and wine from the tax collector; and many others, including the injustice suffered by Diderot, as will be told subsequently.

Rousseau was launched on the sea of social and educational thought by an accident—and a conversion. He was walking in the hot sun for several miles to visit his friend, Diderot, who was in prison on account of charges against the famous *Encyclopédie* of which he was the editor. An example will serve as explanation: State and church were united to prevent the spread of heresy, and the contributors to the *Encyclopédie,* not to speak of Diderot, were not all "safe." They were such men as Voltaire,

D'Alembert, and M. de Buffon, Keeper of the Royal Botanical Garden, who on one unfortunate day was accused of fourteen "errors." One of the problems was the length of the days of the Creation: Were they days of twenty-four hours or might they be taken as epochs?

Diderot and Rousseau were drawn together by their love of music, and Rousseau wrote the article on that subject for the *Encyclopédie*. Matters of business and friendship, therefore, drew them together on that Sunday afternoon in 1750. Stopping in the shade to rest, Rousseau read the current copy of the newspaper *Mercure de France* and saw the notice of a prize to be given by the Academy of Dijon for the best essay on the question, "Whether the revival of the sciences and arts has contributed to purity of manners?" This question struck fire in Rousseau's soul and he received an illumination. He saw that mankind had missed its true goal by traveling away from it and in the opposite direction, away from a simple wholesome life toward a complicated, corrupt, extravagant, and contentious condition that provided no calm satisfaction for anyone.

He had a vision. He was so overcome by emotion that his tears saturated the front of his shirt. He saw that the natural man was good and that civilization had perverted him. Man was fitted to live a simple, natural life, not the artificial, competitive, warring life of contemporary France. He made his visit and told his story to Diderot. There is no evidence that the idea was given him by Diderot. Diderot made no such claim.

Rousseau wrote his essay, the *First Discourse*, or *Discourse of 1750*. He praised a simple, pure, natural life, such as he imagined the life of unspoiled rural people to be. He believed that such a society had once existed but had been destroyed by the arts and sciences, which developed an artificial and insincere culture. It seemed plausible to him and to many but he had no proof. The science of anthropology had not been born, let alone developed. He was captivated by the vision of the Noble Savage. He probably believed that the Indians of French Canada were happier than French nobles in Paris. The Indians had not, at least, been compelled to learn a foreign tongue before they had gained command of their own. His answer won the prize and Jean Jacques became famous. That his writings and his fame, in the end, made him unhappy is a kind of confirmation of his theme.

The *Discourse of 1754*, undertaking to explain the origin and foundation of the inequality that exists between men, gave Rousseau's answer to the new problem set by the Academy of Dijon. It was a better essay than the first but did not win. Rousseau now assumed two basic human traits: a drive for self-preservation and a native feeling of sympathy. He stressed the latter, an answer that immediately brings to mind the contrasting answer of Hobbes (1588–1679). Hobbes declared that primitive existence is "a state of war by all against all" in which life is "poor, nasty, brutish, and short." In his heart, Rousseau could not accept this view; but it might be argued that both may have been right. Perhaps after a beastly beginning, as reported by Hobbes, the food supply would increase, the growth of family life would be settled, mothers would become motherly, and sympathy would even outstrip self-preservation. Life might become pastoral and idyllic, for Rousseau would have the world stand still. This was the mood of the *Discourse of 1754*.

In *Émile*, the Hobbesian theory is scrapped. Some men, including Rousseau in his major educational theory and the account of the Garden of Eden, begin with perfection. Everything including the child is good as it comes from the hands of the Author of Nature; but everything including the child becomes evil in the hands of man. These are the opening sentiments of the *Émile*. How does evil, one wants to know, develop out of good? An able German author has explained that the *idea* of the child—the divine plan of the child—is good, but the actual child is only an earthly copy of the Platonic form or idea. He said Rousseau was not so silly as to suppose that persons individually good become bad just by being brought together.

Perhaps not, but more probably that is just what Rousseau did mean and it is not silly. He meant that there is a divine germ in man's nature. This grows and flourishes if it is not perverted and tempted beyond what it can bear; but society sets up overpowering temptations that pervert the child's original nature. Insufficient food, a scarcity of warm pelts, and lack of room around the campfire may even in primitive life lead to competition, quarreling, and the struggle for mastery and private property. In play also, one is stronger, swifter, or more skilful than all others. Satan slips into the garden bringing in anger, envy, and ambitions. To avoid this outcome, Rousseau educates Émile in isolation. It is in relative isolation that he stays and ends up as a relatively useless country gentleman. But then Rousseau described more than one kind of society; and he proposed a different program for each.

Every educational program, if thought out to its end, implies a theory of human nature and one of society. Rousseau in his three distinct programs covers the entire range of theories from the individualist scheme of *Émile* to complete nationalization. Émile was educated for himself and as far as possible by himself. The *New Héloise* provides an illustration of family education, an intermediate form between the individual and the national schemes. National and public education wholly controlled by the State is proposed in the article on political economy written for the *Encyclopédie* and also in Rousseau's proposed constitution for Poland. His attention was drawn to this variety of education by Plato's *Republic*. Each of these forms is suitable for a different kind of civilization and social organization. *Émile* is intended for the "decadent" society of France in Rousseau's time.

NATURE AND EDUCATION

The scheme of education that Rousseau proposed in the *New Héloise* and especially in *Émile* is based on an array of facts or purported facts. For what he believed about the world and man, he used the word *Nature*. Nature, therefore, is a word of several meanings in Rousseau, but the different senses can usually be gathered from the context and from his writings as a whole. The chief meanings will, however, be set down here.

Nature is, first, the external world by which he sometimes meant the system of the universe and sometimes the physical conditions in which we live. By the system of the universe he meant the sun and the planets, the stars in their constellations, and the seasons of the rolling year. This is the world of Newton who was living when Rousseau was a boy. Rousseau saw a universal reign of law, a vast system of bodies in constant and regular movement. From this he inferred an intelligence and a will, or God. In this he sensed two kinds of lessons for a boy: a series of lessons on elementary observational astronomy and lessons in the deistic religion that was expounded by the vicar of Savoy in Book IV of *Émile*.

In the physical surroundings in which we live on the surface of the earth there were other lessons for the boy, lessons that we shall examine later. This envrionment formed nature in a second sense; and we must at once recall that Rousseau was Swiss and from childhood familiar with the mountains. The aspects of surrounding nature to which Rousseau responded were the wild and the pastoral. The mountains untouched by man called out his strong antisocial feelings as the sea did in that other romantic, Byron. But Rousseau also loved the sweet beauty of the secret nooks and valleys. He was a nature poet without a poet's voice.

Nature may be taken to include man or, on the other hand, we may consider external nature as man's environment. Rousseau usually considers the two separately but in either event we have human nature as a special case. According to Rousseau, men are physical and emotional and, to a lesser degree, reasonable beings. Men differ widely among themselves. Human nature is not uniform and therefore we have, thirdly, not only general human nature but the nature of any one man as compared with another or with the average.

All adults were children at some time and children differ among themselves; and also as a group they differ from adults. Child nature differs from adult nature in many ways; for example, in sex interest, types of play, optimism, continuity of attention, economic judgment, and others. Rousseau criticized Locke for having advised tutors to reason with children. This advice he condemned because "children cannot reason," especially on moral questions, perhaps. Some things, therefore, according to Rousseau, children cannot learn because they are too immature. For this reason, reading should not be taught before the age of ten or twelve. These delaying tactics, given a central place in educational theory by Rousseau, are now known as the *readiness principle*.

Much has been made of these developmental theories by the child, or genetic, psychologists. The famous Jean Piaget, of Rousseau's own city of Geneva, proposed a physical explanation of child immaturity: It is the result of incomplete nerve growth. Now this is no more than a guess. To mechanists everything must have a mechanical explanation. For Rousseau the father of the whole notion, who was no mechanist, the idea of slow growth and delayed maturing was a reflection of his own extended immaturity. His own experience more than anything else led him to advise teachers and parents to do the opposite of what you see others doing. This extreme view and the casual origin of the readiness principle should not lead us to underestimate the idea. The idea of child nature and immaturity as major qualities is of great importance in education. Of equal importance is the idea that by appropriate methods many things can be taught earlier than we thought possible. Education can increase readiness.

We have been thinking of individuals but men live in families, neighborhoods, and nations. But Rousseau did not accept the organic view of society. In analyzing the human past he reverted to the idea of an original state of nature. Here we have another meaning of our word, nature. In the state of nature men were associated in families, clans, or tribes. Usually Rousseau did not refer to the actual beginnings of the race in primitive or savage life. His state of nature is rather a simple, mainly rural, condition. He considered it a more wholesome life than the complex, artificial, and urban way of modern living.

He proposed to take the unspoiled infant and in appropriate surroundings by good education to bring to maturity a natural man, not a spoiled and unnatural man. He did not propose to go back to the earliest conceivable state of nature but to educate for greater simplicity of manners, purer ethics, honest economic relations, and more wholesome corporate living in all ways. If men had followed the correct path they would have developed from the state of nature into a natural civilization, but they lost their way and civilization became artificial and corrupt. But by a good education something can still be done to make civilized life more natural and wholesome.

The preceding uses of the word nature with minor variations will reappear as we examine Rousseau's scheme of education. Two distinctions are of great importance: the differences between the child, with its power to grow, and the adult; and the difference between a corrupt and a natural and wholesome civilization. We cannot return to the original state of nature, nor do we desire to do so; but we can avoid luxury and extravagance, the artificial manners of high society, the deceitful veil of politeness, and the vast gulf between the rich and the poor in our ant-hill cities. We can develop a more sober, simple, industrious, and honest way of life, a more natural way in the open country. This was an idea of 1762.

THE NEWBORN CHILD

Both Locke and Rousseau were opposed to the doctrine of innate ideas, but this does not serve to draw the two men into agreement on the nature of the newborn child. The infant, according to Rousseau, is an organism that carries traits and capacities that will condition its whole career. Its nature, including its physique, traits, and capacities can be cultivated, neglected, or perverted; but it is not clay to be molded at will into this shape or that. Now and later, as child and man, it will respond to some stimuli and opportunities and not to others. It has a character, and the teacher, employer, statesman—its friend or foe—must reckon with that nature. This Rousseau believed.

This has not always been accepted. Locke, when he wrote the first paragraph of his *Thoughts,* did not accept it; nor did Helvetius in Rousseau's own time. Helvetius claimed that a man was completely formed by his environment, that heredity had no part in forming him. Some psychologists and many sociologists of our own time have held views similar to those of Helvetius. Rousseau believed that every child is unique from birth, with a nature all its own.

We are assured (*Émile,* p. 33) that there is an "innate sense of justice and injustice in man's heart," and (p. 252) that "there is at the bottom of our hearts an innate principle of justice and virtue," the skeptical Montaigne to the contrary notwithstanding. Rousseau in words of passion tells the story of the child beaten by its nurse (pp. 32–33). "I thought he was frightened, and said to myself, 'this will be a servile being' . . . a moment later there were bitter cries, every sign of the anger, rage, and despair of this age was in his tones. I thought he would die. Had I doubted the innate sense of justice and injustice in man's heart, this one instance would have convinced me." The account is suspiciously like the story of the lambasting received by young Rousseau, as told in the early pages of his *Confessions.*

THREE KINDS OF LEARNING

A famous passage near the beginning of *Émile* (p. 6) combines the ideas of education as growth and as development from experience. We read,

All that we lack at birth, all that we need when we come to man's estate, is the gift of education. This education comes to us from nature, from men, and from things. The inner growth of our organs and faculties is the education of nature, the use we learn to make of this growth is the education of men, what we gain by our experience of our surroundings is the education of things.

The first of these three kinds of education is merely the gradual maturing of our organs and the sharpening of our faculties. All these, the organs, the faculties, and the power to grow are in the original nature of the child. The concept of three kinds of education came from Aristotle, as we have seen. The development of the child's original nature is not beyond influence from the outside. Control may be too strong a word but nourishment, hygiene, exercise, and stimulation can be supplied to aid growth. The organs and faculties are, indeed, given but since Rousseau's day much has been learned about the conditions of growth. Nature controls the order, manner, and the possible degree of growth, but she can be encouraged and aided in doing her best. This is the chief subject of Rousseau's book.

The education of men is given by the child's association with others in work and in play, in conversation, by cooperation and conflict, and in all the ways in which persons come into mental and physical contact. Thus the education of men is carried out through institutions, in school, church, scouting, and clubs. This kind of education is to be postponed by keeping the child out of society until the age of fifteen. Education for citizenship is a later phase of this education and we will treat it several pages hence when we come to the proposed constitution of Poland.

The third kind of education, that of things, comes from the physical world, nature in its elementary sense. The child may learn, for instance, that snow is white and cold and can be made into snowballs. These may be hard and if hit with one the child may be hurt; but the snowball, and all things, is relentless, it does not care. Later the child may learn that glass is brittle and can be fused at high temperature—the beginnings of science. The relations between phenomena will lead the boy to the idea of cause.

The three kinds of education by nature, men, and things are to agree; but Rousseau does not show how this agreement is to be achieved, except by saying that because nature is beyond our control the other two kinds of education must be made to agree with it. He admits that this is difficult. And because the education of men is postponed we need only adjust that of things to that of nature. This simplifies the process considerably and this is the plan Rousseau advises.

Education, like all effective processes, requires the application of means; here, those that enable the child to grow. These include physical care, exposure to external nature, the setting of scientific problems, and in time, social contacts. Like all processes, education takes place in time and exhibits a serial development. Rousseau divides the education of a child into five periods: infancy, early childhood, later childhood before adolescence, youth, and early manhood. Speech marks the end of infancy. When the child can talk he no longer needs to cry. The first period of childhood extends from two to twelve years; the second ends at fifteen.

About age fifteen, with the onset of adolescence, we come to the great division in this process of growing up. The change is one of emotional stresses when the youth is angry and sorry at the same time, when he weeps without cause, and when conscience awakens but he becomes deaf to the voice he has hitherto obeyed. Rousseau's view of this disorder leads him to introduce into his scheme some of its most unusual features: negative education, natural punishments, and the isolation of the boy. Negative education meant "shielding the heart from vice, the mind from error," to delay the maturing of the boy, "not to gain time but to lose it."

The formal teaching of morals by commands and warnings tends to promote the bad conduct we would prevent. The child cannot understand ethical lectures. The true course is to prohibit nothing, command nothing, to protect against serious injury, and to let him suffer the pain and discomfort of any foolish action that he may undertake. Let him suffer the natural punishment of ignorance, carelessness, and wilfulness. He will learn from nature's instruction. And, thirdly, to keep him from developing too rapidly we must keep the boy away from parties, towns, and society—high and low—especially that of the opposite sex.

Many have disagreed with Rousseau on the social isolation, but he may have under-, not over-, estimated the dangers of the social milieu in the eighteenth century; and they are even greater today. The extreme evils of a great portion of urban life: divorce and desertion, disorderly schools, the automobile, liquor, narcotics, tobacco, money-madness, and poverty, to name a few, lend support to Rousseau's contention that good young people can be ruined by bad society. His paradox of the good man destroyed in an evil society has become a sobering fact.

INTELLECTUAL EDUCATION

To protect Émile from the evils around him, he is to be educated apart from a single tutor who received him from the nursery. In the preceding pages of Book III there is a servant who among other duties acts as the diplomatic agent who links Émile and the tutor. Rousseau had not forgotten his troubles with the de Mably boys. Elsewhere in the book, Émile comes into direct contact with a gardener, a magician, and numerous playmates. In spite of the plan, Émile was not self-educated; he was under constant direction, artifice, and deception. The tutor sets the stage, but the chief actor does not always know his lines and has to be prompted. That is, the boy is not as eager to attack intellectual problems as we had been told; or, rather, it was that Rousseau from time to time realized that his plan was too ideal.

Comparison with Locke will be useful at this point in the story. Both sharply separated the several departments of education, and they agreed in valuing a virtuous life more highly than intellect and learning. Both used a tutorial plan, but Rousseau in contrast with Locke removed the boy from the family and the servants, which had bothered the Englishman. This decision by Rousseau affected the intellectual education for, because society is evil, Rousseau decided to delay the introduction of the social studies and history. Also, he thought that a small child could not understand such studies. Even reading is postponed to age ten or later. The intellectual program will long deal only with external nature, which is morally neutral—neither good nor bad.

Rousseau planned to have objects presented in a suitable order so that memory would later recall them in the same order. He neglected the selective attention that rearranges experiences according to purposes. Rousseau's plan reveals a certain mechanical quality, but the association psychology is itself mechanical.

Thinking begins with the excitement of the senses, we learn; and objects presented to the senses and the sensory experiences become the materials of thought. The child is eager to touch, taste, and handle things; in this way he learns about temperature, weight, size, shape, color, sound, and smell. Rousseau thought smell was the last of the five senses to develop. Because our knowledge of nature enters through the senses, Rousseau thought the senses should be "trained." He had an extraordinary notion of the height to which sensation could be improved. He had heard and apparently believed that the Indians in Canada had trained their sense of smell to such a degree that they needed no hunting dogs to follow the trail of game. He was more rationally impressed with the improvement of touch by the blind. Much of Rousseau's sense-training is more a development of judgment than improvement of the senses.

Geometry provided opportunity to exercise the senses, especially the sight. His plan for the teaching of geometry was inductive and experimental; it became an art of seeing rather than proving by demonstration. If the boy draws circles with a pencil and string he will need no separate proof that the radii of a circle are equal; it will be evident. The corners of a paper triangle snipped off can be placed to show that they fill the space around a point on one side of a straight line. For a small boy such inductive or observational geometry will be of interest; but if Rousseau thought that it could have the same values as demonstration he was mistaken. The tutor, he said, will not teach geometry; he will lead Émile to discover it; and this was one of Rousseau's best ideas, itself a discovery.

The principle we have just now repeated is the key to Rousseau's plan of science-teaching and, indeed, of his entire plan of intellectual education.

And even though he mentions problem methods (p. 110), he too often secures information merely, rather than understanding. Sports and drawing are other means of sense-training. The chief defect of this plan is the idea of training instead of having children inquire and investigate in their efforts to understand.

We turn to Book III for the main treatment of science-teaching. The object according to Rousseau is to develop a taste for science, not to cover the subject and not to prepare a scientist. Rousseau seems to have had in mind a modern type of liberal education. Science, he said, is unlimited, an unfathomable and shoreless ocean; but the best period for intellectual education is contained within three years, between the ages of twelve and fifteen. This imposed other limitations: the exclusion from the course of study of all that is erroneous, or useless, or merely showy; of social and moral questions for which the boy is too immature; and, finally, of what does not interest him (p. 129). The idea of a process of elimination in order to reduce the content to a manageable amount may have been suggested by Abbé Claude Fleury who has a comparable scheme, but without the plan to limit intellectual education to a few years. Rousseau labored under the difficulty that in France in his time a boy's schooling ended at fifteen or sixteen.

The pupil's progress in geometry, said Rousseau, may be a true measure of his growth in intelligence. This is an acute remark, but the intelligence tests include several kinds of materials, not mathematics alone. As motives Rousseau proposed curiosity, a present drive, and utility, a future advantage. As soon as the boy can distinguish between the useful and the useless the teacher must, with skill and discretion, lead his pupil to see the need for theoretical studies.

Curiosity is the first motive as we have seen. It is easily aroused by natural phenomena but, if we would maintain it, we must not too easily satisfy it. Rousseau began with problems and thus became the herald of a revolution in the teaching of science. But he began with extremely difficult problems: the sun set over there last night and now it is rising over here. How did it get from the west to the east? This is a tough beginning, but the second problem is tougher. The boy is to explain why the sun rises and sets further to the south in winter than in summer. Rousseau tried to help with leading questions but would not tell the boy anything. It took all mankind a long time to answer these questions. And no globes, maps, or other equipment are to be used. "The earth is his globe, let him use that." But the whole earth is hard to see and to manipulate. We can be sure that Rousseau did not himself work out the answers in this way. Instead of analysis and scientific investigation we get a burst of eloquence (p. 131). Books also are unnecessary. The only book mentioned in connection with science instruction is *Robinson Crusoe*.

Geography offers a much easier beginning in science than astronomy.

We should begin with the neighborhood, with home geography or *Heimatkunde*, as the Germans say. The boy will first draw a map to show the road from his father's country house to his residence in town. We are to forget for a moment that the boy is an orphan. It will be a very simple map at first but he will gradually add the bridges, farms, and villages on the way between the two places. Perhaps it is to be drawn to scale, which would be a difficulty. Rousseau did not show how this becomes a problem; it reads much like an exercise. He has better success with the problem of finding the way home when they got lost in the woods.

The boy is introduced to physics (p. 135 ff.) and there is a chemical problem about the adulteration of food and drink. However, it is not made clear how a small boy could attack these. At this point (p. 148) the discussion turns to the industrial arts. Everywhere there is the insistence on the use of only the simplest instruments or none at all. It seems to him that only what is visible or tangible or otherwise concretely experienced is truly scientific. This principle would exclude the abstractions and inferences that make up a great part of science; but Rousseau is educating a man, not a scientist.

Rousseau had no scientific training. He read and "reread a hundred times," two books by Father Bernard Lamy, a popularizer: the author of one book of "Conversations" on the sciences, and a second on "Elements" of mathematics. It is important to know that in the study of algebra Rousseau was not satisfied with the identity $(a+b)^2 = a^2 + 2ab + b^2$ until he had constructed diagrams illustrating this proposition. There is perhaps no reason to think that Rousseau was unable to complete this very simple figure. Geometry he liked but did not pursue far and for analysis he showed a distaste. He dabbled in astronomy and anatomy and made some progress in Latin, but more in music, and usually without a teacher. One result is the conclusion that solitary study is slow and laborious work. He lacked the power to continue. The story of his self-study is told in Chapter VI of the *Confessions*. He was twenty-five years old, too old to begin self-discipline for the first time.

THE LANGUAGE ARTS

If Émile did not learn to read before he became ten or twelve years old, Rousseau was pleased. In this, as in most matters, he controverted custom and informed opinion before his time and since. Learning to read is the schoolchild's first occupation, except where Rousseau and Froebel have introduced reading-readiness ideas. In such schools the teacher talks with the children and carries on exercises with them for some weeks or months before they learn to read. This is a continuation of the activities of the kindergarten, which has always shunned reading. But we are today turning back to an older view and voices are heard to say that some children should learn to read at five, four, or even three years of age. Some children do this with very little help. Others do poor work at school because they have not learned to read well, and there are teachers who think that such children need more practice and teaching; hence they should begin early. This most recent view is also ancient. Quintilian said, "All that is learned early need not be learned later." Headstart is only one example of a present trend.

All this is anti-Rousseau. He placed the teaching of things before words, and as far as possible without words, from nature herself. "I hate books," he declared, "they only teach us to talk about things we know nothing about" (p. 147). We recall that Robinson Crusoe, perhaps the first do-it-yourself manual, was the only exception. As for the problem of teaching reading—according to Rousseau, there is no problem. In his book on education there is never any lack of any skill and competence in Émile when they are needed. Émile learned to read at twelve with hardly any teaching. And penmanship was beneath notice as a school problem. "Shall I proceed to the teaching of writing? No, I am shamed to play with such trifles in a treatise on education!" (p. 81).

In late adolescence when the boy is rapidly growing into manhood the whole scheme suddenly changes. "Now is the time to read pleasant books." He supplies no names or titles. "Now is the time to teach him to analyze speech and to appreciate all the beauties of eloquence and diction," as if that could be achieved at a gallop and without having learned to ride. More and worse is to follow:

It is a small matter to learn languages, they are less useful than people think; but the study of languages leads us on to that of general grammar. We must learn Latin if we would have a thorough knowledge of French; these two languages must be studied and compared if we would understand the rules of the art of speaking (p. 308).

His enthusiasm mounts. The ancients are the best authors, he said, for simplicity of taste, sober judgment, and excellent matter. Contemporary authors talk much and say little. "If Émile has the least glimmering of taste for poetry, how eagerly will he study the languages of the poets, Greek, Latin, and Italian" (p. 309). He wrote, in conflict with his own experience, as if these three languages could be learned, as Milton said of Italian, "at any odd hour." But Milton meant any daily or weekly hour not otherwise assigned. Lastly Rousseau thought that Émile would acquire two or three modern languages in his student travels (p. 435).

All this is mere day-dreaming by an author who had labored fitfully and unsuccessfully on Latin. Of that labor he said, "I found this my most difficult task, and I never made much progress in it." He was first introduced to the Latin language in childhood and at least twice in youth resumed the study but he never persisted in it. He never attempted Greek. His knowledge of the ancient authors was obtained from translations. Plutarch, the story-telling biographer and moralist, was his favorite, not Aristotle or Thucydides. Of Plato, he knew the *Republic*, and he calls it a work not on politics but "the finest treatise on education ever written" (p. 8). This is the wrong view; it is a political work but education, as in Aristotle's *Politics*, is an important aid to the maintenance of the state. He did not mention the *Phaedrus*, *Protagoras*, *Meno*, and others of Plato's dialogues that also deal with education. How much his views on this subject were influenced by ancient authors would be a difficult inquiry that could yield only speculative answers.

Every ounce of Rousseau's power and influence in the world was exerted solely through his pen. He was a teacher and tutor for only short periods and in private situations; he held no office; made only one public speech; and directed only one concert, and that was a failure. Without his writings few would have heard of him and yet he gave no place in his educational scheme to the language arts. This is one of several paradoxes in his system. If by this stepmotherly treatment of language-teaching he means to say that the use of words is a free gift, an inborn facility that cannot be improved by cultivation, he is making a wrong guess. His own practice belies it, for he labored over his manuscripts. It was perhaps the only hard and persistent work of his life.

Like Hobbes he always carried writing materials as he wandered in the lanes and fields, so that—we are quoting Hobbes—"if a thought should dart, for thought is quick," he could write it down before it escaped him. "The moment I stop, I cease to think," said Rousseau, "and as soon as I am in motion again my head resumes its work." He sometimes had several writing projects in hand at the same time and worked at them by turns. For this reason also he needed to keep a pen at hand.

The thoughts he recorded had to be arranged, worked over, and polished for the final composition. He composed with great difficulty, but he persisted until the form pleased him. He failed in a number of occupations, often because he would not persevere and undergo the necessary discipline. At writing he at least succeeded, but he was thirty-seven years old when he made his first great strike. His later opinion of that *First Discourse* shows that his judgment was sometimes quite accurate; he said that although it was tense and passionate, it lacked in logic and unity "for the art of writing is not learned at once." After this he should have seen the necessity of close, constant study by children of the mother tongue; and to enable the student to understand foreign peoples and distant times the necessity of other languages also.

MORALS AND RELIGION

Adolescence, which is taken to begin at age fifteen and to end at maturity about five years later, is the subject of Book IV. These limits cannot be determined with exactness; children differ and the sexes differ. Girls begin to grow into womanhood about two years sooner than boys into manhood; and in boys the transition may become noticeable at twelve or thirteen years. Adolescence is, however, more plainly marked than Rousseau's other periods—except infancy, which ends when the child learns to talk. This also does not occur at any set age or particular moment. Book IV deals with the adolescence of boys only but according to Rousseau, the education of girls presents no problems. As her name may imply, Sophy is born wise and, therefore, docile and needs to be taught only a few simple skills.

In *Émile* we have a new and important interpretation of adolescence. No earlier writer had given the period such significance. The adolescent is born into life, and the child becomes a man, a portentous change. "As the roaring of the waves precedes the tempest, so that murmur of rising passions announces this tumultuous epoch whose suppressed excitement warns of the approaching danger. A change of temper, frequent outbreaks of anger, a perpetual stirring of the mind, make the child almost ungovernable. . . ." Notice the figures of speech and the adjectives.

Every education library now has shelves filled with books on the psychology of adolescence and other shelves with books on secondary education. We can believe that much of this began with Rousseau. No one before had so extolled and magnified the power of sex in life and education; but Rousseau's eloquence made a beginning only. He only provided the provocation for psychologists, psychoanalysts, psychiatrists, and Havelock Ellis, who exploited Rousseau's ideas after him.

Mankind, Rousseau continued, is driven by many powerful passions and these are the means of our self-preservation or our destruction. The primary passion for our self-preservation, the one that never leaves us as long as we live, is self-love. This is naturally good but—note this—external influences are likely to transform it into other and harmful forces. External influences—luxury or an artificial civilization—can turn self-love into selfishness, which can lead to deception, treachery, war, and all human evils. Here we come back to the main theme of *Émile*, a new statement of its first pages: Man is good, civilization makes him bad.

To control the growth of selfishness in a boy we must control his surroundings, curtail his wants, limit his acquaintances, and simplify his total environment. Because Rousseau admired the *Republic* of Plato we should recall that the great author of that famous work espoused the same idea. He said that a healthy community will be satisfied with bare necessities and the simple life; but if people insist on luxuries and display, they will need more land and a multitude of callings: actors, dancers, tutors, wet nurses, dry nurses, confectioners, and others. In such a mercenary and unhealthy city, two other professions will be needed, the medical and the military; disease and war will be inevitable. Plato wrote thus more than twenty-three centuries ago.

Self-love, which is necessary and good, according to Rousseau, gives rise not only to selfishness but to most of the other passions including sex. This seems to pose an unsolved problem. Perhaps he means that self-love is translated into the desire to maintain the human race. He believed that sex develops earlier in cities, especially among the rich, the educated, and the highly civilized. This is not what William James believed. Rousseau held that the early satisfaction of this drive ruins character and health, emphasizing the need for restraint and delay; hence, throughout, Rousseau's doctrine and policy of delayed maturing. Love, that is conjugal love, restrains desire and reduces the dangers of social life, all of which validates monogamy. The tutor holds off the marriage of Émile and Sophy for about two years after they have joined their hearts.

During that period, Émile's social education is completed through travel under the guidance of the tutor. The young man is to learn to love all men, even those who do not love him. The "clever teacher" develops in his pupil a warm and tender heart, shows him the world gradually, and teaches him pity and a horror of vice. Rousseau's clever teacher needs a way to educate his pupil for society without submerging him in society. For this purpose history is valuable and biography even more valuable. This last idea is an echo of the author's reading of Plutarch's *Lives*. His views on history, on the ancient historians, and on the teaching of history range from the true and useful to the clearly false. Rousseau had only an amateur's knowledge of history.

By travel, by visiting workshops, hospitals, and other resorts of men, from history and the tutor's views and information, Émile learns to know mankind in society. And in adolescence he must also be introduced to religion. Rousseau favors a natural religion, a faith that can be demonstrated to reason—one that does not depend on miracle. To be sure, in the end, this religion must include the greatest of all miracles—namely, God, Freedom, and Immortality. However, Rousseau thinks these can be demonstrated as one demonstrates a geometric proposition. It is to be remembered that a geometric demonstration also uses assumptions and definitions, principles that for the moment we do not question.

To show how he would develop his ideas on religion for the instruction of Émile, he introduces the vicar of Savoy who, in fifty of the most eloquent and interesting pages of the book (pp. 228–278), outlines the method. Finally, through a transparent artifice, Émile is led to meet Sophy, the obedient and not too clever daughter of a rural family, and they fall in love at sight. Her education has been limited and entirely conventional but this is what Rousseau approves for women. The book continues for many pages, but its message has been delivered.

SUMMARY

The rationalism that the eighteenth century inherited from Descartes and Locke was followed by romanticism, in education as well as in literature. Both the evangelism of Wesley and the doctrine of fraternity, although differing in other respects, supported the growing humanitarianism that reformed prisons and asylums, created schools for the deaf and the blind, and improved the care of children. The natural right of the individual to liberty and equality was considered to justify the democratic revolutions against kings who claimed to rule by divine right.

The eighteenth century was a period of diverse trends in education. Humanism, although it had become traditional, was still dominant, but a young and vigorous Realism was opposing it. The church schools for the common people were beginning to feel the hostility of democrats and nationalists demanding universal education for citizenship. Political and scientific advances led from the uncritical optimism of the writers of Utopias to a definite but still uncritical theory of progress. Although the philosophers favored education, they did not fully realize the central place the school should have occupied in this program. Civilization was expected to produce a perfected society easily and quickly.

Rousseau thought otherwise. He believed that man had been perverted and enslaved by a civilization that had fostered oppression, corruption, injustice, and artificial and extravagant urbanism, and "those ridiculous institutions called colleges." Men had been happier in simpler conditions. He also disagreed with his contemporaries on the nature of the world and man. Nature gave sufficient grounds for belief in God, freedom, and immortality. Man should guide his life not only by reason but also by feeling and conscience.

According to Rousseau, the first task of the teacher is to study the child. True education is self-education, which is a dual process of growth in native capacity and the discovery of truth. It will be the teacher's function to provide the environment that will be best for the growth of the child's body and mind and that will stimulate in him the spirit of investigation. Growth and discovery can take place only where there is no constraint. The child's freedom must not be circumscribed, and he must be placed in a rich and stimulating environment. Rousseau's key idea that it is the environment that provides the conditions for education is important and has been influential. Through Pestalozzi and Froebel it influenced the schools that the Western nation-states were beginning to establish.

QUESTIONS

1. Why did Rousseau propose to have his pupil "educate himself"? Make a list of exercises, activities, and projects that would do this better than anything Rousseau suggested.
2. What ideas and educative processes that may come from Rousseau have you noticed in education courses, such as philosophy of education or methods of teaching?
3. How can one evaluate Rousseau's criteria, in the early pages of *Émile*, for the selection of the pupil who is to be taught?
4. Can the statement that "the poor man has no need of education" be justified?
5. Why did Rousseau assume only two basic human traits? How many can you name? Are any basic to learning?
6. If reasoning and learning of various kinds are natural activities, why cannot children be trusted to carry them on without much direction?
7. Why does Rousseau include the growth of our powers by increasing maturity under the general word *education*? Growth is a physical change, an increase in height, weight, and strength, not an intellectual or emotional change. Is he confusing different changes under a common name?
8. Why the opposition to the use of globes and other equipment in geography while in geometry tools and devices are recommended?
9. Why *Robinson Crusoe*?
10. Why should the teacher study the child; and can this be fruitfully accomplished?
11. Why should all children be educated under state systems and only a few carefully selected on the main plan of *Émile*?
12. Is it true, that, as Rousseau seems to claim, indoctrination is always wrong? Give examples on either side or both sides.

NOTES AND SOURCES

Few writers have evoked as much discussion as Rousseau. All over the civilized world his ideas are still "living thoughts" that call out either the acclaim or the criticism of partisans or opponents. Among the following books, those of Babbitt, Davidson, and Maritain are critical if not hostile. In the same vein is Paul Elmer More's "Shelburne Essay" on Rousseau, which is not listed here. Rousseau is also considered in most of the collections of essays on educational reformers by Frank P. Graves, R. H. Quick, and others. These have been mentioned in the reading lists in previous chapters. The paper on Rousseau by Quick is especially illuminating. We do not list Rousseau's *Confessions*, but there are many editions in French, English, and other languages. The publication of a condensed text of *Émile* by the Rousseau specialist, William Boyd, deserves particular notice. The book, *Émile For Today*, published by Heinemann, London, contains introductions to the separate Books of *Émile* and an editor's epilogue of about thirty pages.

ARCHER, R. L., *Rousseau on Education*, New York, Longmans, Green and Company, 1912, 278 pp.

BALLANTYNE, ARCHIBALD, *Voltaire's Visit to England 1726–1729*, London, Smith, Elder & Company, 1893, 338 pp.

BOYD, WILLIAM, *The Minor Educational Writings of Jean Jacques Rousseau*, Glasgow, Blackie & Son, Ltd., 1910, 159 pp.; *The Educational Theory of Jean Jacques Rousseau*, New York, Longmans, Green and Company, 1911, 368 pp.; *From Locke to Montessori*, London, George G. Harrap & Co., Ltd., 1914, 271 pp. The collection of Rousseau's minor educational writings by Boyd should not be neglected. *From Locke to Montessori* has short passages on Pereira and on Condillac. Also by Boyd, *Émile for Today*, mentioned here, London, 1964.

COLE, G. D. H., *The Social Contract and the Discourses by Jean Jacques Rousseau*, New York, E. P. Dutton and Company, 1950, 330 pp.

DAVIDSON, THOMAS, *Rousseau and Education According to Nature*, New York, Charles Scribner's Sons, 1898, 253 pp.

FOXLEY, BARBARA, *Émile*, New York, E. P. Dutton & Company, Inc., 1925, 444 pp. In the Everyman's Library. Complete translation.

GRAHAM, H. G., *Rousseau*, Philadelphia, J. B. Lippincott Company, 1883, 227 pp.

GREEN, F. C., *Jean Jacques Rousseau, A Critical Study . . .* , Cambridge, University Press, 1955, 376 pp.

HAVENS, GEORGE R., "Diderot and the Composition of Rousseau's First Discourse," New York, *The Romantic Review*, Vol. 30, December, 1939, 369–381.

HENDEL, C. W., *Citizen of Geneva, Selections from the Letters of Jean Jacques Rousseau*, New York, Oxford University Press, 1937, 405 pp.

JOSEPHSON, MATTHEW, *Jean Jacques Rousseau*, New York, Harcourt Brace and Company, 1931, 546 pp.

MARITAIN, JACQUES, *Three Reformers: Luther, Descartes, and Rousseau*, New York, Charles Scribner's Sons, 1929, 234 pp.

MORLEY, JOHN, *Voltaire*, London, Macmillan & Company, Ltd., 1913, 365 pp.; *Diderot and the Encyclopedists*, London, Macmillan & Company, Ltd., 1914, 2 vols.; *Rousseau*, London, Macmillan and Company, Ltd., 1915, 2 vols.

PAYNE, WILLIAM H., *Rousseau's Émile*, New York, D. Appleton & Company, 1914. An abridged translation first published in 1892 in the International Education Series.

TOZER, HENRY J., *The Social Contract*, New York, Charles Scribner's Sons, 1895, 247 pp.

VAUGHAN, C. E., Editor, *The Political Writings of Jean Jacques Rousseau*, Cambridge, University Press, 1915, 2 vols.

Chapter 10
BASEDOW AND PHILANTHROPIC EDUCATION

After Rousseau a new type of school, to which Basedow gave the name *Philanthropinum,* was developed. He may have used the name to designate schools that would cultivate the love of mankind and would also be maintained by lovers of mankind that is, philanthropists. These were to be boarding schools for boys, schools with enriched curricula, including Realist studies and many activities. They would, necessarily, be expensive, calling for high fees, gifts, endowments, or all three. Although the ages of the pupils would vary, these were to be secondary schools, not intended for small children.

Small children were the especial interest of a second founder of new schools in the eighteenth century, Pestalozzi, who was devoted to the very poor of both sexes, many of whom had no earlier schooling. These were elementary or primary schools. We shall see that as things turned out, Pestalozzi made room for all kinds of children. His work will be treated in the next chapter, but we mention him here because both Basedow and Pestalozzi were much affected by the great social changes of their own and earlier times: the revolutions in England, America, and France, the rise of constitutional government, the Enlightenment, natural science and scientific agriculture, and the spread of new ideas by Locke, Voltaire, Rousseau, Franklin, and many others. This is a preface to our chapter but another preface is needed here.

Since we introduced our succession of schools by mentioning the invention of the writing school in ancient Sumer we have noticed the development of twenty-five or more new or partly new schools in many countries. The new schools were not always entirely new—the mere fact that all were schools would guarantee that—but they served new needs, taught different studies, and prepared pupils for a changing society. The Philanthropinum was different from the English dissenting academy and the German *Realschule*. This will become clear. It was the result of a more secular outlook and a wealthier clientele than those schools.

NEW TIMES

In the eighteenth century the influence of Locke on philosophy, politics, and education became strong and spread far. His *Thoughts on Education* was published in 1693. It was soon translated into German, French, and other languages. It was cited fourteen times by Franklin in preparing his *Proposals for the Education of Youth in Pennsylvania*; and the school that resulted from his efforts was called an academy, the Philadelphia Academy. The school had two branches, but Franklin's heart was on the modern branch and not on the classical. He felt to the end of his life that he had been misled by his cofounders.

A more fortunate pioneer in the founding of a new school was the Swiss pastor and schoolmaster, Martin Planta (1727–1772). The Swiss were beginning to apply science to agriculture, new industries were being developed, the first guidebook to the country was published, and Swiss engineers were starting to build the roads that would make its scenery accessible.

Martin Planta came from a peasant family in the Grisons. His older brother, who was a pastor, supervised his early studies and then sent him to Zürich where he learned mathematics, the sciences, languages, and divinity. He was ordained at an early age and was for a short time the pastor of a church in London. Before he was twenty, he began to plan a new kind of school, which received government approval in 1760 and was established in the following year at Haldenstein. Pupils came even from foreign countries, and a number of prominent men received their early education there. One of these was Frederic C. La Harpe, statesman and tutor of Czar Alexander I. The aims of the school were to develop Christian and patriotic men of affairs thoroughly imbued with the need and desire for Swiss unity. The curriculum included three modern languages and Latin, arithmetic and advanced mathematics, physics, history, geography, drawing, dramatics, bookkeeping, music and dancing. Observation and independent thought were encouraged and the curriculum and methods were adapted to individual capacity and need. Gymnastic exercises and mountain climbing in the Alps were features of the school. Excursions were taken to collect minerals and plants, and these collections were used in the school. There was a shop for work in glass, woodturning, and cabinetmaking. A system of student government was used to prepare the pupils for participation in democratic political life. Thus it is seen that Planta developed a sort of Philanthropinum more than a decade before Basedow. After the founder died no one could be found to carry it on successfully and in 1777 it was closed.

INTRODUCING BASEDOW

Johann Bernhard Basedow (1724–1790) became the leader in the "progressive education" of the eighteenth century. The idea that he was a disciple of Rousseau is incorrect. He was more nearly a disciple of Locke, but Rousseau also influenced him, most by his opposition to memory work. In emotion, temperament, and artistic feeling he was entirely different from Rousseau.

Basedow was born in Hamburg where his father was a wigmaker. As a boy he delivered to his father's customers the products of his workshop, a task he despised. Throughout life, also, he disliked any work that required steady application. The father was harsh and Johann ran away. He shipped for the East Indies, but the boat ran aground and he came home. For one happy year he was tutor to a little boy, the son of a nobleman in Holstein. The family governness taught Johann French by conversational methods. His employer told the father that his son had ability and should be given an education.

In the gymnasium, between the ages of nineteen and twenty-two, he did very well under superior teachers. Reimarus, the author of the "Wolfenbuttel Fragments," which Lessing finally published, was one of his teachers. From this or some other source, perhaps Rousseau, Basedow acquired deistic ideas. His manner was worse than his meaning. His scornful treatment of other people's opinions offended many who themselves held liberal views. Goëthe's account of his journey with Basedow makes this very clear.

Basedow attended the universities of Leipzig and Kiel, receiving the doctor's degree from the latter. His dissertation dealt with language-teaching, and some of his ideas were later used in schools. This occurred ten years before *Émile* appeared and shows clear independence from Rousseau. Like Rousseau, however, he never really mastered the Latin language, and this made trouble for both.

He showed his independence further in 1768 by issuing an educational manifesto that, in his inflated manner, he called *A Memorial to the Friends of Mankind and Men of Means on Schools and Studies and Their Effect upon Public Welfare.* To this he attached a proposal to prepare a book for elementary-school teachers that, when completed, was to be called *Elementarwerk*, that is, an elementary book or work. Basedow was working under the idea of a countrywide reform of schools, inspired, no doubt, by the writings of Locke and La Chalatais. *Émile* had been out only six years when he published his *Memorial*. Even before the *Memorial*, Basedow, in minor essays, advised teachers to begin with objects not abstract words, to use games, and to avoid compulsion. He attacked the attention given to Latin and advised the constant use of the mother tongue in teaching Latin so that both languages would be learned at the same time. He urged the preparation of systematic schoolbooks, an echo of his idea of an *Elementarwerk*.

Although Basedow is to be treated as the founder of a new school, he should also be heard on other matters. The *Memorial* was addressed to philanthropists, men of good will and men of means, who were to provide

Visual education according to Basedow. (Courtesy of the Bettman Archive.)

for schools that would further the public welfare. This was a call neither for public schools nor a school tax; but he did propose a state schoolboard. Prussia established a *Schulcallegium* in 1787, nearly twenty years after Basedow proposed it, but it is unlikely that his writing influenced the action. Württemberg had a state system in the time of the Reformation and Luther had favored it. Besides, Basedow's plan to support semipublic schools with private funds, really donations, was illogical and unworkable.

The *Elementarwerk*, which he proposed along with the *Memorial*, was completed in four parts in six years by Basedow and a group of assistants with the aid of great sums of donated funds. In the middle period of his life Basedow was a successful propagandist. Through letters, announcements in the papers, and actual visits and appeals to the wealthy, he collected the considerable sums that were needed to maintain his staff and to print the expensive illustrated volumes. If the first campaign did not yield enough he started another, and another, and succeeded.

In the *Elementarwerk*, one finds detailed directions on the care and treatment of children. This kind of information is found in Aristotle (*Politics*, Book VII, xv, xvii), who had without a doubt gathered it from earlier writers on child care, one of the oldest subjects of general interest in the world. Exercise, sleep, food, drink, and teaching the child to meet small hardships bravely, to stand up to wind and weather, are sample topics. Basedow in desiring to say new and striking things also included some absurdities.

In dealing with methods and curriculum he followed Locke, and sometimes, Rousseau. He was, as they were, a Realist. The language problem was a difficult one and he would not accept Rousseau's summary solution. He had little that was new to say about it.

Part One of the *Elementarwerk*, which dealt with methods of teaching, came out in the spring of 1771. The whole work, complete in four parts, as we have noted, was completed and furnished with numerous illustrations prepared by a famous Polish artist and engraver, Nikolaus Chodowiecki. The year was 1774. The book was an early landmark in visual education. One fears that many teachers were unable to afford a copy of the book written especially for them; the price was twelve taler.

BASEDOW'S PHILANTHROPINUM

Basedow foresaw that with the completion of the big book he would be fifty years old and unemployed. In his earlier years he had been a tutor and a teacher but his public appeal for contributions to finish the *Elementarwerk* had brought his greatest success. He turned to the same device. He announced that he would be prepared to serve as an educational consultant to families or institutions; or he would receive subscriptions for a new school.

Prince Leopold, of the small German state Anhalt-Dessau, was interested in the second proposal and his family tutor urged him to invite Basedow to a conference. First impressions were unfavorable. Basedow seemed impulsive, reckless, and even violent; but the ruler's opinion changed and because "education was an Augean stable and he had no Hercules," he decided to support Basedow in the establishment of a "new" school. The prince, a man of honor, put first things first, and demanded that Basedow do the same. Basedow promised to devote all his efforts, before beginning in the new school, to the completion of the *Elementarwerk* for which he had received large sums; but he failed to keep his agreement. While the assistants labored, he wrote *An Entertaining Arithmetic*.

In 1774 the conditions had been met. The new school was to be opened. Prince Leopold had arranged to help Basedow with funds; but floods and other disasters had swept over his little country making it difficult for the prince at once to meet all his engagements. Basedow would have left if a better chance had offered. He tried to find such an opportunity. He visited Halle, the scene of Francke's ancient achievements, but found no help there, or elsewhere. During the period of isolation, his public had become indifferent. He returned to Anhalt-Dessau and opened the school he named Philanthropinum.

The printed rules, in twenty numbered paragraphs, together with an introduction, covered four pages. Such documents were not unusual even in American colleges. Basedow's school was not to be a school-republic, but older boys were given some voice and privileges. Corporal punishment was not excluded but perhaps not practiced. School life was to resemble life outside "for we do not know what may befall us." The toughening processes in physical exercises came from Locke's *Thoughts*.

Three classes of pupils were invited: the academic, looking toward the university; future teachers who were to be taught pedagogy, but were not so taught; and attendants, stewards, and servants in the houses of the great. There was a school uniform. Every hour of the twenty-four was prescribed and sleep received a meager allotment. Sitting down was to be limited as much as possible. There was to be no formal memorizing and Basedow particularly invited pupils who had been spoiled in other schools by too much memorizing. He wanted to show how by his method they could be made into fine, enthusiastic students; but few such came. The fees were high but there was a great reduction for the poor. It was, of course, a boarding school. The school was not privately owned, in theory, but was to be a public trust with Basedow its only trustee; and there was no board, no legal transfer, and the building was firmly planted on Anhalt-Dessau soil.

The prince took no part in the opening of the school in December, 1774. Basedow delivered an address asking for money from the friends of mankind. There were three teachers and three pupils, two of them being Basedow's own children. In April, the famous Von Rochow, a philanthropic landlord, sent two children and a letter filled with advice and warning. Basedow gave no lessons, but his devoted and incredibly industrious assistant, C. H. Wolke, surprised everybody with the progress made under his instruction by Emilie, Basedow's daughter. A young adult who had just completed an apprenticeship came to fill up some academic oversights in his education and remained for a short time as a teacher. New students came in slowly, but no money. Basedow threatened, if no help came, to close the school and also dreamed of a new establishment elsewhere.

In a lucky turn of mind they thought of a new kind of publicity: they would hold a public examination of their dozen pupils. The date was set, three days in the middle of May, 1776. Basedow sent out notices and invitations. Many came from Berlin, Magdeburg, and even Switzerland, professors, authors, pastors, and teachers but not the ones most eagerly solicited: not Goëthe, J. K. Lavater, a Zürich preacher and mystic, and certainly not J. G. Harder, a scholar and philosopher who might be considered an enemy. On the other hand, Pastor Jean Frederic Oberlin (1740–1826) from his mountain valley wrote a letter both pathetic and enthusiastic, regretting that lack of means made it impossible for him to come. Oberlin was an early founder of infant schools. The examination, planned and conducted by the teachers, was a success. Emilie and others performed brilliantly. A new enthusiasm brought more money and new pupils; the Philanthropinum continued.

Although it continued, renewed opposition and real defects hindered its progress. The success of the examination roused the hostility of the Humanists and university professors. Herder called Basedow the *Pontifex Maximus*, the most elevated high priest and said that the examination proved that the Philanthropinum was not a school at all but a frightful forcing bed in a hothouse. He said that with God's help his own son should be kept away from the place. This was "an unkind cut" for a forcing bed was just what Basedow disapproved of most.

The failure to teach the art of teaching, pedagogy, was one of the defects criticized by supporters. Von Rochow's pupils came back without having any lessons that would enable them to organize and administer schools on the philanthropist's estates. Basedow endured the great man's complaints. A Danish father said his son, back from Dessau, had failed an examination given him at home. Others feared that young men returning from the school had acquired heretical religious views that would prevent their appointment as rural school teachers.

After two years the pupils numbered only twenty-nine; the contributions had attained no greater ratio to Basedow's expectation. A new era was to begin with the arrival, in 1776, of the Reverend J. H. Campe, an army chaplain, with unusual mental gifts. His titles were removed because Basedow would not tolerate any churchly office or garb; and a new title, that of Educational Director, was given him. Campe had attended the examination in May and had been completely hoodwinked, a bad omen. Apparently he had made no investigation or assessment of the situation.

When he arrived in September he had difficulty in locating the institution. No place of residence had been set apart for him. Teachers and pupils were scattered about town in rented houses and rooms. What had happened to the building occupied at first is in doubt. The Philanthropinum had neither property nor financial credit; and the deficit was twelve thousand taler. There were now forty or fifty pupils and half as many teachers and employees, but no equipment, materials, or collections. The teachers, for the most part, had been appointed without inquiry into their record or competence. To Campe it appeared that everything was still to be done in organizing the school; and Basedow seemed not disposed to help.

In this sea of trouble, Campe proposed to abandon ship, to close the school. Von Rochow was opposed. Once closed, he said, it could never be reopened. Prince Leopold also refused to let it die. He helped to reduce the debt and to meet the new expenses.

Basedow chose this moment to retire from the directorship. If he had only cut all ties and left Dessau permanently, Campe and Wolke could probably have made the school a success. Campe showed later that he had the skill. But Basedow insisted on staying to lead the religious services and, naturally, on the greater privilege of interfering as he pleased. First of all he insisted that the school must drop the old name, Philanthropinum, and call itself the Dessau Educational Institute. This was done. The founder's resignation did not kill the school. It flourished. Even professors and Humanists seemed to grow kinder. Immanuel Kant chose this moment to publish a favorable article in a Königsberg paper. He had been friendly before. The two principals, Basedow and Campe, established an educational magazine with the title, freely translated, *Pedagogical Review and Philanthropic Journal*—for them and the time, an economical use of language. This earliest of educational papers in Germany, to be issued at regular times, continued for seven years (1777–1784).

The prosperity and apparent peace were an illusion; there was war within. After each petty quarrel and brotherly reconciliation, sometimes mediated by the prince, there would be a lull, never a secure peace. One day, Campe left and refused to return for all the promises, penitence, and wheedling of Basedow and the solicitation of the prince, who even went to Hamburg to persuade the fugitive. The wise man would not reconsider. Even Wolke, who had suffered most, and others also resigned but were replaced.

With Campe gone, Basedow advertised in his *Pedagogical Review* for a replacement, a teacher who was to be fitted by experience and training to become the principal of the school for, as he said, quite consciously, but profanely, quoting St. John, "He must increase but I must decrease." The list of requirements is too long and elaborate to quote. There must have been few people who could have filled them at five hundred taler a year there were no applicants. Eventually he greatly reduced the qualities demanded and slightly lowered the salary and in 1780, Christian G. Salzmann (1744–1811) applied and was appointed.

In Salzmann, the Institute had a man of substance and quality. He remained about three years. He had been a pastor in Erfurt and had already written some educational pieces and was to write other and important ones. At Dessau he suffered, like Campe, from the lack of order in the school and of respect for regulations by both staff and pupils. In February, 1784, he, like Campe, abandoned the school that was to provide a perfect education, to serve as a model for others, and thereby to assure the happiness of all mankind. It never at one time had a sufficient number of pupils or the stability and general support to carry out any appreciable part of so great an objective.

JUDGMENT OF A NOVICE

The greatest of Basedow's several errors was his attempt to put play in place of work: to have teachers teach and pupils learn without intensive, continued effort. This was the judgment of Karl Pilger, who became a well-known writer under the pen-name of Spazier, a word that might suggest a walk for pleasure. Pilger, like many others, was fascinated by Basedow's showy speeches and his promises. He found that the school, without any examination of his credentials, would and did accept and install him as a teacher. He had no experience, no preparation. After a few days he was fitted with a new uniform by the school tailor. It was interesting to see citizens come to their windows when the boys marched through the streets. They no longer paraded with drums and banners as in former days but they made noise enough. The neat, clean uniforms and the courteous and even friendly relations between pupils and teachers and among the teachers themselves were very pleasing. Later he found that some of this was surface show, that there was dissatisfaction and spiteful quarreling underneath.

He was favorably impressed with the physical exercises. The gymnastics, sports, and competition in the open air gave the boys a healthy and even robust appearance. This was fine, but it soon appeared that gymnastics were more important than language lessons, which could be interrupted or even omitted for trivial reasons.

Soon he was given full charge of six and then of ten boys, all thirteen-years old. He was their sole academic teacher. If he did not teach them the French language they were not taught the French language. It was a staggering assignment for a greenhorn. He tried to get help from Wolke, who was cooperative and gave the class a lesson from pictures in the *Elementarwerk*. It was too elementary. These courteous youngsters hid their amusement from Wolke, but it was evident to Pilger. He sought help from others but they merely offered useless advice. He went to Basedow, who would certainly know how to teach. Basedow hid himself in "a smoke-filled room" and all he would say was, "It is not a Philanthropinum, only an Institute." This is the key to his insistence on the change of name. The school had not come up to his lofty unrealistic ideals; therefore, it was not a Philanthropinum. Pilger found an easy book, read it to the boys, explained the words in little lectures now from mythology, then from natural science, and gradually developed his own methods.

Pilger, or Spazier, approved the religious exercises conducted by Salzmann; and he described the little chapel, the services aided by a small orchestra, and Salzmann's impressive sermons. He thought they were, however, too much directed to the heart alone. He considered religion a matter of belief and doctrine. One may properly infer that Pilger thought the heart or sentiments and the physical body were well developed at Dessau but the intellect was undernourished. When Salzmann left in 1784, the school was again reorganized and became something quite other than it had been and quite similar to a conventional school.

Such success as the school had was the result in part of Basedow's assistants. The one indispensable teacher was C. H. Wolke (1741–1825). Kant, who was greatly interested in this school, said of Wolke that he was unassuming, indescribably industrious, and not to be deterred by difficulties. He was in fact a gifted man, skilled in drawing, painting, and etching, and an independent thinker. J. H. Campe (1746–1818) was on the staff for a short time. In earlier years he had been the tutor of two boys who became famous, the scientist and diplomat Alexander Von Humboldt and his brother William Von Humboldt, a scholar who became Minister of Public Instruction of Prussia and played a leading part in organizing the University of Berlin. Campe was a voluminous writer. One of his books was his *Robinson the Younger*, an imitation of DeFoe's classic. *Robinson the Younger* outlived its hundredth edition and was read by children in all languages from Gibraltar to Moscow. The development of a literature for children was promoted by the Philanthropinum movement. Another Dessau teacher was E. C. Trapp (1745–1818), who worked with Wolke to develop a more systematic plan of lessons for the Dessau Institute. Afterward he became professor of pedagogy at the University of Halle and director of the practice school (1779). This seems to have been the first example of a university practice school for the training of teachers. He published a *System of Education* in which he took psychology to be the essential foundation for a science of education. The hostility of the rest of the faculty at Halle made his university career unhappy and after four years he resigned.

SALZMANN'S PHILANTHROPINUM

Although several attempted it, Christian G. Salzmann (1744–1811) was the only one of Basedow's staff who succeeded in establishing a permanent Philanthropinum. Like Pestalozzi, he was moved by ideals of social reform. He was for three years the chaplain and teacher of religion and other subjects at Dessau and always acknowledged his indebtedness to that experience. The school that he opened in the duchy of Saxe-Gotha with the help of its ruler, Duke Ernest II, celebrated its centennial in 1884.

Salzmann's first criticism of the Dessau Institute was directed against the teaching of physical education. He thought more attention should be given not to teaching about health but to forming health habits and maintaining cleanliness. The dancing, riding, running, jumping, and swimming that the school carried on were good, he admitted, but all this seemed to him to be mere play. Physical education should include work, hard and useful labor. Perhaps it would not be unfair to say that Salzmann wished to interchange the roles given to work and play in the old schools: the classroom lessons were to be taught through play; but in the physical education, work and the acquirement of manual skills were to be included. Shops with tools and materials were an essential part of the scheme. Every teacher was to have a skilled trade.

Every child, Salzmann said, is a born naturalist, and the streams and fields of the beautiful Thuringian land "offer us so many interesting things that we shall not have time to examine them all." Nature itself, he said, is my science cabinet. The school should have fields and gardens to satisfy the children's passion for activity. It must be located in the country for reasons of health, morals, and intellectual education. The pure air and the vigorous outdoor occupations of the country make for health. Life in the country avoids the temptations that the city spreads before youth. Only in the country are geographical and botanical excursions and the study of nature at firsthand possible. Like all the philanthropinists, Salzmann was opposed to the rising "new Humanism" with its emphasis on Latin and Greek and its preoccupation with distant lands and ancient peoples. The immediate surroundings and the life of the present should engage the children's attention.

Salzmann gave advice to teachers as follows: Be healthy; always be cheerful; play and work with the children; strive to form clear ideas and to make them clear to the children; learn to use your hands skilfully; become well educated yourself and keep on learning; and, in all you teach, be an example. In the conduct of his school, he was aided by able assistants, among whom was C. F. Guts Muths, the organizer of school games and founder of systematic school gymnastics. The first pupil to be admitted to the school was Karl Ritter, who became the founder of the *natural method* in geography and a famous professor of that subject at the University of Berlin. Salzmann was an important contributor to the children's literature that the Philanthropinum movement developed. In his *Carl of Carlsberg,* which appeared about the same time as Pestalozzi's *Leonard and Gertrude,* he painted a picture of the school evils of the time. He proposed to collect into a pile, which would reach the clouds, all catechisms and spelling books and into another, equally high, all rods and canes and to set fire to both at once. His once popular *Stories for Children and Their Friends* was begun in 1778 and was continued until the collection filled seven volumes.

PUPIL SELF-GOVERNMENT

Among the early schools that had systems of pupil self-government we list those of Martin Planta and Emanual Fellenberg in Switzerland; Friedrich Froebel in Germany; and, in England, Hazelwood School, directed by Thomas Wright Hill and his four eminent sons. These were precursors of many that were to follow in the nineteenth century.

The arrangements at Planta's school are not fully known; but Fellenberg's Hofwyl had a complete system with constitution, laws, and officers. All was prepared and operated by the pupils themselves. A contemporary who described the system also expressed the opinion that self-government was mainly responsible for the success of Fellenberg's establishment. The financial arrangements were not permanently successful. The schools absorbed and dissipated Fellenberg's large fortune.

Froebel's first school at Keilhau in 1816 was opened long before he thought of the kindergarten. It was a school for boys who intended to enter a university. The school had a student-government system with a student court. After Froebel left, the school was conducted by J. Arnold Barop.

A pupil of this later time wrote,

If any act really deserving of punishment . . . was committed by one of the pupils, Barop summoned us all, formed into a court of justice, and we examined into the affair and fixed the penalty ourselves. For dishonorable acts, expulsion from the institute; for grave offenses, confinement to the room . . . for lighter misdemeanors, the offender was confined to the house or the court-yard. If trivial matters were to be censured, this Areopagus was not called.

The description raises the question whether the court may not have been controlled as well as convened by the principal. This is indicated also by the statement that "Barop in later life told us that he was frequently compelled to urge us to be more gentle"; and Barop added that, "Old Froebel regarded these meetings as means of coming into unity with life."

Hazelwood School in England was nearly contemporary with the schools already described but the organization of its student government was much more elaborate. The founders, Thomas W. Hill and sons, shared the liberal and utilitarian principles of Joseph Priestley, Jeremy Bentham, and the Mills, James and John Stuart. It is reported that Thomas Jefferson used a copy of the Hills' book on *Plans for the Government and Liberal Education of Boys in Large Numbers* when he was developing his plan for the University of Virginia where he introduced a self-government plan. We do not have the space to describe the elaborate student government at Hazelwood, but it has been remarked that the founders had before them a copy of the Constitution of the United States. One criticism we must not omit. Four pupils later in life complained that the Hazelwood system placed too much responsibility on the boys; "the spring, the elation of youth" was crushed by the weight of the decisions they not infrequently had to make. Perhaps Barop had done better.

JUDGMENT OF THE PHILOSOPHER

Neither Oberlin nor Kant visited Dessau. They formed their opinions and nurtured their enthusiasms in part on reports but also on expectations and promises. Now neither real estate nor educational prospectuses are to be blindly trusted. Kant certainly knew this, but his enthusiasm over *Émile* showed that he was vulnerable. He too believed that the obvious evils of a bad past could be corrected, simply and at once; but he also asked for facts and knew that facts could be gained by experiment.

Immanuel Kant (1724–1804) having completed his studies at the University of Köningsberg, began to earn a living by his services as a family tutor and continued for a number of years until he became a university teacher and eventually developed into a scientist and a great philosopher. He was a stimulating lecturer and a delightful host at dinner parties in his bachelor quarters. His friends found him entertaining.

He lectured on many subjects as was the custom of professors in the eighteenth century: on geography, the solar system, including his own projection of the nebular hypothesis, on education and, of course, on philosophy proper.

The lectures on education, as they have come down to us do not report Kant's exact words but only the sense as reported by students. His lectures, *Über Pädagogik*, were repeated more than once with numerous variations in content. Naturally, Kant did not treat education as a well-developed science. His doctrines are empirical; he argued from observed facts and conditions. For example, he pointed out that we learn by gathering information from books, teachers, our own collected information and then, by sudden insight, we may hit on a new and revealing hypothesis or, perhaps, conclusion. Here there were two ways of learning, one way to acquire knowledge, another to gain understanding or even wisdom and foresight.

Kant sometimes explained that philosophy cannot be taught as history or science is taught, largely by accumulation; but he also had great respect for information and he was widely informed in a variety of fields and enjoyed such discursive subjects as geography and anthropology were in his day. In connection with these two ways of learning, he pointed out that we can discover only by extensive experiments how great man's capacities are. Education, he said, holds the secret of human perfection.

He held that animals achieve all their gains by nature; they follow a reason not their own. We call it instinct. Only man needs to develop and to follow his own reason; but to develop the reason that becomes his own, he needs help, education. It is through education that man becomes man.

Each generation, he continued, educates the next one. This can be done by custom and haphazardly or with care and wisdom. The process of education can itself be improved in each generation that teaches the next how to teach. A correct view of education and the methods of teaching require thorough culture and experience [the education of teachers].

Education, he held, consists of two main processes: discipline—which is negative and restraining—and instruction—which is positive and stimulating. Without discipline men become capricious and maladjusted to social life. Discipline must precede instruction, for when children grow up and develop too great a love of freedom they become less amenable to instruction. Savages show this lack of restraint by a lawless freedom, not the noble freedom of Rousseau. It is, however, evident that Kant did not wholly approve of the innovations of Rousseau and Basedow. Lawless child becomes lawless man, or miseducated man, said Kant, a condition often exemplified by members of the ruling classes [or as is sometimes claimed, by the children of affluent moderns].

Kant speculated on the course of educational advancement. It may come not by conclusive experiments but bit by bit and by experience that will only gradually reveal the great secret of what human nature will be like when it is perfected. People were only then, it seemed to him, beginning to strive for a better education; and this gave him and others of his time the hope that a race of men, nobler, happier, and more perfect would develop. Men, he said, are developing a new theory of education and we should welcome their efforts.

Kant was thinking of Basedow and of the Philanthropinum group. He continued the thought that man's hidden nature might be revealed and perfected by better education. He used the anology of cultivated plants, which reveal perfections unsuspected in the wild state. This analogy would be much stronger but hardly convincing even today.

Men who aim to form comprehensive plans for education, Kant continued, must plan for the future and for the perfection of humanity. Parents, also, should educate their children not merely for the day or hour but for the future. Children should be directed toward the improvement of their surroundings; but parents do not think of this. They merely try to adapt them to conditions as they are, to enable them to make a living, perhaps. And rulers do worse. They try to use the people for their own purposes and this is all wrong. All the good in the world comes by a good education.

The basis for a scheme of education should be cosmopolitan, universal. Rulers care only for the state, but we are to care for humanity. And, besides, before rulers could lead the way, their own education would have to be improved. We must depend on private individuals who have acquired a vision of the whole, of the future, and of perfection. We cannot depend on the state as much as Basedow supposed. Even money voted by the state will be applied to the ultimate benefit of the treasury rather than to the enlightenment of the people.

Kant saw the great power of education but was unwilling to entrust this power to the state. Was he wise? Was he correct? How can the state provide for free experimentation to achieve the advance and the ultimate perfection that Kant desired? Few would now question the wisdom of state activity, but many believe that private initiative and provision are also essential in a democratic society and in society that would be progressive.

SUMMARY

The eighteenth century provided the axis on which education turned from service to the chosen few to a broader opportunity for all children, girls as well as boys, the poor and the wealthy. The turnabout was only the first step toward a distant goal. It was also the first time in history that this goal came into view and was chosen.

The eightenth century provided several kinds of new schools. These were modeled partly on the views of Locke and Rousseau but also on the designs of the several founders, Planta, Basedow, Salzmann, Pestalozzi, and others. The new schools did not separate elementary and secondary schooling; but Pestalozzi, who will be treated in the next chapter, was especially concerned with the elementary phases. He had advanced pupils also.

The eighteenth century also was a time of democratic, scientific, and economic change. The increasing numbers of its great writers, many of whom are now considered modern classical authors, is an indication of the spread of education. We have named only a few of a great number. Without a reading public, no writing fraternity would have existed.

Realistic studies rather than languages formed the central core of the curriculum. There were many activities including, in some schools, pupil self-government, field trips, and work in shops and in rooms for modeling and other skills. The varied activities were in the main new. These more active and practical schools drew a class of pupils different from those who attended classical schools. The new schools, we emphasize, attracted new classes of pupils.

The pioneers, as they have been called, were less noted for originality than for their courage and persistence. It seems to have been the lack of financial support that sapped the courage of the most enthusiastic of them, Basedow. All schools were small in the eighteenth century, as compared with those of the twentieth. The most thriving new schools had one or at most two hundred pupils. Regular financial support for schools came with the adoption of education by the state in the nineteenth century and later.

QUESTIONS

1. Should the university movement rather than the movement for universal education be taken as the beginning of modern education? Why?
2. How did the general aims of education of the classical and the "new" or realistic schools differ?
3. Do political or economic changes affect schools more strongly? Illustrate from history and explain.
4. Why did the movements for the "new" schools and the progressive schools die out after a short period?
5. Evaluate Basedow as an educational leader and promoter.
6. Basedow seems to have set an absolute ban against memorizing education. What sense, if any, is there in such a position?
7. On their attitudes toward memory work, compare Basedow and Rousseau.
8. How does the Fellenberg plan differ from the other schools treated in this chapter?
9. Consider the cases in this chapter in which schooling is directed toward political ends. Is it possible to teach leaving the pupil politically, vocationally, morally, and so forth, free?
10. On the freedom allowed pupils to form their own opinions, compare the French with the English schools.

NOTES AND SOURCES

A good account of Basedow is A. Pinloche's *La Réforme de L'Education en Allemagne au dix-huitiene siècle*, Paris, 1889; also in German, *Geschichte des Philanthropinismus*, Leipzig, 1896. The account by Spazier, abstracted in this chapter is at pp. 152 ff. in the French version and at pp. 131 ff. in the German version. Goëthe's account of a meeting with Basedow is in *Dichtung und Wahrheit*. A popular translation of this is by R. O. Moon, *Goëthe's Autobiography*, Washington, D.C., 1949, pp. 544 ff.

The story of Hazelwood School is told by the founders, Thomas W. Hill and his sons, in their anonymous book, *Public Education, Plans for the Government and Liberal Education of Boys in Large Numbers, As Practiced in Hazelwood School*, second edition, London, 1827.

French efforts in the period reviewed are treated by F. de la Fontainerie in *French Liberalism and Education in the Eighteenth Century*, New York, 1932; and American efforts by A. O. Hansen, *Liberalism and American Education in the Eighteenth Century*, New York, 1926.

Henry Barnard's *American Journal of Education* has pertinent material. It is indexed.

Kant on education has been translated by Anne Churton and her book, now a University of Michigan paperback, is entitled *Immanuel Kant, Education*, Ann Arbor, University of Michigan Press, 1960, 121 pp. It is mentioned here because Kant was greatly interested in Basedow's efforts. Others, including Theodor Vogt (1901) and Edward F. Buchner (1908) have also edited Kant's writings on education.

BOSSE, RICHARD, AND J. MEYER, Christian G. *Salzmann's Pädagogische Schriften*, Leipzig, 1886–1888, 2 vols.

FRITSCHE, THEODOR, *J. B. Basedow's Elementarwerk*, Leipzig, 1909, 3 vols., with the famous artist's engravings.

GORING, HUGO, *J. B. Basedow's Ausgewählte Schriften*, Langensalza, 1880, 519 pp.

Chapter 11

PESTALOZZI AND THE NEW ELEMENTARY SCHOOL

Before Pestalozzi the poor were offered a poor education, if any. He found that the children responded with love to his love of them and that his interest in them and in the high mountains, the running streams, in counting and singing games inspired their interest. He discovered, what everybody should have known but did not, that experience is interesting for all children, all people, and the lack of experience is dull. By discovering a new continent of children's inquiries, observations, activities, and experiences he became the Columbus of elementary education. Herbart said it best, "Pestalozzi did not assume that children already had all necessary experience; he provided the means by which they would gain experience"; and experience, so Pestalozzi claimed, should be the foundation of education and the material for further inquiry and increased understanding.

HIS CHILDHOOD

John Henry Pestalozzi (1746–1827) like Martin Planta, a Swiss contemporary, had an Italian ancestor in the male line. He was born in Zürich and his close connection with that city continued even though his work took him away for long periods. He gained a knowledge of the country roundabout early in life. Pestalozzi's grandfather was the pastor of a rural flock and the future teacher often went with him on his visits to the poor of his parish. In this way the boy gained valuable experience and perhaps his life's inspiration.

The mother, who early became a widow, had three brothers who were physicians in outlying areas, but for the sake of her children's education she remained in the city. She may have been too solicitous and protective. Henry did not acquire skill in games or engage in boyish rough-and-tumble play; and besides, his clothes might have been torn and soiled and could not have been easily replaced. Even in his own home he early became acquainted with poverty. Looking back, it seemed to him that he had spent his entire boyhood in the schoolroom and his mother's sitting room. His mature judgment was that he had been too closely confined, too exclusively directed by women; but his judgment often came into conflict with his feelings. In some moods he was apt to place the highest value upon family education. In the first volume of his famous novel *Leonard and Gertrude*, and in many statements elsewhere, he ranked family education and the influence of the home in the forefront of all means of education. His own mother and a pious servant, Barbara, led him to this conclusion.

His family's religious belief was one of the strongest influences on his early life. He was brought up in the old Reformation doctrines and in home piety. When the father died the family remained in the city for both church and school privileges. Thereby, Henry was enabled not only to complete a classical education in the Carolinum, or university, of Zürich but also to grow up in the orthodox church and faith.

YOUNG MANHOOD

The last half of the eighteenth century was a stimulating period in Swiss history, and although Pestalozzi was for many years held to his manuscripts, he longed every day and hour to become active in the world. It was a time when old feudal and guild regulations were loosening their hold on property and industry. The Industrial Revolution was invading the land and political liberalism was growing in Switzerland. Religion was not exempt. Rationalism was entering the churches, both pulpit and pew. Pestalozzi's professors in the Carolinum, especially John Jacob Bodmer, were liberals. The old order was still too strong to be dislodged, but Pestalozzi responded to all these voices, most of all to the humanitarian call for aid to the poor, the prisoners, those bodily or mentally ill, and all the neglected. Most numerous and also most open to improvement were the neglected children of the poor. These were to become Pestalozzi's particular care.

Among his student friends was John Henry Füssli (meaning Littlefoot) who became a painter. One of his celebrated pictures shows a bust of Homer in the background and posed before it Füssli in a brilliant red coat listening to a vigorous exposition by the gray and aged Bodmer, professor of the history of Switzerland, who was no doubt pointing out the inequities of the country's legal system. Another friend was J. Casper Lavater, famed as a writer but more important as a preacher, who was to have an influence on the future educator's life.

Pestalozzi, also, when he was a student was much influenced by the Enlightenment, which carried him away from his family's Reformation piety to a new this-worldly view of humanity, freedom, and culture. Gradually and almost imperceptibly he accepted a natural religion that was valued because it was morally and socially useful. There was no clear and definite break with his past, and even after his marriage he continued his former religious practice; but from the diary of the newly formed family it

John Henry Pestalozzi (1746–1827)

is clear that Pestalozzi more and more found reasons to omit, or to absent himself from, religious exercises. He later came to an only moderately liberal position.

In action and associations, Pestalozzi showed his interest in the people and in responsible government. He joined the Helvetic Society, founded by Bodmer and students—all "patriots" and some, revolutionaries—for the evils that were to bring on the French Revolution were becoming notorious and Zürich was not free from problems. Switzerland, adjoining France and partly French, was affected by every current of passion that swept over Paris.

Pestalozzi began to write in his student days and some of his early work is not uninteresting; but we shall begin with his part in the Helvetic Society's propaganda. They published a weekly paper to which Pestalozzi contributed. This, when the government banned the publication, put a slight mark on him. Soon a young friend, C. Henry Müller, wrote a political document entitled *Farmer's Conversation*, which the authorities considered to be criminal. Müller escaped to Berlin and in time became a noted scholar, no revolutionary! Pestalozzi was arrested on the suspicion that he had aided Müller in his escape. He was twice examined and after several days in jail was released after payment of the costs. If he was innocent, as it appears, the government should have paid him but this, evidently, was not the custom.

Social reform and education were not separate concerns for Pestalozzi. He became a great educator but this was not clear from the beginning. First of all he was a social reformer, deeply aware of harsh laws and the injustices suffered by the people; and at the other end of the social scale, the poverty, drink, crime, disease, unemployment, and unhealthy work in factories. The poor peasants especially enlisted his sympathy. He saw them living on barren wasteland or driven back into huts in the mountains. He was aware of the Industrial Revolution developing in Switzerland, a country rich in mechanical power. The factory tended to treat the worker as a thing, a machine.

The integration of social reform and education in Pestalozzi's life work was not foreseen at the beginning. It has been said that his statement, "All my politics is education," would be equally true if reversed and made to read, "All my education is politics." To raise each of these concerns to the boiling point required time; to get them to coalesce demanded experience.

GETTING SETTLED

When he faced the choice of a vocation, Pestalozzi turned away from the ministry and the law for reasons that are apparent from what we have already noted. Although he had near relatives who were physicians, there is no evidence that he was drawn to medicine. His unexpected decision to become a farmer is only partially explained by the rise of scientific agriculture in his time. Chemical experiments, rotation of crops, and the use of fertilizers were transforming agriculture in England, France, and Switzerland. Pestalozzi conceived the idea that by developing a model farm and cultivating madder, a plant yielding a red dye and some medicines, he could show the country people how to live and make a living on their small farms. This was for several reasons not a good idea. Pestalozzi, a city boy, now a young man, with ideas of social and political reform, went to live for too short a time, part of a year, with a reputable farmer in order to learn the business. A young man in a hurry! On borrowed money he built an overly expensive house and began on land he called Neuhof, or "new farm."

And a farmer needs a wife. After an almost public courtship, Henry Pestalozzi, aged twenty-three, and Anna Schulthess, eight years older, were married on September 30, 1769. Her father was a businessman in Zürich and for reasons that can be surmised he did not want his beautiful Anna to marry plain Henry. His friends, the famous preacher Lavater, already mentioned, and John Heidegger, the mayor of Zürich, interceded for him. Anna took him "for richer, for poorer" and it proved to be for the latter all the way.

They were not blind. During the engagement, a steward on the farm where Henry was studying agriculture with his farmer-adviser, told Anna, "Of his exterior I say nothing, but his heart is right." This was no news to her; but she at once showed him both sides of the coin and added that she kissed his portrait including the pock marks. On a different occasion she said that his large dark eyes both revealed the goodness of his heart and redeemed the plainness of his face. She also tried to get him to dress more carefully and to cultivate the social graces but without marked results.

He was equally direct with her. In a letter he listed his faults as he saw them: improvidence, heedlessness, and haste. He is trying to overcome these but still suffers from them to a degree that will not permit him to hide them from the maiden he loves. He said he was irritable and apt to go to extremes in both praise and blame. He revealed that a common friend, Casper Bluntschli, known as Menalk, on his deathbed warned Pestalozzi that he should always take the advice of a prudent friend before every serious decision.

Now the climax:

I am further bound to confess that I shall place the duties toward my fatherland in advance of those to my wife, and that although I mean to be a tender husband I shall be inexorable even to the tears of my wife if they should ever try to detain me from performing my duties as citizen to the fullest extent. My wife shall be the confidante of my heart. . . . One thing more, my life will not pass without great and important undertakings . . . I shall risk everything to mitigate the misery and need of my countrymen.

NEUHOF

After the failure of his farm experiment Pestalozzi began those educational experiments that were to occupy him, although with a long interruption, nearly to the end of his life. The interruption was caused by another failure in management. He spent the long period, in deepest poverty, writing. He did not greatly value words as compared with deeds or examples. Social, especially economic, reform on these matters was only the pursuit of the shadow of a phantom. Before taking up the pen he carried out one educational experiment with his small son and another with poor children at Neuhof.

The education of his only child Hans Jacob, called Jacobli, meaning "Little Jacob," began when the boy was three and one-half years old. The record is in the form of a biographical diary kept by the father. It is one of the early examples of this instrument for child study. On January 27, 1774, Pestalozzi wrote,

I showed him water, how it briskly ripples down from the mountains; it pleased him. I went a stone's throw further down; he followed me and said to the water: "Wait for me water, I will soon come back." I led him, at once, somewhat further down to the same stream. "Look papa, the water also comes, it comes from up there; it runs away, more up there." We followed the stream of water and I said to him several times: "The water runs down the mountain."

I mentioned several animals to him, for example: "the dog and cat are animals; but not your uncle, Titi, Claus, they are people"; and then I asked him: "Which is the ox, the calf, a mouse, our Claus, the maid, Miss Roth, the elephant, the pastor, the lamb, goat?" and so forth. He answered correctly most times and when he gave a wrong answer it was always connected with his peculiar smile which indicated the purpose not to give the right answer. This deliberate not-giving-the-right-answer seems to be a playful attempt to see how fancy may work and what can be done by individual caprice to make things be what one desires them to be, and so it requires carefully watching.

What the danger was that Pestalozzi seemed to see is not clear. That so small a child would hit on the idea that things could be changed by renaming them seems very doubtful. Such notions are found in primitive religions but they are not invented by children. The education began in the spirit of Rousseau but it soon developed into a lesson. Worse was to follow.

On the very next day Pestalozzi reported,

Spelling was somewhat boring to him because I had firmly resolved to devote a fixed period of time to it and to do this daily. Since he was to occupy himself with this task even against his will, I determined to make him feel the necessity at once the very first time in the firmest possible manner. I gave him no way to escape this exercise without my displeasure and his confinement. Only after the third check did he become patient and, thereafter, we pursued spelling and Latin with jest and liveliness. . . .

Latin also! and at three and one-half years! This may be the correct way, but it was not Rousseau's; it disagreed with Pestalozzi's principle that children and men should exercise their eyes, ears, and hands, rather than their tongues.

The diary continues: "I showed him that wood floats on water and by contrast stones sink to the bottom. In the afternoon he went with the servants to Brunegg." Two days later, "the severity of the working hours was moderated by the fear of his night-time coughing. I taught him the Latin names for most of the outer parts of the head. . . ."

Evidently Pestalozzi had just almost everything to learn about teaching small children. A few days later he taught the boy the names of the counting numbers, 1, 2, 3, and so on, without any exercises to show their use and meaning. When the lad was hopelessly confused, Pestalozzi lamented his own stupidity. "How natural it would have been to teach him the meaning of two with any convenient objects before speaking of three. How naturally he would have learned to count and how seriously I have gone off the path of Nature in my haste."

Pestalozzi was proud of his child's intelligence. He said to the servant, Claus, "Don't you think Jacobli has a good memory?" The reply was, "Yes, but you are overworking him." Pestalozzi responded by going to the opposite extreme and giving up all lessons. The boy was skilful in mimicking people; and he was diplomatic in heading off a possible refusal by a preceding promise; "I will take only one"; "I will not break it"; "I will bring it back, right away." The anxious father did not quite know what to do with such adroitness. More and more he turned to Rousseau; he accepted his principle of freedom but with reservations; he devised ways of going from things and experience to words; he practiced teaching playfully, not joining his own will against the boy's. The record, and probably the experiment, ended in a few weeks.

The same year, 1774, Pestalozzi began at Neuhof the much greater effort to improve the condition of poor, neglected, even derelict children. Both he and Anna were deeply interested in this project and set up a plan of work and study to develop untaught children into useful men and women. Neuhof was to be home, school, and place of industry—the original Pestalozzi Children's Village.

The children carried on spinning, weaving, farm work, and studies. They were expected to produce marketable products. On paper, Pestalozzi was able to convince himself that in two years the establishment could be made self-supporting. This conviction shows that he had not gained practical wisdom from his farming experience. Wisdom would have counseled a slow start with a few carefully selected children; but there were many neglected children growing up in rural slums and too many were admitted until there were eighty. The staff had to be increased in proportion and expenses mounted, some parents took away their children as soon as they were given new clothes, and the early supporters refused to continue their contributions. The experiment had to be discontinued after about five years.

Discouragement and failure were ideas that Pestalozzi refused to contemplate. His deep compassion would not allow him to admit that some of his wards were so defective mentally as to be almost ineducable. After everyone but Pestalozzi saw that the failure was complete and irretrievable,

Pestalozzi Village. (Courtesy of Adelaide Lohner. Photograph by Anita Niesz, Baden, Switzerland.)

he wrote to his friend, the liberal-minded publisher and educator, Isaac Iselin, "Truth, freedom, and the love of mankind have not been vanquished; this is not youthful optimism [he was thirty-three], no, it is the assurance of a man who can carry out the plan, who for this cause would live in a lonely thatched hut on bread and potatoes," for many years.

Those who had supported him did not question the goodness of his heart or the purity of his purpose. They saw that he had little practical sense, judgment, or skill in management. All this and more he admitted with utter frankness in writing to his patrons. Some of these supporters also wrote to Iselin. One said, "Everything including much that is noble is built on sand. He [Pestalozzi] hurries too hastily toward his proposed goal without any preparation and now [June 13, 1778] breath and power fail him."

There was another reason why his support dried up. Some of his contributors were in favor of public institutions for the relief and education of poor children. Pestalozzi argued that such institutions were too lavish, put too little emphasis on work, and did not prepare the poor for poverty. Besides, he claimed that the managers and teachers of public institutions were government officials and did not know the poor, and only those who knew and loved them and truly sympathized with them could help them. He argued that the number of public institutions was wholly inadequate. Private ones were better and if made self-supporting would fully satisfy the need.

There are some questions to be asked about this theory. Should the poor be educated for continued povetry or for self-support in order that they may rise above poverty? It seems that Pestalozzi himself, as has been said, was determined to remain poor. At a later point in his career, a wealthy philanthropist, Emanuel von Fellenberg, offered to support the experimental school that Pestalozzi was developing but naturally he held on to the purse strings. Also, naturally, this would have affected the educational program and Pestalozzi refused. This was the right choice because it led to the greatest educational achievement of his life—but also ultimately to financial and institutional ruin, as we shall see later.

He wanted to help everybody to attain a decent, comfortable poverty through educational institutions that were self-supporting. This leads us to a second question: Could a self-supporting school for the poor offer the best care and education? The answer is clear. A wise administrator would tend to admit only children who could contribute to their own support and perhaps to that of others. Children weak in body or mind, the sick, and the incorrigible would not be admitted or helped. At the other end, our wise administrator would trim expenses to fit his income providing only such supplies, equipment, and help as his resources would buy. Pestalozzi gave slight attention to practical considerations and his disillusioned supporter gave his judgment: that he hurried too heedlessly toward his proposed goals. Pestalozzi once quoted an old saying to the same effect, as follows: "He who looks too far into the distance may easily fall downstairs."

We shall inquire a little into his method of operating: first about the kinds of strays and orphans he took into his home, which he had converted to new uses as a workshop and schoolhouse. One of the most promising pupils was Francis Joseph Husinger, age fourteen, of good capacity, courteous, but very poor. Others were Clara Waser, twelve, a beggar, ignorant, but healthy; Jacob Baggenstoss, fifteen, stupid, just able to spin cotton; two four-year olds who would not be able to contribute to their self-support before the age of eight years; and Maria Bachli, an imbecile. Pestalozzi hoped to find a few more of the latter kind because be belived they could be educated.

He found that it was difficult to keep his beggars and waifs at work; they had been too long accustomed to idleness and vagrancy. Food, sanitation, and health in general were problems. A physician, J. F. Koller, gave medical aid and counsel. The diet was sufficient in quantity but apparently lacking in sufficient protein. Twenty-four of the children were down with measles at the same time but all recovered without bad after-effects. The school was troubled by the itch. Pestalozzi said that when warm weather came he would arrange for regular bathing. Lice and other vermin not mentioned cannot have been wholly absent.

Of the six children mentioned, only the Husinger lad and Clara Waser, perhaps, were good risks. He recklessly admitted too many. At one time when there were between thirty and forty children he had fourteen workers. A better administrator would have used care in his selections, knowing that if he tried to help everybody the whole project would fail and nobody would be helped; but Pestalozzi pitied "poor children hired out to farmers who exploited them, nearly ruining them, body and soul." They came to him, "abused, frightened, undernourished"; but at Neuhof they soon became "cheerful, confiding, civil." He could not refuse them. He was a poor manager but we should not judge him harshly. It was his kind heart, his love for the poorest, and his sympathy with their trials that made him a great educator. He inspired others, smaller and stonier souls, to do what he would not.

We must not forget his desire to educate Maria Bachli and other idiots and imbeciles. The belief that this could be done was not based on an ignorance peculiar to him. He had given some attention to the patients in mental hospitals. On such a visit he had a long conversation with one of the guards. In the issue of his journal *A Swiss Paper* (*Ein Schweizer-Blatt*), for April 25, 1782, he printed a dialogue between himself and a guard in an asylum who furnished a portrait of the mind of a patient.

It was widely believed that education could overcome mental deficiency. Twenty years after the publication just mentioned, a noted physician, Jean Itard, who served the Institution for Deaf Mutes in Paris, undertook such an experiment. The patient or pupil was a "wild boy" found running about in the woods without human associates and unable to speak a word. He was doubtless an idiot or imbecile but he was regarded as "a child of nature" like those mentioned by Comenius in Chapter VI of *The Great Didactic*. Doctor Itard after four years gave up his exercises because the results were insignificant. It is now held that ineducability is the substance and evidence of mental deficiency; it is what the words mean. This view was not held in Pestalozzi's time.

Pestalozzi in writing to a rich patron of his Neuhof Institute to confess his faults and mistakes was completely frank; and he was outspoken in defending his serious convictions. He said the Institute must not prepare children for leisure, pleasure, or plenty, but must accustom them to active, skilful, and constant work. The children must learn not to be afraid of the damp weaving cellar, the cotton dust, the bad smells. . . . He added, "I will avoid further details." The sciences of hygiene and sanitation were almost unknown. The Institute or school, he claimed, must be like their later dwellings. "A hard bed, alone or with others, this must be all alike to them. Noble sir! I know your kind heart finds this hard doctrine. I also desire their welfare but I find it in their preparation for hard living-conditions." He could be firm, as we see here; but surely, one thinks, he was wrong in settling for so low a standard of living.

We already know the result. The Institute for the poor had to be closed for want of support. His philanthropic friends in Zürich, Basel, and other places saw no prospect of ultimate success. This second failure and the closing of all roads leading toward his goal plunged him into dark discouragement. He ceased to attend the annual meetings with his friends of the Helvetic Society. His self-confidence was shaken and the confidence of others in his administrative capacity vanished. A few constant friends, especially Isaac Iselin of Basel and John Henry Füssli, tried to encourage him. It was to be twenty years before he secured another opportunity to direct an institution. Meanwhile he won a great but temporary success as a writer.

AUTHORSHIP

When the Institute had to be closed, Henry Füssli advised him to take up the pen. He had recently learned that a journal article he had read and admired had been written by Pestalozzi. Up to that time most of Pestalozzi's writing had been directed to the promotion of his practical projects, and authorship as a career lay entirely outside of and was contrary to his purpose and desire. This man whose written words were to fill many volumes had a fine contempt for talkers and writers and their accumulations of unused and probably useless knowledge. Instead of dealing in words he wanted to help people, to help them directly, especially the most helpless and most depraved children for whom no others cared. Except as an aid in promoting his humanitarian aims, fame had no value for him; but he became famous as a storyteller.

We may say that fame overtook him in 1781 when he wrote *Leonard and Gertrude*, "A Book for the People." It was a combined family idyll and problem novel. Like his plans and reports on the economy of his Neuhof Institute for poor children, it was writen for a practical purpose. The Swiss and Germans who read it loved Gertrude, hated and cursed the corrupt village bailiff, and admired the Junker who set matters right when shown how wrong they had come to be. People wept and laughed by turns as they read but they cared nothing for the purpose of the story. In that age of the many-volumed novel, Pestalozzi was encouraged to continue; he added a second part in 1783, a third in 1785, and a fourth and last in 1787. With every addition there was a further decline in public interest. Sociology and schooling had crowded out the love and laughter. Rousseau had been able to gain wide applause for a so-called novel with hardly a crumb of romance but this was perhaps beyond Pestalozzi's powers and certainly outside his design. He was a social reformer.

Pestalozzi seems to have changed his plan while composing *Leonard and Gertrude*. In the early parts, Gertrude was the only teacher; there was no school. The instruction was combined with the children's work and play, and was entirely oral. Gertrude was in no hurry to teach reading and writing but was careful to cultivate the ability to speak because, she said, it is of little use to read and write if one cannot speak plainly and to the point, because reading and writing are only an artifical sort of speech. In her custom of having children practice the pronunciation of syllables we may see the first elements of Pestalozzi's method. So in counting the two rows each of five panes in the window we may have the germ of his *table of units* arranged in groups of ten units each.

We have said that the instruction was incidental to their activities. They counted the threads while spinning and the turns of the reel as they wound the yard into a skein. Gertrude taught them without seeming to do so, for she gave her instruction as there was need during the meals, work, worship, and play of family life. Her verbal instruction seemed to be a part of her practical activity. Thus the children sang morning and evening hymns that they had learned by imitation; and they repeated the Bible verses she read or recited for them.

In the later parts there was a schoolmaster who tried to model his school on Gertrude's plan, but he was of a very different spirit and the school became formal. He was a retired army lieutenant who gave orders and, although kind, demanded obedience. This, it will be recalled, was also what Pestalozzi had done with little Jacob. The lieutenant began by classifying the pupils into those who did not know their letters, those who knew some words, and last, those who had learned to read. So Gertrude after all taught reading! In addition, all were to learn to write and work sums, skills that formerly were taught, according to Pestalozzi, only to children of the wealthy. Girls were taught to sew and spin by a special teacher, a woman who also looked after the children's hair, clothes, and general cleanliness. The schoolroom was to be clean, windows whole, everything shipshape.

The extended studies and the formality were not the chief differences between Gertrude's home education and the lieutenant's system. The chief change was a spiritual one. The lieutenant was a worldly wise exponent of rationalism. Gertrude was a deeply pious and saintly woman of childlike faith. Was she perhaps modeled on Pestalozzi's mother? Paul Wernle has asked another question, "Was the faith of Gertrude also Pestalozzi's when he was writing the First Part?" It is unlikely. He began with the religious views and feelings of his home and the older people of his youth and gradually as he wrote substituted progress for Providence. His schoolmaster was a Realist. He no longer taught the catechism; the village and especially the old schoolmaster called the new school pagan. Once the school had been an appendage to the church, the schoolmaster a pastor's assistant; but these relations were reversed under the new order of things.

Pestalozzi was not happy with the result. In a second edition he made definite changes in Part Three and elsewhere. The lieutenant took on some of the qualities of Gertrude. Religion was again considered necessary in order to curb selfishness and the pastor plays a more active and vital role.

OTHER EARLY WORKS

As a writer, Pestalozzi was best in stories such as *Leonard and Gertrude* about the villagers whom he had learned to know from his grandfather or in his farming operations and his Neuhof Institute. He had a homely natural wit that served him well in his fables in *Figures from My ABC Book* and his journal the *Schweizer-Blatt*, or *Swiss Paper*, often translated as *Swiss News*. This was not a newspaper but a weekly filled with ideas, opinions, stories, and accounts of social ills.

Pestalozzi in another dimension felt a divine vocation to seek clarity in a philosophy of life and to teach the world the true answers to such questions as: "What is man and what is his destiny? What is my own nature and my destiny?" In the *Evening Hours of a Hermit*, composed near the time when his Institute for the poor was closing, Pestalozzi offered his own view of man and man's development. He asked himself, "What is man; what are his needs; what elevates and strengthens and what degrades and weakens him?" The answer was: truth, not all truth and knowledge, but the truth that is applicable to his condition. This truth is needed by all, by the shepherds of the people and by those who dwell in the humblest cabins. It is found not in faraway places but in the heart of man himself and in the everyday relations and duties of life.

That thought led him to a polemic in the manner of Carlyle against the pursuit of an abstract and indefinite knowledge of things in general. Useful knowledge is truth that will apply to the concrete problems of life. The book of nature and human nature deals with the actual conditions of man and schooling, and abstractions and generalities will merely mislead the pupil. He declared that the usual school curriculum was artificial and would not help people living in this century; much that was taught was confused as well as useless. He demanded a simple, elementary course that would serve the simple, innocent person at his work, in his family, and in society.

Thus Pestalozzi passes beyond Rousseau. The word *society* is the key to the next step. According to Pestalozzi man is by nature social. The family, community, and nation are natural groups. "Man, you do not live on earth for yourself alone," he said. The domestic life of man provides the model and cultivation for life in the larger society. The father furnishes the model for the prince, the brothers for the citizen, the family for the organization of the state.

The theme can be gathered from the *Evening Hours*. The *Hermit*, by examining nature and human nature, tried to understand man's destiny, here and hereafter. He warned against the word lore and facile verbalizing of the philosophers and other people from the schools, and he demanded a fresh inquiry unsullied by ancient error. By "waiting upon nature" and studying "the simple, innocent man" he found that all human beings are fundamentally alike.

He wrote a prize essay. The Economic Society of Berne was disturbed by the rapid increase in public and private expenditures for goods and services formerly considered unnecessary. They set the prize-essay subject as, "To What Extent Is It Desirable To Limit Luxurious Expenditures in a Small Commercial State?" There were twenty-eight competitors, and the prize was divided between Pestalozzi and a Professor Meister.

Pestalozzi argued that the manufacture of luxuries increases employment, develops new, refined skills, broadens domestic and foreign markets, and the products can be taxed. He admitted that there were limits to his program but claimed that sumptuary laws did not provide the remedy. They create ill-will and cannot be enforced. Education beginning in the home, self-restraint, and patriotism are better controls.

Another essay of those years, when the American Revolutionary War was in progress, was entitled "On the Freedom of My Fatherland." He said freedom and civic duty are complementary. The State assigns duties but the government is for the people and not conversely. Different countries have different laws and rights but only an enlightened people can either secure or safeguard its freedom. The spirit of freedom rests on the dignity of man, and free constitutions rest on the patriotism of their citizens, on their self-conquest, self-sacrifice, and love of their fellow citizens. Habits, customs, and traditions, he considered as important as laws. In the spring of 1782 he printed an anonymous contribution to the effect that America had won her independence.

Another work of this time must not be omitted for it reveals his interests before the time when "all his politics became education." In the eighteenth century so many unwedded mothers destroyed their children at birth that the practice became a public issue in many countries. The practice was related to economic conditions, factory work, and harsh laws against illegitimate sex relations. Great writers including Schiller wrote on the subject. A prize was offered in Germany, and Pestalozzi intended to compete but his inquiry continued too long and resulted in a considerable book *Legislation and Infant Murder*.

As a by-product of this investigation he published his views on the proper treatment of criminals (*Swiss Paper*, May 30, 1782). Those views in summary form follow:

1. The offender should not be lightly discharged before being improved. Former criminals must be directed toward a regular law-abiding life.
2. Offenders when punished and released must be provided with employment and accepted by society without prejudice.
3. No arrested person should be discharged without a thorough investigation of his conduct.
4. No one is to be imprisoned for an indefinite period unless the individual is a danger to the State. No one must be deprived of hope.
5. All prisoners must be on the same footing, none to be treated particularly harshly or kindly.
6. The children of convicts must be cared for and educated by the State.

It seems that Pestalozzi was opposed to the death penalty; but this is only an opinion.

We have shown something of the breadth of Pestalozzi's interests—something but not all of it—before he became almost solely an educator. He wrote on many topics for his weekly paper, on epidemic diseases, quack doctors, mental hospitals and their patients, servant girls and their trials, and even on land values and farming. Now and then he wrote and inserted a story. He had become a publicist but his deepest interest was always in the people and especially in the poor and helpless. These were his people and he belonged to them; the rest could look out for themselves.

STANZ EPISODE

Early in the 1790s, Pestalozzi wrote *Yes and No*, a political tract on the French Revolution in which he blamed both sides; and, also, an Inquiry into the *Course, Nature, and Development of the Human Race*, in which he admitted that man is often controlled by circumstances. However, he claimed that by education he may become able to control circumstances. He again transcends Rousseau.

He wrote some smaller pieces in which he dealt with the struggle that was tearing apart the French people and nation. He was always a liberal, never a radical. In 1792, along with Joseph Priestley and others, Pestalozzi was made an honorary citizen of France. He told the older Fellenberg that women when they met him crossed themselves, but he reminded his aristocratic friend that the author of *Leonard and Gertrude* had in that book proved, to each and all, his friendly regard for a benign aristocracy. This was also indicated by his repeated efforts to gain support for his projects from princes and emperors and by the adoption of the Pestalozzian system in "benevolent despotisms" such as Prussia.

When the French invaded strife-torn Switzerland they, in severe fighting in the forest Cantons, left many homeless people and several hundred fatherless children. Pestalozzi was on the side not of the French but of those who made terms with the French. The new Swiss government sent him to Stanz in the devastated region at his own request as schoolmaster. In the buildings of a war-damaged monastery he took care, with the help of a single housekeeper, of a flock of poor orphans, about eighty at the high point in enrollment. They varied in age and previous economic status, but most of them were destitute and ignorant. They had to be persuaded to cooperate and, even more than at Neuhof, Pestalozzi had to meet the interference of a hostile population.

Without equipment at first and very little at any time he combined labor and learning in his program. The domestic economy provided some work and for learning he developed oral exercises in the spelling of syllables and words. The experiment lasted only six months, for the French army was driven back by the Austrians who reoccupied the village in June, 1799. Only toward the end did he have books and a few spinning wheels. According to Pestalozzi the children became cooperative, industrious, and were much improved morally; they also learned to use their minds in writing and thinking. The judgment of others was less favorable. Living conditions must have been very unsanitary; and this cannot be charged wholly against Pestalozzi.

At both Neuhof and Stanz, Pestalozzi showed what he was, not a mere teacher, but a character-builder, whose purpose it was to "Train up a child in the way he should go." In Germany they consider him one of the great *erzieher*, or molders of character. If our language permitted, we might call him a great upbringer. He was now to become also a schoolmaster striving to find better methods of teaching small children.

THE METHOD

Worn out by his nerve-shattering ordeal, Pestalozzi was given a brief vacation high in the mountains overlooking one of his country's most beautiful lakes and valleys. It was fortunate that the ordeal had not lasted longer, but he recovered quickly for he was still in the prime of life and had a sound physique. After resting for three weeks he could rest no longer. He was so eager to try some of his ideas on a group of children that he could no longer enjoy the pleasures of the mountain resort.

He had the support of the government, now more than ever, but they had some difficulty in finding an appropriate place for him. At last, near the end of July, 1799, he was installed as assistant to a cobbler-schoolmaster who had charge of the poorest children of Burgdorf, a village of Canton Berne. This may seem to have been an appropriate place, because his chief interest was in the improvement of schools for the poor, but the shoemaker interfered with his investigations. He was transferred to other schools and in a few years, having secured some assistants, Herman Krüsi, J. Georg Tobler, and J. Christoff Buss, he was enabled to conduct an institute of his own. The government sent a commission to study his program and they made a highly favorable report. For this commission, Pestalozzi prepared "An Account of the Method," before October, 1800. This was the first broad statement of his views on primary education; and most of its ideas and some of its language are repeated in his more formal book, *How Gertrude Teaches Her Children* (1801).

In his "Acount of the Method" we read,

I am trying to psychologize the instruction of mankind . . . to bring it into harmony with the nature of my mind. . . . I start from no positive form of teaching but simply ask what I must do to give a single child all the knowledge and practical skill he needs. . . . I think, to gain this end, the human race needs exactly the same thing as the single child.

All forms of instruction, he wrote, must be made to agree with those eternal laws by which the human mind is raised from sense impressions to clear ideas. He said he had tried to simplify all elements of human knowledge according to those laws. "Sense impression of Nature is the only true foundation of human instruction because it is the only true foundation of human knowledge." The art of instruction involves the use of speech, drawing, writing, reckoning, and measuring.

The "Account of the Method" was solely Pestalozzi's composition, for it was prepared before he had any assistants. Although it was not published during his lifetime, Niederer who gave it to the press in 1828, seems not to have altered it. It contains the germ of the more extended treatment of elementary method in his *How Gertrude Teaches* to which we have referred. This book has nothing to do with the heroine of his popular novel, and the title was apparently chosen because it was thought attractive.

How Gertrude Teaches continues the account of Pestalozzi's investigation of elementary methods and his opinion of the work he was doing. The condition of Europe about this time after the Revolution greatly disturbed Pestalozzi. At the century's end, wars and rumors of further wars, devastation, and numbers of hungry and homeless people, including many child refugees and the associated social disorders, seemed to him to be the result of bad education. The poor were ignorant and suppressed; the rich miseducated, greedy, and cruel; the schools and the want of schools, both together, separated people into hostile classes; and everywhere there was a lack of Christian faith, and hope, and love.

Education had taken the wrong tack long before and especially in the fifteenth century when printing developed and books became cheap. The school had become "the house of the book"; this was a great mistake. Thereafter the young were taught words they could not understand instead of live and usable knowledge, gained from experience firsthand. This was one of Pestalozzi's early and constant convictions. The second mistake was made at the Reformation when the catechism was made the chief means as well as the end and object of schooling. Children were considered educated when they were able to repeat the abstract language of church doctrine. In higher education the attention given to the ancient languages led to a similar error, the substitution of books for experience. Pestalozzi proposed to marry the school to life.

It was Pestalozzi's original idea to unite learning and labor, first at Neuhof and also in *Leonard and Gertrude*, with the mother as teacher of spinning and housework, of the school arts, and of manners, morals, and piety. But in the later parts of the same story he brought in a school, perhaps because most families and mothers were not as he had described them. Family education could not become general. At Stanz he faced scores of unkempt children of various ages and conditions. For much of the time he had, as already noted, hardly any equipment. He was able to develop cooperation and attention and to teach spelling, although by wasteful oral methods, number work, and other skills. His chief success lay in civilizing the half-wild children.

At Burgdorf he was for the first time put in charge of a conventional school with class-teaching. He devoted his efforts to the development of better methods of instilling the ordinary and some then extraordinary school arts and knowledge. *How Gertrude Teaches* was, as already shown, the record. It also contains some personal information and impressions, as most of his books do. As his nature dictated, he proceeded bit by bit, empirically.

Because an abstract verbalism seemed to be a major defect of the schools he tried to provide for basic experience involving real things that children could see, hear, and handle, but especially could see. This led him to the use of sense impressions and, based on these, lessons in language, number, geography, and other subjects. School journeys were an excellent means to bring children into contact with natural and fabricated things. Trips had been used before, as by Martin Planta in his own Switzerland and by the philanthropinists in general. But they were expensive in time and money. Pestalozzi, therefore, often turned to common objects, as in teaching children to count the threads in spinning or the window panes in their room. When the objects were not readily available he turned to drawings, pictures, models, and even descriptions. Once when he was using a picture of a window a child asked, "Couldn't we study the window itself?" The answer is not recorded.

In his effort to develop a science of teaching Pestalozzi accepted, as anyone would, those principles that formed the common fund of knowledge. One of these accepted principles was the doctrine that mind and body mature in gradual stages as a plant grows in the garden. Sir Thomas Elyot and others had used the same figure. Pestalozzi emphasized the gradualness, the imperceptible steps, of mental growth. It was necessary, he believed, to make every step in learning secure so that no gaps would remain; and this led him to the endless repetition of spelling and number exercises. We now know that the child learns by discovery and insight as well as by slow accumulation from patient practice. Pestalozzi was an impatient experimenter apt to generalize too quickly. As we noted before, he was a man in a hurry.

The law of the daily accumulation of knowledge in a progression without leaps may contradict another of his discoveries. He held that instruction should follow the steps in the original development of the subject he was teaching. Thus he described the steps that mankind must have taken in creating language, or articulate speech, and he proposed to repeat these steps in teaching children to speak. This is a form of the *culture-epochs theory*. The culture-epochs theory is the doctrine that each person in his growth parallels the history of mankind in passing through such epochs as the primitive, savage, nomadic, tribal, early civilized, and so forth. Now by his account there were great gaps in the evolution of language; but in teaching he began with the vowels, to which he added consonants to form syllables, joined syllables to form words, and combined words into sentences. Considered as stages in the evolution of speech this is highly improbable and, of course, Pestalozzi knew nothing about the history of language on which he quite inconsistently based his practice.

The law of physical distance is another false step, but of a different kind. The problem was that of securing clearness in the observation of objects. The law said that clarity of vision varies with the distance of the object from the eyes.

Our learning grows from confusion to definiteness; from definiteness to plainness; and from plainness to perfect clearness. But Nature in her progress towards this development is constant to the great law that makes the clearness of my knowledge depend upon the nearness or distance of the object in touch with my senses. . . .

This is from the sixth letter of *How Gertrude Teaches*.

There is certainly a proper distance for clear vision or audition. For sight it varies with the light, size, and color of the object, the structure of the viewer's eyes, and other factors as well as the distance. The catalogue could be made much longer and similar lists prepared for the other senses. With circumstances so varied and indefinite it is inappropriate to speak of a law.

Although we must reject this law of physical distance, the careful consideration of the conditions that affect observation is not to be neglected; it is the key to his method. In the account of his method he often admits that what had been considered advances were later seen as errors. It is hard to quarrel with one who is so ready to admit his mistakes; and we accept his claim in a note in the eighth letter of *How Gertrude Teaches*. He said, ". . . the ABC of *Anschauung* [observation] appears to be the only essential and true method of instruction for the just appreciation of the forms of things. But until now, this method has been entirely neglected and ignored. . . ." Perhaps not entirely. *Anschauung* is an observation of things that yield a clear mental image and true knowledge of things observed. We saw an example of it when Jacobli was shown the water running down the mountain. It is more than looking; perhaps looking with care and with a purpose is what should be said.

Like Francis Bacon in his account of scientific method so Pestalozzi, in the method of instruction, paid too little attention to the purpose of the learner. It is now also clear that numerous methods can be used in science and in elementary teaching and should in all cases be methods promoting discovery. As the scientist seeks to discover new truth, the child should be encouraged to discover truth new to him. Pestalozzi insisted that there is not only *Anschauung* but also *an art* of *Anschauung*. We may admit this and may call it skill in presenting things for the various educational purposes. Since 1801 the instrumental equipment for such presentation has increased so greatly that it is no longer useful to consider the matter in his terms. He was, however, a pioneer who in this area helped to make our schools.

Observation provides the matter for speech, and speaking must and, therefore, always does precede reading. Teachers have taken up this idea and have made much of observation, speech, and mental maturity as preparation for reading. This phase of primary education is important, but it has often been extended beyond need.

In his search for the elements of the art of speaking, Pestalozzi came upon three that seemed to apply to all objects. These are language, form, and number (Letter VI of *How Gertrude Teaches*). Before we can speak of an object we must know its name, and Pestalozzi, at this point, introduced a long list of names that children were to learn as preparation for use later, an error into which his formalism led him. He chose these three: language, form, and number because they alone seemed to apply to all objects.

We shall admit the need for language if we are to refer to objects, or to qualities, or even to feelings and other mental states. We shall not make an exception in the case of gestures or mere pointing. These are also a form of language. For communication, language is necessary; and in the present context it is especially necessary in directing observation.

The view about form and number is questionable. They are not applicable to all objects. A swarm of bees has no determinate form or readily ascertainable number of components. Wordsworth's daffodils as seen in an aerial photograph would probably show an indefinite distribution of form and they, like the bees, could be actually but not usefully counted. The educational uses of form, number, and measurement are great but limited; on the other hand, color, if we include the grays, is more universal than clearly distinguishable form. The position of an object is often important and so is its variability. But in all this we are not questioning what Pestalozzi was trying to do but only his statement of it.

Even if all the preceding criticisms, and several other possible ones, are valid we must not miss the main point of Pestalozzi's quest. The main point is that his intuitions, namely (1) that experience must precede or accompany speech; (2) that language is a means of thought; and (3) that mere words without experience or thought are only "chatter," which interfere with real education, are correct and basic in teaching and learning. In this as in other cases, Pestalozzi succeeded in the discovery of an educational problem of great importance. How much experience, of what kinds, shall the school provide? The full answer is not yet known. But Herbart, Froebel, Dewey and others who followed in the footsteps of Pestalozzi have provided important leads.

NEW STUDIES

Geography, nature study, and, more generally, science can be regarded as studies supplementary to Pestalozzi's language, number, and form as the elements of knowledge. We have already noted that there are other elements beside the three. Geography interested Pestalozzi particularly because of its social content and he gave the study a new definition. He said geography is the study of the earth as the home and workshop of man. The earth provides the materials and the forces such as heat, sunlight, and gravity by which man works and lives. This concept, it seems, was new and it inspired the labors of a great geographer and the founder of modern geography, Karl von Ritter. It seems that the "old geography" studied directions and distances from the map—mail-carrier geography. Rousseau in *Émile* taught this kind of geography; so did the Hills at Hazelwood and Herbart, whom we will meet in the next chapter.

Karl von Ritter (1779–1859) was in early life a tutor in a nobleman's family and he was accustomed to take his pupils, William and Alexander von Humboldt, on long journeys for their education, health, and recreation and his own as well, we may believe. On two such tours he visited Pestalozzi at Yverdon, the school to which Pestalozzi moved after Burgdorf and a few months with Fellenberg. When Ritter visited Yverdon the school was at its height. On his first visit he stayed for a week examining every phase of the institution. A few years later he found the scope of the school much expanded, but the same "powerful, original, and indefatigable" assistants were in charge of the different departments.

"The good old Pestalozzi," he wrote, "remains [although in his sixties] still a youth in heart and spirit, full of fire and restlessness, his wife the model of womanly purity, modesty, and good-heartedness, cultivated and refined. The freedom which prevails here brings people together at once . . . at supper I had to sit between 'father and mother' Pestalozzi while all our friends sat in nearby chairs for the simple meal." Cheerful conversation and sallies of wit made time pass rapidly and pleasantly.

The Institute, Ritter said, had grown to "colossal proportions, so that the founder can no longer look after all the interests centered here"; but when we learn the numbers we see that this account merely shows how our estimates of school enrollments have changed in a century and a half. Yverdon had one hundred and fifty pupils, about forty more young people who also helped with the instruction, and possibly twenty-five full-time teachers, such as Krüsi, Tobler, Buss, and others. There was also a girls' school and two schools for teacher-preparation. Pestalozzi explained to Ritter that he had a very imperfect preparation in language, arithmetic, and other school arts and that his head teachers would laugh "if I should say that I was their teacher. . . . I am merely the first mover here; others must bring into active use what I think out; I am merely an instrument in the hands of Providence." Ritter added that this was entirely true but that "without Pestalozzi none of this would have existed." Ritter wrote,

> He is in a measure without a language, for he speaks neither pure French nor pure German, and yet he is the soul of society, whether in earnest or sportive talk. His morning service, the prayer, and the address to the pupils are very effective. He is loved and honored like a father.

One of Pestalozzi's pupils, Roger de Guimps, has recorded Ritter's testimony to the educator's concept of geography. "Pestalozzi," we read, "knew less geography than a child in one of our primary schools, yet it was from him that I [Ritter] gained my chief knowledge of this science, for it was in listening to him that I first conceived the idea of the natural method."

We learn from another pupil, Vullimein, how geography was studied at Yverdon: not mainly from books in the early lessons. He wrote, "The first elements of geography were taught us from the land itself. We were first taken to a narrow valley not far from Yverdon, where the river Buron runs." After studying the valley in general and then in greater detail, they took clay and in their workroom in the school made a complete model of it. "Only when our relief was finished were we shown the map"; and then map and relief served as checks each upon the other. Rousseau had proposed that the teacher should begin with local or home geography, but Pestalozzi made improvements on both the method and the purpose of earth study that went beyond the suggestion in *Émile*.

Pestalozzi also taught lists of facts about the earth and sets of geographical locations. Thus he ran into formalism. He began with large cities, rivers, and other features and added less important ones to these. The second phase of his plan was the study of the earth in connection with the cultural history of man. This was the idea that inspired Ritter. One is surprised that it was entirely new to him. The teaching processes, the school journeys, exploration, and modeling were not entirely new. Such ideas were not entirely new but were more often treated in books than used in schools. The rural school of that day, with children of all ages from six to sixteen years, without equipment or money, was restricted to work with book, pencil, and chalk.

Arithmetic was a second subject to which Pestalozzi gave special attention. This could be taught with a book, paper, and the blackboard. It fitted ideally into the small school with pupils of different ages; it could be taught individually or in classes; and in those times its value for formal discipline was considered very great. Pestalozzi laid great stress on the mental manipulation of numbers without writing them at all. This was called mental arithmetic and was practiced in classes separate from written arithmetic; many pupils recited in both subjects on the same day. This excrescence disappeared from American schools in about 1900; but it is still useful to gain a ready skill in handling numbers both on paper and "in the head." Of the "new mathematics" as a logical system nothing was known. Arithmeitc was calculation and problem-solving.

Pestalozzi came to his views on teaching slowly over long periods of time. We remember the mistakes he made in teaching his son to count. He and his successors made great advances in the sources from which they drew their arithmetic problems. Until the nineteenth century practically all arithmetic taught in schools was business arithmetic; and the subject was rarely taught in primary schools. It was studied by adults who were or would be employed in commerce. This had not always been the case. From the ancient Babylonians we gained our measures of short periods of time—sixty seconds made a minute and so on. Plato (*Laws*, vii, 20–21) has the Athenian say that all freemen should know the elements of numbers and their use in games, sports, and household and military matters. Such sources were used by Pestalozzi and he helped to simplify arithmetic and to make it interesting to children.

INFLUENCE

The latter years of Pestalozzi were not his happiest ones, although that period and the following one after his death became the time of his greatest influence. We previously saw him about 1800 in his government-aided school at Burgdorf. He was no longer a solitary teacher but had gathered a staff of assistants. The first one was Hermann Krüsi, a village schoolmaster, who brought his flock and joined them to Pestalozzi's class. He was self-educated and came to learn the art of teaching. He succeeded so well that after Pestalozzi's retirement he became principal of a Swiss normal school at Gais.

Pestalozzi and Comenius earlier were concerned with the loving care of small children and their instruction, and these two opened the way for Froebel and the kindergarten. They were not the only, nor the first, to deal with the infant years, but they were most explicit and practical. To say that they opened the way to the nursery school and kindergarten seems just about correct.

At Burgdorf, Pestalozzi began to acquire his European reputation; many visitors came, some perhaps merely to see him and some to learn. Georg H. L. Nicolovius (1767–1839), who was to become a prominent school administrator in Prussia, met Pestalozzi while he was still at Neuhof and was deeply impressed. He told his experience to the aged Kant who urged him to work for school improvement in Prussia. This he did;

and he became instrumental in sending many young Prussians to study the work and aspirations of Pestalozzi. Others, Johann F. Herbart and Gottlieb Anton Gruner, came to Burgdorf. Froebel was connected with Gruner's Pestalozzian school at Frankfurt, but he came for a long visit and study period at Yverdon a few years later.

As the Burgdorf school grew it became more expensive; and when the building was requisitioned for other uses, Pestalozzi and the wealthy Emanuel Fellenberg formed a plan to carry on their work together. Fellenberg, the son of Pestalozzi's old friend Daniel Fellenberg, was engaged on a plan of vocational education for poor boys. The scheme resembled the Neuhof experiment, but Pestalozzi was now working on the reform of the common school. This was only one difference that hampered cooperation. It required only a few months to convince the principals that they could not agree. Even Fellenberg, although a good manager, so expanded his institutions that he dissipated his large fortune.

The government gave Pestalozzi a life lease on a castle and grounds at Yverdon and there he and many new and old assistants developed the methods and studies described here. More and more, others carried on the work and Pestalozzi became the titular head. He remained the chaplain and spiritual guide. More and more also, dissension in the staff made the school something other than an example of good school administration.

Before its decline, Yverdon became a magnet for visitors. Pestalozzi's ideas spread far and wide in Germany and became so popular in the largest German state that the program was called the Prussian-Pestalozzian system. In Great Britain the new schools helped to overcome the deficiencies of the monitorial system and to develop the infant schools.

The Pestalozzian movement came to the United States in a series of waves, but the first one was quite weak. A disciple of Pestalozzi and an assistant in his school, Joseph Neef, established a school near Philadelphia and in 1808 wrote a book on the *Plan and Method of Pestalozzi*. He also taught at New Harmony, Indiana, and other places, but his influence is not easily traced. There will be more on Neef in the following chapter.

A second wave developed after 1820, with Warren Colburn's *Intellectual Arithmetic*, using the ideas of Pestalozzi and rose higher through the work of George B. Emerson and Horace Mann. Lowell Mason of Boston taught music on the Pestalozzian plan. The object-teaching movement after the Civil War can be considered a third Pestalozzian wave. Actually, none of these efforts approached the spirit or the vitality of the master's ideals. The kindergarten had the spirit but not the vitality or intellectual elements of those ideals. We have, doubtless, in some ways gone beyond the great Swiss teacher; and this may suggest a comparison between Pestalozzi and John Dewey; but Dewey was far more interested in the work of Froebel, especially in his use of materials, than in Pestalozzi. We shall continue the story of Pestalozzi's influence in the following chapter.

SUMMARY

In his advanced studies, Pestalozzi heard enough criticism of social injustice to arouse a keen interest in reform. The "new schools" at home and abroad might have led him to adopt school reform as the first and best means to improve the condition of the poor, but this did not occur. His earliest efforts misfired; and after a few days in jail, he chose a positive means—model farming—to lead the rural poor to a better life. When he failed again, he stumbled, as one may say, into teaching at his farm home at Neuhof. The idea was to teach the most neglected children work skills and work habits, health care with cleanliness, and basic literacy. Led astray by his deep sympathy for the poor and his great confidence in the support of the rich, this work-study-play-and-bathe school had to be closed.

It will not do to say that with the advice of a practical assistant or steward, he might have succeeded. Later in his career he had such an arrangement with Emanuel Fellenberg, but Pestalozzi would not continue it. He would not be practical and cautious. He chose to remain poor because only so could he understand and help the most helpless.

For many years he was a writer and practicing journalist. He had a great success with the problem novel *Leonard and Gertrude*, in which a school for little children was a leading institution. In the several parts and versions of the story, the school passed through many transformations or experimental patterns. With the mass of Pestalozzi's writings during a period of twenty years, we shall not deal. His next opportunity to work with actual children came at Stanz in central Switzerland, where a group of war orphans were collected. Pestalozzi offered himself as housefather, mother, nurse, and teacher. Henceforth for a quarter-century he was to be a teacher and educator.

As an educator he wrote and spoke about the teacher, his teaching or method, and what was or should have been taught. At an earlier period he had written about his teaching of his own son; and, absolutely honest as he was, he did not conceal his early mistakes after he became sophisticated and skilled.

Soon after Stanz, the fame of Pestalozzi began to attract assistants, some of them skilled in music, drawing, or other arts, thus expanding the course of study. Pestalozzi directed his efforts largely to the improvement of content and method in the basic school skills: reading, spelling, arithmetic, nature study, and geography. He tried to overcome the great fault of schools, mere verbalism, by introducing concrete materials and direct experience. His book *How Gertrude Teaches Her Children* is a record of his growth in practical schoolwork. In later years the assistants did the teaching and Pestalozzi devoted himself to the religious and moral cultivation of the children.

QUESTIONS

1. Why did the rich and powerful, as well as the poor, applaud *Leonard and Gertrude*?
2. Why did Pestalozzi change his methods of teaching from Neuhof, to Stanz, to Burdorf and Yverdon?
3. Is there a serious conflict between Pestalozzi's views on the nature and purpose of geography and history in education? Can it be resolved?
4. In what chief respects has education changed since the eighteenth century?
5. Why did Pestalozzi call *Émile* "a dream book"?
6. Why was Pestalozzi's program quickly introduced into German countries?
7. Why was Pestalozzi's program slowly and imperfectly assimilated in the United States?
8. Why, with Pestalozzi's high opinion of the educational gifts of women and mothers, did he employ only men as assistants?
9. After Neuhof, Pestalozzi wrote, "Truth, freedom, and the love of mankind have not been vanquished. . . ." What did he mean and what does it show?
10. How do you evaluate Pestalozzi's proposal for the treatment of convicts?
11. Switzerland warmed up to its great educator very slowly. Now the Swiss are engaged in publishing every scrap of his writing. Who was right?

NOTES AND SOURCES

Two centuries have not dimmed the fame of the great and versatile Pestalozzi but have spread and increased it. The most ambitious effort to make him as fully known as possible is that of publishing *Pestalozzi, Sämtliche Werke*, under the editorial direction of three famous scholars: Artur Buchenau, Edward Spranger, and Hans Stettbacher. The publisher, W. de Gruyter, Berlin and Leipzig, brought out the first volume in 1927. Volume 21 contains the writings of the year 1809. Some of the original promoters are no longer living.

Another recent collection of Pestalozzi's writings in a beautiful set of eight volumes has been edited by Paul Baumgarten, *Heinrich Pestalozzi, Werke*, Zürich, Erlenbach, Rotappel Verlag, 1944–49. It has the most important writings and excellent notes.

Kate Silber's *Pestalozzi, The Man and His Work*, London, Routledge and Kegan Paul, 1965, marked the appearance of a new and excellent life of Pestalozzi and is an event in the history of education. The German edition was published at Heidelberg, in 1957. The translation was made by the author. There are many older lives and a few are mentioned subsequently.

Escher Hermann, Editor, *Pestalozzi and His Times, A Pictorial Record*, New York, G. E. Stechert & Co., 1928, contains about 80 pages of text and 165 plates, several in color. It is a beautiful and valuable book.

Arthur Bill, Director, has written "The Pestalozzi Children's Village," *School and Society*, December 9, 1967, pp. 502–503, an illustrated and up-dated account of the famous international school. The number of cottages has increased and the children are no longer World War II orphans. There are other small errors in the account in the text. Next year there will be further changes in the village.

BARNARD, HENRY, *Pestalozzi and His Educational System*, Syracuse, N.Y., C. W. Bardeen & Co., 1906, 751 pp.

BOYD, WILLIAM, *From Locke to Montessori; A Critical Account . . .*, London, G. G. Harrap & Co., 1914, 271 pp.

COOKE, E., *Pestalozzi's How Gertrude Teaches Her Children*, Syracuse, N.Y., C. W. Bardeen & Co., 1898, 391 pp.; *Letters on Early Education, Addressed to J. P. Greaves*, Syracuse, N. Y., C. W. Bardeen & Co., 1898, 180 pp.

GREEN, J. A., *Pestalozzi's Educational Writings*, New York, Longmans, Green & Co., 1912, 328 pp.; *Life and Work of Pestalozzi*, London, W. B. Clive & Co., 1913, 393 pp.

KRÜSI, HERMANN, JR., *Pestalozzi, His Life, Work, and Influence*, New York, American Book Company, 1875, 248 pp. It may have been the only biography of Pestalozzi written in the United States at that time.

PINLOCHE, A., *Pestalozzi and the Foundation of the Modern Elementary School*, New York, Charles Scribner's Sons, 1901, 306 pp.

VON RAPPARD, IRMEGARD, *Die Bedeutung der Mutter bei J. H. Pestalozzi*, Bonn, H. Bouvier & Co. Verlag, 1961, 156 pp.

Chapter 12

FROM PESTALOZZI TO PUBLIC EDUCATION

This chapter will deal with the spread of Pestalozzi's doctrine and practice in Europe and America and with the views of three pioneers who, although they were inspired by Pestalozzi, developed original views and founded new institutions. These were Fichte, Herbart, and Froebel.

The Pestalozzian era in the eighteenth and early nineteenth centuries is notable for the rise of several social and economic movements that changed the world in ways that have continued to the present time.

We already know that the English Bill of Rights of the seventeenth century was a great political landmark. In the next century the American Revolution, the Declaration of Independence, and the Constitution framed in Philadelphia showed that the Colonists had learned from the mother country. In 1763, La Chaletais, in his *Essay on National Education,* attacked the Jesuits as a foreign power that was interfering with the proper education of the French for service to France. The French Revolution, striving for liberty, equality, and fraternity, led to plans for national education prepared by Talleyrand, Condorcet, and many others. Out of these and later schemes a plan of education for France was developed and adopted. Although changed in important ways, it continues to exhibit the centralized control, dual organization, and high technical standards introduced into the system by its founders.

Religious and humanitarian emotions drove Pestalozzi forward and eventually he directed his efforts toward the salvation of the children of the poor. After Neuhof, during his writing epoch, he championed many causes; but Stanz led him to concentrate on one, the education especially of the poor. Meanwhile many great movements, social, economic, scientific, industrial, and technical, swirled up around him, without attracting his attention. And yet, several of these were to have a powerful effect on the education of the poor and the rich. The antislavery movement, although it fell far short, at least pointed toward human equality. Prison reform had once attracted his attention. Whether he continued to believe, as he did at Neuhof, that feeble-mindedness could be overcome by education is perhaps uncertain. The Industrial Revolution, which was transforming Switzerland and Europe, was to provide the means to make universal education economically possible; but it was the lowest level, the poorest of the poor, that attracted his attention. He regretted to the end that he had been unable to help the most helpless.

EARLY DISCIPLES

As we have noted, even at Neuhof, Nicolovius discovered Pestalozzi and became his friend for life, as well as an effective promoter of the new education in Germany. The Pestalozzian movement had a great influence on the teachers' seminaries in Germany and the normal schools of the United States.

Among the visitors to Burgdorf, we must name G. A. Gruner of Frankfurt, who persuaded Froebel to try his skill in teaching; and J. E. Plamann, who developed a famous Pestalozzian school at Berlin in which the young Otto von Bismarck received his early education. By teaching in Plamann's school, Froebel earned the money to pay his fees at the University of Berlin. "Father" Jahn promoted his famous gymnastic system in Plamann's school. Jahn and his exercises were factors in rallying German patriotism in the last and finally victorious struggle against Napoleon. Among those who enlisted was Froebel, who thereby gained two long-time friends and fellow teachers: William Middendorf and Henry Langenthal.

The German habits and speech of Pestalozzi and of his schools were doubtless strong reasons why his system was more readily accepted in Germany than in France. Napoleon was another reason. He told a Swiss delegation that he had no time for ABC. Pestalozzi was a member of the delegation, but he saw that nothing could be accomplished and went home early. He never saw the First Consul. Napoleon helped to maintain the gulf in the French national system that separated the working-class schools from the really important secondary and higher institutions. Napoleon said girls should be educated by their mothers, and that would be enough for them. There were Pestalozzian schools in Paris and elsewhere in France, but they had no great success. Even after Napoleon, public education made little progress for a generation.

BRITISH PESTALOZZIANS

Britain was more fertile soil; and British knowledge of Swiss activities, although hampered by the Napoleonic wars, was not entirely cut off. The famous Irish writer Maria Edgeworth met Pestalozzi early and again later, when she wrote her father, "He recognized me and I him; he is, tell my mother, the same wild-looking man he was, with the addition of seventeen years. The whole superintendence of the school is now in the hands of his masters; he just shows the visitor into the room, and reappears as you are going away with a look that pleads irresistibly for an obol of praise." This, no doubt, she gave willingly. The important book on *Practical Education* written by Maria and her father R. L. Edgeworth gave the English some knowledge and also criticism of Pestalozzi.

The war with Napoleon interrupted the flow of knowledge from the continent to England, and most of the Irish and English visitors to Yverdon came later, after the quarrel between Schmid and Niederer, two of Pestalozzi's leading assistants. The Irishman, John Synge stayed with Pestalozzi for three years (1819–1822). Like so many others, he fell in love with Pestalozzi but wished the great teacher's philanthropy had been tempered with more prudence. Also, like others, he brought a number of boys to be educated. His letters home gave accounts of Pestalozzi's school and teaching.

The introduction of the monitorial systems of Bell and Lancaster hampered the introduction of Pestalozzianism into England, but the infant schools of Robert Owen may have helped. Bell, visiting Yverdon was not impressed. He said, "I have now gained an understanding of Pestalozzi's method. Believe me, in twelve years' time nobody will speak of it while mine will have swept over the earth." For the children of his mill hands, Owen independently developed a method similar to Pestalozzi's kindness and step-by-small-step cultivation of children's interest, capacities, and skills. It was not simple or others would have done it frequently; but Owen showed that others could approach the Swiss master's skill.

Object-teaching and infant schools in Britain owed something to Pestalozzi, but his influence was more important in the training of teachers. The Home and Colonial School Society established a model infant school that applied Pestalozzian methods and educated several thousand teachers in the new way. J. P. Greaves was an assistant in the school and Charles Mayo one of the founders of the society. Both became effective promoters of the new method in Britain. The Battersea Training College followed Swiss ideas. It had a model school for experiment but more for demonstration and practice. Battersea was especially noted for its use of Pestalozzi's reforms in the teaching of arithmetic. As we have noted, Britain acquired a late and somewhat formal type of Pestalozzianism, and it was this variety that was introduced still later into the United States at Oswego, New York.

AMERICAN PESTALOZZIANS

The new spirit and method came to the United States, as we have stated, in three waves: early through the importation of a Burgdorf assistant to Pestalozzi; in the middle years through American visitors to European centers of the movement; and after 1860 by borrowing from England as we have noted here and in Chapter Eleven.

The assistant who was imported was Joseph Neef (1770–1854), who had been a soldier—a veteran of Napoleon's early Italian campaign—and had been wounded in the crucial battle of Arcole in mid-November, 1796. Mustered out, his wounds had time to heal before he could begin with Pestalozzi at Burgdorf as a teacher in the school. He had a rather rough exterior, a booming voice, and loved to lead in singing, not always choosing the most appropriate songs. He was a lively leader in games and marching exercises and the children accepted him as a leader. He called himself a coadjutor of Pestalozzi, but he cannot have been at Burgdorf very long for he was soon conducting his own school in Paris.

Neef was found at Paris by a Scottish-American politician and geologist, William Maclure, who was on a mission to the French government from President Jefferson. Maclure persuaded Neef to come to America and paid his way while he learned to speak English and prepared himself to introduce Pestalozzian ideas. He first opened a school in the city itself and then at a place named Valley Green, near Philadelphia. Pupils came from different states, including Ohio and Louisiana. One boy who was to give a favorable report of the school was named David Farragut, and as we know he became an admiral of the United States Navy. Farragut spoke of the oral teaching, by a hatless teacher leading his pupils on long hikes through the country, gathering rocks and plants for study, and of the swimming, climbing, and military drill in health education.

All this sounds like a report of the school at Burgdorf and shows that Neef fulfilled Maclure's purpose to introduce Pestalozzian practices and ideas into his adopted country; but he was not able to graft them on the formal system in vogue in the United States. He did not look like or act like the ordinary American teacher. The hatless leader of a pack of boys made an odd figure on the streets of Philadelphia where, in 1808 or about that time, men wore hats.

Neef left Pennsylvania to set up schools elsewhere. Perhaps he was not a member of "the boatload of knowledge" that floated down the Ohio River to Robert Owen's colony at New Harmony, Indiana, but he arrived there nevertheless. He taught at New Harmony but he was not able to attract persons who might have helped to win America for the new activities. He wrote an excellent and very informative book, *A Sketch of a Plan and Method of Education* (1808) as carried out by Pestalozzi, but it had little influence and is now rare. Americans at that time still believed that education was acquired almost solely from books while seated at a desk.

Although Albert Picket mentioned Pestalozzi (in his *Academician*, 1818–1820), little was known about him until 1830 and after. A very few textbooks, such as Warren Colburn's *First Lessons in Arithmetic on the Plan of Pestalozzi* (1821), were published early. Lowell Mason is supposed to have followed Pestalozzian ideas in teaching music. The center of the movement moved to Boston where Horace Mann's reports and especially the seventh report and his *Common School Journal* promoted the new idea. Some Swiss scientists in America, Agassiz and Arnold Guyot, although they may have had little direct knowledge of Pestalozzi, yet worked in his spirit.

About the time of the Civil War, a third Pestalozzian influence came from England by way of Canada. This came to be the most widespread, but may have been the least useful of all. Its center was in Oswego, New York, where Edward Austin Sheldon developed schools for the poor children and eventually secured the foundation of a public school system and a normal school. Sheldon introduced from Canada a collection of object-teaching materials. His student-teachers indoctrinated in these methods carried them to many states, near and far.

This third period is also marked by the establishment of normal schools in state after state from New Jersey to Minnesota. The first such institution was founded in Massachusetts, in 1839, under the prodding of Horace Mann; but after 1860 they multiplied rapidly until nearly every state had one or more, and about a hundred state normal schools were in operation at century's end.

Pestalozzi's ideas were spread by men who believed in them, disciples who tried to promote his views and practice without much effort to improve them. Beside these disciples there were also some pioneers who differed from him and tried to go beyond him in several ways. We shall deal with three who were more articulate and perhaps more self-consistent than he: Fichte, Herbart, and Froebel.

PESTALOZZI'S FAME TODAY

In his lifetime Pestalozzi received more recognition in Great Britain and Germany: from the Edgeworths, Nicolovius, Herbart, Froebel, and the Prussians than at home. However, Switzerland has long since made up for the delay in its repeated publication of his works, in the adoption of his principles, and recently by the establishment of a children's village for war orphans near his native city. The story follows.

Pestalozzi, as we know, had great success in dealing with orphans and strays at Stanz. It is, therefore, particularly appropriate that a living monument, the Pestalozzi Children's Village, has been established near Zürich to give aid to children who suffered from World War II. The village was proposed by Walter Robert Coti, a Zürich editor, under the heading, *Ein Dorf für leidende kinder*, a village for suffering children. It was to be at once a home, school, and small community for destitute war orphans from many nations. The war was to be swept from the memory of the new generation and none were to remember who had been friend, who enemy. The children were to receive loving care and a chance to grow mentally, spiritually, and physically under freedom, responsibility, and tolerance. Publicity brought support and also opposition, and in two years, by 1946, a beginning had been made.

The cottage or family plan was adopted. There are now eighteen houses, each with fifteen or more children, presided over by a married couple, who serve as house parents; and all members of each "family" are from the same country. There is a British house, a French, an Austrian, an Italian, and so on. Children are received at the age of six or a few years older, and they may remain until they are fifteen or sixteen. Each house has a large living room with a schoolroom above and a workshop below it. As Pestalozzi in his time advised, the living room is the center of the family life. The national language is spoken there, but the school is conducted in German. This is the language of the surrounding region, and the children learn it by means of songs, games, and plays. They may also, more formally, acquire a second foreign tongue. The school is of the type some would call progressive. There is a community hall for general meetings; it is a gift from Canada's UNESCO and the city of Zürich. Interdenominational Christianity is the religion of the village.

The legal control and government is made up of adults, but the children have a voice in the internal management of the community's affairs. They elect a village council and administrative officials. The residents over whom they rule are between two and three hundred in number. When the children are to be repatriated to their homelands, the village aids in finding places and positions for them. The student of Cecil Reddie's Abbotsholme may see several resemblances between the early progressive school (1889) and the Pestalozzi Children's Village. (See "Notes" for this chapter.) Clearly, good schools are good medicine for troubled minds; and where homes are wanting or faulty, boarding schools may be best.

FICHTE

The chief characters in the rest of this chapter will be Fichte, Herbart, and Froebel, all younger than Pestalozzi and in various ways indebted to him. But we must resist any impulse to call them Pestalozzians. All turned away finally and Fichte first and most decidedly.

Johann Gottlieb Fichte (1762–1814) was a poor boy who, because he pleased a nobleman by repeating a sermon nearly word for word, was sent to a famous school, Schulpforta. Later he paid for his own way through the university by tutoring, although some of these engagements were brief because of his impetuous temper. There were compensations. In one such situation in Switzerland he met Pestalozzi.

He passed through an early liberal period during which he approved of certain phases of the French Revolution, of *The Social Contract* by Rousseau, and of the struggle for freedom of speech and publication. He was against all of these in his book on education, the *Addresses to the German Nation*, delivered in 1807–1808, when he was forty-six years old.

There are fourteen addresses. They were the author's response to the defeat of the German armies at Jena in 1806 and the resulting fear that Germany and its culture and language might be damaged beyond recovery. While he was speaking the heels of the French soldiers clicked on the pavement outside. Although the speaker's words reveal some trepidation, none of the enemy came in and, also, according to report, not many auditors. The book has become famous and is read by many who touch few of Fichte's other writings. Its republication in 1955 is evidence of this, but evidence is not needed.

Three of the addresses, the second, ninth, and tenth, are of special importance in a study of Fichte's views on education. We shall come to these presently. The messages altogether were intended to outline the means of preserving not the German state or states, but the historic community of Germans with their irreplaceable and invaluable culture and language. This is the meaning of the word *nation*.

An entirely new system of education, said Fichte, is the essential means to preserve the German culture and language. Present education merely exhorts children; the new education must compel them to good order, morality, and patriotism—to Germanism. The new education must do away with all freedom of the will; the children must will as they are taught to will. Fichte outlined the means to these results but his plan is not convincing. He was invincibly strong-willed and seems to have believed that a philosopher can compel events to support his convictions.

In the ninth and tenth lectures, the speaker dealt with Pestalozzi's views, but more with his practice. He had met Pestalozzi in Switzerland in about 1792, but he made a special study of his writings after the defeat of Germany. It is characteristic of this philosopher that in judging Pestalozzi's work it was for him sufficient to read the writings and not at all necessary to see the work in progress or to evaluate the results. Theory was more important than process or product.

For his purpose, Fichte thought only complete education would have any value. Pestalozzi was quite wrong in providing a few years of schooling before the children were able to work; and it was a mistake to begin with reading and writing. At this point he agreed with Rousseau, although he did not mention him, saying that after children were more mature they would acquire those insignificant school arts without difficulty. He disagreed with Pestalozzi's high opinion of the value of family life. Fichte demanded that the children must be taken out of the homes and taught in national boarding schools. They must be trained in perception, given vigorous physical education, and taught practical work skills, good morals, civics, and religion.

Future scholars were to be separated from the masses and trained in philosophy. Fichte's almost exclusive devotion to abstract thought is illustrated by his draft of a program of studies for the new University of Berlin established in 1810. In that program he gave almost no place to experimental science. Few philosophers have been so fully convinced that they were capable of simply excogitating a future world, in his case the world of German culture, language, and destiny—the German nation that was to be. But, then, for him only thought, not the external world, was real.

HERBART IN EARLY LIFE

Johann Friedrich Herbart (1776–1841) became, like Fichte, a university professor of philosophy. While Fichte was delivering his lectures on the preservation of the German nation, Herbart was expounding his new educational psychology and quietly spreading from his chair at Göttingen a friendly criticism of Pestalozzi. But we are to speak first of his early life.

Several generations of his family had been connected with Oldenburg in northern Germany where his grandfather had been rector of the Latin School and where his father was a jurist and civil official. The future philosopher was an eager, precocious student. He was, like Fichte, able to repeat a sermon almost verbatim. This seems to have been the German anticipation of the intelligence test! His youthful ability was, however, more reasonably attested by his skill in logic and mathematics, even before he reached adolescence. In his early years he had a tutor and then briefly attended a private school. He completed the six years of the Latin School at the usual age of eighteen. He attended the University of Jena immediately but did not matriculate until the opening of the winter semester. Fichte was called to a professorship at Jena in the same year (1794).

For some time he was associated with Fichte in a dining club composed of "Free Men"; that is, students who did not belong to the regular corps or fraternities. It was one of Fichte's aims to have these exclusive groups disband and this led to one of the philosopher's several quarrels. Herbart attended Fichte's lectures for a considerable period but being of an empirical temper he drifted away, unable to accept the absolute idealism of the master who included all reality in the Ego and the non-Ego.

In contrast with Fichte, Herbart called himself a Realist, believing that things exist independently of mankind. This is the position of common sense. The bricklayer has no doubt that this house and the clock on the wall are there quite without him. The clock ticks and its sound is audible, or would be if anyone were there to hear it. Our absence makes no difference in the clock until it comes time to wind it.

The philosopher Kant added an important thought here: He pointed out that the mind brings to things the *categories* such as quantity, quality, cause, and others. Such ideas, necessary in dealing with objects, are mental only; but the nature of the things, the sweetness of sugar or the toughness of shoe leather, we find in the objects only by experience. This was essentially Herbart's position; but he held also that because a substance, say sugar, has various qualities—granular state, solubility, and others—there are several realities in it. It is this multiplication of realities, of "reals," that has given him the title, Realist.

Philosophy is given the task of making sense out of experience and thought. When discrepancies appear in experience a scientist resorts to experiment; the philosopher is more likely to turn to observation and to the analysis of the concepts derived from experience. Herbart as a philosopher did not carry on any direct experiments but he made good use of his observations. An example will be found in his first experience as a teacher, as we shall soon point out.

HERBART AS TUTOR

Probably Herbart had not intended to become a teacher of small boys; but having reached a dead end in his studies, he accepted the invitation of Herr von Steiger of Berne to serve as tutor to three sons, Rudolf, Carl, and Ludwig, aged respectively, eight, ten, and fourteen. The year was 1797, his age was twenty-one years, and his university studies were unfinished. At Zürich on the way he met Pestalozzi. The meeting was to become significant.

Because there was a six-year span in the ages of the pupils he had to teach many subjects including the classical languages, German composition, history, music, mathematics, physics, chemistry, and also geography. He taught four to six hours daily and made bimonthly reports on the work. Several of these reports and some letters survive and provide an account of his work and experience.

Of the great educators only Herbart has left so full an account of his views and practice in a concrete situation; a wealth of detail of his methods is found in his reports. Others give advice; Herbart tells us what he did and what the results were.

Herbart told the father that by short reviews and by seeking out general ideas he tried to connect his lessons with those of preceding tutors. He hoped in this way to develop a continuous web of knowledge and understanding. By working in his preparation times at the subjects he was teaching, he increased his own current interest, believing that an uninterested teacher is not likely to interest his pupils. And also, to avoid tedium he tried to vary the exercises as much as possible. He knew that one of the

Immanuel Kant (1724–1804)

factors in good teaching is participation by the pupils, and he encouraged them to write out questions to ask during lessons and to make outlines of important passages. He thought teachers are apt to fail by talking too much and not eliciting pupils' questions and objections.

Herbart naturally learned about teaching from his experience as a pupil and student. One does not gather that he had received any instruction on methods or theory but it is probable that he read pedagogical works. Even this is supposition. He clearly learned from his own efforts as the tutor of three boys. We shall relate what he gained in teaching the elements of the Greek language to the younger boys, Rudolf and Carl.

It was and is customary to teach Latin before Greek, but Herbart reversed this order. His reason was that the Greek culture and literature are older than the Latin and that the Romans followed Greek models in their own literature. In teaching, Herbart followed the historical and in a sense the natural development of the subjects. It is natural, one may say, to follow nature rather than to go contrary to her course.

Another idea, an idea on method, occurred to Herbart. The ancient languages had long formed one of the great obstructions in the paths of young students. Ways to avoid or conquer the difficulty had been tried by Ratke, Comenius, and others. Herbart thought of a new way to avoid the great waste of time in the use of the lexicon and grammar and to make language studies practically painless: work with the children, enlist their efforts as much as possible, and help them over every real difficulty as they come to it. He was their lexicon and grammar combined. Between periods the boys did some review work and at every lesson they gained power and confidence until at last they could read unaided. By this method the children did not blunder at almost every step, forming bad habits. Difficulties were solved before they became too serious.

There was a third main factor in this method; the first was Greek before Latin; the second, working with the pupils; and the third was the choice of a world-famous story, Homer's *Odyssey*, as the first book to be read. In about a year and a half the boys had fully mastered it and had gained a great literary masterpiece as a life-long possession. We may add that the *Odyssey* had been used as a school book at Rome in the third pre-Christian century by Livius Andronicus.

HERBART ON PESTALOZZI

Upon leaving the von Steiger family, Herbart went to live in Bremen, not far from Oldenburg, near a friend of Jena student days. He devoted himself to the completion of his university studies at Göttingen University instead of Jena. At Göttingen he received the doctor's degree and became, first, a lecturer, then professor, until he was called to Königsberg to the chair made famous by Kant. Here he established a small boys' school where some of his students carried on apprentice teaching under his guidance. After twenty-five years he returned to the faculty of Göttingen and there he died in 1841.

We shall now devote our space to Herbart's study of Pestalozzi's writings. The first of these compositions was a copy of a speech to some young mothers and their friends in Bremen. It was entitled: "On Pestalozzi's Newest Work, 'How Gertrude Teaches Her Children.'" The address was adapted to his audience, for Herbart was a skillful speaker and a charming writer. First, he reviewed the scene when he had visited Pestalozzi to hear a lesson at an hour when the children should have been in bed; and he recalled his surprise to find them lively and cheerful.

Then he reminded the young mothers that the welfare of wholly ignorant and uncultivated people is Pestalozzi's aim. Not in homes like yours, he told the young mothers, but in the huts of the poor he seeks the crown of his labors. Unless you keep this in mind you will not understand him. Pestalozzi speaks of beggars' children and their culture must include the lowest kind of labor. The materials must be so simple that their beggar parents can teach them. "Perhaps," said Herbart to the young mothers, "you think such matters cannot concern you; we shall see."

We shall inquire whether an education for beggar children has a message for you. We shall look for what is the most important of all instruction. Is it a little nature study, a bit of history, a glance at geography, and so on? No, the most important teaching is that which will enable us to support life, by work; and the next most important teaching is that which will lead us to do our duty, it is teaching of religion, morals, and civil life. This is what Pestalozzi says.

A second study of Pestalozzi's theory was not a speech or short paper but a book of one hundred and fifty pages entiled *Pestalozzi's Idea of an ABC of Observation Scientifically Investigated*. The last words of the title indicate that Herbart considered this to be an important work. Herbart agreed with Pestalozzi that observation can be practiced, taught, and improved. They both maintained that the eyes are the organs of observation, too hastily overlooking the touch and other senses, although there is a reference to hearing.

We see color and from colored patches, we are told, we observe form and space, which leads to mathematics and thus to the discoveries of the greatest minds of all ages. Without mathematics the work of observation would result in useless efforts. Here we see that not only Greek but also, and even more, mathematics belongs to the greatest means of education. This indicates that the plan and practice of observation will be largely mathematical.

In trying to make observation exact, Herbart narrowed its scope as he had already narrowed the sensory means. So when he undertook to make an application to a particular subject, geography, he turned to mathematical geography—to locations and distances. Pestalozzi wisely applied the word *observation* more broadly and with greater educational effect by having pupils make a model of the valley they had observed. It was, furthermore, Pestalozzi who gave Carl Ritter useful hints toward a more modern geography. There is a time for measurement in all sciences but one must first discover what is worth measuring.

HERBART'S PSYCHOLOGY

The active forces in mental action are presentations or, as Locke called them, ideas. The German word is *vorstellung*, meaning to present or introduce someone. The introduction makes him one of the party, no longer an outsider or onlooker but one entitled to take part in the activities, supporting one, opposing another person and his position. The activities of the mind are all presentations, or ideas, impulses, images, conclusions—a multiplicity of forces.

The mind itself is the floor on which this party is held or, perhaps better, the gridiron in which the ideas like players support, oppose, draw offside, outwit, and even knock each other senseless. The figure is not, however, perfect according to Herbart, for the mind does not affect the action of the ideas as the condition of the field may affect the athletes and the game. As ideas compete, weaker ideas will be driven to the margin of consciousness or even over the threshold into the unconscious mind from which, however, they may again emerge when conditions are more favorable.

Psychology, according to Herbart, must, like geography, become mathematical. This was a new idea but, because he entirely separated the mind from the body, he had no means of measuring the strength or effectiveness of the *vorstellungen*. It was Gustav T. Fechner (1801–1887) who, using several of Herbart's ideas, performed what Herbart considered impossible and invented experimental psychology.

Moral character is chosen as the aim of education, and on this, Herbart insisted with all his force and strength. His ethical theory can be taken as a form of intuitionism. He held that we recognize the right and good as we recognize harmony in music. This view has never been accepted in ethical philosophy. On the way in which men become moral, he agrees with the majority. They develop a good character, acceptable conduct, and agreeable manners by living in a pure environment and imitating the best examples. The child, therefore, needs only to find and to imitate the best people.

We end our treatment of Herbart with a quotation from an evaluation of Pestalozzi. Herbart wrote,

A determinate interest may be implanted in the child; but that of a youth, one can only cultivate. The child believes what it is told, accepts what it hears; it imitates what it has observed; one creates for him a world by means of pictures and stories. On the contrary, one can only expand or contract the youth's world. In his world he builds a cabin; he scornfully rejects the palace which we have erected for him contrary to his desire.
If these are well-known truths, I may well ask why one considers the spirit of the Pestalozzian method a puzzle and why people are still doubtful about its value and proper position, that is, where it belongs. . . . With respect to the nature of instruction in the method, one must not expect any pedantic limitations; the entire field of sensory perception, possible as well as actual, lies open before us, and will be used ever more extensively and freely. But its [that of the method] true advantage consists in this: that it is more daring [venturesome] and enthusiastic than any earlier method in undertaking to cultivate the mind of the child and to develop in it a clear and definite experience—not to act as though the child already had a rich experience but to develop one in him.

FROEBEL

Few of the makers of schools, as we have noted earlier, created wholly new institutions. The idea of a school was no longer new after 2500 B.C., and as time passed and additional features were introduced, complete originality became less and less possible. But Plato started out upon a relatively new program and also, perhaps, did Vittorino, Basedow, and Booker T. Washington. Of the comparative originality of Friedrich Froebel (1782–1852) there is no question.

Froebel was indebted to Pestalozzi, but he also disagreed with him in important ways. In spirit Pestalozzi was a scientist, gathering experience and information, bit by bit, and changing his views accordingly. Observation, or perception, is his most important word; he was an empiricist and had a skeptical strain in his constitution.

Not so Froebel. He was a philosopher and knew from the beginning what the answer in general must be. Froebel started with a constitutive idea, the idea of unity: the unity of nature first; then the unity of man and nature; and, finally, the unity of nature, man, and God, with man the middle term. Historically, he had begun with the God of the Bible, but eventually and logically the sequence developed as stated.

We shall quote the philosopher-educator, William Torrey Harris, on this important matter. Harris wrote, "Froebel is in a peculiar sense a religious teacher. . . . He sees the world of physical nature and human history as firmly established in a divine unity which is to him no abstraction but a creative might and a living Providence. God to him is infinite reason." Harris, the Hegelian, had no defences against such a philosophy.

Pestalozzi, as we know, also was deeply religious. His religion, however, was expressed especially in service to the poor, the defective, the oppressed, and those in prison. He took pains to find out what caused their difficulties and sought not a general solution but practical help, as a modern social worker does. Education was to him a practical matter, a means to save the poorest and the least gifted, teaching them sobriety, industry, self-support, and the way to self-respect and a useful life.

Froebel, with his more general and idealistic theory, was less interested in social conditions. He had found a general, universal answer to educational questions. He thought all children needed to be put on the road to an inner and predestined development. His problem was to find the means, exercises, and materials to nourish the divine germ and enable it to grow to maturity.

Here we have two opposed theories of human nature and education; but perhaps neither exponent was entirely consistent in his practice or his philosophy. At all events, Froebel, who was closely associated with Pestalozzi for a few years, remembered him with gratitude. We have the evidence. Thirteen years after Pestalozzi's death, Froebel, in demonstrating his games and gifts at Dresden, met a lady who told him of her visit with Pestalozzi at Yverdon. Froebel wrote to his wife, "Is it not remarkable how this man reappears, either as a link drawing people together, or drawing more closely bonds already existing? I frankly confess that on hearing this [name], I felt a glow at my heart." But why should this surprise him? Did he not know that Pestalozzian ideas were at that moment spreading far and wide?

The answer may be that Froebel no longer recognized his debt to Pestalozzi, whom he now considered outmoded by his own system. Yet Froebel may still be called Pestalozzi's disciple. A disciple is a follower who may not fully agree with his master. The root meaning of the word seems to be "one who stands apart." Froebel is in the Pestalozzian tradition if not completely of it. Many educators have fused their practices and forgotten their conflicting theories.

The life of Froebel tells more than his theories about his system. He was born in a manse; his father had a large parish and was very busy; his mother died before he was a year old and this, he wrote, "more or less decided the external circumstances of my whole life." He did not say, like Rousseau, that "this was the first of my misfortunes." He was not a dramatic writer. With his father away most of the time and a stepmother in charge, the boy's tether was kept short. This may be one reason for his games for young children. Froebel ascribed his habit of introspection and self-examination to this early isolation without space, toys, pets, or playmates.

His life did not continue solitary. He helped in his father's favorite occupation of gardening and began to take an interest in plants and flowers. He also became interested in the religious exercises and meditations of the home and church. He speaks of "delightful hours of heavenly meditation."

Problems arose: In his boyish vivacity he broke and destroyed things, as boys will, got into scrapes, and may have told a few fibs. To his well-educated father's distress he had great difficulty in learning to read. Although his older brothers were sent to the university, Friedrich was thought not worth educating. Was this experience the source of his conclusion that reading should be postponed for unliterary exercises? This might have come from Rousseau but, unaccountably, he seems never to mention Rousseau. Perhaps he had not heard of the new education announced in *Émile*.

In his autobiography, which should be reprinted so that every young teacher can read it, he described his self-education and schooling. It was largely self-education. Not literature, but arithmetic and science attracted him; not the Bible, but religious questions, exercises, and meditation fascinated him. He listened to his father's conferences with parishioners in trouble, particularly sex trouble, and was disturbed. He talked things over with a brother, home on a visit, and one day when little Friedrich expressed his "delight at seeing the purple threads of the hazel buds, he made me aware of a similar sexual difference in plants." This showed him that man and nature are connected. He wrote, "From that time, humanity and nature, the life of the soul and the life of the flower, were closely knit together. . . . I can still see my hazel buds, like angels, opening for me the great God's temple of nature."

This is the voice of a religious poet, one who is beginning to consider the immanence of God as stronger than His transcendence. Froebel's philosophy was largely based on such insights, which were more inspirational than logical in source and quality. In his educational scheme he tried to follow "the divine law of human development."

Froebel's apprenticeship was a hit-or-miss process that began in his early youth in an attempt to study agriculture, as Pestalozzi also had done. It proceeded through forestry, accounting, and architecture, until in his late twenties he came across a Pestalozzian school at Frankfurt. The head of the school, Gottlieb Anton Gruner, convinced him that teaching was to be his forte. He twice visited Pestalozzi at Yverdon and spent two years with him in the good years before the staff became divided and quarrelsome. Pestalozzi gave him abundant opportunity for conferences and all classes were open to him. Froebel has told of what he approved and of what he did not.

Even after two years with Pestalozzi, he still doubted the need to include history and the productions of man's arts and manufactures in the elementary curriculum. Eventually he made this change in his outlook and wrote, "It broadened my inward and outward view considerably when I was able to look upon . . . the works of man as also a part of the 'external world.' In this way I sought . . . to make clear the meaning of all things through man, his relations with himself, and with the external world." We can excuse this early failure to see the need for history and the arts in schooling; Pestalozzi also suffered from the same blindness.

Meanwhile, Froebel was reading the new books dealing with education. He mentions Jean Paul Richter's *Levana*, which was published in 1807. At this time, Froebel was at Yverdon. He wrote,

The Pestalozzian method I knew. . . . What especially lay heavily upon me at that time . . . was the utter absence of any organized connection between the subjects of education. Joyful and unfettered work springs from the conception of all things as one whole, and forms a life and lifework in harmony with the constitution of the universe and resting firmly upon it.

The universe is, however, a large object and our knowledge of it has to be built up, piece by piece. Because our span of attention is limited, Fleury and indeed all teachers, including Froebel, frequently change exercises and studies to suit the child and human capacity.

Froebel refers to Pestalozzi in a number of places. He wrote, "Our greatest teachers, even Pestalozzi himself not excepted, seemed to me too bare, too empirical and arbitrary, and therefore not sufficiently scientific in their principles, that is, not sufficiently led by the laws of our being." He should have included such laws as our need for frequent change of interest and occupation. An assistant, Arnold Barop, referred to Froebel's dissatisfaction with Pestalozzi's object-teaching, which seemed to Froebel to stop short of its proper goal. He wanted to awaken an eager desire for learning and especially for creative activity. He also introduced more handwork and construction into the school. He even at times used the language of Rousseau in demanding that schools and the whole educational system do the exact opposite of what they were doing. Froebel was as little capable of self-criticism as Rousseau.

Intermittently he studied for extended periods at three universities: Jena, Göttingen, and Berlin. He gave most of his attention to the sciences, making good progress in mineralogy and crystallography. At Berlin he was for a time in charge of the collections in Mineralogy. His efforts to master linguistic studies were not successful. He liked mathematics but seems to have studied only its elementary branches.

When he was nearly forty years old he opened a school in his own neighborhood at Griesheim (1816) but moved a short distance to Keilhau (1817). His schools did not suffer from staff-dissension, as did Yverdon, but from mistrust of socialism and atheism by the people and authorities. Froebel was no linguist and the language-teaching was criticized. An associate by marriage, J. Arnold Barop, took the management of the school and made it a permanent institution.

Froebel's book *The Education of Man* deals with elementary education. It was published in 1826, before he had thought of the kindergarten. But only two years later in connection with the ill-starred Helba Plan, which had gained, and then lost, the interest of the Duke of Meiningen, Froebel wrote to Barop, "I shall not call this [division of the proposed institution] an infant school because I do not intend the children to be schooled, but to be allowed under gentlest treatment to develop freely." A school for mothers and work in art and construction were parts of the plan. Here we may see the idea of the kindergarten beginning to grow.

The Education of Man was not Froebel's first publication. Others were to follow but all these were privately an inexpertly printed and not actually published. Only those who were already interested or somehow connected with the Froebel circle heard of the books. And when found they were usually difficult to read. Many young people and even older ones do not know what to make of *The Education of Man*. Only his *Autobiography* has considerable charm and some may think that even this praise is not entirely deserved. The translators' notes add useful interpretation and facts.

School and Society, by John Dewey, is a commentary on Froebel although he is not mentioned. It is an account of the University of Chicago experimental or laboratory school. One of Dewey's stories adds further commentary: When a lady called on Dewey to secure permission to visit the kindergarten at the laboratory school he explained that they had no kindergarten. Upon being pressed he admitted that they had small children and practiced many of the exercises usually associated with the kindergarten. We can safely assume that there was too much routine in the

Frobelian kindergarten to suit Dewey; he objected also to the symbolism, the deductive approach, and the formal gifts and other materials. He turned the group into a miniature society with materials and exercises that prepared one not mainly for rural life but for an urban and industrial democracy. By that time at the century's end, the kindergarten in the United States had given up many of Froebel's exercises; but the purpose and the spirit remained as he had developed them.

CREATION OF THE KINDERGARTEN

Froebel, in 1836, spent some months in Germany in visiting infant schools that had been founded as a result of the impulse given to the movement by Oberlin and his German disciples. He found the schools conducted by teachers without adequate training. Often they were mere day nurseries whose chief purpose was to keep children out of harm's way while the mothers were at work. Eventually, he returned to Blankenburg in his native Thuringia, which became the cradle of his new institution.

The problem was to find the best materials and activities and to organize them so that they should form a regular series that would call out and cultivate the children's powers of observation and understanding and develop their self-activity and self-expression—the living out or expressing in life of the children's natural capacities, both social and individual. Froebel's early names for his institution, a "school for psychological education," a "school based on the active instincts of children," were felt to be unnecessarily clumsy. He sought for a simpler and more expressive name. On May 1, 1840, on a walking tour in the mountains, the desired phrase came to him and he shouted, "Eureka! I have found it. The school is a kindergarten," a garden in which children can grow as naturally as a plant under the care of an expert gardener. It was a fortunate choice. The name has had a widespread acceptance and has been incorporated into many languages as the title of Froebel's school and spirit.

As materials for the children's play, Froebel selected three forms: the sphere, the cube, and the cylinder. These are the basic gifts, as he called them. The spheres of the kindergarten were balls that children rolled and tossed; the cubes were used as building blocks; and the cylinders, a mediating form between the other two, could be used as either stationary or movable elements in the plays. Many elaborate plays were worked out. Squares, triangles, sticks, and rings were included for use in construction. These objects were considered as typical of nature and art, and Froebel held the view that nature and art form a unity and that the highest form of this unity is God. The child has in him a spark of the divine fire and is, in his small way, a creative personality as God is the great Creator. Education as self-expression, *darstellung*, is a creative process through which and in which the child develops. This symbolism, which has been discarded, is best expressed by Froebel himself in numerous passages from which we select the following three:

I have not only forms for the child's eyes which are to make him acquainted with the outward world which surrounds him; I have symbols which unlock his soul for the thought or spirit which is innate in everything that has come out of God's creative mind. If the ripened mind is to know this thought, its embodied image must make an impression on the yet unconscious soul of the child and leave behind it forms which can serve as analogies to the intellectual ordering of things. . . .

We must render perceptible to the child the unity of the world, absolute existence, the world within. . . . Such things we have to give the children through the system of ordered games and occupations which I have created. . . .

God clothed His own image in a mass of clay and was not ashamed of his creation; neither will I be ashamed to set forth in little blocks of wood my ideas upon the nature of man.

These passages are quoted in Susan E. Blow's *Educational Issues in the Kindergarten* (Appleton-Century-Crofts, 1908, pp. 52–53). In regard to them even that loyal Froebelian asked, "What must any sane person think of an effort to render perceptible not only the unity of the world, but absolute existence? And is not any educator clearly daft who attempts to set forth in little blocks of wood his ideas upon the nature of man?" In our workaday and secular civilization there is little room for mysticism, and Froebel's symbolism has disappeared from the modern kindergarten.

As the kindergarten developed, not only were features that Froebel had regarded as essential, such as symbolism, dropped out, but also some new features of which he would not have approved were introduced. Charles Dickens, as early as 1855, pointed out the dangers of formalism in the kindergarten. One type of formalism that Froebel would have opposed grew out of the mingling of Pestalozzian and Froebelian ideas. Froebel never intended that the stories, collections, and nature materials should be used for object lessons. His aim was not knowledge about things, especially not verbalism, but rather the use of things for the accomplishment of the child's or the children's purposes. Yet object lessons were introduced. Nor did Froebel intend that the kindergarten should develop free and unregulated play. His thought was the exact opposite of chance or chaotic self-expression. "In all things," God and man and nature, he had said in the opening sentence of his first book, "there lives and reigns an eternal law." This, one of his key ideas, would, if taken to heart, have prevented the free play that for a time characterized the American kindergarten. Free play is perhaps analogous to busy work in the elementary school.

SPREAD OF THE KINDERGARTEN

The Prussian government, through its minister of education, proscribed the kindergarten. The edict delivered on August 7, 1851 was probably based on a confusion in the official mind between Friedrich Froebel and his nephew Karl Froebel who held socialistic views. However, once issued, the prohibition was not withdrawn in spite of all that Froebel and his influential friends could do. Even a direct appeal to the king was ineffective. Because Germany was not yet united, the prohibition did not apply to the other German states, but it made the institution suspected everywhere. And from the Prussian official standpoint the suspicion was, doubtless, justified for the new school leaned toward democracy; and as Georg Ebers, a Keilhau pupil, remarked, in any German legislative assembly the Froebelians would have sat on the Left. Froebel died in the following year (1852), but there is no evidence that the blow, although he felt it keenly, shortened his life as has been asserted. The prohibition was withdrawn in 1861, and the new school for very young children spread rapidly.

The opposition at home may have aided the extension of the kindergarten abroad, for its missionaries had to find open doors and sought for them beyond the borders of Prussia and even of Germany. The most famous of these foreign missionaries was Bertha von Marenholtz-Bülow, a titled and well-educated lady with fine personal qualities. She had made Froebel's acquaintance in 1849 and devoted the remainder of her life to the spread of his ideas. Her *Reminiscences of Friedrich Froebel,* translated into English by Mrs. Horace Mann, and others of her numerous writings were read in many countries, and her personal labors were almost as widespread. She worked in Germany for several years, but in 1854 went for six months to England, where Mrs. Ronge had already established a demonstration kindergarten at Prince Albert's Exposition in London. These two women enlisted the support of Charles Dickens, who expressed his high approval of the kindergarten in a paper he conducted, *Household Words* (1855). Eleanore Heerwart, who later aided in the founding of the International Kindergarten Union, and Adele von Portugall established kindergartens in Manchester. Bertha von Marenholtz-Bülow visited France in 1855, won the approval of the historian Michelet and other well-known French leaders, and through her addresses aroused interest in the kindergarten. The Low Countries had already received the message from other hands but, beginning at the Hague, she worked in Holland and Belgium also. In the latter country, she with others wrote a *Manuel des Jardins d'enfants,* which had great influence. Henriette Breyman, who assisted in the preparation of this manual, was called to Switzerland in 1864 where the two cities of Lausanne and Geneva particularly became centers of kindergarten propaganda. The Baroness von Marenholtz-Bülow also worked in Italy where, at Florence,

Elizabeth Peabody found her in the winter of 1871. Many of the leaders of the newly unified Italy, including Garibaldi, showed much interest in the new education. In several of the larger cities, Florence, Rome, and Naples, kindergartens and training schools were established.

After all, the kindergarten was first spread in the land of its birth. Froebel, we saw, left Switzerland in the spring of 1836 after establishing his schools at Willisau and Burgdorf. After four months at Keilhau, he moved into a house at Blankenburg where he collected and invented his gifts and handwork occupations, experimenting with the village children. This school was called a school for the psychological training of young children. From 1837 he published a small weekly called the *Sonntagsblatt*, the Sunday sheet, to spread his ideas. During the following year, Barop and Adolf Frankenberg took some Keilhau pupils to Dresden on a trip and gave a demonstration of the future kindergarten exercises with small children of Dresden. At Leipzig, where Langethal had prepared the way, they gave a further demonstration. Froebel himself gave demonstrations in Göttingen and Frankfurt. Many visitors came to Blankenburg. In December, 1838, Froebel and Middendorf helped Adolf Frankenberg open a "play school" at Dresden, which he ably conducted for twenty years. The queen of Saxony expressed interest in the movement and asked for a demonstration; and a "christening" of the new institution was held in June, 1840, at which a Women's Kindergarten Union was formed. The well-known *Mutter-und Kose-Lieder*, actually suggested by seeing a mother carrying her child about the farmyard and singing to it, was published in 1844. It had been in preparation for years and the first edition, like the early kindergarten, had a bulky title, *A Family Book for Developing the Self-Activity of Children*.

Assistants, chiefly young women, began to leave Blankenburg to establish kindergartens of their own. There were a half-dozen of these before 1844 in different parts of Germany. Articles began to appear in journals. Diesterweg, the great educator, came and was convinced and his favorable influence was important; and Froebel's travels and addresses helped. Froebel's later years—after 1845—were mainly devoted to the education of young women as kindergartners. The kindergarten as a private institution was well established in numerous places in Germany during Froebel's lifetime.

Creative self-activity through social participation is the basis of Froebel's psychology. His concept of the individual is genetic. The child grows into maturity. He made out five stages: infancy, childhood, boyhood, youth, and maturity, but these are not sharply separated from each other. His concept of the individual is, secondly, an activist concept. The child is by nature a doer; and learning is secondary to doing, out of which it grows. Formal training of the senses, of which Rousseau or Pestalozzi approved, is to be discarded. The senses are used and perception is developed in the course of creative self-activity. Creativeness implies purpose. The individual is partly determined from without— else why a kindergarten—but he also has his own purposes, which he works out as far as conditions permit. The child's purposes must not be too closely controlled, yet civilization—the achievements of the race—must guide the growing individual.

Froebel's psychology, therefore, is less analytic and less mathematical and mechanical than that of Herbart or Locke. Biological and evolutionary ideas were becoming prominent, although Froebel lived before Darwin. The child, according to Froebel, is "replete with all the active tendencies of human nature" and, in John Dewey's phrase, is "spilling over with interests." These active tendencies and interests first manifest themselves as play.

SUMMARY

New schools for children and for their teachers developed out of the work of Pestalozzi. These schools were marked by new methods and new studies but especially by a new spirit of friendliness. The disciples of Pestalozzi carried his message throughout much of the western world, in most cases without great changes or new ideas. Joseph Neef, young Ramsauer, and many others were such promoters of the system worked out by the master.

Others can be set apart as pioneers, with new ideas that may or may not have come into conflict with the Pestalozzian views. Thus the theories of Froebel, in spite of his claim to originality, were absorbed into the thought and system of the common school; but this was accomplished by dropping out some of Froebel's teachings as unessential. John Dewey at Chicago showed clearly how this might be done. In fact the kindergarten was largely reconstructed in the United States and without loss of Froebel's essential ideas.

Fichte, on the other hand, in his early liberal period was highly favorable to Pestalozzi; but later he turned away although continuing to profess support for the Swiss master. Perhaps Fichte should not be included among the great educators; Bertrand Russell even denies him the title of philosopher. But Fichte's *Addresses to the German Nation* is still being reprinted and is worth attention for its extreme views on education.

Herbart is to be classed among the great educators who were also scholars, such as Plato, Aristotle, and perhaps Erasmus, Vives, and others. The group is not a large one. Rousseau and Pestalozzi were not great scholars. Kant was a philosopher and a scholar and he wrote on education. Was he a great educator? The question can be asked about others. One may even inquire whether scholarship may sometimes interfere with insight into educational problems. Great minds may have difficulty in understanding little minds.

Herbart invented an ingenious way of teaching the elements of an inflected language such as Greek. It seems that he did not receive any lessons on how to teach. He accepted the culture-epoch theory and, therefore, taught Greek to his pupils before Latin. It is, perhaps, remarkable that so intellectual a man as Herbart should recognize the genius of Pestalozzi, whom he understood more fully than Froebel did. He said correctly that the welfare of an ignorant people was Pestalozzi's aim. He saw that this education of beggar children had a message for the upper classes. He agreed with Pestalozzi that the ability to observe should be trained. He prepared the way to experimental psychology but did not succeed in inventing it. At the university of Königsborg he had a practice school for teachers. In this not very successful project he had been anticipated in 1779 and later at the University of Halle where Professor E. C. Trapp's practice school had been forced to close by the assaults of the rest of the faculty. The preparation of teachers could be condoned; the sin consisted in the introduction of such work into a university.

QUESTIONS

1. How may we account for the widespread publicity and the meager results of Neef's work in both Pennsylvania and Indiana?
2. Why were teachers' seminaries accepted in Germany while professorships of pedagogy were rejected?
3. How would the future of the Germans have been affected by the adoption of Fichte's program?
4. How much of Pestalozzi's theory did Herbart accept; and, especially, did he accept the democratic implication?
5. Set up the views and practice of Herbart's teaching at Berne into plus and minus columns.
6. Why should Herbart, who denied the possibility of experiment in psychology be, after all, given some credit for the development of experimental psychology? (See E. G. Boring's *History*).
7. In what did the originality of Froebel consist? Trace the evolution of the teaching of young and younger children through Plato, Comenius, Pestalozzi, the infant school, nursery school, Froebel, Headstart, and others.

NOTES AND SOURCES

The book by Joseph Neef on Pestalozzi is mentioned in this chapter. On Fichte there is the translation by R. E. Jones and G. H. Turnbull of the *Addresses to the German Nation by J. H. Fichte,* Chicago, 1922; and the German, *J. G. Fichte, Reden an die Deutsche Nation,* Hamburg, 1955, with introduction by Alwin Diemer.

The *Sämtliche Werke* of Herbart in nineteen volumes, edited by Kehrbach and Flügel, was published at Langensalza, in 1887 and in later years. It was reprinted in 1964.

The Bartholomai-Sallwürk edition of the pedagogical writings with a biography was published as *Johann Friedrich Herbart's Pädagogische Schriften*, Langensalza, Beyer & Mann, 1905–1906 in 2 vols., 456, 467 pp.

An excellent study of Herbart's practitce school at Königsberg, called a seminar, in Germany, is the following by Harold B. Dunkel of the University of Chicago: "Herbart's Pedagogical Seminar," *History of Education Quarterly*, Vol. vii, No. 1, Spring, 1967, 93–101.

BORING, EDWIN G., *A History of Experimental Psychology*, Second edition, New York, Appleton-Century-Crofts, 1950, 777 pp.

COLE, PERCIVAL, R. *Herbart and Froebel, An Attempt at Synthesis*, New York, Teachers College, Columbia University, 1907, 116 pp.

ECKOFF, WILLIAM J., *Herbart's ABC of Sense-Perception and Minor Pedagogical Works*, New York, D. Appleton and Co., 1896, 288 pp.

LANGE, ALEXIS, *Herbart's Outlines of Educational Doctrine*, Annotated by Charles de Garmo, New York, The Macmillan Company, 1901, 334 pp.

RANDELS, GEORGE B., *The Doctrines of Herbart in the United States*. No publisher, place, or date. A dissertation written at the University of Pennsylvania.

REDDIE, CECIL, *Abbotsholme*, London, G. Allen, 1900, 640 pp.

The extensive and still-expanding periodical literature on Froebel and the kindergarten cannot be listed here, but the *Reader's Guide, Education Index*, or other indexes will provide access to American sources. There is a biographical literature on American kindergarten leaders. The Germans have written extensively on Froebel and his influences. Froebel's own writings are relatively unimportant. His chief book, *The Education of Man*, was written before he thought of the kindergarten.

FLETCHER, S. S., and J. WELTON, *Froebel's Chief Writings on Education*, New York, Longmans, Green & Co., 1912, 246 pp.

FRANKS, FANNY, *The Kindergarten System*, London, S. Sonnenschein & Co., 1897, 253 pp.

LAWRENCE, EVELYN, Editor, *Friedrich Froebel and English Education*, New York, Philosophical Library, 1953. Five essays on kindergarten history in England.

MARENHOLTZ-BÜLOW, BERTHA M., *Reminiscences of Friedrich Froebel*, Boston, Lee and Shepard, 1877, 359 pp.

MICHAELIS, EMILIE, and H. K. MOORE, Translators, *Autobiography of Friedrich Froebel*, Syracuse, New York, C. W. Bardeen and Co., 1889, 167 pp.

Part IV
ADAPTING EDUCATION TO NATIONAL AIMS

Chapter 13

NATIONALISM, INTERNATIONALISM, AND EDUCATION

We have now reached the great divide in our history that separates the older education: ancient, medieval, and early modern from those schools and forms of educational control familiar to us by personal experience. The institutional mountain range that divides the older past from the present is *nationalism*, and its individual peaks and great plateaus are the nation-states, which use the school as an instrument of nationalism. We see around us inclusive educational systems that are maintained and directed by the states. These form a close network of related and connected agencies that cover the entire area and embrace the whole population of the country. All of us as children were compelled, in the absence of legal exemptions, to attend such public schools. In the Western countries, and not in them alone, these schools are now so firmly supported by public opinion and established by statute that other possible arrangements hardly come to mind. Yet they are a new phenomenon in history. Inclusive and powerful systems of public schools did not exist anywhere in the world even two centuries ago; and now those earlier conditions have passed away so completely that some historical knowledge and a vigorous use of the historical imagination are needed to understand the transformation caused by the rise of nationalism.

We shall at this point, then, with profit briefly recall how children were educated and how schools were managed before the national era. In all the classical world except Sparta, education was the concern of the family and was conducted according to custom, not law, by tutors in the home or in private schools. State aid was sometimes given, especially in the higher branches, in the Roman Empire, but no general attempt was made to promote the education of the people or to regulate the schools. The Emperor Julian during his brief reign attempted to eliminate Christian teachers and teaching; and two centuries later, the Emperor Justinian decreed the closing of non-Christian schools. But in general the ancient laws and decrees merely served to offer inducements or privileges to teachers and to provide salaries for a very few or to regulate school hours or the conduct of pupils. Roman cities established chairs of letters, rhetoric, and law; but neither the cities nor the Empire developed a general system.

With the dominance of Christianity, cathedral, monastic, and other church schools came into being. The church was far more active in the establishment of schools than the state was or had ever been. Charlemagne, however, harbored a conception of the civil importance of education and he even attempted to spread the benefits of church schools to the lay public. His efforts were not permanently or deeply effective, but they can be considered to have been a slight anticipation of the later collaboration of state and church in education.

After Charlemagne and particularly after 1100, the church greatly expanded its educational efforts. Important cathedral schools developed in the cities and, in the thirteenth century, universities operating under charters and struggling for freedom from external control helped to make an epoch in the competition of state and church for the support of the rising intellectual classes. Schools under municipal, guild, and other corporate auspices also multiplied. And in the Renaissance-Reformation era, a new period of cooperation and competition between church and state for the promotion of education was begun. The growing nations and their national churches developed joint policies for the support and regulation of schools, not only for the ruling classes but also for the common people. This was the era of parochial schools, of semipublic secondary schools, and of the territorial-confessional universities.

The next step in this evolution no longer involved collaboration between state and church but instead led to the displacement of the church as a main educational agency. Schools became public—that is, they were established and controlled by the state; and to church-controlled schools there was reserved only a minor place in the whole system.

As we noted in our discussion of Aristotle, he taught that each form of state—the aristocratic, democratic, or monarchial—has a particular form of education that is most appropriate to it. In this and the following chapters the truth of this teaching will be demonstrated by showing the impact of nationalism on education generally and then tracing the evolution of the educational systems of five nation-states. Our treatment will be both historical and comparative.

THE RISE OF NATIONALISM

Nationalism developed out of community of custom, feeling, belief, and the sense of a common origin and history; and its most effective carriers are language, religion, and education. In the medieval universities the students who came from particular regions organized themselves into "nations." In more recent times nationalism has added to the older foundations a common political organization and political patriotism, and these have led directly to the nation-state. States based on nationality hardly existed in ancient and medieval times. The loyalty of the ancient Greeks was given to a city-state, not to Greece. The Roman Empire was not a nation but an imperial system imposed on peoples of many nationalities. The Middle Ages had little sense of nationality; and they could not have it because of the dominance of a universal church and a universal language, and the lack of a cultivated vernacular language and a common culture.

To understand modern education, it is important to realize that nationalism is a cultural product that is developed by propaganda and education. The nation and the state are objective facts, but nationalism is a condition of the mind. A nation is a people connected by real or at least accepted racial unity, such unity being shown by language, religion, customs, and apparent destiny. The Poles form a nation. The individuals who compose a nation are sometimes called its nationals. A state is a sovereign political body, occupying a definite territory and having a central government. The Swiss state includes nationals of the Italian, French, and German nations. Nationalism, in contrast with these concrete terms, means devotion to national interests and unity, and a nationalist is such a devotee. The height of nationalism would be reached if each nationality constituted an independent state that commanded the complete obedience and loyalty of all its nationals. It is such extreme nationalism that Hitler, Mussolini, and the "one hundred per centers" of all nations have had as an ideal. Nationalism, therefore, implies patriotism, and it is the joining of an accented patriotism with nationality that is new. This is a state of mind that is developed by propaganda and education; and this is the reason why nationalism is an important issue in education. Modern states have used the schools not merely to cultivate loyalty and patriotism, but also to develop chauvinism and an aggressive militarism.

Modern nationalism developed first in Europe. The Crusades, in which Frenchmen took a most active part, helped to develop a sense of solidarity in the West, particularly in France. The wars of the Christians against the Moslems in Spain stimulated a strong nationalist feeling among Spaniards, especially in the time of Ferdinand and Isabella. The strong monarchy that the Conquest of 1066 introduced into England was modified by the Magna

Charta, which the nobles extorted from King John. In the struggle of Parliament with the Crown a high degree of nationalist sentiment was generated also. These three countries were among the first to become great nation-states. However, nationalism is a world-girdling universal movement and its impact on education was not limited to Europe.

Absolutism, although it both fostered and was fostered by nationalism in France, is not a necessary stage in the development of national patriotism. It may even be a hindrance to unity when the government becomes, as the French government in the eighteenth century became, high-handed, capricious, and extravagant. The result was the French Revolution, the First Republic, and a messianic enthusiasm in spreading world democracy.

The essential relations between nationalism and democracy are not altogether clear. "No patriotism without liberty," said Rousseau. And it would seem that a people that governs itself would have a more intense loyalty to state and nation than one that is governed by a class, a party, or a dynasty; but the intense nationalism of National Socialist Germany and the devotion of many nationalities to Soviet Russia perhaps tend to refute this notion of a natural alliance between democracy and nationalism. In France, however, it was the Revolution that blazoned to the world the doctrine of national democracy and threatened the thrones of half of Europe. John Locke had developed the theory of popular government and he was followed by the American patriots of 1776. Rousseau performed a similar function in France.

NATIONAL SYSTEMS OF EDUCATION

The national school systems of Western Europe and the Americas belong to a common family. They differ in many ways, but these ways are like those that distinguish the children of a common parentage; and it is not strange that all of their languages belong to the same far-ranging Indo-European speech. It is even less surprising that these school systems have a common foundation in the culture of the eastern and northern Mediterranean countries of Judea, Greece, and Rome. Much of the culture of those ancient lands was transmitted by the medieval Church and Empire.

On this road came the Judean-Christian religions and practical ethics; Greek philosophy, literature, mathematics, and science; and Roman law and government. Would that the destiny assigned to Rome by Vergil—to rule the nations and to maintain a lasting peace—had been attained; but Rome, although she did not establish perpetual peace, did well by the future otherwise. The civilizing elements brought to the West were molded into new forms by the Renaissance, the Reformation, the Enlightenment, and the democratic revolutions of the seventeenth and eighteenth centuries. These are the foundations and the forces of the school systems of France,

Germany, England, and the United States. Local conditions and particular peoples have given the systems their special forms. If to these four we add a fifth, the system of the Union of the Socialist Soviet Republics, most national systems of education can be related to one of these five in terms of the degree of centralization of educational control at the national level and the degree of local participation in the administration of the state schools.

France can serve as the prototype of a democratic nation-state in which control of education is highly centralized in a national government. There is little or no local participation in the administration of state schools in Spain and Italy; and most of the new and developing countries, such as Indonesia, the African states and Israel, as well as most of the countries of Latin America, incline toward the French pattern of centralization in control of their state systems of education.

Since 1949 the German Federal Republic (West Germany) has represented a pattern in which control of education is centralized in the individual states of the Republic. The local subdivisions of the states have little direct influence on the schools. This same pattern existed throughout German history except for the twelve years under National Socialism. The educational system of a German state is a state system as completely centralized within the state as the French system is within the nation. Australia exemplifies this German pattern of a centralized state system.

The Union of Soviet Socialist Republics can serve as the model for a system of national education in which control is highly centralized in a single political party. Administrative details have been decentralized to the republics and local government units. The People's Republic of China adopted this Soviet model as a basis for its system of education. Although there is an appearance of decentralized control, the real authority is centralized in the monolithic Communist Party.

England reflects a pattern of control divided between the national government and local units. Local authorities have a large measure of freedom in the administration of the schools. Financial support is provided largely by the national government. The Republic of India reflects this divided control of education in that the state ministries of education have decentralized responsibility for elementary schools to local governing authorities while retaining control over secondary education. The 1957 plan for reorganizing the Swedish school system also exemplifies this divided control of education in that local communities are encouraged to reorganize their schools in accordance with the plan by means of grants from the national government. Wales, Scotland, Northern Ireland, Norway, Denmark, and the Netherlands also exemplify this divided control of education.

The United States represents a pattern of decentralized control of education with strong local responsibility. The fifty states and the Federal Government provide financial and other assistance to local school districts to which the states have delegated much of their authority. Canada, Switzerland, and Japan reflect this pattern of strong local control of education.

These groupings of nation-states into five patterns according to the degree of centralization or decentralization of control of their educational systems is admittedly incomplete and overgeneralized in many respects. For example in Latin America, Mexico, Argentina, Venezuela, and Brazil could easily be placed in the pattern of divided national and local control exemplified by England. Also it is difficult to generalize concerning no less than thirty-two countries of middle Africa. Or even within the same country, provinces, such as Quebec and Newfoundland in Canada, would show exceptions to our generalized pattern. In spite of these deficiencies in classifying the educational systems of the nation-states according to a single criterion, such a scheme is believed to be useful in achieving a better understanding of the influences affecting the character of national systems of education. The grouping should assist in our study of the relative roles played by nationalism and other factors, such as racial, geographic, linguistic, political, social, cultural, economic, religious, and secular forces, in determining the form of education that is most appropriate to a particular nation-state, as Aristotle believed.

In order to clarify these relationships, in subsequent chapters we shall trace the historical evolution of the five national systems of education that we have used as patterns for our grouping. However, before concluding this chapter we need to consider the effects on education where the potentially aggressive spirit of nationalism leads to wars among the nation-states and the possibilities of moderating this aggressiveness by developing the counterforce of internationalism.

NATIONALISM, WAR, AND EDUCATION

We have noted that nationalism is a condition of mind leading a people to believe that they belong together; such a state of mind can also lead a people to believe that they are superior to other peoples. It is this latter state of mind that can lead to an exaggerated patriotism, which the French call *chauvinisme*, that often results in war.

Men, women, and children of all ages and conditions suffer in the violence and chaos of war. The children suffer most because they are robbed of nearly the whole of life and of the opportunity to work in building a world of order under law. War destroys the means of learning. Libraries, laboratories, shops, and whole cities are reduced to rubble, and treasures are destroyed that can never be replaced. The world will forever be the poorer because a bomb was dropped in a given place. War scatters teachers and pupils, damages bodies and morals, and destroys the peace of mind needed for fruitful study.

We need go only to World War II to illustrate the disastrous effects of war on education. The Germans found it much more difficult to Nazify the people of their conquered countries than they had expected. The people and the teachers of Norway formed a brilliant example of refusal to take orders from the enemy. The Quisling government, on February 8, 1942, promulgated a law requiring all teachers to join a new teachers' association that was specially designed to promote Nazi principles. Dismissal from their positions was to be the penalty for refusal to join. Twelve thousand of the fourteen thousand teachers of Norway refused, and within two months two thousand of them had been put into concentration camps. Five hundred were deported to the shores of the Arctic Ocean. From time to time school strikes broke out in Oslo and elsewhere. Children refused to take German as their foreign language and elected English instead. The Norwegian Church supported the teachers and pupils in their opposition to the foreign invaders. (See Höye, Bjarne, and Trygve M. Ager, *The Fight of the Norwegian Church Against Nazism*, New York, The Macmillan Company, 1943, 180 pp.) After continued failure to secure a pliant teaching staff, the Nazis, in 1942, closed the schools on the grounds of a fuel shortage. They actually closed them because of the resistance of the population. There were some native collaborators in Norway and others in the coastal countries of Denmark, Holland, and Belgium. France had its Vichy government but also had a vast Resistance movement. In these countries the Germans frequently resorted to the abduction of children from the streets and then shipped them to Germany to be converted into Hitler Youth. In the words of Professor Walter Kotschnig, the Nazis held that "slaves need no leaders"; and they intended not to leave any among their subject peoples.

When the bombing raids over Great Britain developed, both England and Scotland devised plans to evacuate school children, teachers, and also mothers with infants from London, Glasgow, and other large cities. The movement was voluntary, but large numbers from the poorest sections of the towns streamed into villages and country districts. In this way the "two nations" of which Disraeli spoke came face to face with each other. The meeting was not always a mutually agreeable one. Many people were shocked to find that some of the slum children brought with them vermin, bad manners, and the speech and morals of the street.

City schools and homes had, meanwhile, in some cases been bombed. Other schools had been taken over for war purposes, and the available school buildings became overcrowded when the children drifted back, as they soon did. Many of the returning children simply returned to the streets. The problem of the waifs plagued England and all the war-torn countries. The authorities tried to provide schools, and they set up hostels for troublesome youngsters. Youth benefits, which had been started in the nineteenth century, were expanded. Health inspection, medical and dental care, play facilities, and food for the hungry and underfed were supplied through the schools.

On the Continent also there were large-scale evacuations toward the east and away from the cities and military installations. Food was often difficult to obtain and the evacuees' diet was lacking in milk and other sources of calcium. As the war developed, many of such ordinary necessities of life as fuel, soap, shelter, and medicines became scarce. People, and especially children, became more subject to infectious diseases. In 1945 the children of France were on the average three and a half inches shorter and weighed ten pounds less than the comparable young people of 1939. Before the war ended and as the Russian armies approached, many thousands of those who had fled eastward came back and escaped into western Germany. These and the constant stream of those who continue to escape from Communist countries have burdened West Germany with vast numbers of displaced persons. In these and many other ways the children of Britain and the Continent have been deprived of what in a peaceful world would have been considered the normal opportunities of youth.

Many of the minds of Europe's scrambled people have been the victims of racism and war. They are the refugees, waifs, and delinquent youngsters. The refugees are still coming. The daily paper reports a steady stream of farmers, engineers, doctors, and teachers, including one former rector of a university, coming through barbed wire into West Germany. The first eight months of 1958 brought 130,000 because the Communist Party of East Germany had new orders to crack down on nonconformists. These are people who were long tolerated because they were needed; but they will not be tolerated any longer unless they submit. Refugees began coming westward before the war ended and have continued ever since.

Figures tell only the least part of the story. The children among the refugees are not like the calmly self-confident youngsters whom one sees in school in times of peace and prosperity. They are the survivors from a much larger number of the victims of brutality and near-starvation. Many are marked in body and suffer from deficiency diseases. They have been hiding in cellars and ruined buildings by day, fleeing by night, foraging for food, stealing whatever seemed of value. Numbers had joined the underground, thus gaining the chance to retaliate upon their persecutors. They had acquired the immoral code of war, and after the war their teachers had difficulty in again instilling the morals of peace.

Those who escaped, leaving parents and friends behind, often developed feelings of guilt. They felt that they should atone for their desertion. Many who survived persecution, the disappearance of friends, and the experience of deception by those whom they had trusted developed nervous and mental disorders.

Suspicion showed itself in peculiar ways in young refugees. They were not disposed to place confidence in their fellows, but they distrusted the camp management even more. When a new arrival came it was customary for two or three to accompany him when he was interviewed for assignment. They wanted to be assured that he got a square deal.

Although the numbers were so large that a severe burden was laid on the government, the psychiatrists and teachers, and the communities, they formed only a small proportion of the whole body of refugees. The report of the United States High Commissioner for 1953 said, "One of the most serious problems in postwar Germany is posed by the refugees who form one fifth of the Federal Republic's population." The commissioner might have added that they composed a political force strong enough to gain respectful consideration from the government for their demands.

Many of those who would now be in middle age were killed in the prison camps and in the war, and, therefore, the old and the young are most numerous among the survivors. The child refugees in the schools in 1956 numbered about 1,300,000, and they composed about one fifth of the nation's entire school population. They are found in all types and at all levels of schools, including the technological institutions and universities. They are helping in the restoration and development of the country.

Many countries, including America, have gained excellent citizens through the admission of those who were not wanted elsewhere. The Pilgrims of early New England were refugees. Mrs. Carl Schurz, who introduced the kindergarten into the United States, was the wife of a refugee who became a national figure. The Revolution of 1848, the two World Wars, the Nazi coup of 1933, and the Hungarian revolt of 1956 caused many to flee to more hospitable countries, and among these were scientists, scholars, and physicians. Canada and other American countries have given asylum to many, but probably no country in modern times has admitted as many in proportion to its population as West Germany.

The wars have, doubtless, also increased juvenile delinquency. This has, in any event, been growing in many countries. Some would say that programs exhibiting violence on television have contributed some cases. Guns and narcotics are too easily obtainable. The lack of jobs and recreation for youth in the cities must be other causes. Russia has not escaped. Her young hoodlums are ridiculed in *Krododil* and castigated in the newspapers. England suffers from the "Teddy Boys," who were the instigators of race riots in 1958. In the United States, vandalism in school and church buildings and crimes of violence, gang warfare, and even murder are reported in the press. Early diagnosis and special schools are being tried, but the rate of delinquency is still rising.

Many countries have large numbers of people who have no permanent homes or who can spend very little time in their homes. Such are the migrant workers, some theater people, gypsies, and others. The children of the workmen who built the early railroads of Massachusetts troubled the conscience of Horace Mann. Today the fruit-pickers, weeders of the onion fields, the circus people and gypsies, and the "children of the roads and rivers" make a difficult educational problem. The solution is not easy but a scheme of national registration and boarding schools with scholarships might provide the answer. But few countries care enough, it seems, to make such provisions.

Waifs, gamins, and hooligans seem to form a more or less permanent element of society, but the numbers have increased in the postwar years. A psychoeducational study made in Italy lists parental neglect, poverty, mistreatment of the children, and family dissension as the chief reasons why children take to the streets of the less respectable parts of the cities. They live by begging, pilfering, trading, shining shoes, and doing odd jobs. The study showed that most of these adolescent wanderers were practically illiterate and had been badly corrupted by lawless associates. They were very suspicious but could be won over by amusements, games, companionship, and, finally, by offers of a home. An extended description of children of this class has been prepared by a noted Russian educator, A. V. Lunacharskii (1875–1933), who was the first Commissar of Education for the Russian Republic (RSFSR), which is by far the largest of the fifteen republics composing the Soviet Union. His book, *The Waif* (New York, Pantheon Books, Inc., 1955, 292 pp.), seems to be a synthetic account from the early Communist period. It is told in the first person by a "waif" and was published as the work of one, named Nicholas Voinov. Lunacharskii was a cultivated person, and it was he who persuaded Lenin to save the art treasures of Russia. He was removed from office in 1928.

INTERNATIONALISM, PEACE, AND EDUCATION

What are the possibilities of moderating the potentially aggressive spirit of nationalism that leads to war? Some have proposed international education. In professional books and papers international education is a term of several meanings and indefinite scope. A few of the meanings will be indicated and illustrated in the following paragraphs. And by "the plain historical method" we shall try to show that one definition should have preference over others. This definition says that international education is education for peace, the education of nations not to learn the arts of war any more.

This idea will not be universally accepted, but it is at least not new. As World War II was drawing to a close, George F. Zook of the American Council on Education wrote that "a major responsibility for preventing future wars" rested on education, and he claimed that American educators believed that the failure of the League of Nations to stress education for peace was partly responsible for World War II. Every effort should be made, he said, to bring to the world and the framers of the new world organization—the United Nations—the information and ideas that can be used in leading the world to a lasting peace. It was this line of thought, held by many, that led to the establishment of the United Nations Educational, Scientific, and Cultural Organization (UNESCO).

This latter view also is not shared by everyone. Friedrich Schneider, a noted German educator and the founder and editor of the *International Review of Education* (The Hague), believes that the setting of a practical goal for international education will turn it into a biased or prejudiced kind of propaganda. Usually, we commend teachers when they develop definite aims and state them plainly; and in the search for peace a certain degree of prejudice can be excused.

International education as frequently understood is a formless sort of concept. From the earliest times education has tended to spread across both natural and social barriers. Neither mountains and seas nor the differences in the languages and customs of tribes and nations have been able to contain it. Soldiers, merchants, travelers, and missionaries have both incidentally and deliberately carried ideas, knowledge, and practices to those whom they have touched. This is plain from the earlier chapters of this book.

The Christian Church through its propagation of the faith has transmitted much beside its religion. The Moslems, who in the eighth century and afterward conquered portions of Europe, introduced new concepts in arithmetic and trigonometry, chemistry, medicine, architecture, and education. All modern nations use the schools to instill their way of life and to justify their policies before the world. International Communism is one of the most assiduous promoters of so-called international education.

The distinction is that such education is directed by the agent and imposed on the learners. They do not seek it; it seeks them. To call it propaganda is not useful because the line between propaganda and education is too faint. The means to carry on this kind of propaganda-education has been greatly increased by modern inventions, including printing, the post office, and all the newer kinds of communication. Francis Bacon could today take all knowledge for his province if he had the capacity to absorb all of it. It could all be put before him.

The contrasting form of international education in this broad view requires inquirers and students to seek out notable centers and teachers. Such centers were ancient Athens with its Socrates and Alexandria with its library; medieval Europe with the development of its universities; and the Renaissance with the cities of Italy attracting the students of classical learning. Such a center was Germany for the young scholars of the United States in the nineteenth century. The direction of the movement is not, however, the chief difference between this form and the preceding one. The difference is that in this second form the students are the seekers and they are free. In the former case the teacher seeks the students, corrals them, and instructs them. We must not completely separate the two forms for they often coexist, but the difference between them is real and important.

A special example of the second form must be particularly noticed because writers have described it as an important phase of international education. This phase is the study and importation of foreign educational philosophy and practice. As an example we can take the schools of Pestalozzi. These drew from various countries many inquirers who spread his philosophy and methods. His books, especially *Leonard and Gertrude*, made him known; but it was visitors and students of his work at Burgdorf and Yverdon who in some cases converted practically whole nations to the Pestalozzian system. The early visitors inspired the later ones. Thus, Anton Grüner's assistant, Froebel, followed his master in visiting Pestalozzi and then went to live for a few years at Yverdon. Froebel in his turn became the leader of a succession of admiring disciples in Germany, Switzerland, England, and the United States who carried the kindergarten into the most distant lands. Americans usually have been borrowers instead of lenders of educational programs, but the views of John Dewey have been widely disseminated by his books, by foreigners studying in the United States, and by his activity as an educational adviser abroad. Other Americans have been influential in foreign countries, but we need not list them.

International congresses, conferences, associations, fairs, and expositions spread both educational and other knowledge, through formal meetings, through exhibits, and by conversation in the corridors. The three ways are arranged in what is often the order of increasing importance. It was at the international exposition at London in 1851 that Henry Barnard saw his first kindergarten demonstration and realized that the new institution was an improvement over the infant school he had promoted. The International Kindergarten Union was formed a little later. Gradually education won a recognized place in the programs and exhibits of international expositions, such as the one at Paris in 1867 and the World's Fair at Chicago in 1893. There are international student federations, a World Federation of Educational Associations, and in the United States the Institute of International Education (1919) and the International Institute of Teachers Colleges, Columbia University (1923). Further listings would not lead us to our goal, a definition of international education. We must, meanwhile, look at another subject that is sometimes equated with international education, that of comparative education. This is not a new field. A French scholar, Marc-Antoine Jullien, in 1817, published a *Sketch and Preparatory Survey of a Work on Comparative Education*. This pamphlet has only recently been translated into German, and only in part into English. It contains a plan for collecting and disseminating educational information. Fifty years later the United States created the Bureau of Education with just these

Marc-Antoine Jullien, who supported Pestalozzi and suggested the idea of comparative education.

functions, to be exercised, however, in and for the United States. The first head of the Bureau was Henry Barnard, who was giving large space in his *American Journal of Education* to the school systems of Europe.

At least fifty years ago courses on comparative education were offered in the larger American universities by professors of the history of education. Classes were usually small and good textbooks were not available. But gradually some of the large publishing houses such as Longmans, Green and Company and The Macmillan Company provided series of volumes on English, German, French, and other national systems of education. The comparison had to be supplied by the teacher and the students; otherwise, the real subject of the course was not comparative education but foreign school systems. Twenty-five years ago Professor I. L. Kandel, the leading

American authority in the field, brought out his *Comparative Education* (Houghton Mifflin Company, 1933, 922 pp.) which, although now quite old, is still excellent if suitably corrected by later publications.

But what is comparative education? A short answer is found in the title of another book, namely, *Contemporary Education, A Comparative Study of National Systems*, by J. F. Cramer and G. S. Browne (Harcourt, Brace and World Inc., 1965, 598 pp.) Comparative education usually deals with national school systems as they presently are, and *contemporary* is a more truly descriptive word for it than *comparative*. Perhaps the chief question that such a book or course tries to answer is, "What makes the systems 'tick'?" Comparison must be based on knowledge of the forces that propel and direct each of the systems being considered. These forces reside in the physical features, institutions, character, ideals, and economic resources of each country and people; and they can be understood only in the light of their history. A national school system is an instrument of the nation for the formation of the national will and the cultivation of the people's capacities to make that will effective. One key question asks how much freedom a particular nation allows individuals to control their own education and to use it for their own purposes. The last few years have seen a remarkable increase of interest in this subject among professors. The Comparative Education Society has been organized, and its official organ, the *Comparative Education Review*, appeared first in 1957.

Some would identify international education with comparative education; but if they are the same we need only one name. Others would include comparative education under international education as part of a larger whole, but this would be to subordinate a fairly well-defined subject with a method of its own to an area of studies that has neither limit nor system.

The study of the pedagogy of several countries is, as we have seen, sometimes taken as a phase of international education; but it is more appropriately considered as a part of the sections on teacher education in courses in comparative education. The same kind of reduction of lesser topics to parts of large subjects can be pressed much further. Most of the matters that have been included under international education can be assigned to some better-established discipline. The history of education already includes a great many, as any book in this field will show. Geography and world history will absorb what remains after the usual professional subjects have enforced their claims. In that case, we should for international education substitute the education for international peace, not as another subject but as one of the great goals of all education. This goal is about as old as modern nationalism.

Education for peace has been promoted by leading educators since the time of Comenius. He proposed the establishment of a pansophic college where students from many nations were to gather universal knowledge to be applied to the harmonizing of international discord. Comenius was not the first but he was an earnest advocate of this idea. He held that until a universal language could be perfected, a knowledge of languages, especially those of one's neighbors, would be useful. He would have favored the international exchange of teachers and students, the study of comparative education, and the abolition of class privileges in education and other areas of life. He would have applauded Point Four, UNESCO, and other forms of international cooperation. He overemphasized the power of knowledge, but he desired much besides. He proposed to educate everyone in knowledge, virtue, and piety; he hoped to transform people.

To transform people by moderating the aggressive spirit of nationalism and chauvinism is the problem. This problem involves several tasks. To provide a fuller, rounded education of heart and soul as well as of intellect is necessary although difficult. The difficulty is increased by the fact that public schools do not stand outside the emotional currents that move a nation and are apt to carry a full load of nationalist prejudice. Even when educators favor a changed spirit, the public may be hostile, as was demonstrated by the attacks in sections of the United States on the United Nations and UNESCO and on all efforts to teach pupils about these organizations.

There is also the condition that it needs only a single nation to start a war, rendering the best educational efforts of other nations ineffective. Any of the little wars ignited by the "peace-loving nations" can blaze up into a big war. On the other hand countries with popular governments are subject to emotional storms that may sweep across even old-line republics and create the danger of a military explosion. For all these reasons international agencies and diplomacy must carry forward the peace-making and peace-keeping processes to which the schools must also contribute.

Something along educational lines was attempted even before World War I. Fannie Fern Andrews in America worked for the International Conference on Education at The Hague in 1914. Sixteen governments had prepared to send delegates, but the outbreak of war canceled the plan. At war's end there were unsuccessful efforts to commit the League of Nations to the promotion of international education. When these failed, the Committee of Intellectual Cooperation was formed by private efforts in 1921 and later was associated with the League.

After World War I, German and French historians attempted to displace the biased and nationalistic history taught in their schools with objective national accounts. During the 1920s they made great progress in developing more scientific history textbooks, but Hitler (1933) put a stop to this; and, quite in character with his policy, he published the "lies" that the French had admitted but suppressed the corresponding German "lies." The American historian Carleton J. H. Hayes published a survey of nationalism in a hundred French schoolbooks of the 1920s in his *France, A Nation of Patriots* (New York, The Macmillan Company, 1930).

The International Bureau of Education in Geneva was formed in 1926 as a private venture but soon became an intergovernmental body. It served as an international clearing house of educational information. The World Federation of Educational Associations was founded at Oakland, California, in 1923. Governments—France, Great Britain, and the United States included—developed national programs of cultural relations with other countries. Under its Department of State, the United States began a policy of cultural cooperation with other nations in 1938. The preceding are only a few samples of the many international bodies that dispense educational and cultural services. In the following paragraphs we shall deal mainly with the exchange of persons for educational purposes. This is believed to be an effective form of international education.

International scholarships and teacher exchanges are part of a larger class of arrangements for foreign study and teaching. The Rhodes Scholarships at Oxford University were established by Cecil Rhodes, the African diamond king and empire founder, to make war "impossible" between the English-speaking and German peoples. They have, unfortunately, not accomplished this purpose, but according to Frank Aydelotte, American Secretary of the Rhodes Trust for many years, they have developed many hundreds of "world citizens," promoters of international friendship. The exchange of professors has been promoted by the Institute of International Education (1919), which for many years was directed by Stephen Duggan.

Student and teacher exchanges have developed in many countries since the beginning of the present century. A small-scale but interesting example along this line has been promoted by Peter Manniche, long the head of a special kind of Danish folk high school, the International People's College of Elsinore. A newspaper item in the *Times Educational Supplement*, London, on its summer vacation project in 1947 tells the story. It said, The College "has this month [August] entertained about ninety teachers from England and an equal number from eight European countries and British Guiana in South America."

In Europe there are international federations of teachers to promote the exchange of their members and of pupils also. An international federation of teachers' associations and an international federation of secondary school teachers held a joint meeting in Edinburgh in 1947. They made arrangements for the exchange of teachers and pupils, worked for the improved study of languages, and attempted to lay a better foundation for cooperation and understanding among the nations. A resolution was adopted asking UNESCO to develop plans and principles for the exchange of students and teachers. The second of these associations (*Fédération Internationale des Professeurs de l'Enseignement Secondaire Officiel*, or FIPESO) has also undertaken the important task of creating a more democratic outlook in secondary education, a plan from which many European boys and girls could greatly profit.

In the United States, several thousand persons are exchanged annually with corresponding persons from as many as ninety countries to teach, study, lecture, or engage in research under the International Educational Exchange Program carried out by the Department of State, with the help of the Office of Education and voluntary groups such as the National Association of Secondary School Principals. The exchanges were made possible by the Fulbright Act, Public Law 584, the 79th Congress, and the Smith-Mundt Act, Public Law 402, the 80th Congress. Private foundations, universities, and associations also make arrangements for the exchange of educators and students. The Guggenheim Fellowships have long been useful for this purpose.

The Fulbright Scholars are carefully chosen, and according to reports they compare not unfavorably with those sent out with the support of the Rockefeller, Guggenheim, and Ford foundations. The numbers also are not small. Since the beginning, in 1947, a total of about thirty-seven thousand students, teachers, investigators, and technical specialists have received Fulbright aid. Senator J. William Fulbright has said that although the scheme has not yet remade the world, given time it may do so. Values such as those of religion, he has said, are intangible. Senator Fulbright himself was a Rhodes Scholar. One of the values of the program results from the fact that many of the Fulbright and also of the Rhodes Scholars become teachers after their return to America.

In the colleges and universities of the United States the number of foreign students has been growing rapidly, and there are annually, at present, over forty thousand here. They distribute themselves very unequally among possibly fourteen hundred institutions. This is a form of international education in reverse. They come to America, but they return home after completing their program; and their reports cannot but be an important factor in the international reputation of the United States. They should be met by active helpfulness and good will.

Perhaps the most ambitious project for moderating the aggressive spirit of nationalism is UNESCO, to which we have already referred. UNESCO was formed to apply the resources of education, science, and culture in attacking those problems of the world's peoples that might threaten international peace and security. There was an altruistic and humanitarian motive behind this action, and the thought was not entirely new. The League of Nations (1920) was aided by cooperating committees, one of which was the International Committee on Intellectual Cooperation (1924) with aims somewhat like those of UNESCO. Both were to promote education, the exchange of scholars between nations, the rights of intellectuals, and peace. One difference is plain: UNESCO tries to help the have-not persons, peoples, and nations as well as (if not rather than) intellectuals. It also receives better financial support.

The leaders of both bodies have been more distinguished than the leadership they were able to give. They were far greater in other fields than in administration. At the head of the International Committee on Intellectual Cooperation were Gilbert Murray, Chairman, and Albert Einstein, Henri Bergson, and Henri Bonnet. It would be difficult to find a more eminent quartet of intellectuals, but this was a case where administrative skill was needed. Yet the labors of the committee were not without fruit. It investigated the teaching of history and history textbooks, and the teaching of art and music, the two international languages, as they may be called. One result of its activities was the International Bureau of Education at Geneva, already mentioned. The committee was liquidated after World War II, and UNESCO, with a broader mandate, took its place.

The United Nations (1945) provides in its charter for an organization to promote peace and security by intellectual and moral means. A convention with delegates from forty-nine countries met in London in November, 1945, to form such a body. The resulting constitution of UNESCO argues in the memorable words of the Prime Minister of Great Britain, Clement Atlee, that ". . . since wars begin in the minds of men it is in the minds of men that the defences of peace must be constructed." The criticism, sometimes heard, that the "mind" is not as important a cause of war as the Prime Minister supposed is flippant, for the constitution goes on to give due emphasis to economics and politics.

The tasks of UNESCO are, however, intellectual and moral. The constitution would have it promote mutual understanding, equal educational opportunity, the diffusion of knowledge, extended library opportunities, exchange of teachers and students, and respect for justice, law, and fundamental freedoms. In applying these words from its primary law, UNESCO frequently uses education, science, and culture to fight poverty, hunger, dirt, and disease, and, on the mental level, racism and national greed and chauvinism. Certainly wars begin in the minds of men, and the absurd nationalism of the present can be moderated only by changing the minds of men. Incidentally, the word *racism* is found in the newer dictionaries only.

Membership in UNESCO is open to nations, and the present member-nations number eighty-two. Each member has one vote in the General Conference, which is the legislative body, and which directs the work. Delegates are chosen by national commissions formed in each state. Instead of the annual meetings of the early years, the General Conference now meets every two years. The first meeting at Paris was followed by other early convocations in Mexico City, Beirut, and Montevideo. An Executive Board and a Secretariat of some hundreds of international civil servants carry on the day-to-day business. The chief executive office is that of the Director-General. Early incumbents were Julian Huxley, British biologist, J. Torres Bodet of Mexico, Luther Evans of the United States, and Dr. Vittorino Veronese of Italy. The interposition of national commissions between the member-nations and UNESCO was intended to reduce national pressures on the international body; but in the Senator McCarthy period in the United States the device seemed ineffective.

In the beginning UNESCO had difficulty in settling on a plan and program. So many projects were submitted to it by delegates and such diverse views were held of its proper functions that much of its energy was spent in program-making. The danger that UNESCO might become another scientific society or one dispensing social theory and propaganda was avoided. Fortunately, UNESCO has found ways of helping backward peoples through practical education to help themselves. This thought was developed by Bodet who, when he was Director-General, proposed three yardsticks for all projects as follows: (1) Will the project promote the welfare of the masses and improve their living conditions? UNESCO is not "an assembly of mandarins." (2) Will it enlist the cooperation of intellectual leaders everywhere to work for humanity? If it can be done without educators, scientists, scholars, let it be done elsewhere. (3) Will it produce results quickly? UNESCO must succeed early if it is to survive.

Program, support, and permanent membership all were in doubt for some years. When the first General Conference met in 1946, the administration hoped for an $8,000,000 budget, but this estimate shrank by one fourth. It has since been increased a great deal. There were only forty-three nations represented at the first General Conference. Some early members, being Russian satellites, soon withdrew or, we should say, were withdrawn. Russia remained away until 1954, when she joined as the seventieth member, and her satellites returned. At the time there were those who predicted that she was joining merely to make trouble. They were mistaken, but this is no proof that Russia is in full sympathy with the aims of UNESCO. In late 1958, the General Conference defeated Russia's efforts to gain a seat for Red China and her proposal to grant full accreditation to the delegates from her satellite Hungary. The chief Russian delegate replied to these rebuffs by raising the question whether Russia was getting from UNESCO the value of her contribution to it. The budget then (1958) was about $25,000,000, and Russia contributed 13 per cent, the United States, over 32 per cent.

UNESCO spent much time in the early years making pronouncements and was critized for talking instead of acting. Some statements, although not effective at once, were significant. The Universal Declaration of Human Rights was much criticized but significant. The Declaration's thirty substantive articles affirm (1) that all persons are born free and equal in dignity and rights; (2) that all are entitled to the essential human rights and freedoms without respect to race, color, sex, religion, or property; and (3) that among these rights are life, liberty, security of person, freedom from slavery, torture, cruel or inhuman and degrading treatment and from attacks on the honor and reputation of any person. It would seem that such statements are demanded because the promises of 1776 and 1789 have not in two centuries been fulfilled. The Declaration is not a legal but an educational instrument.

The spread of fundamental education is the primary means selected to aid peace and security. To remove illiteracy is an essential part of fundamental education. If the removal of illiteracy were easy, it would have been achieved long ago. Over one half of the people of the world are unable to read and write in any useful degree. Many illiterates are found even in countries that take pride in their public school systems, such as in the United States of America. For this there may be no sufficient excuse. But in parts of Asia and Africa where the rates of illiteracy are highest, tax yields are low, the birthrate high, and life expectancy short. The result is that there are few producers of economic goods and no margin of capital savings to pay for schools. UNESCO has made and published many studies of such conditions.

An opportunity to attack the problem in a Western nation occurred in 1947 when the General Conference met in Mexico. This is a country with a highly cultivated upper class in the capital and elsewhere but with many illiterates, low living standards, and poverty in rural areas, especially among the Indian population. When the Mexican government offered opportunity and facilities to institute a fundamental education scheme, UNESCO decided to make it one of a series of pilot experiments that might serve as models for other areas and countries.

The place chosen for the project is in the small state of Nayarit on the coast in west-central Mexico. The whole state is about as large as Vermont, but it has only half as many people. The area chosen is also a tropical plain drained by the Santiago River that winds its way from the sierras on the east to the Pacific Ocean. The district has a small city, about thirty villages, and a population of fifty thousand made up of businessmen, farmers, fishermen, laborers, Indian tribes, and their dependents. The experiment is an enlarged version of the cultural missions that have been carried on in many countries. Those also were intended as examples to the neighbors, examples of a method to develop socially and economically backward communities.

The fundamental education experiments directed by UNESCO are new only in the sense that they are large, well financed, and expertly administered. In the present case the promoters dealt with the occupations and economics of the people; they built a road across the sierras to provide access to markets and contacts with the socially advanced world outside; they showed how houses should be built; they attacked the causes of malaria and other tropical diseases; and with a well-drilling outfit they provided pure water. Schools were established in all villages, many with kindergartens. Personnel trained in the Mexican pilot project and a similar one in Egypt are working in five South American countries and in the Near East.

Parallel to the promotion of fundamental education is UNESCO's aid to the establishment of free and compulsory public school systems. Korea and Libya are among the countries aided in this matter. A third UNESCO activity is the provision, with the help of other specialized agencies of the United Nations, of technical assistance. Other agencies such as the United States Department of State, through the Point Four program, also work along this line. UNESCO's greatest success in recent years has been in giving technical assistance to education in less developed countries. "Education is the big push in UNESCO," said Luther Evans.

The library program is another activity that is likely to have helpful results. Few countries of the world, perhaps about ten, have modern library systems. UNESCO has led in establishing pilot libraries in New Delhi, India, and in Medellin, Colombia. The plans include not only modern processes in a central library but also branches and bookmobiles to take books to prospective readers. Not wholly unrelated to library developments is UNESCO's work in promoting a universal copyright convention that went into operation in 1956. Other activities such as arid zone studies to make the once fruitful deserts bloom again and the hope of conquering the Amazon Basin cannot be treated here. It was, no doubt, the former of these to which President Eisenhower referred in his speech to the Near East during the 1958 diplomatic and military crisis.

SUMMARY

Before the rise of nationalism, schools were usually conducted either by private or by church agencies. The imperial and municipal schools of the Roman Empire form only apparent exceptions, for they were not controlled by the state or specifically intended to promote its interests. In the later Middle Ages and after the Reformation, newly founded municipal schools became numerous and state activity became pronounced; but only in the last two centuries have the great national states created public schools for the education of all.

These national systems of schools generally exemplify the patterns developed by five of the great nation states: France, Germany, the USSR, England, and the United States. The historical evolution of these five systems will be traced in subsequent chapters.

The great wars have done great harm to schools and children, but by revealing the weak spots in education they may have also helped to bring about some improvements. Nazi fanaticism and the war and, on the other hand, the Resistance movement exerted the most evil influences on many young lives. Schools and other mental and moral agencies have had a hard and not always successful task to bring them back to physical and mental health. Education should do what it can do to prevent war and so to make unnecessary the repair of its destruction, not to speak of its irreparable wastes and horrors. Education for peace should be carried on in schools; and UNESCO is a practical agency putting into effect what schools teach by bringing the means of self-help to depressed countries, by helping to cure present ills, and by raising a vision and a hope. References are given subsequently to magazines that carried the violent American criticisms of UNESCO and objections to American participation in it. Educational and general periodical guides provide further citations.

QUESTIONS

1. Why has nationalism become strong and aggressive in recent times, when it was almost unknown in earlier days? Consider changes in economic conditions, in modes of communication, in science, invention, and the conduct of war, and the complementary effects of nationalism and education on each other.
2. How could an adequate view of a nation's schools be presented to the people?
3. Why does secondary education everywhere pose greater difficulties than elementary or higher education?
4. What is the meaning of the phrase, "Slaves need no leaders"? Is the statement, as you interpret it, true?
5. If a nation contributes to the support of church schools, should it not also aid the independent schools? And if it provides support, should it not also inspect and license them?
6. Should special public schools be provided for talented young people, and can you recommend other ways of cultivating and directing their capacities?
7. If international education and UNESCO are accepted and promoted, as it seems, mainly in the "democratic and peace-loving countries," how can they advance the cause of peace? Which are the "democratic and peace-loving countries"?
8. Should language-study aim at a speaking knowledge mainly, or a reading knowledge? Consider the several values of language study for people today.
9. By what tests can a school system be shown to be mature? Compare certain school systems with respect to their maturity.
10. If television is extensively used what roles should be assigned to teachers?

NOTES AND SOURCES

The quarterly *International Review of Education*, The Hague, Holland, has been revived since its release from Nazi control. The founder, Friedrich Schneider, has returned to the publication. Professor Karl Bigelow from Teachers College, Columbia University, is on the editorial board. The *Comparative Education Review* is published in New York. The London *Times Educational Supplement* and *School and Society* have been of great value in the preparation of this chapter.

The publications of UNESCO, including documents, reports, pronouncements, directories, and studies, many of them pamphlets, are far too numerous to list. One of its publications is the quarterly *Fundamental and Adult Education*, which with others that are still in print can be obtained from UNESCO Publications Center, New York, New York. For some idea of the hostility aroused by UNESCO, see *Saturday Evening Post*, October 2, 1948; *American Mercury*, January, 1954, February, 1954, and August, 1956; and *Commonweal*, May 27, 1954. The article last cited deals critically with the outburst in Los Angeles.

"International Education," by W. W. Brickman, *Encyclopedia of Educational Research*, New York, The Macmillan Company, 1950; and "Intergroup Education" by Lloyd Allen Cook, in the same volume, and their references will carry the student of these topics a considerable distance.

The *Year Book of Education* was founded in 1932; and since 1953 it has been prepared under the joint editorial care of the Institute of Education, University of London, England, and Teachers College, Columbia University. It is published by Evans Brothers, Ltd., Russell Square, London, and the World Book Company, Yonkers-on-Hudson, New York.

ASCHER, CHARLES S., *Program-Making in UNESCO 1946–1951*, Chicago, Public Administration Service, 1951, 84 pp., double-column.

BEACH, FRED F., and ROBERT F. WILL, *The State and Nonpublic Schools*, Washington, D.C., United States Government Printing Office, 1958, 152 pp.

BENJAMIN, HAROLD, *Under Their Own Command, Observations on the Nature of a People's Education for War and Peace*, New York, The Macmillan Company, 1947, 88 pp.

BRICKMAN, W. W., "The World Challenge to Elementary and Secondary Education," *Educational Forum*, XVIII, May, 1956, 477–481.

CRAMER, J. F., and G. S. BROWNE, *Contemporary Education, A Comparative Study of National Systems*, New York, Harcourt, Brace and World, Inc., 1956, 598 pp.

HAYES, CARLETON J. H., *Essays on Nationalism*, New York, The Macmillan Company, 1926, 279 pp.; *France, A Nation of Patriots*, New York, Columbia University Press, 1930, 487 pp.; *The Historical Evolution of Modern Nationalism*, New York, Richard R. Smith, 1931, 327 pp. The second work cited here is an important study of nationalist education as conducted by schools and other agencies.

LAVES, WALTER H. C., and CHARLES A. THOMSON, *UNESCO: Purpose, Progress, Prospects*, Bloomington, Indiana University Press, 1947, 469 pp.

LINDEGREN, ALINA M., *Germany Revisited, Education in the Federal Republic*, Washington, D.C., United States Office of Education, Bulletin, 1957, No. 12, 107 pp. Bibliography, pp. 101–107.

MALLINSON, VERNON, *An Introduction to the Study of Comparative Education*, London, William Heinemann, Ltd., [1957], 249 pp.

PILGERT, HENRY P., *The West German Educational System*, Frankfurt-am-Main, Office of the United States High Commissioner for Germany, 1953, 136 pp.

REISNER, EDWARD H., *Education and Nationalism Since 1789*, New York, The Macmillan Company, 1922, 575 pp.

SAMUEL, R. H., and R. HINTON THOMAS, *Education and Society in Modern Germany*, London, Routledge and Kegan Paul, Ltd., [1949], 191 pp.

SCHWARZ, LEO W., *Refugees in Germany Today*, New York, Twayne Publishing Company, [1957], 168 pp. Bibliography.

TANDLER, FREDRIKA, *Teaching About the United Nations . . .* , United States Office of Education, Bulletin, 1956, No. 8, 40 pp.

Teacher Exchange Opportunities, 1959–1960, Washington, D.C., United States Office of Education, 1958. Pamphlet issued annually.

UNESCO, *Flight and Resettlement*, [Paris, 1955], 281 pp. Illustrated. First-hand stories and scientific studies by several contributors.

UNESCO, *Fundamental Education*, New York, The Macmillan Company, 1947, 325 pp.

WALSH, HENRY H., *The Concordat of 1801: A Study in the Problem of Nationalism in the Relations of Church and State*, New York, Columbia University Press, 1933, 259 pp.

Chapter 14

NATIONAL EDUCATION IN FRANCE

It was in France that nationalism developed most rapidly and reached its highest point. Intellectual and political forces aided its growth. The revival of the study of the Roman law had a considerable influence on the French judicial system. The position obtained by a body of professional lawyers who derived their powers from the king increased the growing might of the monarchy. During the same period, the right of the king to impose taxes without the consent and against the will of the papacy was affirmed by the Estates General. That body, the system of national taxation they ratified, and the standing army that was then created were all instruments of centralization. This tendency became much stronger during the Hundred Years War. If the Estates General had seized the opportunity during the anarchy that followed the French defeats at Crécy and Poitiers, they might have developed into an institution able like the English Parliament to set limits to the power of the crown; but they were unable to do this and the French monarchy continued in its course toward absolutism. Louis XIV admitted with royal candor that the love of glory took precedence over everything else in his soul. His ministers sought to stimulate the intellectual life of France for the exaltation of the crown, to encourage art, literature, and science, and to refine the civilization and culture of the nation. In this period France occupied the center of the European stage as the leader in thought and action. At last, the centralizing process reached such a point that Louis XIV could pertinently declare, "*L'État, c'est moi*"; and the cultural eminence of that state was likewise unchallenged. The French Revolution swept away the autocratic monarchy, class privileges, and local provincialism and united the French-speaking people into a democratic national state that undertook the task of spreading democracy throughout Europe and the world. And it was the Revolution that called out the *Report of Condorcet* and other schemes for universal, secular education.

LA CHALOTAIS ON NATIONAL EDUCATION

In France, where the Jesuits were in control of education, the idea of national education received little support until the latter part of the eighteenth century, when La Chalotais, Condorcet, and many others began to promulgate it. The *Essay on National Education* was written by La Chalotais in 1763. It was an attack rather than a program. It was directed against political and religious privilege and especially against the Jesuits and their schools rather than toward national education. Yet it contained an argument for a secular system of public schools and it offered a regular plan of studies. There was the usual attack on the decadent humanism of that period and the charge that the Jesuits taught little but Latin and that ineffectively. Their pupils, he declared, cannot tell a bad argument from a good one, or set forth the principles of their religion, or even write a letter. He went on to maintain that more important still, the Jesuits, who are presuming to prepare citizens of France, give their allegiance to a foreign power, the pope in Rome. He demanded, instead, a national system of education, because every state, he claimed, has the right and duty to educate its own citizens. Yet he was an educational reactionary, for he restricted schooling to the upper classes. As a mercantilist, he wanted to limit the number of the clergy and lawyers, whom he regarded as economically unproductive. Considering the opposite end of the social scale, he condemned any extended education of the working classes because it would make them discontented with their lot as laborers.

THE PLAN OF CONDORCET

In the generation following La Chalotais, interest in national education increased rapidly in France. Turgot, who was for a short time the capable finance minister of Louis XVI, proposed in 1775 the creation of a Council of National Education that would control all schools, including those of the primary grades. In the primary school, he proposed to have instruction given in manners and customs and the social duties of citizens, with a schoolmaster in every parish to teach the usual elements and also elementary geometry and the principles of mechanics. Diderot, in his plan of a university, proposed schools that would be open without distinction to all the children of the nation, where publicly paid teachers should instruct them in an elementary knowledge of all the sciences. But it was Condorcet

(1743-1794) who prepared the most careful plan for the education of the French people along modern lines in his *Report on Public Instruction*.

The Marquis de Condorcet was an original mathematician, a philosopher, and one of the leaders of the Revolution—an aristocrat by birth but a democrat by conviction. He was also one of the great exponents of the theory of historical progress. One of his finest achievements was a life of Turgot, whose plan for the financial rehabilitation of France he had ardently supported. Living in times of social upheaval, he was a friendly spectator of the drama of the American Revolution but a tragic actor in the French Revolution. He was chosen a member of successive national legislatures and was commissioned by one of them, the National Assembly, to prepare a report on education. This he presented in the spring of 1792. It was a document of about fifty pages containing a plan for a complete system of national education; but it was meant to be more than that— namely, a charter of freedom, self-realization, and happiness. Condorcet was possessed by two ideas: the idea of liberty and the idea of human perfectibility.

The aim of national education is a part of the larger aim of every social institution—namely, the general and gradual improvement of the human race. This desired improvement of all would be attained, he continued, by offering to all individuals the means of securing their welfare and their rights, of satisfying their needs and fulfilling their obligations; by giving to each the opportunity of perfecting to the fullest extent all those talents with which nature has endowed him. Then each will be able to perform his political duties; and only then will the political equality of the citizens guaranteed by the law become a fact. The individualistic spirit and the optimistic tone of this statement are apparent. The counterpart of this interest in the individual was his cosmopolitanism and interest in the welfare of all mankind. The needs of mankind impose on governments the obligation to establish schools in which every individual can develop fully all his natural talents; and this, given the opportunity, everyone will do. The direction of such a view diverges at an angle of practically one hundred eighty degrees from the usual nationalist position that governments should support education for the sake of national unity and economic and military power. Condorcet would have the government serve the people; and the people were to him, not a mass, but a group of individuals.

The outlines of his plan are clear and logical, as one would expect from a mind like Condorcet's. His basic principles demand universal education with equal opportunities for everyone and with curricula and facilities as complete as money and time will allow; as much freedom as possible from political control, from political propaganda, and from the political suppression of truth; and continued opportunity for adult education throughout life. He proposed four grades of schools: the primary schools, one in every village to teach the elements including measurements, morals, and some agricultural and industrial instruction; the secondary schools, one in each town of four thousand inhabitants, in which the sciences and social studies were to be taught; the institutes, one or more in each of the ninety departments of France, in which the applied sciences such as agriculture and the mechanical arts were to be taught; and the lyceums, corresponding to the university in grade, of which there were to be nine in the whole country. Education was to be free in the primary and secondary schools; scientific, social, and civic studies were to be emphasized at the expense of the languages and the fine arts; the courses in the institutes and lyceums were to be elective; special attention was to be given by the teachers to methods of teaching—the use of demonstrations and other illustrative materials and the preparation of good textbooks—all for the purpose of making the student as soon as possible independent of the teacher and school. In his faith in the common man's desire and capacity for knowledge and enlightenment, Condorcet was one of the most optimistic of all educational writers. Comenius believed that the average man had great, practically unlimited capacity to retain what he had been taught; but Condorcet believed that the average man would ardently and persistently pursue knowledge, if only the means were made available. Not only in the lower schools but even in the institutes, a certain number of chairs were to be reserved in each classroom for those citizens who had not been able to receive a complete education but who, although not being regular students, might yet wish to follow a course of instruction or even merely be present at a few lessons.

To make it possible for poor but talented children to continue their education beyond the primary schools, Condorcet proposed to have about four thousand national scholarships created. Each of these was to maintain a national scholar for a year. The plan was to open to the poorer classes an "abundant source of prosperity and learning" and to society a "powerful means to maintain the natural equality of man." The plan has no provision for normal schools or teacher training.

The final proposition of Condorcet's plan was quite unrealistic. To protect the schools against political interference, he proposed to place the system under the control of a self-perpetuating board of scholars that he called the National Society of Sciences and Arts. It was to be their duty to supervise the schools, to perfect the sciences and arts, and to disseminate useful discoveries. We can applaud his purpose but surely no government would continue to support a full complement of national schools over which it was not allowed any sort of control. A nonpartisan board, either elected or appointed, would have been a more reasonable suggestion.

The actual French school system will be separately considered. The hopes of the Revolution were long deferred, but during that period there were drafted many, a score or more, plans for a system of schools for the

French nation. For the most part they asked for publicly supported and controlled secular schools with a practical, civic, and largely scientific curriculum. Education was to be free and universal in the lower grades at least. In general they proposed a centralized system of state administration and some scheme of normal schools for the preparation of teachers.

FRENCH EDUCATION TO 1830

The programs of the Revolution could not be put into effect immediately. The disorder of the times, the lack of resources and of an effective tax system, the lack of professional lay teachers, and the absence of a national educational consciousness delayed the establishment of universal free education for almost a century. Meanwhile, France was working at this task. The actual achievements of the Revolution were in secondary and higher education. A radical bill by Lepeletier de Saint-Fargeau to create a system based on that of ancient Sparta was not adopted. The law of Lakanal to establish elementary and secondary schools was ineffective. One of his proposals led to the brief opening in 1795 of the *École Normale Supérieure* and this, when it was reestablished by Napoleon, became permanent and is still a part of the University of Paris. It has always been a higher school of science to prepare teachers for lycées. Another law of 1795, named for Daunou and sponsored by the middle class, led to the organization of some primary schools and more especially of secondary or central and higher schools in which the bourgeoisie was particularly interested. The central schools this law established had a distinctly modern and practical curriculum and were later patronized by Napoleon, but they were too few in number and too poorly organized to compete with the lycées. Daunou's law might have been more effective but for the foreign wars in which France became involved. However, its failure also shows the bankruptcy of revolutionary radicalism that had demanded elementary, not secondary, education. The same conservative trend is shown by the dozen or more technical schools, bureaus, and conservatories that were opened in Paris by the Convention. The Convention also adopted the newly devised metric system of weights and measures. From these revolutionary beginnings a national system of education was developed in the course of the nineteenth century.

The interest of Napoleon was in secondary and technical, not in primary, education. One of his first acts was the creation of four military schools out of the endowments of the sixteenth-century Humanistic school, the Collège of Louis le Grand. He also instituted a system of colleges and lycées and within a few years more than four hundred of these were opened or reopened in the whole country. These taught about fifteen subjects including Latin, French, science, and mathematics. They were boarding schools, and although the law defined their curriculum the state, beyond providing the buildings, gave little financial help.

Yet, although private schools continued, this was the beginning of modern secondary education in France. The noted chemist, Fourcroy, was made Director-General of Public Instruction with three superintendents of secondary studies. The same law of 1802 established special schools of medicine, law, and science. And Napoleon created a School of Arts and Trades and fostered two schools of engineering and mining that had been opened earlier. French engineering schools took first rank under Napoleon, and the American West Point and Rensselaer Polytechnic were indebted to them. The same is true of the Paris schools for the deaf and blind that became models for American schools at Hartford (1817) and Boston (1832). For primary education, Napoleon did little more than to reenact Daunou's law and to enjoin that teachers should not carry their instruction beyond the rudiments. The state did not support them, and after the Concordat of 1801, by which Napoleon made his peace with the Catholic Church, the Brothers of the Christian schools again came in as teachers of the primary schools.

The most spectacular and influential work of Napoleon in the whole field of education was the creation of the University of France, at first called the Imperial University. This is not a school but an administrative system to direct and control all grades of schools. The decree that created it, with a Grand Master at the head and a council of twenty-six members, was issued in 1808. Its functions were to govern the schools, appoint the teachers, disburse the funds, and set the school examinations. "No school, no establishment of instruction whatsoever," the decree declared, "may be set up outside the Imperial University and without the authorization of its head." With various changes of powers and even of name, this highly centralized system of educational control lasted until 1940. The nearest American analogy is to be found in the University of the State of New York.

Napoleon considered education to be a primary function of the state. He declared that education is of all political questions perhaps the most important. Unless there is a teaching body with definite principles, unless the child is taught from infancy whether he is to be a republican or a monarchist, a Catholic or a freethinker, the state will not be a nation but will rest on shifting foundations constantly exposed to disorder and change. He saw clearly the political use that could be made of national education. In creating the University he said,

It was necessary for me to create a civil profession, disinterested, grave, which would work in the interests of science and letters. That is the ideal of my University. . . . Above all I insist that it shall devote itself to letters. I love the mathematical and physical sciences; algebra, chemistry, botany are excellent though partial applications of the human spirit; but lettetrs are the human spirit itself. The study of letters is the general education which prepares for everything; it is the education of the soul.

By letters he meant French and Latin literature. In this ideal of classical education as in his centralizing system of control, Napoleon expressed the spirit of France, and these two ideals have been dominant in French education from that time to the present.

During the period of the Restoration (1815–1830), French industry and agriculture prospered; but little was done for education. The very small annual appropriations were gradually increased and by 1830 somewhat more than half of the thirty-seven thousand communes (or townships) had established primary schools. An effort was made to improve the qualifications of the teachers by requiring certification, but the Brothers of the Christian schools resisted this demand and were excused from the requirement. Thirteen normal schools for primary teachers were established. The monitorial system was introduced from England and, as in the parent country, it aroused great enthusiasm. The infant schools, first developed by J. F. Oberlin in the previous century in eastern France, were now modified to follow the English pattern. In the next reign they were accepted by the government as part of the public system.

UNDER THE JULY MONARCHY

The Restoration government fell because the king, Charles X, like a true Bourbon, attempted to alter the constitution to increase his own power. The middle classes, who had been partially disfranchised by royal ordinance, with the help of the Paris workingmen overthrew the government in July, 1830. Louis Philippe of the House of Orleans became king. The July Monarchy was not a popular but rather a businessman's government. The working classes, who had ensured the success of the July Revolution, went unrepresented. But the country increased in wealth and population. Industry was fostered. The state aided in the building of roads, canals, and railroads; and agriculture was rapidly improved. The "internal improvements" of France paralleled those of the United States in the same period; and in both countries the increasing wealth provided the economic foundation for the extension and improvement of schools. The French Revolution had developed the theory and created the demand for national education and the Industrial Revolution created the means that made it practicable.

The greatest educational achievement of the July Monarchy was the Primary School Law of 1833. The primary and higher primary schools that the law created were intended for the common people; and the old colleges and lycées continued to furnish secondary instruction for the upper, the wealthy, and the professional classes. There was no attempt to combine the primary and secondary schools into a ladder system that would have enabled the children of the common people to enter the secondary schools and to prepare for a profession. The July Government was conservative and bourgeois and was the friend of popular education to this extent and on these lines only. It did not intend to open the higher professions to common people.

The new government immediately increased the annual appropriation for primary schools; required all teachers to hold a certificate from the state, even those who belonged to religious orders; and opened thirty new normal schools. To find a model for the new primary school system that was proposed, they looked to Germany, which had recently reformed its schools. Victor Cousin was sent as a special investigator to gather the results of that country's experience. His *Report on . . . Public Instruction in Germany . . .* was issued at Paris in 1831 and an English translation appeared in London and New York. This was one of the important educational documents of the century. Cousin favored local school control, but the centralizing tendencies of France were too strong to permit the use of this idea. He did not recommend compulsory attendance because he was sure the French people were not ready for it. He insisted that every commune must have a primary school and proposed the establishment also of higher primary schools. These ideas were adopted.

By the law of 1833, the primary schools were required to teach the French language. This teaching was to include work in reading, writing, spelling, grammar and composition, the elements of arithmetic, and the metric system of weights and measures. Church schools were to be allowed if the teachers held legal certificates and if the schools submitted to state inspection. Other important concessions were made to the church. Religious bodies were to be represented on the local school committee, but a child was to receive religious instruction only when it was approved by the parents. These provisions show how the religious difficulty was solved, and they reveal the extent to which France had receded from the secularizing tendencies of the Revolution. The schools were allowed to charge fees, but these were to be remitted to poor children the teachers' salaries were guaranteed and the cost of the schools was to be met, according to a formula written into the law, by the communes, the departments, and the state.

The administration of the schools was apportioned among the same units. There was to be a local committee of the commune with slight powers; and a committee of the arrondissement with more general powers. The arrondissements are the largest political divisions of a department and are themselves divided into cantons and these into communes. The committee of the arrondissement appointed the teachers and reported to the national ministry on the condition of the schools. The power of the central government was supreme. Through inspectors, the minister could control the schools, the teachers, and the officers of the arrondissements and communes. By the end of the reign of Louis Philippe about one hundred and fifty inspectors were in service and were exercising delegated powers similar to those of an American superintendent of schools.

The law required the establishment of higher primary schools in the chief cities. These admitted pupils who had completed the work of the lower schools. They taught practical mathematics, including the elements of geometry; drawing; design; some measurements and surveying; some physical and biological science; singing; and the history and geography of France. Where possible, instruction in a modern language and other additional subjects might be offered. But the higher primary schools were primary rather than higher, for they did not prepare their pupils to enter a university. Adult classes were organized, and by 1848 a hundred thousand persons were receiving postprimary instruction. Despite this auspicious beginning, the higher primary schools soon began to decline. Their greatest success was achieved after they were revived by the Third Republic.

The infant schools that had been established under the Restoration were accepted as a part of the public system in 1837. The industrial development of France and the employment of women in factories made them a useful adjunct of the primary system. They were placed under the management of the existing school committees. They admitted children up to the age of six and taught singing, needlework, and manual activities, together with some work in the elementary school subjects.

Within a few months after the passage of the law, the Minister of Public Instruction, Guizot, sent a body of special investigators to report on the condition of primary education throughout the country. The reports were compiled by P. Lorain and published as *A Survey of Primary Education* (1837). This survey called particular attention to the educational ills of the poorer rural districts and showed that whole communities were illiterate and many communes entirely without schools. Where schools existed, they were often poorly housed and conducted by teachers whose main business might be the selling of liquor or the mending of shoes. Some teachers were paid in provisions that they collected by going from house to house. These were only the worst cases and it would be easy to point to similar conditions in other countries. The purpose of the report was to arouse the French people to the need for immediate improvement. France in 1851 had sixty-one thousand primary schools, but there were even at that time twenty-five hundred communes without schools; the number of normal schools for men had been greatly increased, and a parallel system of normal schools for women had been begun.

The secondary schools, lycées and *collèges*, remained under government supervision. They were the classical schools that prepared for entrance to the universities, admiting students at the age of eleven and graduating them as *baccalauréats* at eighteen. By 1850, France had about fifteen hundred public and private secondary schools with a total enrollment of eighty-five thousand pupils. From these the future civil servants and professional classes were drawn, opportunities that to the parents justified the considerable expense involved. These facts perhaps sufficiently explain the initial failure of the higher primary schools, which could offer no such privileges.

UNDER NAPOLEON III

The Second Republic lasted from 1848 to 1853, but during the last of these years Louis Napoleon was actually in power and in December of the latter year he was proclaimed Emperor of France and took the name Napoleon III. The revolutionary year of 1848 was followed in France, Germany, and other countries by a strong reaction from liberalism toward autocracy; and the French education law of 1850 was a reactionary statute. Carnot, the Minister of Public Instruction under the provisional government, had appealed to the primary teachers to work for the election of liberal-minded representatives. Looking back to the great Revolution, he declared: "It is not now a matter, as it was in the time of our fathers, of defending the Republic against foreign foes, but rather of defending it against ignorance and deception [from within]; and that task belongs to the teachers." We do not know whether the teachers followed Carnot's suggestion and electioneered for liberal candidates; but the conservatives won. And a noted English observer, Matthew Arnold, remarked that "the conquerors of the Revolution of 1848" did not fail to remember that Carnot and his party had made the schoolmasters their missionaries.

It is perhaps not hard to see why teachers should and why some of them do in fact support a liberal political policy. They usually come from the lower and lower middle classes and have a great deal to gain from a wide distribution of power and from liberal policies. One ought to expect also that teachers would be liberal-minded and liberally educated persons. If this were the attitude and disposition of the French teachers, they were disappointed. Both Carnot's bill and that of Saint-Hilaire, which was substituted for it, had provided for a full complement of infant, primary, higher primary, normal, and trade schools with liberal curricula, free tuition in part, and compulsory attendance until the age of fourteen. But such a program had no chance of adoption in the legislature, with its strong monarchist majority. An education committee of the new government led an attack on the normal schools and their curriculum. They declared that the outlook of the primary teachers should be limited to the local school and community; and that they did not desire, as did teachers in French primary schools, the budding scholars who had been coming from the normal schools. They limited the courses in history and geography in the normal schools and made them strongly nationalist in tone. They objected to normal students' browsing in libraries. Broadly educated teachers with liberal ideas were not wanted. In France, as in Prussia at this time, political reaction came into power and circumscribed the outlook of the teachers and their pupils. A slighter but similar trend was noticeable in Massachusetts and in other American communities.

The law of 1850 made numerous concessions to the church, in both primary and secondary fields. It also combined the administration of both levels of schools under a Minister of Public Instruction and an advisory Superior Council of twenty-eight members, who represented all the educational interests of the country. It increased the force of inspectors and established the academy as a unit for the administration of secondary and university education. France was divided into sixteen, later with the inclusion of Algiers into seventeen, academies. Since then the chief administrative units for the administration of education have been the whole state, the academies, the departments, and the communes. Only minor functions were given to the arrondissements and the cantons.

Under Napoleon III the power of the University of France became almost absolute, and the new ruler became an autocrat. The press came under complete governmental control. Teachers were allowed to read only *The Monitor*, the official newspaper. An official order required them to shave off their moustaches so as to remove from "their faces, as well as their minds," every trace of the Revolution of 1848. By the Organic Decree of 1852, the emperor through the minister could name and dismiss teachers and practically all educational officials. Teachers were required to take an oath of loyalty, and prominent university professors were dismissed "in the interest of public peace." This centralized system, the University of France, was taken over by the Third Republic, but its powers have not been exercised as tyrannically as in the days of the Second Empire. As the Revolution of 1848 receded into the past, educational support became more bountiful and educational administration more liberal, even under Napoleon III. France was prosperous, the salaries of the teachers were raised, many new schools were opened, and many primary schools were made tuition free. Under a famous minister, Victor Duruy (1811-1894), the normal schools were improved and given a greater degree of freedom, and education became more professional. Under Duruy, who was a noted historian, much attention was also given to the advancement of higher studies.

NATIONAL EDUCATION COMES OF AGE

The defeat of France in the short Franco-Prussian War once again transformed the government into a Republic. The Third Republic was proclaimed on September 4, 1870, when the news of the disaster of Sedan reached the capital; but the danger that a monarchy would after all be reestablished was great. In fact, the National Assembly, which was elected to make the peace, was sharply Royalist in composition. The Socialists and Jacobins of Paris feared that one of the Bourbons would again be enthroned. Then came the Commune, an insurrection of the poverty-stricken masses of the capital, which was put down, after a siege of two months, in seven days of ferocious street fighting, the "Bloody Week." In the summer of 1871, the hard treaty with Germany was signed and France was again at peace, except that an army of occupation remained and would remain until the heavy indemnity was paid. The most repugnant part of the treaty required the cession of the two provinces of Alsace and Lorraine to the harsh conqueror, who at once proceeded to Germanize them. German, which was a foreign tongue to many, was made the official language of the courts and the schools. It was this change that gave Alphonse Daudet the setting for a pathetic little story, *La Dernière Classe*, the last French lesson. It is not without meaning to a study of nationalism in education.

The difficulties of the first days of the Republic were staggering. Twenty-six departments were occupied by German troops, the horrors of the Commune were fresh in mind, the public services were disorganized, and party intrigue hampered the new government. The first task was to get the enemy out of the country; and under the leadership of Thiers, the chief executive, this was done so speedily that victor and vanquished were both surprised. The last German soldiers were evacuated in September, 1873. The opponents of the Republic hoped to establish a monarchy, but they were divided among themselves and could not agree on who was to occupy the throne. As Thiers said, "Those who want a monarchy do not want the same monarchy"; and, "There is only one throne but three claimants." The three were a grandson of Charles X, a grandson of Louis Philippe, and the son of Napoleon III. Thiers used his influence in favor of democracy, and by applying the principle of "divide and conquer" he saved the Republic.

The new government adopted the parliamentary system. The president was elected for a fixed term, but the ministry remained in power only while it retained the support of the lower house, the Chamber of Deputies. This was essentially the English system. As a result of this plan, coupled with the unstable party alignments in French politics, the ministries changed frequently. The average term of the Minister of Public Instruction was less than a year. But because the laws did not change with the ministry and because the details of school administration were carried out by permanent civil servants, these changes did not affect the schools as much as one might suppose. The Republicans came into power in the elections of 1878. They celebrated their victory by repealing much restrictive legislation against the freedom of the press, the right to form labor unions, and the right to hold public meetings.

One of the great leaders in the new order was Jules Ferry (1832–1893), who was a member of several ministries and was twice Prime Minister. The Republicans were especially eager to nationalize primary education, to consolidate the administrative system, and to reform secondary education. As the state was now based on manhood suffrage, primary education acquired a new importance and the most significant new legislation dealt with the primary schools. A law of 1881 made these schools free; and another law of the next year made attendance compulsory between the ages of six and thirteen and prohibited the teaching of religion. Increased financial support was provided. A law of 1883 required every town and village to erect and maintain public primary schools and, two years later, the government granted state appropriations to support them more adequately. The main laws of this period are often called the Ferry Laws after Jules Ferry, the statesman mentioned, who was Minister of Public Instruction from 1879 to 1880 and again in 1882. The educational activity of this creative period was also extended to the normal schools. Each department was required to establish two such schools, one for men and one for women, for the preparation of primary teachers. Two higher normal schools were created at St. Cloud and Fontanay-aux-Roses for the education of teachers of the departmental normal schools, but these have not been as well patronized as it was hoped. Public lycées and *collèges* for girls were established. The Higher Council of Public Instruction was reconstituted and provision was made for the inspection of the schools. The system of administration of the French schools will be more fully explained subsequently.

The dominating idea of Jules Ferry was that education, especially in a democracy, is a function of the state. "Let it be understood," he said in an address on July 4, 1876, "that the first duty of a democratic government is to exercise control over public education." His nationalism did not go so far as to prohibit private schools, but these were to be subject to state inspection and regulation and he held that any delegated educational power must be revocable at the will of the state.

Such principles were certainly not accepted by the Catholic Church, which had been officially recognized by the French state ever since the Concordat of 1801 between Napoleon and the pope. According to that agreement, the state paid the salaries of the clergy in return for the privilege of nominating them for appointment to their positions. The new leaders were now becoming more and more dissatisfied with this century-old settlement of the religious difficulty. The Catholic party had from the beginning opposed the Republic and joined forces with the Monarchists. On the other hand, in 1871, the fiery republican orator Gambetta had declared, "Clericalism, that is our enemy." Three decades later, Waldeck-Rousseau, the Prime Minister, declared that the church was a rival power, hostile to the state. He claimed that unauthorized orders of monks and nuns had increased until their membership exceeded a quarter of a million and that they held property in excess of a billion francs. But the most serious element in the situation was their teaching, which he said was hostile to the principles of liberty and equality, the very foundations of the Republic. This was a new version of the argument of La Chalotais in his *Essay on National Education*. Waldeck-Rousseau, in 1901, secured the passage of a law that made all religious orders illegal unless they were specifically authorized by Parliament. In 1904, the members of even authorized religious orders were excluded from teaching in public schools, and in the following year, the separation of church and state was made absolute and complete. The French state schools, like the French state, became entirely secular.

This does not mean that private schools were outlawed. It must not be forgotten that France is still a Catholic country and that the private, mainly Catholic, primary schools are still formidable competitors with the public schools. This fact is best exhibited by a few figures. In 1886, out of a total of five and a half million French primary school children nearly two million, or about one third, attended private schools. In 1906, the proportion had dropped down to about one in five and is now about one in six. As a result of the falling birth rate, the whole number of children in all primary schools dropped from five and a half million in 1886 to less than four million in 1926, a decrease of about thirty per cent. The French call their private schools free schools, which is to indicate freedom from government control; but they are after all not entirely "free" in this sense. Their teachers, the curriculum, and their textbooks must meet all the state qualifications. They may teach religion, but even the catechisms that are used must be approved by the Minister. As a result, the private schools are largely patterned after the state schools, and set the same examinations.

The following table (from Carleton J. H. Hayes' *France, A Nation of Patriots* New York, Columbia University Press, 1930) shows the curriculum of the public primary schools.

TABLE OF STUDIES, PRIMARY SCHOOLS
(hours per week)

	Ages			
	6 and 7	8 and 9	10 and 11	12 and 13
Morals and Civics	1¼	1¼	1¼	1½
Reading French	10	7	3	2½
Writing French	5	2½	1½	¾
Language Study		5	7½	7½
French History and Geography	2½	2½	3	3
French Songs	1¼	1	1	1
Physical and Military Exercises	1¾	2	2	2
Mathematics	2½	3½	4½	5
Science	1¼	1½	2½	2½
Design	1	1	1	1
Manual Training	1½	1	1	1½
Games	2	1¾	1¾	1¾
	30	30	30	30

THE UNIVERSITY OF FRANCE

The organization of education in France is of particular interest to citizens of other democracies because it is so highly centralized in comparison with their agencies of control. The present description applies to conditions as they were under the Third Republic. The President of the Republic appointed a Minister of Public Instruction and Fine Arts as a member of his Cabinet. He was a member of Parliament, qualified to address either House, initiate educational legislation, prepare the budget, and issue regulations within the law. Because he was responsible for educational policy and had many legislative and ceremonial duties, he did not concern himself with details. This limited the powers with which he was legally and theoretically invested. The actual work of administration was carried on by a permanent civil service staff organized in four divisions: higher education; secondary education; primary education including higher primary and teacher education; and finance. There were also two sections that dealt with physical education and vocational education. This staff further served to limit the actual exercise of ministerial power. And the Higher Council of Public Instruction formed a third limiting factor: The members of the council represented the several branches of education and the larger number were elected by their colleagues in the teaching profession. The advice of the council on such subjects as courses of study, methods, examinations, textbooks, and supervisors was regularly given and almost always followed, although there have been exceptions. There was also a Consultative Committee that dealt especially with appointments and promotions. And there was, lastly, a staff of twelve national inspectors who supervised the field inspectors and reported on the conditions of education throughout the country. The general effect of this distribution of functions was that the several parts of the central organization served as checks upon each other and that each function was carried out by experts in the field.

The remainder of the system was largely an extension of the same pattern to the subdivisions of the country. For educational administration only, all France including Algiers was divided into seventeen academies. At the head of each was a rector appointed by the president. He was responsible for the whole educational system of his academy, but in practice he dealt mainly with the university, the secondary schools, and the normal schools. An Academic Council advised the rector, and a group of inspectors supervised schools and reported on their work. Actually, the academy inspectors dealt mainly with the secondary schools. Another group of primary school inspectors dealt similarly with this level of education. They made recommendations on appointments, discipline, attendance, buildings, and similar matters.

In each of the ninety departments, the prefect was the head of the primary school system. He was aided by an elected departmental council.

With their advice he appointed or transferred teachers, supervised expenditures, and located schools. The departments provided the normal school buildings and contributed to the salaries of the primary inspectors and the cost of education in the commune.

There are in France, as we have said, about thirty-seven thousand communes or townships. Each was administered by a mayor and a council, but except to supervise the school buildings, maintain a school census, and encourage attendance, there was little left for them to do. The communes had no authority over the teacher of the area. The system was nearly as national and centralized as possible. There was no opportunity for direct action or influence or even representation of the people themselves.

This is the nature of the University of France. First established by Napoleon I, reestablished and clothed with autocratic powers by his nephew Napoleon III, and taken over by the Third Republic and equipped with various "checks and balances," it has been the prevailing system of school administration in France through most of the nineteenth century and down to 1940. The French believe that education should be national and should be administered by experts and not by laymen who would represent either the local community or the people at large. The French are noted for orderly organization and for the clear definition of the functions of officials and institutions, and the University of France reflects French character or at least the character of the French intellectual classes. The American system, on the contrary, reflects our localism, our individualism, our regard for the wishes of the parents and the pupils, and our feeling that government should not interfere more than is necessary in social and educational matters. Our schools began as local and private institutions and, although centralization has made great progress in the last hundred years, the schools are still close to the local community. Under the laws of the states, the cities, counties, or other districts, each headed by one of our one hundred twenty-seven thousand American school boards, directly elected by the people, still control our schools. There is no greater contrast in the field of educational administration than that between France and the United States. Even in France there has been opposition to the uniformity of the system and a demand has been voiced that local and community interests should be considered. An organization of reformers, called *Les Compagnons de l'Université Nouvelle*, favored greater adaptation of the schools to local and individual needs but, as will be shown here, without marked success.

SECONDARY SCHOOL REFORMS

We should recall that the French system is a dual scheme of primary and higher primary schools, for those pupils who have no intention of attending or at least no opportunity to attend a university, and of secondary schools for those who are to be prepared for university entrance although not all do in fact enter. By the age of eleven the matter has to be decided, for at that age secondary studies proper begin. Two characteristics of French secondary education must also be singled out for special mention. Ever since the Renaissance it has been strongly classical; and it has been devoted to the preparation of a relatively small class of intellectual leaders and to the maintenance of a high level of culture.

Criticism of both of these features began to appear long before the Revolution. In the opening pages of his *Émile*, Rousseau referred to the "ridiculous colleges" of his time and, except for the contemptuous tone of his reference, he merely repeated what Descartes and the Abbé Fleury had said before. La Chalotais attacked not only the Jesuit control of the schools but also the absence of French modern languages, science, and industry from the program of studies. Five years later Rolland proposed a state system of secondary schools that was to give attention to the history and language of the French nation and people and to include also modern languages, mathematics, and physical education. The authors of the cahiers of 1789 and Talleyrand, Condorcet, and others favored and attempted to introduce similar changes. An unsuccessful effort to do this was made through the decree of 1852, which established a common course of three years to be followed by two parallel series of studies, the one classical, the other scientific. Each was to lead to the university. But such a program was only actually achieved in 1902. Within a decade the compromise of 1852 with the modern, practical world was again abandoned because it did not really meet the demands of that world. It merely directed toward the university a group less well prepared than the graduates of the classical course to do what the conservative higher schools required. The reform had gone too far for the classicists and not far enough to prepare for business, industry, or agriculture.

The demand for reform did not grow less, meanwhile, but instead was fast becoming irresistible. "Authority does all that can be done in favor of the old classical training," said Matthew Arnold after a study of secondary education on the continent. "Ministers of state sing its praises. Still in the body of society there spreads a growing disbelief in Greek and Latin, at any rate as at present taught, a growing disposition to make the modern languages and the natural sciences take their place." This was a correct analysis of public opinion. The demand for reform came from the lower and middle classes, not from the secondary teachers or the ministers of state. But at this point the demand for reform struck a second snag. For centuries the French secondary schools had been not only classical but also highly selective and devoted to the preparation of an intellectual elite. The people themselves were now asking to be allowed to share directly in the benefits of this education.

Under the Third Republic six successive reforms of the curriculum were undertaken. Because all of these turned on the question of the classics *versus* the modern subjects, it will be possible to deal with them somewhat generally without going into the details of each one. Jules Simon, Minister of Public Instruction under Thiers, increased the time given to modern language and reduced the amount of grammar and composition in the classical studies in favor of a broader reading program. "Modern languages," he held, "are to be spoken and dead languages to be read." This lasted about three years. Jules Ferry, in the important reform of 1880, made a radically different attack. He postponed the beginning of Latin by several years in order to make it possible for pupils from primary schools to enter the secondary schools later; and he also increased the attention given to the sciences. The time of the special classes in modern subjects that were taught in some of the lycées and *collèges* was increased from three to four and even to five years; but these classes were not part of secondary education proper. These efforts were, however, made to increase the opportunities of the common people.

The Ribot Commission of 1898 was appointed to study the whole question of secondary education. It concluded that the classical tradition should be maintained and even strengthened. But to do this it was declared essential that only suitable pupils, those with linguistic ability, should be enrolled in the classical courses and that a parallel modern course with equal rights and privileges should be set up. This was done in the reform of 1902. The new scheme provided for four sections of seven years, from the age of eleven to that of eighteen, in all full secondary schools. These can be designated as Latin-Greek, Latin-modern languages, Latin-scientific, and modern languages-scientific. Each of these, when successfully completed, led to the university. In all sections great attention was given to the study of the mother tongue. Modern foreign languages were to be taught by direct methods and in Latin the emphasis was to be placed on reading and literature rather than on grammar. Thus, in 1902, the modern subjects won their long struggle for equal treatment and recognition in comparison with the classics. They did not succeed in winning equal prestige among the French people.

There was after all some question about the conclusiveness of the victory. It will be noticed that three of the four parallel courses included Latin and two included or might include Greek also. Only one had no classical requirement, but this one did give all the rights and privileges of university admission. Except for the abortive attempt of Minister Bérard in 1923 to bring back compulsory Latin and Greek, the reform of 1902 stood until 1925. It was not satisfactory to all classes, or perhaps to any in all respects. One of the most valid criticisms of the scheme was that it required a too early and too complete specialization, that the classical student did not get enough scientific education and the scientific student did not get enough literary education. The reform of 1925 attempted to remedy this. The studies required of all secondary students by this act can best be exhibited in the following table, which is taken from Carleton J. H. Hayes' *France, A Nation of Patriots*.

TABLE OF STUDIES COMMON TO ALL PUPILS IN
BOYS' SECONDARY SCHOOLS (1931)
(hours per week)

	Year					
	VI	V	IV	III	II	I
French	4	4	3	4	3	3½
History	1½	1½		2	2	
Geography	1	1	3½	1	1	3½
Modern Language	3	3	3	3	1½	1½
Mathematics	2	2	3	3	4	3½
Natural Science	1½	1½	1	1		
Physics and Chemistry					3	4
Drawing	2	2	1½	1		
Art				½		
	15	15	15	15½	14½	16

But the table shows only a part of the requirements. The boys took six or seven additional hours per week in languages and literature. For this work they were divided into three groups, according to their election to study Latin and Greek, Latin and a modern foreign language, or two modern languages. For the seventh and final year all the boys were divided into two sections, a philosophy section and a mathematics section. In the former they studied principally philosophy, history, and literary subjects, and in the other, principally mathematics and the sciences. The total program involved twenty-one hours of class work in each week in the early years and twenty-three to twenty-five in the later years of the course. There were also private secondary schools, but their curricula and work were very similar to those of the public ones. Boys, whether from private or public schools, had to pass the same state examinations for "graduation" and again later when, as men, they wished to be allowed to practice their profession.

Until within our own generation, secondary education in France remained a privilege of the ruling and the upper middle classes. And, because secondary education provided the only avenue to the university, the same statement applies to higher education. France carried on two separate school systems within one centralized administration, a primary system for the millions and a secondary higher system for the elite, although there were scholarships for the brilliant among the poor.

In World War I, the *Compagnons de l'Université Nouvelle* was formed to secure for all classes of children the privileges that had been restricted to a few. They succeeded in 1925 in establishing the *école unique,* or common school, on the elementary level, although only in a few towns. Preparatory classes for secondary schools continued to exist, but fees were gradually abolished and children were admitted from the *école unique.* In 1933, the number of scholarships in the secondary schools was increased and fees abolished. But with few and unimportant exceptions the curricula remained as they had been. The reform had not gone far enough. It had opened the secondary higher education to many poor and brilliant children, but it had not diversified the offerings. Secondary and higher education still led only to the professions and the professions were already overcrowded.

When Jean Zay became Minister of Education in the middle 1930s, an attempt was made to correct this condition. He proposed to develop technical and industrial schools on secondary and higher levels to enable large numbers of young people, excluded from the professional and purely intellectual fields, to serve France in practical vocations and to provide means for personal advancement. He realized that a democracy must provide opportunity for all kinds of abilities. Guidance classes were established in the secondary schools and handicrafts and extracurricular activities were introduced. However, the war in 1939 stopped all these efforts to make French education more fully democratic.

FRENCH EDUCATION SINCE 1947

French educational experiments since 1947 have concerned the secondary schools and vocational education chiefly. These are the phases of the French system that have been long and severely criticized. They are indeed two of the phases of education that have been vigorously attacked in many countries. In France the *Compagnons de l'Université Nouvelle,* which came after and in part out of World War I, were the active proponents of free secondary education. They worked also for orientation classes in the early years of the secondary programs. These classes have aims that parallel some of the purposes of the American junior high school: to study the capacities and interests of individual pupils, to introduce more modern studies, and to provide educational guidance.

After the recommendations of the Commission for Educational Reform (1944) failed to win general approval, the government appointed a new commission headed by Paul Langevin, a famous physicist, and Henri Wallon, an eminent psychologist, with other noted scholars as members, to bring in a new report. This, the Langevin plan, was published in 1947.

It proposed raising the leaving age to eighteen. The educational system was to consist of three cycles: basic cycle, ages six to eleven; orientation cycle, eleven to fifteen; and determination cycle, fifteen to eighteen. Americans would call the third cycle the period of specialization. Economically, the most ambitious part of this proposal was the raising of the leaving age for all children to eighteen years; and the three-year orientation cycle was the most striking educational innovation.

The plan included new proposals for the preparation of teachers. Elementary teachers were to complete a secondary school course and two years of pedagogical study. More active teaching methods were recommended, and all external examinations were to be postponed to the end of the secondary school course—a radical change from practice. The commission was able to agree on the content of the syllabus for moral-civic education—an achievement. Adult education was to reach out to the villages and farms.

The Langevin plan implied that too many had been excluded too long from proper educational opportunity. In the opinion of the commission, other forms of education, such as technological studies, were as good for their own purposes as the classics and were equally necessary in modern society. The plan may have threatened the social prestige of the classicists, who form a large part of the educated public in France. The plan, if adopted and fully carried out, would have tended to erase the line between those who read Euripides and those who build steel and concrete bridges. This thought was not acceptable to educational conservatives, and they launched a vigorous attack against the whole program. Across the Channel the papers reported that the Langevin reforms were tabled and spoke of them as being "ambitious" (*Times Educational Supplement*, London, November 15, 1947, p. 613). We shall see that the supporters of the English grammar schools were similarly exercised over the new views and provisions on secondary education in the Hadow report and the Education Act of 1944.

Although the Langevin plan was not adopted, it was not without influence. Many of its proposals were not new, but it was of value because it gave the support of distinguished men to previous demands for improvements. The violence of the attacks on it showed that it was gaining support.

The new trends that received the most support were (1) the extension of the opportunity for secondary school education to pupils from the primary schools; (2) the improvement of teaching in secondary schools; and (3) the introduction of technical education on the secondary school level. After World War II, the urban higher primary schools were transformed into modern secondary schools, *collèges modernes*, parallel to the *collèges classiques*. In theory this change enables a child of thirteen who has taken only the common school subjects to complete a secondary school course in modern languages, the sciences, and technical studies. Even village schools with only the one-year extension known as the *cours complémentaire,* instead of the higher primary school, can fit a pupil for transfer at age fourteen to a neighboring *collège moderne* where he can complete a secondary school course. The new *collèges* have been taken out of primary school administration and added to that of the secondary schools.

The second improvement was a reform in teaching and the internal administration of secondary schools. It will be necessary to say that in France there has been much complaint of overpressure in the secondary schools. Children in some lycées are in school nine hours a day and as many as forty-eight hours a week; and they do a great deal of homework. The teachers are officially given the title of *professeur;* and most of the teaching is done by means of lectures. The teachers have no out-of-class duties and few face-to-face meetings with the students. Examinations are difficult, and many pupils fail. It is perhaps not necessary to say that the teachers have had no training in child study or psychology. The effort to improve these conditions is carried out in what are known as *classes nouvelles,* new classes.

The new classes are the outgrowth of a movement that began before World War II. The Ministry of Education began in 1937 to promote the use of school exercises and activity methods, including some slight elements of pupil self-government, and to advise the correlation of subjects such as history, literature, and geography. Centers of interest with projects are used. "Forests" might be one such center from which the work would go out toward biology, art, industry, and other topics. The classes were limited to twenty-five pupils. A school psychologist equipped with test and interview charts made a study of the aptitudes and progress of each pupil. The experiment was started in the first year of the secondary school course and was moved up one year at a time for four years. The three upper classes were left untouched. The ministry was careful from the first not to let this experiment get out of hand. The number of new classes was limited to eight hundred; and in recent years the program has been much diluted.

The proposal to teach psychology and education to those preparing for secondary school positions has not been carried out. Educational guidance has been introduced into some of the lycées, and there are some school psychologists in Paris and other cities to investigate cases of maladjustment among pupils. There are ways of enlisting the cooperation of the parents when their children do not do well at school. Vocational guidance is in the hands of the state, which requires tests and an interview before a child is assigned to a center of apprenticeship or given a job. Educational guidance was demanded by the Langevin Commission, but in the land of Rousseau and Binet it is not yet well developed.

The promotion of technical education is the third of the postwar movements. There are two phases, the creating of *collèges techniques* and the development of centers of apprenticeship. The former has made great progress, and apprenticeship was expanded in the rearmament effort of the

1930s. The centers embody plans very similar to the scheme introduced into Munich by Georg Kerschensteiner. According to the scheme, the young person spends a part of his time on a job, a part in school, and the rest in whatever way he pleases. Boys and girls may choose any available trade. Some learn the fundamentals of several trades and become capable of independent work in one. This provides insurance against trade obsolescence. Each apprentice also pursues academic study in French, mathematics, civics, and geography. This scheme was recommended in the Langevin report, but in its essentials it was not new.

The continued high birth rate has given France another problem, that of finding schools and places, teachers, and books for the growing body of youth. We have seen that the struggle of the state against "clericalism" and for a secular school system was fought out and won in the nineteenth century. The separation still exists, but conditions are not the same as they were even twenty years ago. Today one fourth of all primary and two fifths of all secondary school pupils attend private schools, mostly Catholic. The church is asking the state for financial help in maintaining and operating her schools and is getting it.

The Vichy Government in 1941 passed a law granting aid to private schools, up to three fourths of the cost where needed. In 1945, this arrangement was sharply condemned by the Consultative Assembly. Catholics, liberals, anticlericals, and Communists fought over the issue for years. Radical Socialists and Communists advocated a single, entirely secular school system and the banning of all private schools. This is the Russian policy. It would obviously not be acceptable to the French. In 1950, the Minister of Education appointed a new commission to bring in still another report on the position of the nonpublic schools. The Catholics explained once again that they found it difficult—especially so in the postwar inflation—to pay for their own schools and also the state school tax. They presented figures on the number of children for whom they care. They pointed to some parts of France, wholly Catholic, where the state had provided no schools. It was doubtless not the strength of these facts and arguments but the weakness of the postwar governments of a badly divided France that caused the state to yield. France has adopted the plan, also followed by England with its much smaller Catholic population, of giving financial aid to private schools. What effect this will have on the public system we cannot tell now.

FRENCH NATIONALISM AND EDUCATION

Devotion to the nation and the state is always, in any country, a product of the contemporary culture. It is not inherited. It can be transmitted only as the knowledge of arithmetic is transmitted, by teaching each generation and individual; but, unlike arithmetic, it is not a matter of knowledge and skill only but of a knowledge that is highly charged with emotion. Love of country is a fit and frequent theme of story, poem, and drama, and it is taught not only in set lessons but also through popular works of literature and history, through songs, ballads, slogans, national holidays and ceremonials, by service in the army and the offices of the government, and through the activities of patriotic societies and deliberate propaganda of many kinds. Many of these means are employed in schools. Competent students have reported their conclusion that the French people were more nationalistic than most of their neighbors, but this is a view that in the nature of the case cannot be demonstrated. Certainly this love of France was not able to produce unity in politics and national policy. It will, nevertheless, be useful to see how the schools contributed to French nationalism.

The national system of primary schools brought about one result, at least. The schools taught nearly everyone to read and write the national language. Literacy is a word of various meanings but, if it means some ability to read and write, then illiteracy in France was reduced from forty per cent in 1850 to about three per cent in 1940. The schools did their utmost to bring about this result. No nation has given more, or more careful, attention to the teaching of its national language. Since about 1880, French primary school children have received about thirty hours of instruction per week, and two fifths of this time has been given to language instruction—to the reading, writing, and study of French. But there were always pockets of non-French who resisted these efforts of the schools. There were the Germans of Alsace, which had been returned to France after World War I; the Basques north of the Pyrenees; and the Bretons of the northwest. The autonomist movement in Brittany was at first purely cultural in character. A group of loyal Bretons agitated for the preservation of their ancient language and for its cultivation in the schools. Before the outbreak of the war in 1939, each of these three regions became centers of anti-French propaganda.

Not only the language instruction but also the history, geography, civics, and the French songs were made vehicles of nationalist influence. Nearly all the history taught in the primary schools was French history and almost all the heroes who were held up for admiration by the children in the lower grades were French heroes. Columbus, Franklin, and Livingstone were included and may seem to be exceptions and the only exceptions. Of these, however, Franklin as United States Ambassador was the friend and idol of France, and Livingstone was the explorer of the African continent where France's most extensive colonial possessions lie. This leaves Columbus, who discovered America—once the seat of a great French empire and still the home of many who speak French. The history textbooks, including those used in Catholic schools, were all approved by the Ministry of Public Instruction and were so far official. Not all of them were equally nationalist, but in the main they taught that the glory of France had been dearly bought and that all her children should early learn to love her and to sacrifice for her so that she might continue to hold her position in the world as the leader and champion of civilization. Except for the claim in this last clause this seems to be a reasonable patriotism.

Patriotism was also one of the main topics in the books on morals and citizenship, and many of the school songs were patriotic and nationalist in character. As early as 1883, the Minister of Public Instruction issued a circular on the then new branch of civics. He urged the teachers to teach it in a simple and concrete way through examples and illustrations. The children were to be taught good habits, respectful manners, and such virtues as obedience and loyalty in the home and school. The personal virtues of cleanliness, honesty, and temperance were extolled, and the dangers of alcoholism were explained. The religious teachings were to be such only as would not offend the leading faiths, the Catholic, the Protestant, and the Jewish—that is, they were to be general and nondoctrinal. There were also lessons on the greatness of France and her claims on the youth. A wide variety of books written on these lines was prepared. They generally stressed French nationality, the republican government, and the duties of the citizen to the nation. The necessity for a large army was explained and the children were taught that it would be their duty to pay taxes for its support and for the security it would provide.

Both the history and civics books in later times went much further. The wrongs of France in the war and peace of 1870 and 1871 came to be emphasized and a hatred against Germany was sometimes instilled. This tendency was greatly increased by World War I. Many of the newer books taught that Germany had deliberately caused the war and had waged it in a barbarous manner. The largest of the teachers' associations of France defended this account of the war. In a statement on the question of chauvinistic teaching that they made in 1927, the teachers declared that Germany, without question, had wanted, prepared for, and begun the war and had indulged in barbarities and atrocities as long as she thought that she could win. Not all French teachers agreed with this verdict and the government itself on several occasions undertook to discourage chauvinism in the schools. But the patriotic societies and some of the influential newspapers, including *Le Temps*, denounced all attempts to moderate the language of the textbooks as "school pacifism." The table of studies for the primary schools in 1938 shows that from one half to two thirds of the work of the primary schools was admirably adapted to promote nationalism. And, although this cannot be in equal degree asserted of the secondary curricula, the product of these schools, the secondary school *bacheliers*, were even more nationalist than the average French citizen.

The effect of the teaching should be examined from a broader standpoint. Nationalism was not enough. Even though the school system helped to unite the people in their admiration for their language, history, and culture, it did not sufficiently unite them in other respects. The conditions in France preceding the disaster of 1940 would embarrass anyone who should assert the irrefragable unity of the nation. There were numerous groups and parties—Communist, Fascist, industrial, proletarian, Catholic, Royalist, Socialist, and Republican—that in the latter years of the Third Republic fought with each other for control. Most of them were ready to shout for the *gloire de la belle France,* but each of them wanted a different France. After 1936, the Republic was further undermined by a vicious German propaganda supported by Berlin and directed from Paris itself. Nationalistic the French people were, but they were not united in support of their government.

The French school system will always be a profitable subject of study and especially so for those who live under so different a plan and organization as do the Americans and the English. From the foregoing it is evident that France did not have any profound influence on American education. Particular institutions, such as Jefferson's university plan, several military and engineering schools, schools for the blind, deaf, and mentally defective, and certain devices such as the Binet tests have been borrowed or modeled on French antecedents. But in school administration, in contrast with the French policy of central control, we began at the other extreme, with the local community, and we have not yet attained any very high degree of centralization. From the next country to be studied, Germany, we have borrowed a great deal more.

SUMMARY

Since the French Revolution had the most far-reaching effect in spreading an aggressive nationalism, we have considered the French schools system first of all.

To reduce the theoretical educational proposals of the French Revolution to practical form and to incorporate them in the political system of France required almost a century. Napoleon outlined the administrative system, the University of France; the government of Louis Philippe laid the foundations of primary education; and in the Third Republic, primary, secondary, and higher education became secular and nationalistic, well supported and efficient, and centralized in administration. Both primary and secondary education became free and the former bacame practically universal. The French schools have become especially effective in teaching the national language; and also in instilling nationalistic sentiment. The French child learns to write well and to believe in French culture and its civilizing value to Europe and the world. France is a Latin country and its secondary schools tend to emphasize classical education. An elaborate system of public professional schools for teachers has been developed. With all these public provisions, one fourth of the primary and two fifths of the secondary school pupils attend private, usually Roman Catholic, schools; but these also are required to meet state standards.

Although the schools and other institutions of France succeeded in developing a strongly nationalist sentiment, they were not able to prevent internal disunity or to repel foreign propaganda in the years before 1940.

QUESTIONS

1. What nations have followed the French pattern of a highly centralized national system of education? Explain any differences you find between these national systems and the French system.
2. Why is French educational control highly centralized?
3. Why was it logical for the July Monarchy to develop primary and higher primary schools?
4. Compare the meaning of the phrase secondary education as it is used in France and in the United States.
5. Why were the French primary school teachers more likely to be politically liberal than secondary school teachers?
6. Compare the plan of Condorcet with the system developed by the Third Republic.
7. Why should a unitary (ladder) system be more appropriate for a republic than the parallel system that France retained after 1870?
8. What objections do you see to an administrative organization such as the University of France? What advantages may it have?
9. Does French education seem more nationalistic than American education? If you think it is, how can this be explained?

NOTES AND SOURCES

The following sources deal in the main with education in France since the eighteenth century. In the brief introduction to his *French Liberalism and Education*, La Fontainerie contributes important information on conditions before the Revolution. If to the four documents he has translated we add *Émile*, we shall have the materials for a fair understanding of educational thought in the *Ancien Régime* and the Revolution. The *Yearbooks of the International Institute* are essential for the period between the two World Wars.

ALLAIN, ERNEST, *L'Instruction primaire en France avant la Révolution*, Paris, Société Bibliographique, 1881, 304 pp.
AUTIN, ALBERT, *L'École Unique*, Paris, Libraire Felix Alcan, 1933, 158 pp.

BARNARD, HOWARD C., *The French Tradition in Education. Ramus to Mme. Necker de Saussure*, Cambridge, University Press, 1922, 319 pp.

BROWN, ROLLO WALTER, *How the French Boy Learns To Write; A Study in the Teaching of the Mother Tongue*, Cambridge, Harvard University Press, 1915, 260 pp.

BUISSON, FERDINAND, *Dictionnaire de Pédagogie et d'Instruction Primaire*, Paris, Hachette et Cie., 1880–1887, 4 vols.; *French Educational Ideals of Today; An Anthology*, Yonkers-on-Hudson, N.Y., World Book Company, 1919, 326 pp.

COMPAYRE, GABRIEL, *The History of Pedagogy*. Translated and edited by W. H. Payne, Boston, D. C. Heath and Company, 1891, 598 pp.; *Histoire critique des doctrines de l'éducation en France*, Paris, Hachette et Cie., 1911, 2 vols.

DICKINSON, G. LOWES, *Revolution and Reaction in Modern France*, London, George Allen, 1892, 300 pp.

FARRINGTON, FREDERIC E., *The Public Primary System of France*, New York, Teachers College, Columbia University, 1906, 303 pp.; *French Secondary Schools; An Account of the Origin, Development, and Present Organization of Secondary Education in France*, New York, Longmans, Green and Company, 1910, 450 pp.

GAY, P., and O. MONTREUX, *French Elementary Schools: Official Courses of Study*. With an introduction by I. L. Kandel, New York, Teachers College, Columbia University, 1926, 270 pp.

HALLS, W. D., *Society, Schools and Progress in France*, New York, Pergamon Press, 1965, 194 pp.

HASSALL, ARTHUR, *Louis XIV and the Zenith of the French Monarchy*, New York, G. P. Putnam's Sons, 1925, 444 pp.

HUDDLESTON, SISLEY, *France*, New York, Charles Scribner's Sons, 1927, 613 pp.

HYSLOP, BEATRICE FRY, *French Nationalism in 1789, According to General Cahiers*, New York, Columbia University Press, 1934, 343 pp.

KANDEL, ISAAC L., *The Reform of Secondary Education in France*, New York, Teachers College, Columbia University, 1924, 159 pp.; *Comparative Education*, Boston, Houghton Mifflin Company, 1932, 922 pp.; *History of Secondary Education*, Boston, Houghton Mifflin Company, 1930, 577 pp.; Editor, *Educational Yearbook of the International Institute of Teachers College, Columbia University*, New York, Teachers College, Columbia University, 1934, 564 pp. Under the title "The Educational System of France," this contains (pp. 1–290) a translation of the *Atlas de l'enseignement en France*, prepared by the *Commission française pour l'Enquête Carnegie sur les Examens et concours en France*. It has an extensive bibliography. The Yearbook has been published annually since 1924 and each volume to and including that for 1932 contains material on French education. See especially the volumes for 1929 and 1930.

LA FONTAINERIE, FRANÇOIS DE, *French Liberalism and Education in the Eighteenth Century; The Writings of La Chalotais, Turgot, Diderot, and Condorcet on National Education*, New York, McGraw-Hill Book Company, Inc., 1932, 385 pp.

For the period since 1947, in addition to the book listed by Halls, consult the *Comparative Education Review* for the article by Charles H. Dubinson, "French Educational Reform," in Vol. III, No. 1, pp. 5–14, June, 1959 and that by William R. Fraser, "Reform in France," in Vol. XI, No. 3, pp. 300–310, October, 1967; the publications on education of the French Cultural Service, New York; and the reviews of the literature in international and comparative education in the *Review of Educational Research*, such as that in Vol. 37, No. 1, February, 1967.

Chapter 15

NATIONAL TRENDS IN GERMAN EDUCATION

The history of Germany provides the material for a second study of the national trends that characterize education today. That country was a loose confederation of states until Bismarck welded them into an empire, but even then the states retained their autonomy in education. Complete unification and subordination resulted when the National Socialist party came into power in 1933.

After the Reformation, each state gradually developed its own school system; but the church, the Lutheran State Church in the north and the Catholic Church in Bavaria and the south, remained strongly entrenched in educational matters. Cooperation between state and church marked the earlier systems, but the actual management of the schools long remained in the hands of the clergy, who did not favor strong civil control of education and who were in intimate contact with the people.

IN THE EIGHTEENTH CENTURY

Although the Reformation inspired the organization of elementary schools, it was the eighteenth century, and partly the influence of Frederick the Great, that laid the foundations of the Prussian and other state systems that were later held up for our admiration. Compulsory attendance had been proposed by Luther and was enacted into law in Weimar in 1619. A century later Frederick William I of Prussia issued an order requiring attendance at school. His son, Frederick the Great, in 1763 prescribed detailed regulations for rural schools. This decree marked an educational milestone. Compulsory attendance from the age of five to fourteen was ordered and arrangements were made to relieve the poor from excessive financial burdens. The school year, the hours of the school day, and the curriculum were fixed. Supervision was prescribed but was left in the hands of the clergy. There were other difficulties. Funds and means of enforcement were lacking. Similar but somewhat broader regulations covering the urban schools also were made for Catholic Silesia. And a parallel code for normal, secondary, and elementary schools in Austria was prepared by J. E. Felbiger (1724–1788), who had been appointed Minister of Education by Maria Theresa. The normal schools were model practice schools in which teachers were to be prepared.

Prussia took further measures in the eighteenth century. A national board of education or *Oberschulkollegium* was instituted in 1787. The Prussian code of 1794 included the principle of state control of education, declared schools to be state institutions, and established local school committees. Supervision was still left to the clergy and even the members of the *Oberschulkollegium* were taken from the same profession. No religious discrimination was to be permitted. But these advanced measures were mere paper reforms. Frederick the Great had revealed his real intention when he said that "in country places a little reading and writing will be enough, for if the peasants learn too much they will want to move into town and become clerks." The schools were not much improved and this explains why neighboring countries paid so little attention to Prussian education until the next century. When progress began in earnest, not only in the law books but in the actual schools, Victor Cousin of France, Henry Brougham of England, and Alexander Bache, C. E. Stowe, and Horace Mann of the United States made the world acquainted with the new developments.

The eighteenth century was the period of the "benevolent despots": Frederick the Great, Catherine II of Russia, and Maria Theresa and Joseph II of Austria. They all understood the educational strategy of autocracy based on the cynical observation that highly educated officials do not easily become revolutionaries but that to educate the poor spells danger. Frederick the Great, like Napoleon after him, was most interested in the education of leaders. He reformed the classical gymnasiums and also the old knightly academies, a task he committed to J. G. Sulzer. Upon the advice of Frederick Gedike (1755–1803), the gymnasial leaving certificate was introduced. This certificate, which was granted after a comprehensive examination and which admitted its holders directly to the university, raised the level of instruction and guaranteed its quality. The measure had far-reaching effects on both the gymnasium and the university.

If the government had provided financial support, the lower schools also might have been improved. Under existing conditions, reform in elementary education often depended on the initiative of humanitarian landlords. Such a landlord was Eberhard von Rochow (1734–1805). In the preface to his *School-Book for Country Children* he said "I live among country people and I pity them for the wretchedness of their condition and their ignorance and prejudices. They neither know how to make good use of what they possess nor how to give up cheerfully what they lack. They are not at peace with either God or king." This condition he ascribed to defective education. On his estate he demanded and attempted to supply educated teachers, good buildings, and adequate salaries, and set up a curriculum that included arithmetic, nature study, letter writing, and enlightened religious teaching. He was personally acquainted with Basedow and accepted his aims of happiness, utility, and reasonableness and his principle that schools should be public institutions. His reforms and ideas did not spread and the effort to introduce them in Brunswick in 1786, with J. H. Campe as superintendent, was wrecked by the opposition of the clergy and nobles. The ideas of Basedow and the Enlightenment were adopted in private schools and affected national education when it actively developed in the Napoleonic era. The real beginnings of modern public education must be placed in the nineteenth rather than the eighteenth century, and only a generation before similar measures were taken in France and the United States.

BIRTH OF THE FATHERLAND

Napoleon routed the German armies in the battles of Jena and Auerstedt in October, 1806, while Hegel, with the thunder of the guns in his ears, continued to write his philosophy. The incident can be taken to mark the lack of nationalist feeling of the greatest Germans then living: Hegel, Goethe, Beethoven, and others. Nine months after the defeat, France imposed the severe peace of Tilsit on the humiliated Germans. Prussia lost vast territories, assumed a heavy indemnity purposely left indefinite, and agreed to support the armies of occupation and to limit her own army to forty-two thousand men. When Napoleon later needed soldiers for the Spanish campaign he was compelled, fortunately for Prussia, to withdraw many regiments from the occupied areas.

The defeat and the drastic peace treaty aroused the patriotism of the Germans. Fichte, who in his lectures of 1805 had declared himself a citizen of the world, now became a nationalist. His *Addresses to the German Nation*, delivered while French soldiers patrolled the streets of Berlin, were a call to regeneration and the use of the child as an instrument in building the new Germany. It might be easy to overemphasize the influence of Fichte but not of these ideas, which many held in common with him. Within eight years after Tilsit, the allies were in Paris and Napoleon was on his way to St. Helena.

The German fatherland was a creation of the youth under the lead of von Stein, Hardenberg, Scharnhorst, and Gneisenau. The collapse had revealed the fault of the state to von Stein: it was built from the top downward. He saw new forces arising from below, from the common people, and he turned to them. If the state could develop and enlist their talents, it would become invincible. This was von Stein's program for the regeneration of the nation: "To bind everyone to the State by conviction, sympathy, and cooperation in the affairs of the nation, to give the forces of the nation free play and direct them toward the common good." And if this sounds like the voice of revolutionary France, the answer is that von Stein was not deaf. Nor were the principles of the French Revolution altogether French or new. Government by the people was a principle of Calvinism that had been asserted in the English Commonwealth, the English Revolution of 1688, and the American Revolution of 1776.

The first law of von Stein freed the serfs, and he attempted to provide land for the peasants. Civil rights were promoted and internal improvements were begun. When the French secured von Stein's dismissal, Hardenberg carried on. He abolished guild monopolies and developed commercial freedom and he annulled the restrictions on the Jews. Scharnhorst created a citizen army by evading Napoleon's limits on its numbers. Greater than any specific measures was the moral renewal of the nation.

The political and social reforms implied educational reforms and of this the leaders were well aware. Education, said von Stein, must develop love of country, of fellowmen, and God, and must avoid all merely decorative, borrowed, artificial culture. Such an education, the Pestalozzian, was waiting to be adopted and it was in this period that Pestalozzi's ideas became fruitful in Germany. Ernst Moritz Arndt (1769–1846), the patriotic writer, was to some extent a disciple of Rousseau and Pestalozzi. Friedrich Ludwig Jahn (1778–1852) was the founder of a propagandist German physical education. He was at this time a teacher in Plamann's Pestalozzian school in Berlin, as was Froebel. Eighty-four gymnasiums of the Jahn type were established in Prussia and most of the young men who attended them enlisted in the War of Liberation.

The reorganization of the central educational administration and the founding of the University of Berlin testify to Prussian concern for education. The old *Oberschulkollegium*, a sleepy and reactionary body, was abolished and a new bureau was set up in 1808 as a division of the Ministry of the Interior. William von Humboldt (1767–1835) was the first chief of the division. He was a scholar whose appointment to a government post was about as remarkable as that of Henry Barnard to a similar position at Washington in 1867. With others, Humboldt organized the University of Berlin. He secured for Prussian students the right to study at non-Prussian universities, introduced a state examination for all prospective secondary school teachers, and reformed the gymnasium on a more thoroughly humanistic plan.

FOUNDERS OF SCHOOLS FOR THE COMMON PEOPLE

The greatest changes in education occurred in the elementary schools. Prussia in the north and Bavaria in the south were the leaders, but all states became active. Two members of the Prussian Bureau of Education were G. H. L. Nicolovius (1767–1839) and J. W. Süvern (1775–1829). As we have noted, Nicolovius met the young Pestalozzi while he was still at Neuhof and wrote, "I have made the acquaintance of a man who is really a man, Henry Pestalozzi, the author of *Leonard and Gertrude*." The great Swiss was equally drawn to the young visitor. Upon returning home, Nicolovius was advised by the philosopher, Kant, to devote himself to education and to aid in adapting the schools to the new needs of the nation and people. Nicolovius and Süvern were able to persuade the government to send young men to study with Pestalozzi, expenses paid, in order that they might acquire a similar zeal for the education of the common people. These young men, when they returned, became the nucleus of a corps of Pestalozzian teachers. Pupils of Pestalozzi were put in charge of seminaries for teachers. One of these was Karl A. Zeller (1774–1840) who, as principal of the teachers' seminary in Königsberg, educated hundreds of young elementary school teachers. Another great leader was William Harnisch (1787–1864), who had come into intimate contact with Jahn in Plamann's Institute in Berlin. He published his first work, *Schools for the People, on Pestalozzian Principles*, in 1812. "I have been inspired," he wrote, "by the ideal of a popular education for the development of a community which shall include the whole nation and all the people." Because no one else has written on this subject, therefore, he declared, "I write upon it." Jahn found him a kindred spirit and Walt Whitman, if he could have known him, would have acclaimed him.

His book made Harnisch, at twenty-five, head of the teachers' seminary at Breslau, but officialdom and the aristocracy did not share his views. When the reaction caught up with him, the *Turnplatz* he had opened was closed, his nature-study excursions were suspended, and he was moved to another seminary at Weissenfels, which he also made into a model institution. It was this second seminary directed by him that was visited and praised by Bache and by Stowe from the United States. During the next period of reaction in 1840, he was permanently retired. His influence was continued by his writings and by the teachers' association he had founded at Breslau.

The extension of the Prussian-Pestalozzian system was largely due to the one who gave it this name, F. A. W. Diesterweg (1790–1866). Diesterweg was a teacher and was successively director of two teachers' seminaries, but it was as a liberal educational publicist and a champion of the common schools and their teachers that he was most significant. He campaigned for improved teacher education and for better salaries, and he organized educational associations, directed conferences, delivered speeches, and conducted institutes. He fought for professional and against clerical administration and opposed the teaching of sectarian religion in the schools. On these latter points he had against him the full weight of the church, the government, and the Holy Alliance. In his later years he made the acquaintance of Froebel and became a promoter of the kindergarten. His services to Froebel were of doubtful value because he was suspected of socialism and the Prussian bureaucracy retired him. Even then he was not completely silenced, for he continued to write and speak for the cause of broader and freer education.

The success of the new schools was retarded by the opposition of the officials, the clergy, and the landlords who had the legal privilege of selecting the teachers of schools on their estates. We have incidentally referred to several waves of reaction. The first came in 1819, the year when Süvern proposed an education law outlining a ladder system that would have opened the way for even peasants' sons to pass through the elementary schools to the gymnasium and into the university. This was the plan of Comenius come to life and shows the height to which educational liberalism rose after the defeat by Napoleon. Such a scheme might have received serious consideration a decade earlier when the government was in desperate straits, but it had no chance after the danger passed and the princes breathed freely again.

REVOLUTION AND REACTION

We have seen how liberals such as Harnisch and Diesterweg were moved from one position to another and finally retired from active service during periods of conservatism. We must look a little further into the revolutions of 1813, 1830, and 1848. During the hundred days before Waterloo, the thoroughly frightened Prussian king promised his people a constitution and popular assembly. This pledge was forfeited after Napoleon was interned. A national association of students, the *Burschenschaft*, was founded at Jena in 1815 and chose for its motto, "honor, liberty, and fatherland." Two years later, meeting at the Wartburg to celebrate the third centennial of the Reformation and to claim its liberties for themselves, they burned the writings of a reactionary university professor. But when, in 1819, a student killed Kotzebue, the dramatist and journalist, the government seized the opportunity to suppress all student associations and all liberal movements. Teachers charged with liberalism or socialism were thrown into prison. One of the victims was Father Jahn. He was arrested in his child's sickroom and, although the accusations against him could not be proved, he was carried from prison to prison, and shut off from communication with his friends until even his tenacious spirit was broken. The reactionaries were in complete control.

The Greek revolt against Turkey in 1821 aroused anew the liberal conflagration that had been damped down by the Holy Alliance. Free peoples everywhere sent sympathy and aid. In 1830, the Revolution broke out in France and the Bourbons were for the last time driven from the throne. When the storm passed through Germany, many of the princes were compelled to grant constitutions to their people, but a few years later some of these were again revoked. When this occurred in Hannover, seven Göttingen professors, including the historians Gervinus and Dahlmann, and the Brothers Grimm, protested against the arbitrary act. All seven were removed by the Duke of Hannover and some were banished. A Prussian Cabinet Minister declared, "It is not becoming for subjects to judge the actions of the Head of the State by the measure of their limited understanding." This *cause célèbre* should not be forgotten when we hear of the boasted *Lehrfreiheit* of the German universities.

Some of the objectives of the liberals in the Revolution of 1848 were free speech and a free press, the right of assembly and petition, and popular representation in government. Although the army soon had complete control of the situation, the king was irresolute because he swayed between a romantic desire to be regarded as the father of his people and a firm faith in the Divine Right of kings. His promises were worth no more than those of his father had been. The common school teachers were in general of peasant or working-class stock and were on the side of freedom; but the common schools had not prepared the people for participation in politics. As a result, there was no cohesion among the liberals and they were unable to work out a plan that the majority would support. Frederick Engels called it "playing at revolution." Much of the social legislation that was proposed in the Frankfort Parliament (1848) was, however, enacted later.

The authorities demanded changes in the work of the elementary schools as early as 1840. In December of that year a beginning was made in the effort to curb liberalism by placing restrictions on teachers' seminaries. Teachers were not to instill in the children hopes that could not be realized. The schools should emphasize religion, a modest vocation indusrtiously pursued, simplicity, and loyalty. Future teachers were to read only "safe" books. Horace Mann visited Germany in 1843, and the student can read in his *Seventh Report* not only his praise of the schools but also his criticism of the government of that period.

During the revolutionary movement of 1848, the teachers took fresh courage. They attempted to return to the earlier program of Süvern, which proposed to frame the lower schools, town schools, gymnasia, and universities into an educational ladder; and they urged the establishment of continuation and infant schools. Nothing came of it at the time. The king appeared before a meeting of the teachers' seminary leaders to threaten and scold. All the misery of Prussia, he said, was the result of the false and godless education of these schools. "As long as I hold the sword-hilt in my hand," he boasted, "I shall know how to deal with such a nuisance." The king won; but one suspects that it was after all a somewhat nervous hand that grasped the royal weapon. A new Minister, a bureaucrat who knew how to govern by edict and decree, Karl von Raumer, was placed over the schools. He prohibited the circulation of the writings of Diesterweg and Froebel and proscribed the kindergarten in Prussia. In the October Regulation of 1854, he prescribed the curriculum of the teachers' seminaries. Broad cultural education was to be avoided. Educational theory was a powder keg for which school management had to be substituted. The elementary curriculum was to be similarly limited and was to aim at the development of loyal, submissive subjects who were not to have or to expect political influence. Thus it becomes evident that in Prussia each liberal movement was curbed by an autocratic reaction that laid its heavy, repressive hand on the schools and teachers.

THE UNIFICATION OF GERMANY

The unification of the German states, with the exception of Austria, was accomplished through the Franco-Prussian War in 1871, and the king of Prussia became the head of the new German empire. Neither in the violent methods used nor in its outcome was it such a unification as the liberals had proposed. They had worked for a union under a democratic constitution; but the constitution of the empire gave Prussia the controlling voice in foreign affairs, and even in domestic questions the representatives of the people had little power.

The empire was a union of the governments of twenty-six states. Its chief administrator was a chancellor who was responsible only to the emperor and not to Parliament. The imperial Parliament was composed of two bodies with very unequal powers. The upper house of *Bundesrath* represented the states of the federation and had extensive powers over foreign affairs, the army and navy and the issue of peace and war, and over commerce and communications. The members were appointed by the governments and Prussia sent nearly one third of the whole number, far more than any other state. Action on important questions including all constitutional changes could be blocked by fourteen votes and Prussia had seventeen. Theoretically the *Reichstag*, the lower house, which was elected by the people, had a veto in legislation. However, the efficiency of this was greatly limited by the condition that the Cabinet, that is, the active government, was not responsible to the people's representatives. It was proposed during the process of unification to make the Ministry responsible to the *Reichstag*.

This would have given the people powers similar to those exerted in Britain through the House of Commons; but the princes, governments, and Bismarck would not consent. Because the empire was a federation, many matters of local concern and internal administration were, as in the United States, left to the state governments. Education was one of those political functions that were left to the direction of the separate states.

In her economic and industrial development, Germany in 1870 was almost a century behind England. It was in 1874 that Queen Victoria took the title of Empress of India and England reached out for the Suez Canal; but in Germany at that time only the first signs of colonial ambition and the earlier stages of the Industrial Revolution were to be observed. Bismarck declared Germany to be "a satiated state," for he needed peace to consolidate the recent gains. Industry developed with unexampled rapidity after 1871. The output of coal, a good index, quadrupled between 1860 and 1880 and increased to six times the 1860 output by 1890; and this rate of expansion was maintained for two decades longer. Within the single year of 1872, nine thousand miles of railroad were under construction in Prussia alone and, instead of importing it, the rolling stock was now manufactured within the country. A part of this huge expansion was financed from the indemnity that France was forced to pay after the war. The chemical and electrical industries showed similar vigor. The good times were interrupted by a severe business depression, partly caused by the flow of French gold into Germany. Bismarck declared that "next time" he would insist on paying the indemnity instead of receiving it. Although the panic of 1873 brought severe losses and great disillusionment to workers and capitalists alike, German industry recovered and with few setbacks continued to expand until 1914. This industrial expansion led to a pronounced and increasing emphasis on vocational education.

Administration under the empire was bureaucratic, that is, it was carried out by appointive officials and boards who were not directly responsible to the people. This, taken with the extensive social welfare and relief legislation that was passed, makes it an apt comparison to say that the policy of the empire was a continuation of the patriarchal and benevolent despotism of Frederick the Great and his contemporaries. An aggressive nationalism developed and led to German colonial expansion and to competition for world markets. And nationalism had important domestic consequences, for it brought the government into conflict with all agencies that competed with it for men's loyalties, and especially with the Catholic Church. The Lutheran Church, being a state institution, was more amenable to pressure from the government. The struggle, known as the *Kulturkampf*, began about 1850 and was resumed in an intensified form under Hitler, although the same name was not applied. In the earlier phase of this German cultural war, Bismarck secured legislation that drove the Jesuits from Prussia in 1872, suppressed the Catholic bureau in the ministry of education, withdrew all schools from church control, and provided for their inspection by qualified, nonclerical officers of the state. These are known as the May Laws of 1873. They were given a moderate interpretation. Falk, the Minister of Education of Prussia, removed only a minority of the clerical inspectors. Ultimately, Bismarck had to give way. When Leo XIII became pope in 1878 Bismarck opened negotiations with him and the cultural war ended in a truce with the church.

Nationalism was also attacked from the opposite side by the radical socialists. Although socialism of many kinds had existed for centuries, the Marxian form that developed in Germany in the Bismarckian period was new, vigorous, and hostile to the nation-state and the church as well as to private capital. There were some considerable social evils. Some of these resulted from Bismarck's policies, the hegemony of conservative Prussia, royalism, a strong army not subject to the will of the people, and bureaucratic government; and others, as in all countries, were the evils growing out of the Industrial Revolution. The factory divided the work of each laborer into the smallest possible fraction and robbed him of all joy in it. Every boom period drew a new labor supply into the towns, which enabled the employers to cut wages, increase hours, and employ women and children. Stupefying drudgery and inhuman living conditions in the best times alternated with periods of unemployment when only the soup kitchens barely prevented starvation. There was no adequate provision for illness and old age. These conditions contributed to the development of socialism in Germany. Ferdinand Lassalle (1825–1864), a revolutionary of 1848, founded the Socialist party; and Karl Marx (1818–1883) promoted the international working-class movement and a somewhat different brand of socialism. In 1875, a fusion was effected; the platform, adopted at Gotha, demanded public ownership and control of industry. The Socialists insisted on universal suffrage of men and women by secret ballot, a free press, a progressive income tax, health legislation, the prohibition of child labor, and other social reforms. The Socialist vote increased rapidly between 1880 and 1890.

Bismarck replied to the Socialists with the weapon he had already used against the church, repressive legislation. A murderous attack on the life of the emperor gave him the needed opportunity. He dissolved the Reichstag; and the newly elected house agreed to a law prohibiting all Socialist meetings and publications with severe penalties. Yet the Socialist vote kept on increasing in successive elections. Then the attempt was made to draw the teeth of the opposition by extensive social legislation. Old age and disability insurance and government aid in sickness and accidents were voted but without conceding the main point that the people should have a greater voice in government. The state benevolently relieved distress but its authoritarianism prevented it from securing the loyalty of the laboring class. And the greatly extended social legislation after Bismarck also suffered from the same basic defect.

EDUCATION UNDER THE EMPIRE

In educational legislation also the attitude was similarly paternal, cautious, and restrictive. The effort was not to make people critical and independent but on the contrary to make them orderly, vocationally efficient, satisfied with conditions and their position in life, and submissive to the authorities. In vocational education, especially, Germany became a leader. There were already, from 1850 and earlier, a great many local vocational schools and classes and most of the new vocational schools were developed by the towns, the employers, and the local authorities in general, not by the empire or even the states. In the later nineteenth century, the vocational continuation or part-time school for young people who already had jobs became widespread. Even before the formation of the empire, the old North German Confederation made it compulsory for workers under the age of eighteen to attend continuation schools for a specified number of hours a week and for employers to release them from work for that purpose. This law was retained by the empire.

One defect in the situation was that there was no law requiring the establishment of vocational continuation schools, and even in 1918 about half of the states had only permissive laws on this subject. Where there were no schools with classes in the particular trade in question, the young workers could not, of course, be required to attend. Most localities had some schools but few had so full a complement and so extensive and effective a system as the one developed by Georg Kerschensteiner in about 1898 in the southern German city of Munich. Kerschensteiner was one of the leading educators of Europe in the period before World War I. In 1913 he visited and lectured extensively in the United States. Upward of fifty somewhat distinct trades and vocations, including the commercial vocations, were taught in the public schools of Munich. Besides the trade schools there were others for preparing foremen, superintendents, and personnel workers in general. A second defect of these schemes was that they continued class education.

Meanwhile higher vocational education in science and its applications had an extraordinary development. The universities, beginning with Liebig in 1826 or earlier, gave more and more attention to the sciences and, through their emphasis on research, made many fundamental discoveries. German medical education was world famous and, at a time when our medical schools were undeveloped, they served as examples for the United States. Besides the universities, Germany also had great technological schools in agriculture, engineering, mining, and other applied science fields. The industrial growth and technical competence of Germany rested squarely on an excellent system of education for the learned vocations and professions.

Teaching in the lower schools was one of the vocations to which special attention was given in the legislation of Prussia and other states. The Prussian general regulations of 1872 dealt with the curriculum of the seminaries in which the future teachers of the elementary schools received their professional and much of their general education. In comparison with the regulations of 1854, these were liberal and enlightened. However, in making the comparison we must remember that the earlier rescript had been an angry response to the Revolution of 1848. Under the regulations of 1872, the reading of the students was broadened to cover general history followed with German history, the classical German literature including such un-Prussian authors as Goethe and Schiller, and the great educational classics. There were courses on logic, psychology, and the history of education. The German language, grammar, and composition were studied thoroughly; and foreign languages, including French, were offered as electives. The work in science and mathematics covered what would be included in a good American high school in these areas. The biology and earth science had a considerable resemblance to general science. Religion, because it was one of the subjects in the common school curriculum, was taught in the teachers' seminaries. Bible history, the gospels, the parables, hymns, and church history were stressed and, although the instruction was less confessional than it had been, the emphasis on memory work was retained. There is a diverting but unfriendly account of the work of the teachers' seminary in the autobiographical works of the schoolmaster-author Otto Ernst.

At a later date the curriculum was further extended, but the teachers' seminaries were not made a part of the secondary higher education of Prussia. Common school teachers were kept apart from the higher professional class of society and, except in Saxony, had no opportunity to attend the universities. A boy who wished to teach in the elementary schools was first sent to these schools, then to a seminary for six years and, after a trial year as an assistant, was installed in his own school. Now and then one left this employment to attend the secondary school and the university—Kerschensteiner is an example—but in that case he never returned to the lower schools unless, like Kerschensteiner, he became an administrator.

Until the establishment of the Republic in 1918, Germany had a dual system of schools, one path for the common people down in the valley and another on the heights in the bright sunlight for the professional and official classes. This was, evidently, a necessary element in the system of caste and privilege that had been written into the imperial constitution.

One small dent in this armor of the privileged classes was made by the pressures of social democracy. The general regulations of 1872 permitted the erection of a new type of expanded and elevated common school, called the middle school. Although the common schools were entirely free, the middle schools charged a tuition fee. The name was doubly appropriate because educationally the middle school occupied an intermediate position between the lower and secondary schools and socially it was the school of the lower middle class—of minor officials and retail businessmen. The schools provided for these a more extensive and socially exclusive education than the common schools, but it had other qualities to commend it. The course varied in length from three to nine years. In the former case, children transferred to it after a certain number of years in the common schools. In the upper years of the middle school courses, work more advanced than that of the lower schools and, in particular, English, French, and Latin, was offered. It was this that made possible the pupils' transfer from a middle to a secondary school and thence to the university. Few took this path, so difficult for the children of the poorer classes; but boys who completed the full middle school course, having studied two foreign languages, got off with one year in the army and had access to skilled and semiprofessional occupations. These schools were found only in larger cities, and before 1914 about one child in twenty-five in Prussia attended a middle school.

By the end of the nineteenth century, three types of secondary schools had been developed. All were boys' schools although there were also comparable schools, much fewer in number, for girls. Coeducation on the secondary level was practically unknown in nineteenth-century Germany. Each of the boys' schools had a nine-year course and their graduates were admitted to the university without examination. The oldest type was the *Gymnasium*, an early example of which was established by John Sturm in 1538. We have seen that Humboldt helped to standardize this type in the second decade of the century through a leaving examination and certificate. A second type was the *Realgymnasium*, a Latin-scientific school that in some cases taught Greek as an elective but never as a required subject. The time saved by the omission of Greek was given to modern foreign languages. The *Realgymnasium* was more popular in southern Germany than in Prussia. It was an intermediate school between the gymnasium and a third type, the *Oberrealschule*. This latter school, in which neither of the classical languages was studied, emphasized mathematics, science, and modern languages. The type goes back historically to 1747 when a *Realschule* was opened in Berlin. This was only a six-year school and when the type was changed to a full nine-year school the word *ober*, or higher, was prefixed to the name.

All of these types also existed as part-course or six-year schools, with slight changes of nomenclature that we need not specify. The reason for these part-course secondary schools will appear in a moment. In addition to the major subjects we have named, all of the schools taught religion,

German, history, singing, handwork, physical education, and other subjects—twelve to sixteen in all. The average weekly schedule comprised about thirty recitation periods, but not all of these subjects required outside preparation. The course, however, was stiff beyond the dreams of the average American high school boy.

After three years in a common school or in a public or private preparatory school in which elementary subjects were studied, the boy at the age of nine entered a *Gymnasium*, or a *Realgymnasium*, or an *Oberrealschule*, and at eighteen he was ready to enter the university. This assumes that he completed a year's school work in each year without repeating. None of the ten or twelve subjects assigned to the year could be omitted, nor were substitutions allowed. However, if a pupil stood high in the major subjects—German, foreign languages, mathematics, and science—the staff would exercise some leniency in its rating of the minor subjects. But the promotions were annual events and the pupil who was considered to have failed was compelled to repeat the work of the whole year. Let us note again that all subjects were prescribed. Electives, if any, were extras and were not required for graduation. As a result of this system, the pupils at graduation were on the average about twenty years old. Pupils who completed the first six years of a secondary school course were required to spend but one year in military service, instead of the customary two or three years. A large number of pupils who had difficulty with their studies, or who were poor, or who for other reasons could not go to the university, consequently left school at the end of the sixth year. This was one reason for the popularity of the six-year school; and another reason was that many towns were too small or too poor to support a nine-year school.

EDUCATION UNDER THE WEIMAR REPUBLIC

The constitution of the German Republic, adopted after World War I at Weimar, contained (Art. 1) this declaration: "The German Reich is a Republic, the political power emanates from the people"; and this admirable general statement (Art. 148) on education: "In all schools effort shall be made to develop moral education, a sense of responsibility for the public welfare, personal and vocational competence in the spirt of German nationality and reconciliation with the nations." Unfortunately, "the nations" and powerful sections within the country did little to promote this reconciliation. Germany had lost her colonies and her markets; economic conditions were unpropitious; and the German people soon became so divided politically that it was difficult for the nation to pursue a progressive policy. The constitution went on to say that the central government, "may define the guiding principles for the educational system, including higher education; that the public school system is to be developed as an organic whole, and the middle and higher, that is, secondary schools, are to be extensions of a common school."

These sections provided, for the first time, the basis for a national school system on the plan of an educational ladder that would open the universities to the common people and to the teachers of the elementary schools. The most liberal among the educational leaders tried to revive Süvern's proposal of 1817 for the development of a single school system that would provide a common education throughout the elementary school years and would open freely the various vocational, liberal, and professional doors to the young adolescent. This program, which would have abolished the dual system, was not to be realized. The General School Law of 1920 did, however, provide for a four-year public elementary school that was to be common to all children. The new institution was called the foundation school (*Grundschule*). The public preparatory schools to prepare the children of the wealthy for entrance to secondary schools were closed in 1924; and the private schools of the same kind were to be abolished in 1929. This would have lengthened the course for secondary school pupils from twelve to thirteen years. In 1925 the General School Law was amended to permit capable children to transfer to the secondary schools after three years in the *Grundschule*.

Although the constitution prescribed that the education of youth should be carried out in free public institutions, it permitted the establishment of private schools that would fully meet the standards and appointments of the public schools. Private elementary schools were allowed only for experimental or conscientious reasons, and all private schools had to be approved by the state. The constitution both guaranteed religious freedom and decreed that, except in the comparatively few secular schools, religious instruction must be a part of the regular curriculum. This suggests the fact that there was a serious religious problem in education. Several unsuccessful attempts were made, the last in 1927, to authorize the establishment of sectarian, interdominational, and secular schools as a community might decide. But comparatively few parents exercised their right to withdraw children from all religious instruction. The right to inspect schools was taken away from the clergy. Attendance was made compulsory for eight years full time; and, beyond that period, for four years part time at free continuation or vocational schools. The lack of schools and of money for their establishment prevented the enforcement of the latter clause in many communities. The constitution provided that the central government, the states, and the local units were to cooperate in the promotion of education. In actuality, each of the states developed its own system as in the United States although, also as in the United States, there was considerable similarity in these systems.

In Prussia the Ministry of Public Education had the general direction of the schools and also of the cinema, stage, public museums, and the fine arts as its responsibility. Some phases of child welfare and other activities related to education were controlled by other departments. The spirit of educational administration was greatly liberalized. Instead of authoritative decrees, the ministry now set up standards, offered guidance and suggestions in matters of curricula and methods, and gave opportunity for local adaptation to community and individual needs. Within this pattern a new type of secondary school, the six-year *Aufbauschule,* was organized for those gifted children, chiefly from the lower classes, who were unable to begin secondary classes at the age of nine and to carry them on for nine years. Through the *Aufbauschule* such pupils, entering the secondary school at the age of twelve and finishing at eighteen, were enabled to prepare for the university in six years. Finally there was also created a fourth type of nine-year secondary school called the *Deutsche Oberschule.* Some schools of this type were established in all the states except, apparently, Bavaria. These schools based their curriculum on German culture rather than on classical or mathematical-scientific subjects; and they were given a coordinate place in the system beside the *Gymnasium, Realgymnasium,* and *Oberrealschule.*

The training of teachers was to be conducted according to the principles that applied generally in higher education and teachers were to have the status of public officials. These provisions of the constitution were intended to apply particularly to teachers of the elementary schools. It was intended that future elementary teachers should first complete a secondary school course and that their further and professional preparation should be completed in the university; but economic conditions and party politics prevented the realization of this ideal. In those states where a liberal party was in power for a time after the Revolution of 1918, the necessary transformation of the teacher-education program was begun. However, all this was swept away later when the conservatives returned to power. In some states teachers were prepared partly in the university and partly in a teachers' seminary. In general the attempt to make teacher education a part of the secondary university system was not successful.

The productivity of German writers in the fields of psychology, philosophy, history of education, and of methods of teaching is well known. No other language has so extensive a literature of books, monographs, and magazines on these subjects. Several of the factors that were at least partially responsible for this educational ferment were the bureaucratic management of the schools, the decline of interest in school and university work among the students themselves, the German youth movement, progressive education, and the collapse that eventuated in the formation of the Republic.

During the late nineteenth century, it was frequently noticed that pupils in the secondary schools and students in the universities no longer had the enthusiasm for study that had characterized their fathers and their grandfathers in 1830 or 1870. The reasons were found in the formalism of the schools and the academic and the purely intellectual and abstract nature of their work. Music, the arts, social problems, manual and constructive activities, and the development of the will and of individual responsibility were neglected. Rigid standards and great overpressure militated against the development of personal interests. When the students entered the university, they found themselves completely free from all control and even guidance. The tendency grew among them to waste their time during the early years of the university course and to attempt to make up for this by cramming for a few semesters before the final examinations. Alcoholism and other vices had made great inroads among students.

There was also an economic-vocational problem. Thousands of young men after achieving a doctor's degree found that they could not find a secure place in the professions or could do so only after many years of waiting. The country had become oversaturated with "learned" men and an academic proletariat was forming. This body of the disillusioned and discontented formed fertile ground for social revolution and radical measures of many kinds. Even the elementary schools, although they were set apart as the schools for the lower classes, tended to become authoritarian and to be guided by the intellectual aims of the higher schools. German education, so highly admired by much of the outside world, was ill. Industrialism; the great cities with their luxury and their slums; the insecurity, not only of the poor; bureaucracy and repression; and the worship of material success, which plagued other countries also, were basic causes of social ill health.

The German youth movement was one of the most spectacular protests against these conditions. It was begun by Karl Fischer, a pupil in a Berlin Gymnasium, with the organization of the *Wandervogel* in 1896. The *Wandervogel* was a hiking club whose members wished to come into close contact with nature and the peasants. They attacked the compulsions of the school with its *Wissensballast* of dead information and its success philosophy. They opposed themselves to the social and secret associations that were analogous to American Greek-letter societies. They stood for simplicity, physical health, and wholesome human associations. Other societies were formed on similar lines. The Hamburg *Wanderverein* of 1905 cultivated folk songs and dances, conducted walking tours to come in contact with peasant life, and held discussion meetings. Most of the youth societies in one way or another stressed the simple life and fostered a "back-to-nature" movement.

When the first Liberal Congress of German Youth was held in 1913 on a mountain top near Cassell to form a closer union and to celebrate the centennial of the liberation of Germany (1813), the delegates from thirteen youth associations numbered several thousand. The congress declared that youth must chart its own course without adult interference, although most of the speakers and leaders were adults, some of them teachers. One of the most influential was Gustav Wyneken, founder of a radical progressive school. Physical fitness, self-control, community spirit, and love of the fatherland were set up as goals, and a pledge promising not to indulge in alcohol and tobacco was exacted.

Under the Republic, political purposes came to play an increasing role. Girls had come into the movement early and a great many girls' associations were formed. The German youth movement spread throughout the country but became less and less harmonious as political activity grew within it until 1933, when all the various societies were by command merged into one, the Hitler Youth.

In scouting and in the gradually developing youth hostels and trails, we have the slight beginnings of a similar movement in the United States. We have no autonomous youth movement, however, although in the colleges there are a number of associations with political aims. The German youth movement might well be studied by us as a symptom and, in its outcome, as a warning.

An attempt to show how some of the defects of the schools might be overcome was made by the founders of experimental schools. Hermann Lietz, one of the pioneers of the new education in Germany, was much influenced by Herbart and directly by Cecil Reddie at whose school in England, Abbotsholme, he taught for one year. When he returned to Germany he developed his own "country home schools," Ilsenburg first (1898) and others elsewhere. Manual labor, music and the fine arts, hiking, projects, a varied curriculum, and comradeship between teachers and pupils were some of the features. Teachers whom he had trained established other schools. One difficulty, the matter of expense, kept such an education from spreading.

Most of the recent educators in Germany have been concerned with the place of the individual in the social order. Most of them have been individualists—even those like Spranger and Litt, who derived their values from a theory of culture, and those who began with the demands of society and community as Gaudig and Kerschensteiner did. Friedrick Paulsen, the beloved teacher of many American students at the University of Berlin, was for a generation the most uncompromsing foe of bureaucracy and was bold enough to brave the wrath of Kaiser William II. More recently and far more radically, Paul Oestreich has preached the complete freedom of the child from all prescription. All this was wiped out in 1933 and Germany returned to uniformity and authoritarian control of the most extreme kind.

One victory for democratic education was won by the Republic through the establishment of the *Grundschule,* which brought all classes of the people together for four years in their early childhood and which led to the closing of the separate preparatory schools for future secondary school pupils. But this was the only important victory. The *Aufbauschule* and

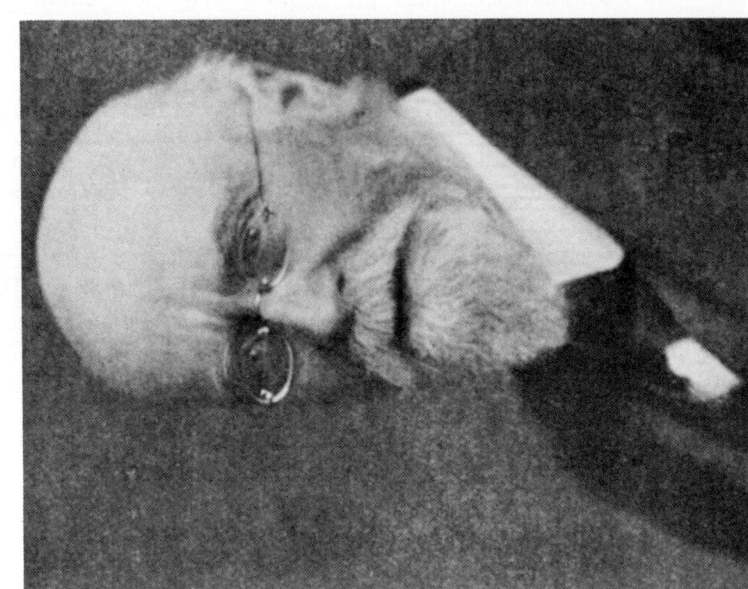

Wilhelm Rein (1842–1929)

Nineteenth-century German educators who greatly stimulated philosophy in the United States.

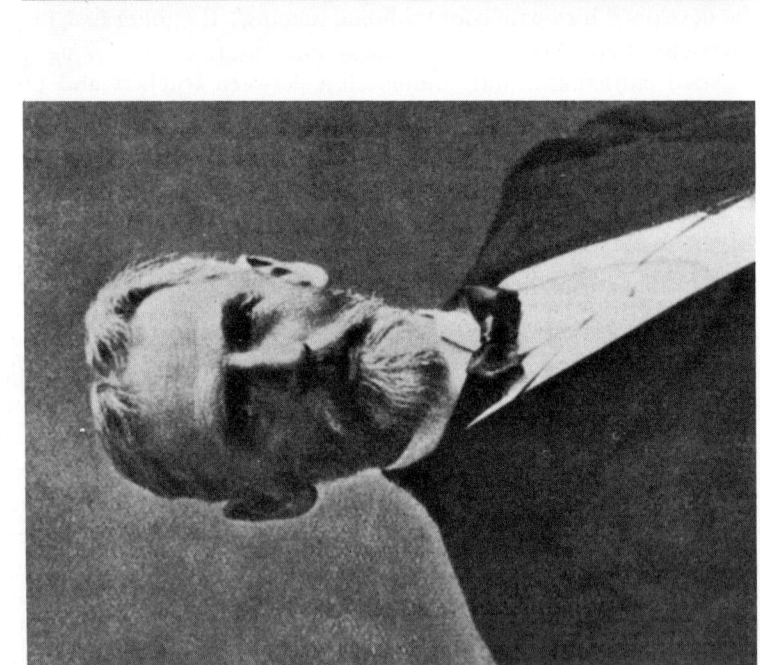

Otto Willmann (1839–1920)

Ernst von Sallwürk (1839–1926)

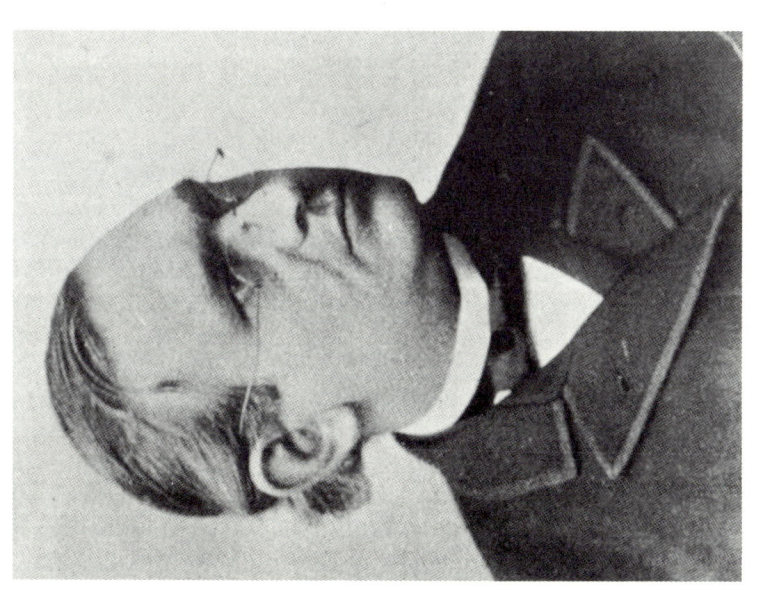

Friedrich Paulsen (1846–1908)

Deutsche Oberschule were to make secondary education more accessible to the people, but few of these were successful. Fees for secondary education were not abolished. Most of the secondary school teachers were hostile to the principles of the Republic. Even though many more pupils attended the secondary schools than before, they were, as in France, prepared only for the already overcrowded professions. The secondary schools did not offer a cultural and vocational education for practical life.

The result was inevitable. It has been estimated that in 1932 there were fifty thousand unemployed professionals in Germany, and many of this intellectual proletariat accepted the promises and assumptions of Hitler. Neither Germany nor France did enough to bring culture and vocation together or to open a way for people of all classes to raise themselves to the level appropriate to their abilities. Both were hampered by the philosophy and institutions of a stratified society. A democratic system should unite the people and not set them against each other. To do this it must be flexible, enabling those who may have made wrong vocational choices to correct their errors, assisting those who are poor but capable to raise themselves to higher levels, and aiding the adventurous and the gifted instead of suppressing them. In these respects the German system, even under the Republic, was not sufficiently democratic.

GERMAN EDUCATION UNDER THE NAZIS AND THE AFTERMATH

In Germany at the end of the most destructive of all wars (1945), education had to be started afresh and under the direction of the military governments of the conquering nations. The new authorities had to work with a system that had been reorganized twice in a generation. The National Socialists had integrated the whole school and university system into a vast military and propaganda organization; and, contrary to all German history, they created a national, or Reich, Ministry of Science and Education to control all the schools. Under the preceding republican constitution and the still earlier empire the separate states had been the chief educational agencies. The existence of the numerous political parties and distinct religious groups had caused the development of school systems with general similarities and many individual peculiarities.

Religion had always been an important element in German life and education. It stood first on any list of the elementary or secondary school studies, and yet educationally and politically it was often a divisive influence. The people grouped themselves into Evangelical, Catholic, and Jewish confessions with many smaller faiths and unfaiths. There were many denominational schools, and these have been reestablished and continue to form exceptions to the even structure of the system. Politically also, education has gone back to the pre-Nazi status. Each of the states had a long political past of independence or semi-independence, but all were politically dominated by one masterstate, Prussia. Her school system was at times an example, but she did not impose it on other states. The Republic proposed a Reich education law but did not succeed in adopting it. Only the Nazis did that and Germany has now gone back to the separate state systems.

Germany was one of the most literate nations of Europe and the world; but she lacked an active and powerful middle class. German localism did not lead to democracy. Even in the Republic, convinced democrats were doubtless in the minority. It may be this distrust of popular rule and also self-distrust by the common people that make them unwilling to shoulder responsibility for the enormities of the Nazi regime. They really feel that they could do nothing about the matter. And who in the democracies can say that he has done all that he could have done for peace, justice, and decency? At any rate, the roots of National Socialism, often not recognized, were deep in the soil, and the economic collapse of 1929 gave them the opportunity to grow.

German education had long been celebrated and was frequently admired by the rest of the world; but obviously the new masters of occupied Germany would not wish to restore the Nazi or the pre-Nazi system. They did not have a clean slate to write on. The war damage created a difficulty. It had come gradually, but at the end the destruction was, in many places, complete. Schools had continued in the usual way for several years, but in 1943 a sudden decline began. The difficulties were both material and spiritual. In Hamburg the schools were closed in July, 1943 and remained closed for exactly two years. By the end of the war, schooling in Germany had practically ceased.

Physical facilities were, as we have noted, lacking when the war ended. Great numbers of school buildings and all but nine of the universities had been damaged. The destruction of the University of Giessen, which is in the Russian Zone, was almost total. The University of Jena and the famous University of Berlin are also in the Russian sector of the city. To make good the loss of the latter, the Free University of Berlin was founded in 1948 in West Berlin, but about forty per cent of the student body come from Soviet parts of Germany. Frankfurt, Munich, and Würzburg had half of their buildings damaged. Heidelberg, the oldest German university, was intact. Many libraries and laboratories were destroyed. Large parts of the cities had been rendered uninhabitable, and usable structures were needed to shelter the homeless and fugitive or were requisitioned for military or hospital use. Schoolwork had to be conducted in shifts for lack of rooms to house the pupils.

In the American sector of Berlin, one fourth of the more than six hundred school buildings had been demolished. Ninety per cent of the schools of Cologne were hit and many were totally destroyed. Even in semirural Schleswig-Holstein there were great losses. Everywhere there were shortages. The lack of light bulbs was unimportant because there was no electric current. Coal was lacking as were housing, shoes, soap, and other necessities. The food shortage reduced the effectiveness of both teachers and pupils.

Despite such difficulties, the schools in the British Zone were reopened in July, 1945, and those in the American Zone the following October. There were many mental blocks and difficulties. The children were listless and purposeless. Like the older people they had no feelings of remorse. "What could we have done?" they said. They lacked the powers of concentration and decision. At the once progressive Odenwald School, one third of the pupils were refugees. They had already been in several, some in as many as five, schools. The principal reported that they were thin, constantly hungry, and could not be quickly restored to a normal condition.

War had for several years been the main business, and as the British and American bombers had become more effective many people had been moved from the target cities to places of greater safety. Women, children, and the aged fled eastward and from the cities to the country. Toward the end they were again driven back by the approach of the Russian armies. The chaos that resulted hampered the reestablishment of the schools. With one matter that might have been judged a probable cause of difficulty there was none: Compulsory school attendance is so much a part of German life that it was easy to get the children back into the schools.

The Potsdam Agreement (August, 1945) of the occupying powers declared, "German education shall be controlled so as completely to eliminate Nazi and militaristic doctrines and to make possible the successful development of democratic ideas." The powers did not all understand this in the same way, but the British and Americans made a strong effort to dismiss National Socialists from their teaching staffs. Two thirds of the thirty-six thousand elementary teachers in the American zone and eighty per cent in some districts were disqualified. Their places were taken by retired teachers or imperfectly trained persons. As a result the age of the staff exceeded fifty years. Many of these older teachers were like other Germans in holding a low opinion of democracy, and they had no stomach for an active crusade to make the schools democratic. Yet this was demanded of them. Schoolbooks, especially those in history, were filled with Nazi propaganda. Even arithmetic had been slanted in the Nazi direction. The process of de-Nazifying the books consumed time, and paper to print new editions was almost unobtainable. For a time, photographic reproductions of pre-Nazi books were used. With the return of the children and the arrival of refugees the schools became overcrowded. Classes averaged about seventy members, and the teachers were constantly overworked.

Schools in West Germany in general follow the organization developed after World War I. The *Grundschule*, or common school, which was instituted at that time is now accepted, but the length of this common school course varies from state to state. It is always given at least four years, ages six to ten, but the Liberals and Socialists who favor a one-class society want a longer course. A long common school course naturally reduced the time that can be devoted to secondary education. Those of the political Right wing and Roman Catholics usually favor the short course. The states of North Rhine-Westphalia, which are mainly Catholic, transfer the pupils to the secondary school at the age of ten; the farmer-Socialist state of Schleswig-Holstein keeps all pupils in the common school for two years longer; and the Socialist administration of West Berlin has completely integrated elementary and secondary education, deferring the choice of the academic courses until the pupils are fourteen years old.

Where the short common school course is in vogue, pupils who are not planning to stay in school beyond the leaving age are transferred at age ten to an advanced elementary school course of four years. This takes them to the age of fourteen and the beginning of an apprenticeship or a vocational school program, or, more often, a combination of these two. Pupils who can remain in school longer can enter a middle school with a six-year course including a modern language. Those destined for a profession or an upper social status will attend a secondary school, with a course of eight years, that prepares for a university.

There is a variety of vocational schools and adult educational opportunities. Apprenticed youths must be excused for attendance at part-time schools. There are nearly two hundred folk high schools that provide opportunity for a combined liberal and vocational education part time, for older youth and adults.

Russia in the eastern zone and sector of Berlin is imposing her own form of one-class school system. All private schools and all religious teaching are suppressed. The state is the only educator, and the school system is uniform in all phases from the kindergarten through the university. Study of the Russian language is required.

Democratic processes were not emphasized in the schools of old Germany. Under the Republic some efforts were made in that direction, and parent councils and student government were tried. In some localities, such as Hamburg, they had a fair success. Where they had none or little it was frequently because the public, teachers, and pupils had not been prepared for the change and because new organizations, abruptly introduced, were given too much power and too free a hand at the outset. The Nazi government killed whatever democratic growth had taken root.

In the Occupation a new beginning was attempted and something was accomplished; but few general statements will apply to the whole country, because education is again administered by the separate states (*länder*). The Reich, or *All*-German, Ministry of Science and Education that the Nazis erected was abolished and each state in West Germany has its own laws, institutions, and practices. There are naturally many similarities. Practice varied also between the American, British, and French Zones; and the Russian Zone of East Germany was entirely different.

Although the states manage their schools, there is a Basic Law of the German Federal Republic (West Germany), and Article 7 deals with education. It provides that all schools are to be supervised by the state, but private schools that satisfy state requirements are permitted. There are reservations about private primary schools. The second main provision of Article 7 says that parents and guardians can decide what religious teaching, if any, the child is to receive. Private primary schools can be established if they are necessary to provide the desired religious instruction or if they are likely to make a contribution to the science and art of education. In any case all schools must satisfy state demands before they can be licensed.

The laws in the German states are much more explicit on the aims, methods, and curricula of the schools than are English laws. England leaves such matters to the teachers and the local authorities. We shall underscore this. The Act of 1944 says nothing about what must be taught, does not require a democratic or patriotic school, and is generally careful not to infringe on the prerogatives of teachers and masters.

The educational directives of the American Military Government were framed in specific terms. They directed that the states were to provide equal educational opportunity for all, to stress education for civic responsibility and the democratic way of life, and to provide opportunity for the people to cooperate in the reform of education. The Germans correctly interpreted this as a criticism of their former practice.

The introduction of social studies into the schools, even into the vocational schools, is one of the new trends in West Germany. The teaching of citizenship and the cultivation of civic interests and skills are stressed. After much hesitation and some hostile objections, discussion groups have been organized in some schools. New teaching methods involving pupil activity are encouraged. Moving pictures showing how elections are conducted in Britain and the United States have been shown in the schools. For many years there has been a radio broadcast for schools. Aid has now been given for the further development of broadcasting, and radio receivers have been supplied to schools that had none. Encouragement has been given the organization of student councils and a new youth movement.

School counseling and guidance, almost unknown in old Germany, have a special importance because they will doubtless moderate the authoritarian school discipline that has been traditional. They also have a particular use in a dual school system. At the end of the *Grundschule*, the child must choose between preparation for the university, the middle school, or continuance in the upper elementary grades. This choice has usually been made without scientific information about the child's abilities, interests, health, and other qualities or with insufficient consideration of the vocational or professional opportunities for which he might qualify himself. In Europe the so-called vocational guidance is not real guidance but a mere assignment to an apprentice's job. It is done by the government, not the school, and is, therefore, poisoned at the source. Seminars and workshops on both social studies and counseling have been held and were opened to West Germans as well as others. They have been well attended.

Thousands of Germans, including many teachers, have traveled and studied in the United States, Britain, and France. The hope is that on their return home they will influence their friends and neighbors to support a more democratic school—one without fees for tuition, books, or supplies —one that offers an open road to all. This will take time, especially the open-road idea; the direction of the change is important now. The universities are even more conservative than the secondary schools.

Secondary school teachers were from the eighteenth century prepared in the universities. Under the Republic several states began to send also their elementary teachers to the higher institutions. The Nazis promised to continue this policy, but, as in many other matters, they failed to honor the arrangement. Anti-intellectual as they were, they even shortened the long-established secondary school course and limited the attendance of all classes and of women at the universities. Under the military occupation, teacher training tended to go back toward the practice of the nineteenth century.

Elementary teachers were again prepared in pedagogical institutes and secondary teachers in the universities, thus reopening the social and intellectual gap between them. Secondary school teachers receive an exacting scholarly preparation, and they study their teaching fields intensively. Their pedagogical study is, however, wholly theoretical, containing little that will have immediate application to their work. Both elementary and secondary school teachers must take two state examinations, one on completing their period of study and another after several years of teaching in a regular school. After these alternating periods of study, teaching, and passing examinations, they become eligible for permanent appointment. The requirement of a trial year or years is not new and surely has merit.

The educational system in the Russian Zone has a compulsory attendance period of twelve years, two more than in Russia itself. The German period of a *Grund* or foundation school of four years (or six in some states) has also been lengthened. It is eight years. As in Russia, every child has to study the Russian language, and the secondary school is continuous with the elementary. There are various types of vocational schools that lead off from the elementary, some part-time, some full-time. The curriculum emphasizes native and foreign languages, mathematics, and science. Religion is omitted and the treatment of the church and religious groups is becoming more harsh and intolerant. All prospective teachers must qualify for entrance to the university, and they are prepared at the university.

The de-Nazification process was much more thorough in the Russian Zone than in the others. The Russians made a clean sweep by dismissing all university teachers and then reappointing those deemed satisfactory. The authorities in West Germany temporized, dismissing only flagrant Nazis at first; and they found difficulty in getting rid of the rest. Hardly any action was taken in the French Zone. We must also notice that some anti-Nazis are as undemocratic as former members of the party.

The effort to democratize the German universities gradually and by an internal process alone reveals in the authorities a certain blindness to the realities of the case. Only when Germany becomes democratic and develops an active and vocal middle class can the universities become democratic. They may be among the last institutions to resign the Prussian authoritarian spirit. And the secondary schools also were not greatly transformed in the occupation. Japanese schools likewise were not changed radically under American tutelage. There are some clear lessons in these negative experiences.

Schools are conservative institutions. In fact the conservation of a way of life is one of the chief reasons for schools. The public often tends to resist the efforts of native leaders to "improve" the schools. And a nation resents much more the interference of a foreign and conquering power in its institutions. Also the Americans have for one hundred years praised German education, studied in German universities, and copied their methods. It is really not surprising that the Germans did not readily abandon their own educational program for the American, which they have never greatly admired.

GERMAN INFLUENCE ON AMERICAN EDUCATION

German immigrants brought new educational ideas and institutions to the United States, such as the outdoor gymnasium, the *Turnkunst*, and the kindergarten. They also provided a tough Americanization problem that is not yet altogether solved. Other influences came through books and magazines and through visitors—either Americans visiting in Europe or Germans spending some time in the United States—but most of all by American students returning after a period of study at a German university. We should remember that Alexander Dallas Bache, Calvin E. Stowe, and Horace Mann wrote influential reports of their visits to German schools, that many important American chemists were trained in German laboratories, that the historical seminar and the doctor of philosophy degree were imported from Germany, and that the German language was for many years the modern foreign language most studied in our high schools and colleges.

The *Turnkunst* has been carried on chiefly in the greater German centers in large cities. There were, however, a few examples of Jahn's system and outdoor Gymnasiums introduced early into New England by refugees after the revolutionary movement in 1830. The names of Charles Beck and Charles Follen are connected with this effort, which aroused great enthusiasm for a short time and then came to an early end. The same can be said of the private secondary schools in New England that were modeled on the German Gymnasium. Among these were the Round Hill School established by George Bancroft and others and Sereno and Henry E. Dwight's New Haven Gymnasium. Our four-year college and the public high school precluded the wide adoption of a nine-year secondary school.

The German teachers' seminary affected the American normal school by its example, but its program and curriculum were not closely followed. The effectiveness of the German teachers' seminaries became known in the United States through Cousin and several American investigators. That knowledge clearly furthered the establishment of the state normal schools, but without affecting their curricula or administration to any marked degree. The normal school was an American institution. But, through Horace Mann, the methods of the elementary schools and, through S. G. Howe and Mann, the education of the deaf, were influenced by German example. Early state administration of schools and the centralization of educational authority in the state were frequently attacked by American publicists on the ground that they were borrowed from autocratic Germany. This argument was used in 1840 in Massachusetts against its State Board of Education and has often been confused with the contemporary attack on the normal schools. The chief charges against the latter were that they were ineffective, unnecessary, and expensive, not that they were foreign importations. The American elementary school organization owed little or nothing to Germany. However, the methods of teaching were affected somewhat by German example and much more by the theories and demonstrations of Pestalozzi, who was an Italo-German-Swiss, and of Herbart and Froebel, who were wholly German. The playground movement, physical education, and music education show German influence; and the kindergarten was a direct importation from that country. The American kindergarten, however, soon diverged from the path marked out for it by Froebel.

Of all our educational institutions, Germany had the greatest influence on the college, for it was to a considerable extent German example and teaching that transformed our colleges into universities emphasizing advanced study, investigation, economic and technical applications, and the development of research and independent graduate work. A new and great era of university history was opened by the establishment of the University of Berlin in 1810; and it was at that moment in their evolution that the influence of the German universities on American education began.

German influence was introduced by students returning from German universities, where they had been welcomed and accorded all the available educational facilities. And the American students seem to have done very well, although they lacked the severe training that the German Gymnasium provided. The results of that rigorous course were sometimes criticized even by the Germans themselves. One such criticism was reported by a young American, James Henry Breasted, who studied at the University of Berlin in about 1890. Breasted wrote home,

> Yesterday, I heard Virchow's inaugural speech as Rector of the University. His intensely interesting address touched German education in general, and disapproved of many features. One statement especially interested me: he said that many foreigners have come into the universities without having had the benefit of the severe training of the German Gymnasium and have done just as good work as the Germans. Something, he therefore argued, is wrong with the Gymnasium.

The influence of the German universities on the American when it got fully under way was potent, widespread, and in the main beneficial. It was transmitted by students who went to Germany: one in 1799; another in 1811; four in about 1820; and ten thousand altogether in the course of the century. These, after shorter or longer periods of study at one or more institutions, returned home, many of them with a doctor's degree, to become college or university research workers, scholars, and professors. Beside the higher degree, they came back with a fund of knowledge, with new methods of work in investigation and teaching, and with a devotion to learning and its uses in private and public life such as our own meagerly equipped institutions were unable to give or to call out.

Several hundred Americans had studied in Germany before 1850 and the numbers increased very rapidly decade by decade until 1890. They then began to decline and, with the outbreak of World War I in 1914 and the American entry into it in 1917, dropped to zero. The University of Berlin enrolled the largest number with Leipzig, Heidelberg, Halle, Bonn, Munich, and Göttingen, in about that order, attracting smaller but still considerable contingents. Several of the early migrants, George Ticknor for example, studied literature and languages; but the development of Liebig's laboratory at Giessen, opened in 1826, and Wohler's and other laboratories elsewhere attracted some young American chemists soon after 1830. The younger Silliman and others of the School of Applied Chemistry at Yale followed German examples. The doctor of philosophy degree, first granted in the United States at Yale in 1861, was imported from the same source. Eventually, all the liberal arts and sciences and the old professions—theology, law, and medicine—drew American students. As a temporary but important phase of this migration, the Herbartian pedagogy attracted about fifty American students, chiefly to Jena and Leipzig.

There were no graduate schools or advanced and research courses in American institutions before the nineteenth century. These were to a great degree a result of German influence. The first well-organized and adequately staffed graduate school was Johns Hopkins, opened in 1876, although Yale and Harvard had been making efforts in the same direction. Through the example of Johns Hopkins, aided by the vast expansion of higher education, the increase in the number of colleges, and the development of the state universities, the field for collegiate and graduate instruction in the United States expanded at a phenomenal rate. The German university seminar, research work, the doctor of philosophy degree, and the expansion of laboratories and libraries were all introduced or greatly stimulated by students returning from Berlin, Leipzig, or their sister institutions. One of the fields of study that was entirely transformed and rapidly expanded by the movement was the field of psychology. Shortly after Wundt opened his psychological laboratory at Leipzig in 1879, American students flocked to it. G. Stanley Hall and J. McKeen Cattell were among the first, and they and their contemporaries developed new phases, such as educational, differential, and functional psychology, and founded psychological laboratories and journals.

American students attended German universities because they were freer, more accessible, and had more to teach them than those of other countries. Academic freedom, however, was never as unqualified as has sometimes been asserted. On political and social questions, the professors usually agreed with the state. The faculties and the state usually saw to it that unsafe men were not appointed to professorships. But outside this danger zone, *Lehr-* and *Lernfreiheit* were great indeed. Not only was there freedom of teaching, but the professors were qualified to teach by their learning, industry, and capacity in their fields. When George Ticknor, after graduating from Dartmouth and living under the shadow of Harvard among some of the best American scholars, went to Germany, he was astounded by the depth, breadth, and originality of the scholarship of his Göttingen professors. The same experience was repeated by many of Ticknor's successors. Many Americans went to secure special training in research or to use the great European libraries and laboratories; some went to secure the advanced degree and prestige of foreign study; and some merely combined study with travel and a period of residence aboard. An important item is the fact that residence at German universities was less expensive than at Oxford and Cambridge; and the English institutions did not offer the advanced work or the degree of doctor of philosophy that was becoming a prerequisite for appointment to an American professorship. Before World War I, the United States had learned many of the lessons that Germany had to teach us, and our facilities in scholarship and equipment had in many fields begun to rival and even to excel theirs. Even so it is still true that foreign study in England, France, or elsewhere provides stimulation and a broadening experience.

SUMMARY

The German states began to take an interest in the schools at the Reformation; and did so to a greater extent in the eighteenth century, when the "benevolent despots" began to direct education toward national purposes. But it was in the nineteenth century that they created universal public education in Prussia and Germany. Accepting many of the principles of the French Revolution and Napoleon's policy of universal military service, the youth of the country united to repel the conqueror and to create a liberal Germany. In education their success was hardly greater than it was in politics, yet something was accomplished. Taking Prussia as our example, they formed a central educational administration, established the University of Berlin (1810), reformed the secondary schools, and, most important, remodeled the common schools and the teachers' seminaries on Pestalozzian principles. There was a galaxy of democratic leaders that rivaled the American group of the same period (1810–1850). However, the first conservative reaction (1819) came within a decade, and the subsequent history of German education oscillates between successive waves of liberalism and autocracy.

Under the empire, the May Laws (1873) made the schools more secular and repressed Catholic and, in general, clerical influence. In that period of rapid industrialization, Germany became the leader in vocational education. This development was aided not only by the demands of industry but also by the sharp division into social classes that made it easy to direct working-class youth into a definite vocation at an early age. In the nineteenth century also many secondary schools were opened and the *Realgymnasium* and *Oberrealschule* acquired the right to prepare pupils for the university. A new type of school, called the middle school, was established in some cities. This made it somewhat easier in the favored localities to transfer from the common school to the secondary school.

The Weimar Republic took the creation of a unitary, or ladder, system as one of its goals; and it actually established a four-year common school for all children. This school, the *Grundschule*, brought all classes of children together for a short period, after which they were separated as in previous times. Beginning as early as 1850 and continuing under the Republic, education was agitated over many serious problems: bureaucratic administration, overpressure of pupils, decline of interest in school, increased youthful vice, the overcrowding of the professions, and the hostility of many secondary school teachers to the Republic. The National Socialists integrated the German educational system into a vast military and propaganda organization under highly centralized national control. With the fall of the Nazis, education in West Germany tended to return to the pattern established by the Weimar Republic. However, the attempts to democratize the schools have not been too successful. In East Germany, Russia has imposed her own form of one-class school system.

Through German literature and official reports, through immigration, and especially through the thousands of Americans who studied in Germany, that country has exercised a potent influence on education in the United States. This influence has been greatest at the extremes of our system—in the lower grades and in the university; the high school has been much less affected.

QUESTIONS

1. Why did the German states introduce compulsory attendance requirements earlier—and how much earlier—than other states?
2. How does the "educational strategy" of autocracy differ from the policy of democracy?
3. Compare the educational conditions and policies after military defeat in Prussia after 1806, in France after 1870, and in Germany after 1918.
4. Consider the complementary effects of education on politics and of politics on education during revolutionary crises.
5. Why was it easier to carry out a scheme of compulsory vocational education in Germany than it would have been in the United States?
6. Using Russell's *German Higher Schools*, or Kandel's *Comparative Education*, compare the amounts of work demanded in the German secondary school and the American high school. How do you explain Virchow's judgment quoted in this chapter?
7. Why, in your opinion, were German secondary schoolboys of 1900 less interested in schoolwork than their fathers and grandfathers had been?
8. In what respects, if in any, do you agree that German influence on American education was beneficial? Was this because of the excellence of the German schools, to the weakness of ours, or to our wisdom in borrowing?
9. Study and evaluate the education experience of George Ticknor in American and European schools and universities.
10. How do you explain the relative failure of efforts to democratize the German school system since 1945?

NOTES AND SOURCES

There are many German encyclopedias of education that cite the literature on each important topic. We shall name only two of the more recent ones, as follows: Ernst M. Roloff, *Lexikon der Pädagogik*, Freiburg-im-Breisgau, 1913–1917, 5 vols.; and Hermann Schwartz, *Pädagogisches Lexikon*, Leipzig, 1928–1931, 4 vols. *The History of Secondary Education* and the *Comparative Education* by I. L. Kandel and E. H. Reisner's *Nationalism and Education Since 1789*, which were given in the two preceding chapters, apply also to this one and to the chapter on England. We include here some works by Kandel, Kneller, Lindegren, and others that deal with recent phases of education in Germany. The periodical literature such as the article by Smart cited here and especially the various issues of *Comparative Education Review*, should be consulted for the recent period.

ALEXANDER, THOMAS, *The Prussian Elementary Schools*, New York, The Macmillan Company, 1919, 511 pp.; and, with Beryl Parker, *The New Education in the German Republic*, New York, The John Day Company, 1929, 387 pp.

BARNARD, HENRY, *German Educational Reformers*, Hartford, Conn., Brown, Russell and Gross, 1878, 724 pp.

EDDING, FRIEDRICH, *Okonomie des Bildungwesens: Lehren und Lernen als Halshalt und als Investition*, Freiburg, Rombach, 1963, 440 pp.

FLETCHER, ARTHUR W., *Education in Germany*, Cambridge, England, W. Haffer and Sons, 1934, 61 pp.

HEMAN, FRIEDRICH, *Geschichte der neueren Pädagogik*, Leipzig, A. W. Zickfeldt, 1921, 588 pp. Revised edition.

HENDERSON, ERNEST F., *A Short History of Germany*, New York, The Macmillan Company, 1902, 2 vols.

HILLARD, GEORGE S., *Life, Letters, and Journals of George Ticknor*, Boston, James R. Osgood and Co., 1875, 2 vols.

HUEBENER, THEODORE, *The Schools of West Germany*, New York, New York University Press, 1962.

KANDEL, ISAAC L., *The Making of Nazis*, New York, Teachers College, Columbia University, 1934, 143 pp. Also found in the eleventh *Yearbook* (1934) of the *International Institute of Teachers College, Columbia University*. A bibliography is given. Each volume of the *Yearbook* from 1924 to 1934, excepting that for 1930, contains one or more articles on Germany.

KNELLER, G. F., *The Educational Philosophy of National Socialism*, New Haven, Yale University Press, 1941, 299 pp.

KOTSCHNIG, WALTER M., *Unemployment in the Learned Professions; An International Study of Occupational and Educational Planning*, London, Oxford University Press, 1937, 347 pp.

LEARNED, W. S., *The Oberlehrer; A Study of the Social and Professional Evolution of the German Schoolmaster*, Cambridge, Harvard University Press, 1914, 150 pp.

LEXIS, W. H., *A General View of the History and Organization of Public Education in the German Empire*. Translated by G. J. Tamson, Berlin, A. Ascher and Co., 1904, 182 pp.

LILGE, FREDERIC, *The Abuse of Learning; The Failure of the German Universities*, New York, The Macmillan Company, 1948, 184 pp.

LINDEGREN, ALINA M., *Education in Germany*, Washington, Government Printing Office, 1939, 145 pp. Bulletin No. 15, 1938, Office of Education. Useful for its collection of secondary curricula as well as its brief treatment of National Socialist education.

MOOG, WILLY, *Geschichte der Pädagogik: die Pädagogik der Neuzeit vom 18 Jahrhundert bis zur Gegenwart*, Leipzig, A. W. Zickfeldt, 1933, 540 pp. This is the second volume of a general history of education from the Renaissance; but it is especially complete on German education.

PAULSEN, FRIEDRICH, *Geschichte des gelehrten Unterrichts*, Leipzig, Veit and Co., 1896–1897, 2 vols.; *German Education, Past and Present*. Translated by T. Lorenz, New York, Charles Scribner's Sons, 1908, 310 pp. Paulsen was an educational liberal and the inspiring teacher of many Americans who studied at the University of Berlin. His little book on *German Education* is a classic in the field. He also wrote several important philosophical works and was a constant contributor to periodicals.

PINNOW, HERMANN, *History of Germany; People and State Through a Thousand Years*. Translated by Mabel R. Brailsford, New York, The Macmillan Company, 1933, 473 pp. A good short history in English giving special attention to social and popular developments.

RUSSELL, JAMES EARL, *German Higher Schools; The History, Organization and Methods of Secondary Education in Germany*, New York, Longmans, Green and Company, 1899, 455 pp.

SAMUEL, R. H., and R. HINTON THOMAS, *Education and Society in Modern Germany*, London, Routledge and Kegan Paul, Ltd. [1949], 191 pp.

SCOTT, JONATHAN FRENCH, *Patriots in the Making*, New York, D. Appleton & Company, 1916, 262 pp.

SMART, K. F., "Education in East Germany," *Educational Forum*, vol. 25, pp. 463–471, May, 1961.

THUT, I. N., and ADAMS, DON, *Educational Patterns in Contemporary Societies*, New York, McGraw-Hill Book Company, 1964, chap. 4.

THWING, CHARLES F., *The American and the German University. One Hundred Years of History*, New York, The Macmillan Company, 1928, 234 pp. Sketchy but containing information not otherwise readily available.

WALZ, JOHN A., *German Influence in American Education and Culture*, Philadelphia, The Carl Schurz Memorial Foundation, 1936, 79 pp.

Chapter 16

NATIONALISM AND SOVIET EDUCATION

The West has been deeply moved by historical forces that hardly touched Russia. She was not affected by the revival of Greek and Latin learning and art or the Humanism and the new history and archaeology of the Renaissance. The devotional movements in the Roman Catholic Church did not reach her, nor did the Protestant Reformation with its powerful incentive to strive for the education of the common people. The Enlightenment and the democratic revolutions did not shake the autocracy, the orthodoxy, or the imperialism of the country of the czars. Even after the Revolution of 1917 Russia did not change as much as some observers imagined. The new autocracy is that of the Presidium and Premier; the new orthodoxy, that of materialism and Communism; and the new imperialism swallowed the Baltic nations and holds its neighbors in its powerful grip.

In this chapter we treat the educational system of the Union of Soviet Socialist Republics (USSR) as the pattern for a third type of highly centralized national school system. Whereas in France educational authority is centralized in the federal government and in Germany in the states, in the Soviet Union it is concentrated in the Communist party. Because the party is not decentralized, it effectively controls every phase of education throughout the USSR. This was the pattern of control in Germany from 1933 to 1945 under the National Socialist (Nazi) party. It also served as the model in education for the Communist party of the People's Republic of China. Thus the educational systems of the two largest land masses on earth are under highly centralized party control.

The aim of Soviet education is to destroy the old nationalism with its devotion to the czar and Russia and to develop a new nationalism with its devotion to the Communist party and its ideology. Thus the study of Soviet education can serve to illustrate the deliberate and planned use of an educational system to propagandize in order to develop a new social order. In order to better understand this transition from the old to the new order we must first trace the development of nationalism in Russia under the czars.

RUSSIAN EDUCATION BEFORE THE REVOLUTION

The largest of the fifteen republics that constitute the USSR today is the Russian Soviet Federated Socialist Republic (RSFSR), which includes three fourths of the area of the Soviet Union and a majority of its people. Strictly speaking the name Russia should be used only for this republic with its capital at Moscow. Even this republic includes over one hundred linguistic groups and nationalities. Aided by the Eastern Church, these Russian peoples were united by a series of absolute monarchs beginning with Archduke Ivan IV (the Terrible) who became the Russian Caesar (czar). With the support of the clergy, Ivan consolidated the powers of the Crown so securely that only the Communist Revolution of 1917 could destroy it.

Czarist Russia was strongly nationalistic and a policy of "Russification" was pursued ruthlessly. Many minority groups resisted these attempts to prevent the use of native language and native religions. Many of the minorities were without a written language and about three fourths of the people were illiterate.

The Russian czars were not only nationalistic but were also imperialistic. They extended the power of Russia across Asia to the Pacific Ocean. In their Eurasian conquests they embraced additional peoples with many varied colors, languages, and religions.

Early in the seventeenth century the Romanov family came to power and continued to rule until 1917. Among the Romanovs, the three who did most to advance a national system of education were Peter I (the Great), 1672–1725; Catherine II (the Great), 1729–1796; and Alexander II, 1818–1881. Peter attempted to "Westernize" his people, founded several schools of engineering including a naval academy, developed "cypher" schools to stress arithmetic among children of the nobility, and planned an Academy of Science that was founded in the year following his death. Catherine ascended the throne in 1763 and broadened Peter's interest in Western science and technology to include other aspects of education. With the advice of Diderot and Friedrich von Grimm she established Charity Committees and charged them with the founding of schools in all cities. Alexander freed the serfs and authorized elected county councils (Zemstvos) to levy taxes and establish schools. But the combined results of these reforms fell far short of meeting the educational needs of the people.

Thus the Russian Empire entered the twentieth century with a people largely illiterate and unprepared for the reasonable and responsible exercise of freedom; with many nationalities without a written language; with an underdeveloped technology unable to meet the problems of hunger and poverty; with crusading liberal thinkers attracted to the writings of Karl Marx and other materialistic writers; and an army of peasants repeatedly rioting against the abuses of an autocratic monarchy and an insensitive bureaucracy. Then came World War I ending any hopes for bettering the condition of the common people. The result was a general uprising and the overthrow of the monarchy in March, 1917. After a period of confusion under a revolutionary government headed by Alexander Kerensky, the Bolsheviks under Lenin and Trotsky seized control in November, 1917 and gradually unified the sprawling Russian Empire into the USSR.

FORMATIVE IDEAS OF SOVIET EDUCATION

Changes in the Soviet school system are nothing new. The system passed through an experimental phase in the period following the Revolution. It did not emerge full-grown. In that early phase there was considerable fumbling, as one would expect; and the leaders were active in borrowing, trying out, and adapting the ideas and practices of other countries, particularly those of Germany and the United States. They were also fertile in educational invention and the end result of their efforts is unlike any other system.

From the first they were interested mainly in methods and organization rather than in goals, which have always been those of the Communist party of Russia. They found the liberal and progressive practices of the West unsuitable for their purposes. The school system was changed after 1928 and became fixed and rigid by 1938. It was organized under Stalin who has been charged with the "betrayal of an ideal," the ideal of brotherhood in a classless and stateless society. It is more probable, however, that the monolithic state and the inflexible schools are the natural results of radical socialism. The school system has some strongly marked features, as will appear, but its efficiency does not come only from its structure, curriculum, and methods of teaching. Intangible forces have been effective. The pupils are the children of peasants or of parents removed from peasantry by a generation only, and they have seen a vision of a new world of ideas and opportunity for intelligent people. The political education they receive in school and in the youth organizations fosters this ideal. In a little book, *I Want to Be Like Stalin*, we read, "Education for us is a vital public concern and is directed toward the strengthening of the Socialist State." That state that is the Soviet Union respects brains in those who will serve the regime. Even old czarist Russia had a distinguished intelligentsia: novelists, historians, and scientists. The new Russia, as in so many other lines, carries forward old Russia's intellectual tradition also and, with greater resources and skill, tries to cultivate talent wherever it appears. But autocracies, old and new, although they reward genius and use it, are careful not to trust it too far.

The Soviet schools are organized, directed, and supported by the state, that is, by the Communist party. Although a collective farm or a labor union can conduct a kindergarten or vocational school, these must be uniform with the state system in organization, curriculum, methods, and theory. There are no private schools in the Soviet Union; but the Russian Orthodox Church is allowed to maintain seminaries to train its priests, and Moslems and Jews have corresponding institutions.

In the schools for all pupils, the materialistic-scientific philosophy of man and nature must be taught from kindergarten days on. The party ideology provides a complete philosophy of life that is imposed on everyone in school, in youth organizations, and in the system of political education for adults. Russian party members not only know the required answers to the fundamental questions, but they are fully committed to the task of "building socialism." This greatly simplifies the educational problem. The social studies cease to be a controversial area. The answers to social questions become nearly as exact as those of physical science.

In the process of changing the people, the instrument used—that is, the educational system—was itself changed. Lenin had insisted that the infant can be molded easily, the child or youth less easily, and older persons hardly at all. From the first, therefore, the Soviets laid great importance upon the education of the smallest children. They established infant nurseries for children as young as six weeks, nursery schools for those between two and three years, and kindergartens for three- to seven-year-olds. Communist indoctrination begins soon after the child leaves the cradle.

There was another reason for these state institutions for the very young. Lenin wanted to free women from petty household tasks and the poverty that crushed, stifled, and degraded them. Women were to be given the same privileges as men, including the privilege of helping to build socialism. Another and truer way of putting this is to say that by freeing mothers from housekeeping, the labor force was greatly increased. It has been estimated that a million women were thus enabled to join the working force in the early 1930s when the industrialization drive began. These were found mainly in cities, for that is where nursery schools and kindergartens were established. Even today these institutions are available to only a small proportion of the appropriate age groups, and in this respect Russia does not differ from other Western countries.

Waifs, the homeless and fatherless children, made another problem. Such unfortunates by the thousands resulted from the famines of 1921 and 1933, from war, and from the early practice of easy divorce. Many boys and not a few girls roamed the streets, seeking food and shelter, stealing, and committing depredations. The Communist theory of the ultimate "withering away of the family" proved as mistaken as the parallel theory of the "withering away of the state." The former theory and the practice of free love produced a generation of children left by their unmarried or divorced mothers to be cared for in children's homes, if cared for at all. The situation was described in *The Waif* by "Nicholas Voinov."

In the pages that follow we shall trace some of the steps by which the fluid school system of the 1920s became the hard, autocratic system of today. In the 1920s, a three- or four-year elementary school was established, and this was expanded into a seven-year and then a nine-year school. Compulsory attendance regulations were announced in 1930 and extended in 1933. At first, school attendance began at the age of eight, but this left an awkward gap of one year because the kindergarten program ended at seven. The ten-year school, taking children at seven, closed the gap. Lenin had died in 1924, and the views of Stalin—the name means steel—began to affect the schools, at least by 1928. In the middle 1930s the present rigid and autocratic system became fully established, although there have been some temporary changes. The separate education of the sexes, completely contrary to standard Communist theory, was one of these.

In Lenin's time school practices were compartively free and easygoing. Russian theorists, in the manner of John Dewey, declared that there could be no final system or universal philosophy of education. Each school was a sort of soviet with the pupils largely in control. The curriculum was often made up from day to day. This has been called the experimental period, and it continued in one phase or another until the 1930s. Great emphasis was laid upon ideological and political indoctrination in socialism, sovietism, and Marxism-Leninism. This object is vigorously promoted not only in the "people's schools," but also in the special Party Schools and by every means of mass communication.

Polytechnical education, which Karl Marx had envisioned, was introduced. It involved the participation by the children in work processes: learning the uses of various tools, the qualities of materials, and the methods of constructing various simple objects. A related scheme introduced somewhat later has been called the activity program. It was, however, a Soviet creation and did not follow the ideas of John Dewey or Georg Kerschensteiner of Munich, who developed a Western activity school. According to the Russian plan, children were to help in building socialism. They went out from school to harvest corn, kill potato bugs, carry lunches to workers, or to "liquidate illiteracy." The activity program, sometimes called the project method, was especially emphasized after the First Five Year Plan was undertaken in 1928. According to the brigade method a group, rather than individual children, was held responsible for the completion of a task.

Parallel to such schemes there was also a foray into educational psychology or rather pedology, the study of child growth and development. An extensive program of testing and charting the qualities and growth of children was carried on. This was based on the theory, soon to be repudiated by the Communists, that what a child becomes is determined not by environment and education but by native ability. The program came to a sudden, and for participants, unhappy end. The Central Committee of the party decreed in 1936 that the entire pedological experiment must be abandoned. The use of intelligence tests was forbidden, and some of the leaders in the testing program were purged.

THE SOVIET TEN-YEAR SCHOOL

The educational task as thus simplified is carried out in a single-track school, uniform throughout the entire country. It has been a day school. The schedule in Table 16-1 shows what is taught in it.

This schedule must be supplemented with further information if we are to grasp its meaning. Small towns may have only a seven-year incomplete school and some rural sections only a four-year elementary school, which may be compared with the German *Grundschule*. As in other parts of the world, there is a considerable gap between city and country school provisions.

The complete ten-year school is an elementary and secondary school on a 4-3-3 plan. It is a comprehensive school covering all studies offered to children between the ages of seven and seventeen; it is coeducational; it is supposed to be classless, and it is intended to promote the abolition of social classes in the population. Bureaucracy, however, and education itself, tend to form new classes in Russia. This condition is the subject of strong complaints in the Communist party press (*Times Educational Supplement*. London, January 1, 1954, p. 7).

The comprehensive elementary-secondary school of Russia forms a contrast with the parallel elementary school for the common people and secondary school for the elite in such countries as France and Germany. But in the latter countries there is a tendency toward the integration of the parallel systems, and in England as we shall see that this was accomplished in theory by the act of 1944. In Russia, on the contrary, there are new plans—the Khrushchev reforms, to be mentioned again—that may tend to develop a laboring proletariat on the one hand and a scientific-technological elite on the other.

A comparison with the American high school, which is different from the schools just mentioned, may prove instructive. The high school is comprehensive in its subject offerings, and it admits all qualified children of its district; but it separates pupils into different groups by assigning them to somewhat specialized curricula. In a large school a vast number of adjustments is possible so that some pupils may have an individual scheme. We sometimes call the high school a single-track school, but this term may be

TABLE 16-1. SCHEDULE OF SOVIET TEN-YEAR SCHOOL

	Number of Class-Periods per Week										
Subjects	Primary			Junior				Senior			Total
	1	2	3	4	5	6	7	8	9	10	
Ages:	7–8	8	9	10	11	12	13	14	16	16–17	
Russian Language and Literature	13	13	13	9	9	8	6	5	4	4	84
Mathematics	6	6	6	6	6	6	6	6	6	6	60
History	—	—	—	2	2	2	2	4	4	4	20
USSR Constitution	—	—	—	—	—	—	—	—	—	1	1
Geography	—	—	—	2	3	2	2	2	3	—	14
Biology	—	—	—	2	3	2	3	2	1	—	12
Physics	—	—	—	—	—	2	3	3	4	4	16
Astronomy	—	—	—	—	—	—	—	—	—	1	1
Chemistry	—	—	—	—	—	—	2	2	3	4	11
Psychology	—	—	—	—	—	—	—	—	—	1	1
Foreign Language	—	—	—	—	4	4	3	3	3	3	20
Physical Education	2	2	2	2	2	2	2	2	2	2	20
Drawing	1	1	1	1	1	1	—	—	—	—	6
Drafting	—	—	—	—	—	—	1	1	1	1	4
Singing	1	1	1	1	1	1	—	—	—	—	6
Labor and Excursions	1	1	1	1	2	2	2	3	2	2	17
Total	24	24	24	26	32	32	32	32	33	33	293
Number of subjects (carried by each pupil)	6	6	6	9	10	11	11	11	11	12	—

NOTE: This schedule is a modified form of one in George S. Counts, *The Challenge of Soviet Education*, New York, McGraw-Hill Book Company, Inc., 1957, p. 77. By publisher's permission.

more correctly restricted to schools like the Russian or the German Gymnasium in which all pupils do the same work. But Germany also has alternate schools, as we have shown. Russia offers no choice, an appropriate scheme for an autocracy, and also a comparatively inexpensive plan.

The Soviet single-track is not without barriers or gates. The completion of the seventh year marks an important step in the child's progress. At that point there is a critical examination. Those who pass can proceed to the senior school and ultimate graduation, perhaps even to the university. At that point also, or even at the end of the junior division, special examina-

First-year pupils in Moscow during an arithmetic lesson. (Courtesy of UNESCO. Photo by Sholomovich.)

Moscow tenth-graders learning to calculate with the use of a slide rule. (Courtesy of UNESCO. Photo by Sholomovich.)

tions may admit those who pass them to *technicums,* a variety of practical schools, usually on the secondary level, that prepare pupils for skilled and semitechnical occupations.

The ten-year school is, therefore, a terminal school for some and a preparatory school for those who will continue in advanced institutions. Not all children are able to complete the course, but all must attend the school to the end of the compulsory period. Before 1949, attendance was compulsory only in urban districts; from 1949 to 1960 education was compulsory from age seven through the junior school at thirteen or fourteen; and in 1960 the compulsory period was extended everywhere to age seventeen.

Below the elementary school there are nursery schools and kindergartens. These are directed not by the department of education but by the department of health. As in other countries preschool institutions are lacking in many rural parts. The technicums, as already mentioned, are mainly secondary institutions, drawing off students from the main system. Above the ten-year school there are many higher and technical institutions including the universities, many technical and professional schools, research institutions, military and naval academies, and special schools for political enlightenment in Communist theory and doctrine. These latter prepare party leaders and functionaries.

Barring the foreign languages where large schools can offer the pupils some choice between English, or German, or French, for example, all studies as listed in the preceding schedule are required and as far as possible are uniform in content and method throughout the Union. The Russian tongue is required either as the native tongue, as shown in the schedule, or in non-Russian-speaking republics, as an additional foreign language. Most of the world's leading languages are offered in different schools. The reading selections in Western languages are not usually taken from the literature of the country whose language is being studied; they are often synthetic pieces praising the great Soviet land and sounding its virtues; or they may be the writings of Communists from the country being studied. In contrast with some small countries like Holland or Luxembourg, which may require a pupil to study five or more foreign languages, the Soviet Union requires only one. Yet Russian educators claim that their aim is to give children an understanding of the cultures of foreign countries.

We should notice that most studies are pursued continuously for several years, not, as in many cases in the American high school, for a single semester or year. Russia follows the European habit of demanding continued application, not the American scheme of course credits that permits the pupil to "cash in" his work for graduation even though he may have forgotten what he has learned. In the European and Russian system the number of class exercises per week in a given subject is reduced and the subject is in most cases kept before the pupil until graduation day. In the ten-year school, physics is studied for five years, biology for six, history for seven, and mathematics for ten.

Instruction in mathematics begins with primary arithmetic and includes algebra, geometry, trigonometry, and some references to non-Euclidean geometry, one of whose several inventors was a Russian, Lobatchevskii; and the teacher is required, by party regulation, to make this fact clear to the pupils. The mathematics course includes a brief introduction to the history of elementary mathematics; but the mathematical content and methods are formal and conservative in comparison with advanced teaching practice in the West. The purpose is mainly practical, not the cultivation of independent thinking. With able pupils the scheme is effective in attaining the selected goal.

Recent information raises questions about the effectiveness of the methods with less able pupils. Soviet educators are said to be much disturbed by poor teaching and poor learning in mathematics and physics. In *Izvestia* (June 7, 1958) a Soviet teacher reported that high school pupils are losing interest in schoolwork because they find that they will have to work in factories and on farms (*The New York Times*, Editorial, June 16, 1958). One teacher's report is not conclusive, but there is further evidence of the situation subsequently described.

For some unexplained reasons, oral examinations prevail in Soviet education. The judgment of a former student on this practice is as follows:

> From personal observation the system of oral examinations seems one of the poorer aspects of the Russian educational system. Since there is a limit to the problems that one can solve orally, the examinations emphasize too much procedural knowledge (i.e., give the *rule* for multiplying fractions) and place a heavy premium upon memorization. The examinations when I took them were recitations, not discussions. It seems to me that this examination system contributes to "formalism" as much as anything else. (*Documentary and Reference Material on Education in the Soviet Union*, Cambridge, Massachusetts Institute of Technology, 1956, p. 10, no name given.)

Some Russians claim that the secondary schools are overloading the pupils. Thirty-three periods a week in the upper years, the heavy emphasis on mathematics and science, and the excessive demand for memory work place great burdens on young people, most of whom, as in other countries, will not be geniuses. The same kind of charge has been laid against the German and French schools, as we have shown. In both countries the same causes may have been at work, namely, high competition for scholarships and even for places in the higher institutions. The latter, at least, is a fact in the Soviet Union. The university system is expanding but not rapidly enough to absorb all or even a majority of the secondary school graduates. We return to the schedule. It shows that the child will be exposed to seventeen subjects. The exposure is brief in some cases: one hour a week for a year on the Soviet constitution, and the same for astronomy and psychology; but it is extended in other cases as the schedule indicates. The number of subjects carried at any one time by each pupil varies from six in the early years to eleven or twelve later. The number of class exercises also rises from twenty-four per week to thirty-three. Exclusive of examinations, the school year extends to thirty-three of class work and one week of excursions. The student can make the needed comparisons with American practice. As in some other European countries, the schools are in session six days a week.

The schedule reveals three main points of concentration in the curriculum. Native and foreign languages are given one hundred and four week-hours, mathematics and science are given one hundred, and history and the constitution are given twenty-one. This omits geography, which is partly a social study but is taught as a natural science. Langauges will be difficult for some, but we can assume that mathematics and science will be the most difficult for many and that not all pupils complete the course. A large number of these are drawn off at the end of the seventh year, and others will fail in the senior school. Figures by Nicholas DeWitt show that only about one third of the four to five million seven-year-olds who enter the system remain to graduate from the tenth grade. (*Comparative Education Review*, June, 1958, p. 9.) This is one measure of the success of the system; but we must recall that the ten-year school is not found everywhere.

Teachers for the elementary schools are prepared in training schools in a two-year course. The course for secondary teachers extends over four years and is offered in teachers' colleges. These are organized into faculties and departments. The term *faculty* has the sense frequently given it in Europe and is approximately what Americans call a school, as in School of Fine Arts. It is a major specialized division of a university. The faculties in teachers' colleges are physics and mathematics; natural sciences and geography; language and literature; foreign languages; and, in the larger colleges, a faculty of history. Not all teachers' colleges have a complete program, and they vary greatly in quality. All students must take the required courses in education and in the principles of Marxism, which are taught in special departments serving the entire college. It is to be noticed that there is no faculty, or even a department, of philosophy.

Teachers' colleges are classified as higher institutions along with technical schools and universities, but those in the smaller cities do not always justify this ranking. The colleges are distributed over the Union, and large cities may have more than one. Graduates who make the highest grades or who are members of the party are assigned to ten-year schools, and less able students to seven-year schools. A former professor in a teachers' college has written:

Exceptions are made in the case of students who are party members. Regardless of their academic accomplishments they are assigned to ten-year schools. Students who fail the state examinations are classified as "course auditors" and assigned to teach in elementary schools. In all my experience, I have never known the State Examination Commission to fail a student who was a Party member. (From a report by Ivan Rossianin in *Soviet Education*, edited by George L. Kline, London, 1957, p. 79.)

Similar reports are not infrequent, but Russian teachers deny their substance when Western visitors inquire.

Most officials, but not most teachers or students, are party members. Higher institutions seem to have less autonomy now than they had under the czar; and the surveillance of the universities and spying on students were cultivated as an art and practiced as a vocation under the old regime.

SOVIET EDUCATION SINCE 1956

We have described the Soviet ten-year school in detail because it is the prototype from which the present Soviet school system evolved. It performed its function effectively until the mid-1950s when the Khrushchev reforms, which we have mentioned, altered its function somewhat. Moreover, it is necessary to understand the ten-year school as the foundation for the introduction of boarding schools in 1956 and the polytechnical reform of 1958.

Because the man who proposed these changes in the functions of the ten-year school is now discredited by the Communist party, we can only speculate on the reasons for changes in Soviet educational plans. The following anecdote illustrates this difficulty. In 1951 a London newspaper commented on some of the "revolutions" in Soviet education: the dropping of intelligence tests and coeducation (since restored), projects, and activity methods and the reversion to lessons delivered by the teacher and discipline administered by him. The newspaper said,

The reason for this reversal of policy was strictly pragmatic. Russia badly needed an educated population, and the more advanced methods were simply not producing it. Sterner, more disciplined techniques were found to be necessary. (*Times Educational Supplement*, London, August 3, 1951, p. 613.)

In the following issue a correspondent replied that the new Soviet plan demonstrated simply "that if you wish every member of a population to think alike you dare not teach them to think for themselves."

Nikita Khrushchev while Premier of the Soviet Union and head of the Communist party proclaimed two reforms of Soviet educational policy, both of which are critical of the ten-year school. In 1956, in his speech to the Twentieth Congress of the party, he demanded boarding schools where the children could be confined to a Socialist environment for twenty-four hours a day. He gave no clear explanation of his demand for such schools. Did he want to appease the upper classes who had attained position under Stalin, or was he looking forward to the preparation of a new privileged group? It was not clear.

More than two hundred boarding schools were formed within a year (1956–1957). These do not seem to cater to an upper class of parents nor to be preparing an elite group. Perhaps the groups of children are to become partly self-governing collectives, small soviets, and their work is to consist of a combination of mental and manual labor.

The manual labor part was emphasized in a criticism of the whole system by Khruschhev in 1958. He declared that Soviet education was making pupils unwilling to work with their hands, and he called for a work and study program through which youth would earn its right to a chance in higher institutions.

A correspondent's account of Boarding School No. 16 near Moscow hardly supports any of the preceding ideas. This English visitor found an old building, previously used for a day school, now housing one hundred and eighty boys and girls, aged seven to twelve. The wood and metal shops were moderately well equipped; but the laboratories for biology, physics, and chemistry could not provide for much individual work. The library was well furnished with books, newspapers, and maps, and the reporter especially noticed translations from English works. There were tables for chess and other games. The rooms were comfortable, the food good and substantial. The director was a photography addict who lost no time in having his visitors pose for him. There were numerous pupil groups: an orchestra, a cinema club, sports organizations, and others. The teachers were young. They had "full control over the children." The curriculum was identical with that of every other elementary school in the Union. The director reacted with "shocked scorn" to the idea that party members' children were given preferential treatment. (See the *Times Educational Supplement,* London, November 22, 1957, p. 1491.) The preceding information is only what one man saw and saw fit to report, but it adds concrete detail to a subject that is often buried under generalizations.

Before his downfall, Khrushchev had envisioned all children having the opportunity to attend boarding schools. Now its future is uncertain.

The 1958 plan introduced manual work into the lower grades. After the completion of the seven-year school all children, except a small group of intellectuals, are put to work in field or factory. If they want to proceed with their schooling, they must attend night classes or take correspondence courses. Only the highly talented will be allowed the privilege of continued full-time schooling. Russia's need for a great labor force may be the reason for the change. Perhaps the boarding schools will, after all, be used to train an elite.

SOVIET AND AMERICAN EDUCATION

The Soviet educational system has aroused an extraordinary degree of interest in the West and especially in the United States. This interest has been increased by the observation of Russian technological progress. The effect might well be an overemphasis on science and technology in American education. The question deserves the fullest consideration by those who guide pupils and frame curricula.

The technological success of the Soviet Union is of interest with respect to many fields and especially to two fields: war and trade. The governments of the world pay attention to Russia's fleets of planes and submarines, long-range weapons, and growing steel industry. And Russia is offering to supply India, Egypt, and other countries with agricultural, industrial, and military equipment and to build the Aswan Dam on the Nile. She will continue her bid for a larger share of the world markets. These activities are neither new nor surprising, but her priority in putting into orbit two satellites—the Sputniks of 1957—was both. The United States was astounded by a result so contrary to her expectations, and American prestige abroad suffered an abrupt decline.

Because of the great interest at present in engineering education, we shall deal with it first. We shall then give some attention to the literacy problem. The Soviets have a variety of schools that run parallel to the ordinary elementary and secondary schools. Thus, there are opportunities to receive elementary and secondary instruction by correspondence. There are schools for the blind, the deaf, the dull, and those who are crippled or in poor health. We have already mentioned the technicums, which prepare their pupils for practical work of various kinds. There are schools with curricula of two or three years for industrial and transport workers who have only an elementary education. Education is provided in children's homes; there are evening schools for rural youth; and until recently there was an apparatus for the removal of illiteracy. No group seems to be overlooked by the Soviets, but how widely these various facilities are available is not readily discovered.

Soviet higher education has grown out of the czarist school system. The numbers of both institutions and students have increased rapidly. Women are admitted on an equal basis with men, and this was not done in old Russia. There is also a much greater degree of specialization in Soviet technical education than there was before the Revolution. The Soviets criticize the old Russian education as having been too general. They seem to have gone to the opposite extreme.

Under the czars there were nine universities, attended almost exclusively by members of the upper classes. The present regime in 1957 opened its thirty-seventh university at Ufa near the Urals on the eastern edge of Europe. There are universities far east of the Ural Mountains also. There are eight or nine hundred polytechnical, engineering, and special schools and institutes giving higher technical education. There are higher schools for workers in the food and fish industries, in oil geology, in electric power, in light industry of various kinds, and in many other specialties. A recent report claims that there are about four thousand specialized secondary schools in the Union.

Specialists produced by these various institutions are said to be in great demand. Many are mainly technicians who work under the direction of engineers and scientists who understand the theoretical foundations of the techniques used. Russian institutions of higher and especially of technical and semitechnical education have had a decisive effect on the rapid industrialization of the Soviet empire. It has been noticed that the technical schools have been moving eastward to aid the rapid growth of cities and industries in new regions. We have just noted also the eastern location of the newest university. The making of engineers out of peasants has been a great political achievement. In view of the fear frequently expressed that Russia is outpacing the United States in the preparation of engineers, a few figures are given here from a recent publication.

TABLE 16–2. COMPARATIVE NUMBERS OF GRADUATES IN RUSSIA AND THE UNITED STATES

	USSR	U.S.
Number of Higher Education Graduates Empolyed in the National Economy	2,750,000	5,800,000
Estimated Number of Above Trained in Engineering and the Sciences	1,730,000	1,600,000
Total Number of Engineering Graduates	720,000	600,000
Number of Engineering Graduates per 1,000 Population	3.6	3.6
Per Cent Engineering Graduates Are of All Higher Education Graduates	26.0	10.4

NOTE: Information from Nicholas DeWitt, *Comparative Education Review*, June, 1958, p. 10; see also R. J. Havighurst, "Is Russia Really Out-producing Us in Scientists," *School and Society*, April 26, 1958.

Some considerations not included in the table or not apparent after a cursory view should be mentioned. The Soviet population numbers about two hundred million and the American, one hundred and seventy-five million. The numbers of engineering graduates are exactly proportional to the two populations, but the United States has twice as many college and university graduates as the Soviet Union. The broader sweep of higher education in America is one reason for this difference. Soviet education is largely practical and technical; it does not stress the humanities, the arts, social studies, philosophy, and other liberal and cultural disciplines to the extent that American education does. Even some engineering courses in the United States are partly liberal and are becoming more so.

The United States can prepare more engineers if more should be needed, but the present situation is confused. As in Russia, women could be induced to enter the technical fields, and many young men who do not go to college might make good engineers. Preparation for a technical profession requires time, and failure to act now might be costly. But one should not forget that the great numbers of engineers prepared after World War II found positions only because unforeseen conditions arose. It was the fighting in Korea, together with the rising industrial production, growing air transport, and missile and rocket research that have made many new jobs for technically educated men.

The present drive to increase the number of engineers almost without limit is contrary to the spirit of American education, which has never failed to emphasize, along with technical objectives, the ethical and humanistic components of life. The drive is not effective. College enrollments have increased annually since 1952, but engineering freshmen in 1958 were fewer than in 1957 by 7.6 per cent (*School and Society*, December 6, 1958, p. 427). We should also remember that the quality of engineering talent is far more important than numbers. If the American people wish to copy the technical education and materialistic philosophy of Russia, they should do it with full knowledge. Even the Soviets admit that they have about reached the saturation point in engineering.

We have treated the growth of technical education first because of the present great interest in it. Historically, however, fundamental education had the priority. Russia claims to have reversed the figures on illiteracy. From a population of whom four fifths were illiterate, she has raised the proportion of literate persons to four fifths of the whole. This claim may be questioned if, as is asserted, the average numbers of years of school attendance in the Soviet Union as a whole is only about four years. This is hardly enough schooling to assure functional literacy.

The West may have underestimated the Soviet educational achievement also. There is little doubt that the schools have had a share in the material advances of the Soviet Union. How great the share has been and how it has been accomplished are difficult questions. The freer access to that country in the last few years and the large number of Americans who are studying the system will produce more accurate answers. At the same time Russian students, athletes, farm leaders, and intelligentsia are visiting the United

States. This is encouraging in more than one way, but one is the better understanding of Russian education that will be formed. Critical voices have recently begun to spread the opinion that there are flaws in the Russian system. The changes that are being introduced into it, such as the boarding schools and the manual labor period, also suggest a cautious attitude.

SUMMARY

The educational system of the USSR represents the pattern of a highly centralized national school system with control vested in a single political party. It illustrates the deliberate and planned use of an educational system to build a new social order whose blueprint is the Communist ideology. The educational system of czarist Russia operated under a policy of "Russification," whereas that of the USSR promotes Marxian socialism. Both are aggressively and ruthlessly nationalistic. The Soviet school system did not take its present form immediately after the Revolution of 1917, but evolved as a result of a series of "revolutions." Even now at the half century of its birth it is undergoing changes as evidenced by the growth of boarding schools and the emphasis on manual labor. However, the single-track ten-year school served as the foundation for the system. All of the changes are aimed at making the school a more effective instrument of indoctrination and a conditioner of human behavior. At the same time the Soviet school system has been extraordinarily successful in producing scientists and engineers and in reducing illiteracy generally.

QUESTIONS

1. Which nations have followed the Soviet pattern of a highly centralized national system of education under control of a single political party? Explain any differences you find between these national systems and the Soviet system.
2. Why was it logical for the Soviets to develop a single-track school system?
3. Distinguish between education and propaganda. What is the relation of each of these concepts to indoctrination? Illustrate these concepts from Soviet educational policies.
4. Why did the early Soviet reformers concentrate on the elimination of illiteracy? Compare their aims with those of the early Protestant reformers.
5. Do you think that Khrushchev's criticisms of the Soviet ten-year school were justified? Explain.
6. Is it more difficult to develop an educational system in accordance with

the aims of American democracy than with those of Soviet Communism? Defend your position.
7. Both the Soviet ten-year school and the American high school have been described as single-track schools. Do you agree? Why?
8. How do you explain the success of the Soviets in producing scientists and engineers in an atmosphere of political and social conformity? What is the meaning of this success for the teaching of science and engineering?
9. Since the Soviet launching of the Sputniks in 1957, critics of American education claim that the Soviets have higher educational standards than the U.S. and place greater stress on quality. Do you agree? Why?
10. Read the book by George S. Counts cited at the close of this chapter. What is the challenge of Soviet education to American education?
11. Bowen, in the book cited at the close of the chapter, says that the failure of the Soviet experiments in education during the 1920s came from much the same reasons as the failure of progressive education in the West during the same period. What were these reasons?
12. Anton Makarenko was to Soviet education what John Dewey was to education in America. Compare and contrast their views.

NOTES AND SOURCES

There is an abundance of material on Soviet education but much less on Russian education under the czars. The work by Hans cited here is a pioneer study and has a bibliography of both Russian and English sources. The books listed for the Soviet period include only those that have been useful in the preparation of this chapter. Because Soviet education is subject to periodic and sometimes violent change, bulletins of the U.S. Office of Education on the USSR, such as those by Apanasewicz and Rosen cited here, should be consulted.

APANASEWICZ, NELLIE, and SEYMOUR M. ROSEN, *Soviet Education: A Bibliography of English Language Materials*, Washington, D.C., U.S. Office of Education, Bulletin 1964, No. 29, 42 pp.

BEREDAY, GEORGE Z. F., WILLIAM BRICKMAN, and GERALD READ, Editors, *The Changing Soviet School*, Boston, Houghton Mifflin, 1960, 514 pp.

BOWEN, JAMES, *Soviet Education: Anton Makarenko and the Years of Experiment*, Madison, The University of Wisconsin Press, 1962, 232 pp.

BRICKMAN, WILLIAM W., "John Dewey's Foreign Reputation As an Educator," *School and Society*, LXX, October 22, 1949, 257–265, with a bibliography.

COUNTS, GEORGE S., *The Challenge of Soviet Education*, New York, McGraw-Hill Book Company, 1957, 330 pp.

Documentary and Reference Material on Education in the Soviet Union, Cambridge, The Massachusetts Institute of Technology, 1956, 2 vols.

Education in the USSR, Washington, D.C., U.S. Office of Education, Bulletin, 1957, No. 14, 226 pp. With a bibliography of English and Russian sources.

GRANT, NIGEL, *Soviet Education*, Baltimore, Md., Penguin Books, 1964, 189 pp.

HANS, NICHOLAS, *History of Russian Educational Policy, 1701–1917*, London, P. S. King and Staples, Ltd., 1931, 255 pp.

JOHNSON, WILLIAM H. E., *Russia's Educational Heritage*, Pittsburgh, Pa., Carnegie Press, 1950.

KLINE, GEORGE L., Editor, *Soviet Education*, London, Routledge and Kegan Paul, Ltd., [1957], 192 pp. A collection of papers by Russian contributors; the Foreword is by George S. Counts.

KOROL, ALEXANDER, *Soviet Education for Science and Technology*, New York, John Wiley & Sons, Inc., [1957], 513 pp.

LONDON, IVAN D., "Evaluation of Some Current Literature About Soviet Education," in *Proceedings*, Fifth Annual Conference on Comparative Education, School of Education, New York University, April 25, 1958; bound with *School and Society*, November 8, 1958, it is also separately available.

ROSEN, SEYMOUR M., *Significant Aspects of Soviet Education*, Washington D.C., U.S. Office of Education, Bulletin, 1965, No. 15, 22 pp.

SHALIN, A. F., "Technical Education in the Union of Socialist Soviet Republics," chap. 7, in *Year Book of Education, 1956*, Yonkers-on-Hudson, New York, World Book Company, 1956.

Chapter 17
EDUCATION IN ENGLAND

English education has been less consciously nationalist than that of France, Germany, or Russia but, as in the continental countries, it has suffered from the division of the people into social strata. The English have achieved the difficult task of forming a stable society of such conflicting elements as social and economic aristocracy, political democracy, and religious freedom. It is especially remarkable that they have done this in a situation that has shielded them from direct attack. But the political democracy and religious freedom of England have not been altogether favorable to the development of schools and to the free and generous provision of education for all.

The national system of schools in England reflects a pattern of control that is divided between the national government and the local districts. Unlike France, Germany, and Russia, education was long considered to be the province of the home and the church. Religious toleration and the growth of large bodies of dissenters made the religious question in education a difficult problem. Traditionally, the English have held that the activity of the government should be restricted to essential matters of state and should not interfere in such a social, church, or private interest as they conceived education to be. This traditional feeling, although now declining and perhaps disappearing, was strong within recent times. Finally, the considerable, although partial, success of private and philanthropic agencies in providing schools operated to restrain vigorous public effort. As a result of all these factors, England trailed the continental countries by as much as a half century in the development of public schools.

EARLY BEGINNINGS

The first schools were probably established in Roman times. Roman Britain sent three bishops to the Council of Arles in A.D. 314 and because there were churches there were, no doubt, also schools. These were destroyed after the Romans withdrew from the island; but before A.D. 800

Christian schools had again been established and had become notable. They produced such scholars as Aldhelm, in the seventh century, and Bede and Alcuin, in the eighth. The red ruin of the Danish invasions interrupted progress again, but King Alfred encouraged the founding of schools. Schoolbooks in both Anglo-Saxon and Latin were prepared by English scholars in that and later times. Testimony to the flourishing condition of learning a century after Alfred is furnished by Aelfric, a teacher of about the year 1000. His schoolbooks, including a glossary, a Latin colloquy with an Anglo-Saxon gloss, and a Latin grammar in Anglo-Saxon provide firsthand evidence of the educational vigor of that time.

The advent of John Wycliffe in the fourteenth century marked not only a religious reformation but also a democratizing movement. The Black Death and the heavy taxes made necessary by the foreign wars of Edward III helped to produce a social revolution that gave greater privileges to the laboring classes. In religion itself we can see the contrast between an England that was building great cathedrals and a second England that listened hungrily to Wycliffe's "poor priests." The common people were becoming a social force, and the English language after a long period of neglect, which had begun at the Norman Conquest, was again coming into use not only in common life but also in law and in religion.

To reach the common people, teachers and propagandists had to give up the Norman-French and use the vernacular. That is what Wycliffe did. The evidence also shows that many of the common people were sending their boys to school. That "low-born" Englishmen were claiming this privilege as a right is indicated by a petition of 1391, which asked the king to ordain that no villein should be allowed to send his children to school. The object of the petition was to prevent such children from rising in the social scale *par Clergie,* that is, by becoming priests. The king denied the petition; and the Statute of Artificers in 1406, which can be called the first education law in England, confirmed his denial. That law said, "Every man or woman, of whatever state or condition he may be, shall be free to set their son or daughter to take learning at any school that pleaseth them within the realm." The student can follow the subject further in the third volume of Bishop Stubbs' *Constitutional History*.

In the fifteenth century Lollardry, as the Wycliffe movement was called, was crushed. In the process many schools were destroyed and the effort to democratize education came to an end. Instead, the great public schools for the privileged classes were established in those years. Among the most famous of these are Eton, Harrow, Shrewsbury, and Winchester. Many schools that had been intended for the poor were taken over by the rich. An example would be the hospital school of St. Anthony's, which was attended by Thomas More and John Colet. The revival of classical learning in the following century led to the founding of new grammar schools and the reform of others. Some were founded by businessmen and several were placed under the control of lay boards. St. Paul's was one of the most famous of the schools that were reformed in the classical direction and placed under a lay governing board. This was done by John Colet, the Dean of the cathedral. This fact will enable us to view Colet as school reformer, in truer perspective than is sometimes done. He introduced into this ancient cathedral school "clean and chaste" authors both classical and Christian. He was not, however, a radical innovator, although it is somewhat remarkable that the dean of a great cathedral should establish a secular governing board.

The educational influence of the English Reformation has been described. There was a certain slight impulse toward elementary education and Mulcaster urged universal education in the common tongue. The change from a Latin to an English church service was an important result. The Bible and the catechism were introduced into schools, even into grammar schools. John Colet prepared an English catechism for St. Paul's School. But neither the church nor the state actively promoted elementary education; and on the secondary level, the Reformation did not increase but rather reduced the facilities for learning. The Reformation did little for the education of the ordinary poor and for a time less than nothing for the well-to-do; but through the apprenticeship laws it accomplished something for the poorest of the poor.

The second English Reformation, which was carried out by the Puritans in the seventeenth century, promised an educational revival. The Puritan Parliament of the Commonwealth proposed to educate the children of the nation. In 1649 it voted twenty thousand pounds for elementary education. But political conditions prevented the execution of the program and the Restoration (1660) put an end to all efforts in this direction for nearly two centuries. The Restoration laws, which were passed to suppress all nonconformist teaching, were partly undone by the Acts of Toleration under William and Mary, which again gave the dissenters religious freedom under certain conditions. The court cases of Bates (1670) and Cox (1700) further loosened the hold of the Church of England, and a law of 1719 removed the last restrictions from dissenting teachers of elementary schools. But the people still occupied opposing educational camps, the Puritans and other dissenters fighting the Anglicans. This made agreement on a unified national system difficult and delayed the establishment of such a system. It has been truly said that three promising opportunities to establish national education in England were blighted and destroyed, the first after King Alfred, the second in the time of Wycliffe, and the third, by the reaction against the Puritan movement. As a consequence England relied upon church and private efforts to educate her children until well into the nineteenth century.

PHILANTHROPIC EFFORTS

An extensive system of charity schools developed in London and surrounding towns and suburbs near the beginning of the eighteenth century. These provided free education for poor boys and girls, furnished them with clothing, and helped them to find work. It seems that the charity schools of London were influenced by the similar work of Thomas Gouge (1609–1681) in Wales. Gouge had been a clergyman in London but, having turned Puritan, he lost his pastorate as a nonconformist in 1662. Ten years later, with the permission of the bishops, he began to evangelize and educate the people of a section of Wales. The costs were met by subscription, and a society to spread the schools was formed. Schools on this plan developed in many parts of the country, but their later history is somewhat obscure.

In Anglican circles a similar but more active agency, the Society for the Promotion of Christian Knowledge (SPCK), was formed by Thomas Bray and associates in 1698. The SPCK aided members "to set up catechetical schools for the education of poor children" in reading, writing, and especially in the principles of religion. It is almost certain that the founders were influenced by the work of Gouge and that of the German Pietist, August Hermann Francke of Halle. In a charity sermon of 1706 by Dr. White Kennet, it was asserted that the schools were directed not only against indifference in religion and dissenting faiths but also against Roman Catholicism. Every charity school was to be "a fortress and frontier garrison against popery." A secondary aim was to prepare children to earn a livelihood: girls were taught to sew, spin, and knit, and boys were apprenticed to trades. The schools, like those of Gouge, were supported by subscriptions and from the proceeds of annual charity sermons. They grew rapidly in numbers and had forty thousand children under instruction by 1740. Joseph Addison called them "the glory of the age we live in." Bernard Mandeville, the cynical Dutch physician of London, thought differently. In his *Fable of the Bees* he argued that "To make society happy and people easy under the meanest circumstances, it is requisite that great numbers of them should be ignorant as well as poor." Mandeville's attack is a witness to his belief that the schools were effective. Francis Place (1771–1854), the London tailor who became a utilitarian reformer, condemned the charity schools because they "taught poor children next to nothing, and nothing likely to be useful to them." All of these were prejudiced witnesses and the true verdict seems to be that the schools were a useful agency at a time when a national system and even good private schools were not yet possible.

To carry on the same work in the British Dominions a daughter society, the Society for the Propagation of the Gospel in Foreign Parts (SPG), was formed and Thomas Bray came to America to found schools and to provide libraries for the clergy, the teachers, and their pupils. Although thousands of children in New York and the southern states received at least the elements of an education in the charity schools, the work of the SPG aroused the antagonism of many who had come for religious freedom. Fear of an American episcopate and an established church was one of the factors in the Revolution, and the SPG helped to keep alive that fear. The society remained active in the American Colonies until the close of the Revolution. A further extension of elementary education was made by the Sunday School movement, which was widely publicized by Robert Raikes, a newspaper publisher of Gloucester, England, and was more directly promoted by the Methodists, the Friends, and other religious bodies. Many, who might have had no teaching otherwise, learned to read in Sunday Schools. Attendance at Sunday Schools also carried no stigma of pauperism; and the Bible, as interpreted by workingmen, became an important introduction to social democracy.

TOWARD A PLANNED EDUCATION

Public opinion was becoming more favorable to the idea of universal education as the eighteenth century unrolled. At the beginning of the century few were interested; at the end, it was becoming a national question. The whole argument had moved into a new phase. Earlier generations had asked whether the poor should be educated but now the leaders, at least, were asking how the common people, not merely the very poor, could be educated. Not all had arrived at this point. Many still feared that education would make the industrious classes discontented with their lot, disobedient, extravagant, and politically radical. In spite of these prophecies of doom, humanitarian and libertarian opinions came to prevail, partly because of the increase of industry and greater material welfare. Although England was gaining the conviction that the people should be educated, she was not yet ready to lay taxes for that purpose. And education was not to be secular or to violate anyone's conscience. How could this be done?

The answer seemed to have been found in about 1800 when Joseph Lancaster published a new method of conducting schools cheaply by having the older boys teach the younger. The system was not new, having been brought from Madras, India, by a British army chaplain, Dr. Andrew Bell. It had also been used by the Jesuits, by John Brinsley, and others; but it seemed novel and as simple and inevitable, once it had been thought of, as the discovery of America or the invention of the steam engine. Indeed, its similarity to the mechanical operation of power machinery and the factory system was one of its chief recommendations to a practical, industrial people. Actually, it was only the first of the modern plans that have so often promised short and easy solutions.

Bell was imitated by Joseph Lancaster. When he was a boy of fourteen, Lancaster was prevented from sailing to Jamaica where he intended to teach the slaves of the sugar plantations. He therefore determined to gratify his passion for teaching in his native country and opened in about 1796, when he was sixteen, a school for poor children in his father's house. There he taught reading, writing, and arithmetic for a weekly fee of fourpence. He soon had sixty children and twice that number in the summer. Members of the Society of Friends, which he joined about this time, aided him with funds and his school prospered. In about the year 1800 he read a pamphlet published in 1797 by Dr. Andrew Bell entitled, *An Experiment in Education Made at the Male Asylum of Madras, Suggesting a System by Which a School or Family May Teach Itself.* In the absence of competent teachers, Bell had used those pupils who knew a little to teach those who knew less and now Lancaster enthusiastically adopted the same scheme and vigorously advertised it. The pupil-teachers were called monitors and the scheme the monitorial system. Lancaster's schools were nonsectarian and Bell's Anglican; and that was the chief difference.

By this plan the teacher met his monitors each session and taught them in a class the lesson of the day. Each of them then relayed the lesson to the small group of perhaps ten children to which he had been assigned. The school was carried on in a single large room equipped with benches, blackboards, and other materials. Lancaster collected and invented a good deal of simple equipment and many devices for use in instruction and discipline. Competition and rewards were used to excess. The schools were organized along military lines. The monitors received for their reward only the lessons that the head of the school gave them and, sometimes, the hope of becoming masters of other schools. They were not paid in money. A large school could be maintained for a whole year for the rent and heating cost of a building and a single salary, the master's. The annual cost per pupil might be as low as one pound or even ten shillings.

A witness from Dr. Bell's schools testified before the Brougham Committee (1816). The following colloquy ensued:

How many can one master superintend, according to your system? I conceive I do not exaggerate when I say 1000. What would be the expense? The room being given, the expenses are, salary to the master, and the expense of books, which is a mere trifle, say £80 a year. The room being given I conceive, 4s. 2d. ($1) a head abundantly sufficient for 500 children. What is the longest time that you take a boy for education? I conceive two years abundantly sufficient for any boy.

Such was the cost and such the conception of education in high quarters.

Although the instruction was mechanical, it succeeded in teaching children the elements of reading, spelling, and arithmetic. Apparent efficiency and the low cost explain the enthusiasm with which the system was received. Henry Holman, a critical historian of English education, has described the reception that was accorded the monitorial system as follows:

> The greatest popular enthusiasm was aroused. If it were possible to teach poor children next to nothing for next to nothing—a reasonable equation—by all means let it be done. The king, members of the royal family, nobles, gentry, all subscribed to so pleasing a project. Lancaster was a public hero, and almost every city erected a monument to him, in the shape of a Lancasterian school.

Lancaster had solved, or appeared to have solved, the question of the cost of popular education. He was not so successful in dealing with the religious question. The religion that was taught in his school was too undogmatic, Holman said—too purely religious—for some members of the Church of England. Some became obsessed with the notion that Voltairean ideas and a covert attack on Christianity lay concealed beneath the smooth surface of Lancaster's system. When the schools began to spread, Dr. Bell, who had taken little interest in the matter, was drawn out of his retirement and whipped up to lead a campaign for monitorial schools in which the catechism and formularies of the Church of England were to be taught. A controversy over originality and priority also arose. Was Lancaster or Bell the inventor? Which one had stolen the other's idea? The controversy may have had a good deal to do with the spread of both systems, but it was a dispute that never should have arisen. Neither was the inventor. Dr. Bell had seen the monitorial system in operation at Madras in India. Lancaster had acknowledged his debt to Dr. Bell in the first edition (1803) of his *Improvements in Education As It Respects the Industrious Classes*. After the fight became hot, he not only ignored his indebtedness but claimed to have invented the monitorial system. Really, he had only improved it; and some of his additions, such as the excessive use of emulation, rewards, medals, decorations, and of humiliating punishments, were serious defects, not improvements.

Improvements in Education was an important book because it discussed a scheme for a national system of popular education. The education of the people as a whole is a matter of national importance and the greatest obstacle, he believed, was the proselyting spirit of the religious bodies. This could be removed if people would consent to have only "general Christian principles" taught in the schools. Such an education could be made universal; but he was opposed to compulsion. To make the system universal, public funds would be required. Although each sect was permitted to maintain its own schools, a compromise similar to the one Lancaster had suggested was actually adopted. It was followed by the government down to 1870, when the public school boards were instituted by the Forster Act.

The monitorial schools performed a useful function and even the controversy over the discovery was fruitful. Combining forces with the SPCK and Sunday School movements, the monitorial systems prepared the public for the final step toward public education. Two societies were set up to promote the two systems: the British and Foreign Society (1810) to establish Lancasterian schools; and the National Society to spread those of Dr. Bell, also called the Madras system. Each set up a model school and provided some training for its teachers, but as the courses were short, averaging only about three months for each prospective teacher, the training dealt chiefly with the organization and management of schools. By 1835 the National Society had trained about two thousand teachers and had about three thousand schools under its nominal charge. The British and Foreign Society had far fewer, perhaps not over five hundred schools, but many of these were large schools in London. The National Society had established schools in rural parishes, had introduced the Madras system into Sunday Schools, and had taken over some of the SPCK charity schools. Although there are no accurate statistics, it has been estimated that all three of these types—the SPCK, the Sunday, and the monitorial schools—in 1835 enrolled about sixty, perhaps only fifty, per cent of the children of the working classes of England.

The Lancasterian system was introduced into New York City in 1806, from whence it spread to most of the larger and many of the smaller cities of the United States, including those as far west as Cincinnati and Detroit. Joseph Lancaster himself came to the United States and an idea of the honor accorded him is to be found in the fact that he was invited to address the two Houses of Congress in a joint session and did so. Philadelphia, in 1818, established a city training school for teachers on the Lancasterian principles. The monitorial system remained in use in New York City until 1853, but its active life was much shorter in most American cities. In both England and the United States the system did a great deal to spread the ideal of education for all.

INFLUENCE FROM ABROAD

From the beginning of the nineteenth century English educationists began to study the developments that were taking place on the continent. Robert Owen visited Switzerland and established, in 1815, at his mill town of New Lanark the first British infant school, which received children "at one year or as soon as they could walk" and retained them until the age of six when they were transferred to the elementary school. Within four years, Henry Brougham and others opened an infant school at Westminster; and in 1824 the London Infant School Society was founded and Samuel Wilderspin became its superintendent. Through his activity, infant schools were rapidly established in England and they have remained a permanent part of the English system. Later the infant school was also influenced by Froebelian ideas. It has, however, with some notable exceptions, remained comparatively formal, more like a school in its emphasis on reading and other school skills than like a kindergarten.

About the same time, David Stow of Glasgow was working out his system of preparing teachers; and other students of popular education were introducing the ideas of Pestalozzi and Fellenberg and of their German disciples. The *Quarterly Journal of Education* (1831–1835) performed for England a function similar to that of W. C. Woodbridge and later Henry Barnard in the United States in acquainting the English with new developments in France, Switzerland, and Germany. The *Quarterly Journal* showed particularly that the elementary curriculum in England was meager and formal compared with that of the best schools abroad and that English teachers lacked the professional preparation that was becoming usual in progressive countries. One who was soon to become the real founder of national education in England, Dr. James Philips Kay (1804–1877), later known as Sir James Kay-Shuttleworth, visited many European schools where he made the acquaintance of Father Girard of Fribourg, of Fellenberg, and of Wehrli, who had conducted Fellenberg's school for poor children before becoming the principal of a Swiss cantonal normal school. Through Kay-Shuttleworth's work in developing teacher-training, the ideas of David Stow and of Wehrli were embodied in the English system. From Stow he learned the virtues of the *criticism lesson* in which a skilled teacher taught a class while normal school pupils observed the work, which they later analyzed for the purpose of deriving principles. Wehrli taught him that future elementary teachers should develop habits of frugality, patience, and sympathy by sharing the conditions of life of the pupils whom they were later to teach. The Battersea Training School for teachers was founded on these lines in 1839.

Pestalozzian methods were introduced into England and the United States about the same time. In England, Elizabeth Mayo published a book on Pestalozzian object-teaching in 1830, the famous *Lessons on Objects*. Her brother Charles Mayo had spent three years at Yverdon following 1819, and on his return established a Pestalozzian school. The Mayos and others, in 1836, organized the Home and Colonial School Society, which brought a famous Pestalozzian, Herman Krüsi, Jr., to England. Krüsi later taught at Oswego, New York, but he was not responsible for the Oswego method, which was a direct importation (1860) of English Pestalozzianism.

RISE OF THE NATIONAL SYSTEM

Education in England as elsewhere had long been the function of the church and the family. To propose now in the nineteenth century that the government should establish and support schools for all the people represented a radical break with this tradition. And, in the second place, not only education but other social matters were considered to be outside the sphere of government and contrary to the individualism expressed in such phases as "Government is a necessary evil," and "A man's house is his castle." English democracy, because it had to create a public opinion in favor of education, made slower progress than highly centralized governments such as the Prussian. And the very success of the voluntary effort by the SPCK, the monitorial schools, and other private agencies in some cases delayed national education by raising the hope that additional similar efforts might be able to provide opportunity for all without governmental action. Finally, there was no easy solution of the religious question. For all these reasons, national education was achieved a generation or perhaps a half century later in England than in the advanced countries on the continent.

Some of the steps were the following. The Factory Act (1802), called the Health and Morals of Apprentices Act, limited the daily hours of labor for apprentices in textile mills to twelve, prohibited night employment, and prescribed that "every such apprentice shall be instructed, in some part of each working day, for the first four years of his or her apprenticeship, in the usual hours of work, in reading, writing, and arithmetic, to be paid for by the master or mistress of such apprentice." The law was evaded by refusing "to apprentice" the child workers; but it was a beginning in the area where there was a precedent, established by the old apprenticeship legislation.

Further advance was blocked for thirty years. One cause was the fear that the education of the masses would lead to a wave of radicalism, such as had engulfed France. The Napoleonic Wars occupied the attention and emotions of the country until 1815 and after Waterloo came the conservative reaction led by the Duke of Wellington. The Lords rejected Whitbread's Parochial Schools Bill of 1807, which would have provided two years of free education for every child. In the year after the final defeat of Napoleon, as frequently happens after a war, the people were for a moment willing to give serious attention to education. Henry Brougham was, in 1816, appointed chairman of the committee to investigate the condition of the poor in London. Witnesses testified that they lived in a "very dreadful state" from overcrowding and lack of sanitation, that large masses of children received no education, and that those who attended school received little benefit. But in spite of this evidence, Brougham's education bill of 1820, a tax measure, had to be withdrawn.

Not until 1833, one year after the passage of the Reform Bill that abolished the "rotten borough" representation and extended the franchise to the middle classes, did Parliament vote any money for schools—namely, twenty thousand pounds for building schoolhouses, to be used by the two monitorial societies, the National, and the British and Foreign. It was a time of serious financial difficulty, but in the same year England purchased and freed all slaves in the British Dominions at a cost of two million pounds. The education grant became an annual one and the yearly amount was from time to time increased: to thirty thousand pounds in 1839, to one hundred thousand pounds in 1846, and to eight hundred thousand pounds in 1860. The year 1839 was also memorable because it was then that a Committee of Council was created that was to function as a department of education. The chief function of the Committee of Council was to allocate the government money grants. In 1846, the further policy was adopted of appointing school inspectors on whose reports the allocation of funds could be based. It will readily be seen that the powers of the committee were expanding. From allocating money to inspecting schools is itself a big step. Matthew Arnold was for most of his life one of Her Majesty's Inspectors of Schools.

The first secretary of the Committee of Council was a man whom we have named, James Kay-Shuttleworth. He was educated as a physician at Edinburgh and his fellow student, Charles Darwin, later recorded admiring regard for his ability and particularly for his skill as a public speaker. As an administrator he was discreet, self-sacrificing, energetic, and progressive. Matthew Arnold, who had every opportunity to know the basic facts, called him the founder of the system of public education in England. Kay-Shuttleworth, like Horace Mann, began as soon as possible to make provisions for the education of teachers. The first effective appropriation for training colleges was made in 1841, five thousand pounds to the Borough Road College and smaller amounts to two other new schools.

Following the Chartist agitation and the increasing strength of the labor movement, the demand for a local tax for schools kept growing, but the opposition of the friends of the voluntary system and of those who would have to pay heavily was too strong. Meanwhile, without a clear plan or national decision, the school system kept forming itself. English democracy has always laid great store by fact-finding and publishing, believing that the facts when known will convince the public and lead to well-informed action. Thus, in 1858, the first national education commission was appointed to study the "state of popular education in England, and to consider what measures, if any, are required for the extension of sound and cheap elementary instruction to all classes of the people." It was called the Newcastle Commission, for the Duke of Newcastle who was its honorary chairman, and made its report in 1861.

The Newcastle Commission reported on all sorts of elementary schools: dame, infant, Sunday, evening, and day schools, and both private and public schools in any of these classes. Public in this case means conducted by a society or board and not managed by an owner for his personal support or profit. The commission recognized the public day schools as the most important provision for the education of the poor; and they recognized too that the quality of any school depends most on the capacity and education of the teacher. They found also that schools of some sort, often of a very bad sort, existed everywhere and that there were very few children in 1860 who did not attend school at some time in their lives. On this point the commission was probably much too optimistic, because it was shown ten years later (1870) that in Liverpool one fourth of the children attended no schools at all. Less than half the children were in schools that were receiving the government grants. The commission report also showed that in England and Wales thirty-two training colleges for teachers were in operation.

The commission did not recommend any organic change in the system that was growing up; but one matter that might seem a detail had striking consequences. This was the scheme of "payment by results," which provided that the government grants were to be allocated to schools on the basis not only of average daily attendance but also on the basis of the number of pupils who annually passed a state examination in reading, writing, and arithmetic. The system of payment by results was apparently first suggested long before by Dr. Andrew Bell and used in his monitorial schools. The plan was, of course, an unfortunate experiment. It placed a premium on the bald teaching of facts by cramming and drilling for examinations and it tended to restrict the curriculum essentially to reading, writing, and arithmetic. No grants could be earned for work in geography, history, or drawing, however excellent, because these subjects were not included in the examinations. Kay-Shuttleworth argued against the adoption of payment by results, declaring that it would be "ever remembered with shame." So it has been, although it remained in use in English schools until the middle 1800s when it was gradually abandoned; it was completely abolished in 1890. A suggestion by Archbishop Ireland that payment by results should be introduced into American schools was brilliantly answered by B. A. Hinsdale (*Studies in Education*, Chicago, 1806).

The next great step, and the greatest yet taken, came in 1870 with the passage of the Elementary Education Act of 1870. This law is also known as the Forster Act after the author W. E. Forster. The Reform Act of 1832 had extended the vote to the middle classes, but it still left the numerous working class and the poor generally without the ballot. A new Reform Act passed in 1867 extended the suffrage further and formed the foundation of a long campaign that led to manhood and, after World War I, to adult suffrage. The return of the Liberal party in 1868 was the opportunity for a great deal of social legislation: laws on child labor, on hours of labor, on sanitation, and on accident prevention and acts permitting trade unions to hold property and another introducing the secret ballot. It was the influence of the workingmen when they were given representation in Parliament that formed the balance of power between the dissenters and churchmen and enabled the Forster Act to pass.

The central provision of this act was that it established school districts and elective school boards for the purpose of providing and supervising elementary schools in all places where the existing supply was insufficient. The school boards had the power to levy taxes for schools in their districts.

The government continued to aid private schools; but it now could and did establish its own public schools for the education of the "schoolless multitude," of children, as Matthew Arnold called them, whom the private schools had not reached. Acts of 1867 and 1880 introduced compulsory attendance; and in 1891, elementary education was made free. By that time, where elementary education was not supplied by voluntary bodies, it was public, free, and supported by local tax and government grant. Everywhere attendance was compulsory. The Committee of Council was not an efficient agency, and in 1899 Parliament created a national Board of Education with a president as the excutive officer directly responsible to Parliament. The Bryce Commission of 1895 reported in favor of public secondary schools closely connected with the elementary schools, and this recommendation was embodied in the Balfour Act of 1902.

By 1910 there were nearly twelve hundred secondary schools supported by local tax or government grant or both, in addition to the old grammar school and public school foundations. The Fisher Act of 1918 attempted to weld into one system all the public educational agencies, all the elementary, secondary, technical, and higher schools under public control. And in 1944, in the midst of another war, England was again engaged in further democratizing its educational provisions. To this we shall return immediately.

DEMOCRATIZING THE SYSTEM

About two thirds of England's children attend public or "provided" elementary schools and the rest attend the "nonprovided" or private and voluntary schools, which are conducted by the Church of England, the Catholic Church, or other smaller denominational bodies. Many of the nonprovided schools are located in rural England and have smaller average enrollments than the public schools. Religious instruction is sectarian in the nonprovided schools, whereas, in accordance with the Cowper-Temple clause of 1870, in the provided schools, only nonsectarian Scripture knowledge, in which "no religious catechism or religious formulary which is distinctive of any particular denomination," can be taught. Bible reading without comment and prayers are permitted.

The infant schools for children between the ages of five and seven are separately organized. Above these ages the elementary school proper, with seven or eight classes, can enroll either boys or girls or both. It was usually organized into the junior, intermediate, and senior grades, but some schools had only one or two of these departments. Until recently most children did not continue in school beyond the elementary period. Compulsory attendance ended at age fourteen, after which there were opportunities in evening classes and adult education. As will be seen, the Butler Education Act of

1944 changed these conditions. Earlier attempts to raise the compulsory attendance age had failed.

England has made two recent attempts to reconstruct its educational system. The Fisher Act of 1918 contemplated raising the compulsory age to fifteen but, for financial reasons, it was not possible to bring it into operation. The same fate overtook the provision for compulsory continuation schooling. In the years between the two World Wars the question of improved education for England was under continuous study. This is best shown by the issue of the Hadow Reports on *The Education of the Adolescent* (1926), on *The Primary School* (1931), and on *Infant and Nursery Schools* (1933) and on the Spens Report on *Secondary Education* (1939). The student of English educational history cannot afford to neglect these reports, which are valuable not only for their recommendations but also for their historical sections written by Robert Fitzgibbon Young, the learned and judicious secretary of the Consultative Committee that conducted the extended hearings on which the reports were based.

The Hadow Reports defined the limits of infant and nursery, primary, and secondary education in England more clearly. Secondary education was to include all schooling between the ages of eleven-plus and eighteen years. Many English people understood secondary education to include only pre-university training that was given in the great public schools and the more prominent public and private grammar schools. These schools were selective and offered an extensive classical curriculum in which only very bright youth could succeed. Because the complete curriculum occupied the pupils to the age of about eighteen years, only the leisure classes were able to take full advantage of it. Others had to go to work several years earlier.

There were various stopgap measures to provide some postprimary schooling for those who were excluded from the grammar schools or who needed a more immediately useful education. The public central school, an institution somewhat like the junior high school of the United States, was the most widespread example of these. For reasons that will now be apparent, the Hadow Report of 1926 carried the phrase "Education of the Adolescent" in its title instead of the words *secondary education*. Its purpose was to draw a plan for the education of all English youth. This report had a great effect on educational discussion and was a major step toward the formation of the Butler Education Act of 1944, which will be discussed later.

The elementary schools all taught religious knowledge, English, physical education and hygiene, arithmetic—which received one fifth or one sixth of the total time and attention—nature study and geography, history—which received little emphasis—writing, drawing, and practical subjects such as manual or domestic instruction. Each school made its own schedule which, however, had to meet the regulations of the Board of Education, and each school was given considerable freedom in arranging its courses and determining its methods of teaching. There was and is little effort to use the schools for nationalist indoctrination.

This last topic is of great and growing importance in the world. The English people seem to be no less loyal and patriotic than those of other nations, of France, for example, where great efforts are put forth in the primary schools to instill nationalist sentiment. Do the situation of France and the history of her relations with her neighbors explain and provide the motives for her nationalist indoctrination? Is nationalist feeling more effectively instilled in adult years than in childhood and through public communication and ceremony than through schoolbooks? These questions merit study. If schools have ever tended to increase chauvinism they should do so no longer.

Above the elementary schools there were the central schools, already mentioned, that gave advanced elementary and prevocational courses and were public and free, and a great variety of public and private secondary schools. The secondary schools gave a general liberal education and usually charged fees, but to receive government aid they had to provide a certain number of free places, usually one third of the enrollment. Entrance to the secondary schools was obtained through the free place examinations that were taken at the age of eleven. The examinations covered English and arithmetic and, frequently, history and geography. Intelligence tests were sometimes also used and consideration was given to the pupil's school record. Because there were not enough free places to accommodate all the children who might qualify, the examinations were made rigorous and became, in fact, not qualifying but competitive. It was said that only ten per cent of the children were able to pass the free place examinations. Those who did not pass with the highest averages might be admitted to a central school.

The central schools provided a considerably lower and easier form of education than the secondary schools, which prepared for the university. They were called by this name because each central school served a number of the surrounding elementary schools. Because the best of the senior pupils from the elementary schools attended the secondary schools the work of the central schools was often further lowered in quality. This was a weakness of the system. And another problem arose from the variety of schools and curricula that made transfer and promotion from school to school more difficult. The central schools offered general, industrial, commercial, domestic, and fine arts courses. These were four years in length, and some pupils were permitted to remain an additional year. It was often possible to enter a secondary or technical school from a central school.

The reader will remember that in England the terms elementary and secondary were not clearly defined. Some schools for girls or boys took pupils from the primary grades to the door of the university. Some secondary schools admitted pupils between the ages of nine and twelve and retained them to sixteen or eighteen. From twelve to eighteen was regarded as the secondary period; and to be eligible for government grants, a secondary school was required to have a stated proportion of its pupils in continuous attendance between twelve and sixteen. But the Board of Education said only that a secondary school was one in which most of the work is secondary, which is not a model definition. Usually English secondary schools, like those on the continent and unlike the American high school, have offered only academic and not activity and vocational curricula; but this does not apply to the experimental schools, then or now.

The English secondary schools were of four kinds. Established under the Education Act of 1902 there were public secondary schools maintained by counties and county boroughs. These were required to teach the English language and literature and at least one foreign language, unless there was special provision to give adequate linguistic and literary training by means of English only. Most schools taught two foreign languages, and, in that case, one was to be Latin. By permission a second modern language could be substituted for Latin. These provisions reveal the flexibility of the controls over secondary curricula. The other required subjects in the public schools were geography, history, mathematics, science, drawing, and physical, manual, and musical instruction. In girls' schools domestic studies had to be taught. In some schools Greek, German, French, Spanish, or Italian were offered. In subject matter and in the percentage of the adolescents attending, the English public secondary schools before World War II were similar to the American ones of about 1890. They did not offer the technical, industrial, and commercial courses that were common in the larger American high schools; but one must remember that of the subjects just named only the commercial course was almost universally offered in the American high school.

The second class of English secondary schools was composed of local day schools managed by a private board like an American academy. Many of these are old grammar schools with a classical curriculum. Because they are local day schools, they are somewhat responsive to local demands. These schools charge fees.

The Great Public Schools form the third class. Only nine such schools were originally recognized, but the definition has been broadened and new ones have been founded so that the *Public Schools Handbook* includes about two hundred, many of them nineteenth-century foundations. These are expensive schools for the richer and upper classes. They are managed by private boards.

There is, finally, a wide variety of entirely private secondary schools that are conducted by the owners. Some of these are conservative, but included in this class are some of an experimental or "progressive" type. A once-famous school of this kind was established early in the nineteenth century by Thomas Wright Hill at Birmingham, but it did not become permanent. Abbotsholme School was founded by Cecil Reddie in 1889, and it has inspired numerous other schools with a modern-activity curriculum. Bedales is a coeducational school that was established in 1893 by J. H. Badley, who had been an Abbotsholme teacher. Abbotsholme has other daughters in France and Germany. Schools of this type usually have a flexible curriculum and emphasize the physical, manual, intellectual, moral, and aesthetic development of their pupils. The curricula are broad as well as flexible and are intended to promote the development of the children rather than to transmit a set body of knowledge. Because these schools are experimental and have the most various facilities, no simple description will apply to all of them; but like other secondary schools they prepare some pupils for admission to the university and others, perhaps in greater number, for practical life.

The variety of the English schools is the result of freedom and group planning as we shall see. The Education Act of 1944 made the system more uniform without changing its basic character. English education like English life and history is the result of compromises and changes introduced as new classes of people came into the programs. It has not been possible, in our limited space, to give a precise outline of a system that contains so many irregularities, but I. L. Kandel's *Comparative Education* (Boston, Houghton Mifflin Company, 1933), from which much of the preceding information also is taken, shows the general relations of the schools.

English educational freedom is even embodied in the legislation that has consistently sought to protect existing institutions and to preserve existing interests. Schools have grown up or have been provided by law to take advantage of opportunities and local needs or to fill gaps in the arrangements previously made. It was on this basis that the Education Department and the Department of Science and Art were created in the nineteenth century. Their functions were at the turn of the last century assigned to a single body. Thus England, in 1899, created a central authority for education, the Board of Education. Its power consisted in the fact that it disturbed and allotted the public money to the schools; but it did not control the schools through rigid and general regulations, as is done in France and Germany. Instead, it called on the local authorities to submit their programs and to make reports and it also inspected the grant-receiving schools. There are general regulations on buildings, class size, the number of days when the schools must be in session, and other physical matters, but the prescriptions on what should be taught and how it should be taught are flexible and are couched in terms of suggestions and minimal essentials merely. The Board of Education and the schools have generally cooperated and exchanged views on the best ways of using the available resources. This ideal plan permits a maximum of local planning and adjustment to local need.

EXTENDING NATIONAL CONTROL OVER THE SYSTEM

Two world wars and the Education Act of 1944 were the most important educational events in England in our century. They were not unrelated. Ever since World War I the English people have tried to improve their schools. National committees worked over the problems and proposed solutions, the people were informed and aroused, and World War II presented the final unanswerable argument for reform.

If it should seem strange to speak of wars as educational events, a brief glance backward will help. The Boer War and the Balfour Education Act of 1902, World War I and the Fisher Education Act of 1918, and World War II and the Butler Education Act of 1944 were directly connected in pairs. In each case a war revealed deficiencies and impelled the people and Parliament to seek remedies. But this is a costly and otherwise undesirable method of achieving educational progress. In fact, today's wars are more likely to destroy than to improve education.

The way to improve public education is to secure the moral support of the people. The Butler Act of 1944 was adopted and has been fairly, although not completely, successful because the people were gradually informed of the needs by means of a series of able and readable official studies and reports and by newspaper and professional discussion. The Fisher Act had failed. Mr. R. A. Butler, President of the Board of Education, and his colleagues were skillful strategists; all parties were represented in the government; the rural people saw that many of their schools could not go on without public aid, and some of them had come into contact with the slum children of the evacuation; and business and industrial leaders were convinced, as they had not been in 1918, that a nation that depends on industry and trade cannot survive without effective schools. For all these reasons the new bill was enacted into law in 1944.

The act was intended to achieve the following purposes:

1. To provide stronger central direction of education while preserving local initiative.
2. To make each administrative district large enough to supply all kinds of educational services.
3. To raise the leaving age by one or more years as a condition of effective secondary education.
4. To treat secondary education as a continuation of primary education and to supply appropriate kinds of secondary education, free to all youth.
5. To offer "further education" for working youth.
6. To preserve church, voluntary, and independent schools insofar as they could be made efficient.

Richard A. Butler, leader in framing English Education Act of 1944.

The law provides for a Minister of Education and empowers him "to control and direct," new language in English educational administration. The early ministers have been discreet, but there has been some partisan criticism of their official acts and language. The local school districts, as they would be called in the United States, were reduced to the number of one hundred and forty-six for the whole of England and Wales with forty-four million people. They have since been increased to one hundred and sixty-five.

The law extends the compulsory attendance period to age fifteen and permits further increase. Extension to fifteen years had been a provision of the Fisher Act and was reenacted in a law of 1936 but had not been generally enforced. Enforcement after the war was made especially difficult by the extraordinary increase in the number of children to be accommodated. The increase in the birth rate during the war years was the reason why an unusual number of new five-year-olds was ready for school in the later 1940s. At the other end of the school years there were the thousands whom the law kept in school one more year. Each of these "bulges" required additional buildings and teachers, the two most expensive elements in the operation of schools.

This time the nation was determined to raise the leaving age. The Prime Minister's statement in Parliament on November 12, 1946 was applauded for its courage. He said, "We are straitened in our manpower. We must make up in quality what we lack in quantity. We are, therefore, raising the leaving-age." On April 1, 1947, the Minister set it at fifteen years.

In England, as in many other countries, elementary education is more fully developed than secondary. In England it consists of three stages: the nursery school, before the age of five; the infant school, from five to seven; and the junior school, from seven to eleven. The nursery school has grown during and since World War II, but many children under five are enrolled in infant schools. The compulsory period begins at age five. This seems to be an inheritance from the Industrial Revolution when children were put to work at early ages. The infant school has been much influenced by the Italian educator Doctor Maria Montessori. The American student is surprised to learn that there is an active Montessori Society in England. Montessori influence was slight in the United States and died out about the time of World War I, but was reborn following World War II.

The junior school enrolls children of the ages seven to eleven. In American schools these would be in grades two to six. There is no nationally required curriculum, but language, arithmetic, geography, elementary science, history of England, local history, and community and homemaking studies are common fare. The last three on this list were products of the evacuation and the war.

After the war the schoolbuilding problem and the teacher shortage troubled England and other warring countries. The International Conference on Public Education held in Geneva in July, 1957, twelve years after the last gun was fired, was devoted to the world-wide schoolbuilding shortage. By using temporary buildings and starting a one-year training program for teachers, England was able to meet the 1947 deadline for the raising of the leaving age. All the children at age eleven or over were to receive secondary schooling. Even before the introduction of the bill to reform the general system it was secondary education that received most attention, and it was most radically changed by the act. In deciding to have it begin at age eleven and to include all youth, England assumed a liberal position. Conservatives favor a long elementary school course to age fourteen or beyond and a secondary school for a different and socially privileged class of people. If they cannot retain this oldest plan, they will move for a short elementary school course for all, preferably not over four years, and a division of the whole body of children about age ten into two groups, one of elementary and the other of secondary school pupils.

In England all the children are directed at eleven-plus into three kinds of secondary schools: the academic or grammar school, the technical school, and the modern school. This tripartite system is not in the law but was proposed by the Norwood Committee in 1943. It is not followed everywhere. Psychologists have opposed this early division, on the ground that there is no scientific way of forecasting at the early age what capacities may develop. They cautioned the local authorities against erecting buildings for these three types of secondary schools without fuller assurance that the plan would work.

About the same time, many Englishmen made an old discovery over again: namely, that the intelligence quotient can be improved by coaching and that intelligence test scores reflect the subject's experience, not his native ability alone. Two other ways of classifying the eleven-year-olds were available: a selective examination and the pupils' elementary school records. The examination plan was attacked as leading to cramming and coaching and to anxieties and tensions. Both parents and teachers, it was said, concentrate too much on it, and this perverts the children's sense of values. Both failure and success have unfortunate effects. Some writers in the press proposed copying the American comprehensive high school (*Times Educational Supplement*, London, February 8, 1952, p. 113). There are multilateral schools with a number of parallel courses, in London and elsewhere, but England is proceeding with the tripartite scheme. According to this plan the brightest and most literary children are selected for the academic or grammar school; those endowed with mechanical and scientific abilities are chosen for the technical school; and the rest, about sixty to seventy per cent, are gathered into the modern school.

The law looks toward the division at age eleven without competitive tests by using school records and teachers' opinions. Research groups and teachers' associations also stress guidance in all periods of schooling and a general review of all factors at the time when children are to be assigned to the special schools.

The modern schools have a wide field for experimentation. Provided with facilities for group activity, practical exercises in shop and garden, community projects, drawing, music, and drama, fewer academic children find schoolwork interesting and rewarding. Teachers who will cautiously experiment, small classes, varied equipment, and freedom should be the appropriate formula.

There is also political objection to the tripartite scheme. The Labor party favors the comprehensive school and objects to schools that tend to preserve the class structure of society. Labor holds that the prestige of the public schools and grammar schools is unwarranted; and even some friends of those schools admit that school influence is exaggerated, that Etonians gain high office not because of Eton's virtues but because those who go there come from great and influential families. The Labor party wishes to explode this so-called artificial prestige, and Labor is not alone in that wish.

School prestige is, however, built up over the years and will not be quickly overcome. Only when the pupils from other schools receive equal treatment with classical students at the universities and equally desirable positions in life will the prestige of the grammar schools be overcome. No one can say how much time this will take. It required a century in the United States where the classical tradition had not become firmly rooted.

A better example is found in Prussia, where the modern language *Oberrealschule* established in 1885 was officially given equal status with the ancient classical *Gymnasium*. The pupils of each were admitted to the universities. The middle classes, who had demanded the *Oberrealschule*, continued to send their sons to the *Gymnasium*. The General Staff of the army in 1905 had one hundred officers with a *Gymnasium* education but only four from the *Oberrealschule*. This example (from R. H. Samuel and R. H. Thomas, *Education and Society in Modern Germany*, London, 1949, p. 45) speaks for itself.

An idea of the degree of selection exercised by the grammar schools can be gained from a review of the examination system. At eleven-plus the children of the elementary schools take an examination that may determine their future. About one third will pass with marks that will permit them to go to a grammar school or a technical school. The other two thirds will go to modern schools or remain in the elementary school until age fifteen. At fifteen another examination of the third that passed at eleven-plus will eliminate all but about twenty per cent, who then enter the sixth form for specialized training. Two or three years later there is an examination that qualifies for university admission and, if passed with high grades, may earn a scholarship. Very few reach this goal. In proportion to population there are two and one-half times as many university students in Scotland as in England. This is an indication of the relative selectivity of the English and Scottish universities. At the end of the English university course there is a last examination requiring a three-hour paper each day for ten days. It is competitive, and a First Class or a high Second is required of those who hope for a civil service appointment or any high academic position. That is a map of the ten-year journey marked out for the brilliant grammar school boy who begins it at the age of eleven.

The proposal to establish large numbers of modern schools aroused the fears of the grammar school masters, although the new schools were to cater for a body of pupils whom the grammar schools would not take—not a generous position. The charge was made that Mr. Butler was willing "to jettison the traditions of the grammar school for the sake of uniformity." The fact is that he appointed the Fleming Committee to report on the place of the grammar schools in the system. The report (1945) was not unfavorable to those schools. The upper-class English view is that classical education is the best and that other forms are good in the degree to which they resemble the classical. In the debate over modern versus classical education for the academically most gifted pupils, the grammar schools had an able spokesman in Doctor (now Sir) Eric James, High Master of the Manchester Grammar School. He argued that a grammar school education fits gifted pupils equally for the university or for their lifework. This formal discipline argument was also used by the American Committee of Ten in 1893, as we shall see in the following chapters.

English independent schools and especially the public schools are now in a difficulty that has little to do with their virtues. They have always been expensive. With reduced fortunes and rising living costs, many who would wish to send their sons to exclusive schools are no longer able to afford the expense. How this may affect English politics can be gathered from the fact that Prime Minister Macmillan was an Etonian and all but two of his eighteen-member Cabinet were public school men.

As noted here, the law gives the Minister "control" over education; and the central government is increasing its financial contribution so that it sometimes pays as much as two thirds and the local authority as little as one third of the whole cost of education in a local area. Americans will be apt to ask whether this will lead to greater central control and even dictation. Judging the future by the past and present will cause almost everyone to doubt such an outcome. England has a long history of central and local cooperation in education.

Each local authority prepares a development plan to be submitted to the Minister. This shows how the local authority intends to meet its obligations and promote education in its area. After review and approval, this becomes a program.

THE SPREAD OF ENGLISH INFLUENCE TO AMERICA

English education has influenced the schools of foreign countries and of the British colonies and the Dominions. The views and practice of Rousseau and the philanthropinists were shaped by the doctrines of John Locke. The English cooperative movement played a part in the development of the Folk High Schools of the Scandinavian countries. The Hazelwood School of the Hills was copied in Sweden; and Cecil Reddie's Abbotsholme became a model for both French and German school reformers. But the British Dominions feel that influence most strongly. In Canada, Australia, and South Africa and in the British colonies, one finds modified extensions of the English system. A comparison of these shows family likenesses that stem from the education of the mother country.

Similar resemblances stemming from common centers of origin can be traced into other parts of the world. Latin-American systems are similar to each other and different from the English because the Latin-American countries borrowed the outlines of their civilization from Spain and Portugal and followed the French pattern of centralization in control of their state systems of education. The Scandinavian countries are so closely united by language and religion, and by the similarity of their political and economic systems and ideals, that their school systems also have developed along similar lines—although they follow the English pattern of divided control. And, to give only one more example, it is well-known that schools in the countries within the Soviet bloc have taken on many of the characteristics of the education of the dominant nation. Modern education is carried forward on national lines as the last three chapters have shown. Because we are next to take up American education, it is appropriate to close this chapter with a brief survey of English influence on American education. This is especially pertinent because we were colonies of the British Empire in its early stages.

In Virginia and Massachusetts, the early schools were established by Englishmen and followed the pattern of education that prevailed in England in the seventeenth and eighteenth centuries. The English language became the language of the American people, government, and schools, and so it has remained. The early textbooks were written in England and many of the teachers for two centuries came from England. The Latin grammar school was imported from England. The English SPG was active in the Colonies, especially in those in which the Anglican Church was established. The *Thoughts* of John Locke were widely read; and they impressed even so original a man as Benjamin Franklin when he came to promote the establishment of the academy. In other ways, also, the American academy was affected by English writings, and by English experience with a similar institution; but it did not entirely follow its English model or Franklin's idea. It became, as we shall say later, the first important educational invention to be developed in America.

Other English influences were of a local or temporary character. The monitorial system of Lancaster and the English variety of Pestalozzian object-teaching have already been mentioned. The mechanics institutes developed by George Birkbeck in about 1820 and the scheme promoted by Albert Mansbridge early in the present century for the education of organized labor were both copied in the United States, but they never attained the success they had in England. The nursery school is an even more recent importation. It remains to be seen whether it will become a general feature of the American system.

The American colleges also were at first modeled on the colleges of England. Harvard College was founded by graduates of Emmanuel College, Cambridge, and was named for one of them, John Harvard. Even the town in which the new college was opened was named for the city on the Cam where its promoters had studied. William and Mary College, Yale, Princeton, King's College in New York, and others followed. But the wide dispersion of our people did not permit the association of these colleges into a university of the Cambridge or Oxford type. Religious diversity also divided them. Some were Anglican, others Congregational, Presbyterian, Baptist, or Dutch Reformed. Because there was no overarching university to hold them together and direct their ways they each gradually developed into independent universities. One important feature of the English college we have retained: namely, the idea that there should be a period of broad liberal education interposed between the secondary school and the specialized study and investigation of the professional and graduate schools. The continents of Europe and Latin-America do not have any institution resembling the American or English college.

The examples that we have already given illustrate a general truth about the diffusion of culture and its institutions. It is this: Unless the conditions in the borrowing country are very similar to those in the lending country, the imported culture and institutions either fail to take root or are quickly and often radically modified. One or both of these results followed in most of the cases named here. Even our language is no longer quite the language of England. The Latin grammar school, although imported, was not suited to American conditions. The academy never closely followed its English prototype. And so with most of the other importations.

American democracy was one of the conditions that tended to limit the introduction of English schools and educational practices or that transformed them when they were brought over. By democracy we here mean merely the greater equality in the social status of the American people, the absence of an aristocracy and of great landed estates, and the extension of the suffrage. Even in England the aristocracy was not a caste, but there were ruling classes. Her Prime Ministers were not like Jackson or Lincoln, drawn from the self-educated "common" people. Her educational leaders were drawn from the public schools and the old universities. The open frontier and the scattered population were other American conditions that tended to transform borrowed institutions. Our rapidly expanding economy made necessary the extension of elementary and some secondary education to the general public. This need in its turn promoted the education of girls who in many cases became teachers in our fast-growing school systems. The separation of church and state and the development of schools from which sectarian instruction was banned both eliminated from American public education much of the religious dissension that long hampered the development of public education in England. These American conditions will be considered further in the following chapters. Those chapters will show that, although we borrowed from England and many other countries, the American people have developed their own system of education.

SUMMARY

The development of national education in England makes an especially interesting historical study because conditions hindered it that, abstractly considered, should have promoted it. English individualism, a restricted view of the functions of government, political democracy that could not use compulsion or royal fiat, religious freedom, and the growth of a class of wealthy and influential dissenters all tended to delay nationalization. We must add to this that the English, like other Western peoples, had to overcome a tradition of family and church education, and that the partial effectiveness of philanthropic efforts often made public education seem less necessary.

The monitorial schools of Bell and Lancaster played an important part in demonstrating that universal education would not be too expensive. They also developed methods of administering large schools, of grading the classes, and of organizing and teaching the subject matter. They convinced many that teaching was a skilled, if not a professional, occupation for which some preparation and training were necessary. They formed an important stage in the movement for universal education.

The early nineteenth century was notable for a fruitful interchange of educational ideas with the continent. While the monitorial system was being introduced into France and other countries, the English and the Scotch schoolmasters borrowed and spread the infant school, the teacher-training school, and a series of Pestalozzian practices and ideas. The English variety of object lessons was widely spread in the United States.

After three failures at widely separated intervals: in the time of King Alfred, of Wycliffe, and of the Commonwealth, the English government in 1833 adopted the promotion of education as a public policy. Parliament granted a sum of money for building schoolhouses to be used by the two monitorial societies; and it shortly instituted the inspection of private schools and established training colleges for teachers. The Newcastle Commission drew the map locating the evils of English elementary education in 1861 and added another to a chapter of errors, "payment by results." The Act of 1870 established local elective school boards and assigned them the power to levy taxes for schools in their districts. Compulsory attendance followed a decade later. The elementary curriculum has been greatly expanded, health services and vocational and technical courses and schools have been developed, and an extensive system of partially free secondary schools has been created. The Act of 1944 was intended to unify, extend, and modernize the comprehensive system of national education that England has developed. The passage of this act in the midst of war was indicative of an increasing public interest to pay for it, and this changed attitude has continued into the present decade.

QUESTIONS

1. Why was it difficult for the English to agree on a national system of education?
2. Compare and contrast the philosophies of philanthropic and of public education as these were developed and held in England.
3. Do you agree with the statement in the text that the charity schools

were useful? Why or why not? Would the period to which this question is taken to refer influence your answer?
4. If Napoleon's plan to invade England had succeeded, would public education have developed as rapidly as it did in Prussia?
5. Why did the monitorial schools develop in England rather than in Prussia, Switzerland, or France?
6. Examine Lancaster's *Improvements in Education* and estimate its significance in its own time and country.
7. Compare the methods and stages of educational progress in England and France.
8. Why was payment by results a mistake? Give other examples in which public money payments had, or have, to be "earned."
9. Private secondary schools have occupied a strong position in English education. Why had this been true? Has it been advantageous to England or to the English people?
10. Examine C. Reddie's *Abbotsholme*. How do you account for the fact that his early "modern progressive" school arose in an educationally conservative country such as England? Why can England be called educationally conservative?

NOTES AND SOURCES

The literature on the Great Public Schools must be omitted here, but this note will apprise the student of its existence. There are special volumes dealing with individual schools and also more general treatments. The histories of the English universities must likewise be passed over. The following list is intended to amplify the history of national popular education in England. Particular mention should be made of the extended series of Board of Education reports, including the *Special Reports on Educational Subjects*, which began in 1897. Noteworthy publications include the Hadow Reports on *The Education of the Adolescent* (1926), on *The Primary Schools* (1931), and on *Infant and Nursery Schools* (1933) and the Spens *Report* (1939). Other major reports are the Crowther Report (1959) of the Central Advisory Council for Education; the Newsom Report (1963) of the Central Advisory Council; and the Robbins Report (1963) of the Committee on Higher Education Appointed by the Prime Minister. The Yearbooks of the International Institute of Teachers College, Columbia University, have many articles on English education as do the issues of the *Comparative Education Review*; such as the one by Peterson cited subsequently.

ADAMSON, JOHN W., *English Education, 1789–1902*, Cambridge University Press, 1930, 519 pp.

ARCHER, R. L., *Secondary Education in the Nineteenth Century*, Cambridge University Press, 1921, 363 pp.

ARNOLD, MATTHEW, *Reports on Elementary Schools, 1852–1882*, London, Macmillan & Company, Ltd., 1889, 306 pp. Nineteen reports on elementary schools by the poet and critic who was also one of Her Majesty's inspectors of schools.

BIRCHENOGH, CHARLES, *History of Elementary Education in England and Wales*, London, University Tutorial Press, 1938, 572 pp. Second edition.

DE MONTMORENCY, J. E. G., *State Intervention in English Education; A Short History From the Earliest Times Down to 1833;* Cambridge, University Press, 1902, 366 pp.; *National Education and National Life*, London, Swan Sonnenschein and Company, 1906, 287 pp.

DOBBS, ARCHIBALD EDWARD, *Education and Social Movements, 1700–1850*, London, Longmans, Green and Company, 1919, 257 pp.

DRESSLER, BRUNO, *Geschichte der Englishen Erziehung*, Leipzig, B. G. Teubner, 1928, 340 pp.

FIELD, LOUIS F., *The Child and His Book. Some Account of the History and Progress of Children's Literature in England*, London, W. Gardner, Darton and Company, 1895, 358 pp.

GREENOUGH, J. C., *The Evolution of the Elementary Schools of Great Britain*, New York, D. Appleton & Company, 1903, 265 pp.

GROSS, RICHARD E., Editor, *British Secondary Education*, London, Oxford University Press, 1965, 589 pp.

HOLMAN, HENRY, *English National Education: A Sketch of the Rise of Public Elementary Schools in England*, Glasgow, Blackie & Son, Ltd., 1898, 256 pp.

KELLY, THOMAS, *George Birkbeck, Pioneer of Adult Education*, Liverpool, University of Liverpool Press, 1957, 380 pp. Illustrated.

LEACH, ARTHUR F., *English Schools at the Reformation, 1546–1548*, London, Constable & Company, Ltd., 1896, 346 pp.; *The Schools of Medieval England*, New York, The Macmillan Company, 1915, 349 pp.

LOCHHEAD, JEWELL, *The Education of Young Children in England*, New York, Teachers College, Columbia University, 1932, 226 pp.

MANSBRIDGE, ALBERT, *An Adventure in Working-Class Education, Being the Story of the Workers Education Association, 1903–1915*, New York, Longmans, Green and Company, 1920, 73 pp.

NEWTON, ALFRED W., *The English Elementary School*, London, Longmans, Green and Company, 1919, 299 pp.

OGILVIE, VIVIAN, *The English Public School*, London, B. T. Batsford, Ltd., [1957], 228 pp. Illustrated.

PARMENTIER, JACQUES, *Histoire de l'Education en Angleterre; les doctrines et les écoles depuis les origines jusqu'au commencement du XIXe siècle*, Paris, Perrin et Cie., 1896, 302 pp.

PETERSON, A. D. C., "Educational Reform in England and Wales, 1956–1966," *Comparative Education Review*, Vol. XI, No. 3, 288–299, October 1967.

REDDIE, CECIL, *Abbotsholme*, London, George Allen, 1900, 640 pp.

SNELL, REGINALD, *Progressive Schools, Their Principles and Practice*, London, L. and Virginia Woolf at the Hogarth Press, 1934, 197 pp.

TRUSCOTT, BRUCE, *Red Brick University*, a Pelican Book, 1951, 375 pp. On the English provincial universities. The author is said to have been Professor E. Allison Peers of Liverpool University.

WARD, HERBERT, *The Educational System of England and Wales and Its Recent History*, Cambridge University Press, 1935, 256 pp.

WATSON, FOSTER, *The English Grammar Schools to 1660: Their Curricula and Practice*, Cambridge University Press, 1908, 548 pp.; *The Beginnings of the Teaching of Modern Subjects in England*, London, Sir Isaac Pitman & Sons, Ltd., 1909, 554 pp.

WEBB, SIDNEY, *London Education*, New York, Longmans, Green and Company, 1904, 219 pp.

WILSON, J. DOVER, *The Schools of England; A Study in Renaissance*, Chapel Hill, University of North Carolina Press, 1929, 388 pp.

Chapter 18

EVOLUTION OF AMERICAN STATE SCHOOLS

The fifth and final pattern for the development of national systems of education is that of the United States of America. Unlike the French, German, and Soviet patterns, and more like the English pattern, the American pattern of control is one of extreme decentralization. Like their English ancestors, the American people originally regarded education as a proper function of home and church and not of government, either Federal or state. It is no accident that the Federal Constitution makes no mention of education at all. Gradually, however, in the period preceding the Civil War, after attempting to extend education to larger numbers through philanthropic agencies and private institutions, the American people began to recognize education as a proper function of local government and to a lesser extent of state government. During the same period they envisioned new educational objectives and introduced new materials and methods to achieve these objectives. In this chapter we shall trace this developing awareness of education as a legitimate function of government. In the two chapters that follow we shall outline the main features of the American national system of schools as it has evolved.

The early Colonial period was an era in which the Colonists copied European schools as closely as American conditions permitted. We sometimes call it the period of transplantation. But even so the schools were gradually adapted to the needs and circumstances of the frontier. The break with tradition that resulted from the migration and the mingling of many peoples gave occasion for innovation. The first great innovation was the development of the American academy.

Thirteen Colonies, extending from New Hampshire to Georgia, were founded in a period of one hundred and eighty years. By hard work a living was obtained from the soil, the sea, and the forests. In savagely fought wars, the Indians were driven inland and the strip of English civilization along the Atlantic was gradually widened. By 1750, in Pennsylvania and Virginia where the strip was widest, the settlements reached up into the Alleghenies and were spilling over the crest. The French and Indian War (1755-1763) assured the frontiersmen that the Ohio Valley would be English and not French. By 1770, the people of the thirteen Colonies numbered two and a quarter millions and, from natural increase and continued immigration, they grew so rapidly that, as Burke said, "While we spend our time in deliberations on the mode of governing two millions, we shall find that we have millions more to govern." This growing body of people became ever more restive under English control, especially after the French menace was removed; and in 1776 they declared their independence and their intention to build up a separate American civilization.

During the Revolutionary War, the common danger led to a certain unity among the states; but when the war was over, sectionalism and state sovereignty again strongly asserted themselves. The period between the close of the war and the adoption of the Constitution was an era of political confusion when the new sovereign states competed among themselves and on several occasions threatened armed hostilities within the confederation. Even before the Constitutional Convention, education was proposed as an important means of forming a more unified nation. With the establishment of the Federal Government, the need for education to promote national unity and citizenship became apparent to all thinking men. Washington and other leaders argued that education should be fostered and employed to overcome sectionalism, to prepare the young for the duties of citizenship in a republic, and to maintain the spirit of liberty. Many urged also that practical education would aid agriculture and commerce and would in this way promote the general welfare. Nor could the individual need of education be neglected in a country that claimed to be the land of opportunity for the common man.

THE EARLY SETTLEMENTS

The period when the British formed their early American settlements was a time of low wages, unemployment, and social unrest. The famine of 1595 was the beginning of a long depression. Many people were obliged to find new ways of making a living and some of these turned toward foreign lands. The destruction of the Spanish Armada in 1588 had established the sea power of England, and the East India Company was founded in 1600. Others looked westward to the little known lands across the Atlantic. How little the English knew of America, even after the voyages of

Hawkins and Drake and after Raleigh's attempted settlement, is shown by the account of George Weymouth who visited the coast of Maine in midsummer of 1605 and thereupon reported a climate suitable for tropical fruits. Much of the difficulty that the early English settlers encountered came from mistaken notions about the resources and conditions of the country.

The band of one hundred and five Colonists who landed on the banks of the James River in 1607 did not find the gold and immediate wealth for which they had hoped. Starvation and disease carried off half of them in six months and would have destroyed the rest but for supplies and replacements supplemented by greater attention to agriculture. A few years later, when the Puritans came into control of the company that promoted the settlement, they sent over a new govenor with instructions to hold an election for members of a representative assembly in Virginia. The first American legislature met in the church in Jamestown in 1619. The new government lasted only five years, for Virginia was made a royal province in 1624.

The Virginia settlements became permanent through the discovery of a profitable crop suited to the climate, tobacco. The tobacco plant rapidly exhausted the soil so that new land had to be constantly brought under cultivation. The plantation system that developed demanded a supply of cheap, unskilled labor. This demand was met by transporting debtors and criminals from English jails, children from English poorhouses, and persons kidnaped in London alleys. English paupers came as redemptioners and paid for their passage by a term, usually four years, of labor in the tobacco fields. Some of the redemptioners were skilled mechanics, bookkeepers, or schoolmasters. The first shipboard of slaves from Africa was brought over in 1619, the year of the first legislative assembly. Thus there were two classes in Virginia, one consisting of the planters, the clergy, and a few other professional people and the other the working class, many of them employed at forced labor as slaves or redemptioners. There was no large middle class.

The population of Virginia was widely scattered on the plantations fronting on the rivers. There were no cities, few villages, roads, industries, or stores. Cooperation and the assembling of people was difficult. The center of the planter's life was still in London where he disposed of his crops and purchased his clothes, furnishings, and implements. The planters' families were frequently refined and their homes were furnished with books, musical instruments, and English furniture. The children were educated by the parish clergy or in schools maintained on the plantations. There were a few Latin grammar schools and some of the boys in wealthy families were sent to English schools. For the poor, neighborhood or "old field" schools were established, in which itinerant teachers taught on occasion. The system of apprenticeship provided opportunity for vocational training. Many children received little or no schooling.

The first settlements in northern Virginia, or New England as it came to be called, were made at Plymouth in 1620 and at Boston in 1630. In the latter year the great emigration of Puritans began, for civil war was imminent in England. In that single year more than a thousand and within ten years not less than twenty thousand Colonists came to Massachusetts. No such peaceful mass migration had taken place in historic times. The Colonists settled in compact villages, and the New England town, that is township, became the center of their political life. There was no large-scale agriculture and no plantation system. Diversified farming, which demanded varied knowledge, skill, and business ability, became the rule. And because New England could not maintain her growing population by agriculture, she turned to industry and fishing. Cod and herring from the waters between Marblehead and Newfoundland were exchanged for the products of the West Indies and Europe. Fishing boats and seagoing ships were needed. There were great forests of timber and the resourceful Colonists readily learned to build their own vessels. Within twenty years of the settlement of Boston, more than a thousand boats were engaged in the fishing industry. Masts for the Royal Navy were frequently exported to England. Thousands of skilled workmen were employed in shipbuilding and in navigation. The New England system of farming and industry was built upon the skilled and semiskilled labor of a dominant middle class.

Economically, New England was democratic. By industry and intelligence it was usually possible for the poor to become landowners, artisans, shipowners, or merchants. Scores of trades developed. The wealthy class was often alarmed because of the high wages that enabled artisans to own houses and gardens and threatened to break down the social classes. There were few slaves, but the slave trade was profitable and many slave ships were owned by New Englanders. Business and the town meetings provided training for democracy.

Political democracy developed very gradually. In the beginning, society in New England was neither democratic nor tolerant. But Puritanism was a leavening influence, a transition movement, tending to dissolve the medieval system of class and status and to produce free and equal individuals. A dozen men held all the powers of government in Massachusetts in 1630. The next year one hundred and sixteen others were admitted to the company. The leaven was working; but the freemen were still only a small part of the population. Thomas Hooker, who founded Connecticut, declared that "to leave power in the hands of rulers who are not responsible to the people is to invite tyranny." The numbers of the freemen were increased and a form of representative government was worked out; but it was in the annual town meetings and by serving on town committees that the people received the most useful political education.

Tolerance also developed slowly. The Puritans had chosen a post of danger in the wilderness, instead of their quiet homes in a civilized country, to establish a "godly commonwealth," free from error; and now they were dismayed to find error both springing up within and assailing them from without, threatening ruin to their "holy experiment." They tried to defend by mistaken means that for which they had sacrificed home and native land. Their executioner burned heretical books; they censored the output of their printing press which, established in 1639, remained for a generation the only one in America; and they did worse in driving Roger Williams into the wintry forests and in banishing Ann Hutchinson. But the persistency of the Quakers, whose opposition to a regular clergy made them especially obnoxious to a theocracy, led to the strongest measures: Four were hung.

The theocracy could not continue on this road. Sympathy for the victims, a growing sense that ideas cannot be destroyed by force, and a growing fear of interference from England put an end to the killings. Charles II did interfere; and the "glorious revolution" of 1688 further strengthened the principle of toleration throughout the English world.

The most advanced position was taken by Roger Williams. In 1631 he became pastor at Salem and ascended the pulpit to denounce the union of church and state and to declare that the civil authorities had no right to punish violations of religious commandments, Sabbath-breaking for example. This was the position later taken by John Locke. Williams founded his colony in Rhode Island on civil equality, the separation of church and state, and complete religious freedom; and these principles became foundation stones of government and public education in the United States. Close approaches to religious liberty were also made in the colonies of Maryland and Pennsylvania.

The settlers of the Middle Colonies, with their confused intermingling of languages, faiths, and nationalities, were much more diverse than those to the north or the south of them. New Amsterdam, before the English conquest in 1664, was a mere village, yet in its streets more than a dozen languages were heard. The Swedish and Quaker settlements on either side of the Delaware attracted men from the British Isles and almost every country of western Europe. The Dutch, after winning their struggle for independence from Spain and after the decline of Spanish sea power, turned even more vigorously than before to commercial and maritime pursuits. They became enterprizing traders rather than colonizers. Because they found religious toleration and reasonable economic opportunity at home, they did not emigrate in large numbers. New Netherland was governed not by the mother country and not in the interest of the Colonists but by the Dutch West India Company for the financial enrichment of its members. The fall of New Netherland and its occupation by the English seems to have been welcomed by most of the inhabitants. In the last quarter of the seventeenth century the colony, favored by its excellent location and by the development of representative government, began the rapid growth that early in the nineteenth century made New York the largest American city. During the eighteenth century, however, Philadelphia, not New York, was the largest city in British America.

The active settlement of the Middle Colonies to the south of New York was held back by Dutch claims and Dutch control of that region until 1664. After that the vacant spaces on the Atlantic coast between the southern and northern Colonies were rapidly filled up. The great increase in population that took place in the two decades following 1690 was the result in considerable part of the new immigration into Pennsylvania, New Jersey, and other Colonies and in part to the high birth rate in Colonial families elsewhere.

The people who were coming into the Delaware Valley in those years were of many stocks and faiths. Small settlements of Swedish Lutherans and Dutch Calvinists had been there long before. The Dutch social reformer Plockhoy established a small colony far south on Delaware Bay in 1663. Puritans escaping from the unfriendly England of Charles II, English and Welsh Quakers, and Welshmen who were not Quakers, to the number of several thousand, had come before William Penn arrived in the ship *Welcome* in 1682. Some of the Welsh moved out into the country and Welsh names such as Brecknock and Caernarvon are found far from Philadelphia in Pennsylvania. A small number of Huguenots came in the same year (1683) as did Francis Daniel Pastorius and the Mennonites who founded Germantown. Pastorius was a scholar, university bred, and a Pietist. He was for several years a teacher of a Friends' school in Philadelphia and later a teacher and town officer of Germantown. The statement is sometimes made that he was the most learned man of his time in America, not excepting Cotton Mather. Among the half-dozen languages of which he had a command was English, and he prepared a little primer, *The True Reading, Spelling, and Writing of English*, which was printed by William Bradford of New York in 1697. German, Swiss and some Dutch Mennonites came in large numbers into the counties of southeastern Pennsylvania. Twenty families of Dunkards, now the Church of the Brethren, arrived in 1719 and others followed. Influenced by John Huss, Caspar Schwenkfeld, a nobleman of Silesia, founded the sect that bears his name. In the first half of the eighteenth century, some Schwenkfelders settled in eastern Pennsylvania where they much later founded the Perkiomen School. The Moravians, who were the direct disciples of Huss, and who had settled in the new colony of Georgia, were aided by George Whitefield in moving to Pennsylvania where they settled at Nazareth and Bethlehem in about 1740. They have been noted for their work as missionaries to the Indians, for their activity as founders and teachers of excellent schools, and for their devotion to music, especially the music of Bach. The Scotch-Irish, grievously oppressed in Ulster and cordially hating their English oppressors, began to arrive some time before the German and Bohemian groups and settled in the mountain valleys of Pennsylvania and Virginia. They were mainly Presbyterians and they played an important part in the Revolution and the politics and education of America. Catholics, both from Germany and from Ireland, also migrated to the middle Colonies; and Maryland was for a time a haven for English Catholics. Episcopalians came in large numbers into New York and Pennsylvania. Many of these groups developed their own church schools so that the middle Colonies became a parochial school region.

Many motives served to send people across the Atlantic. Redemptioners came because they were out of work. Ship captains could sell the time of a healthy and especially of a skilled immigrant for more than the regular passenger fare and even found it profitable to delay transportation, holding emigrants at embarkation ports until their savings were used up, when they could be taken as redemptioners. Some were transported from English jails where they had been confined for debt, for political offences, and for many worse crimes. Others came voluntarily to escape political or economic or domestic involvement, some for travel or adventure, and some to Christianize the Indians. Many came to escape religious persecution, especially during the horrors of the Thirty Years War; others, such as the Puritans, the Quakers, the Moravians, and Roger Williams, intended to found an ideal church. As in other conditions of human life, economic motives were usually also involved: to find gold or to work at high wages and to return; to engage in trade or to develop a new country and to make a fortune. But perhaps the most frequent reason for the great migration, which to the majority meant a complete severing of all ties with the old country, was a keen desire to found quiet and comfortable homes under easier conditions than Europe could offer.

None came for educational advantages for these were not to be found in a wilderness, except that in a negative sense the New World might help them to escape some of the disadvantages of the traditional, and at that time decadent, schools of the Old World. But apparently they had no idea of the shortcomings of the schools of the seventeenth century. It is a striking fact that none of the Colonists were dissatisfied with the educational institutions or with the opportunities that would have been theirs in those institutions if they had remained in Europe. They were seriously dissatisfied with their religious, political, and economic opportunities, but for the schools of their mother countries they expressed the sincerest admiration by imitating them and attempting to transplant them to the new soil.

With some exceptions they were satisfied with a moderate degree of education for their children. Some of the planters of the South, some of the official class, and those who looked forward to professional careers for their sons demanded secondary and higher schooling. But the vast majority of American settlers were less ambitious. Women and the mass of unskilled laborers were at best taught little more than reading and writing. The slaves expected no education and received none. The Puritans, the Presbyterians, the Quakers, the German sects, and all those aroused by the Reformation to a living sense of religious issues demanded literacy and a knowledge of the catechism and Bible. Some, but not all of these, also required an educated ministry. The small businessmen and skilled artisans and even the farmers needed some arithmetic, practical measurement and calculation, and elementary training in drawing up legal documents. The land surveyor was an important functionary in every community in the seventeenth century; and a knowledge of navigation had to be acquired by ship captains and of handwriting and bookkeeping by merchants. The general effect of frontier life was to reduce both the demand and the supply of schools. By 1700, or soon after, the lands nearest to the coast and to the larger rivers were pretty well occupied and the Indians less menacing. The peace of Utrecht in 1713 coincided with the conquest of the Tuscarawas by the Carolinas. Soon the strong Scotch-Irish immigration was to begin. As a result of all these factors, a broad and spreading band of frontier settlements began to develop westward. In seventeenth-century America the real frontiersman, like the unskilled laborer and most women, was likely to be illiterate.

TRANSPLANTING EDUCATIONAL INSTITUTIONS

Four main types of educational endeavor characterized the seventeenth century: apprenticeship to the manual vocations; reading and religious instruction directed by churches and missionary societies, or obtained in dame schools, or otherwise; the formal secondary and higher education of the Latin schools and colleges, although until near the end of the period Harvard was the only college; and practical schooling in mathematics and its applications to accounting, navigation, and surveying together with supplementary work in English. Only the first three of these were transplanted and will be discussed in this section. The last was in the main a native development and will be discussed in the next section. Every one of these four types of education was found in each of the Colonial regions: New England, the middle Colonies, and the South. The cultural similarity of all the early Colonies, in spite of their economic differences, has not been sufficiently noticed and has even been denied. It is a true statement, however, that the educational differences between the different social classes and the different regions of any one colony were greater than those between the different Colonies.

We shall discuss apprenticeship education first. In the laws and the practices of apprenticeship training, English legislation and precedent were directly followed. The English laws on apprenticeship education were from the first closely related to poor relief. The first such act was voted in the reign of Henry VIII, and the series of enactments came to its climax in the code of 1601, just as the colonizing trend was beginning. The English guilds were declining. The state, therefore, took over some of the most necessary of their activities, including the relief of the poor and the vocational education of poor children. The laws in England provided for the compulsory apprenticeship of such children at public expense and made it the obligation of the local government to supply the necessary materials and facilities. Those laws were copied by the Colonies. Apprenticeship was one of the most widespread forms of education in Colonial America and all the Colonies passed laws to facilitate it.

The word *apprentice* comes from an old French verb that even in the Latin from which it was derived meant "to learn." An apprentice is one who is bound to a master to learn a trade. The legal instrument, which specified the duties and privileges of the master and the apprentice, was called an *indenture*. The indentures frequently contained a clause that required the master to provide opportunities for a small amount of schooling, sometimes in an evening school. In such cases we have a combination of the two types, trade training and elementary literary education.

One of the early acts of the Virginia Legislature ordered that the English "statute for artificers and workmen" should be published in the colony. A law of 1646 further provided for a workhouse school to teach spinning and knitting to young children. A third Virginia act in 1661 required the justices of the peace to apprentice poor children. Various other acts dealt with the same subject and with the literary and religious education of poor and orphaned children. The repeated reference to orphans in the laws demands a word of explanation. All youths and minors whose parents remained in England, as well as those whose parents were no longer living and all illegitimate children, were by law classified as orphans, and for the education of these the state attempted to provide. Others were voluntarily apprenticed by their parents if they were to learn a trade. The apprenticeship system was most widespread in the northern Colonies but it was found in Virginia, as indicated, and in the other southern Colonies also. The system was frequently abused. Masters sometimes exploited their apprentices, employing them at common labor without teaching them the specified trade. In such cases the laws provided redress through fines or by reassignment to more responsible masters. The laws of New York introduced a new element by providing that the completion of an apprenticeship should entail the right of full citizenship.

The first general education law in New England, that of Massachusetts in 1642, was in part an apprenticeship law. The law was passed to remedy "the great neglect in many parents and masters in training up their children in learning and labor and other employments which may be profitable to the commonwealth." A later clause in the law explains that by "learning" was meant "ability to read and understand the principles of religion and the capital laws of the country." Any parents or masters who neglected to teach these abilities together with a trade were subject to a fine; and the selectmen of the town were commanded to remove children or apprentices from the custody of neglectful parents or masters and to commit them to the care of others who would perform their duty under the law. In this first New England school law, as it is sometimes called, schools are not mentioned. It was not a school law but a law on the proper upbringing of children among the poor and the lower middle classes. We should notice particularly that it required training in "learning and labor," joining apprenticeship to reading and religion as many indentures also did. Court records in the several Colonies show that the apprenticeship laws were sometimes enforced but not how strictly this was done.

The power of legislation in Colonial times was in the hands of the rich and well-to-do. The apprenticeship laws were therefore an example of one class legislating for another class—the rich for the poor, partly for the benefit and the control of the poor and partly for the benefit and relief of the rich. These motives can be exhibited best in a summary of the arguments for such laws and for the apprenticeship system. Apprenticeship, it was held, tended to reduce the burden of poor relief and to prevent pauperism and crime; to avoid probable distress; to prepare capable workmen for employers; to teach the elements of learning and religion in addition to a trade; and to aid in maintaining the traditional, or as they would have said the natural, order of society. Obviously apprenticeship and the legislation related to it were not entirely, perhaps not even chiefly, intended to benefit the apprentice and his social class.

Apprenticeship declined in importance in the Colonial period and even more rapidly afterward. The abundance of land, the mobility and freedom of the people, the willingness of the frontiersman to do with makeshift implements and furnishings, and the immigration of mechanics and craftsmen who had been trained in Europe all worked against the apprenticeship system. The heaviest blow was delivered by the factory in the nineteenth century, but the system had been declining in Colonial days.

Another general type of transplanted educational institution were the schools for reading and religious instruction. Everywhere in the Colonies the common people were seriously concerned that children should be taught reading and the principles of religion; but frequently their interest in education did not go much further. Everywhere education was still accepted as one of the functions of the church, although it was felt that other agencies, such as private bodies or the state, might properly support or at least supplement the church in the performance of this duty. The Virginia statute of 1631, which required the clergy to instruct the youth in the catechism and the *Book of Common Prayer*, also laid an obligation on the parents and all those who had the charge of children: that they should send them to the church to receive this instruction. Many of the Virginia churches established parish schools and a few maintained charity schools. In the eighteenth century the Church of England missionary body, which was called the Society for the Propagation of the Gospel in Foreign Parts, established charity schools, imported orthodox schoolmasters from England, opened libraries, and provided entirely or in part for the support of these institutions.

The interest that parents took in the education of their children is proved by the wills of the period. Many testators provided not alone for the education of their own but also for the children of others. There were Virginia wills bequeathing funds for the education of "six poor children"; or for the schooling of the poor children of the testator's county; or giving five hundred pounds in trust for the salaries of schoolmasters; and providing for the maintenance of a free school in the County of Lancaster. Wills and letters also show that indentured servants were employed in teaching. From the very end of the Colonial period we have the diary of John Harrower, an indentured servant from the islands far north of Scotland, who served as teacher in the Daingerfield family near Fredericksburg. The last entry of the diary, made after the news of the Battle of Lexington had reached Virginia, speaks not of teaching but of getting a supply of lead, perhaps for bullets, from the roof of one of the buildings on the estate.

Families with means frequently employed a tutor or established a family school in the mansion house or in a separate building erected for the purpose. It would not be possible to distinguish clearly between the tutorial plan and the family-school plan. The one merges into the other, but in the latter there was often a separate building close by the residence, especially erected for school purposes, and the children of the plantation and those from neighboring plantations were taught together. Graduates of northern colleges or Scotch schoolmasters were sometimes employed. There is an excellent account of such a family school, as it was at the end of the Colonial period, in the diary of Philip Fithian. Fithian was a graduate of Princeton and taught for a year in the Carter family in eastern Virginia. The boys of the school followed an English and classical course, including some Greek, but the girls were given merely an English education. Fithian described not the school alone but also the social life of the period and region.

Another nonchurch type of school was the neighborhood or, as it was usually called, the old field school. The historian Beverly speaks (1705) of the habit of the people of Virginia of joining together to form little schools for their children; and Jones in *The Present State of Virginia* (1724) says that "in most parishes there are schools, little houses being built on purpose where English and writing are taught." The latter of these passages almost certainly and the former probably refer to the old field school. In these buildings, usually located on some plot of abandoned or wasteland—whence the name—itinerant teachers "kept school" when they were able to gather a sufficient flock of pupils. Such teachers were good, bad, or indifferent in ability and character. Their reputation in history is certainly not high but some historians think injustice has been done them, pointing out that almost every advertisement for a teacher demands one of sober and correct life and good character. But even this evidence is really ambiguous. The unanimity with which such qualities were demanded may actually mean that they were hard to find. We know that some of these itinerant teachers were learned and reputable men and that some were not, and this seems to be all that we do know.

In Pennsylvania, and in the middle Colonies generally, educational conditions were not so different as they have been painted from those of Virginia and the South. There was no established church, there were many sects, and the people lived in more compact settlements. They engaged in diversified farming and, in the towns, in a great variety of occupations. The middle class of free and independent workmen, farmers, and small businessmen formed the bulk of the population. In this region also the locally organized and democratic neighborhood school was a familiar and frequent institution. It was most frequent where, as in Pennsylvania, the settlers were divided into many sects and where the number of any one sect was too small for a church school. In Philadelphia and other large towns, in the southeastern part of the colony, and wherever whole communities were composed of a single denomination, there were church schools. Elsewhere the neighborhood schools predominated and served the children of all faiths. They were commonest in the region toward the Susquehanna and beyond in the valleys of the Cumberland and Juniata rivers and in the region across the Alleghenies. There a common school, established by the people themselves, religious in its tone but undenominational in its teaching, grew up on the frontier and formed the basis for the public school when the time arrived. Wickersham has estimated that in 1834, when Pennsylvania voted to adopt the public school system, there must have been at least four thousand schoolhouses in the state built by the contributions of the people themselves. They were not closely modeled on any previous institution, but were the simple response of farmers and frontiersmen meeting a need with the resources at hand. The fact that the Scotch-Irish settled in the central and western parts of the state aided the movement because, although interested in education, they did not usually favor church schools.

The third type of transplanted educational institutions provided secondary and college education. Our early secondary schools were Latin grammar schools that prepared boys for college and were closely connected with the colleges. Some Latin grammar schools were public, others were private. Most of them were independent, but some were merely the preparatory departments of colleges. The curriculum was always classical, but the role of the Greek studies had shrunk so greatly that only the simplest elements of the language were taught. The instruction in Latin was more extensive and consisted of drill in grammar and composition and the reading of Cicero and other authors. Rhetoric, declamation, and ancient history were sometimes added.

Many of the American Latin schools were local day schools that enrolled the children of the community, but there were some boarding schools. Obviously the boarding school, a little world in itself that shuts out the great world beyond its walls, erects a greater barrier between its pupils and those who are excluded than the day school. The day school is not so far removed from everyday interests; and after school hours the children of the whole neighborhood mingle freely with each other. The typical Colonial grammar school was a small day school in a middle-class community; and it frequently taught the common branches to one group and Latin to another and smaller group who intended to go to college. To cite just one example: the school of Roxbury, Massachusetts, at the end of the Colonial period had eighty-five pupils, and only nine of these were studying Latin. The rest were enrolled in the common branches. Only in the largest towns were there many Latin pupils. In small places the master was compelled to teach reading and arithmetic to ten boys before he had the chance to introduce a single one into the mysteries of the Latin tongue. The aristocracy of the Latin grammar school of which we sometimes read is a good deal of a myth; but educationally it was not well adapted to the frontier. Before the end of the Colonial period a new institution, the academy, began to take its place because it was a more flexible institution and better adapted to a new country. Very few of the Colonial Latin schools remain, but among these are the Boston and the Roxbury Latin Schools and the William Penn Charter School.

As early as 1621, a free school called the East India School was planned at Charles City, Virginia. Perhaps it was never opened because the whole settlement was wiped out in the following year by an Indian massacre. The Symms School, endowed by a will of 1634, and the Eaton School were not in constant operation, but here is a slender thread of continuity leading to the present Symms-Eaton Academy, a public school at Hampton in which the two old foundations have been merged. Several other private and endowed schools offered classical education in Virginia. The school at Norfolk was a public school controlled by the town council. Thomas Jefferson prepared for William and Mary and James Madison for Princeton in private grammar schools, and such schools became numerous in the later Colonial period when Scottish schoolmasters migrated to Virginia. One of these was Donald Robertson who maintained a prosperous school in the period from the French and Indian War to the Revolution. The College of William and Mary, named for the sovereigns brought in by the "glorious revolution," was the only Colonial college south of Philadelphia; but this section rapidly developed new colleges after 1776.

Several efforts were made by the Legislatures of North Carolina and of

Maryland to encourage the founding of grammar schools, but conditions were very similar to those in Virginia. As Governor Calvert of Maryland said, "the remoteness of the habitation of one person from another" was the great obstacle. The government of North Carolina aided several grammar schools with grants of land and funds; and Maryland provided for a school at Annapolis, which later developed into St. John's College, and also a county system of Latin schools, each county school system to be governed by a board of trustees. Only a few of the twelve schools projected by the latter act were successful.

The Penn Charter School was the first permanent Latin school in Pennsylvania. Several elementary charity schools were connected with it; and the central school itself was in two divisions: a Latin school and an English and mathematical school. The former was strictly classical throughout the Colonial period and long after; but the latter was a practical school that taught a range of subjects: arithmetic, bookkeeping, trigonometry, navigation, surveying, and others. The French and German languages were taught from 1742. This early school differed from Franklin's academy in that it was conducted by a religious society and was not connected with a college; but otherwise the two were very similar. Eastern Pennsylvania had many private grammar schools in the eighteenth century. Several of these, which were designed to prepare young men for the ministry, were established by Presbyterians and resembled the Puritan academies of England. They taught the classics, which received the main emphasis, but also included mathematics, some of the sciences, and theology. There were grammar schools conducted by several of the churches, and there were a few neighborhood grammar schools managed by groups of interested citizens. Most of these were classical, but from the Penn Charter School and some of the schools of the Presbyterians we gather a hint of an important truth: that even in Colonial times grammar schools in the middle Colonies tended to introduce modern subjects. This statement applies to the schools of New York and New Jersey as well as those of Pennsylvania. Life was less ecclesiastical west and south of New England, and medical and scientific interests were more widely diffused.

The settlers of Massachusetts began to set up grammar schools in the first years of the Bay Colony. Because conditions were more favorable than in the other Colonies, their success was much greater. Seven or eight grammar schools in the towns of Boston (1635), Roxbury, Ipswich, Dorchester, Cambridge, and other were begun within a few years of the settlement; and the law requiring every town of a hundred families to maintain a school where boys could prepare for college was passed in 1647. Connecticut enacted a similar law in 1650, although a few grammar schools had been established earlier. Two of these were located at New Haven (1641) and Hartford (1642). The bequest of Edward Hopkins was applied in aid of these two schools and another one at Hadley. The Hopkins Grammar

The Colonial Colleges

```
1600      1620      1636 1640      1660      1680      1693 1701 1700      1720      1740   1746 1754 1755   1760   1764 1766 1769   1780      1800
```

The Venerable Nine

1636 Harvard	1755 Pennsylvania
1693 William and Mary	1764 Brown
1701 Yale	1766 Rutgers
1746 Princeton	1769 Dartmouth
1754 Columbia	

In New England
Harvard
Yale
Brown
Dartmouth

In Middle Colonies
Princeton
Columbia
Pennsylvania
Rutgers

In Southern Colonies
William and Mary

Early Time Schedule, Harvard

Classes		8:00–9:00	9:00–10:00	10:00–11:00	1:00–2:00	2:00–3:00	3:00–4:00
M	Freshmen	Logick, Physicks	Ethicks, Politicks	Arithmetic and Geometry	Disputations[3]	Disputations[3]	Disputations[3]
	Junior Sophs						
	Senior Sophs						
T	Freshmen	Logick, Physicks	Ethicks, Politicks	Arithmetic and Geometry	Disputations[3]	Disputations[3]	Disputations[3]
	Junior Sophs						
	Senior Sophs						
W	Freshmen	Greek Etymology and Syntax	Greek Prosody and Dialects	Greek	Greek Grammar	Greek Poetry Disputation	Greek Composition and Verse
	Junior Sophs						
	Senior Sophs						
Th	Freshmen	Hebrew Grammar	Chaldee	Syriack	Bible	Ezra and Daniel	Trostius on New Testament
	Junior Sophs						
	Senior Sophs						
F	Freshmen	Rhetorick[1]	Declamations[2]		History (in winter) Botany (in summer)		
	Junior Sophs	As above	As above		As above		
	Senior Sophs	As above	As above		As above		
S	Freshmen	Divinity	Commonplaces				
	Junior Sophs	As above	As above				
	Senior Sophs	As above	As above				

[1] Collectively. [2] Everyone, once a month. [3] Each in his art.

School of New Haven is still in operation. In most of New England the zeal for a grammar school education declined in the late seventeenth and eighteenth centuries. According to the Massachusetts court records, some towns that had been favorable to education neglected their schools and deliberately incurred the penalty of the law of 1647 because it was cheaper to pay the fine than to pay the master. Many grammar schools also became mere elementary schools because there were no advanced pupils.

Four colleges were established in the New England Colonies: Harvard, Yale, Dartmouth, and Brown; four in the middle Colonies: The College of New Jersey, now Princeton, King's College, now Columbia, the College of Philadelphia, which grew out of Franklin's Academy, now the University of Pennsylvania, and Queen's College, now Rutgers; and one in the southern Colonies: William and Mary, at Williamsburg in Virginia. For fifty years after the settlements, Harvard was the only American college and it was long a small and mediocre institution. It began to grow in numbers and importance in the eighteenth century and especially after the Revolution. Something of its early scope and purpose can be gathered from the accompanying diagram. Evidently its early curriculum was composed of three historical strata of materials taken respectively from the Middle Ages, the Renaissance, and the Reformation. The diagram also reveals the significant fact that six of the nine Colonial colleges were founded within the last thirty years of the Colonial period.

The Colonial colleges were regarded as societies of ministers and prospective ministers. The only profession for which they specifically prepared was the clerical. Many destined for other callings, however, attended and only about forty per cent of the graduates of the colleges became ministers. Only the College of Philadelphia was to any great degree independent of church affiliation; but the head of that school throughout the Colonial period was a clergyman, and the school was accused of teaching Episcopalian and Tory doctrines. Besides the clergy, lawyers and physicians became intellectual leaders in the years before the Revolution. No Colonial college maintained a law school; but the College of Philadelphia, located in the city that had become the greatest medical center of America, established a medical school in 1765.

INVENTING EDUCATIONAL INSTITUTIONS

The schools in America made numerous adjustments to the special conditions of the new country, but in the eighteenth century they effected an invention—a distinctly new institution—that developed into the American academy. Among the adjustments that have been mentioned were public control, the district system, the neighborhood schools, and—contrary to the English practice of grouping colleges in universities—the distribution of our colleges in widely separated population centers. The new invention was the incipient academy, often called the private school in the city, or the advertised school. With the increase in population, new business and construction needs arose, and the gap between what the grammar schools taught and what practical life demanded became constantly wider. Enterprising teachers sought to satisfy these growing needs where they were more insistent: namely, in the towns of Boston, Newport, New York, Philadelphia, and Charleston. Such teachers opened evening and day schools, offered practical subjects, and advertised their programs in the papers. Evening elementary schools had appeared in New Amsterdam before 1650, but these practical evening or day schools on the secondary level did not become very numerous until 1725. Philadelphia alone had one hundred and sixty teachers of such advertised schools between 1722 and the end of the Revolutionary War. City directories tell a similar story. In the period following the Revolution, New York City had one private teacher for every ninety families. About one fourth of these teachers were women. Many of the advertised schools for girls were well stocked with ornamental branches, but those for boys were more likely to offer mathematics and its applications. The schools usually followed the quarter plan; and, being without endowments, if they were to prosper they had to meet the needs and wants of the pupils.

To show the emphasis on mathematics and the variety of the branches and topics in that field, we give a list made by combining the offerings of several of the schools. Each of the subjects named here was taught or at least advertised by one or more private schools in eighteenth-century America. The list is as follows: algebra, geometry, mensuration, logarithms, plane and spherical trigonometry, fluxions (also called calculus), the quadrant, navigation, astronomy, surveying, dialing, gauging, geography, maps, use of the globes, bookkeeping; and also engineering subjects such as leveling, hydraulics, hydrostatics, pneumatics, optics, perspective, architecture, fortification, and gunnery. Bookkeeping was advertised to be taught according to "the Italian method of double entry." The modern languages were not omitted. There were teachers of French German, Spanish, and other subjects that the grammar schools and colleges of that time ignored almost entirely. These were new schools meeting practical needs.

The foundations of the American academy were laid by the private schools we have described. The academy is distinguished from these by the fact that its control was vested in a board of trustees that often operated under a charter from the state. In the present account both the chartered secondary schools with a realist curriculum and those without a state charter will be included under the term *academy*. It was a more flexible and variable institution than the English academy. It frequently admitted girls and sometimes was open to girls only. In the latter case the term *female seminary* often was used. The English academy was a boys' school and usually taught theology to ministerial students, whereas in America the academy frequently had no church connections. Many American academies prepared teachers for the common schools and indeed these institutions became the models for both the normal schools and the public high schools. The Americanism of the academy is suggested by its development during the movement for independence and its general acceptance during our first national period. The pre-Revolutionary period belonged to the Latin grammar school; and soon after the Civil War the high school became dominant; but during the intervening century from 1770 to 1870 our needs for secondary education were served mainly by the academy.

The chief defects of the academies as institutions in a democracy are that they were not free and were not controlled by a public board. Many tended to become expensive and exclusive boarding schools, but in the beginning they furnished educational opportunity to the boys and girls from the farms and villages. They were not free, but in the thousands of country academies the costs were low. To maintain themselves these schools had to teach what the public demanded at a cost it could afford. The curricula were broad and flexible and included many courses in mathematics, the sciences, English, and history. Logic, ethics, geography, and civics were offered. The great subject fields were divided into short courses. The English branches might include reading, elocution, grammar, composition, rhetoric, word study, declamation, debating, literature, and literary history. Mathematics and the sciences were similarly divided into short courses. As many as one hundred and fifty distinct courses were offered, although most of these were subdivisions of a few large fields. Like the "advertised schools" from which they stemmed, the academies taught many subjects that led to engineering or business employment; but the idea of a general liberal education was also present. Gradually, as the weaker academies were displaced by the public high school, those that survived tended to become college preparatory schools.

School equipment had not yet become extensive in the age of the academy. Libraries and laboratories were lacking in most cases, although there were usually little-used cabinets of minerals and apparatus. Most of the courses were taught from textbooks and the spread of the academy must have greatly encouraged the writers of the flood of schoolbooks that came from the press after 1800. Many of the academies were small, one- or two-teacher schools, and textbook recitation was the usual method, although field work and simple experiments were not entirely unknown. It should be remembered that the boys and girls of that rural age had more direct contact with nature and more knowledge of her ways than the city-bred youth of today; but, in itself, academy education was both bookish and discursive, even superficial.

Secondary schools were sometimes called academies early in the eighteenth century if not before. There was a South Carolina Academy in 1712;

and the "log college" of Pennsylvania, opened in 1726 by Reverend William Tennent, was not only sometimes given the name but had the characteristics of the English dissenting academies. As early as 1743, Franklin drew up a proposal for establishing an academy in Philadelphia. Six years later he returned to the project, secured the help of a number of active supporters, wrote a pamphlet entitled, "Proposals Relating to the Education of Youth in Pennsylvania," and started a subscription for funds. A board of trustees was agreed on, and in November, 1750 they ordered "that the Academy be opened on the seventh day of January next," and it was opened on that day. Although not incorporated until 1753, it may have been the first chartered academy in America. It was Franklin's intention to found a completely nonsectarian school and one in which modern subjects, especially English, history, and mathematics, were to have the chief places. He was to be disappointed in both objectives, as it was inevitable that he should be. Of the twenty-four trustees about two thirds were Episcopalians. And after the College of Philadelphia was established in 1755, an active clergyman of the same church, Reverend William Smith, became provost. Neither the original academy charter nor the new charter of *The Trustees of the College, Academy, and Charitable School of Philadelphia in the Province of Pennsylvania* mentioned the religious affiliations of the trustees or staff and the nonsectarian character of the school was, in the legal sense, preserved; but at any rate some very prominent Episcopalians felt that the school leaned to their side. The academy, like the old Penn Charter School, was divided into a classical and an English school and the chief teacher of the classical division became the administrative head of both classical and English schools with the title of Rector and a salary twice that of the English master. Perhaps these were the best terms that even the diplomatic Franklin could get from the board for his cherished English school; but it is not surprising that the Philadelphia Academy laid more stress on the classics than on the modern subjects, especially when we consider its close affiliation with the college. It was in the public high school that Franklin's educational ideal finally came to prevail. As the high school developed many academies were closed, others were turned over to the public school boards, and the rest became a minor but not unimportant agency in the whole field of American secondary education.

EDUCATION FOR A MORE PERFECT UNION

The Constitution was framed to strengthen the central government, to bind the states together, and to overcome sectional feeling. The preamble proposed, as the first aim, the development of a more perfect union. Other aims would, indeed, become possible only if this one were attained. Many of the framers of the Constitution believed, with Washington, that education would be an additional means of drawing the people together. There were, however, obstacles to closer union that neither the Constitution nor the school was able to reach. Such obstacles were the wide dispersion of the population, poor roads, difficult communication, and property qualifications for the suffrage. These tended to divide the people and, because they were hindrances to the development of schools, they tended to keep the people apart by hindering the formation of agencies that would have drawn them together. We shall illustrate some of these statements.

In about the year 1800, the entire population of Great Britain was fifteen millions, that of France almost twice that number, while the United States with its vast area had only five and one-third millions. Manhood suffrage existed in only four states, and the one million voters of the Republic were fewer in number than the slaves. Many felt that the new government gave them no more voice than the British had done. The center of population was northeast of the city of Washington; but there were already a half-million settlers in the Ohio valley, separated by a hundred miles of mountain and forest from the civilization of the East. Transportation, everywhere, was slow, costly, and laborious, and the West found it easier to reach her markets through New Orleans than by crossing the mountains. There was a good deal of sentiment and some intrigue, fostered by Spain and by Great Britain, for a separate nation in the Great Valley.

Communication was equally unsatisfactory. Franklin had organized an inter-colonial postal system in 1753, but in 1800 it still required twenty days to cover the one mail route from Maine to Georgia. Letter postage varied with the distance, and the cost of sending a letter from Boston to Philadelphia was twenty-five cents. As a result few letters were sent, in the year 1800 fewer than one per white inhabitant. The tri-weekly stage from Boston to New York took three days to reach its destination and the daily stage from New York to Philadelphia took two days. Stagecoach travel with hotel charges cost about twenty cents a mile. These were the conditions where roads existed; that is, in the neighborhood of towns and between the cities. In many settled parts of the country there were no roads. Jefferson wrote to his Attorney-General that five of the eight rivers that had to be crossed between Monticello and Washington had neither bridges nor boats.

The people and the government realized that improved communication and transportation were essential to the success of the union. They did not foresee the steamboat or the railroad, but they set about building the Cumberland Road from the Potomac to the Monongahela, another road south west toward Knoxville, and a third from Philadelphia to Pittsburgh. The era of the canals also was just beginning. Towns were still small in 1800. Philadelphia, the largest, with seventy thousand people and New York with sixty thousand people were about three times the size of Boston, Baltimore, or Charleston. Educational facilities in these and even in much smaller towns were far better than among the dispersed rural population. Rural education in Europe is village education, but the American farmer lives in an isolated home at some distance from all neighbors. This dispersion, greatest in the new West and the South—but a basic fact also in the East—was one of the most difficult educational problems. It is one that has not yet been solved, for the country school is still the weakest link in our educational system.

In the period of eighty years following the Revolution, the cities with a population of more than eight thousand increased in number from five to one hundred forty-one; and the percentage of the total population in cities of the size stated increased from three per cent in 1780 to sixteen per cent in 1860. After the war with England (1812–1815), American industry developed rapidly. Cotton spinning became a New England industry and Pennsylvania became the center of iron and steel production. The steel, in turn, made possible the construction of the railroads and manufacture of the newly invented farm machinery. In 1844, when the telegraph was invented, there were about eight thousand miles of railroad lines in operation.

With the increasing demand for labor, immigration rose to a flood. Most of the newcomers found homes and work in the cities of the North and on the prairies of the West. The children of the migratory workers who built the railroads, canals, and telegraph lines and those of the new immigrants who did not speak English made difficult educational problems. As in England, slums and various social maladies such as pauperism and juvenile delinquency marred life in the factory towns. To mitigate such evils and provide a little education for the children before they entered the factory, first monitorial and charity schools and then public schools were established.

More important in determining the future of the nation than the industry of the East was the westward migration of the people. Between 1800 and 1820 the population of the country increased by nearly two million, and the extending frontier presented a staggering educational problem. It was a problem not solved in one generation, for illiteracy in the United States as a whole increased rather than diminished in the middle decades of the century. Frontier life was without luxuries and was scanty in comforts. The frontiersmen were or became self-reliant and self-assertive individualists. The period of nationalism (1815–1825) was followed by the revival of sectionalism and the rise of the grass-roots democracy that characterized the party of Andrew Jackson. Before the Civil War, thirty-one states, six of them beyond the Mississippi, had been admitted into the Union. To a moderate degree at least, the educational needs of this empire were met through its increasing wealth and the resurgent democracy of its people.

Education became a matter of popular and public concern after the Revolution: popular as shown by a growing volume of writing on the subject; and public through the action of state and national legislatures. Even during the war Pennsylvania, Massachusetts, and other states introduced sections on public education into the new state constitutions adopted at the time. The old Congress of the Confederation also acted. The Ordinance of 1785 provided that "there shall be reserved the Lot No. 16 of every township for the maintenance of public schools within said township." Ohio became a state in 1803 and was first to benefit from this clause. One section for schools for each township became the rule as new states were admitted into the Union; but some of the later states were given two sections and the last few states, four sections for each township. In each state the people, through their legislatures, were the ultimate custodians of the school lands. In some states, especially the new ones, which profited by the mistakes of others, the lands were carefully managed and yielded large endowments for public education; but in many the lands were dissipated through inefficiency and dishonesty, both the results of a too-easy public morality. Even when this was not the case, land was plentiful and cheap in early times, and the financial returns were meager. Even after 1860, the standard price of public lands was only a dollar and a quarter per acre. Yet there was some return and some aid to schools; and one can argue that, if the lands helped to make a beginning in public education, an important service was rendered. Later generations could provide for the support of schools more easily than the early pioneers could establish them.

Another far-reaching act was passed by the old Congress. The Ordinance of 1787 for the organization of the Northwest Territory excluded slavery from the entire region north of the Ohio River. This ordinance also included what can be called a charter for public education in this large area from which five states were to be carved. The charter is in Article Three and is expressed in these words: "Religion, morality, and knowledge, being necessary to good government and the happiness of mankind, schools, and the means of education shall be encouraged." This is intended to mean, and it is so stated in the sentence that follows, that the Government shall encourage education, for the ordinance was a scheme of Government.

State governments also took action. Their aid to the academies has been mentioned. Their constitutions frequently included clauses on education. By an act of 1787, the legislature of New York set up a permanent Board of Regents to charter all secondary schools and colleges and to control the education, on these upper levels, of the entire state. This idea of the centralized control of education, especially of secondary and collegiate education, cropped up at about the same time and later in several of the states including Georgia, Louisiana, and Michigan. As noted in Chapter 12, the University of France was established by Bonaparte. In the United States, however, the nation was not yet ready to undertake an educational program. The only discussion of education at the Constitutional Convention concerned a proposed national university that was to promote national unity. The Constitution does not mention education, but its adoption profoundly, although indirectly, fostered educational progress.

THE LANCASTERIAN SCHOOLS

The actual next step did not tend to help the rural children directly. They had to wait another century until the modern elementary and high school, scientific agriculture, good roads, and the autobus were developed. The next step was an effort to aid city children by the introduction of the Lancasterian monitorial system. The main agencies of this movement were private; and for decades after 1800, progress continued to be made chiefly not through state action but through the labors of private persons or groups, incorporated societies, and churches. The Lancasterian schools were promoted by each of these; but one result of the movement was to further public education. In many cities the Lancasterian schools led directly to the establishment of public schools. Cincinnati, Louisville, and Detroit, in the far West of that time, and New Haven, Albany, and Baltimore, in the East, were only a few of the scores of cities that welcomed the Lancasterian monitorial schools. The system continued in use in many places until 1830 or later; and we must not, because it was finally discarded, suppose that it had no value.

In about 1805, New York outdistanced Philadelphia to become the largest city in the country. There the first Lancasterian school was opened in 1806 and there the monitorial system received its most extended trial. A small group of Friends and others formed a Free School Society, later called the Public School Society, and secured a charter for the purpose of providing schooling for children "who do not belong to, or are not provided for by any religious society." They developed and operated a number of monitorial schools; but although active for almost half a century the Society was never able to reach all the children, nor could any other system, without a compulsory attendance law, have reached all the children of a rapidly growing city. For a time the Society attempted to charge those who were able to pay a very moderate fee, but this proved to be a mistake. The attendance immediately declined because the poor refused to "confess their poverty." For a time, the Society received financial aid from both the state and the city, but this also led to difficulties. Various churches insisted on sharing the funds on the ground that the Lancasterian schools were also sectarian. They argued that if the state or city supported the schools of one sect it should also support the schools of every other sect. As a result, in 1842, New York City established a Board of Education and laid the foundation of a public school system. The Public School Society continued to operate monitorial schools until 1853, when it transferred its property to the city school district and ceased to exist.

Elsewhere the monitorial schools had disappeared twenty years earlier, but not before they had taught several useful lessons. They were, first of all, inexpensive. In New York City the per pupil cost was one dollar and twenty-two cents per year in 1822; but by reason of higher prices and greatly reduced classes the per capita cost rose to almost six dollars in 1852. The Lancasterian schools convinced many doubters that the cost of universal education would not need to be prohibitive, and they accustomed many parents to pay something at least for the education of their children. The schools were fully organized and prepared the way for grading and class management. Lancaster used sand tables, charts, slates, and slate pencils, even setting up a factory to make this and other equipment. He also familiarized teachers with the idea that schools should not depend exclusively on books. The *Manual of Instruction* he prepared was a teacher's handbook. Teachers in the system were usually given a short course of instruction and apprenticeship before being given charge of a school. The idea of professional training was fostered in this way. In Philadelphia, where the Lancasterian schools were received with as much enthusiasm as in New York, a city normal school grew out of the Lancasterian training classes. In Philadelphia, and in many other cities, free public schools resulted directly or indirectly from the Lancasterian movement. These were useful services to education, but the schools themselves, as compared with the best schools even of that time, were poor. The routine, the rigid organization and semimilitary discipline, the mechanical instruction, and a curriculum restricted to the formal elements of the different branches were all bad features. Yet the general influence of the monitorial schools was favorable to the extension of education; and both their introduction and their early disappearance after they had made their contribution were forward steps in the path of progress.

RISE OF STATE SYSTEMS

The Constitution guarantees a republican form of government to each state; it was not thought necessary to guarantee to each a democratic system of education. Although certain beginnings had been made early, it was in the second third of the nineteenth century that our system of democratic education began a vigorous growth. It was then that the states actively undertook to educate their children for democracy.

From early times the Colonies, and later the states, passed a large volume of laws dealing with education; but the administration and enforcement of this legislation were left to the courts and the ordinary officials. As public education grew the need came to be felt for a state agency to interpret school laws, to spread ideas and information, to supply professional leadership, and to exercise some supervisory and administrative functions. Such duties were assigned *ex officio* to an officer, usually the secretary of state, or to a newly chosen officer who was variously styled superintendent of free schools, or of common schools, or, in a few states, superintendent of public instruction.

Strong traditions impeded the development of the powers and prestige of the new office. The old historical tradition that the education of children should be directed first by their parents and then by the church was against public education and still more against state-administered education. But a second party, that of the frontier democracy, held that if education were not to be private then the local community should be allowed to manage it without state control. In several states the superintendency, after having been established at a politically favorable moment, was again abolished when its enemies had mustered their strength. The arguments against the office were sometimes opposed to each other and frequently contradicted the facts. The office was declared to be too expensive for a state that may have counted a half-million people, or too ineffective when the officer was given almost no powers, or Prussian in origin or tendency, although it was, with slight exceptions, American in both respects.

New York, which had long before placed a Board of Regents over secondary higher education, was in 1812 the first state to create the office of State Superintendent of Common Schools. The first and only appointee under this law was Gideon Hawley who, after an able and successful administration, was for political reasons removed from office in 1821. The secretary of state acted as superintendent until 1854 when a separate office of Superintendent of Public Instruction was again created. Fifty years later, in 1904, the administration of elementary and of secondary higher education was combined under one executive with the bulky but historically interesting title of President of the University of the State of New York and Commissioner of Education.

Maryland established the office of state superintendent in 1826, abolished it in 1828, and reestablished it in 1864. For Ohio the corresponding dates are 1837, 1840, and 1853. The history of the office in Connecticut, Rhode Island, Iowa, Missouri, and other states shows similar advances and retreats and finally permanent establishment. Elsewhere, as in Illinois in 1825, Louisiana in 1833, and in other states at other times, *ex officio* officers were provided before the state superintendency as a separate office developed. But Michigan in 1836, while it was still a territory, Massachusetts in 1837, and Kentucky in 1838 created state school superintendencies that have continued to function without a break. This list could be extended. Of the thirty-six states and organized territories existing in 1861, thirty had provided state school officers.

The movement was far broader than we have indicated. The decades before the Civil War were marked not by the revival but by the birth of public education as we know it today—a broad and generous extension of educational opportunity to all the children of all the people in a school system created by the people themselves. This was the ideal at least, and on this plan the states proceeded. We should honor our Colonial forefathers for their efforts to provide schools, but of such an educational ladder they had no conception. This is a program developed in the nineteenth century, not the seventeenth. The development of the state school office can be regarded as an index to the growing will of the American people to develop public education.

Public education is usually financed through local taxation, state appropriations, and Federal aid. Small amounts, less than ten per cent of the total in most states, are obtained from other sources such as income from permanent funds, fees, and donations. The process by which the public has educated itself to consider taxation and the appropriation of public funds as the fairest, most dependable, and most adaptable method of educational support can be regarded as an historical experiment that has now been carried on with varying success for more than a century.

A century ago there was no such agreement on the best methods of supporting schools. Most schools were private then and charged tuition or depended on contributions from the wealthy or from organized groups such as churches. Usually there were also numerous special charges, for firewood, for supplies, and for candles in evening schools. Books were provided by the pupils or their parents. Lotteries were a common source of support for schools and colleges and were frequently authorized by state legislatures. As we learn from sober history, and not only from school stories and poems such as *The Hoosier Schoolmaster, Ichabod Crane,* and Whittier's *Snow-Bound,* many teachers "boarded round" among the families of their district. Boarding the teacher was a form of school support, and it was not the only example of "payment in kind." An Ohio teacher in 1825 contracted to accept Indian corn at thirty cents a bushel; and a governor of Massachusetts paid the expenses of his son at Harvard College in the same commodity. Rents from lands or fish weirs, income from herds of cows, contributions, bequests, license fees collected from banks, theaters, liquor sales, and marriages, occupational taxes, the rate bill, and other items were among the sources of funds applied to schools before taxation was fully accepted. Clearly such financing did not assess the costs fairly and such sources were not dependable or readily adaptable to changing needs.

The monitorial schools rendered a service by demonstrating that a little education could be provided very inexpensively to large numbers. Another effort to support a general system of education was based on the Federal land grants. The initiation of these was contemporary with the introduction of the monitorial schools. It was soon discovered that the land grants were also inadequate, although this was already well known to those who were familiar with the history of rents and land endowments for schools from early Colonial times down to the period in question.

Those states that had come into the Union before Ohio did not share in the Federal land grants for schools, and many of them formed state school funds from other revenues. Connecticut, in 1795, sold her vast and rich "Western Reserve" of nearly four million acres for the trifling price of about thirty cents an acre and through this transaction added over a million dollars to a school fund that had been established almost fifty years earlier. As a result the state was for a time so wealthy that she could pay for the simple and meager schools of that time without taxation. The people, consequently, almost forgot the existence of their schools, neglect bred contempt, the "better people" patronized private schools, and it required the statesmanship of Henry Barnard to teach them their duty to provide good schools for all the children. Most of the permanent school funds in the older states were established in the first third of the nineteenth century. By themselves they were everywhere inadequate; and if, as in Connecticut, they were sufficient to pay for a short annual term of school, the unfortunate result was that the people went into an educational coma. One can perhaps declare it as a principle that when people regularly pay at least a substantial portion of the cost of a public service they will take a more active interest in its management.

The early idea was that schools and especially public schools should be cheap. When improvements were made, even poor schools whetted the appetite of the people for good schools and then for better schools, and their willingness to pay for improved education for their children grew with their experience. A very slight tax, often left to the option of the districts, was the entering wedge to a low mandatory tax and this to heavier and more adequate taxation. Cities, because of their concentrated wealth and population and the greater need for highly educated men, were more willing and better able to raise taxes than the rural districts. The example of the wealthier cities exerted a potent influence on their neighbors, and from this competition better support for all schools emerged. A special stimulus was also deliberately applied. The states offered aid to local areas on condition that these should levy a specified tax or on condition that the district should, out of its own funds, maintain the schools for a specified number of months in each year. Such aid then enabled the district to keep its schools open longer or to pay better salaries or otherwise to improve its educational program. By these means the principle was eventually established that property taxation was the most equitable, dependable, and sufficiently flexible method of supporting public education. This essential lesson was learned gradually and at different times in the several states, but it can be said to have been driven home well by about 1870. By that time the public schools not only were supported by local taxes and state appropriations but also had become generally free.

Important improvements in the application of the principle have been made. The standards that districts must meet before state aid is granted have been made more inclusive and the levels have been raised. The idea has been accepted that state aid should be used to assure a basic minimum of educational opportunity to every child and also to stimulate further improvement of the schools. Not the equalization of education but the greatest opportunity for all is the ideal. To assure to each the basic minimum of opportunity, the state may, after the district has met its obligations, guarantee a certain amount of money per child per year. The details of such *foundation programs* vary in different states. The contribution of the Federal Government, except for the early land grants, has generally been given in support of vocational and technical education.

Without the support of an enlightened and united public, the schools of the pioneers could not have become the instruments of democracy. And although this unity of the public was never completely attained, as sentiment became more favorable the schools were given increased funds; but they needed, more urgently even than money, systematic organization and scientific administration. These advantages were lacking in the district schools that prevailed in the Jacksonian era.

The district system was widely employed even in the cities until the middle decades of the century and much longer in sparsely settled regions. By definition it required an individual trustee or a separate board of trustees for each one-room school, and until about 1830 or 1840 almost all schools were one-room schools. To these district boards the broadest powers were allowed. They had the right and duty to levy the school tax; to fix the length of the term; to make all contracts for buildings, repairs, and equipment; to select textbooks; to determine the curriculum; to certificate and employ the teacher; and to settle on and pay his salary. But they did not always carry out all these functions. The standards of school administration were so low that many of the powers committed to the district boards were neglected through default. And when they were exercised, practice varied from district to neighboring district because each board was an independent agency. One school might, therefore, have a three- and another a six-month term, and similar variations were to be found in salaries, books, and other elements of the school program.

Because the district schools were small and the pupils were frequently not classified the teaching was carried out by individual recitation. It is true that the graded-class system was coming in here and there before 1840, and skilful teachers in larger schools had been using it for some time, but it was not in vogue where most of the people lived—that is, in the country and small towns. Not only were the schools generally small, but the attendance was very irregular also. Starting in the fall with a few pupils, a school might swell to fifty or more during one or two winter months after the corn had been husked and the hunting season had ended. A single teacher was expected to care for the entire number; and against truancy or simple absence he was helpless. Under such conditions individual teaching, or rather individual reciting, was practically unavoidable.

School discipline was authoritarian, sometimes capricious and often harsh, even according to the standards of that time. The punishments, which included a sentence to occupy the dunce block and other forms of school disgrace and corporal punishment in several forms and all degrees, reached a maximum in expulsion from school. The pupils retaliated by insubordination and by breaking up the school. Edward Eggleston's *The Hoosier Schoolmaster* is not the product of a novelist's imagination alone but was based on actual conditions. In New England it was found advisable to have cases of flagrant disobedience and violence in schools reported in open town meeting, naming names and giving the facts. There are few boys, said Horace Mann, who will not recoil from such a public report. Repeated and gross infractions of schools discipline were to be finally entered into the public record that the pupil's ignominy might be transmitted to future ages. It was a great satisfaction to Horace Mann to be able to report in 1842 that the number of schools broken up by the insubordination of the pupils was not more than one tenth of what it had been for the preceding year; but the record for that preceding year seems to have disappeared. A century ago the district schools were frequently disorderly, badly organized, and educationally ineffective. One should not be surprised to learn that the "better people" refused to send their children to such schools and, therefore, took little interest in their improvement.

The teachers themselves knew no better way. There were no normal schools, teachers' institutes, or summer schools for professional education. Even the necessary academic education for teaching could not be obtained in public schools but had to be secured in academies or colleges. More than one half of the teachers of Massachusetts, and probably a larger proportion in other states, were allowed to teach without any examination whatever, and of course without a certificate. Teachers' wages, too, were low, beginning about on a par with the wages of farm laborers. Accurate statistics are not available, but in about 1830, men teachers who "boarded 'round" with their patrons received about fifteen dollars per month, and women received from one third to one half of that amount. Farm hands were earning ten to fifteen dollars with board, lodging, and other services such as washing and mending, although in the haymaking and harvest season the wages of day laborers were higher. Mill hands earned rather more than teachers or farm laborers but not as much as skilled artisans. Henry Barnard in 1842 reported that men teachers in Connecticut received seventeen dollars per month. The wages of the same class in Michigan were slightly below that, and in Pennsylvania and New York they were slightly above the Connecticut level. However, men teachers in Massachusetts were in 1842 receiving rather more than twenty-five dollars per month. This latter group of figures represents cash wages. In addition, teachers often received board and room by "boarding 'round."

Another great and almost universal evil of the common schools was the variety of the schoolbooks that the children brought into the schools. The diversity of textbooks was itself reason enough for the individual methods and the absence of grading. Simply because such action was likely to give offense, school boards did not perform the function of prescribing the books. *The North American Review*, in 1841, proposed to solve the difficulty without demanding uniformity by persuading the publishers of approved books to furnish them at reduced prices. The same writer remarked on the very general absence of apparatus, blackboards, maps, globes, and the means to illustrate the common weights and measures. The schoolhouses, as will be explained in a later section, were often quite unfit to shelter the children.

The natural result of the poor condition of the public district schools followed: namely, the establishment of numerous private schools that gave instruction in the same branches that the public schools taught or were expected to teach. To these private schools, the minister, the doctor, the lawyer, and others who could afford it sent their children; and in this way they reduced still further the prestige and standards of the common school. Horace Mann estimated that, in 1840 in his state, thirty thousand pupils making one sixth of all the children between the ages of four and sixteen were attending private elementary schools; and he figured that the cost of teaching those thirty thousand children in private schools was six to eight times what it would have been if all had together attended the common schools. He showed from enrollment figures that by reason of this division of the children and the funds both the private and the public schools were too small for economy, and also too small to provide the socializing advantages of a good school.

All of this was no doubt true and discouraging, but there is another side. Some of the private schools and their teachers served as models and provided leadership for the common schools. Such men as Ebenezer Bailey, George B. Emerson, and G. F. Thayer were far in advance of the district schools and provided excellent examples for imitation; and we know that they were imitated. The proverb about the ill wind applies here, yet it remains true that the private schools were both effect and cause of the unsatisfactory condition of the public district schools. The obvious solution was to improve the public schools, to raise them to such a level that private schools could no longer compete with them; and because the resources of the whole public must always be greater than those of a few, this would seem to be a general solution, applicable in a democracy at all times.

It was in these circumstances that Horace Mann became Secretary of the Massachusetts Board of Education in 1837; and the greater part of his notable achievement was the overcoming of the defects of the district system. But to gain the true perspective of his work and of the entire period, it is necessary to see that the improvement was not the result of individual effort alone, whether that of Mann or Barnard or another, but to the increasing density of the population, the commercial and Industrial Revolutions, and the growing wealth and the rising standard of living of the American people. It is important to see, secondly, that the reform of the schools had already begun years earlier and was spreading, in 1837, from widely separated centers of influence, such as New York, Pennsylvania, Ohio, Indiana, and Michigan.

Horace Mann carried forward a program that had already made great progress in Massachusetts under the leadership of James G. Carter and many others. The law of 1827 had been in operation for a decade before Mann took any interest in public education. Gideon Hawley had for a quarter of a century served public education in New York, first as Superintendent of common schools and then as Secretary of the Board of Regents. State school officers were being chosen in the East and the West as we have already noted, the governors in their messages were urging legislatures to attend to public education, and teachers and citizens were beginning to organize in the interest of this cause. Education had a long road ahead but it was making progress. If we keep this background in mind we shall be able to understand better the development of the common schools for democracy and the work of Horace Mann.

Mann began to attack along the entire front. His first task was that of informing and educating not only the teachers but the people. Most of the citizens had themselves been educated in district schools alone and knew of no better system of education. Mann traveled from county to county holding educational conventions in the more important towns. He spoke often and secured the aid of other speakers, including John Quincy Adams, Daniel Webster, and Edward Everett, to arouse interest in school improvement. After his return to Boston, having covered the state for the first time, he wrote in his journal that, in spite of weariness and some irritation caused by a few "miserable, contemptible, deplorable" meetings, the tour had been successful. He had on the whole met with unexpected and extraordinary encouragement. This, he wrote, shall be only a beginning. "I confess life begins to have a value which I have not felt for five years," he declared. He also knew the value of printer's ink. He established the *Common School Journal*, writing much of its contents with his own hand, and he prepared twelve annual *Reports* in which he took up the defects of the schools and proposed remedies.

During his term (1837–1848) great changes occurred in the schools of Massachusetts and the country. In some of these he played an important part. He was a reformer and a prophet, but like some other prophets he was without much aesthetic feeling or a saving sense of humor. He had great faith in the common man and a very practical understanding of the value of useful knowledge in such fields as physiology, bookkeeping, drawing, surveying, and applied sciences. For science beyond its more immediate uses, for history, even the history of his own country, for ideas as ideas, he had little use in his educational scheme. He was a man of action, a propagandist, and a publicist; but in judging his achievement one must consider not only his own gifts and defects but also the difficulties of his

Horace Mann (1796–1859)

office. For years he was hardly ever free from attack and had to fight to maintain his position. A more sensitive and less devoted man would have retired from the storm. Mann fought on for twelve years and by that time the amount of money appropriated for schools by the state was double that of 1837, the average school term was longer by a month, teachers' salaries had risen fifty per cent, four normal schools and fifty high schools had been opened—the latter without direct help from Horace Mann—and the private schools were improving in equipment, curriculum, and teaching. Pestalozzian ideas and a growing faith in American institutions and in our national destiny had begun to build schools for democracy.

The Pestalozzian influence was brought in through official reports, accounts by travelers, and the personal contributions of European teachers such as Agassiz and Guyot. To American teachers, Pestalozzi represented two principles: The first was that the child should be governed by love and not fear—that whoever was unable to gain the affections of a child was unfit to teach. The second principle was that lessons should as far as possible be concrete and objective in order to lead the child to understand what he was asked to learn.

The *Common School Journal* as early as 1840 published a series of model object lessons. It also proposed the "elliptical" method, which had a curious history. According to this Pestalozzian elliptical manner of teaching, the pupils had to supply words that were omitted from the sentence that was given them. Thus the teacher, referring to an object before the class, might expect the child to supply the italicized word in, "Glass is *brittle*," or "Water is a *liquid*." A further step was taken when language books incorporated composition exercises that required the pupils to complete the sense by providing the sense by providing the missing words. Then Ebbinghaus, in 1897, and other psychologists who followed his lead, devised completion tests using the same idea. Unfortunately several words often could be used to complete a given sentence, for glass is not only brittle, but also transparent, useful, hard, and so forth. But by controlling the recognized completions as in the item, "Northern flowers that bloom in the spring include (1) asters (2) tulips (3) goldenrod (4) chrysanthemums," an objective test could be constructed. Thus a device used by Pestalozzi contributed, after a century of development, to a purpose that was much in his mind and that he called psychologizing education, or, as we should say, making education scientific.

Along with object lessons, the Pestalozzians, as we have just noted, stressed composition through both oral and written language lessons and with reduced attention to formal grammar. The attack on formal grammar was not at once successful, and indeed the schools of the early nineteenth century were a grammarian's paradise. Webster, Lindley Murray, and Kirkham wrote several of the most popular school grammars used at that time. The Pestalozzians also favored oral teaching and an expanded common school curriculum including local geography, nature lessons, drawing and modeling, mental arithmetic, and music. Mental arithmetic was so called because the problems were to be solved without the use of a pencil and the pupil was asked to explain the reasoning he followed in the solution. Warren Colburn's *First Lessons in Arithmetic on the Plan of Pestalozzi* (1821) went through numerous editions. Mental arithmetic became a fad that lasted in some parts of the country until 1890 or later. Perhaps it is unfortunate that it has died out. It seems reasonable that all arithmetic teaching, whether with a pencil or "in the head," should be "mental." Pestalozzi's demands for the systematic teaching of music and a direct approach to music through singing were accepted by those who introduced the subject into the common schools.

How far Pestalozzian ideas penetrated the American educational frontier, and what their permanent influence was, it is difficult to say. The normal schools were few and the institutes, which by 1850 reached a great many teachers, were in session for very short periods. Besides, they were likely to be of the "Do as I say and not as I do" variety. Through magazines, teachers' meetings, and all the intangible ways by which ideas spread, and especially through textbooks, Pestalozzianism was diffused. Horace Mann judged that Pestalozzi's "influence has been felt where his name even has not been heard."

Professional supervision of education had begun to develop before the Civil War, the grading of schools was under way, and our school system with, in many cases, an eight-year elementary school leading to a four-year free public high school was beginning to take form. Among the notable city superintendents of schools in the nineteenth century were William T. Harris (1835–1908) of St. Louis and William N. Maxwell (1852–1920) of Brooklyn and Greater New York. At first the schools were loosely graded, often into four levels of three years each. These levels were sometimes called the primary, secondary or intermediate, grammar, and high school grades. Many of the early high schools were three-year schools. The elementary school years also varied, being at a time six in Newark, New Jersey, seven in Rochester, nine in Oswego, and ten in Louisville. In the South and in Kansas City the elementary school was usually a seven-year school, and in Maine it was a nine-year school. The most frequent number was eight.

Closer grading began to develop and the result in the cities was the familiar year-by-year grading. On this plan each elementary teacher was put in charge of a room in which all the children were doing the same work and aiming to complete a specified year's course in each school year. In a later chapter we shall see how this iron-clad system of grading, which was called the "greatest invention in education in several centuries," came into conflict with the new ideas of the twentieth century.

SUMMARY

The plantation system of Virginia and the South was much less favorable to school development than the compact settlement, skilled industry, and town government of New England. Both of these sections were settled by Englishmen; but the middle Colonies had a mixed population of many languages and faiths. As a result of these differences, three types of school administration were developed: The South depended largely on private education; New England on a simple form of semipublic schools under the legal and extralegal control of both church and town; and the middle Colonies largely on parochial and neighborhood activity. The South, therefore, followed the ancient classical custom, the middle Colonies the medieval practice, and New England adopted the rising idea of state action. Examples of all these types of school administration existed in Europe and, in fact, in the British Isles. Religious toleration and freedom and political democracy, as they slowly developed, gave increasing support to the growing public school idea.

Some of the schools themselves, like the administration, were transplanted. There were four main types of schools and educational effort: namely, apprenticeship, the elementary school of the four R's, the secondary and collegiate scheme that was carried on by the Latin schools and colleges together, and practical schooling to prepare youth for simple engineering and business occupations. A noteworthy achievement of the period was the development of the American academy. Each of the main types of institutions was found in all sections.

In retrospect, the Colonies are seen to present almost every variety of educational system and institution, each competing for social acceptance and survival: parochial, sectarian missionary, private, neighborhood, town, district, and still other elementary schools; medieval, humanist, and realist secondary schools; schools and apprenticeship for vocational preparation; and Old World colleges in the towns. To maintain all these educational endeavors, various kinds of administrative devices, numerous forms of financial support, and several ways of securing public attention and interest were employed. It was as though some educational Francis Bacon had set up a giant experiment to determine which types of schools and school management could best survive and prosper in a wilderness developing into the United States of America. One of the most conclusive phases of this experiment is that having to do with modes of support. However, although much has been learned from this and the other phases of the whole great adventure, it is important to notice that the "experiment" has not ended. It is still in process and the evaluation is continuing.

In the Colonial period, then, the foundations were laid for our public schools systems, for our numerous types of private schools, and for the public policy that permits private education to continue and to compete with public education.

With the formation of the new nation, education to overcome sectionalism and to promote citizenship became important. Educational needs became greater also from the rise of industry, the growth of cities, the westward movement, and the increasing immigration. Even before the adoption of the Constitution, land was granted for the support of elementary schools; and the encouragement of schools by the Government was demanded by the Northwest Ordinance. The states gave their adherence to the theory of public education but delayed effective action. A favorable public opinion was developing, however.

Instead of the French system, we introduced the English monitorial plan. All the cities along the coast and inland as far as Cincinnati welcomed the Lancasterian schools because they were inexpensive. These schools also taught us something about grading subject matter, classifying children, equipping classrooms, and preparing teachers. Although the education they provided was somewhat meager, they helped to convince the people that universal schooling was feasible. Educationally, as in other fields, the time preceding the Civil War was a creative era.

The most important educational achievement, however, and the most notable reform of that reforming age, was the free public school system in the northern and western states. There was a great wave of propaganda in favor of more schools and better schools. Teachers' magazines and teachers' associations, citizens' promotion societies, the Workingmen's Party, legislative lobbies, and the favorable section of the press urged the creation of the state school office and the passage of laws for the establishment, support, and administration of public schools. New York led the vanguard, to be followed later by Michigan, Ohio, Massachusetts, and other states. Even with state action, the most serious defects of the private schools were only gradually overcome. But in the more progressive sections of the most advanced states, and especially in the cities, there were better curricula, some use of the Pestalozzian methods, higher salaries, longer terms, and better textbooks in 1860 than in the preceding decades. Education was beginning to aid in forming a more perfect union.

QUESTIONS

1. Educational differences between Colonial New England and the South are supposed to have been the result of different physical, economic, political, and religious influences in the two sections. What effects can be assigned to each kind of influence?
2. Civil control of schools, support by public taxation, and nonsectarian (or, perhaps, secular) teaching can be considered as cornerstones of public education. How much progress toward achieving each of these was made in Colonial days? What would you choose for the fourth cornerstone? Would it be compulsory attendance, or some other feature. Why?
3. Using Wickersham's *History of Education in Pennsylvania*, consider the statement that William Penn was a Realist.
4. Why was it easier for New England than for other parts of the country to approximate public education?
5. Why did the district system develop and why was it found unsatisfactory? What is a district school?
6. Why must the academy in late Colonial and early national times be considered an important development?
7. Using Woody's *Educational Views of Benjamin Franklin*, show why the Academy of Philadelphia did not accomplish what its chief promoter intended.
8. What are the conditions that aid, and the others that hinder, educational borrowing by one country or culture from another? Consider the chief examples mentioned in this book.

9. Why, in your opinion, is there no direct reference to education in the Constitution?
10. What educational provisions are found in the constitution of your state?
11. Does "demand" tend to call out "supply" in education, as it does in economic matters; or, more specifically, did the growing need for education in the period 1780 to 1860 tend to promote more and better schools? Illustrate.
12. If you have access to early teachers' journals, study the issues of two or three consecutive years between 1820 and 1840. What topics and problems are most frequently treated? Have these been solved or are we still debating them?
13. Why was Pestalozzianism probably less evident in America at this time than in Prussia? Read Horace Mann's *Seventh Report* (1843) on this question.
14. Had education by 1860 succeeded in binding the people together to any great degree? Had it succeeded in doing so in the North?

NOTES AND SOURCES

About ten per cent of the fourteen thousand sketches in the *Dictionary of American Biography*, New York, Charles Scribner's Sons, 1928–1936, deal with educators, teachers, scholars, and others whose lives form a part of the history of education. The work, in twenty-one volumes and an index volume, was cited by Allen Johnson and Dumas Malone. Volume 21 (1944) is a supplementary volume edited by Harris E. Starr. The *Dictionary* will be useful for all periods of American education, as will Monroe's *Cyclopedia*, which has been mentioned before. The Circulars of Information issued by the United States Bureau of Education between 1887 and 1903 as "Contributions to American Educational History" cover all of the thirteen Colonies but give the chief emphasis to higher education. A list of the *Circulars of Information* is found (pp. 253–254) in Donald W. Tewksbury, *The Founding of American Colleges and Universities Before the Civil War*, New York, Bureau of Publications, Teachers College, Columbia University, 1932, 254 pp. The Colonial colleges are, of course, treated in this latter work and there is an extensive bibliography. An illustrated list of arithmetic texts and other mathematical books published or reprinted in the American Colonies is found in Louis Charles Karpinski, *Bibliography of Mathematical Works Printed in America Through 1850*, Ann Arbor, University of Michigan Press, 1940, 697 pp.

Educational journals began to appear in the period covered by this chapter. They contain a great deal of firsthand information on conditions, ideas, movements, and textbooks. The most important early ones are William Russell's *American Journal of Education* (1826); W. C. Woodbridge's *American Annals of Education* (1831); Henry Barnard's *Connecticut Common School Journal* (1838); and Horace Mann's *Common School Journal* (1839). Volume 19 of Barnard's *American Journal of Education* contains a study of curricula, especially those of the early high schools (pp. 463, 465–576), and of illiteracy between 1840 and 1860 (pp. 802–835).

ADAMS, JAMES TRUSLOW, *Provincial Society, 1690–1763*, New York, The Macmillan Company, 1927, 374 pp. In the "A History of American Life" series.

BRIDENBAUGH, CARL, *Cities in the Wildnerness, The First Century of Urban Life in America, 1625–1742*, New York, The Ronald Press Company, 1938, 500 pp.

CLEWS, ELSIE, *Educational Legislation and Administration of the Colonial Governments*, New York, 1899, 526 pp. A Columbia University dissertation, also published in "Columbia University Contributions to Philosophy, Psychology, and Education," Vol. 6, Nos. 1–4.

EARLE, ALICE MORSE, *Child Life in Colonial Days*, New York, The Macmillan Company, 1899, 418 pp. Mrs. Earle has written many other popular books that would furnish useful background. Among them are *Costume in Colonial Times, Curious Punishments of By-gone Days, Home Life in Colonial Days, and others*.

EGGLESTON, EDWARD, *The Transit of Civilization from England to America in the Seventeenth Century*, New York, D. Appleton & Company, 1901, 344 pp.; *The Hoosier Schoolboy, The Circuit Rider, Roxy, The Hoosier Schoolmaster* and other novels.

FITHIAN, PHILIP VICKERS, *Journal and Letters of Philip Vickers Fithian, 1773–1774: A Plantation Tutor of the Old Dominion*. Edited by Hunter Dickinson Farish, Williamsburg, Va., Colonial Williamsburg, Incorporated, 1943, 323 pp.

FORD, PAUL LEICESTER, *The New England Primer*, New York, Dodd Mead & Company, Inc., 1899, 78 pp.

GRISCOM, JOHN, *A Year in Europe*, New York, William Collins Sons and Company, Ltd., 1823, 2 vols. Contains an early American account of Pestalozzi and other European men and movements that were influential in this period.

HANSEN, ALLEN OSCAR, *Liberalism and American Education in the Eighteenth Century*, New York, The Macmillan Company, 1926, 317 pp.

HINSDALE, BURKE A., *Horace Mann and the Common School Revival in the United States*, New York, Charles Scribner's Sons, 1900, 326 pp.

JENKINS, RALPH C., and GERTRUDE C. WARNER, *Henry Barnard, An Introduction*, Hartford, The Connecticut State Teachers Association, 1937, 118 pp.

JOHNSON, CLIFTON, *The Country School in New England*, New York, D. Appleton & Company, 1893, 102 pp.; *Old-Time Schools and School Books*, New York, The Macmillan Company, 1904, 381 pp.

KRAUS, MICHAEL, *Intercolonial Aspects of American Culture on the Eve of the Revolution, with Special Reference to the Northern Towns*, New York, Columbia University Press, 1928, 251 pp.

LANCASTER, JOSEPH, *Improvements in Education*, London, Darton and Harvey, 1805, 211 pp. Editions are several and various.

MANN, MARY, *Life and Works of Horace Mann*, Boston, Walker, Fuller and Company, 1867, 5 vols. Republished, Boston, Lee and Shepard, 1891, 5 vols. Volume I is a life of Horace Mann by his wife and the other volumes contain his writings and official reports.

MULHERN, JAMES, *A History of Secondary Education in Pennsylvania*, Philadelphia, published by the author, 1933, 714 pp. This detailed study covers the Colonial and later periods.

REIGART, JOHN FRANKLIN, *The Lancasterian System of Instruction in the*

Schools of New York City, New York, Teachers College, Columbia University, 1916, 105 pp., Teachers College Contributions to Education, No. 81.

SEYBOLT, ROBERT FRANCIS, *Apprenticeship and Apprenticeship Education in Colonial New England and New York*, New York, Bureau of Publications, Teachers College, Columbia University, 1916, 121 pp., Teachers College Contributions to Education, No. 85; *Source Studies in American Colonial Education: The Private School*, Urbana, University of Illinois, Bureau of Educational Research, 1925, 96 pp.; *The Evening School in Colonial America*, Urbana, University of Illinois, Bureau of Educational Research, 1925, 68 pp.

STEINER, BERNARD C., *Life of Henry Barnard, The First United States Commissioner of Education, 1867–1870.* U.S. Bureau of Education, Bulletin No. 8, 1919, Washington, D.C., Government Printing Office, 1919, 131 pp.

THWING, CHARLES FRANKLIN, *A History of Higher Education in America*, New York, D. Appleton & Company, 1906, 501 pp. The first six chapters deal with the Colonial colleges.

WARFEL, HARRY REDCAY, *Noah Webster, Schoolmaster to America*, New York, The Macmillan Company, 1936, 460 pp.

WOODY, THOMAS, *Early Quaker Education in Pennsylvania*, New York, Bureau of Publications, Teachers College, Columbia University, 1920, 287 pp., Teachers College Contributions to Education, No. 105; *Quaker Education in the Colony and State of New Jersey; A Source Book*, Philadelphia, published by the author, University of Pennsylvania, 1923, 408 pp.; *A History of Women's Education in the United States*, Lancaster, Pa., The Science Press, 1929, 2 vols.; Editor, *The Educational Views of Benjamin Franklin*, New York, McGraw-Hill Book Company, Inc., 1931, 270 pp.

WRIGHT, ARTHUR D., and G. E. GARDNER, Editors, *Hall's Lectures on School-Keeping*, Hanover, N. H., The Dartmouth Press, 1929, 192 pp.

Chapter 19

THE AMERICAN NATIONAL SYSTEM

By the close of the Civil War most of the northern states had developed the outlines of their systems of public schools. Progress in that section had not been easy or uniform, but those states generally were committed to the program of developing a state-wide common school. The South had made similar but more tentative beginnings; and there a period not of reconstruction but of primary organization and educational construction paralleled and followed the political and economic phases of the Reconstruction era. Beginning not much before 1873, the state school office, the school tax, and laws for the organization of common schools were generally introduced in the South. That section also demanded a dual system, one set of schools for the white and another for the Negro children, and this made the problems of finance and organization extremely difficult.

In the North the period from 1865 to 1900 was marked by the rapid development of common schools, high schools, and normal schools; the grading of the schools, the expansion of their curricula, and the passage of compulsory attendance laws; and a great increase in expenditures for buildings and equipment. The foundations for this expansion, which formed the subject of the preceding chapter, were laid in the three or four decades that came before the outbreak of sectional strife. The kindergarten was introduced into the public system after 1873, and at the other end of the ladder, the state universities, then for the first time aided by regular appropriations, and the new land-grant colleges established through the Morrill Act, completed the system. The junior high school and the junior college developed later, but they are only links inserted into the chain. The American national system consists of the state systems each of which, when fully formed, comprises the kindergarten, the elementary school, the high school, the teacher-education school, and the state university and land-grant college; and it offers the pupils the opportunity, at public expense, for a complete education beginning in the preschool years and continuing until a graduate or professional degree is attained.

THE CIVIL WAR AND ITS AFTERMATH

We do not have the space to describe the effects of the war and its terrible consequences. Time was needed to heal its wounds, to revive the spirit of the people, and to lay the foundations for future progress. Four years of conflict had ruined industry and agriculture and demoralized the labor system. The political evils of the congressional plan of reconstruction increased the sectional hatred aroused by war; and the fear of Negro control, the burning issue of mixed schools, and outright opposition to Negro education even in separate schools tended to paralyze the agencies that might have developed public education.

The agencies that first attempted to provide education for the South were private and church associations; and they wrote a chapter that we are likely to forget but ought to remember. Even before the end of the war, northern teachers in large numbers went into the occupied sections and established schools for Negroes or for both races. Others followed after the war until many towns had schools for the freedmen. There were nine thousand teachers in these schools by 1869, and more than half of them were from the North, sent and supported by freedmen's aid societies and educational associations. Two of the latter were the American Freedmen's Union, composed of Unitarians and other religious liberals, and the American Missionary Association, which had been founded by the Methodist and other orthodox churches. The two bodies did not cooperate with each other because the former insisted on secular and the latter on religious schooling. The Freedmen's Bureau, which was created by Congress in 1864, was a public agency to provide medical and hospital services, to supervise labor contracts, and to establish schools in cooperation with the private associations. The head of the Bureau, General O. O. Howard, believed that education was the most urgent need of the freedmen.

The emotional force that abolitionism had generated furnished a part of the motive power for the education of the Negroes. They would not really be free, it was held, until they had been equipped to take their places as full citizens of the Republic; but there were also partisan, economic and, as we have seen, religious motives. Many of the teachers came from the centers of abolitionism and former stations of the Underground Railroad. Others who had strong political interests attempted to lead their pupils safely into the fold of the Republican party. And much of the support came from northern industrialists who hoped to develop markets for their products by educating the freedmen.

The quality of the schools varied, but very poor schools seem to have been the most numerous. The buildings and equipment were inadequate. At first the pupils were eager and not only children but older men and women attended. The attainment of an education proved to be a long and tedious process, however, and in a few years the enthusiasm declined. The southern whites were at first helpless against the new invasion, but they soon became violently hostile to the "Yankee schools." They refused to board the teachers or to rent them buildings for schools and frequently they engaged in real persecution. The attempt to establish mixed schools for the two races, as the American Freedmen's Union tried to do, especially provoked southern ire. By 1870, the northern teachers had begun to withdraw, and by 1873 radical reconstruction had lost the day. There are those who see in the work of the northern teachers and politicians the origin of the public school system of the South, but this contention cannot be supported by sound evidence.

The Presidential plan of reconstruction from 1865 to 1867 attempted to enlist the cooperation of the white citizens of the South; but under the Congressional plan from 1867 to 1876, the freedmen and northern carpetbaggers controlled the attempted reconstruction. Under Presidential reconstruction at least five states had made efforts to reestablish schools; but these attempts were nullified by the radical members of Congress who in 1867 passed the Reconstruction Act over President Andrew Johnson's veto. This act formed the southern states into military provinces under martial law. As the state governments were reconstructed, educational clauses were included in the state constitutions, boards of education and state and local supervision were provided, and state appropriations and the property tax for schools were authorized. Much of the legislation was taken from the laws that existed in the same states before the war, although it was made more mandatory and more detailed. By 1870, public school systems had again been created in outline, but the financial difficulties and the hostility of many of the people prevented the effectual administration of the laws.

The extent to which some northern elements were willing to go in order to force educational reconstruction on the South was shown by the attempt to institute a Federal system of education in those states. Representative Hoar, in introducing a bill with this purpose, dwelt on the failure of the South to provide free public education before the war. The Hoar Bill (1870) was written to apply to all of the states of the Union, but its terms would actually have applied to the Southern states only. The bill provided that the President should appoint a state superintendent of national schools for any state that did not provide an approved system of schools for all children between the ages of six and eighteen; and that the Secretary of the Interior should appoint division and local superintendents of national schools for each such state. All textbooks were to be prescribed by the state superintendent and the United States Commissioner of Education. Local, division, and state superintendents were to report to the Federal Government. And the schools were to be supported by an annual direct tax to be collected by Federal agents. The bill failed to pass. Superintendent J. P. Wickersham of Pennsylvania, reviewing this bill in an address to the National Education Association in 1871, declared that the country could not endure half republic and half despotism any more than it could endure half slave and half free. The Association passed resolutions favoring national aid for schools with local autonomy in educational administration.

There was agitation for national aid for some years after the failure of the Hoar Bill, but without tangible result. It was proposed to create a national school fund from the sale of public lands and to divide the income among the states for the support of public schools. When this plan also failed, the Department of Superintendents formulated principles that were embodied in a bill introduced by Senator Blair in 1881. The Blair Bill provided for the distribution of seventy-seven million dollars to the states in proportion to the number of illiterates in each. This would have given large proportional amounts to the Southern states. The bill allowed each state almost complete freedom in the application of its share. The Senate of three successive Congresses passed the bill, but each time it failed in the House. For many years thereafter there was no revival of the proposal to secure Federal aid for general education.

Private funds were, however, devoted to this purpose in the South, and these were used to stimulate self-help in certain sections and cities. The first great donation was made by George Peabody, who provided two million dollars to be managed and applied by a board of trustees. The first general agent of the Peabody Fund was Barnes Sears, who had followed Horace Mann as Secretary of the Massachusetts State Board. He, therefore, came with large experience in educational promotion. He was succeeded after some years by an able southerner, J. L. M. Curry. The income of the Peabody Fund was used to cooperate with state authorities in aiding free public schools for either race, especially in communities where the people were already doing all that they could to help themselves. Because the annual income from the fund was only from ninety thousand to one hundred and thirty thousand dollars, it was deemed better to give considerable help to a few places to become models for neighboring towns or schools rather than give small amounts to a large number of places, in which case the effects would hardly be seen. The Peabody board also followed the policy of aiding normal schools for both white and Negro women teachers. The agents of the Board spent much of their time in developing sentiment for education, allaying antagonisms, visiting schools, and conferring with state departments of education. One of the schools for teachers that was aided was the Nashville Normal School, which with this help developed into the George Peabody College for Teachers, incorporated in 1909. A few years earlier (1898) the Conference for Education in the South had been organized, and the Southern Education Board developed out of this conference in 1902. The General Education Board (1903) and a number of other privately endowed boards cooperated with these agencies.

The conquest of illiteracy, the development of high schools, the improvement of living conditions and health, and the raising of the economic level through a more scientific agriculture were among the leading aims of the southern educational revival. One effort to reduce illiteracy in the country was begun in eastern Kentucky by Cora Wilson Stewart through her "moonlight schools," first established in 1911. Although greatly reduced since then, illiteracy has not been stamped out; the rate per thousand is still high in the rural parts of the South. The public high school also developed slowly in that section. Apparently no Southern state had as many as one hundred four-year rural or small-town high schools in 1910. This number has been increased many fold, the standards have been raised, and the curricula have been greatly enriched. Many consolidated schools have been developed and some states have numerous public junior colleges. But this does not mean that all sections are served by adequate schools. Indeed in the last half-century, educational progress in the South has not everywhere kept pace with that of the rest of the country.

INTEREST OF NATIONAL GOVERNMENT IN EDUCATION

In the decades following the Civil War, the national government took increasing interest in education. As a result of these efforts a more truly national system of education gradually evolved. Three of these early efforts will be treated here and more recent evidence of this interest will be discussed in Chapter 21.

The first of these early efforts resulted in the development of the land-grant or agricultural and technical colleges. These were created as the result of the Morrill Act, which was passed by Congress and signed by President Lincoln in 1862. We must distinguish between the state universities and the land-grant colleges, especially because in several states the land-grant colleges have been incorporated in the state universities. The state universities were formed to provide a liberal higher education and preparation for the old professions, especially those of law and medicine, under public, that is state, auspices. The land-grant colleges are also administered by the states, but they receive national support; and, as they have developed, they furnish a higher education in agriculture, engineering, and many of the newer professions and vocations. In those states in which the older and newer functions have been combined in one institution, the name *state university* has usually been adopted; but the second group of functions is subsidized by the national government under the provisions of the Morrill and supplementary laws. In such states the name *land-grant college*, or *agricultural and mechanical college*, or *state college* is not used. We shall briefly trace these developments.

Even the Colonial colleges, although they were private corporations, were frequently given public aid in money or land. Such an investment of public wealth was understood to impose a responsibility, but the nature and limits of the obligations were not clear. In the Revolution and intermittently for a period of forty years, several attempts were made by different states to secure control of private colleges and to transform them into state institutions. Such efforts were made in the cases of Yale, William and Mary, Pennsylvania, Columbia, and Dartmouth. At that time all maintained their private status. The last attempt occurred between 1815 and 1819 in New Hampshire and led to the celebrated Dartmouth College case before the Supreme Court of the United States. The decision (1819) reached far beyond the immediate issue to declare that a charter is a contract that a state legislature is not competent to annul. This decision gave legal protection to private property and business agreements in general; and, in particular, it guaranteed the endowments and chartered rights of private colleges. The New Hampshire State Legislature was compelled to return Dartmouth College with all its former rights and property to its old board, and the college has continued as a private institution. The decision may have stimulated the founding of private colleges by assuring their continued private status; and it has been asserted that it convinced the public authorities that they would have to establish their own state colleges and universities in order to complete the public school systems. This they proceeded to do.

They had already begun. Nine state colleges and universities had been established by the year of the Dartmouth decision: by Georgia in 1785, by North Carolina in 1789, by Virginia in 1819, and by other states. Twelve more state universities, making twenty-one in all, were founded before the Civil War. Most of them did not at once acquire the later characteristics of state universities. The early institutions were hardly of college grade, were not secular, and were not given regular support by the parent states. The University of Virginia (1825) and the University of Michigan (1837) became the leaders in developing university standards of scholarship and teaching. Eventually the state universities and the land-grant colleges became what the constitution of Indiana in 1816 had indicated that they should be: the top rung in our education ladder, or, in the language of that document, the highest stage in a "general system of education ascending in regular gradations from township schools to a State University wherein tuition shall be gratis, and equally open to all." These phrases well describe the ideal of the American state systems of education. It should, however, be noticed with great concern that state universities and land-grant colleges, by charging fees and often by piling one fee upon another, have come more and more to violate this early principle of gratuitous instruction. This is a policy that cannot be harmonized with the ideals of free public education.

We turn now from the early state universities to the land-grant colleges. The Morrill Act had a distinct purpose: to provide advanced education for working farmers and mechanics and other members of the "industrial classes." The older colleges and the state universities prepared students for the older professions; the land-grant colleges prepared them for scientific agriculture, engineering, homemaking, and the growing industry and commerce of the country. The act required each state that accepted its benefits to maintain "at least one college where the leading object shall be, without excluding other scientific and classical studies, and including military tactics, to teach such branches of learning as are related to agriculture and the mechanic arts . . . in order to promote the liberal and practical education of the industrial classes in the several pursuits and professions in life."

For this purpose the act made available to the states, in proportion to population, about ten million acres of public lands. As a result of the gift, almost every state established such a college. They developed slowly at first because they lacked the prestige of older types of institutions and because both the sciences and the teaching of agriculture, home economics, and engineering were not well developed at that time. Not until about the end of the century did they begin to grow rapidly both in size and effectiveness. Nine of them have developed into state universities, and the rest are usually designated as state colleges. However, many of these are also universities in fact. This latter development was natural because advanced technical and vocational education cannot be imparted except to those who have the necessary basic preparation in the arts, languages, mathematics, and sciences. Meanwhile, these institutions have exercised great influence on the high schools by preparing teachers, developing new sciences and materials, and enabling the schools to serve the common people's needs. We have fought against early vocational stratification by means of comprehensive high schools, state universities, and liberal land-grant colleges and by educating future lawyers, teachers, and physicians in the same schools and up to a point in the same classes. The Morrill Act in these and other ways has been a powerful democratizing force that has been felt throughout the American system.

In the Congressional debates on the Morrill Act, it was freely predicted by its opponents that the initial appropriation would be only the first of a series of "raids on the treasury." One may object to the words and to the philosophy underlying them, but this was a true forecast. Not only are the land-grant colleges receiving regular support from the national treasury, but a whole series of supplementary acts, all carrying further appropriation, have been passed. The agricultural experiment stations were created in 1887. A "Second Morrill Act" in 1890 provided fifteen thousand dollars a year for the maintenance of each of the original institutions and this amount has now risen considerably. An act was passed to provide seventeen separate land-grant colleges for Negroes in the southern states. Other national acts that may be considered to be supplementary to the original Morrill Act, because they are intended to carry out its purposes among those whom the colleges could not reach directly, are the Smith-Lever Act of 1914 for the extension teaching of agriculture and home economics, the Smith-Hughes Act of 1917 for vocational education in high schools, and the George-Deen Vocational Act of 1936. The Smith-Hughes and George-Deen Acts carry appropriations of twenty-one million dollars a year for agricultural, home economics, and vocational education in the states.

That this series of laws would raise many questions is evident. Three of these problems will be mentioned. When the Morrill Act was passed in 1862, it was widely believed that the new colleges could directly reach their objectives: the teaching of agriculture, home economics, the mechanic arts, and the related subjects by enrolling future farmers, homemakers, and industrial workers in their campus classes. This was a double error. It was soon discovered that the required teaching methods and means, and to a great degree the sciences themselves, were undeveloped and often were still to be created. Hence the need for experiment stations, experimental laboratories, shops, and research workers to discover and to organize the knowledge and techniques that were to be taught. In two or three decades considerable progress was made in solving this problem and scientific agriculture, home economics, and the several technologies were developing their present forms. In the second place the colleges did not reach the working farmers and mechanics in large numbers. Those who completed the college courses went into technical and government employment rather than to the farm or factory. Hence the need for simplification and the extension of the new practical knowledge to those who would directly apply it. Much of this was done through the publications of the United States Department of Agriculture; through the Smith-Lever, Smith-Hughes, and George-Deen Acts and the resulting high school and extension teaching; and through the county agents, the Four-H Clubs, and other organizations. The whole complex program is an instructive example of popular education and can be studied by educators in all fields with profit.

A third problem concerns national educational administration: If we are to develop a national system of education, what parts in the total scheme are to be played and what controls exercised by the local community, by the state, and by the nation? Only a part of this whole question has been raised by the legislation supplementary to the Morrill Act. The original act provided for national aid to the states for a specified purpose, the foundation of new colleges. But it did not supervise state plans to carry out the purpose. The Smith-Hughes Act for the first time introduced a measure of national supervision over the expenditure of national funds for education. That law provided that the money assigned to a state under the act must be matched by an equal amount of state funds; and it created a Federal Board for Vocational Education with the power and duty to examine the state programs of vocational education. A state may be required to modify its program to meet the judgment of the board before it is allowed to draw on the Federal funds. We have called this a measure of national supervision over vocational education. There is evidence that it has not worked to the satisfaction of all. The proper integration of national aid and supervision with state and community interests is a more inclusive problem to which the future may be required to find a satisfactory answer.

Federal aid for vocational and technical education is now a well-established policy. Every year Congress appropriates large sums for vocational education and for each land-grant college; and so far there has been little evidence of any undue Federal influence. But Federal aid for the improvement of general education in the elementary and secondary schools is a different matter. When it is proposed to use Federal funds to equalize educational opportunity among the states, the cry of states' rights is raised and the fear of possible Federal interference or control is expressed.

An example in World War II was Senate Bill 637, which was debated in 1943 but did not come to a vote. The bill would have appropriated annually two hundred million dollars to the states to meet educational emergencies caused by the depression and the war and an additional one hundred million for equalizing elementary and secondary school opportunities among and within the states. The bill was only one example of several in a series of similar bills that have been before Congress periodically since World War I. The need has long existed and was recognized more than a third of a century ago when the Smith-Towner Bill, the first of the series, was introduced. State inequality of educational opportunity arises from the fact that the states vary in wealth and in the number of children for whom they have to provide. Those states with the highest proportions of children of school age, many of them in the South, are also the states with the lowest per capita wealth.

Federal aid for general education in elementary and high schools would be a means to resolve the preceding paradox. This would be merely the application of a principle that many states have long applied to their poorer districts. Such grants would probably lead to a degree of Federal regulation. Such regulation should be carefully circumscribed, but if the national government is to furnish money for general education it should have the power and duty to require that the money will be used by the states for the intended purposes. In the past the state governments have amassed power over education; and it is a fair question whether reasonable regulation by Federal agencies is less necessary or desirable than state regulation. It is in the local community where citizens and parents can influence the school directly. Such educational democracy as we have—and we have a great deal more than the people of most nations—resides primarily in the local community. But some governmental regulation of public education there must be, and it should probably be distributed between the community, the state, and the nation. It should not be too difficult to devise a scheme of Federal and state cooperation that will give each unit its proper share in the direction of public education. In this matter the nation is moving slowly, but it is moving as we shall see in Chapter 21.

A third effort by the national government looking toward the development of a more truly national system of education was made by the creation of the Federal Office of Education. This movement also attained its early form shortly after the Civil War. The national government conducts some special schools of its own and renders important services to schools in the states. The Military Academy of West Point, conducted since the early years of the nineteenth century, the Naval Academy, founded in 1845, and the Air Academy, founded in 1953, are national schools. Many of the departments of the government, such as the Department of Agriculture, carry on extensive educational activities. The Smithsonian Institution and the Library of Congress are national agencies. The Federal Department of Education, later called the Bureau, and since 1933 the Office of Education, was established in 1867 to promote education by collecting and disseminating information. The first Commissioner was Henry Barnard, who had been active in securing the establishment of this agency. Further duties have from time to time been assigned to it. The Office of Education promotes vocational education and aids in the administration of the funds set aside by Congress for this purpose, conducts investigations including fundamental research studies, issues numerous periodical and occasional publications, and maintains in Washington a national library of education. Upon request the Office of Education conducts educational surveys of national, state, or local scope. An example is the National Survey of Secondary Education whose findings were published in about 1932 in a series of monographs. The Office issues many bulletins a year and publishes a monthly magazine. Its *Biennial Survey of Education* is a primary source on education in the United States for each two-year period, and its also prepares and publishes many studies of education in foreign countries.

FROM NORMAL SCHOOLS TO TEACHERS' COLLEGES

Public schools for the preparation of teachers are an essential part of the American system. A few public normal schools had been established before the Civil War, but the period of expansion began with the conclusion of that struggle. In earlier times, it was often considered that teachers were sufficiently prepared when they had completed the work of the school in which they were to serve. Of the principles of school administration, of educational psychology, and of the real functions of the profession they were entering, they knew almost nothing, and knowing little they were doubtless hardly aware of their professional ignorance. The special schools for teachers have improved these conditions, at least as they relate to elementary and secondary teachers.

Lacking special schools, other means had already been used in Europe to acquaint prospective teachers with their future duties. Handbooks and some forms of cadet teaching were used by the Jesuits, the Brothers of the Christian Schools, Joseph Lancaster, and others. The educational works of the great writers were not very suitable for this purpose because they were not practical handbooks but broad, theoretical treatments. With the rise of systems of public education, teachers were gradually expected to show competence in teaching as well as knowledge and moral character. Professional schools and the modern systems of universal education have developed together. The elementary normal schools of France, from which we apparently derived the name of the American schools for teachers, were first established during the Bourbon Restoration (1815–1830). A normal school is literally one that maintains or sets forth a norm or standard of teaching ability. The American normal school is a native institution, and this applies to the similar schools in other Western countries also. They were all similar in purpose, closely associated with the elementary schools, and formed of native materials. The one international influence that affected them was the influence of Pestalozzi. His methods and spirit, although variously interpreted, permeated them all.

The American normal school did not come without preparation. It was exactly fifty years from 1789 when the idea of such a school was first proposed by a writer, probably Elisha Ticknor, to the opening of the first state normal school at Lexington, Massachusetts, in 1839. During this half-century many plans and propaganda articles appeared. One of these by Thomas Hopkins Gallaudet in 1825 anticipated the most essential features of the schools that were established, including the idea of a practice and demonstration school. Travelers returning from Europe published their observations of such schools in books, magazines, and official documents.

There had also been more concrete anticipations. The academies had long been preparing teachers in the knowledge of the common and more advanced branches and a few had begun to give some attention to the principles and practice of teaching. The well-known schools for girls established at Troy, New York, by Emma Willard and at Hartford, Connecticut, by Catherine Beecher prepared many women for teaching, but they did not give courses on methods. A course of three years for the preparation of teachers, in which the common branches were reviewed and special lessons in the art of teaching and class management were given, was instituted by Samuel Read Hall in a private academy in Concord, Vermont, in 1823. He also published his *Lectures on Schoolkeeping* (1829), an elementary work on teaching that was based on the lessons that he gave in his normal academy. The report of the principal of the Canandaigua Academy in New York for 1829 shows that prospective teachers in that school were formed into a class to study Hall's *Lectures* until the book had been "finished and thoroughly reviewed." The defects of common schools, the methods of teaching the several school subjects, the making of pens, the government of schools, the construction of schoolhouses, the formation of lyceums and school libraries, and "Pestalozzi and his mode of instruction" were among the topics of the teachers' class in this New York academy in 1829. In New York also an act appropriating funds to promote the education of teachers in the academies was passed in 1827; and this act was followed by a stronger law in 1834. These laws seem to have been the first legislative provisions by an American state for the professional education of teachers. But they fell short of establishing a special institution for that purpose.

The first state normal school was opened in Massachusetts in 1839. It combined instruction in the common branches with work in methods and management and in a practice school. The same year a second, the following year a third, and a few years later a fourth state normal school was opened in Massachusetts. The state of New York, influenced by the report of a committee of it legislature on the Massachusetts schools, abandoned its academy program and opened a state normal school at Albany in 1844. But less than a dozen similar schools were established in all the states before the Civil War. The first thirty years of the schools formed an experimental period; but after the close of the Civil War, state normal schools were established at the rate of about twenty-five in each decade until nearly every state had one or more. Populous states, such as New York and Pennsylvania, each had ten or more so located that the various sections of the state would be served. By the end of the century more than a hundred state normal schools were in operation.

Meanwhile the normal schools developed internally, in number of students, in the qualifications of the staffs, and in their courses of study and equipment. The typical state normal school of 1860 was carried on in a single building that contained the dormitories and also housed the model school. There was a staff of five teachers and less than a hundred students who were seventeen or eighteen years old and whose only preparation was a common school education. The one-year curriculum included reviews of the common branches, methods of teaching, class management, some elementary psychology, and some work with children in the model school. Twenty years later the typical school of 1880 had two hundred and forty students, and the model school was conducted in a separate building. The curriculum had been increased to three years and the staff had grown to ten or twelve. Some academy and college preparatory subjects were usually taught, and this led to an unexpected result. Many of the students were no longer preparing to teach but were in preparation for college instead. The normal school, which had evolved out of the academy, tended to turn back toward its earlier academic functions. This tendency continued until the state normal schools became teachers' colleges. But meanwhile other changes had made this development seem natural and indeed necessary. To this we shall return.

From the first, many of the normal schools were led by able men, most of whom have not received the attention that their work for American education merits. Cyrus Peirce, the first principal of the Lexington school, David P. Page, of the Albany school, James Pyle Wickersham, Nicholas Tillinghast, Richard Edwards, and Joseph Baldwin are only a few of the great leaders of that age. With few resources and against great odds they succeeded in building serviceable institutions.

Meanwhile other means were tried to improve the services of those who were already engaged in teaching and who, for the most part, had no professional preparation. One of these means was the teachers' institute, which was a teachers' meeting conducted for professional instruction and continuing usually for a week. The normal institute had the same general character but continued for four or six weeks. Henry Barnard organized a normal institute in Connecticut in about 1846 and J. S. Denman of New York apparently first developed the short-period teachers' institute. Another medium with the same purpose was the summer school for teachers. One of the first and most famous was conducted by Louis Agassiz on the Island of Penikese on the coast of Massachusetts in the summer of 1873. One with a more distinctly professional purpose was conducted at Martha's Vineyard about ten years later. Wisconsin, Indiana, and Cornell University instituted summer schools in about 1890. The Summer School of the South at Knoxville was established in 1902 by Charles W. Dabney and enrolled two thousand students. Thereafter, many other colleges and universities throughout the country began to conduct summer schools, and a large proportion of their students were teachers or prospective teachers.

Professional courses for elementary teachers were given in some of the midwestern state universities before the Civil War. These were usually of the normal variety and were administered in special normal departments. The standards were low and the universities, at that time weak, marginal institutions, were competing with the state normal schools. The competition was frequently effective. At the State University of Iowa the teachers' courses for many years had a larger enrollment than the collegiate departments.

When the attendance and the support of the universities increased they abandoned their normal departments, and after an interim of ten or fifteen years, during which they gave no professional work, they began to offer courses for high school teachers in "the science and art of teaching." At the State University of Iowa, which was first in the field, the transition to education courses for secondary school teachers was made in 1873. At the University of Michigan, courses for elementary teachers had been given at intervals from the opening of the university in 1841, but in 1879 a new "chair of the science and art of teaching" was established to prepare school administrators and high school teachers, to develop teaching as a profession, and to promote cooperation between the secondary schools and the university. These purposes acquire special meaning when we notice that they were framed only a few years after the university began to accredit high schools and after the Kalamazoo decision. These matters will be further noticed in Chapter 20. By the end of the century, one half of the recognized colleges and universities reported that they were teaching education courses, and today almost all are doing so.

As the departments of education grew in size and importance in the large universities, they were reorganized into university schools or colleges of education. Teachers College in New York was chartered in 1889 and became affiliated with Columbia University in 1898. A school of Education was established at the University of Chicago in 1900 with a famous educator, F. W. Parker, as Director. Similar developments occurred in the growing state universities between 1890 and 1920. Bureaus of educational research were frequently established as divisions of the colleges of education. At Indiana University this took place in 1915, at the University of Illinois in 1917, and at many other universities in the following decade.

During the same period it became a marked tendency for the stronger state normal schools to develop into four-year degree-granting teachers' colleges. About one fourth of the previous two- or three-year normal schools had become teachers' colleges by 1920, and one half of them by 1925. There still are county, city, and state normal schools and a number of private normal schools, but rising standards of certification, competition with university and college departments and schools of education, and rising teachers' salaries after World War I practically compelled the normal schools, especially in the more opulent sections of the country, to raise their facilities and standards to the college level.

With all this progress teacher education is still very defective. One major difficulty is the condition that teachers' colleges, universities, private colleges, and indeed all institutions that prepare teachers are in competition with each other for students and are therefore unwilling to apply any strict selective principles in the admission of students. Nor is there any accepted prognostic scheme that will with certainty or near certainty predict future teaching success. Secondly, there is too little relation between supply and demand as teacher-training is now conducted. Under war and postwar conditions there is likely to be a serious shortage and in periods of economic depression a vast oversupply of teachers. This is, of course, due not only to the numbers being graduated from teachers' schools but also to conditions of appointment and terms, which the professional schools do not control. The schools do in a large measure control their own courses. It is admitted by almost all, faculty and students, that the courses are too theoretical and that in any given institution there is unjustifiable duplication of content between courses with widely different titles and professed aims. There are, on the other hand, large gaps in the curriculum. Practical questions in school management, in planning lessons, courses, and programs, in guidance, and in personal relations are often treated briefly, theoretically, or not at all. The courses also deal with conditions in large schools and metropolitan centers, although some graduates spend the first years of their teaching in small schools in rural or village surroundings. Finally, not to make this arraignment too long, there is often a lack of scholarship in the faculties, not only a lack of present knowledge and training but also a lack of the investigative spirit and the scientific scholarly interest that would fill up gaps and remove present deficiencies. But it would be unfair to end on this critical note. Teacher education has been created in the last hundred years, has improved greatly in quality and scope in the last fifty years, and is still developing. It must continue to improve if it is to serve the future well.

COMPULSORY ATTENDANCE

The United States very gradually developed the conviction that an educated citizenry could be developed only if all the children attended school. This conclusion was not accepted until the later decades of the nineteenth century. It was seen that no country had attained universal education or even general literacy by merely setting up schools and encouraging the parents to send their children to school. The church schools, the philanthropic and neighborhood attempts, the Lancasterian schools, and the public schools had all failed at this point. It came to be recognized that only an agency such as the state, which includes everyone and which can act directly on individuals, can secure general school attendance, and then only by specific legislation. Some degree of the increased attendance and greater regularity of attendance at school that we have attained is certainly the result of the growing recognition of the need for education in modern life; but wherever society has concluded that universal schooling is a necessity, it has been found necessary to enact compulsory attendance legislation in order to attain it. Most of the more democratic states long resisted this necessity and it was not until the latter nineteenth century, about seventy or eighty years ago, that France, England, and the United States began, as Guizot, French Minister of Public Instruction, phrased it, to exercise "this coercive action of the state upon the domestic economy of the family."

Nearly one half of the states of the Union enacted compulsory attendance laws between 1870 and 1890, and within thirty years after the latter date the other half had slowly and somewhat reluctantly followed their example. One state, however, anticipated the rest by more than a decade.

Massachusetts, as early as 1852, passed a law that embodied the essential features of such legislation; and that law will be used here as a convenient illustration. These features were the age limits, the annual period of attendance required, the necessary exemptions and allowance for alternative instruction, the provision for enforcement, and a penalty for noncompliance. According to the Massachusetts law of 1852, all children between the ages of eight and fourteen years were required to attend school for twelve weeks a year, and for six of the twelve weeks the attendance had to be continuous. The legal exemptions were specified. Children who were too poor, or too weak in body or mind, or who were otherwise receiving instruction, or who had already completed the school course were not required to attend. The selectmen and the truant officers were to examine the merits of each case and, if any refused to obey their summons, a set fine was to be imposed on the parents. This law with its easy requirements was a beginning, but even these moderate demands were not rigidly enforced.

The compulsory attendance laws provide an excellent illustration of the general truth that in education the American states, while following similar historical patterns, are, at any one time, at very unequal stages in the evolution of the program. Every state has now for more than twenty-five years had some kind of compulsory attendance law, but the provisions of the laws are not alike in any two states. Massachusetts and Mississippi, and even two adjoining states like Ohio and Kentucky, differ in the provisions and in the enforcement of their laws. This unfortunate diversity in our compulsory attendance requirements is the natural result of the differences in the past history of the states, in their economic and industrial condition, and in the character and distribution of their people. The industrial states and the new western states were the first to pass such laws: Massachusetts, Connecticut, and New York led in the industrial East; and in the West, Washington, while still a territory, Nevada, and California all fell into line before 1875. The southern states were the slowest. The last twelve states, almost one fourth of the entire number of states, were all south of the Mason-Dixon Line, and all but two were east of the Mississippi River— that is, in the Old South.

The general tendency of the growing legislation has been to strengthen both the compulsory attendance and the related child labor laws and the means of enforcement. By 1890, Massachusetts was requiring seven and one-half months of schooling each year between the ages of eight and fourteen. Apparently, however, no other state then demanded more than five and some only three months a year, while one half of the states still had no laws on the subject. The trend since then has been to lower the age when attendance must begin, to raise the leaving age, to increase the number of months of attendance per year, to stiffen the requirements for work permits, and to improve the methods of enforcement. Ohio now requires children to be in school from age six to eighteen, a twelve-year period extending from the first year of the common school to the normal age for graduation from high school. This is at present the longest period of required attendance in any state. One half of the states demand attendance for nine years and some for less time.

The laws allow reasonable exemptions. Children who are ill and whose physical-mental condition is such that they cannot profit from schoolwork, or who live at a distance from the nearest school, or who are receiving adequate instruction otherwise are, in most states, not required to attend the public schools. However, the exemptions vary from state to state and the attendance ages and other provisions of the laws also differ. The last-named exemption, which permits parents to send their children to private schools, has been challenged. A referendum in Oregon, actively supported by the Ku Klux Klan and adopted on March 7, 1922, would have required all children between the ages of eight and sixteen to attend the public schools whenever they were in session. This act would have had the effect of permanently closing all elementary private schools in the state, and this was no doubt the object of the referendum. The Supreme Court declared this act unconstitutional. A somewhat analogous attempt was made, about the time of World War I when a wave of "Americanism" swept the country, to legislate on what private schools may teach. Laws were passed in several states prohibiting the teaching of foreign languages in elementary schools, both public and private. The Supreme Court declared these laws unconstitutional in the case of Meyer v. Nebraska. In the third case, the state of New Jersey has held that home education cannot be accepted in lieu of school attendance. These cases have both a practical and a historical interest because they mark the present frontier between the power of the state and the liberty of the family in the matter of education and school attendance.

FORMING A LADDER SYSTEM

The school-attendance movement was closely related to two parallel developments in the organization of the schools. These were, first, the classification and grading of the children according to their progress in school; and, secondly, the articulation of the schools themselves. By articulation is meant the fitting together of schools and courses so that pupils can go in a regular progression from the lowest to the highest. The public kindergarten, elementary schools, junior and senior high schools, the teachers' college, and the state colleges or state university form such a closely articulated series of institutions because the completion of a properly selected course at each level is the necessary and adequate preparation for undertaking an appropriate course at the next higher level.

Both the grading of the children and the closer articulation of the schools came about gradually in the United States; and they developed together. Evidently when the student body becomes large and the courses of study complex, grading becomes necessary; and the increase in population and compulsory attendance produced these conditions. It was in the cities where the graded school first attained its full development. Conditions varied so widely that the organizing process followed various patterns in different cities. One or two illustrations will show this: An irregular but very minute grading of pupils was introduced into the Lancasterian schools of New York City where the reading classes were divided into nine stages and the arithmetic classes into seven. This minute division was not retained when the public schools were established in 1853, but yet the public board maintained thirteen grades. The highest of these, however, included some secondary school work. In Chicago, a fully graded course of study was adopted in 1861. The elementary schools of the city were organized into ten grades that, together with the high school course established in 1856, made a fourteen-year system. Kansas City developed a seven-year elementary school that, with the high school, created an eleven-year system. These examples show that there was no uniformly graded system at the midcentury and for some years thereafter. To this point we shall return when we consider the history of the high school in the next chapter.

Almost as soon as the schools had become fully, although variously, graded there arose a chorus of opposition to the system. Teachers and citizens protested against the school machine, the lock step, and the consequent retardation of children in school and their elimination from school by the rigid grading, the fixed curriculum, and the stiff promotion examinations at the end of each year of work. The opposition really arose, in part, from a new theory of education. Close grading had been satisfactory in monitorial times, but it became unsatisfactory later because there had occurred a shift in psychology and in educational principles. The new views had been derived from many sources, but they came to us from Pestalozzi and Froebel. They placed greater weight upon the children's interests and needs and demanded a more flexible organization to provide for these individual variations. They helped to prepare the way for the new elementary school that is described in Chapter 20.

The outlines of the American system were practically complete by the end of the nineteenth century. It consists of the kindergarten, in many cities; of a practically universal elementary school; of a widespread public high school, sometimes divided into junior and senior schools; of many public junior colleges very unevenly distributed; of teachers' colleges, and of state universities and land-grant colleges. Because of a great increase in the population many state universities have established branches in nearby cities. Some of these are likely to become independent universities in time. There are also several municipal colleges and universities. The outlines were practically complete by 1900, but the kindergarten in the United States, because of its influence in developing a "new elementary school," and the junior high school and the junior college, because they are mainly twentieth-century institutions, will be treated in the next chapter.

The American system is a ladder system. Its aim is to provide appropriate education for all, at all levels, and to require the regular attendance by children at the lower levels at least. The aim is also to provide these opportunities at public expense and without fees, and to articulate the schools so that there can be a series of easy transitions from the kindergarten and the elementary school to the professional and graduate studies at the top. Education for teachers, in this system, has been articulated with the rest of the system and is no longer set apart as it was in the early normal schools.

The American system permits the operation of private schools and welcomes their contributions. They have made many important contributions in the past and will doubtless make new ones in the future. The Catholic Church and other churches and many secular agencies operate a large number of schools in the United States. Many adult educational services also are outside the public system. Many private organizations of parents, teachers, and citizens, who do not maintain schools, contribute their wisdom and energy for the improvement of the system.

From the administrative standpoint the American system is not yet unified. There is instead a series of state systems, but all of these bear a strong family resemblance to each other.

SUMMARY

In the last hundred years, the public institutions that had grown up independently, each to meet a specific need, were joined together to form the American system, a unitary scheme to provide educational opportunity under public auspices from the kindergarten to the graduate school. Besides this public system there are in all states numerous private schools also. After the Civil War, northern efforts to impose a system on the South having failed, that section gradually developed public school systems on the common plan.

The Morrill Act of 1862 led to the creation of an entirely new type of school, the land-grant state colleges of agriculture and the mechanic arts. These, and the complementary experiment stations, have aided in developing the sciences and their practical uses, have furnished aid to farmers, homemakers, and engineers, and have prepared teachers in these areas for the high schools. Meanwhile, the state universities, which originated earlier, had developed and in some states the land-grant college and state university were combined in one institution. Seventeen Negro land-grant colleges were established in the southern states. A series of laws was passed, supplementary to the primary purpose of the Morrill Act, and to achieve its purposes more completely. Among these laws are the Smith-Lever, Smith-Hughes, and George-Deen Acts.

The Federal Office of Education is mainly an information gathering, disseminating, and promotion agency. But it also administers the allotment of Federal appropriations for education. It does not have the power of some foreign ministries of education, but neither do they exercise the democratic leadership of our Office of Education.

The state normal schools began in 1839, but they were not established in numbers until after the Civil War. The earliest normal schools were mainly advanced elementary schools with a few professional courses added; but later they were raised to a secondary school or junior college level and recently they have become degree-granting teachers' colleges.

The public kindergartens and elementary schools, the high schools, the state normal schools and teachers' colleges, the state colleges and universities, and the public junior colleges and special schools were gradually joined together in a sequence that presents an unbroken highway to the student. The formation of the American system also involved legislation on administration and especially on attendance. Other essential phases were the classification of the children, the better articulation of the schools, the elevation of standards, and the distribution of schools among the people in order that educational opportunities might be extended to all as fully as possible. This American ideal is the objective of the American system.

QUESTIONS

1. What do you take to be the meaning of the title of this chapter? Do we, in law, have an American National system?
2. What are the chief points of dispute in the interpretation of the educational history of the South?
3. Why was the Hoar Bill an educationally unwise measure?
4. Why did the high school have a slow growth in the South? Find several reasons.
5. Is state control of education to be preferred to national control, and why? What is meant by democratic control of education? Why is it to be desired?
6. Which should be most jealously preserved, local control or state control of education? What does history have to say about the defects of each?
7. What important lessons have been learned from the development of the land-grant colleges?
8. Does the early history of the normal schools justify the claim that they were intended as part of the working-class schools whereas preparatory schools and colleges were intended for professional people? How was this incipient dualism overcome?

9. Why did the early western state universities establish normal courses for elementary teachers?
10. What changes in American teacher-education that have taken place in the past do you regard as improvements; and what are its remaining defects? How can these be removed or lessened?
11. Would it be desirable to extend the compulsory attendance requirement in your state, and to what extent? Why? What are the limits of desirable compulsory attendance?
12. Should private schools be abolished as intended under the Oregon law of 1922; or rigidly controlled as in France; or allowed considerable freedom as in most states of the Union?

NOTES AND SOURCES

On Negro education and race questions see the *Journal of Negro Education*, issued since April, 1932; and on school buildings, see the early *Proceedings* of the American Institute of Instruction and the issues in 1831 and later of the *American Annals of Education*. Considerable attention has recently been given to the systematic study of school law. *The Colleges and the Courts*, an important work on the law of higher education in the United States, by E. C. Elliott and M. M. Chambers appeared in 1936 and several annual supplements have been added. The subsequent list contains two manuals on school law, one by Edwards and the other by Hamilton and Mort. The case of Meyer v. Nebraska, mentioned in the text, was argued before the United States Supreme Court on February 23, 1923 and was decided June 4, 1923. See *U.S. Reports*, Vol. 262, pp. 390–403. The Oregon Compulsory Attendance Case, Walter M. Pierce, Governor of Oregon, et al. v. Society of Sisters, and Hill Military Academy, was argued March 16, 17, 1925 and was decided on June 1, 1925. See *U.S. Reports*, Vol. 268, pp. 510–536.

AGNEW, WALTER D., *The Administration of Professional Schools for Teachers*, Baltimore, Warwick and York, 1924, 262 pp.

BOYDEN, ARTHUR C., *The History of the Bridgewater Normal School*, Bridgewater, Mass., Alumni Association, 1933, 156 pp.

DABNEY, CHARLES WILLIAM, *Universal Education in the South*, Chapel Hill, University of North Carolina Press, 1936, 2 vols.

EDWARDS, NEWTON, *The Courts and the Public Schools; The Legal Basis of School Organization and Administration*, Chicago, University of Chicago Press, 1933, 591 pp.

FINEGAN, THOMAS E., *Teacher Training Agencies*, Albany, University of the State of New York, 1917, 439 pp. This is Volume II of the Eleventh Annual Report of the New York State Department of Education.

FRENCH, WILLIAM MARHSALL, and FLORENCE SMITH FRENCH, *College of the Empire State. A Centennial History of the New York State College for Teachers at Albany*, Albany, N.Y., New York State College for Teachers, 1944, 271 pp.

FROTHINGHAM, PAUL REVERE, *Edward Everett, Orator and Statesman*, Boston, Houghton Mifflin Company, 1925, 495 pp. As scholar and teacher, Governor of Massachusetts, and President of Harvard College, Edward Everett had considerable influence in educational matters.

HAMILTON, ROBERT R., and PAUL R. MORT, *The Law and Public Education, With Cases*, Chicago, Foundation Press, 1941, 579 pp.

HAMPTON NORMAL AND AGRICULTURAL INSTITUTE, *Twenty-two Years' Work of the Hampton Normal and Agricultural Institute*, Hampton, Va., Normal School Press, 1893, 520 pp.

HANUS, PAUL H., *Adventuring in Education*, Cambridge, Mass., Harvard University Press, 1937, 259 pp.

HARPER, CHARLES A., *Development of the Teachers College in the United States with Special Reference to the Illinois State Normal University*, Bloomington, Ill., Macknight and Macknight, 1935, 384 pp.; *A Century of Public Teacher Education. The Story of the State Teachers Colleges as They Evolved from the State Normal Schools*, Washington, D.C., American Association of Teachers Colleges, 1939, 175 pp.

HUBBELL, LEIGH G., *The Development of University Departments of Education in Six States of the Middle West*, Washington, D.C., Catholic University of America, 1924, 125 pp. A doctoral dissertation.

HUTCHINS, CLAYTON D., *Federal Funds for Education, 1954–55 and 1955–56*, U.S. Office of Education Bulletin, 1956, No. 5, 163 pp. With notes on history and legislation.

JAMES, EDWARD JANES, *The Origin of the Land Grant Act of 1862 . . . and Some Account of Its Author, Johathan B. Turner*, Urbana-Champaign, Illinois University Press, 1910, 139 pp.

JUDD, CHARLES N., and S. C. PARKER, "Problems Involved in Standardizing Normal Schools," U.S. Office of Education Bulletin, 1916, No. 12, Washington, D.C., Government Printing Office, 1916, 141 pp.

LOOMIS, B. W., *The Educational Influence of Richard Edwards*, Nashville, Tenn., George Peabody College for Teachers, 1932, 213 pp.

MATTHEWS, J. C., *The Contributions of Joseph Baldwin to Public Education*, Nashville, Tenn., George Peabody College for Teachers, 1932, 184 pp.

NORTON, ARTHUR ORLO, Editor, *The First State Normal School in America; The Journals of Cyrus Peirce and Mary Swift*, Cambridge, Mass., Harvard University Press, 1926, 299 pp.

PARKER, WILLIAM B., *The Life and Public Services of Justin Smith Morrill*, Boston, Houghton Mifflin Company, 1924, 378 pp. Potter, Alonzo, and George B. Emerson, *The School and the Schoolmaster*, New York, Harper & Brothers, 1842, 552 pp.

RICE, JOHN ANDREW, *I Came Out of the Eighteenth Century*, New York, Harper & Brothers, 1942, 341 pp.

RUSSELL, JAMES EARL, *Founding Teachers College. Reminiscences of the Dean Emeritus*, New York, Teachers College, Columbia University, 1937, 106 pp.

SCOTT, EMMETT JAY, and LYMAN BEECHER STOWE, *Booker T. Washington, Builder of a Civilization*, Garden City, N.Y., Doubleday & Company, 1916, 331 pp.

SWINT, HENRY W., *The Northern Teacher in the South, 1862–1870*, Nashville, Tenn., Vanderbilt University Press, 1941, 221 pp.

TEWKSBURY, DONALD G., *The Founding of American Colleges and Universities Before the Civil War*, New York, Bureau of Publications, Teachers College, Columbia University, 1932, 254 pp.

WASHINGTON, BOOKER TALIAFERRO, *Twenty-five Years of Tuskegee*, New York, Doubleday, Page & Company, 1906, 18 pp.; *Up from Slavery; An Autobiography*, Garden City, N.Y., Doubleday & Company, 1913, 330 pp.

WESTFIELD STATE NORMAL SCHOOL, *Semi-Centennial and other Exercises of the State Normal School at Westfield, Mass., June 25, 1889*, Boston, Wright and Potter, 1889, 79 pp.; *The State Teachers College at Westfield*, compiled by workers of the Writers' Program of the Works Progress Administration in the State of Massachusetts and sponsored by the State Teachers College at Westfield, 1941, 114 pp.

WOODSON, CARTER GODWIN, *The Mis-Education of the Negro*, Washington, D.C., The Associated Publishers, 1933, 207 pp.

WRIGHT, ARTHUR D., and G. E. GARDNER, *Hall's Lectures on Schoolkeeping*, Hanover, N.H., Dartmouth College Press, 1929, 192 pp.

Chapter 20

NEW SCHOOLS FOR A NEW WORLD

In this chapter we shall show how the old elementary school has been transformed into a new school and how the high school was created in the United States. The new elementary school of which we shall speak is the school of today; but since our treatment is a historical one, we must recognize that the newest institution of any age is never entirely new. The old elementary school was the school of the three Rs and of Whittier's *In School Days:*

> Still sits the school-house by the road,
>   A ragged beggar sunning;
> Around it still the sumachs grow
>   And blackberry vines are running.
>
> Within, the master's desk is seen,
>   Deep scarred by raps official,
> The warping floor, the battered seats,
>   The jack-knife's carved initial.

The old elementary school was the school of Ichabod Crane and *The Hoosier Schoolmaster,* the school of rote memory and brute strength. With honorable but not very numerous exceptions, the new school began to supersede the old little more than a century ago.

The elementary school of the present differs widely from that of a century ago both in its external relations and management and in its internal conditions and teaching. The transformation began about 1830 and has continued to the present day. It is still continuing and the future will certainly see great improvements in elementary education. Externally, the elementary schools are now organized into a network that reaches all parts of the country. There are new teachers equipped with professional preparation; and professional administration and supervision are provided. The school term has been extended from three months to eight or nine. Systematic methods of financing the operation of the schools and laws to secure the regular attendance of the children are in force. Better buildings and more adequate equipment are provided for child and teacher. These matters were considered in earlier chapters. Efforts are being made to draw school and community into a closer alliance and a more helpful relationship. All of this progress has occurred within a century.

There have also been many internal changes brought about by a new philosophy, new methods of teaching, and a new curriculum. It is these changes that we propose to describe here. For the old doctrine that mere literacy—an education in the elements of reading, writing, and arithmetic —is sufficient, there has been substituted the Pestalozzian view that the elementary school, by providing a rich and stimulating curriculum and intelligent teaching, can develop a genuine popular culture even among those whose regular school attendance ends at fourteen or fifteen.

The elementary school has come to draw its materials from the resources of science, literature, history, and the arts. The industrial and the expressional arts have been made to yield their contributions. Instead of merely verbal exercises based on formal textbooks the schools teach children to investigate, to gather knowledge and ideas from many sources, to think and evaluate, and to take an active part in their own education. For the old rigid grading of fifty years ago a more flexible organization has been substituted. Equipped with tools, shops, kitchens, well-planned auditoriums, medical aid, playgrounds, and libraries, the better elementary schools carry on work of a quality that was not possible in earlier days. S. R. Hall, writing a little more than a hundred years ago, stated—and this was the almost universal fact—that the teacher did not even have a dictionary to aid him.

We shall deal first with the influence that originally was derived from Pestalozzi and then with those influences that stemmed from Froebel and Herbart. But we must not assume that American education is merely an application of European ideas. Every borrowed idea was quickly changed to fit local conditions, and our elementary school is a thoroughly American institution. Our curricula and our methods are our own, but we eagerly and wisely adopted promising suggestions wherever we found them.

There were three Pestalozzian movements, or rather three phases of one movement, in the United States. The earliest efforts to introduce the practice of the great Swiss educator, which center about Joseph Neef on the one hand and the manual-labor education concept on the other, were only slightly effective. The second Pestalozzian development, which occurred in the three decades preceding the Civil War, was locally effective but did not spread widely. It was in the period following the Civil War that Pestalozzianism made its greatest impression, not only through the object-teaching of Oswego but also through nature study. We shall begin with the second of these three periods.

THE INTRODUCTION OF ELEMENTARY SCIENCE

Elementary science, object-teaching, and nature study were widely introduced after 1860, but there were earlier beginnings in the use of such subjects. The ideas of Pestalozzi had been filtering into the United States since the first decades of the nineteenth century. There were parallel influences such as that of the *Orbis Pictus* of Comenius, which was republished in New York in 1810, and the writings of Bacon and Locke. There was a growing interest in agriculture and in the applications of chemistry to practical life. That theories should be based on facts, that real things should be studied along with words and ideas, and that children should learn to understand as well as remember were doctrines that had long been familiar; but the time for their more general application had now arrived. Teachers were coming to realize that children should acquire meanings from words, and that expressionless oral reading is a sign that the passage is not understood. They began to introduce the word or sentence method and to discard the usual alphabet and spelling method in teaching beginning reading. Arithmetic was now to be developed intelligently by the pupil, where before the memorizing and mechanical application of uncomprehended rules had been in vogue. In grammar there had been a like slavish adherence to rules, and a more inductive, active, and intelligent method of teaching language and composition came to prevail. A beginning had been made when teachers came to see that pupils cannot learn effectively what they do not understand, and when they began to analyze the pupils' difficulties, to illustrate their lessons, and to provide exercises and applications.This was a considerable part of the Pestalozzian message.

Another part of that message concerned the use of objective materials, concrete things, pictures, and drawings. When Horace Mann returned from Germany he was more than ever convinced that skill in drawing and sketching was a necessary acquirement for teachers. David P. Page condemned mere book-learning in which the pupil was a passive recipient. The teacher, he felt, must inspire the pupil with the desire to know and to find out for himself not from books alone but also from nature and life. He proposed to have the children observe nature, question their parents, review their own experiences, and also read books and report to the class what they had learned. This was a phase of Pestalozzi's doctrine of learning through observation and it came into use in American schools in about 1830.

A third Pestalozzian influence of the period concerned the teacher's relations to the pupils and the spirit of the school. By 1830 and 1840 many educational leaders insisted that the school should be a pleasant and har-

Louis Agassiz (1807-1873)

monious company. The old harshness was to be outlawed. Only teachers who could inspire love and cooperation were to be considered worthy of their office. There was a close connection between this notion of discipline and concrete, intelligible teaching; and both together made some headway in the better schools a century ago.

Teachers were urged to deal with concrete things, to teach orally and visually, and to avoid the tyranny of the textbook. Henry Barnard urged schools to provide "cabinets of real objects as subjects of oral instruction in the field of pupils' everyday observation and experience." Horace Mann had given many similar suggestions by word and pen. Warren Burton, an early institute lecturer and the author of a quaint little book, *The District School as It Was* (1833), urged that the school should no longer fasten the child to his chair or offer him mere words, "little black images that he can not get his fingers under." This book has recently been reprinted (New York, T. Y. Cromwell and Co., 1928, 213 pp.). Louis Agassiz, addressing a class at a teachers' institute in Massachusetts, said to the young women before him: "I see before me many bright eyes, but alas! these eyes cannot see!" He then began to explain some natural object, a grasshopper, for example, and every member of the class held a specimen in her hand while she followed his instruction.

The authors of *The School and the Schoolmaster*, which was mentioned earlier, pointed out that a great part of infancy is spent happily in learning the names, properties, and uses of common things. This, they said, should be a cue for the teachers in the school. The teacher should aid the children in doing better what they were already doing and what they loved to do. Listen, they advised, to the questions that children ask, such questions as: Why do the birds come back in the summer? What makes the rain? Why does the smoke go up in the sky? They said teachers should be familiar with elementary science so that they could answer such questions and could teach children to observe correctly, to draw, and to measure. They gave a list of sixty subjects for lessons in easy science, agriculture, physiology and health, and the useful arts.

The Massachusetts normal schools at Westfield and Bridgewater began to build up science collections and to employ demonstrations and object-teaching. This Pestalozzian drift was supported by the natural interest of their rural pupils in the problems of the farm and the household. These normal schools developed what they called the analytic, objective method by which pupils were taught to observe, to analyze, and to think. John W. Dickinson (1825–1901), who became the Secretary of the Massachusetts Board of Education, had been connected with the Westfield State Normal School for a quarter of a century and he believed that this school was "the first to show that all branches of learning can be taught by the same objective method."

This early form of elementary science and nature study is also revealed by the children's literature of the time. Elementary science books and books giving common-sense information about nature, rocks, plants, animals, and the farm were prepared for use in school and home. Such titles as *The Young Chemist* and *Familiar Lessons*, in one or another subject field, were numerous even twenty years before the Civil War. An example is David Blair's *Catechism of Common Things*, which was in its fifth edition in 1825. Most of the books of this type were by undistinguished authors. One of the writers, however, was David A. Wells, later a prominent economist, who had studied under Agassiz and who in his earlier years wrote *Familiar Science* and the *Science of Common Things*. The flood of such nature and easy science books can only be suggested here, but even this brief notice shows that in the literature for children and schools a scientific current was then beginning to flow beside the older moralistic and patriotic streams. The Pestalozzian influence, as we have already indicated, was also seen in the school subjects of arithmetic, geography, and music. The growing interest in nature and in children led to the development of inductive and object-teaching. We shall now show that these sound early methods were perverted by the introduction of a less flexible and a less natural method, the Oswego system of object-teaching.

The highly formalized scheme of object-teaching that was developed and spread by the State Normal School at Oswego, New York was an importation from England. At least two earlier efforts to introduce it had been unsuccessful, one by Horace Mann, who in 1840 had published some of the English object lessons in his *Common School Journal,* and another by A. J. Rickoff, Superintendent of the Cincinnati public schools. Both efforts failed. But a similar attempt by Edward A. Sheldon, founder of the Oswego Normal School, was successful. Sheldon was an enthusiastic promoter for whom difficulties were steppingstones. Having already established a "ragged" school for Oswego's neglected children and having served as superintendent of schools in Syracuse, he was in 1853, recalled to a similar position in Oswego. There he established Saturday classes for teachers and these developed into a training school. He felt that the schools were too mechanical and that the children were asked only to memorize, not to observe and reason. The work, he thought, should be more objective. "For this purpose," he wrote, "we wanted collections of objects of all sorts, charts of color and form, natural history, pictures, objects for teaching number, and reading matter in quantity, suited to the ages of the children."

In his search, Sheldon in 1859 visited Toronto where Egerton Ryerson, the well-known Canadian educator, had placed a full set of the lesson materials and teachers' guidebooks from the English Home and Colonial School Society. These materials, it should be noticed, were not in use and had not been introduced into the Canadian schools; but to Sheldon they seemed to be exactly what was needed.

By convincing his board of education that the venture would "not cost the taxpayer one cent" he was permitted to bring an English critic-teacher, Margaret E. M. Jones, to Oswego to introduce the Home and Colonial version of Pestalozzianism. Sheldon secured the necessary one thousand dollars by dispensing with the services of one teacher, by charging the teachers a fee for the lessons Miss Jones gave, and by soliciting contributions from his teachers. Miss Jones remained only one year, but that was sufficient time to establish in Oswego the formal object-teaching that she sponsored. Because it was formal it was easily transmitted by means of outlines, lesson plans, and manuals. Object-teaching became a fad. In 1866, Sheldon was able to secure recognition of his training school as the second New York state normal school. The first had been established at Albany twenty-two years before.

Oswego graduates carried its system into nearly every state during the twenty-five years (1861–1886) when it was in favor. They were to be found in large numbers in New York and all the states north of the fortieth parallel, but few entered the Old South or the West. Other normal schools also spread the system including those at Trenton, Kirksville, Terre Haute, and Winona. But object-teaching was not approved by everyone. In the methods of the Home and Colonial School Society, and of Oswego, the objects were such things as leaves, colors, and geometric forms. These were selected and arranged by the teacher, and frequently there was only one object before the class. It could not be handled and could hardly be observed by each child; and it was even more unfortunate that no real motive for dealing with this object was established in the child's mind. The description was abstract and usually confined to the number, shape, size, color, and the parts of the selected objects. Stilted language was standard in the Oswego system, which had copied the errors rather than the inspiration of Pestalozzi. Most important of all, the teachers often knew too little science to deal intelligently with the materials they employed.

The faddism of the Oswego movement seems to have irked Henry Barnard. He remarked that educators had for a quarter of a century urged that schoolwork should be based on the pupils' own observation and experience. Now, he said, within two years (1860–1861) a host of model object-lesson books have been published with such titles as *Manual on Object Teaching, Lessons on Objects, Primary Object Lessons, Outlines of a System of Object-Teaching,* and *Child's Book of Nature.* The danger now, he said, is that teachers will copy the methods of some manual without understanding the principles, without considering the ages and attainments of the pupils, and without adapting the work to the pursuits of the people. Object-teaching, said Barnard, can be made as verbal, mechanical, and monotonous as any other teaching. And it often was.

While the British object lessons were spread from Oswego, the older and more informal study of nature continued in many schools. William T. Harris prepared a syllabus of oral science lessons for the schools of St. Louis. Agassiz continued to teach until 1873 and during his last year he conducted his famous summer school at Penikese. Two years later Francis W. Parker began his work at Quincy, Massachusetts, which is treated subsequently. H. H. Straight, who is sometimes regarded as the founder of organized nature study, had been a student at Penikese and was to be a teacher under Parker at Chicago. Several of the normal schools were carrying on the earlier tradition that has already been described. New influences also came into play. The kindergarten and child study that had begun independently reinforced each other in opposition to formal object lessons and in favor of more active and more natural methods. A wave of interest in the rural school, which was set in the midst of nature, and in the improvement of agriculture fostered the new movement. Out of all these tendencies a new nature study, which greatly improved elementary instruction, was born.

Nature study is not altogether easy to define. It is allied to the older natural history. It is simpler and less formally organized than science and attempts to consider the children's interests more. The sciences of that day often concerned themselves with classification and names and with the structure of animals and plants. They emphasized laboratory methods and dissection and paid little attention to the questions children ask about natural objects. Nature study, which tried to correct these trends in elementary instruction, was directed toward a more informal science. It dealt extensively with living things, both plants and animals, and with their environment. It attempted to answer the children's questions somewhat as an old field naturalist would have done.

Several phases of nature study can be distinguished. One was a humanistic and literary interest in nature, its color and poetry, its seasonal rhythms, and the interdependence of its living forms. This type had a tendency to become a sentimental study rather than a scientific one. The practical study of nature formed a second phase, and here the purpose was to introduce the children to agriculture, home economics, health studies, and the conservation of natural resources. And, thirdly, there were those who used nature study as an introduction to science, or as a kind of general science; and books proposing to deal with physics and chemistry or with elementary biology by homemade apparatus and simple experiments were called nature study books. Although the subject is difficult to define, it will be most helpful to think of it as elementary school science and as closely allied to the natural history of earlier times.

If we leave that earlier period out of consideration, Henry H. Straight (1846–1886) can be regarded as the founder of nature study. He was born near Chautauqua, New York, grew up on a farm, and began to teach at sixteen. As a student at Oberlin, then still in its frontier stage, he became interested in languages. To earn money to study these subjects in Germany, he took a position as principal of the public school in the small town of Galena, Ohio. Experience in teaching object lessons led him to substitute lessons in elementary science and natural history; and his entire life's program was changed by his success and by the growing conviction that scientific knowledge and training were essential in fitting children for life. Instead of going to Germany, he continued his studies at Cornell University where he received a strong scientific and educational impulse.

After a year as principal of a new state normal school at Peru, Nebraska, Straight resigned to take the more congenial position of science teacher in the same school. There he developed a plan of education based on science and the industries, a scheme he attempted to work out more fully in later years. The following year he was first on the list of Agassiz's students at Penikese (1873). He continued to work with N. S. Shaler and other Harvard scientists and at Cornell University until 1876, when he became professor of natural science at the Oswego Normal School. He had at Peru turned the basement of the school into a number of laboratories; and Agassiz had made it clear that it was feasible to handle large numbers of students in experimental work. But at Oswego he attacked another problem. He tried to transform the old formal object-teaching into the study of living plants and animals in their natural habitat. He believed that laboratory work was not suitable for children and instead substituted nature study, especially field excursions to the woods, swamps, and lake shore, where his young naturalists used the pencil and brush rather than the forceps and scalpel. Although some members of the Oswego staff, Hermann Krüsi, for example, valued his work, he was not able to make his ideas prevail. The decadent object lessons had become too firmly entrenched. Meanwhile, at the Martha's Vineyard summer school for teachers where he lectured, he came under the notice of Francis W. Parker who, in 1883, invited him to the Cook County Normal School. He accepted and there he spent his remaining years. Parker credited his own use of the principle of correlation to Straight, who stressed the connections of natural science with geography and other subjects. This principle, independently developed by Straight, was an outgrowth of his great theme, the unity and interdependence of all nature.

After Straight's death, one who is even better known, Wilbur S. Jackman, was chosen to succeed him. Jackman's *Nature Study for the Common Schools* (1891) was a teachers' guide, not a book for pupils although, because it was composed mainly of questions on direct observations and experiments, it could have been used as a laboratory and field manual. The lessons, drawn from nine different sciences, consisted of the regular gathering of materials and the discussion and systematic arrangement of them, followed by the reports of the pupils' observations. The subjects were arranged in a month-by-month series throughout "the rolling year." Like Pestalozzi, he placed great stress on the expression of the children's observations and conclusions; and he proposed varied reports by means of gestures, music, modeling, drawing, and painting, as well as oral and written language.

Before the end of the century the nature study movement had spread far and many higher institutions had begun to prepare teachers for work in this field. Cornell University and the Illinois Normal University were prominent in the promotion of the agricultural phase, and Clark University and the University of Chicago were also important centers. Interest in nature study for farm boys and girls grew out of the severe agricultural crisis of the early 1890s when many farm families became destitute. The agricultural colleges considered plans for the relief of the rural population. It was agreed that the improvement of the rural school was an essential step in the program and that one means for the improvement of the rural school was nature study pointed toward farm life and farming as a vocation. Among the leaders in nature study at Cornell were Liberty H. Bailey in the administration of it, Anna B. Comstock in the preparation of materials, and John Walton Spencer in the development of nature study clubs. Bailey was also important as a writer. In his *Nature-Study Idea* (1909) he declared that, if anyone were to plan schools for a rural section that had no schools of any kind, he would certainly include something about plants, animals, fields, and people. He could not conceivably plan purely academic rural schools in which the work of the children had no visible connection with the habits of the people and the immediate needs of the community. Yet the purely bookish elementary school was not only conceivable; it too often was a fact.

One of the outstanding books produced by the entire movement was prepared at Cornell by Anna B. Comstock. Its title is *Handbook of Nature Study*. Originally issued in 1911 as an outgrowth of her leaflets for teachers, this work attained its twenty-fourth edition in 1939. In that form it contains nine hundred pages, eleven hundred illustrations, and an extensive bibliography. Part One is pedagogical, dealing with the teaching of nature to children. The remainder of this important work treats of animals, plants, earth, sky, and weather and presents materials from which exercises and courses of study can be developed by the teacher. Even though it is a teachers' book, it can easily be read by upper-grade children. A more vocational presentation of the same idea developed in the black-soil country of the Middle West. This was the *Practical Nature-Study and Elementary Agriculture* (1909) by Coulter and Patterson of the Illionis Normal University. The title was accurately descriptive, for it deals with trees, insects, weather, weeds, pollination, plant breeding, and rural school gardens. "In an agricultural community," the authors said, "the lessons must be primarily agricultural." The general movement also gave rise to a national society and many local nature study societies and to magazines such as the *Nature Study Review*, which was started in 1905.

As formulated by Straight, the new subject developed as a reaction against object lessons. It was clear to him that nature study should be elementary science and this was in the main the view of Jackman also. In Jackman's writing one may notice the influence of the kindergarten and the child-study movement. To others, nature study appeared to be especially appropriate for the rural school and the children from the farms, and had special importance for agriculture and life on the farm. By 1900 a more sentimental phase had begun. A critic of this "effeminate" nature study put his judgment in these words:

> Nature study is science. The idea that it is not science leads to serious results. The responsibility for accuracy seems to disappear and much of the nonsense and sentimentalism that has brought discredit on the subject is due to this fundamental error.

There can be no doubt that where nature study was seriously pursued, either as a subject with practical applications to agriculture or as an easy natural history introduction to science, it was a valuable addition to the work of the schools. It was easily possible to link it with geography and with elementary handwork and this was often done.

THE KINDERGARTEN IN THE UNITED STATES

The founder of the kindergarten considered his system and philosophy to be of general application to education at all levels and not to be confined to the education of small children; and in the course of time the new institution has come to influence the work of most of the elementary grades. Perhaps the first Froebelian to work in the United States was Caroline Frankenberg, who came to Columbus, Ohio, in 1838. According to a family tradition, which it is difficult to verify, she in that year established "a school based upon the active interests of children." This title, which had been chosen by Froebel for his new institution, was discarded in 1840 when he thought of the name, *Kindergarten*. At any rate, Caroline Frankenberg had been in the Froebel circle for some time before coming to America; and after a year in this country she returned to Dresden to help her brother in developing the kindergarten there. Her brief early American visit had no definite influence.

A notice of Froebel's "infant-gardens" was printed by Henry Barnard in his *American Journal of Education* in 1856. He described the Froebelian gifts and a kindergarten that he had seen at the London Exposition. He declared the new institution to be "by far the most original, attractive, and philosophical form of infant development that the world has yet seen." At the same time (1855) Mrs. Carl Schurz opened a small family kindergarten for her own child and the children of her neighbors at Watertown, Wisconsin. A native American, Elizabeth Peabody of Boston, opened a kindergarten in 1860 on information furnished by Mrs. Schurz. In her own opinion this effort was a failure and she left for Germany to study the kindergarten in its native land. She later declared, "It was Emma Marwedel who in 1867 first introduced me to Froebel's genuine kindergarten in the city of Hamburg and inspired me with the courage to make the extension of the kindergarten in my own country the main object of my life." In this decision she persevered. The kindergarten became for her a sacred cause. By editing magazines, writing books, and delivering addresses she became an important propagandist for the new education.

When Elizabeth Peabody returned from Germany in 1868, she found that a school to prepare teachers for kindergartens had just been established in Boston by Matilda and Alma Kriege. Mary J. Garland, who became another kindergarten promoter, was educated in this school; and she and her own pupils found a patron in Pauline Agassiz Shaw, who aided not only the kindergarten but also the manual training, vocational guidance, and other educational movements.

The foundations for the spread of the kindergarten in America were laid by the schools for kindergarten teachers that the disciples of Froebel established here, by the Krieges in Boston (1868), Maria Boelte and John Kraus in New York City (1872), and Emma Marwedel in Washington, D.C. (1872). All of these were German immigrants who had been prepared by the immediate pupils of Froebel. Maria Baelte (1836–1918) was the most successful of all, and in the course of a long life she sent out about twelve hundred kindergartners from her school. With Dr. Kraus she published an important early book, *The Kindergarten Guide* (1877). William N. Hailmann (1836–1920) came from Switzerland and was judged by G. Stanley Hall to have been "by far the most eminent of all men in this country devoted to the interests of the kindergarten." Hailmann made the well-known translation of Froebel's *Education of Man* in 1887.

The crucial step of incorporating the kindergarten into the public school system was taken in St. Louis in 1873. Before that the kindergarten had been a private institution promoted by philanthropists, churches, and welfare agencies. In New York the Ethical Culture Society under the leadership of Felix Adler established a kindergarten in their school for workingmen's children. Mrs. Shaw supported thirty or more private kindergartens in Boston until the city finally took them over. Great industrialists sometimes supported the new institution in the belief that it would make children more skillful with their hands and thus develop skilled workers. Many were supported as a means of providing social relief and moral training. But in St. Louis the kindergarten was made a part of the public school system. The initiative was taken by Susan E. Blow (1843–1916). Having secured the support of Superintendent Harris, she prepared for her work under Maria Boelte and opened a training class and one kindergarten in a public school building. By 1880 there were fifty-two kindergartens in the schools of the city.

The public kindergarten spread slowly at first but more rapidly after 1885. As early as 1880 there were reported to the United States Bureau of Education more than two hundred public kindergartens. They enrolled nine thousand children in fourteen states. Five years later the numbers of the institutions and their pupils had doubled and were found in thirty-five states. Between these two years Milwaukee, perhaps influenced by its large German population, sent a committee to study the St. Louis arrangements. Upon receiving a favorable report from its investigators, that city introduced the new institution into its public school system. Boston established the public kindergarten in 1888 by incorporating the large number that had been privately supported in the city. This rapid progress continued at an even greater rate throughout the cities of the country until the early 1890s. As a result of the financial depression of 1893 many were again abandoned. Then, and in every financial crisis since, the kindergarten has been one of the services that school systems have sometimes been too easily persuaded to give up. The kindergarten has never become common in the rural sections; but in the cities it has maintained itself quite well. According to recent official figures, only a little less than one half of all five-year-old children are enrolled in the kindergarten, and the proportion is still increasing. This does not support the opinion of some otherwise well-informed persons that the kindergarten is losing in popular estimation. It is, however, true that it is not getting enough financial support. The classes are too large, the salaries too small, and the space and arrangements are often inadequate.

When the National Education Association in 1884 organized a kindergarten department, William N. Hailmann became its first chairman and was several times reelected to that position. The topics considered by this department provide an index to the questions that interested kindergartens in those pioneer days. Some of the most frequent topics were the following: child study, education for parenthood, how to fit the kindergarten into the primary school system, handwork and industrial education, and the physical development and health of small children. Consider the third topic: The integration with the elementary school has not always been successfully carried out. The kindergarten has often remained apart. Where integration has taken place, its methods have often to a startling degree modified the primary school. Even where the kindergarten remained apart, and in spite of its insecure position in American systems, the kindergarten influence has been one of the main agencies in the development of the new education.

INTRODUCING NEW METHODS OF TEACHING

The new methods were named the Quincy methods after a suburb of Boston where Francis W. Parker (1837–1902) was superintendent of schools in the latter 1870s. The methods of teaching favored by Parker at Quincy and afterward were based, like the Oswego system, on observation. Parker acknowledged his indebtedness to Sheldon, but the methods were also influenced by nature study, child study, and the kindergarten. At Quincy, observation was to lead to further experience because the classes were to be more active and informal and the materials were to be more appropriate and interesting to the children than in the Oswego object-teaching. And Parker succeeded in this. The textbook-recitation routine was overcome; but in steering away from the precipice of formalism, the Quincy schools sometimes sailed close to the whirlpool of triviality.

A product of the American frontier democracy, Parker was to a great degree self-educated. Except for the Civil War period when he fought in the Union armies, he had been from the age of sixteen a teacher and a schoolman. "I do not remember the day," he once said, "when I did not believe that I should be a teacher." From the war, which made him a Colonel, he gained a fierce hatred of war and militarism. From the hardships and narrow opportunities of a pinched boyhood in rural New Hampshire he derived his love of nature, his interest in the common people, and his militant democracy. He was a part of the developing new education at home, but for three years he also studied at the University of Berlin (1872–1875).

The "selfish aristocracy" that attempted to subject the common people to the domination of the few was Parker's greatest enemy, and he never ceased to assail it. He hated the dual educational systems of Europe and all schemes to confine people in fixed classes and by class education to keep them in ignorance and thereby in subjection. He held that in building a democracy we must begin with the children; we must give them both freedom and responsibility; and, therefore, we must make the school a working democracy. And the freedom of the child, in his view, implied the freedom of the teacher; but with the possible conflict that is implicit here he did not deal. There were to be no fixed course of study, no numerical records, and no inflexible classification of pupils. Instead of report cards the children's drawings, compositions, and models were themselves taken to the parents. The *social factor* he declared to be the greatest factor of all: more important than the subjects taught, than the methods, and than the school itself. That which children learn from each other in play and work is the highest that is ever learned. Altogether in the spirit of Lincoln, he insisted that in school the strong and clever must serve the weak, for the sake of the social education of the strong and not only that the weak might be served. In democracy, he held, there can be neither masters nor slaves.

It appears, however, that Parker's analysis was inadequate. He nowhere dealt with the basic economic questions, nor with race; nor apparently did he realize that the lessons learned in a school democracy may be all too quickly forgotten in the stress of practical life and business. Like Horace Mann he hoped for an easy victory over the devils of our modern society. If such criticism, sixty years later, is easily made and unfair it is nevertheless important that we make it in order that we see our own duty more clearly. Our duty is to attempt to use the school more effectively to build democracy; and we shall not be able to do so if we ignore economies, racial discrimination, and the power of ordinary human selfishness.

Parker returned from his European studies in 1875 and was chosen superintendent of schools in Quincy, Massachusetts. The changes he made in the elementary schools of the city are indicated in a well-known book by Lelia Patridge, *The Quincy Methods Illustrated* (1885). Mindful of the formalism that had developed in object-teaching, Parker wrote, "These lessons should not be copied. Imitation never leads to creation." The basis of the Quincy methods was, however, a new form of object-teaching in a more natural setting and using a much greater variety of materials from common life and the sciences. The elementary curriculum of the Quincy schools was greatly enriched and much greater emphasis was placed upon the activity of the children, upon counting, measuring, calculating, drawing, coloring, modeling, conversation, and written composition. Indeed, so much emphasis was placed upon activity itself that some of the projects became, and were in fact called, Quincy Busy-Work. This was one of the diseases that afflicted the new method. To find time to make the teaching more personal the children in each class were divided into smaller groups; and while the teachers worked with one of these groups each of the other groups worked on its own exercises. Some of these activities with pegs, splints, or beads were merely ways to keep the hands occupied. The children sometimes complained that they "had beans" in every room.

The curriculum was reformed. The schools paid more attention to physical education, for the harmonious development of the child was, according to Parker and Pestalozzi, "the guiding principle of the New Education." A combination of local and human geography was introduced. The plan of concentrating as much of the instruction as possible around a geographical core was developed. This was similar to Herbart's idea, whether obtained from him or, as Parker thought, from H. H. Straight. The concentration of studies no doubt resulted from the attempt to unify the materials of an enriched program. Parker agreed with the Pestalozzi-Froebel emphasis on varied self-expression, not only through speech and writing but also through drawing, modeling, and other means. Like Froebel he introduced the principle of the culture epochs and used primitive industries, myths, and folklore as bases for manual work, history, and literature.

At the same time the course of study was flexible in the hands of the teacher, who was given freedom to experiment in selecting and arranging the materials. Textbooks were little used, subjects were fused, and the school skills such as writing and arithmetic were taught through use and not in separate classes. But there was an excess of recitations. The teacher was so much the center in the Quincy methods, there were so many questions and answers, that the children had too little chance to think and work consecutively. The object lesson had come back in a revitalized form. And as we already indicated, the greatest significance of the Quincy method lay in its emphasis on education for democracy and on cooperation between the school and the home. Parker's best phrase was, "The ideal school is the ideal community."

For a brief period, Parker became supervisor of the primary schools in Boston. During these years he gave several series of lectures at an early summer school for teachers at Martha's Vineyard, which had perhaps grown out of Agassiz's school. There Quincy and Oswego met. One day in 1882, after an enthusiastic lecture on Pestalozzi, in walked Hermann Krüsi, Jr., who had been an Oswego professor for twenty-five years and was the son of Pestalozzi's first assistant. Parker was just ready to begin a lecture. Krüsi, who reported the incident, wrote, "The enthusiastic man at once introduced me to his whole class with great warmth, and I was pleased to find that my work on Pestalozzi had found so many intelligent readers." Krüsi referred to his then recently published biography of the Swiss educator. Parker's lectures were published under the title *Talks on Teaching* (1883). He also wrote *How to Study Geography* (1889); and he was one of the most favored speakers at the meetings of the National Education Association (NEA). The last twenty years of his life were spent in Chicago as head of the Cook County Normal School and finally of the School of Education of the University of Chicago. Parker was not a technical philosopher but, more than anyone else before John Dewey, he was the spokesman for the New Education.

But if child development, "free child, free teacher," and education for democracy were to be widely followed as principles in American education, it gradually became clear that the organization of the school would have to be changed. To many it seemed that the rigid promotion system of the graded schools was the greatest of all hindrances in their efforts to promote the welfare and growth of individual children.

BREAKING THE LOCK STEP

In the graded school with its fixed curriculum and annual examinations there were frequent failures. The failing pupils were required to take over not only the studies in which they had failed but all the work of the year. Many pupils were stopped completely, perhaps at the fifth or sixth grade, and continued to repeat the work until they could leave school forever at the end of the compulsory attendance period. Few people thought to inquire what proportions of the pupils failed and why; nor did they ask what were the effects of the failures on the personality of the pupils or how those pupils would respond in the future when, as voters and parents, they had to do with public education.

Questions were however raised, after a while, by a well-known educator, Calvin M. Woodward of St. Louis. He published a study of "the age of withdrawal from school" (1878), based on the figures provided by the St. Louis school report of that year. His indictment received little notice until the subject was revived in the 1890s and his study was republished. Then Woodward returned to the inquiry with a new paper on "When and why pupils leave school; and How to promote attendance in the highest grades." His answer to the latter question was that attendance in the upper grades would be promoted through free textbooks, an enriched course of study including domestic science and manual training, and regional high schools making it unnecessary for pupils to travel across town to attend. He also showed that the problem was much more acute in some cities than in others. The facts that Woodward presented had long been known in a general way, but no one knew precisely what was happening and very few had stopped to think that things might be improved. There was no real child-accounting in education at that time.

To show how pupils of a given city at a given time were distributed by school years and chronological years, a new instrument, the age-grade table, was devised. Such a table was published in a book by Preston W. Search, *An Ideal School* (1901). The table shows that the schools of the city in question consisted of a one-year kindergarten, a nine-year elementary school, a four-year high school, and a year of postgraduate work. The table also shows that in almost every grade a majority of the children was over age. This falling behind the normal rate of progress in the course is called retardation. Reading the totals in the bottom line of Search's table we notice that there were five hundred ninety six-year-olds but only three hundred ninety fourteen-year-olds; and after the age of fourteen the numbers drop abruptly, although the new entrants into the high school partly cover up the facts. This dropping out before the course is completed is called elimination from school.

Within a few years the reports of city superintendents began to present such facts, and in less than a decade a group of young statisticians started to deal with them more comprehensively. E. L. Thorndike's study of *The Elimination of Pupils from School* (1907) was followed by *Child Accounting in the Public Schools* (1909) by Leonard P. Ayres and the same author's *Laggards in Our Schools* (1913). Ayres directed special attention to "the money cost of the repeater" and to the extraordinary difference in degree of retardation between comparable cities. George D. Strayer's *Age and Grade Census* had appeared in 1911. These statistical publications together with J. M. Rice's *Spelling Investigation* (1895) and other studies of teaching efficiency can be taken to mark the American beginnings of the science of education.

Attempts to overcome the evils of rigid grading had been made before accurate information was available: by Parker at Quincy through the formation of homogeneous groups in each room, and by W. T. Harris at St. Louis by a plan of frequent reclassification and promotion. Harris, in about 1868, had the pupils reclassified every six weeks so that none was compelled to remain long in a class doing work that was far above or below his level or capacity at that time. Several other cities introduced modified forms of this frequent reclassification scheme.

Other individualizing schemes were the Cambridge and the Batavia plans, supervised study, and the platoon school. The Cambridge "multiple-track" plan allowed pupils to take a longer or shorter time to complete a standard course of study. The plan requires each pupil to do all the required work of the course but permits him to vary the rate. In other systems bright pupils were permitted to skip a half-year or a year of the course; or they were given extra work to do, thus asking them to complete an enriched or amplified course. Both the double promotion and the enriched course plans assume that the curriculum is adapted to the average pupil but that some adjustment should be made for the keen and aggressive pupils. On the other hand, the Batavia plan and supervised study as well as various forms of remedial instruction are intended to help the slow and the unwilling. Supervised study was very widely introduced about 1915, especially in high schools, but its equivalent was also used in the elementary grades. The Batavia plan was a form of supervised study in the elementary school devised by Superintendent John P. Kennedy of Batavia, New York. Under this plan two teachers were assigned to each room, one to help the pupils in their preparation and the other to conduct the group and class exercises. We have now mentioned three kinds of plans to adapt the schoolwork to the varying abilities of the pupils: to vary the rate of the pupils' progress, to vary the total amount and kind of work, and to aid weak pupils to overcome difficulties they could not master alone.

The most extreme position against rigid grading was taken by Preston Willis Search (1853–1932), who developed the scheme of individual instruction that is usually called the Pueblo plan, after the city in Colorado where it was fully developed. Search varied all three of the factors we have named: the rate of work, the amount of work, and the help given, in accordance with the apparent needs of each pupil. He turned the classrooms into laboratories, studios, and workrooms and abolished all regular classwork except in music and physical education. He did not individualize the course of study. Each pupil followed a regular course, and in each subject, such as algebra, history, or Caesar, the pupil prepared the same series of exercises. He did this at his own gait, going as far as his abilities permitted in the allotted time. The teacher helped the pupils with difficulties and suggested methods of attack.

After Search, the most active exponent of individual instruction versus the lock step in education was his disciple, Frederic Burk (1862–1924). As Superintendent of Schools, research worker under G. Stanley Hall, and Principal of the State Normal School at San Francisco, Burk wielded considerable influence. Like Search, he considered repeating and retardation the cardinal evils in education and individual instruction the effective remedy. His example and his pupils spread the method, especially Carleton Washburne who devised a modified form, the Winnetka plan. The Dalton Laboratory plan, which Helen Parkhurst developed in about 1915, was indebted to Burk but also to Doctor Maria Montessori of Italy and to Edgar J. Swift and his widely read book *The Mind in the Making* (1908). The Dalton plan was intended to give the pupil greater freedom and also greater responsibility for "budgeting his time and fulfilling his contract." Both the Winnetka and the Dalton plans provided some opportunities for group activities and for cooperation along with the individual programs.

This combination of individual and group work also characterizes the platoon school or work-study-play plan that was carried out at Gary by Superintendent William J. Wirt. The more complete and economical use of the school plant is another major objective of the platoon plan. The schoolday is divided into three equal periods, and in any given period one third of the pupils are engaged in work, another third in study, and the rest in play. In this way all the facilities of a school are in constant use. Many cities employ the work-study-play plan or some modification of it.

All of these plans have some merits, but none is a panacea and none has lived up to the early claims of its sponsors. Some of them have been generally abandoned, including the Cambridge, Batavia, Pueblo, and Dalton plans, and the Winnetka plan has never been widely adopted. The present tendency is to use individual and group projects within the class system and the usual social organization of the school. We have learned from all this experimentation to provide for a moderate degree of freedom and responsibility and to increase both as children learn to use them wisely. Schools have not been able to dispense with the judgment and the leadership of the teacher. Teachers, in general, still believe that they should teach their pupils as well as guide them and should use class as well as individual methods.

We shall appropriately close this section with a word from F. W. Parker who, in answer to Search, said:

> The ideal school is the ideal community, an embryonic democracy. The child is not sent to school to acquire knowledge only, but to live. Education is not so much preparation for life as it is real living. The teacher must be the leader in this community in which the child and teacher must learn to live not only for themselves but for others.

Words such as these were accepted and have indeed been repeated by Dewey, who continued the Parker doctrine of democratic education in a democratic school.

PROGRESSIVE EDUCATION

The term *progressive education* has been in common use for more than six decades but, because the complex movement that carries this label has changed from time to time, its various meanings should be gathered from the narrative and description which follow. There is no acceptable brief definition. There were progressive teachers before John Dewey and Francis W. Parker. One can name Amos Bronson Alcott, G. F. Thayer, David P. Page, and H. H. Straight without exhausting the list. Not everything that these great teachers did was progressive, but neither is everything progressive that the present progressives do. Some of the trends of the common school revival fall within the progressive category. All of the movements described in this chapter have some elements of progressivism; and the manual training movement formed one of its introductory stages. The student should have in mind the doctrines of Rousseau and the work of Pestalozzi and Froebel and should read the section on school activities in order to see the scope of the present topic.

Manual training and kindergarten education were combined in two new departures that took place in New York City in about 1880. One of these experiments was made by Felix Adler when he organized a free kindergarten for workingmen's children in 1878. In this undertaking he proposed to form a new type of school "in which the reformed system begun in the kindergarten might be continued through all the higher grades of instruction." The next year the Workingmen's School was organized with handwork, artistic and constructional activities, object lessons, and light gymnastics, in addition to the usual school subjects. Adler was most of all interested in practical ethics, or improved social conduct, and his school became the Ethical Culture School or system that today is one of the leading progressive centers. Unfortunately the schools had to charge fees and they are no longer maintained for workingmen's children.

The other new departure in New York commenced with the effort of Emily Huntington to adapt kindergarten methods to the education of older girls. She substituted domestic utensils and occupations for the kindergarten gifts and developed a curriculum based on household activities. The society formed to promote these classes was called the Kitchen Garden Association. It later was combined with the Industrial Education Association, which was formed to prepare manual-training teachers. The outcome of these movements, as noticed earlier, was Teachers College of Columbia University, with the Horace Mann School and later also the Speyer School as demonstration centers. The early work of Felix Adler and Emily Huntington was contemporary with Parker's work at Quincy, and the three are examples of the new education of about 1880. Parker's later work in Chicago brought him into contact with John Dewey who in 1896 established his laboratory or experimental school at the new University of Chicago. The University Elementary School was its official title.

Several of the current trends in elementary education were integrated in Dewey's new school: chief among them were the ideas of Froebel and Parker that the school should be a community and that learning should be an active and cooperative process involving investigation, construction, and artistic creation. These were supported by the biological and functional psychology of James, Angell, and Dewey himself; by the manual training and nature study movements, each of which underwent important changes at Dewey's hands; and finally by the effort to relate the school to the outside community. This laboratory school thus compounded of earlier elements was Dewey's first great contribution to what was later called progressive education. This was also the beginning of Dewey's philosophical development, which found expression in a long list of works including *Democracy and Education* (1916). We should premise that for Dewey philosophy and education are identical. Each of these familiar but even now still cryptic words means the practical experimental study by man of man himself and of his world. Dewey's philosophy gradually developed into experimentalism.

An excellent account of the school appeared in a series of nine monographs that were published in 1900 under the title *The Elementary School Record*. In one of these, Dewey deals with his debt to Froebel as follows:

One of the traditions of the school is of a visitor who, in its early days, called to see the kindergarten. On being told that the school had not as yet established one, she asked if there were not singing, drawing, manual training, plays and dramatizations, and the attention to the children's social relations. When her questions were answered in the affirmative she remarked both triumphantly and indignantly that that was what she understood by a kindergarten, and she did not know what was meant by saying that the school had no kindergarten. The remark was perhaps justified in spirit, if not in letter. At all events, it suggests that in a certain sense the school endeavors throughout its whole course—now including children between four and thirteen—to carry into effect certain principles which Froebel was perhaps the first consciously to set forth. Speaking still in general, these principles are

1. That the primary business of the school is to train children in cooperative and mutually helpful living.
2. That the primary root of all educative activity is in the instinctive, impulsive attitudes and activities of the child, and not in the presentation and application of external material. . . .
3. That these individual tendencies and activities are organized and directed through the uses made of them in keeping up the cooperative living already spoken of, taking advantage of them to reproduce on the child's plane the typical doings and occupations of the larger, maturer society into which he is finally to go forth; and that it is through production and creative use that valuable knowledge is secured and clinched.

So far as these statements correctly represent Froebel's education philosophy, the school should be regarded as its exponent.

The Chicago school was experimental in two senses: in its constant use of experiment and inquiry as the children's method of learning, and in its purpose to serve as a laboratory for the transformation of schools and of their relation to society. According to Dewey, investigation begins with a difficulty or problem. What was the basic problem that called the Chicago school into being? It was the Hegelian idea of conflict. There were the old oppositions between interest and effort, child and curriculum, and school and society. These phrases are the titles of some of Dewey's early writings. In *School and Society,* he directed special attention to the educational changes that had resulted from the Industrial Revolution. The school he desired was to be a miniature society, in the closest relation to the larger society around it, and an agency for resolving social and intellectual conflicts.

Into such a school the occupations of common life and industry were to be introduced, not as special subjects or for vocational purposes but as the center of the general curriculum and the model for the teaching method. This core-curriculum and method idea was characteristic of the Chicago laboratory school. Children at the age of six began with home activities involving simple domestic and industrial tasks, materials, and implements. Thus, manual training became industrial arts. In the following school years, using the culture-epochs concept of the Herbartians as the organizing principle, the historical development of industry, invention, and group living was followed. The dependence of man on nature and on society led pupils to the study of science and history. Nature study and simple experiments were introduced. Mechanical devices such as the spinning wheel and the loom were used. The study of cotton, for example, was carried through all stages from the seed and growing plant, the matured fiber, spinning and weaving, to the uses of the finished cloth. Thus, the old nature study in new forms was combined with industrial and social studies. Old and new inventions were studied. Clocks and telephones led directly to the consideration of communication and social cooperation. Blind effort, formal drill, recitations, and overt discipline were eliminated by guiding the children in self-education through discovery, construction, and cooperation in engrossing work. The school was in existence for only eight years, not long enough to realize its full promise. Even so it is unfortunate that we do not have a study of the influence it may have exerted on its pupils. The usual assumption, therefore, that this was the ideal elementary school is after all only an assumption. It is, however, one that has been used in many situations by the disciples of Dewey.

There were other new schools at this time. Preston W. Search, in *An Ideal School* (1901), named several of the progressive schools of that day: among the European, Abbotsholme and the École des Roches; and among the American, the George Junior Republic, Felix Adler's Ethical Culture School, The Tome School, and the Casa de Rosa of Los Angeles, as well as several public school systems. But for admission to Search's list it was rather imperative that a school be a promoter of individual teaching, and this may explain why he did not mention the University Elementary School. The new schools that may have been influenced by the Dewey experiment were the laboratory school of the University of Missouri, which was organized in 1904 by Junius L. Meriam, and the Speyer School of Teachers College, Columbia University, into which a strong Herbartian element was introduced by Frank M. McMurry. McMurry developed a curriculum composed of primitive life activities, domestic occupations, nature study, and construction work. Reading and writing were closely related to these activities. Arithmetic was separately organized but it was also connected with the activities as far as seemed feasible. The correlation of materials from different subjects was stressed and problems were employed, but there was provision for drill and subject mastery. The Speyer School under McMurry, therefore, followed a program that was intermediate between the activity and the conventional schools.

The schools named, although all contain new features, were based on the doctrines of Herbart or Froebel, more especially the latter. The School of Organic Education opened in 1907 by Mrs. Marietta Johnson at Fairhope, Alabama, was a still more radical departure from current practice, and it closely resembled the plan of Rousseau. It was, however, a school, not a tutorial scheme. In an ideal school, said Mrs. Johnson, there should be tables and chairs, no desks, and not more than twenty pupils to a teacher. Money would be needed to reduce the size of schools to this number, but we have money for cut glass and silver. One may remark that some people have money for these desirable items. No reading or writing should be taught before the age of nine or ten and "infinite materials" for the children's work and play should be provided. There must be no acceleration and no specialization in the early years—that is, we must, as Rousseau held, lose time, not gain it. Interest, spontaneity, joy, and mental grasp, not knowledge or skill are the goals. There must be no recitations and no assigned lessons, no examinations, grades, failures, or promotions. The children should be outdoors in the midst of nature, but nature study makes children hate nature and is taboo. Music, dancing, singing, games, and handwork, together with stories, are to be the main elements of the early curriculum. All children should be admitted to high school at fourteen and to college at eighteen without examination. This summary of her programs is from Marietta Johnson's *Youth in a World of Men* (1929) and is an example of Left-Wing progressive education.

About the time of World War I and since then, numerous elementary and secondary progressive schools were founded and many older schools turned in the progressive direction. The Country Day School movement of that period was evidence of dissatisfaction with the conventional mass education of the public schools. Wealthy or at least well-to-do parents in many of the large cities cooperated in the establishment of private day schools in the suburban or nearby rural districts. The Shady Hill Country Day School was opened in Germantown, Pennsylvania, in 1912; the City and Country School under Caroline Pratt, in New York, in 1914; the Walden School in New York and the Shady Hill School of Cambridge, Massachusetts, in 1915; and similar schools in other large cities. Many boarding schools and academies with elementary classes developed progressive philosophies and practices. Activity and project methods and core curricula were also introduced more widely in some of the large city systems, including some schools in New York, Denver, Des Moines, and elsewhere. The Progressive Education Association was organized in 1919 by a group of educators and interested citizens for the purpose of uniting those who were experimenting with the new schools and of securing the interest of a wider public for them. At first the association was mainly concerned with elementary education but later, as we shall see in the next chapter, it moved into the secondary field also. In 1932, the association became an affiliate of the New Education Fellowship, which carries on similar work in Great Britain, Europe, and other parts of the world.

At the time of its organization the Progressive Education Association declared that its aims were to encourage the free and natural development of children and for this purpose to study their physical and mental development and to base the education of children on their interests. Many progressives later modified the latter principle to say that education should be based on children's interests and needs. Even this did not satisfy everyone and some within the progressive ranks urged that social needs should also be considered; but one might raise the question whether these were really progressive. On the physical side the association demanded small classes, expanded and improved health-teaching and services, and better and more varied equipment for teaching and learning. They proposed to develop cooperation between the school and the community and to promote the freedom of teachers. These two aims, each good in itself, are not always easy to harmonize. The progressive teacher, however, was to guide and stimulate rather than to control the child or to hear recitations. One of the leaders of progressive education, Vivian T. Thayer of the Ethical Culture Schools, wrote a book called *The Passing of the Recitation* (1928).

The first honorary President of the Progressive Association was Charles William Eliot, President of Harvard University and promoter of the college elective system. He was succeeded in office by John Dewey. For a time the association conducted two magazines, *Progressive Education* and *Frontiers of Democracy*. The latter journal was discontinued in 1943 and shortly thereafter the association took the new name of American Education Fellowship. It would seem that the fellowship took a defensive position to try to hold ground already won and gave up further pioneering. Progressive education had been under attack from the time of Francis W. Parker, and the opposition seems to have increased after 1930. It was reported that the change of name was the result of influences stemming from World War II, and it is a fact that the membership declined sharply after the American entry into the struggle. War always reveals the real or reputed shortcomings of the schools. Similar charges were made in World War I, but the United States participated for only a short time in that conflict and the accusations were quickly forgotten after our early return to "normalcy." In World War II, the continued existence of many remediable physical defects, lack of discipline, inability to write effectively, and great deficiencies in elementary mathematics and science were blamed on the schools. But even if this arraignment is justified, the defects can hardly be attributed entirely to progressive education because our schools had not become widely and generally progressive. The accusers, however, assert that even conservative schools had become soft and flabby through the infiltration of progressive ideas. On the other hand the facts may be quite otherwise. It may be that in our attempt to provide free access to educational opportunity for all, we have everywhere, in the conservative as in the progressive camp, placed too little emphasis on accuracy and thoroughness.

Attempts have been made to evaluate the results of the work of the conflicting types of schools by scientific methods. J. Wayne Wrightstone's *Appraisal of Newer Elementary School Practices* (1938) and J. Cayce

Morrison's *The Activity Program* (1941) are two of these. Both agree that in the fundamental subjects the pupils in the new schools do about as well as those under the older types of teaching and recitation. Pupils from progressive schools may do a little better in reading and writing English and a little worse in spelling and arithmetic, but there is little to choose between them. In more intangible matters such as breadth of knowledge and interests, social activities, initiative, and skill in dealing with new problems, the progessive school pupils excel those from the conventional schools; but again the differences, although significant, are not very great. These results must be profoundly disappointing to both parties. Neither the expert teachers, small classes, rich curricula, varied equipment, and new methods of the one, nor the more rigid standards, drill, and examinations of the other have solved the problem of securing a high level of universal literacy, critical intelligence, scientific knowledge, democracy, tolerance, and social cooperation. This does not mean that our schools have failed, but it does mean that there is no easy road to a high level of national education. It must be the task of the next few years to learn all we can from the great and instructive experiment that progressive education is conducting and has conducted for the last seventy-five years. And our results should also be compared with those of other countries.

As implied in the title of this chapter, the elementary school of the present day whether progressive or more conventional is a new school. Its instruction has a far richer content, its physical facilities and educational materials are better, its teachers have a more scientific preparation and clearer conception of their task, and its treatment of children is more humane and is based on a fuller understanding of child nature than was the case one hundred years ago. The progress of the past is a guide and an incentive to further improvements in the future. But we must always remember that many of our schools in large areas have hardly been affected by the progress in other areas. Although the general level has been raised, many schools are even now poorly equipped and badly staffed, and have narrow, highly traditional curricula. Such uneven conditions set a great challenge before our educational statesmanship.

The old school was almost purely intellectual and bookish, even textbookish. The new elementary school has a far more varied, richer, and better balanced program than the old school employed. Nature study, health care and instruction, domestic activities, handwork, music, drawing, literature, history, and other materials have been added. Child study and educational psychology have supplied a valuable body of knowledge on growth, nutrition, interests, emotional stability and instability, group versus individual conduct, and other school and child conditions and problems. A great deal of knowledge is now at hand for the teacher's use. Social conditions have also, since the time of Pestalozzi and in the first instance through his influence, aided in transforming the old authoritarian relations between teachers and pupils. The older attitudes have largely vanished, and instead one finds greater cooperation and more scientific understanding. Teaching has become more informal and is more directly related to the lives of the pupils. New methods involving investigation by the pupils, group work, projects, and activities have come to be more widely employed. At this point, however, many students of education and prospective teachers sometimes develop a mistaken conception of the actual conditions in the schools. They think progressive education is more widespread than is the case. The activity curriculum, the child-centered school, integrated learning without subject divisions, and freedom for the child within the school have become familiar phrases in descriptions of the new conditions. All these can be found in actual schools here and there, but they are not general. They are still ideals rather than achieved conditions, and many responsible educators do not accept them as ideals. Most of our schools are likely to remain fairly conventional for a long time.

One of the permanent issues that was sharpened by the Depression and also by World War II is that between social orientation and individual interests and development. On the one hand we have those who would stress the demands of society, the problems of American life and culture, or education for democracy; on the other hand are those who consider that the personal interests of children, recognized and accepted by them, provide the only sound basis for a school program. It seems that in the last twenty years the social aims have been given greater attention than they were between 1920 and 1930. Radical progressives would call this a reactionary trend, and it may be in part a reaction against their program. However, it is also a recognition that the elementary school needs to teach the duties and the values of citizenship in a democracy more effectively than either the old school or the new has done. The whole school, not only in the study of history or current problems, should contribute to this end.

FROM GRADED SCHOOLS TO HIGH SCHOOLS

We have already dealt briefly with grading in considering the American system and in other connections, but the subject is so important to an understanding of high school development that further examples will be given. In most states the high school developed without legal authority. However, laws permitting graded schools to be formed were frequently enacted: in Iowa, in about 1850, "central grammar schools" and schools of higher grades; in New York, "union free school districts" with "secondary departments"; and in Pennsylvania, graded schools and the teaching of "higher branches." Many similar examples could be selected. The quoted phrases suggest the fact that the high school developed gradually and that its growth depended on the grading of the schools. After the movement had progressed for several decades—that is, by about 1870 or 1880—the character of the high school became clear. It was seen to be a separately administered and publicly controlled free school offering general education to adolescent youth.

Even the famous Massachusetts law of 1827 was hardly a high school law. It was a reenactment in somewhat broader terms of a still more famous statute, "the old deluder Satan" law of 1647. The new law prescribed that American history, bookkeeping, geometry, surveying, and algebra were to be offered in districts of five hundred families; and in districts of four thousand people, the employment of a teacher who was competent to teach Latin, Greek, history, rhetoric, and logic was demanded. This is a Latin grammar school law, and indeed the subjects named, excepting only the bookkeeping, surveying, and logic, are the exact subjects included in the curriculum of the Boston Latin School at that time. But although in 1647 every town of one hundred families was required to establish a Latin school, in 1827 a similar provision was not demanded until the town had reached a size about eight times as large.

That graded schools formed the necessary base for the public high school must have been clear to many, but it was perhaps clearest of all to Henry Barnard. In 1838, when he had just become secretary to the Connecticut Board of Commissioners of Common Schools, he reported that the state had practically no graded schools, that so much was attempted in ungraded schools with all classes and ages intermingled that nothing was done well, and that the younger children were often neglected. Upon his recommendation, Connecticut passed a graded school law in 1839, and in the following year a rudimentary but, as it turned out, permanent high school was established at Middletown.

The young city of Cincinnati also furnished an early example of grading. An Ohio law of 1829 had made that city an independent school district, but the first public schools were not graded and were conducted in rented rooms. Seven years later, in 1836, the first public school buildings were erected, and the schools were divided into two "grades," called primary and secondary, each comprising several years of work. Albert Picket, who had been one of the advisers of the first staff of public school teachers in Cincinnati, was, in 1840, a member of the school board. With the help of another member, James H. Perkins, he prepared a course of study with five grades extending from the alphabet and "teaching pupils to use their eyes as well as their ears" to high school mathematics and "rural economy" in grade five. The plan could not be fully carried out at once, but by 1847 the system was far enough advanced to permit the opening of the Central High School. Four years later the Hughes and Woodward Funds became available and two high schools bearing those names were established. Many other high schools were opened in Ohio, Pennsylvania, and other states before the Civil War. It has been calculated that New England had one hundred and eighty-five high schools by 1865, but some of these were public Latin schools and others offered only partial courses of two or three years' duration.

Secondary education, both private and public, entered into a period of rapid expansion about the time of the Civil War. In the older states the sparse population, hard living conditions, and a great demand for manual labor had persisted for two centuries from the early settlements, but this pioneer period was progressively shortened as new states developed in the West. Even in the heavily wooded sections, such states as Ohio and Michigan quickly felled their forests and built cities, whose employments gave an opening for secondary education. Ohio, within a half-century after attaining statehood, passed her Akron law (1847), which permitted the grading of schools and the creation of central schools. In Iowa this step took not half a century but hardly more than a decade. And in the Far West many territories provided for general state school officers, public elementary and high schools, and a state university even before they were admitted into the Union. Through the migration of settlers from the older states and the optimism of the pioneers, the new states often started with plans that were in advance of those in operation in the regions from which the people had come. The north central and western states, which did not have as strong a prior allegiance to academies and private schools, accepted the high school more easily, developed it more experimentally, and supported it more ungrudgingly than the East and the Old South.

To report the number of high schools at a given time, say in 1860, is difficult because exact information is wanting and definitions vary. Henry Barnard, using a definition that involved a very high standard, estimated that there were only one hundred sixty. This left out hundreds of small schools, many with partial courses. In New England one investigator, as we have seen, counted one hundred eighty-five high schools by 1865, and two thirds of these were in Massachusetts. In New York several academies had been taken over by the public boards; and union schools and high schools to the number of thirty or forty were in operation by 1860. Pennsylvania had as many. In Ohio, a student found evidence of twenty or more. We can reasonably estimate that by that time there were five hundred public high schools with a separate organization, each offering two or more years of work above the elementary school. But the academies were more numerous and more influential than the high schools until about 1880 or even later.

Although the high school developed as a result of popular demand, it was not a universal demand and there was opposition. The early history of the Norwich Free Academy is instructive in this connection. A strong movement to establish a public high school in Norwich, Connecticut, developed in 1846. However, the opposition proved even stronger and after a delay of eight years the present academy was founded as a private tuition school. In this and similar cases the establishment of an academy prevented or delayed the founding of a public high school. Later, by an arrangement with the school board of Norwich, the tuition of the local pupils was paid out of public funds, and this plan still continues in force. Elsewhere, many academies were from time to time transferred to the local boards and became public high schools. The Utica Free Academy and the Elmira Free Academy, both in New York, illustrate this process. A list has been compiled of about seventy New York academies that, before 1874, became public schools.

In the Kalamazoo case of 1872 the Supreme Court of Michigan declared that a school district could legally use public money to teach branches above those of the elementary schools and to pay the salary of the superintendent. The case became famous because of the eloquent opinion written by Justice Cooley. He supported the decision of the court by the historical, rather than strictly legal, argument that because the Legislature had established public schools and a state university, the Legislature must have intended that pupils should be prepared for the university by the lower schools. He argued that, because the university demanded a knowledge of a foreign language or languages for entrance, the schools below the university had the legal right to teach these and other preparatory branches. Although this decision has been frequently quoted and cited, its effect has probably been exaggerated. Within a decade after the Kalamazoo case, eight or nine other cases against the high schools reached the Supreme Courts of other states and were decided in favor of the legality of the new schools. One of these, which originated in St. Clair County, Illinois, bears a close resemblance to the Kalamazoo case. The main question was on the teaching of foreign languages in public schools. It was decided affirmatively in 1875, and there also the court based its decision on the history of school legislation in the state. Some public controversy over the establishment of high schools has been traced in the same period in thirty or more states.

The opposition to the high school stemmed from various sources. The comparatively higher costs of high schools over elementary schools were frequently cited. The supporters of the high school pointed out that the comparison should be made between the costs of education in high schools and the costs in academies and attempted to show that the former were less. Other economic issues were also raised. The opponents argued that the heavy taxation the high school required tended to discourage business. They also declared that a high school education caused children to despise manual labor. It was argued and denied that the high school courses were superficial, that they benefited only a small part of the population, and that the academies were more adaptable to the needs of the pupils and more thorough in their teaching. The private school interests seem to have mustered their forces against public secondary education for a special effort in about 1885. At that time the high school enrollment in the country passed the total enrollment in private secondary schools; and the United States Commissioner of Education expressed the opinion, which history has confirmed, that the public high school would be the dominant institution in its field. By the end of the century the high schools were far in the lead and at present they enroll more than ninety per cent of all secondary school pupils.

EXPANSION OF THE HIGH SCHOOL CURRICULUM

The high school began with the somewhat broad curriculum of the academy, and this was further expanded as the schools developed. In 1820, the Boston Latin School offered seven subjects, including Latin and Greek; but the English Classical School of 1821, without offering Latin or Greek, taught twenty-one subjects. The Massachusetts law of 1827 specified sixteen subjects and this number rose to twenty-seven in the law of 1858. The high school of Providence, to take another example, in 1855, offered twenty-eight subjects. And Alexander Inglis listed seventy-three subjects as taught in different high schools in Massachusetts in 1861, although no one school offered all of these.

The Boston High School at the beginning offered only a single curriculum, but before long other schools began to organize two or more parallel curricula, and one of these was usually a college preparatory curriculum. The Philadelphia High School began with three curricula. Frequently, in the early high schools a normal curriculum for teachers was also provided. This was usually similar to the general curriculum but included several professional subjects. As the movement developed, the comprehensive high school, offering several kinds of curricula—unlike the specialized school that offered only a single one, such as the commercial, the manual training, or the college preparatory curriculum—became the typical American high school. The Central High School of Philadelphia, as was indicated, was an early example of this important trend.

The colleges had a pronounced effect on the high school program. The great variety of curricula in most colleges in the latter part of the nineteenth century is indicated by the creation of new degrees such as bachelor of letters, of science, of philosophy, and of music. This bloated condition of the college offerings was paralleled by a similar distention of the high school program, which now included several modern languages and Latin; many English subjects such as rhetoric, composition, literature, and the history of literature; several varieties of social studies, including modern and American history and civics; and the sciences that gradually came to be taught by laboratory methods. The high school did not give degrees, but it created a large number of curricula with such titles as English-Latin, Latin-scientific, and English-scientific, in addition to the older general and college preparatory curricula. In 1900 a total of thirty-six curricula, each leading to high school graduation, was observed in different schools. Not many subjects were dropped from the high school program, but Greek was offered less and less frequently. Indeed, it never secured a foothold in the smaller schools and was soon confined to the large city high schools. Logic, astronomy, and the "evidences of Christianity" often given in the early high schools also disappeared. It will be noticed that the expansion up to 1880 mainly involved what are known as academic subjects such as literature, languages, mathematics, the sciences, and the social studies; but beginning about that time a new period of further expansion set in and this involved "things to do" as well as things to learn.

The earlier high schools had devoted themselves to a literary and intellectual program, but before 1900 several imaginative and expressional and several semivocational subjects were introduced. The high school began to emphasize not only knowing and understanding but also doing. Agriculture, commercial studies, home economics, manual training, and music were now taught. Such a classification into knowing and doing is, however, not at all absolute, for language and literature involve speaking and writing as well as reading; mathematics and science, especially when taught by laboratory methods, also involve activity. Yet it will not be denied that the new subjects stress training in skill and physical performance more than the older ones. We do not have space to include the development of all the new activities; but as music was one of the earliest we shall examine it first.

Music instruction books were written in Colonial times, one by Thomas Walter in 1721. Private singing schools began about the same time and continued for a century and longer. These were classes meeting periodically for the purpose of teaching the students to read music, to give them practice in singing, and to cultivate familiarity with hymns, songs, and choral works. It was a form of adult education. Until music was taught in the public schools, the singing school and the church choir were the chief means of music education open to the people.

Music was introduced widely into the public elementary schools in our educational renaissance even before 1830. Boston began to give such instruction regularly in 1838 when Lowell Mason, one of our great teachers, became supervisor of music in the schools of that city. From the elementary schools, music spread to the high schools. An early text, the *High School Choralist*, was prepared by Charles Aikin (1818–1882). Graded series of books for music study were developed after the Civil War, and the normal schools and some colleges began to prepare teachers and supervisors of public school music. The Commissioner of Education in 1886 reported two hundred fifty cities in which music was regularly taught; and so rapidly was it spreading that three years later eighty others were added to the list.

During the years that have passed since 1890, much of the emphasis has shifted from vocal to instrumental music and an extraordinary development has taken place, first of the school orchestra and in the last two decades of the school band. Indeed the band, and the marching rather than the concert band, has tended to win the greatest applause; but the high schools also continue to do not less but more choral and orchestral work. The phonograph and the radio, and the great artists and organizations of national fame, have given music a place in the life and the schools of the United States that could not have been imagined even fifty years ago.

The teaching of drawing as a useful study and especially as an aid in mechanical vocations was urged by Benjamin Franklin and Henry Barnard. To this Horace Mann added that the skill is of value to the teacher in illustrating his lessons. The high schools of Philadelphia and Baltimore offered work in drawing about 1840, and Rembrandt Peale was for a few years the teacher in the former school. Drawing textbooks began to appear. Massachusetts, by a law enacted in 1870, became the first state to develop an effective program of drawing instruction. Few states followed this example, but many of the larger high schools in all parts of the country introduced the subject without a mandate from the state.

For a long time drawing was taught to serve industry and this is still an important purpose, but more recently new ideas and a broader program have developed. Freehand drawing, sketching, illustrating, commercial art, modeling, and even home decoration and home planning have been given a place. Art appreciation in schools may perhaps be dated from a campaign of Ross Turner in about 1892 for schoolroom decoration. The aims of appreciation subjects include the cultivation of taste and of talent and the enrichment of life and leisure. Recent efforts have been made to relate the arts to everyday living and to join usefulness with beauty as well as to teach the best of both old and new art. The teaching of commercial and industrial art has kept pace with these more personal and expressional trends; but American education has not yet become art conscious to the degree that it has become music conscious.

The early purposes of manual training and of drawing instruction were the same, to serve industry; the methods of teaching also were similar, and the two subjects were often taught in close association with each other. In both, a formal method was developed. Both emphasized imitation, exact representation, and a step-by-step procedure. Experiments with shopwork courses were carried on by Calvin M. Woodward of Washington University in St. Louis shortly after the Civil War. Businessmen, hoping to find a substitute for apprenticeship, supported the venture and a manual training school was erected in 1880. The prospectus declared that "the interests of St. Louis demand for young men a system of education which shall fit them for the actual duties of life." This was a repetition, in almost the same words, of the aims of the first high schools opened sixty years earlier. Manual training was now to aid in doing what the older schools had not fully accomplished.

To indicate that he was interested in manual training not only for industrial purposes but also for its value in general education, Woodward used, and perhaps coined, a phrase that swept over the country. He said that manual training made it possible "to put the whole boy to school." Woodward also showed that the high schools were not holding their pupils: that too few of those who entered remained to graduate. He attributed the loss to the narrow academic curriculum and thought the remedy lay in the introduction of manual training, home economics, and other practical studies. This was twenty years before Preston W. Search, in *An Ideal School* (1901), published an age-grade table, and thirty years before Edward L. Thorndike made his pioneer study of retardation and elimination from school.

Private manual training schools were opened in a number of the large cities. The public elementary and high schools rapidly took it up. When the Children's Industrial Exhibition was held in New York in 1886, it displayed the work of all school grades from many localities including some as far west as Chicago. A public manual training high school had been opened in Baltimore in 1883 and other cities followed this example. A few higher institutions had introduced shopwork even earlier. The Illinois Industrial University, now the University of Illinois, had prepared an exhibit of shopwork for the Philadelphia Centennial Exposition of 1876. Eventually the land-grant colleges became extremely effective agencies for the promotion of shop and laboratory work, industrial and practical arts, applied science, home economics, and agriculture, but this influence came only after several decades of experimentation. The most prominent early introduction of manual training into a higher institution was made by the Massachusetts Institute of Technology. This was the Russian system of the Imperial Technical School of Moscow. It consisted of formal drill exercises that never produced any finished objects; but its defects were not seen until later. Its value lay in setting up graded series of class exercises to develop shop skills, which could be easily administered in a school. Only in 1894, in the naming of the Macy Manual Arts Building at Columbia University, was the word *arts* substituted for the word *training* to embrace the ideas of beauty, utility, and skill in one concept.

The United States Commissioner of Education in 1900 noted "a steady increase from year to year in the enrollment in the schools devoted especially to manual and industrial training." There were then about one hundred such schools and some of the largest high schools in the country were in this class. The new Technical High Schools gave considerable emphasis to vocational education without becoming trade schools, but many public trade schools were founded also. The trend, however, was toward the general high school in which the manual training curriculum ran parallel to the home economics, general, classical, and other curricula. The whole great movement toward activities had developed as the result of the convergence of many forces including the demands of a society that was rapidly becoming urban and industrial, the decline of apprenticeship, the introduction of science teaching, the kindergarten and child-study movement, and the growing high school enrollments of which manual training was partly cause, partly effect.

The ideas of Froebel that the school should be a community and that learning should be an active and cooperative process were applied in the elementary school that John Dewey directed from 1896 at the University of Chicago. These ideas had already been given considerable emphasis by F. W. Parker and they were now to be further supported by the biologically functional and evolutionary psychology of "the Chicago school" of psychologists of which Dewey and James R. Angell were prominent members. In Dewey's experimental school, the industrial occupations were not special subjects but became the center of the curriculum. They were also considered to embody the most effective method of teaching; and, accordingly, subject matter and method were regarded as complementary phases of all learning situations. Weaving, for example, studied through the construction and use of a simple loom would involve a different content from weaving studied from a book, a lecture, a film, or even a demonstration by the teacher. The school was experimental in the sense that the children, under guidance, experimentally determined their own curricula and methods. Dewey in 1899 explained the theory and practice of the school in a book, *School and Society*, which quickly attracted wide attention.

Occupations were selected that were considered real for children and not merely those that were typical of adult activities. These were to serve as means through which the school was to become an active community instead of a place set apart for learning lessons. Dewey held with Parker, Froebel, and Rousseau that, through these direct modes of exploring, manipulating, investigating, and constructing, there would arise many opportunities and occasions for the use of numbers, reading, writing, and spelling. These were no longer to be "subjects," but rather organic phases of the child's continuous experience. The natural activities of the child in following out his purposes would effectively correlate all his experiences, thus making unnecessary any special efforts at correlation such as the Herbartians of the same period tried to introduce. The phrase industrial arts was made necessary by the development of mechanized industry and was coined by Charles R. Richards in about 1904. He and Frederick G. Bonser became leading interpreters of Dewey's conception of industrial arts. In the modern high school the work of the industrial arts department has since 1900 become more and more industrial and scientific and has come to use a wide variety of materials. In the high school, however, integration with other phases of schoolwork is often very slight. The aims are turning toward teaching for wise production and consumption in an industrial society.

Active interest in vocational education paralleled the rise of industrial arts education. The report of the Douglas Commission to the Legislature of Massachusetts; the founding of the National Society for the Promotion of Industrial Education by Richards, David Snedden, and others; and the study of the same field by the New York State Department of Labor all came in the first decade of the twentieth century. A few technical schools for boys of sixteen or eighteen had already demonstrated what can be done in teaching the skilled trades. Efforts were not to be made to develop vocational schools either full-time or on a part-time cooperative basis. To study the questions further and to secure public support for the movement, state vocational commissions were appointed in several states in about 1908 and 1910. Laws were also enacted authorizing cities to establish vocational schools. The most complete and detailed act of this kind was adopted by Wisconsin in 1911. This law helped to create a dual system, because the state and local boards of vocational education it established were separate from the local school boards and state education departments that had charge of the ordinary public schools.

Vocational education raised several problems that call for continued attention. The gulf between vocational and general education was widened by the increased activity of the Federal Government which resulted from the Smith-Hughes (1917) and later acts with similar objects. The recent war-training and subsequent programs looked in the same general direction. The possibility that we are turning toward a national and state system of vocational education that will come into competition with the public school system, which has been built up by a century of thought and effort, is unfortunately real. Competition for funds is only one phase of this problem. Another stems from the conviction of public school leaders that young boys who have not completed their high school education are quite unprepared to choose their lifework wisely. This phase has led to the vocational guidance movement, which has been growing vigorously since the early years of this century. A related issue divides capital and management against labor. Labor leaders are disturbed by the prospect of the free and unregulated preparation of skilled and semiskilled mechanics and fear that this would seriously depress that area of the labor market. On the other hand, the lack of trained mechanics assumed almost crisis proportions in the war emergency of 1942 and 1943. Laborers also desire for their children the opportunity to prepare for the white-collar occupations, and in consequence they tend to favor general and academic courses. Furthermore, the rapid mechanization of industry and agriculture is making it more difficult for young workers to secure employment. This social fact is one of the chief reasons why the compulsory school age has been raised, the average period of school attendance has been lengthened, and the enrollment in high school has increased so rapidly in recent years.

Space limitations preclude a complete account of the high school curriculum expansion. Commercial studies have been briefly treated in an earlier chapter. The omission of agriculture and physical education leaves big gaps unfilled. Home economics also has made an important addition to the program. Progress in home economics education occurred in three periods: a long early stage when chiefly needlework was taught; a middle stage when, through philanthropic, health, and welfare movements and the establishment of the state colleges of agriculture, the foundations were laid; and the present period, which began about 1914 and in which the field of home economics teaching has been expanded and diversified. Textiles and clothing, foods, cooking, nutrition, and housing are still the basic subjects, but in this third period other areas also have been cultivated. These include home management, furniture, decoration, fuels, health and home nursing, consumer education, child care and development, and the study of personality and home relationships. In a report of 1939 covering fourteen thousand high schools, it was found that about three fourths of these offered home economics and that the largest enrollments were in the ninth and tenth grades.

Enough has now been detailed to show that a revolution in high school facilities, personnel, and purposes occurred in the latter nineteenth and the twentieth centuries through the introduction of activities and practical subjects. An administrative transition accompanied the changes in the program of studies. In this transition the high school was gradually freed somewhat from domination by the colleges. The early examinations for admission to the high school had long been given up. Now the control that the college entrance examinations exercised on the high school itself was also to be relaxed. We shall turn back to trace the progress of this trend.

STANDARDIZING THE HIGH SCHOOL

Admission to college had always been granted after examination by the individual college. In about 1870, the University of Michigan and a few years later Indiana University began to admit the graduates of accredited high schools without an entrance examination. The University of Michigan sent visitors who inspected and accredited the individual high schools, but Indiana University accepted the graduates of those schools that the State Board of Education certified as standard schools. These arrangements proved so satisfactory to both the schools and the universities that they were adopted by other institutions; and within thirty years similar accrediting systems were accepted by about two hundred colleges and universities, chiefly in the newer states. The new plan did not relieve the school from preparing their pupils in the specific subjects demanded by the particular college they wished to enter. The scheme was otherwise unsatisfactory because both the required standards and the required subjects varied from state to state and the subjects often differed among neighboring colleges in the same state. To correct this condition and to develop a more uniform policy for secondary education, the Committee of Ten was appointed. Later, regional associations of colleges and secondary schools were created to perform the accrediting functions. The latter came to be known as standardizing associations.

The Committee of Ten was appointed by the National Education Association in 1892 with Charles William Eliot as Chairman, and it made its report the following year. In preparing its report it had the assistance of numerous subject committees. The committee in its report agreed that college preparation is not the main function of secondary schools, but what was thus granted was again withdrawn by the declaration that the same subjects taught in the same way form the best preparation for both college and life. Each subject was to be considered equivalent to any other that was pursued successfully for the same length of time. But they set up sample curricula in which the academic subjects were strongly emphasized. And they urged that for purposes of mental training each major subject must be pursued for a considerable period of time. This would be desirable for the mastery of a field also, but if each subject is to be studied thoroughly the number of subjects that any one pupil can take will be clearly limited. Such a program also, like that of the College Entrance Board, did not encourage high schools to experiment with nonpreparatory kinds of work and services. As if to counteract some of the effects of the previous recommendations, the committee proposed to reduce the elementary school to a six-year program in order that foreign languages and high school mathematics and science could be begun earlier. They also favored some degree of subject election by high school pupils.

The work of the Committee of Ten seemed, at that time, to be much more important than it actually was. Even within the committee there was disagreement, and a minority report was prepared by the dissenters. These demanded a larger place for the activity subjects, opposed the doctrine of the educational equivalence of different subjects even for college preparation, and demanded a very different selection of subjects for the ninety per cent of the pupils who would not go to college. There were similar disagreements among schoolmen at large and it was charged that the committee had been overstaffed with college and private school teachers and executives. A study of the effect of the report of the Committee of Ten, made by Edwin G. Dexter in about 1905, found that the expansion of the high school program of studies had been little affected. Indeed the report was immediately followed by a brief trial of the elective system in many high schools. The rising opposition in the country to the doctrine of formal discipline may have been another reason why the report had no greater influence. In fact this outcome was foreseen by Chairman Eliot who predicted that the American high school, as he expressed it, would "diverge from the academy and endowed school, the first working on an information programme, the latter on a training programme."

To secure greater uniformity in entrance requirements, voluntary standardizing associations were formed in several sections of the United States, thus performing by agreement what in some countries was done by government dictation. The associations of colleges and secondary schools were usually formed at the instance of the colleges and were largely directed by them. The New England Association of Colleges and Preparatory Schools (1885) was the first, and it is significant that the term *preparatory* instead of secondary or high schools is used. Others were the Association of Colleges and Secondary Schools in the Middle States and Maryland (1892), the North Central (1894), the Southern (1895), the Northwest (1918), and the Western Association (1930). The associations in their meetings considered not only uniform entrance requirements but also means of improving secondary and collegiate education and of developing helpful relations between secondary and higher institutions.

The North Central Association, in 1900, recommended that member colleges should admit only those students who had completed the equivalent of a four-year course of sixteen units, a unit being defined as "a year's work in a subject for four or five periods a week." Included in the sixteen units there were to be two units of English, two of mathematics, one of science, and one of history. The same idea was a little later accepted by the Carnegie Foundation for the Advancement of Teaching, hence the term *Carnegie units*. The North Central and other associations undertook the inspection of schools. Those schools that, on inspection, met the standards of their associations were accredited. As late as 1940, fewer than six thousand out of a total of about twenty-five thousand secondary schools in the entire United States had met the standards of their regional associations and had been accredited. The standards set up by the different associations varied among themselves, so that although the North Central Association set the pattern and some standards were common there still were no uniform national standards of college admission. The recent cooperative study of secondary school evaluation and standards by these associations will be treated subsequently.

A second mode of college admission, through uniform entrance examinations, was developed by the Association for the Middle States and Maryland from a suggestion by President F. A. P. Barnard of Columbia University; and this led to the formation of the College Entrance Board. This Board, established in 1901, soon became an independent body. Its examinations are held annually at several hundred points in the United States and in foreign countries. The Board has endeavored to bring about "an agreement upon a uniform standard as to each subject required" by the colleges as well as agreement on methods of teaching and the desired preparation of secondary school teachers. It has obviously not tended to encourage high schools to experiment with new types of high school work and services.

REORGANIZING THE SYSTEM

The reorganization of the schools into elementary and junior and senior high schools is often said to have begun in Columbus, Ohio, in 1908 and in Berkeley, California, in 1909. And it was about that time when the idea began to attract attention. But the Committee of Ten had suggested it; the curriculum of the schools of Springfield, Massachusetts, in 1867, partly embodied it; and even the English Classical School of Boston, in 1821, might be claimed having been a junior high school. The Boston school was a separately organized, three-year high school that included the ages from twelve to fifteen and followed a shortened elementary school course; and it offered an enriched curriculum that was supposed to be adapted to young adolescents. Considering still further the date of origin, Thomas H. Briggs in his *The Junior High School* (1920) reports two junior high schools before 1900 and five others before 1909, but without giving the locations.

It is often supposed that we had a fairly universal 8–4 organization before the coming of the junior high school, but this, as we have seen is an error. There were elementary school courses of six, seven, eight, and nine years, and high school courses of two, three, four, and five years, as well as other course lengths and almost every possible combination of these. More than one fourth of the larger cities did not have an elementary school of eight years followed by a high school of four years. So much for the uniformity of our 8–4 plan; although widespread, it was not universal.

The arguments for the reorganization were numerous. Some of the committees of the National Education Association, such as the Committee on Economy of Time, urged a readjustment of the elementary curriculum to enable pupils to prepare for college at an earlier age. This result has not been achieved, for pupils still finish the junior-senior high schools at eighteen in most systems. Bright pupils in the upper grades of an eight-year elementary school, it was claimed, were merely marking time. This "sauntering," as John Locke called it, and the resulting habits of idleness, which the Boston subcommittee of 1821 deprecated, could be overcome by an enriched course. There were precedents for this. In European secondary schools and in good private schools, the pupils at the age of eighteen were one or two years ahead of most American children in their educational advancement. Some subjects such as foreign languages, algebra, and prevocational work should be begun earlier. Pupils above the sixth grade needed broader opportunities and differentiated curricula. This result has been attained in many schools.

The program of studies for youth, it was pointed out by Nicholas Murray

Butler, should be based on the nature and the stage of development of the pupils, and children between the ages of twelve and fifteen are in a transitional stage between childhood and full adolescence. The program should be adapted to them. This is seemingly a reasonable proposal, but there are difficulties in settling on the stage of child development that a given pupil has actually reached and in showing in practical terms how the curriculum can be adapted to the young adolescent. Pupils, it was said, would stay in school longer if the end of the compulsory attendance period, frequently at the age of fourteen, and the completion of the elementary school course did not come at the same time. Costs would be reduced, congestion in elementary schools would be relieved, and the junior high school would be located nearer to the homes of the pupils than the senior high school. The last was an important factor, for experience has shown that many more pupils will attend if schools are made more accessible. Perhaps the most frequently used argument was that the junior high school would help to bridge the gap between the elementary school and the departmentalized high school by providing exploratory courses, by giving more attention to the individual pupil, and by introducing departmentalization gradually.

The junior high school spread slowly after 1910 and more rapidly after 1920. Many grade combinations have been tried and are in use but the 6-3-3 and the 6-6 plans are the most common ones. The reorganization increased the enrollments, especially of boys, it retained pupils in school longer, and it has succeeded in furnishing more varied programs for young adolescents. Most of the large cities and many smaller and rural systems have adopted the new plan. But the factors that give vitality to the junior high school are appropriate methods, courses, equipment, and skilful teachers, not mere reorganization.

At about the time the junior high school was developing, and even earlier, several junior colleges were established. These are institutions that offer two years of work or more above the senior high school and that, therefore, cover somewhat the same ground as the first two years of the university or college course. Some of these regard themselves as terminal schools and offer vocational as well as academic courses; others are preparatory to the upper division of a college. There were junior colleges before 1850, but as the result of a self-conscious movement the institution must be placed in the latter decades of the nineteenth century.

Two ideas were basic: The first was that the university should not dissipate its strength in teaching the elementary subjects of the freshman and sophomore years, but should devote itself to advanced studies and graduate and professional work. This is, of course, the practice in Europe where the secondary schools do the work of the early college years in the United States, and where the university student begins at once to specialize if not in a narrow subject then at least in a field. President Henry P. Tappan of the University of Michigan, in 1852, urged that institution to transfer its lower division work to the high schools. This was not done, but in 1883 the university began to differentiate the work of the first two from that of the last two years and to permit specialization in the upper division. Similar developments took place in Minnesota and elsewhere, but the first real separation of the two divisions was effected at the University of Chicago under President William Rainey Harper, who is sometimes called the "father of the junior college."

The second idea was that many high school graduates who would not attend a college or university should have the opportunity to do one or more years of work beyond the high school. This they would do, it was evident, if local institutions for that purpose were available. President Harper fostered this idea and urged the stronger high schools to establish junior college departments. Such extensions of the work of the high school, although for preparatory purposes, were carried forward in Michigan where the state university began, in 1895, to accept one year of college work from the better high schools of the state. In response to the proposals of President Harper, junior colleges, in affiliation with the University of Chicago, were opened in Joliet, Illinois, and Goshen, Indiana, and elsewhere. Long before this time also a few private academies and seminaries began to offer one or more years of college work; and some struggling four-year colleges reduced their offerings to two years of work. The latter process was especially common in Texas, Missouri, and the Old South. In 1907, the state of California passed a law to permit high schools to offer postgraduate courses of study for their own graduates or those of other high schools; and the city of Fresno in 1910 took advantage of this law to establish a public junior college. Many others have been opened in that state and California is now the home of seventy-one such institutions, enrolling more than three hundred thousand students. In the entire country, over six hundred thousand students were enrolled in 1958 in five hundred and eighty junior colleges. The great majority and the largest of them are public institutions. In facilities and staffs they resemble the high school more closely than a university and form an admirable bridge between them.

NEW GOALS AND FUNCTIONS

The present high school has developed far beyond the ideas of 1890 and in a direction that diverges more and more from the European concept of the secondary school as a selective institution for the preparation of an intellectual elite. By 1910, the high school had come to the smaller towns and the automobile was facilitating the building of strong rural high schools; the junior high school was developing; the program of studies was still growing; and a broader, more democratic, and more practical education was gaining in favor. These trends were supported by the departments and schools of education, by the land-grant colleges and state universities, and by the social-educational philosophies of Francis W. Parker and John Dewey.

A reformulation of high school objectives was made by the Commission on the Reorganization of Secondary Education, which reported in 1918 under the title *Cardinal Principles of Secondary Education.* They decided that secondary education should be based on the needs of society, the natures and capacities of the pupils, and professional knowledge of education. They pointed out that only one third of the elementary pupils reached the high school and that of these only one in nine remained to graduate. They approved the junior high school and declared for the comprehensive senior high school rather than one specialized along technical, commercial, college preparatory, or other particular lines. They proposed the following as objectives: health, command of fundamental processes, worthy home membership, vocation, civic education, worthy use of leisure, and ethical character. As an aid toward the attainment of these aims, they proposed that the curricula should be composed of constants—to be taken by all—variables, and free electives. In language that is reminiscent of Condorcet they declared that in a democracy education "should develop in each individual the knowledge, interest, ideals, habits, and powers whereby he will find his place and use that place to shape both himself and society toward even nobler ends." Whereas the Committee of Ten had made college preparation primary, the commission in planning the work of the high school made preparation for life the primary purpose.

The commission somewhat unaccountably did not call attention to the contemporary movement for the supervision of study in the high school. It has been noticed that high school pupils often did not know how to take notes on their reading, how to make a systematic outline, or how to use the dictionary or the encyclopedia effectively. They were unable to translate problems into algebraic language or effectively to attack a passage for sight reading. In literature they did not sense the mood or the purpose of the writer. In a word they did not know how to study. It was now proposed that the teacher should teach not only in the class but also by supervised study.

Several plans were used. One was the unprepared lesson. This was a period set aside for the preparation of a detailed assignment with the help of the teacher. A second plan was that of the divided period, one half of the usual class period being given to preparation and the rest to group consideration of the material. This had the advantage that it did not interfere with the established daily schedule. Still another plan used double periods, this longer space of time being used as in the divided period plan. If these plans, which were much used in about 1920, helped to emphasize teaching instead of mere reciting and if they enabled pupils to become independent students able to work on their own account they must have been salutary.

Both vocational guidance and supervised study, as well as the Commission Report of 1918, are evidences and effects of the change that was taking place in secondary education. The vast increase in high school enrollments changed the composition of the student body and led to a transformation of the philosophy of high school education. In 1890 there had been less than three thousand schools and slightly over two hundred thousand pupils. The Commissioner of Education reported thirteen thousand, nine hundred and twenty-two schools of secondary grade for the year 1915, and eleven thousand, six hundred and seventy-four of these were public high schools enrolling one and one third millions of pupils. In the quarter-century the high school enrollment, having doubled in each decade, had increased to six times the 1890 figure. Whereas in earlier times only the best of the elementary pupils even considered attending a high school, now the least academic often enrolled. During the transition period from 1890 to about 1910, the schools still took the position that it was their first duty to uphold academic standards. If the pupils came ill-prepared and if they did not succeed in the studies the high school offered, these facts merely showed that they should not have come to the high school at all. But the public now felt that the high school should serve their children, and taking them as they were, it should teach them what was best for them. School administrators, who were in direct contact with the public, and later the teachers also came to take this view, and thus the high school gradually became a higher common school for all adolescent children who presented themselves.

The program expansion continued and curricula were multiplied. In 1929 the Commissioner of Education reported that the high schools of the country were offering two hundred fifty subjects or branches of subjects. The nomenclature and the makeup of the curricula varied, but the most frequently offered were the college or technical school preparatory, the commercial, the general, the industrial arts, and the household arts. Other less frequently offered curricula were named the English, modern languages, fine arts, music, and agriculture curricula. The practice of free election had disappeared, but a similar result was secured by allowing many substitutions and by counting subjects of the most diverse character as equivalent in educational value. Social demands and administrative considerations had driven the old and really vital question of educational values into the background. Extracurricular activities had secured a strong position in the school if not always in the formal program.

Extracurricular activities had sometimes been considered as mere diversions, the froth of student life. On the other hand there is a tendency to give them an increasing part in the work of the school, and in some ultraprogressive schools student-directed activities are tending to displace the formal curriculum. The problem everywhere is to make all activities, whether work or study, or play, serve valid educational purposes.

School athletics and student government are two forms of extracurricular activities that have a long history. Vittorino incorporated games and physical exercises in his fifteenth-century school. Sports have formed a part of English upper-class education from early times. In his school in Silesia, in the sixteenth century, Trotzendorf developed a school republic so that boys by learning to administer and obey laws of their own making might later rule and serve according to law. More elaborate forms of student government were found early in the nineteenth century, in the Hazelwood School in England; in Froebel's school at Keilhau; and in Fellenberg's school at Hofwyl, examples that may have been the result of the rise of political democracy in Europe and America. More or less highly developed forms of student government have been widely introduced in more recent times. Literary societies, debating, public speaking, and dramatics were early cultivated in the schools of many countries. Comenius tried, although unsuccessfully, to embody a whole curriculum in dramatic form.

High schools do much in promoting and guiding extracurricular activities, and teachers who are especially prepared to direct athletics, dramatics, musical organizations, and debating are often employed. The school assembly, which was formerly given over to speeches by the principal and teachers, or to persons brought in from outside the school, is now often conducted by the students themselves and sometimes involves active participation by the audience. Clubs, which take a great variety of forms, and social events are fostered. School authorities often frown on the secret societies that creep into many high schools in imitation of the Greek-letter fraternities of the colleges and try to ban or regulate them. State laws have sometimes been invoked against them. Many activities, which were formerly considered outside the curriculum, have now been incorporated within it and almost all, if skilfully directed, can be used to support educational purposes. The greatest significance of these interests comes from the fact that they are the concerns of the pupils themselves, voluntary expressions of their desire to lead, to cooperate, and to create.

The responsibility of the high school principals to their pupils and communities frequently impressed them with the need for more power to resist unwholesome local interference; and, on the other hand, the old question of high school-college relations, which in spite of many efforts had never been settled to the satisfaction of the principals, was becoming more rather than less irritating as the high schools became stronger. These two conditions were the chief reasons for the formation in 1917 of the National Association of Secondary School Principals. How urgent the latter problems seemed can be gathered from the proposal of one of the founders who said,

I believe in the principle of inspection so firmly that I would extend it even to the inspection of the colleges by the high schools. The colleges inspect us to see whether our product is good enough for them to work with. Now let us inspect the colleges to see whether they are good enough to have the care and direction of our boys and girls.

And Jess B. Davis, a past President of the association, in a review of its history declared, "Twenty-five years ago the National Association of Secondary School Principals was conceived in rebellion." The rebellion began in the Middle West where the high school was most powerful.

One would expect to find extended consideration of the high school-college relation in the meetings of the association, but this did not happen. Instead they were practically ignored and the Principals' Association dealt instead with problems of organization and administration, with the curriculum, student government, extracurricular activities, teaching problems, ability grouping, educational and vocational guidance, character development, the junior high school and junior college, and the function of education in a democracy. Although it may have been "conceived in rebellion," what really interested the association was the question of how the high school can best function as a higher common school. One of its important achievements has been the creation of a National Honor Society of high school students for the encouragement of character development, leadership, scholarship, and service.

An important study was made by the association through its Committee on the Orientation of Secondary Education, of which Thomas H. Briggs was Chairman. The committee began its work in 1932 and made its final report in 1935 during the tercentenary celebration of the founding of secondary education in the United States. The summary of the committee's findings is embodied in the ten "issues" and ten "functions" of secondary education that they formulated. These were submitted to forums of schoolmen throughout the country for consideration and application. The functions are statements of the main tasks of secondary schools, a new and more elaborate set of "cardinal principles." Only once do they even by implication recognize that the high schools are preparing some of their students for college.

The ten issues, on the other hand, raise a whole series of questions, some of which the trend of our history for more than fifty years has been answering. Whether public secondary education shall be given to all youth or only to some, whether it shall work for the welfare of both society and the individual, whether it shall provide differentiated curricula, whether it can offer vocational education, whether it shall be concerned only with knowledge or also with attitudes, whether it has a distinct field of its own—these are hardly issues any longer. The answers that the history of the high school has given to these questions are hardly in doubt any longer. But they have certainly not yet been universally accepted, and they may need modification in the future. The purpose of the formulation was doubtless to have them critically examined, especially by those of the profession who had not already accepted them.

The ninth issue asked, "Shall secondary education seek merely the adjustment of the student to prevailing social ideals, or shall it seek the reconstruction of society?" Clearly all education, even if it does not intend it, actually does something to reconstruct society. But asked, as it was, during an economic depression, this question was doubtless intended to raise the alternative between the existing economic system and some degree of greater social control. In this sense it was a living issue. The seventh issue will serve as a transition to our next topic. It contrasted the usual organization of secondary school work under the conventional subjects with a proposed organization into "functional" topics or fields, such as the social-civic, the economic, the vocational, and other large interests. This was also a central issue in the "Thirty Schools Experiment" of the Progressive Education Association.

The Progressive Education Association was formed in 1918 to work for the improvement of both elementary and secondary education; and in 1930 it appointed a Commission on the Relation of School and College. The main question it was to answer was significantly framed thus: "What would secondary schools do if they were completely freed from all detailed college entrance requirements?" Accordingly, several hundred colleges were pledged to accept the graduates of the selected schools on their records without special examinations and without demanding the usual work in specified academic subjects. The schools were set free to teach those materials and in those ways they considered best for the development of boys and girls, whether they intended to go to college or not. Several University High Schools and many private schools participated, and some of these usually sent eighty or ninety per cent of their graduates to college. But the public high schools of Tulsa, Denver, Des Moines, and Altoona were also included. Several of the schools were known as "progressive," but not all aspired to that designation and some were fairly conventional. It is best to say simply that about thirty schools and systems of mixed character were set free to try what their staffs, students, and clientele wished to attempt.

The "experiment" began in 1933 and continued for eight years until 1941. It touched on practically all phases of secondary school work, but curriculum reorganization was particularly involved. Curriculum study was not new. It had been carried on in American high schools for more than a decade before 1930 and less intensively for fifty years. Many methods of study had been tried: analyses of textbooks, of educational aims, of life needs, of jobs, of studies of the interests and capacities of youth, and of comparative measures of school achievement. The chief difficulty was not in getting facts about youth, life, and the school but in finding any generally accepted principles that could be scientifically applied.

The Thirty Schools tried out a variety of nonsubject curriculum organizations. These might be named the fluid or experimental, the contemporary-problems, the unified-studies, and the cultural-period curricula. The experimental curriculum is made cooperatively by pupils and teachers from day to day and is changed and redirected as the work is going forward. It contains little previously organized subject matter, no formal lessons, and no set recitations. This resembles the practice of the Dewey Experimental School at Chicago.

The contemporary-problems curriculum deals with a living issue. The question of housing would be an example of somewhat restricted scope, whereas that of a planned society would be one of very wide scope. Any such problem will be studied from many standpoints. A study of the home would have to cover family income, housing, home equipment, food, servants, child care, personal relationships, reading materials, and other topics. Usually several teachers cooperate in developing such a *core* curriculum. This is also done in teaching a unified studies curriculum in which several subjects such as English and the social studies, or mathematics, the sciences, and the industrial arts are combined into a single field of study. The cultural-period curriculum finds its core in some epoch or race such as ancient Greece, the Arabs, or Anglo-Saxon civilization. All phases of the period of culture are studied such as the art, politics, literature, science, work, and commerce of the Greeks, for example. The purpose is to understand the life of today by the comparative and philosophical study of an epoch on which somewhat definitive verdicts have been pronounced, as they cannot be in the case of contemporary civilization.

The students who entered college from the Thirty Schools made records that were a little better than those made by equally able students from other schools. They excelled their paired competitors somewhat more in extracurricular and social activities. The methods used in pairing students have been questioned. And one is surprised that the differences were comparatively small when the students from the Thirty Schools had the advantages of a particularly stimulating school environment and excellent teaching. Perhaps college success, although significant, is after all a crude measure of the value of the preparatory work. Given the required mental caliber, it seems that anyone who has studied earnestly in either a progressive or a conventional secondary school can succeed in college. We should now have a careful study of the success in college of students from small and substandard high schools. Do they also do acceptable college work?

In a little more than a century the high school has become more widely distributed and accessible than the elementary school was in 1830. It has also become more firmly entrenched in the good will of the people than the common school was at that time, but this acceptance was not easily won. The colleges, the private schools and their partisans, the business world, and the general public have kept up a fairly continuous fire of criticism. In no period of its evolution has it been free from attack, but it continued to flourish because it continued to give youth opportunities that no other country had provided in equal measure and that we could not have provided by other means that were proposed.

The vitality of the high school is shown by its ability to profit from criticism and to adapt itself to changing demands. Again and again it has taken over the work of private schools and incorporated their services in its own program. When manual training was developing under private auspices, it was quickly adopted by the public school. When an aggregation of business colleges spread throughout the country, the high school established commercial courses. When laboratory science teaching, agriculture, home economics, music, and physical education programs developed, the high school adopted them. When the need for social education, student activities, and guidance came to be seen, the high school incorporated them in its program. But it is only the large and well-equipped school that can perform all these and other functions of a comprehensive high school, and many American high schools are small and are compelled to do the best they can with their limited resources.

The high school has developed as a public school, a local school, and a day school. These three are among the most obvious and also the most important of its institutional characteristics. It is a local, day, and not a state or national boarding school because it is intended to serve the great body of the people who cannot send their children away from home for purposes of education. It must, therefore, be located close to the homes of the children. As a result of this wide distribution many high schools are small schools. How small they are may be shown by a few figures. Three fourths of all the schools are located in towns of twenty-five hundred people or less or in the open country. A few states are closing the very small schools, but many of those remaining have an enrollment of less than one hundred pupils, and another twenty per cent have between one hundred and two hundred pupils. A very large proportion of the smallest schools are not accredited by their regional standardizing associations. President Conant's judgment on these can be seen in his report of 1959 (see the Bibliography). The present condition of a school may be, in the long run, less important than the vigor and intelligence with which it is going forward and trying to improve its work. It was this view that led the standardizing associations to seek better ways of stimulating high school improvement.

The Cooperative Study of Secondary School Standards was carried out by a committee that began as early as 1928; but the study was formally begun in 1934. The committee was aided by advisory members from the American Council on Education and other bodies, and the study was jointly financed by the associations themselves and the General Education Board. Dissatisfaction with the rigid and mechanical standards that had come into use had been felt for some time. These standards usually covered such points as the amount of preparation teachers had received, teacher loads, finances, the number of books in the school library, and laboratory and athletic equipment. The purpose of the study was to discover the characteristics of a good school, the best means of evaluating these, and the best methods by which a school can be stimulated to improve.

By a process of formulating evaluative criteria, trying these experimentally in a number of schools, and criticizing and reformulating them in the light of the experience gained, a definitive scheme for the cooperative evaluation of secondary schools by the staff and with the help of external committees was perfected by 1940. The scheme of evaluation uses both judgments made by teachers and competent investigators and objective measures obtained from the use of tests and scales. More than a dozen phases of the school and its work are covered in a complete evaluation, and a definite program for improvement is the finest result. Among the phases covered are the school's philosophy of education, the pupils and the community, the program and courses of study, pupil activities, the library and its use, guidance, instruction, the staff, the plant, the administration of the school, and also the outcomes of the school's work. Evidently a survey of a high school made on these broad bases will be more qualitative than an inspection, which uses the older quantitative standards. Because the evaluations are made cooperatively by teachers, administrators, and outside experts, they serve an important purpose as means for the professional reeducation of the staff and the improvement of the work and services of the schools. The stimulus that such an evaluation can give may be far more valuable than its standardizing function.

SUMMARY

Considerable interest in school improvement developed even before the elementary schools had become fully established. A part of this concern was the result of the influence of Pestalozzi. Emphasis was laid on comprehension in reading and arithmetic, on the use of illustrative materials such as pictures, drawings, and objects, on the introduction of geography and elementary science into the course of study, and on friendlier relations between teachers and pupils. Many children's books and schoolbooks, dealing with nature and giving practical and scientific information about things in the home and on the farm, were written. The Oswego system of object-teaching was introduced into all the northern states, but it was often merely another memory exercise.

The elementary science movement of the early part of the century led to nature study and back again to elementary science. The two are, indeed, difficult to distinguish from each other for one form of nature study was simply elementary science; but there were also a sentimental or poetical study of nature and a utilitarian study with application to health, the home, and other practical matters. An extended literature was called out by the nature study movement, and schools were made more interesting and informative.

The kindergarten, child study, and handwork came into elementary education together; and this is natural, for they have much in common. They have greatly modified the philosophy and practice of elementary education. It was these three trends, all of them embodied in the Quincy methods, that have done most in creating the new elementary schools. But Parker at Quincy and elsewhere was important not only as a promoter of the "new education" but also as a vigorous protagonist of democracy in school and in society. Thus, Parker laid the groundwork for the progressive education for which John Dewey provided the philosophical justification. Dewey's early writings were an interpretation of Herbartian and Froebelian doctrines; but he soon developed his well-known pragmatic and instrumentalist philosophy. Future historians may find that, in his case as in that of Parker, it has been his Americanism, democracy, and spirit of social reform rather than his technical philosophy that have most deeply affected American education.

The high school is our third effort to develop a serviceable secondary school. It followed the Latin school and academy. It is a public secondary school, closely articulated with the elementary school and offering a general course to practically all adolescents who wish to attend. Generally, the high school was an upward extension of the graded elementary school, but some early high schools were transformed academies. The high schools, early in their evolution, became college preparatory as well as terminal schools. College preparation tended to make them selective; and the effort to serve the community as a terminal school made them comprehensive and coeducational. The cost of the new schools, their selective character, and the interests of the academy were the occasion for strong opposition to high school expansion. After about 1880 or 1890 the schools gradually broadened their programs and began to serve a widening constituency; and the public in turn began to defend and support them more heartily.

The program of studies was expanded first along academic lines and then with vocational and skill studies. Extracurricular activities were added last. Except for bookkeeping and surveying, which were taught in the early high schools, the vocational courses did not develop until late in the century, and vocational guidance began about the period of World War I. The junior high school movement developed at the same time. The public junior college, which has also shown its most rapid growth in recent decades, provides a favorable opportunity for educational expansion.

High school principals long felt that their schools were tightly wedged in between the elementary schools, which directed the children for eight years and the colleges, which restricted the high school program through their entrance requirements. By developing the junior high school below the tenth grade and securing a very considerable degree of freedom from college control, the high school has carved out an area of secondary education that is reasonably free from external domination. But a public demand for greater emphasis on and better work in languages and science is now exerting great pressure on them. Through the National Association of Secondary

School Principals, the Briggs Committee, the Thirty Schools experiment, the standardizing associations, and the leadership of state departments of education, the high school has attempted to decide on a progressive plan for future operations. The task of the high school and junior college will be to provide solid foundations in language, mathematics, science, and social understanding; to give effective vocational preparation and guidance; to establish the character and physical and mental health of their pupils; and to prepare them to deal effectively with questions of public policy and problems of democracy, including world democracy. To do this, or any large part of it, is a challenging task for the high schools of today and tomorrow.

QUESTIONS

1. Did the rise of science and of democracy provide a favorable condition for the introduction of Pestalozzianism? Compare with conditions in Prussia.
2. What is an educational fad? Did the Oswego system of object-teaching have some of the characteristics of a fad? What part did propaganda play in the movement?
3. How were the Quincy methods related to previous and contemporary educational theories and practices?
4. Is Dewey's idea developed in *School and Society* of basing the elementary curriculum on the evolution of industry and society any less far-fetched than the culture-epoch theory?
5. There are said to be thirteen varieties of pragmatism. How many varieties of progressive education can you distinguish? Which variety do you prefer? Why?
6. What are the ten most essential characteristics, such for example as coeducational or public control, of the high school?
7. Study a number of these characteristics to determine why and how they developed. In this process it is useful to compare the American with some foreign secondary schools.
8. Why can the graded school be regarded as a necessary preliminary to the high school? Why not also to the academy and the Latin grammar school?
9. What are the advantages and disadvantages of voluntary accrediting and standardizing schemes as compared with governmental ones?
10. How well has the junior high school fulfilled the claims made for it in the reorganization period?
11. "Shall secondary education seek merely the adjustment of students to prevailing social ideals, or shall it seek the reconstruction of society?" This is the ninth of the Briggs Committee issues.

12. What conclusions can be drawn from the Thirty Schools experiment? Do all of your fellow-students agree with your summary of the results?

NOTES AND SOURCES

Many of the sources for this chapter have been given in the text and these will not be repeated. Several magazines are of special interest here: *The Nature Study Review* (New York, 1905 and after) and *Progressive Education* (Washington, D.C., 1924 and after). For numerous child-study papers and the history of the movement, see the *Pedagogical Seminary* (Worcester, Mass., 1891 and after). The *Yearbooks* of the National Herbart Society provide data on the Herbartian movement in the United States. Paul Monroe's *Cyclopedia of Education* (New York, The Macmillan Company, 1911–1913) has articles on the development of "Child Study," "Kindergarten," "Manual Training" and "Object-Teaching." The *Educational Review*, edited by Nicholas Murray Butler, and the *Proceedings* of the National Education Association contain important historical materials.

Numerous articles dealing with the development of the academy and the high school have appeared in leading educational journals including Barnard's *American Journal of Education*, the *Educational Review*, and the *School Review*. Only slight hints can be given here of the variety of these materials. Volume 19 of Barnard has a table showing the frequency of fifty-nine subjects in the curricula of thirty high schools in about 1867 (p. 463), and a section dealing more fully with the curricula themselves (pp. 465–576). The *Educational Review* and the *School Review* carried numerous articles on the work of the Committee of Ten between the years 1893 and 1895. Special attention is due an article on this topic in the former journal for December, 1896, and another in the latter journal for April, 1906.

BRIGGS, THOMAS H., *The Junior High School*, Boston, Houghton Mifflin Company, 1920, 350 pp.; *The Great Investment, Secondary Education in a Democracy*, Cambridge, Mass., Harvard University Press, 1930, 143 pp. The later volume is the Inglis lecture for 1930.

BROOME, EDWIN C., *A Historical and Critical Discussion of College Admission Requirements*, New York, The Macmillan Company, 1903, 157 pp.

BROWN, ELMER ELLSWORTH, *The Making of Our Middle Schools*, New York, Longmans, Green and Company, 1901, 547 pp. First published in the *School Review* between 1897 and its appearance as a book. Frequently reissued in later years but not revised.

BRUECKNER, L. J., *et al.*, *The Changing Elementary School*, New York, Inor Publishing Company, 1939, 388 pp. This is a volume of the Regents' Inquiry into the cost and character of education in the State of New York.

BURRELL, B. JEANNETTE, and R. H. ECKELBERRY, "The American High School Question Before the Courts During the Post-Civil-War Period," *School Review*, Vol. 42, April, 1934, 255–265; May, 1934, 333–348. The second instalment has a bibliography; "The Free Public High School in the Post-Civil-War Period," same journal and volume, October, 1934, 606–614; November, 1934, 667–675, with bibliography.

CONANT, JAMES B., *The American High School Today, A First Report to Interested Citizens*, New York, McGraw-Hill Book Company, Inc. [1959], 140 pp.

COUNTS, GEORGE S., *Selective Character of American Secondary Education*, Chicago, The University of Chicago, 1922, 162 pp.; *The Senior High School Curriculum*, Chicago, The University of Chicago Press, 1926, 160 pp.; *Secondary Education and Industrialism*, Cambridge, Mass., Harvard University Press, 1929, 70 pp. This title is the Inglis lecture for 1929.

CURTI, MERLE, *The Social Ideas of American Educators*, New York, Charles Scribner's Sons, 1935, 613 pp. Studies of Harris, Bishop Spalding, F. W. Parker, G. S. Hall, William James, and others.

DEARBORN, NED H., *The Oswego Movement in American Education*, New York, Teachers College, Columbia University, 1925, 189 pp., Teachers College Contributions to Education, No. 183. Has a bibliography.

GRIZZELL, EVERET DUNCAN, *Origin and Development of the High School in New England Before 1865*, New York, The Macmillan Company, 1923, 428 pp.

INGLIS, ALEXANDER J., *The Rise of the High School in Massachusetts*, New York, Teachers College, Columbia University, 1911, 166 pp. Contributions to Education, No. 45; *Principles of Secondary Education*, Boston, Houghton Mifflin Company, 1918, 741 pp. Chapter V of the latter volume deals with the history of secondary education in the United States, and Chapter VI with that of foreign countries.

KENDEL, ISAAC L., *History of Secondary Education*, Boston, Houghton Mifflin Company, 1930, 577 pp.; *The Dilemma of Democracy*, Cambridge, Mass., Harvard University Press, 1934, 79 pp. The first title deals with Europe and the United States, the second is the Inglis lecture for 1934.

KENNEDY, MILLARD FILLMORE, *Schoolmaster of Yesterday, A Three-Generation Story, 1820–1919*, New York, McGraw-Hill Book Company, Inc., 1940, 359 pp. Written in collaboration with Alvin F. Harlow, this excellent story deals more with the old school than with the new but is valuable as a corrective to idealized history of education.

KRÜSI, HERMANN, *Recollections of My Life, an Autobiographical Sketch . . .*, edited by Elizabeth Sheldon Alling, New York, The Grafton Press, 1907, 439 pp. Contains materials and judgments on the Oswego system and other topics in elementary education.

MONROE, WALTER S., *Development of Arithmetic As a School Subject*, Washington, D.C., Government Printing Office, 1917, 170 pp. U.S. Bureau of Education Bulletin, No. 10, 1917.

MONROE, WILL S., *History of the Pestalozzian Movement in the United States*, with nine portraits and a bibliography, Syracuse, New York, C. W. Bardeen, 1907, 244 pp. One questionable generalization in this book is that New England was less influenced by Pestalozzian doctrine than other parts of the United States.

MULHERN, JAMES, *A History of Secondary Education in Pennsylvania*, Philadelphia, published by the author, 1933, 714 pp.

PATRIDGE, LELIA E., *Notes of Talks on Teaching, Given by Francis W. Parker at the Martha's Vineyard Summer Institute, 1882*, New York, E. L. Kellogg and Company, 1885, 182 pp.; *The Quincy Methods Illustrated*, New York, E. L. Kellogg and Company, 1886, 660 pp.

SEARCH, PRESTON WILLIS, *An Ideal School*, New York, D. Appleton Century Company, Inc., 1901, 357 pp.

SPAULDING, FRANCIS T., O. I. FREDERICK, and LEONARD V. KROOS, *The Reorganization of Secondary Education*, Washington, D.C., Government Printing Office, 1932, 423 pp., Bureau of Education Bulletin, 1932. No. 17, and Monograph No. 5 of the National Survey of Secondary Education.

STOUT, JOHN E., *The Development of High School Curricula in the North Central States, 1860–1918*, Chicago, The University of Chicago Press, 1921, 322 pp.

TELLER, JAMES DAVID, *Louis Agassiz, Scientist and Teacher*, Columbus, Ohio State University Press, 1947, 145 pp.

THARP, LOUISE HALL, *The Peabody Sisters of Salem*, Boston, Little Brown and Company, 1950, 372 pp.; *Until Victory: Horace Mann and Mary Peabody*, Boston, Little, Brown and Company [1953], 367 pp.

Unsigned articles on "Object Lessons," in the Massachusetts *Common School Journal*, Vol. 2, June 15, 1840, 179–185; July 1, 1840, 193–204.

VANDEWALKER, NINA C., *The Kindergarten in American Education*, New York, The Macmillan Company, 1908, 274 pp.

WELLER, FLORENCE, and OTIS W. CALDWELL, "The Nature Study and Elementary Science Movement." *School Science and Mathematics*, Vol. 33, October, 1933, 730–745.

WOODY, THOMAS, "Historical Sketch of Activism," *The Thirty-Third Yearbook of the National Society for the Study of Education, Part II*, pp. 9–43, Bloomington, Ill., Public School Publishing Co., 1934; *A History of Women's Education in the United States*, Lancaster, Pa., The Science Press, 1929, 2 vols.

Chapter 21

AMERICAN EDUCATION TODAY

The spread of education to almost all the people and its adaptation to their various needs and capacities have been carried out with eminent success in the United States in only three of the twenty-five centuries of Western experience with organized education. Building upon the work that had been done in Europe, we have democratized opportunity far more than the mother countries. Along with our opportunities we have had great problems: to Americanize millions of immigrants; to teach the Negro in a none too genial atmosphere; and to reach an exploding, widely scattered, and often mobile population. The American system has not done its work perfectly, but we have done a great deal to solve these and a host of other problems; we have made and are still making progress. The purpose of this chapter is to report our successes and our failures in handling eight critical problems.

POPULATION CHANGES AND AMERICAN SCHOOLS

To provide teachers and schools for the millions of new Americans in this country is a problem throughout the United States. The number of people in the United States has increased one third in twenty years, and it passed a total of two hundred million during 1967. Twenty years ago no such result was expected; but just when the students of vital statistics had agreed that the population would become stationary at about one hundred and sixty million, a great increase in birth rate began; and this, without much help from immigration, has raised the population to the present level. Other countries are experiencing a similar expansion, suggesting that the guess of Malthus will prove to have been correct. We shall deal only with the educational problem raised in the United States by this population increase.

Several millions of pupils were added to the elementary school enrollment after World War II, and the increase is continuing. At the same time university attendance was high because the veterans in great numbers accepted the educational offer of the government under the GI Bill. Meanwhile high school enrollment was low because of the low birth rate in the 1930s. This accidental interlocking of high and low enrollments made possible some adjustments by shifting high school teachers to elementary schools and in some cases to universities. Such relief was temporary and partial and has come to an end. All levels of the educational system are full, and many institutions are hard pressed for teachers, buildings, books, and operating costs. Total pupil enrollments in public elementary and secondary schools rose from forty-one million in 1963-64 to almost forty-three million in 1965-66, a gain of over 4 per cent.

The war caused a great exodus from the teaching profession. It was reported that three hundred and fifty thousand teachers left the schools after Pearl Harbor. If this number seems incredible, we should recall that many teachers leave the profession every year in normal times. After Pearl Harbor they left to enlist, to work in war industries, and to fill gaps which the war had caused in homes, business, and public life. Not many returned to teaching after the war. They had formed other connections, and teachers' salaries were lagging. There has been some improvement in salaries, but in many cases it was not sufficient to offset the increase in the cost of living. Teachers' college enrollments were low, and great numbers of emergency certificates were issued. Children were put on half-time schedules, or oversized classes were set up. When elementary classes have to hold thirty or even twenty-five pupils, there is a teacher shortage.

A debate has been carried on in the press over the seriousness or even the existence of building shortages. By ignoring such facts it is possible to argue that all is well. But thousands of children are attending school in buildings that are unfit for school use. The White House Conference on Education in 1955 voted, two to one, for Federal aid to provide school buildings but without result. Finally in 1963, a Higher Education Facilities Act became law and was immediately challenged in the courts because of Federal construction grants to church-related colleges. However, the Federal Government has spent 1.6 billion dollars in college construction projects.

Besides the increase in the number of children to be housed and taught, there are other population changes that affect the schools. Immigration, especially from Puerto Rico into New York City, is one of these. Many people also are relocating within the United States, and when they move the receiving districts must provide school accommodations for them. There are four massive trends of this kind: the movement of Negroes from the South into the North and West; the general westward movement, especially into California, which is now the state second highest in population; the movement from the country into the cities; and finally the growth of the suburbs, which in some cases almost surround the cities and prevent their expansion. Everyone of these population changes creates great problems for the schools. One thinks first of the financial and school construction problems and the securing of qualified teachers. Wealthy suburbs often pay better salaries than some of the cities, and the two make it difficult for smaller towns and townships to maintain adequate staffs. The relocation also leads to the intermingling of different classes of people. The Pasadena crisis had several causes, but the influx of new people into that residential community is blamed for part of it.

Juvenile delinquency is another problem of the school and society today. It is not peculiar to the United States; England, France, Russia, and many other countries are similarly afflicted. We shall treat American conditions only.

In the United States, according to the Federal Children's Bureau, juvenile delinquency declined steadily, although slowly, from 1929 to 1939. It increased again during the war and since and seems to be at its highest rate in history. If the schools had the staffs to keep their playgrounds and gymnasiums open all day and every evening, if they could direct more club work, and if every school had a junior republic, some delinquency could no doubt be prevented. Waywardness has many causes including bad and broken homes, slums, the traffic in liquor and narcotics, the unrestricted sale of guns, and the failure of the schools to deal with early indications of future trouble. Considerable delinquency takes place in schools as the city papers make plain, and everyone from the board of education to the custodians has the obligation to prevent it as much as possible.

The study of the ways and means to moderate prejudice and group hostility and to promote cultural unity is called intergroup education or the study of human relations. There is an extensive literature but little scientific knowledge and no formulas for the achievement of the desired ends. Teachers seem to know little about intergroup or intercultural studies, and a course of reading in this field would be rewarding. They would at least learn what some of the causes and early manifestations of group conflict are. Although they might not gain any simple solutions, they would be forewarned; and the old proverb has a measure of truth.

FEDERAL AID FOR EDUCATION

Public schools in most countries derive their financial support from local, intermediate, and central governments or from two of these. In England school expenses are paid from funds of local authorities and Parliamentary grants. In that country, as in most others, there are also miscellaneous funds derived from endowments, tuition, rents, and donations that meet a part, usually a small part, of the total costs. Although Parliament votes large grants for schools and universities, public and private, no one claims that the government does or attempts to influence what is to be taught. In France the communes, the departments, and the nation contribute, but the government does exercise control over the schools.

School costs in the United States are paid from local taxation, state appropriations, and Federal appropriations for some special purposes such as vocational education, the operation of land-grant colleges, school lunches, and others. There are no regular Federal appropriations for general education in the elementary and high schools. This is somewhat strange because the first Congressional action in favor of education was included in the so-called Survey Act of 1785 adopted by the Congress of the Confederation. It began the practice of granting lands for the support of schools and of a university in each state. This beginning was also the end of Federal support for general education in the states.

As the state systems developed it became evident, in the first place, that the rich states are able to support a complete and excellent program with little effort, whereas the poorer states can with the greatest effort offer only a less adequate program. Yet these are sister states in a nation boasting that it offers equal opportunity to all its people. This seems inconsistent and unwise because, in the second place, the half-educated from any state move freely and at will to states with high educational standards. Third, the Federal revenue system draws large sums from even the poorest states but will not return a single dollar to aid in teaching little children to read. Many people in both poor and rich states are opposed to Federal aid because they think it will lead to Federal control. This is not inevitable as England has shown. Also, the difference between state and national control may not be great.

Each of the three greatest wars in which the United States has been involved has been followed by efforts to secure Federal aid. Within the two years following the close of World War I, seventy bills and resolutions dealing with education were presented to Congress. One of these proposed a national Department of Education, "with power to shape national educational policy." These two ideas were not absent from the Smith-Towner Bill, introduced in 1919 and promoted by the National Education Association. This bill also included the matching principle whereby the states provide a sum equal to the amount received from the Federal treasury. But it restricted aid to public schools only. The bill was not passed.

The struggle was repeated during World War II, when a Federal aid bill was reported out of committee and was debated in the Senate (1943). It did not come to a vote. Senatorial opinion has usually been more favorable to Federal aid than that of the House. The powerful Senator Robert A.

Taft, long an opponent of Federal aid, came out in favor of it. A second bill was actually passed by the Senate in 1948 by the decisive vote of fifty-eight to fifteen. This bill called for a subsidy of three hundred million dollars a year, three times the amount named in the Smith-Towner Bill. But most Federal controls had been removed from the bill of 1948. President Truman favored the bill, but the House, as in the case of the old Blair Bill, would not cooperate. Instead, the Congress appropriated about ninety million dollars for school lunches and vocational education.

To secure passage of special and limited appropriation bills is for obvious reasons far easier than to gain approval of a general law. The Congress also, to give another example, votes relief money to communities that are in difficulty from the erection of military, atomic, or other Federal installations within their borders. Such establishments occupy property formerly subject to local taxation and may bring in families with children to be educated in the local schools. The government may provide financial help to local districts that have to carry this extra burden.

The Congress in 1958 was persuaded, by the Cold War, the various hot wars, and the fears called out by the Sputniks, to enact a National Defense Education Act providing for a four-year program of Federal aid to higher education. The title was doubtless intended to make the bill more palatable, and the act did not infringe on the right of the states to protect their children from Federal propaganda. The law did not grant money for the undergraduate scholarships for which the President had asked, nor the much needed aid to school construction that the White House Conference had recommended.

This law provided for loans to college students. Special consideration was to be given to elementary and secondary school teachers and to able students of mathematics, science, engineering, and foreign languages. The law was intended to aid the improvement of language-teaching methods and of the study of modern languages not then popular in American schools. The framers of the bill may have had Russian and other Slavic languages and perhaps Chinese, Japanese, and Arabic in mind. The act provided funds, on the matching principle, for scientific and modern foreign language equipment; and funds to improve counseling, testing, the use of visual aids, and vocational education. It provided for the expenditure on the designated phases of higher education of nearly one billion dollars over four years, the largest Federal commitment to education up to that time.

Following the passage of the National Defense Education Act of 1958, a series of acts was enacted to render categorical, strings-attached Federal aid to education. The categories of Federal aid stressed compensatory, vocational, and technical education as well as support for higher-quality education. The breakthrough in these acts was a reconciliation of the church-state issue on the basis of a pupil-benefit theory. This theory maintains that public money can be channeled through public educational agencies for the use of individual pupils whether they attend public, private, or church-related schools. In accordance with this theory, the Elementary and Secondary Education Act of 1965 continued the type of aid initiated by the national Defense Education Act and added others. Under acts aiding higher education, about one fourth of all college students in the nation receive approximately one billion dollars a year in Federal loans, fellowships, work-study grants, and scholarships. The Higher Education Amendments of 1968 extends these Federal aid programs to colleges and their students and adds other new programs at a total cost of 7.2 billion dollars for a three-year period. If the pupil-benefit theory is upheld by the courts, it is possible that general Federal aid to education will be a reality before the end of the next decade.

PROGRESSIVE EDUCATION IN RETREAT

This section reports the criticism directed against progressive education, and it is to serve as an introduction to the more violent assaults on the schools that led to the organization of the National Citizens Commission to defend the schools. Some opponents of progressive education may not have understood the movement, and it is, in fact, complex and difficult to define.

One way to define it is to say that progressive education is an application in schools of the principles of liberty, equality, and fraternity. Progressive education means freedom to grow naturally, freedom from arbitrary control, and free access to surroundings that will stimulate investigation and construction. It means equality of educational opportunity. And fraternity refers to the friendly society of children and adults. Friends, said Plato in the Phaedrus, can learn from each other with the finest results. This society is the school, a company of learners including teachers, for that is what teachers, as well as children, are—learners.

These are the principles of the Copernican revolution in education of which Rousseau was the proximate author, just as they were also the principles of the French Revolution, which he is said to have inspired. And these are at least some of the essential principles of progressive education; but some think one necessary principle is lacking—namely, that the child must grow up in and for an existing society. We must live in our house, with whatever faults of construction it may have, while it is being rebuilt. John Dewey might not have agreed, and for some progressiveness and disciples of Dewey this concession spoils everything.

Dewey is given too much credit by some and too much blame by others for the rise of progressive education. We grant that he has been the great leader of the movement, but the conditions of the late nineteenth and early twentieth centuries made the movement inevitable. Some of these condi-

John Dewey (1859–1952)

tions were the interpretations of Rousseau by Pestalozzi and Froebel; the kindergarten; the rise of child psychology and the scientific method; the stimulating thought of William James, G. Stanley Hall, and Francis W. Parker; the new elementary school with a broader curriculum and milder discipline; and the growing desires and influence of the common man. We admit that Dewey was the most active and ablest leader, but if he had not appeared there would have been others. There were indeed others, but they were overshadowed by Dewey.

Dewey believed that education should be a process of discovery, not one of instruction and drill. His opponents say children in progressive schools do not gain sufficient command of the fundamentals for further progress.

Such schools they say are not really progressive. Dewey would have the school be a self-governing society, a democracy, that by actual practice prepares children for the practice of democracy in later life. We learn by doing. Opponents want discipline, control by the teacher. They say progressive schools are noisy and disorderly. Some of them claim that the United States is not a democracy; it is a republic. Dewey bases his program on the child's interests. Extreme progressives would allow the child's interests to direct the entire program of the school. Dewey and moderates generally would have the teacher guide, enlarge, and improve the child's interests, but his interests, not the adult interests of the teacher, are to be supreme. Education is life, not preparation for life; and its purpose is more life through scientific investigation. Only within this context do the humanities find a place in education.

American schools, not only the progressive ones, have always been under fire from the Right and the Left alternately, or both together. There seems to be little prospect of a change, and informed and honest criticism is to be welcomed and carefully weighed. The Right had its innings after the break in the stock market in 1929. People were hard pressed to pay their taxes and resented the heavier burden caused by rising high school enrollments. One heard again the proposals of 1895 to abolish the free public high school or to make admission selective, or at least to discard the frills—even foreign languages—and to reduce the salaries of the teachers. Teachers had to wait for considerable periods in some cities for their wages.

Criticism of progressive education was another matter. It increased in the Depression but much more after World War II. A group known as the Essentialists, led by William C. Bagley, charged that in progressive schools pupils did not learn the fundamental school arts well enough. Colleges had to set up remedial classes in composition and arithmetic. Investigators showed that these educational failures were not more numerous in progressive than in conventional schools. But the public demanded that the basic school arts be more thoroughly taught and that the emphasis on drill be increased. Instruction and acquisition, not interest, became the slogan.

The high point of the attacks on the schools was reached in the early 1950s when it, indeed, became strident, irresponsible, and effective. Only the beginning of this hostile campaign could be seen in 1947. One effect, much later, was the dissolution in 1955 of the Progressive Education Association. Two years later the magazine *Progressive Education*, published since 1922, was also discontinued; and this announcement was greeted editorially in a daily paper as "a modest note of cheer in the news." Editors were not always so considerate. Several popular magazines opened their pages to slashing attacks on the progressives.

Teachers' colleges and university colleges of education have been frequent targets of the critics. Because most of these schools are favorable to at least a moderate progressivism, the attacks on them can be taken as, in part, criticisms of the progressive movement. Sometimes these schools are attacked also because they are unlike the liberal arts colleges, but this is a virtue. They have special functions with which liberal arts colleges have little concern unless they prepare teachers. Teachers' colleges are more justly accused of offering too many fragmented courses and often dwelling on the obvious.

Charges of Communist teachers and teaching were frequently made, sometimes in vague general charges, and sometimes by naming particular schools or persons. This was the Senator Joseph McCarthy era of unprincipled propaganda. Often school boards, as in Pasadena, California, were more easily intimidated than private institutions. In many cities, groups of the citizenry were organized in defense of the public schools, and there were also national associations formed for this purpose and for the broader aim of raising the effectiveness of public education. One of these was the National Citizens Commission for the Public Schools.

NATIONAL CITIZENS COMMISSION FOR THE PUBLIC SCHOOLS

A sinister campaign directed not against progressive practices but against public education itself followed World War II. The opening for it may have been created by the attacks on the progressives; and the emotional disturbance of the war, the rise in prices, and the population shifts caused by the demand for workers in war industries roused the hostile elements to action. Some of the leaders talked like real Fascists and used the "big lie" and the underhanded methods of fascism. Some of their organizations, for example, imitated the names of responsible teachers' associations. Only alert teachers were able to distinguish the National Council for American Education from the well-known American Council on Education and took the pains to inquire into the right of the new group to speak for the public schools.

Various "front" organizations issued pamphlets, published periodicals, and attempted to fan any smoldering dissatisfaction in local situations. They called public education Socialistic and teachers Communistic. One of their widely circulated publications was called, "How Red the Little Red Schoolhouse?" The little red schoolhouse was, of course, not red inside. The owner of a chain of newspapers that extends into several states called public education unconstitutional and contrary to the Ten Commandments. He seemed to be most concerned about school taxes. Textbooks in the social studies, some that were in wide use, were attacked and had to be withdrawn. As after World War I, several states passed teachers' oath laws.

There were, as indicated, economic and psychological causes for the dissatisfaction. To the rising costs, changes in the distribution of the population, the difficulties arising from the higher birth rate, and postwar shortages of teachers and buildings must be added the failure of the schools to keep the public informed about school conditions, needs, and plans. Especially unfortunate was the attempt to push new policies before the public was ready to endorse them. And wherever local dissatisfaction became known, the trouble makers, who live and sometimes live well on trouble, moved in.

The National Citizens Commission for the Public Schools was formed in 1949, with Mr. Roy E. Larsen of *Time, Life,* and *Fortune* as Chairman; but the suggestion for such a group was made by President James B. Conant of Harvard three years earlier. President Conant proposed that the leading citizens of the United States should spend at least one tenth of their time and effort on the vital problems of public education that they spend on hospitals or the discussion of foreign policy.

The commission proposed "to help Americans to realize how important our public schools are to our expanding democracy, and to arouse in each community the intelligence and will to improve our public schools." The commission secured the cooperation of the Advertising Council in an effort to reach "every citizen in the United States." Press, radio, public meetings, and even posters in public conveyances were used to tell people about citizens committees in each community. Plans for raising money for school buildings, advice on the proper composition of school boards, and answers to unfounded charges against the schools were developed. The commission reached millions of people and achieved great position results. Other older organizations helped. These included the National Congress of Parents and Teachers, the General Federation of Women's Clubs, and many others.

How much influence the National Citizens Commission may have had on the national administration in Washington may not be known; but President Eisenhower in his State of the Union Message in 1954 called for a White House Conference to report in November, 1955, on the condition of education in the country. Local and state meetings were held throughout the nation to study conditions and needs and to prepare plans for school improvement. Connecticut made one of the earliest state reports; her problems were typical and were indeed the ones already mentioned several times: how to find and retain enough competent teachers, how to keep ahead of growing enrollments with buildings, and how to hold the interest and support of local constituencies. Not all of these could be bought with money, but school taxation and bond issues had high priority among school needs. The question was whether or not the people would shoulder the necessary financial burden, revise the school tax laws, rationalize district boundaries, and provide for financial aid by the rich districts to the poorer ones and Federal aid to the weaker states.

The White House Conference met in Washington in November, 1955. The Chairman was Neil McElroy, a business executive who was later to be Secretary of Defense. The delegates were chosen by state conferences and by a subcommittee of these that added others from labor, business, and welfare organizations from all parts of the country. They were a cross section of middle-class America including housewives, farmers, doctors, executives, and a minority of educators.

The surprising decision of the Conference was a two-to-one vote in favor of Federal aid for school construction. It was probably this unpalatable outcome that caused a conservative paper in the Middle West to make the absurd charge that the conference had been "stacked." The total effect of the resolution turned out to be less important than had been hoped. The Congress passed a wholly unworkable law providing for loans to the states for school construction. The conference also expressed its opinion on educational aims, school districts, school finance, teacher recruitment, and the maintenance of citizen interest in schools. The press covered the Conference (*Saturday Review*, December 21, 1955). The preparation for the Conference and the meeting itself performed an important service in providing a means of communication between the schools and the people in community, state, and nation.

Another effort to improve communication was made by the Kellogg Foundation, which contributed three and one-half million dollars to be spent over a five-year period in the study of the general and professional education of school administrators and of means to protect the schools from those who were attempting to undermine public education. The subsidy was later increased, and the study was continued beyond the five-year period. In its report for the year 1955–1956, the Foundation said that the attacks on public education were the reason it was supporting the study.

INTEGRATION AND STATES RIGHTS

By unanimous decision the Supreme Court in 1954 declared racial segregation in public schools to be unconstitutional. The decision was based on the Fourteenth Amendment, adopted in 1868, which declares that "No State . . . [may] deny to any person within its jurisdiction the equal protection of the laws." The Amendment, therefore, in form and intent, limits the powers of the states.

The judgment of the Court was directed particularly against the segregated schools for whites in the South, but it applies to all races and all public schools everywhere in the United States. Public schools from the kindergarten to the state universities must admit qualified persons without respect to race. This is merely another instance among many in which the High Court has made new application of the Fourteenth Amendment. Nor is the segregation decision a unique instance in which the Court has acted to limit state control of schools. It is, therefore, idle for state officials to claim, as some do, that their states are sovereign political entities.

The Constitution as it is interpreted by the Supreme Court limits the powers and sovereignty of the states. It seems to be the fact that the Federal Government, from its first institution onward, has been extending its powers over the states. Now and then state Legislatures and the Congress have acted to contain this process and have attempted to build a dike for this purpose. So today several states have enacted laws that, in order to prevent racial integration, would close all public schools. If the Federal courts void these laws it will be another proof that the states are not as completely sovereign as some politicians claim. The answer to this question is beginning to appear, as we shall presently show.

A list of several Supreme Court decisions, which restrict each state in its function as public educator, will place the segregation decision in its proper class. In Meyer v. Nebraska, 262 U.S. 390, the Court, in 1923, declared unconstitutional a state law that prohibited the teaching of foreign languages in the elementary grades, a teaching practice now much approved and in use. In the so-called Oregon Case, 268 U.S. 510, the Court denied the state the right to prohibit private schools. The Court has rendered several decisions on religion and matters of conscience in relation to public education. Two important ones were those in the McCollum Case, 330 U.S. 203 (1948), and Zorach v. Clauson, 343 U.S. 306 (1952). It was, perhaps, an unfriendly voice that called the Supreme Court our "national school board," but whether friendly or not the phrase implies the fact that states are not altogether sovereign in school affairs. The citizens whose education the states direct are citizens of the United States and of the state in which they live. On this point see, again, the Fourteenth Amendment. This dual citizenship should receive consideration from those who believe that each state is meeting its full responsibility in educating citizens, and from those who are against Federal aid to education.

The education of Negroes was forbidden by law in many states of the South before the Civil War. During and after Reconstruction, there were some private and public efforts to provide schools for them. When all-white governments again came into control, compulsory segregation laws were enacted in seventeen states. It is these states, reaching from Delaware to Texas, that are principally affected by the school integration decision.

We shall trace the history further: The theory of Negro education was modified in 1896 by the doctrine that school facilities for the two races were to be "separate but equal." This was mainly theory and has remained theory. Negro schools are generally poorly built and equipped and their teachers poorly prepared and paid. Some excellent buildings for Negro children have been constructed in the South in an effort to head off integration, and there are other exceptions, but the difference exists at all levels. The land-grant colleges for Negroes are not the equals of those for whites.

The attitudes toward the Negro that were maintained in the South after slavery, the Civil War, and Reconstruction can be understood. The whites were only human, but their educational policy was doubtless a mistake in economics. Better education would have rendered the Negro population economically more productive and would have offered the South a market such as absentee owners, sharecroppers, and underpaid labor cannot provide. This was the argument of Booker T. Washington. The argument of the Supreme Court in its integration decision has been called sociological, but it is also inherently economic. In all events, the Court did not interpret the Constitution in purely abstract terms, as if it had no concern with social and economic fact.

The Court said,

Today, education is perhaps the most important function of state and local governments. . . . It is required in the performance of our most basic public responsibilities, even service in the armed forces. It is the very foundation of good citizenship.

The Court concluded that "in the field of public education the doctrine of 'separate but equal' has no place. Separate educational facilities are inherently unequal."

In a later statement the Court directed the states and school districts to proceed "with all deliberate speed" in the integration of the schools. The belief has been expressed that, if the Court in 1954 had demanded immediate integration, compliance would have been more general. This is an opinion. It is a fact that in the interval the opponents organized the "white councils" to resist the order. Delay also gave opportunity for disorderly and lawless elements to concentrate in the areas where they could make trouble. There has been some violence in several places. Laws were enacted by Virginia and other states that required the closing of public schools where Federal courts ordered integration. The Virginia laws were declared unconstitutional by the Federal courts in February, 1959. This was a great defeat for the cause of segregation. Small-scale integration proceeded in Virginia in Norfolk, Arlington, Alexandria, and elsewhere in the state. Resistance has been greatest in the southern and eastern counties, which have large Negro populations. The National Association for the Advancement of Colored People (NAACP) moved for further integration in North Carolina, where there had been only token integration. The segregated regions of the South will doubtless be whittled down, but such areas have already remained for too long.

Integration is complete in the District of Columbia and is practically complete in the states of West Virginia, Missouri, and Oklahoma; it is proceeding in parts of Arkansas, Delaware, Kentucky—where Louisville gave an example of early and peaceful integration under the lead of a statesman-superintendent—Maryland, North Carolina, Tennessee, and Texas. It cannot be said that statesmanship could have gained early and peaceable integration everywhere, but it seems evident that selfish politicians have been the fomenters of trouble in some places. Separate schools for Negroes continue in some parts of South Carolina, Georgia, Florida, Alabama, Mississippi, and Louisiana. By their decisions, vacillating Federal judges have given comfort to segregationists. In the Supreme Court all decisions and orders on the issue have been unanimous. Except in the Deep South, which is firmly opposed to integration, the present situation is unstable. The controversy can be followed in the newspapers and weekly news magazines. These are read abroad also, and the harm that has been done to the nation's prestige in Asia and Africa is considerable; the support given to lawlessness at home is another unfortunate result of the struggle.

OPPORTUNITY FOR TALENT

The high school remained selective until the end of the nineteenth century, but then the rise of the junior high school, the lengthening of the compulsory attendance period, and the lack of jobs for youth in a country that was becoming industrialized brought more pupils into the upper schools. They did not all stay; but administrative wisdom as well as public demand led the schools to broaden their program and even dilute it with such subjects as grooming, dating, and table manners. It is not that these are unnecessary skills in civilized life, but only that they were formerly learned in the home, or in school were taught incidentally as needed.

Life-adjustment education is the name given to this type of instruction. It may include some more weighty subjects such as hygiene, family life, thrift consumer education, citizenship, and further teaching of the common branches. Even with this kind of program for the unacademic youth, it is not fair to apply the derisive term "custodial institutions" to the high schools as if they merely kept the youth off the streets until they could go to work.

An exponent of vocational education, Charles Allen Prosser, in a resolution (1947) called on the schools to provide for the education of "all American youth" to the age of eighteen. England has undertaken a corresponding program to age sixteen. The Professor's resolution started from the premise that sixty per cent of the young people are one- or two talent persons who cannot master an academic curriculum, or are persons in such circumstances that, even if they acquired such knowledge, it would be of no use to them in the lives they will lead. The need, he thought, was for life-adjustment education for the sixty per cent. For comparison we may note that the English are finding about sixty or seventy per cent of their youth unable to cope with grammar school or technical school programs. These go to a modern school.

At this point our history tends to become a lesson in current events. Educators are dividing into several groups over the merits and demerits of the life-adjustment program. Publications of the National Education Association recommend it. Some private school leaders declare that such courses are a fraud foisted on the public. Public high school teachers not infrequently oppose the lengthening of the compulsory attendance period to age eighteen and urge the repeal of the law where it is now in force. A half-dozen academic professors in leading universities are both the bitterest and the most vocal opponents, and some of their books and addresses have called out protests and replies from educators. It is difficult to know what the people think, but they pay the school tax and elect the school boards. They seem to favor schools for all the children whatever the number of their talents.

Children with many talents have generally been allowed to find or make their own way. Democracy favors equality and, de Tocqueville thought, mediocrity. What about equality of opportunity? The answer is that the kind of school that suits the one-talent child only irritates and bores the talented. Equal opportunity is not the same opportunity for all; it is simple arithmetic and narrative for some and quadratics and short-story writing for others. The talented are neglected in school because democracy is interpreted as equality of status; or because some schools are weak and many are overcrowded; or because teachers know far less chemistry, electronics, or whatever it may be than some of their bright pupils. The fault lies not in the teacher but in the failure to provide for the talented.

The National Science Foundation is carrying out plans to aid science teachers in improving their understanding of science and science education. There is activity among mathematics teachers also. College professors, sometimes unjustly critical of education in the lower schools, need to become more familiar with the actual conditions and problems of high school teaching. One easy lesson would be that science is not the only field with which pupils should become somewhat familiar. Other areas to be considered would be the Russian language, English composition, American history, and good manners and morals.

School administrators and teachers sometimes suffer from a professional myopia. They see problems near at hand but need the corrections that laymen can provide. One such report was prepared in 1958 for the Rockefeller Brothers Fund. This study held, first, that we are not required to choose between a fair education for everyone and an excellent one for leaders. We must have both, and both must be better than they have been. Teachers must be given better academic and professional education. Salaries must be raised. The United States should not spend only fourteen billion dollars as is now done but should spend thirty billion dollars on public education. A larger share of local taxes should be spent on education. The Federal Government already spends great sums for education but should bear a far larger proportion of the total cost. The report adds that the crisis in science education is real and is caused by the rapid increases in technology.

This report does not tell how education is to be improved. More money by itself will not do it. It does not tell how the education of teachers is to be made better. There are several views on that subject, including the proposal to drop most or all professional education for teachers, which this report would, however, retain.

The Rockefeller Brothers Fund report seems to endorse the present emphasis on the teaching of science and perhaps of technology. For a century technical education has served man's practical interests, guiding him toward the improvement not only of industry but also of agriculture, engineering, medicine, surgery, and alas, warfare also. This so-called second Industrial Revolution began with the discovery of new sources of power, the dynamo that fascinated and shocked Henry Adams (1838–1918), and the gas engine that made the airplane and automobile feasible. Science has been the means that changed man's material conditions in the past few centuries more than in all previous time.

Schools now have the task of bringing science teaching up to the level demanded by the present age. Neither the schools nor the people are prepared for this difficult change. But there is a new seriousness and greater interest in academic work. A survey of the studies chosen in 1958 in the high schools of Maryland shows that the students with a high level of intelligence are choosing to take seven years of mathematics and science. This is a surprising change. If nearly all should continue and complete this program and if the change became general, it would constitute an academic revolution.

To raise the teaching of science and other subjects as well to the level demanded by present conditions should not be too difficult. College students are a little older, more mature, and less "collegiate" than they were. Some have completed their military service; many are married; a greater number are from working-class families; and a considerable proportion are earning part of their expenses. It is unfortunate that some cannot stay to complete their courses. This last condition existed fifty years ago, and many who dropped out for a time returned later and completed their education. All this proves their determination to achieve "success," if not scholarship.

The success of science teaching depends on the intellectual and scientific understanding of the supporting public and on the teacher, textbook, and equipment. The public is the controlling factor. Americans are eager for quick results of a practical kind such as roads, factories, markets, and jobs. They favor engineering at the expense of fundamental science. The teacher is not an independent agent and in his environment he is naturally prone to select the textbook and equipment that the public demands. The public has been satisfied in many cases with teachers who were themselves inadequately grounded in the principles of their sciences. It is in this context that the National Science Foundation chose to attempt to reeducate the science teacher as the holder of the key to the problem. School boards must either employ teachers with adequate preparation and pay them enough to keep them, or the teachers now in the schools must be reeducated. As one means of reeducation, the Foundation uses the science teachers' institutes conducted in universities, either in six- or eight-week summer terms or, for teachers on leave, throughout the college year. Several million dollars are appropriated annually in support of the full-year program. This enrolls fewer teachers but produces results of a more fundamental kind.

The number of summer institutes is large enough to exert an influence on the teaching of the entire country. For the summer of 1959, three hundred and fifty institutes were scheduled. Almost every state had at least one and populous states had many. Others were held in Puerto Rico, Hawaii, and Washington, D.C. Funds were available for the expenses of about eighteen thousand high school and college teachers. The institutes dealt with the teaching of most of the basic sciences and mathematics; in some the instruction was adapted to the needs of junior or senior high school teachers, and in others to those of college teachers.

The Foundation supports other programs also. It bears part of the expenses of the Physical Science Committee, which is preparing a new high school textbook in physics and a set of simple laboratory apparatus as well as accessory manuals to aid pupils and teachers in the use of these new tools. The Foundation carries its campaign into the smaller colleges by sending university professors to give lectures and counsel to teachers and students in the science departments. The preparation of science films for use in school television is another current enterprise. The films have been made generally available to schools through Encyclopædia Britannica Films. The science films of the future will be strictly scientific, avoiding the dramatic and distracting byplay of earlier attempts.

There remains the further problem of gaining greater public interest and the financial support of foundations and professional associations for the improvement of education in the humanities, social studies, arts, and other knowledges and skills that do not bake bread. Not everyone should become a scientist or an engineer. Anyone who has observed the rise and sudden fall of many movements and fads in education knows that this is a real problem. Already it is reported that students have been enrolled in engineering who came to college with no intention of choosing that profession. It is not ten years since the profession was supposed to be saturated. Doubtless, at present more engineers and scientists are needed, and better ones. But science is not enough; knowledge is not enough. The spirit of man must be cultivated through religion, philosophy, literature, music, and all the great arts that interpret the inner life of man. Talents vary and education must be adapted to them, not they to it.

ADULT EDUCATION

All free nations have free institutions for the further education of those who are no longer full-time pupils or students. The exercise of freedom, mental health, and changes in politics and in occupations make adult education necessary. Adult education in the United States has had a varied history. It may have begun in the evening schools of the eighteenth century. The lyceum, the Chautauqua Institution, and university extension began in the nineteenth century. One of the old forms is the public evening school, which is prominent in larger towns. Since World War II, public school adult education has grown at a more rapid rate than the regular daytime schools; but its base to build on was much smaller.

Training programs in banking and other kinds of business and industry are growing rapidly. The increasing number of high school graduates who do not go to college attend private business colleges or trade and technical schools in many cases. Students of this development are predicting great increases in such adult vocational schools.

Correspondence courses were offered in the United States in 1873 and have succeeded beyond any dreams of their early promoters. Private home-study courses are said to enroll more new students each year than the colleges. There are, probably, three hundred such schools in the United States, and they offer courses in almost every kind of subject. The schools are of every grade of competence and vary even in honesty. Only a minority are members of the National Home Study Council, which was organized in 1926 to protect students and reputable schools. The government offers correspondence courses to men in uniform through its United States Armed Forces Institute. The public forum and town meeting type of adult education grew rapidly in the 1940s. Town meetings are often broadcast by radio and television. The American Adult Education Association attempts to promote and coordinate activities in this field. It is a private voluntary body. The *Journal of Adult Education* is one of its publications.

University extension in the United States began in about 1887. Like some other educational institutions for adults, it was borrowed from England; but it has developed in a less academic form in the United States than in the country of its origin. The most elaborate of the early forms of university extension was organized at the University of Chicago, which was opened in 1892 under a President, William Rainey Harper, who was experienced in the teaching of adults, in and out of universities. His subject was the Hebrew language and literature, and he was so expert that at least one university professor of mathematics took his course to study Harper more than Hebrew. Under President Harper, the University of Chicago had not merely a department but a fully organized Division of University Extension. Off-campus classes, correspondence courses, a library department, a lecture-study department, and other services were announced, but only the correspondence department survived the general decline that came over university extension in its first period.

The second period opened at the University of Wisconsin. It was marked by a change from academic and liberal arts subjects to the idea of statewide service on "the broadest basis." The university "Cannot escape," said President Charles R. Van Hise, "from taking on the function of carrying knowledge to the people." This he said is the definition of university extension. It means taking knowledge to the masses; and he might have included practical services to dairymen, industrialists, labor unions, and all who needed any help that the state university was able to give. The theory was that the state is the campus of the university.

As a result of this idea, and the Federal legislation of 1914, the Smith-Lever Act, and of 1917, the Smith-Hughes Act, agricultural extension became by far the largest segment of university extension. It has four times as many enrollments as all other forms of university extension combined. Service to public education is another important form. And through institutes, forums, and conferences university extension aids service clubs, women's clubs, and other sections of the public. It deals also with matters of local and national policy and should probably treat controversial matters of opinion more than it does. Money and staff are other problems. There is a National University Extension Association to aid institutions in exchanging and pooling the knowledge that comes from experience in a field that needs better organization.

It is estimated that the total body of human knowledge may now double every fifteen years. Thus, the knowledge which a student receives in school will be largely obsolete by the time he is thirty years of age. This "knowledge explosion" has emphasized the need for programs of continuing adult education. For example, in Texas the Governor's Committee on Public School Education reporting in 1968 recommended that, "An Adult Basic Education Program should be provided without charge to all persons beyond the age of 18 who have not completed a high school education."

AUDIO-VISUAL AIDS TO INSTRUCTION

Television, in less than ten years, became a significant addition to the equipment of schools. Other recent additions include moving picture equipment, tape recorders, and the radio. History was made by the Federal Communications Commission in 1945 when it set aside the 88–92 megacycle band in FM radio for noncommercial use; and again in 1952 the commission helped the school by setting aside about one in eight of the available television channels for use by educational institutions.

The earliest schools in the ancient world had no special equipment, not even desks; and if they used books, these were literary works. Ancient wordlists that have been found were the early beginnings of the textbook which, in a multitude of forms and in all fields, is the most essential of all special aids to learning. Reference works such as the encyclopedia and the indispensable dictionary form the second attacking column in the battle against ignorance. In the fifteenth century the printing press improved the form and reduced the cost of books and made universal education feasible and also necessary. The list of aids to learning expanded to include writing materials, maps, collections and museums, laboratories, shops, kitchens, gardens and electronic data-processing equipment. From these artificial means the pupil goes out to nature and life, to the panorama of the sky, and land, and sea, and to the activities of man. Television is the most effective means of bringing that panorama and those activities indoors for study.

Television, in one way of looking at it, is only a more effective book, and more effective only in some fields and in some ways of using it. The high school films *Combustion* and *Chlorine* do not include chemical formulae or the periodic table. These are handled in ordinary classwork with textbooks, charts, and teaching machines. The educational world is in the experimental stage in its use of the new instrument. Yale University is reported to have been a pioneer in operating a closed-circuit TV station, heard only on the campus. Others are also using this plan for both entertainment and education. The results already obtained in New York City, Philadelphia, Pittsburgh, Oklahoma City, and many other places, coast to coast, have generated enormous enthusiasm. At the same time many are cautioning against overconfidence. Some fear that it might become an educational toy spreading entertainment rather than understanding. There is the danger that it may stress information too heavily. In the sciences, for example, the pupils will see experiments performed instead of themselves performing experiments. People have long complained that the modern laboratory with textbooks and manuals give the student too much help. How can he become ingenious by merely following directions? Television and radio have the defects that when the performance ends the student has only a memory and memory is a week faculty. The book can be read again, the experiment can be repeated, but the television performance when over is over.

The Fund for the Advancement of Education, a subsidiary of the Ford Foundation, investigated educational television, which was carried on in 1957–1958, in the public schools of several large cities, including Detroit and Milwaukee. The investigation compared the results obtained by the ordinary method with those obtained from the use of television. The balance, according to a preliminary report, was in favor of the television classes. Other comparisons have been made in Maryland, North Carolina, and Oklahoma. In Oklahoma, television was adapted to the capacities of gifted pupils in about fifty high schools. In New York State, television lessons are used in the teaching of English to the Spanish-speaking Puerto Ricans who are coming into the metropolis in large numbers. As with any new device there is the problem of finding the best use of it. Even a blackboard can be used unwisely. It was in such terms that the President of the Fund for the Advancement of Education, Alvin C. Eurich, evaluated the new instrument. He said, "Television is only an educational tool. It makes the best teachers available to more persons, as books make the best writers available. It won't do the whole job—but then books didn't either."

In experimental schools across the nation an "instructional systems" concept of education is being tested. In addition to the learner and teacher, the system utilizes a variety of aids, such as closed-circuit television, direct-access computers, motion picture projectors, tape recorders, and a variety of programmed learning materials.

SUMMARY

The attempts to democratize education in the United States have created many problems. As our population has grown, it has become increasingly difficult to provide trained teachers, adequate buildings, and modern equipment for students. Our highly decentralized system of education permits local control and encourages educational experimentation, but increasingly the states have had to turn to the federal government for financial assistance. As educational costs skyrocket, conservative taxpayers demand retrenchment of newer practices. Advances in technology provide new teaching aids, but usually increase costs. But we have hitched our wagon to the star of equality of educational opportunity for all children and plod confidently ahead.

QUESTIONS

1. In what ways have the influence of science and economics and practical demands affected education since the middle of the twentieth century?
2. Do you think American public education is becoming more nationalistic? More democratic? Why?
3. History teaches that institutions survive long after they become out-of-date. Can you cite some examples?
4. It has been noted that new movements do not sweep away old conditions everywhere at once. How does this generalization apply to the movement toward integrated schools in the United States?
5. It has been said that historical movements grow out of incidents. Do you see any movements growing out of recent critical incidents?
6. How has the use of blackboards affected instructional methods and types of learning?
7. It has been hypothesized that a scarcity of books and writing materials

fostered lecturing by teachers and memorizing by students. What instructional methods and types of learning would you predict will be fostered by the widespread use of radio in the classrooms? Of phonograph records? Of instructional films? Of educational television? Of teaching machines?

8. "Although 'Progressivism' carried its principles to excess, it has contributed much of great and lasting value to education in all countries." (a) What "principles" did "Progressivism" carry to excess? (b) What contributions of "great and lasting value" did "Progressivism" make to American education? (c) Briefly show how "Progressivism" has affected education in one country other than the United States.

9. Select one educational program or institutional pattern of England, France, Germany, or the Soviet Union. (a) Describe the program or pattern briefly. (b) Compare the program or pattern with its counterpart in the United States. (c) What does your comparison reveal that has implications for the improvement of the foreign and/or American counterparts?

NOTES AND SOURCES

Your daily newspaper and such periodicals as the *Saturday Review* and *School and Society* are sources of materials for the problems discussed in this chapter.

BESTOR, ARTHUR, *The Restoration of Learning, A Program for Redeeming the Unfulfilled Promise of American Education*, New York, Alfred A. Knopf, 1955, 459 pp.

COUNTS, GEORGE S., *The Country of the Blind*, Boston, Houghton Mifflin Company, 1949, 378 pp.

DUNHAM, FRANKLIN, et al., *Television in Education*, United States Office of Education, Bulletin, 1957, No. 21, 124 pp. Historical, descriptive, and illustrated.

ESSERT, PAUL L., *Creative Leadership of Adult Education*, New York, Prentice-Hall Book Company, Inc., 1951, 333 pp.

FURMAN, BESS, "Who Killed Federal Aid?" *Saturday Review*, September 8, 1956.

HOFSTADTER, RICHARD, and WALTER P. METZGER, *The Development of Academic Freedom in the United States*, New York, Columbia University Press, 1955, 527 pp.

KANDEL, I. L., *The Impact of the War Upon American Education*, Chapel Hill, University of North Carolina Press, 1948, 285 pp.; *American Education in the Twentieth Century*, Cambridge, Mass., Harvard University Press, 1957, 247 pp.

KELLOGG, FLINT, "Villard and the NAACP," *The Nation*, February 14, 1959, 137–140. An account of the origin of the National Association for the Advancement of Colored People.

MICHELS, WALTER C., "The Teaching of Elementary Physics," *Scientific American*, April, 1958. (This is a highly significant report.)

RICHMOND, KENNETH, *Education in the U.S.A., A Comparative Study*, London, Alvin Redman, Ltd., 1956, 227 pp.

ROSENBAUM, E. P., "The Teaching of Elementary Mathematics," *Scientific American*, May, 1958.

SAETTLER, PAUL, A *History of Instructional Technology*, New York, McGraw-Hill Book Company, 1968, 399 pp.

SAWYER, W. W., *Mathematician's Delight*, Pelican Books, A 121, 1949, 238 pp. The author's view of the proper introduction to elementary mathematics differs from that described by E. P. Rosenbaum in the *Scientific American*.

SCOTT, C. WINFIELD, and CLYDE M. HILL, *Public Education Under Criticism*, New York, Prentice-Hall Book Company, Inc., 1954, 414 pp.

SIEPMANN, CHARLES A., *TV and Our School Crisis*, New York, Dodd, Mead and Company, 1958, 198 pp.

STANLEY, CHARLES J., "Organized Interests and Federal Aid to Education," *School and Society*, January 6, 1951.

State of Texas, *Report of the Governor's Committee on Public School Education*, Austin, Texas, August 31, 1968, 76 pp. (A blueprint to enable Texas to attain national leadership in educational achievement during the next decade.)

Chapter 22

HIGHER EDUCATION UNDER NATIONALISM

We have dealt mostly with primary and secondary education; in this last chapter we shall deal with higher education in the present period of national interest in education.

Language often plays tricks with words including school words. For example, in English a high school is a secondary school, which is not very high; and a higher school as in our chapter title is a university. In German, however, these meanings are reversed and a high school is a university, but a higher school is a secondary school. We shall pursue this line of inquiry only far enough for a certain kind of school.

In Europe a university is usually a graduate school and the preparatory schools—the Gymnasium and comparable schools in Germany—the lycée, which is a French public preparatory school, the ten-year schools in the Soviet Union, and the public schools of England all prepare for the university and for graduate or independent study. In the United States, however, the four-year high school prepares only for admission to a college. After the twelve years from the age of six to that of eighteen the young American begins four years of college. If he is very bright he may gain a doctor's degree at twenty-five years of age but few do. Has he been dawdling and wasting some of the most valuable years of life? Some Europeans think so.

University and universal are, of course, forms of the word; universe is a quantitative, mathematical kind of word. The universe is the All, the Creation, or World. We seem to need capital letters for such words. Although university comes from universe it cannot mean that the university student can know or even study everything; no man can digest the world; he would have to swallow himself. Even Archimedes had to have an outside fulcrum on which to rest his lever in order to move the world.

Reading Room, American Memorial Library, West Berlin.

We must also consider what is possible. A university is a school—or more loosely a society, guild, or corporation—that deals with general, inclusive problems; not special or detailed issues but comprehensive ones. It seeks laws, universal answers. It seems appropriate for a university to pursue the universal. This seems to be something of what it meant in the beginning of universities in the Middle Ages; and this meaning it has kept in view. A trade, a trick, or sleight of hand can be learned in any corner, but the meaning of life and our destiny, the preservation of life and health, and the conduct of life or justice—such great matters—can be learned only in a university where Religion, Medicine, and Law are studied; and these with logic, the art of thinking or simply the Arts, were the four faculties of the earliest universities.

The Germans and the French have pretty well kept the simple organization and sober language of the medieval universities. They study and teach Arts, Theology, Medicine, and Law; in France the fields are Letters, Science, Medicine and Law. Other subjects in many-voiced Academe are somehow attached to one or another of the chief areas of knowledge and lines of inquiry. But in some other countries and especially in the United States, the original organization has been shattered and we have departments of psychology, physical education, animal science, sociology, and social work, which are not the same. There are colleges of several kinds of engineering, and colleges of business administration, of education, of music, and the fine arts and many others.

We are well aware that the title of this chapter would be more appropriate for a volume or a work of many volumes. We actually deal chiefly with the Soviet Union, the United Kingdom, the United States, and France; and we do not systematically treat education in the United States; instead we make various comparisons between American and foreign practices and treat a special topic now and then. We give about equal space to the Soviet Union and the United Kingdom and much less to France. Because the educational system and the policies of Russia are very different from those of the West one might justify an even larger allotment of space to the newest system. But we do not hold that our allotments of space are the correct ones.

Preparatory schools are usually for some children terminal schools; and even those who are qualified and desire to enter the next higher institution may be prevented from doing so by the government or other conditions. But for those who do continue their schooling, the preparatory and higher school become in effect parts of a single institution, whatever the legal arrangements. It seems desirable, therefore, to give attention to some schools below the university level. The same argument will apply to theories and policies such as technological training, which affects academic education in the Soviet Union. But we shall not try to justify the distribution of our space; we merely point out that the topics considered seem significant and interesting. If they are really significant they should be interesting to students of education.

THE SOVIET UNIVERSITIES

The university movement did not begin in Russia, but in Italy at a time in history when Russia hardly belonged to the circle of cultivated nations. Bologna, Italy, developed a law school and received a charter. Paris attained university status in about 1300, and Oxford a little later. At that point the movement turned toward the east to Germany and beyond but did not reach Russia until the eighteenth century. The ruler who helped most to prepare the country for modern times and ways was Peter the Great (1677–1725), who traveled in the West and brought back new ideas and skills that helped his country to develop into a European not an Asiatic nation. He did not found a university. He was a little too early for that.

The oldest and most famous university in Russia is the University of Moscow (1755), now the Moscow State University. This indicates that several other early institutions such as Lemberg and Lwow, which have claimed priority, are now considered to have been only advanced schools and not real universities in the early years.

The same judgment can be formed about certain famous writers who are now claimed by the Communists to have accepted their creed when the fact is doubtful. This applies to Ivan Petrovich Pavlov (1849–1936), who received a Nobel Prize in physiology and is famous also for his experiments in psychology.

Peter the Great prepared the way for the University of Moscow, but the immediate agent in its founding was Count Shuvalov, a wealthy aristocrat, who had absorbed the ideas of the French Enlightenment. The Soviets do not approve of him as the founder of their prize university and they claim that the plans were drawn by a scientific genius, M. V. Lomonosov who came of an appropriate working-class family. His father was a fisherman. Probably both aristocrat and commoner were involved; it would be natural. The original location in the heart of Moscow is retained for the humanities and social studies but a new and massive building complex for the sciences has been constructed southwest of the city in the Lenin Hills, away from the capital. It took five years to build it and the space arrangement is not satisfactory, nor is the style of architecture admired.

Russia now has some forty universities and the number has been increasing at the rate of about one each year. Most of the total number have been established since the Revolution of 1917.

A second class of higher schools in Russia is composed of professional and scientific institutes, many of which are devoted to research. These may number seven or eight hundred. In mathematics, physics, and space and other sciences the Soviet Union is in the front rank. In spite of a heavy defense budget and a mounting population to be educated, she can usually find the funds for research. One of the latest, as yet incomplete, of such institutes is located at Novosibirsk, or New Siberia. It will be a great research city in the far north, isolated from the distractions of politics and economics, entirely devoted to investigation in a great array of sciences. By contrast, in the United States and in Western Europe a great deal of the basic research work is carried on in universities by professors who are also teaching graduate or undergraduate students. We believe that, in general, research activity improves the teaching of the investigator and in some cases teaching stimulates inquiry and research. Perhaps no general conclusion can yet be drawn.

The Soviets have a third class of institutes, those that prepare and upgrade skilled workers in engineering, metallurgy, irrigation, and other technical fields, including teaching. There is a Russian Academy of Pedagogical Science and a large array of colleges or institutes of pedagogy, or education. In these institutes they deal with the application of skill and science to practical affairs. Medical institutes prepare physicians, many of them women, but without requiring the extended and complete preparation demanded by present-day science. Such moderate preparation is, however, extremely useful in mild cases, in the absence of a fully trained physician.

From this policy the United States, it may be, could learn from the USSR. American medical education is probably equal to any in the world, but the supply of these completely prepared physicians is limited. Small towns and rural areas may be without medical services. A drive for the full scientific education of doctors began more than a century ago at the University of Pennsylvania and was increased at the Johns Hopkins University and its hospitals. Early in the present century the report of Abraham Flexner on defective and sometimes actually shabby medical schools led to the closing of the worst ones and the improvement of the rest with the result that they prepare excellent physicians but not enough of them in all parts of the country. (We note here that Flexner also wrote on general education and led in the foundation of a "Modern School" at Teachers College in New York [1915]. We will meet him again.)

Returning to the general system of public education in the Soviet Union, the boy or girl may attend a kindergarten if one is available. At seven the child enters the coeducational public ten-year school. These schools have three successive sections of 4–3–3 years and the upper section is not found everywhere. There are no private schools. The required studies are outlined subsequently and there is another slightly different list in the general chapter on Russian education. (See Chapter 16.) All subjects must be studied, there are no electives. The required number of year-hours is listed in the table. A year-hour is one hour of instruction per week for a school year. The table follows:

TABLE OF SUBJECTS AND YEAR-HOURS

(This compressed table is more recent than the extended one reported from Counts in Chapter 16).

Subject	Year-Hours
Russian Language and Literature	36
Foreign Language	20/21
History	17
Geography	11/12
Physical Education	12
Singing	3
Mechanical Drawing	6
Shop Courses	12
Arithmetic	8
Algebra	17
Geometry	14/15
Trigonometry	2
Biology	9
Physics	15/16
Chemistry	11
Astronomy	1
Psychology	1

There are, we repeat, no electives—a significant fact. Because the curricula of all the secondary schools are alike, the transfer of pupils from school to school is easy; but, on the other hand, it becomes difficult to provide for the special needs of any individual pupil. Education is a State monopoly and it serves the State and not the desires of the people. The system seems to be an application and working out of the principles of Plato's *Republic* and the first large-scale effort of this kind. In the Soviet Union as in Plato, the ruling class by a vote, based on a system of examinations, tells "one to go and he goeth and to another to come and he cometh." The decisions are conjoint or associated decisions for which no one person can be held responsible, nor will they say how the plans were formed. We all know how mechanical and inconclusive examinations are. It seems that Immanuel Kant wisely objected to the complete control of education by the State; but it seems also that there is ample space between the tight system of the Soviets and the lack of system of America for a better plan than either has at present.

Early in the Soviet regime, the control of higher education was assigned to the several republics. After a number of changes the present Ministry of Higher Education in the USSR was created in 1946 to direct all universities —technical, agricultural, and law—and other higher institutions. There are exceptions. Medical schools, teachers' institutes, and some others are jointly directed by the National Ministry and the republics in which they are located. Finally there is still another agency to share control of higher education, the party. All major problems in the field of higher education are discussed by the Communist party of the USSR before they are taken up by the ministry. The internal organization and the titles and duties of the personnel, rector, professor, and assistant professor are common in other countries as well.

To enter a university the boy or girl must bring a very good work and examination record. Those who present a perfect record in studies and conduct are admitted first. From among those who have high marks but not in all subjects the highest may be accepted after an examination. However, priority is given to veterans and to those who have worked for a year or more in the national economy. On the other hand, the authorities try to exclude dissenters and possible trouble makers. Besides, there is an assigned quota set by the Minister of Higher Education. There is some ferment among the youth today. Travelers in the Union are sometimes accosted by those who seek information about the outside world.

Propaganda is universal in the schools at all levels and even more persistent in papers and on radio and television. Communism is taught more vigorously in the Soviet Union than democracy in the United States. As a primary element of communism, great efforts are made also to teach atheism; yet, after fifty years, religion still lives. The Orthodox Church has a few seminaries to prepare priests; there are some small Protestant sects and, of course, many Jews. Anti-Semitism, strong in old Russia, also persists and is promoted despite Kosygin's denial before the living world in 1967 at the United Nations. Anti-Semitism is not essential to communism. Was not Karl Marx a Jew!

The other side of the propaganda issue is the denial of access to foreign papers, magazines, books, and broadcasts. A university student must have written permission to consult *The New York Times* and other foreign writings, but it is perhaps unwise to ask for it. Does this imply that communism is considered a very fragile plant? Are the people so difficult to convince and to hold true that they must be constantly showered with convincing facts and arguments?

Students are a special class. There is growing evidence that they no longer accept all that they hear but are becoming somewhat critical and sceptical; however, the pressure to keep them within legal limits is strong. Education is the only avenue that leads out of a life of assigned labor into one with a chance to acquire a name, position, and possibly power. The young man cannot make his fortune in real estate, invent a new hayloader and form a company to build a factory, or more modestly, open a shoe store. There is no private property but there is developing a slight trend toward a certain economic freedom. It may grow more rapidly in smaller Communist states. At present, education is the best, almost the only way to escape the routine of assigned tasks. Intelligent young people are under heavy pressure to do their homework if they are admitted to a university.

With the great excess of applicants that, through a technical policy change, occurred in 1966, the candidates for entrance into the higher institutions often thought it wise to make some kind of special effort. Sometimes they employed a tutor from the faculty of the institution they hoped to enter. Rural school graduates had a special problem because their instruction had been below average in quality.

If, on the other hand, the student fell into certain unofficially favored categories, his chance for admission might be much improved. The student who could be a beneficiary of a telephone call from someone "higher up," someone considered to be a public servant, or an athlete, or a talented singer, such an applicant was likely to receive special attention. Those with few scruples made use of more flagrantly nonlegal means of gaining entrance.

The evidence also shows that Soviet officials also have difficulties with their job placement plans. (Summarized from Andrew Cheselka, "The Secondary School Graduate Explosion . . . 1966," *Comparative Education Review*, February, 1968.)

Or we cite another kind of clandestine influence in Soviet education. Some large cities have foreign language schools hidden away in quiet nooks.

The Soviet press reports only very sparingly and reluctantly about the activities of these schools. The reason for this silence is that these schools, especially in

Moscow, are attended by the scions of the Soviet aristocracy, and nothing touching the personal lives of this social group in the USSR must ever see the pages of the public press. The author of this essay [David Burg] knows personally that the school located in the Sokolniki section of Moscow, where all instruction is carried on in English, was attended by the children and relatives of Malenkov while he was Premier. The exact location and number of these schools is unknown. We may assume that their number is not great, but because of the importance of the pupils attending these schools, their influence far outweighs their numerical position in Soviet public education.

In the second place, some Soviet intellectual families, carrying on a pre-revolutionary tradition consider it necessary to teach their children foreign languages at their own expense with the help of private tutors. The chief such language is usually English.[1]

POLYTECHNICAL EDUCATION

In turning to the seemingly new subject of polytechnical education—the teaching of a variety of vocational skills—we are not completely deserting the subject of higher education. To know what will not prepare one for entrance to a university and what will probably cause one to drop out is to know something about higher education. Polytechnical education was carried on in the same national system of education as the universities and institutes of research and higher studies, and the separate branches influenced each other.

We have already indicated that polytechnical education is the cultivation of skills that will aid the manufacture of useful goods. This idea was introduced by Robert Owen, a Socialist director of cotton mills at New Lanark, Scotland, in the early nineteenth century. He provided both literary schools and a "factory school" for the children of his operatives. Marx took up the ideas and proposed a triple scheme of physical, mental, and technical education. From Marx the plan passed to Lenin who improved it. Everyone was to learn to work with his hands in a variety of occupations as a means of developing a one-class society, all members of one happy family of workers.

This was the idea of a book by Lenin's wife Krupskaya, who wrote it during the Revolution (1917), which she called *People's Education and Democracy*. Lenin, in his program for the party insisted on polytechnical schools to teach boys and girls the theory and skills of many branches of industry. Two years later, in 1919, the party adopted this policy and demanded such instruction for all, up to the age of seventeen. Immediately Krupskaya pointed to the lack of equipment for such teaching because all available lathes, tractors, gasoline engines, and other machines were needed for production and it was not possible to get a supply for teaching. Others, including educators but also industrialists, called the plan wasteful, claim-

[1] From George Z. F. Bereday and Jaan Pennar, *The Politics of Soviet Education*, New York, Praeger, 1960, pp. 200–201. (The essay was written by David Burg.)

ing that production would be better served by specialized technical education to prepare workmen for particular jobs.

The polytechnical education had to wait. Lenin realized that reading and writing were more important, were indeed necessary for instruction in industrial skills. The people were accustomed to regard the schools as means to white-collar, not factory, work. There were no polytechnic teachers available. Any locality had only a few industries and it seemed far-fetched to acquire unnecessary skills. But the chief reason for delay was Stalin. At a workers' conference in 1931, he said, "We are lagging fifty to one hundred years behind the advanced countries.... We must win this distance in ten years or we will be crushed." The schools were designed to prepare scientists and mathematicians to redesign the industries; and this made it seem absurd to teach the old arts. The process continued and as industry changed, polytechnical education was hard-pressed to keep up with it.

A new era in polytechnical education began in 1952 with a "Directive" from the Nineteenth Party Congress stating that "a start is to be made in introducing polytechnical training into secondary schools, while the ground will be prepared for the transition to universal polytechnical training." Khrushchev at the Twentieth Party Congress (1956) said,

A big shortcoming of our school system is that instruction is divorced from life to some extent; those who finish schools are insufficiently prepared for practical work. Although the directives of the Nineteenth Party Congress (1952) called for measures to introduce polytechnical instruction in the schools, this matter is moving ahead very slowly.

Khrushchev blamed the Russian Academy of Pedagogical Sciences for talking instead of acting. He was correct: the teachers were not entirely favorable to vocational arts. Khrushchev also attacked the parents because they favored intellectual rather than manual studies and arts. It was true; parents wanted their children to rise above physical labor, if possible. They were convinced by the talk of a one-class society. Khrushchev said such views were "insulting to the toilers of a Socialist society." He wanted the youth to "level down" but their parents wanted them to be "leveled up." Industrial managers hesitated to assume responsibility for equipment and personnel. They were not running schools; and besides, modern industry requires highly trained, expert workmen. The managers and personnel would be blamed for any faulty work, spoiled machinery, and wasted materials.

In spite of all objections a new school program was adopted in the winter of 1958. The former seven-year, incomplete secondary school became an eight-year school, the ten-year became an eleven-year school and this plan was to become general in five years. All children, even future professors, were to have work experiences. In the last two years of the secondary school children were to spend two days a week in labor. But the entire plan was changed again after Khrushchev and the ministry confessed its mistake. In 1964 the complete secondary school was cut back to its earlier pattern of ten years. The change was completed in the 1965–1966 school year. When we consider the long history of polytechnical education from Marx to Lenin to Khrushchev we cannot be certain whether or how soon it may be revived. Even in the Soviet Union public opinion eventually influences public affairs including education; but the party may try again after twenty years. The old hunger for equality will return. The Communists still believe that when all are equal people will love each other more. They should know better.

The sudden shifts in policy by the party without the support of the general public make it difficult to anticipate the future course of Soviet policy. It is interesting to note that the Russian Soviet Federal Socialist Republic Pedagogical Society had come to the support of Khrushchev's revival of polytechnical education just before that leader's fall.[2]

POLITICS IN SOVIET EDUCATION

Quantitatively, the Soviet Union is in some areas ahead of the United States. They passed the two hundred million mark in population some years ago; but some of these live in the frozen north and on the barren steppes across the Ural Mountains. The north is being more fully explored and rich deposits of coal and iron have been found.

In science and technology, the Soviets are presenting a great challenge. They already have three times as many engineers as the United States and for every engineer they are training four or five technical experts. It was the Sputnik of 1957 that awakened America and led Congress to pass the National Defense Education Act of the following year (1958) and to support the National Science Foundation for the improvement of science teachers and teaching. We know that genius in mathematics and physics develops early. Our more flexible school systems should enable us to take advantage of the opportunity to increase and improve our scientific and technical education.

Secondary education is more nearly universal in America than in Russia where only one half of the children attend schools, and about eighty per cent of those in the schools finish the course. Those who finish learn more than the American pupils, and in particular, they learn more science. The Soviets are not especially successful with languages, but they work at them longer and harder and achieve more than most Americans. It is supposed that people in large nations do not on the average apply themselves vig-

[2] See the article in *Sovietskaia Pedagogica*, 1962, No. 3, translated in Fred Albin, Editor, *Education in the U.S.S.R., A Collection of Readings from Soviet Journals*, Vol. 1, p. 128. It was published by the International Arts and Sciences Press, apparently in New York.

orously to language study. The Russian schools, it is reported, employ over forty thousand teachers of English, the most popular language. Russian children frequently, but Americans rarely, learn to speak the language they study in the secondary schools.

After an elementary school of four years and a rigid secondary school of six years—we recall that the Russian child has no electives except that he can choose the foreign language he will study—the successful youth can go to a university for five years. The degrees in the two countries are not equivalent: titles in Russia are license, candidate, and doctor; and in America they are bachelor, master, and doctor. The Russian doctor's degree is attained only after the candidate has had years of professional experience and has reached middle age. In America there is also a lower degree than those listed here: the A. A. associate in arts, given after two years of college work. And Russia has a higher degree, that of Academician, conferred on a great professional by the various scientific and governmental academies.

In the Soviet Union preparation for such professions as engineering, medicine, teaching, or scientific agriculture is in the hands of the Minister of Higher Education. He is the manager. Just as we hear of managed economies in various countries, so in Russia they have a managed education. The Minister's power over the lives of young people seeking a professional career has been called awesome; and he admitted that "techniques of persuasion" are used to direct students into the proper studies and graduates into the right positions. They are exceedingly fortunate when what is considered best for the country agrees with their desires.

We have some examples. In 1958 the ministry was disturbed because the system was producing too many engineers. It would have been awkward to send an automotive engineer to manage a collective farm or to teach botany. Five years later the minister reported that they had solved "the problem of engineers." The need for them had greatly increased and they were preparing three times as many as the United States. Now, in 1963, they were increasing the numbers of the students of natural science, such as botany, zoology, and perhaps meteorology or forestry. In a free educational system adjustments are made gradually and there is less likelihood of either a great success or a general disaster. In the United States the growth of state universities and their branches and the multiplication of junior colleges is likely to affect the future of many private colleges, but the results will be discounted in advance and there is no likelihood of calamity. No large number of private colleges will close at one time and students and professors will find welcome elsewhere. We went through this kind of debacle with the private academies with no great harm.

If these forecasts should be realized they will be examples of what has been taking place in this country from its beginnings. A partly public school system was begun in the colony of Massachusetts before 1650, and the movement grew stronger in the newer western territories and states. The elementary schools became public first. The first public high school began in Boston in 1821, and the new trend swept over many of the academies. Thomas Jefferson's University of Virginia became more famous than the earlier University of North Carolina. State universities and private colleges battled for possession of the Midwest from the time of Boston's first high school. In 1862, the land-grant colleges joined in the fray. Today education in the United States is chiefly public, but there are thousands of parochial and other private elementary schools, many private academies, colleges, and great universities such as Chicago, Northwestern, and all those in the Ivy League. The Federal Government is pouring out more and more money for education with a very slight increase in public control. And if all this change during three centuries is bad, the people have not discovered it. They are certain that they do not want an educational czar.

The Minister of Higher Education in the USSR never finds out whether those chosen for admission to the universities were the best ones available. Those who were rejected follow careers so different from those of the students who attended the university. It would be instructive to compare the careers of those who were from one to three marks above a selected critical mark with an equal number who were from one to three marks below it at entrance. It would tell something of the value of marks or the lack of it.

The selection of the professors sets different problems. They stay and become well-known to generations of students and to other professors. They may earn nicknames that are sometimes expressive. The Minister said to his American visitor that both countries should seek to appoint better professors, as no doubt they should do and so should all countries. The Soviet Minister does not have a free hand with the entering students. He makes inquiries, appoints committees, and is even overruled by his advisors and, as the Minister admitted, is informed "that he has erred."

Conditions, however, change and opinions and policies may change with them. Old policies may be revived. We have noted the changes, forward and backward, in polytechnical education; but many leaders still expect the intellectual and manual workers to be united into one social class with every person doing both intellectual and manual work.

Changes are taking place in the internal management of the universities. In the decade opened by 1961 the councils of professors gained new powers. The faculties also can choose their own deans instead of having them appointed by the Minister. The faculties can make some changes in the curricula. Movements to increase learning aids, programming, language laboratories, the use of radio and television, and increased emphasis on the natural sciences are in process; greater pressure is the word. In developing their policies it is noticeable that the Soviets think of the United States as their prime competitor; to overtake will not be too difficult because our system seems loose and easygoing. They prefer "the education race to the armament race," but do not take their eyes off the latter for one moment.[3]

THE SOVIET UNION AND INTERNATIONAL EDUCATION

Economically the Soviet Union is pretty well off; few people are starving and many are in prosperous circumstances. Potentially she is one of the richest countries in the world with vast resources in coal, iron, and oil and some excellent farm lands, especially in the Ukraine: but all of the Ukraine lies north of the forty-fifth degree of north latitude. This difference in temperature was not in the mind of Khrushchev when, standing in an Iowa cornfield, he predicted that his country would soon overtake America in the production of food grain. Incidentally, it was such inappropriate remarks and acts that caused his downfall. The people, however, know how to make use of the cold country, and they even dared to build a great research center, as we have seen, at cold Novosibirsk.

Khrushchev was more successful in his plans to attract foreign students. In a visit to Indonesia in 1960 he announced his decision to build a university expressly for foreign students and mentioned as sources, Africa, Asia, and Latin America. At that time Indonesia seemed to be happily marching toward communism and the installation of Soviet missiles in Cuba seemed to be a safe way to take over all the Americas. These errors contributed to his dismissal, no doubt; but meanwhile, the new institution, called Friendship University, was opened in 1960. Khrushchev expressed the hope that not merely students sent by their governments but also "those who express their wishes personally should study at the new university." In the end he hoped even to draw students from the villages. But would it not have been better to distribute them among the natives rather than to segregate them in one place? The number of students was recorded in hundreds in the first year, but three years later there were two thousand.

Not all foreign students in the Soviet Union have been pleased with the treatment received and facilities offered. This statement would apply to any country that accepts foreign students. From time to time one reads of incidents and withdrawals. It is not very impressive that five or six hundred foreign students have left or been expelled and that others have been dissatisfied. The causes for discontent are numerous, but one stems from an inadequate knowledge of the language of instruction and when to this is added a general ignorance of the subject under discussion, the matter becomes serious. The Soviets have set up foreign and especially Russian

[3] William Benton, *The Teachers and the Taught in the U.S.S.R.*, New York, Atheneum, 1966, 174 pp. This book has been of the greatest use in writing the preceding pages. It should be read by everyone; and it is readable.

language institutes for foreign students, an idea worth imitating. Probably all or nearly all students overestimate their ability to understand foreign speech about an unfamiliar subject.

Like everything else in the Soviet Union, policies for the reception and handling of foreign students is in the hands of the party, perhaps through its Central Committee but more likely through a special committee. At the next level the Ministry of Higher Education would be involved and the ministries of the several republics. Foreign students are accepted at Moscow State University and Friendship University in Moscow, Leningrad State University, Kiev State University, Tashkent Central Asian University, at the Tashkent Agricultural Institute, and at the Georgian Polytechnical Institute in Thilisi. This geographical distribution doubtless indicates differences in the origin and vocation of the students. The great majority of the students, twenty-five to one, come from Communist countries; but this proportion must have changed since the split between the Union and China.[4]

SHOE ON THE OTHER FOOT

At the end of the war against Hitler, a large part of Germany including East Berlin was left under the administration of the Soviet Union. That region was less densely populated and more Protestant than the industrial and largely Catholic people of western Germany. One might suppose that the Lutheran Germans would be at least as compliant as the Poles nearby. One difference is that the Soviet-controlled Germans have a free Germany on their western boundary.

Schools, universities, higher scientific research institutions, and technical schools were badly damaged, needlessly in some cases. Leipzig, now in the Soviet "German Democratic Republic" is the most often mentioned example. The Zones controlled by the Western Allies, after efforts to repair the war damage, returned as soon and as much as possible to the prewar school systems. In the eastern Zone Russia set up a new system intended to make Communists of a conquered people. There was no opportunity to debate the religious issue as it was taken up in the West, where each family could have its children in elementary and secondary schools instructed in the religion—Catholic or Protestant—of the parents.

A professor of Harvard University who was educated in Germany, Robert Ulich, has written on the issue as follows:

And this now leads to the internationally most dangerous factor in the development of postwar Germany. Almost eighteen million Germans, of whom ac-

[4] Stewart Fraser, *Governmental Policy and International Education*, New York, John Wiley & Sons, Inc., 1965, 373 pp. The international student movement cannot be appraised now, it is a question for the future.

cording to careful estimates not more than five per cent would vote for the Communist party if they were free, live under the Soviet-supported regime of the German Democratic Republic and have to send their children to schools about which, in spite of a Democratic façade, they have nothing to say.

The passage goes on to report that in the six years following 1949 an average of three hundred thousand persons a year emigrated or fled to the Federal Republic of West Germany. There was an open gateway until the Communists erected a wall across the city of Berlin. This turned the eastern Zone into a penal colony for anti-Communists. A measure of revenge may be one of the elements of this policy. Many still escape to the West, both liberals and conservatives, the unknown and the famous; Stalin's daughter Svetlana Alleluyeva is now included among them.

The schools provided for the Germans form a ladder that divides into several branches at the upper end. They are, however, used to propagate the Soviet system of ideas and to exclude all democratic thought and free discussion. Pupils who do not absorb this political outlook will not be approved for higher or even upper secondary education; and the same political outlook is imposed on the universities.

The language instruction is not arranged to make it easy for a German student to gain entrance to a university. Many languages are offered, so many that it is unlikely that any school teaches all of them. From the age of eleven, Russian is required. Among the other modern languages, the Slavic are preferred. The ancient Latin and Greek are offered for so few years that they are unlikely to be accepted for university entrance. The number of German students in the universities is declining and the supply of physicians is becoming inadequate.

How far and for how long a period an entire people is to be punished for the crimes of a leader is a question that should not be wholly given over to the will and views of the chief sufferer. Russia's major allies tried to give her some advice in 1957. Britain, France, and the United States said that after twelve years the hopes of the peoples of the world for a true peace had not been fulfilled. They said the continued division of Germany, "which is a grave injustice to the German people," is one of the main reasons why a settlement has not been reached.

In all modern countries, education and the schools have become an agency in national policy, most of all, perhaps, in the Soviet Union. The government invites and provides for foreign students from the wide world but they deal quite otherwise when "the shoe is on the other foot," as in the case of the East Germans.[5]

---

[5] Robert Ulich, *The Education of Nations, A Comparison in Historical Perspective*, Cambridge, Mass., Harvard University Press, 1961, 325 pp.

THREE COUNTRIES MEET

Some further comparison between Soviet and American schools may serve as an introduction to recent changes in education in England; but these changes can hardly be understood and their magnitude can not be measured without some knowledge of the earlier history of the English preparatory schools and of the universities. There are similarities and great differences between the three countries. There are great differences in the antiquity of the higher schools. Only the English universities reach back to the Middle Ages. Age is not the only difference. The early English universities are characterized by a collegiate system not found in America or Russia. The colleges of Oxford and Cambridge are both residence halls and schools. Each of the two ancient universities has some twenty colleges, some nearly as old as the university itself, and each accommodating both students and Fellows. The latter are tutors or teachers; but they are also members of the governing board of the college. The teaching is personal and individual. Each week the student brings and reads an assigned essay to his tutor and receives criticism and direction and a topic for further work. Relations between teacher and taught vary as widely in the colleges as they do outside; but in the United States there is a similar intimacy only in advanced graduate study and tuition. No one supervises a tutor's work and it varies widely from person to person. Students have been known to withdraw from a university because they disagreed with their tutors; but when it is successful the system provides both pressure and skilful guidance.

We shall list a few of the names of the famous colleges of Oxford and Cambridge. University College at Oxford and Peterhouse at Cambridge are the oldest and were established in the second half of the thirteenth century. Balliol and Merton at Oxford arose in the same period; and later ones bear the names Oriel, New College, to be mentioned again, Lincoln, All Souls, and Magdalen. After Peterhouse at Cambridge the list includes Clare, Pembroke, Gonville and Caius, and Trinity Hall. This last name requires us to mention the confusing fact that Cambridge also has a Trinity College as does Oxford. Oxford has a Magdalen College, already noted, and Cambridge a Magdalene College; Oxford has a Christ's Church College and Cambridge a Christ's College; Oxford has a Queen's and Cambridge a King's College.

Reason and sense are diffused in the teaching rather than in the names of the colleges. The universities teach as well; the colleges teach mainly through lectures that are open to all students. These are not well attended because they may not deal with the subjects on which the students will be examined. When the audience is small or missing the speakers do not always lecture. An amusing instance is recorded by James Bryce, famous statesman and author of *The American Commonwealth*. Goldwin Smith was to lecture and Bryce, probably then a freshman, edged into the room where the speaker sat. After a time Smith asked, "Of what did King John die?" Bryce did not know. Smith said, "Of a surfeit of peaches and a new ale." Nothing more was said and each went his own way.

We now take up the further comparison between Russian and American schools. In most highly developed countries, elementary education is now as nearly universal as health, the distribution of the population, and comparable factors permit; but the extension of the highest studies in universities and professional or technological institutions is still limited by sex, social class, mental capacity, and, of course, money. To this list we might add desire or ambition. Perhaps there comes a time to everyone when he begins to resist further tutelage and imposed tasks. But zest for knowledge, perhaps through independent study, continues in many for a long period. Therefore the extension of the school ages both downward over the kindergarten and Headstart into the nursery years and upward into full maturity now covers a third of a man's active years; it may be extended further.

Education above the kindergarten is usually set into three sequences or stages: elementary, secondary, and higher. We have seen how the Soviet system works. Instead of a ten-year school below the university, as in the Soviet Union, American children have a twelve-year span, divided into 6–3–3 year stages or on the older plan an 8–4 year; but the American child in the 3–3 or 4-year high school has many subject choices. One set of choices might lead to college, another to commercial employment, and a third to diversified practical work. The Soviet authorities make the crucial choices for the child at the end of seven and ten years of schooling. Soviet authorities argue that elementary and also secondary schoolchildren, even with guidance and expert advice, are too young to make such fateful choices. Americans argue that mistakes can be corrected, although with some loss of time, and that, in the long run, freedom is worth what it costs.

That difference in the school policies between the two countries is not a snap decision that may soon change. On the contrary, it is based on centuries of ancient authoritarian rule and a new authoritarian philosophy based on a misreading of history that has been imposed on the people by a minority. There is dissent among the young, the writers, and other intellectuals. But knowledge of life outside is carefully controlled. William Benton's question: "When will the Iron Curtain be lifted?" has no answer now. None of the well-known conditions that could fire a military or an intellectual revolution exist. Each country supports its own policies and defends its own system.

Some Soviet educators claim that the Russian youth after ten years of schooling are better prepared for university work than American youth after twelve. This may well be true at the lower ends of the two groups, but there has been a weeding out of weaker students in the Soviet Union in the middle of the secondary school course. And also, the first two years of the

American college make concessions to the less able students that are not allowed in the Soviet Union.

We begin consideration of Oxford and Cambridge, two of the oldest universities in the world, by dealing with an ancient admissions question. Admission to a university is not open to everyone; it is to some degree regulated everywhere. Academic fitness or ability to do the work of the university is a general entrance condition that may be met by an examination or by a certificate from a preparatory school or both. And there may be other conditions.

At least one American state, Ohio, has a law that requires The Ohio State University to admit any graduate from a first-class public high school who applies. Naturally experience has shown that this is not a good law or a satisfactory policy because a large proportion of the students, so admitted, fail in the first year; but the sovereign people have not been willing to repeal it. Perhaps everyone would be willing to admit that the admission standards among American colleges and universities vary widely, many having high standards, but that there is a considerable gap between the easy and the tough.

The Soviet Union, as we should recall, has a special kind of admission policy as a result of the administrative limit that is placed on the number to be enrolled. Being an administrative decision probably means that it has no relation to the capacities of the individual applicants. It means that the state decides on the number and on the placement of those in excess.

We see then that consideration other than the capacities and scholarly interests of the applicants and high marks earned in the lower schools may enter into the question of admission to the university. We see that one such consideration is the need by the economy for greater numbers of technicians and an adequate supply of graduates in the arts and sciences. In a managed economy such matters cannot be left to free choice. There are other considerations such as the family, social standing, race, and the "influence" of the boy or girl who wishes to enter a university.

In an earlier time, those who directed the policy of the English universities of Oxford and Cambridge saw the advantage that would accrue from the admission of many titled or wealthy young men who had no great interest in studies but desired to spend a few adolescent years in shady groves engaging in sports, pleasant conversation, a very moderate amount of reading, and topping it off with a degree. A solution was happily found by the universities. Each institution created two degrees: a Pass degree for a minimum of work and an Honors degree for those who had the gifts, grit, and daring to earn it against severe competition. The Pass degree certified to the residence, conduct, and moderate application of those who had thereby earned an honorable discharge. Requirements for the Honors degree were high and the best students gained First-Class Honors. Those whose marks were high but not quite the highest were given second-class

Honors and there were even third- and fourth-class Honors for those men who were demonstrably better than those who drew a bare Pass.

This ingenious idea of setting up two quite different standards for graduation from a university has called out both humorous and serious criticism, but perhaps neither from holders of First-Class Honors. The scheme saved the universities from the exclusion or early dismissal of all but the most capable. It enabled the universities to attract and reward youth of the wealthy and influential classes; and it reported the academic facts of student life more publicly than the American system under which the same degree is conferred on the best and the poorest of all the graduates. The American plan does not, however, hide anything. Every student's performance is recorded and the record can be inspected by any proper inquirer.

ENGLISH PUBLIC SCHOOLS

Two universities, Oxford and Cambridge, served England for the five hundred years from the thirteenth to the early nineteenth century. The population was much less than it is now and the universities were largely an arm of the English Church. Training for the secular professions such as law and medicine was provided mainly outside the universities. The grammar schools prepared university students and the alliance of Oxford and Cambridge with the so-called public schools began in the latter Middle Ages. William of Wykeham, who founded New College at Oxford in 1379, established Winchester College, five years later, as a feeder for his earlier college. Eton College and King's College, Cambridge also had the same founder, King Henry VI. We must note that in England college can mean either a secondary school or a unit in one of the old universities. Only nine public schools were recognized by the Public Schools Commission appointed in the mid-nineteenth century. Of the number, Winchester had been founded by a cleric and Eton by a king; St Paul's was an ancient cathedral school and Merchant Taylor's had been established in 1561 by a guild. Merchant Taylor's first headmaster was Richard Mulcaster (1532–1611), who was born near the Scottish border. He was educated at both universities and was admitted to the Master of Arts degree by Oxford. He is one of the great, original, but neglected English writers on education. After conducting Merchant Taylor's for twenty-five years he served in the same capacity for twelve at the school reformed by Colet, St Paul's. In his writings, Mulcaster proposed many improvements in education and to one of these, a proposal to reorganize the English universities on the Continental pattern, that is, by colleges of Law, Medicine, and so forth and to include a College of Education. The Public Schools Commission reported after fourteen years; and four years later the Public Schools Act was adopted with "deliberate speed." They supported the provisions of the founders except when they interfered with new purposes. "Reform if we must," they held, but do it conservatively. For further light they looked at newer schools not under official examination by the commission. They found the boys in the old schools intolerably idle; and naturally they could find little that was well learned. They looked abroad and liked what they saw in the German Gymnasium, which had been recently reformed. They adopted the more than doubtful principle that boys should learn the classical tongues as the best way to master their own language. They criticised the snobbery involved in looking down on the mathematics master from a classical elevation. Science was not yet taught. The commission had doubtless been appointed because the famous old schools were losing their race with the many new public schools. These new foundations, Cheltenham (1841), Merlborough (1842), and Rossall (1844) were the earliest of a long list. The answer to the question about the current number of public schools will vary with the respondent. A recent writer has chosen more than seventy.[6]

SCOTTISH UNIVERSITIES

Oxford and Cambridge were, until a few decades before the Public Schools Commission, the only universities in England. The public schools sent their boys to the old universities and received masters and headmasters in return. Scotland, with its hostility to England and leaning toward France, established its own higher institutions: St Andrews in 1411, and before 1500, three others—Glasgow, Aberdeen, and Edinburgh. In the following century the Puritans were excluded from Oxford and Cambridge and many would not on principle attend an Anglican institution. They attended one of their own academies and then matriculated in Scotland. The Scottish universities had a broader list of studies, adopted English as the language of instruction, and introduced the whole extent of the current medical course of studies. In the eighteenth century, Edinburgh attracted students including medical students from England, Europe, and America.

A distinguished American, educated in classics at Princeton and in medicine at Edinburgh, Dr. Benjamin Rush, spent two years (1766–1768) under the tuition of Dr. William Cullen and his four colleagues. Edinburgh attracted many American and even more English students. One of the latter was Charles Darwin who studied medicine in Edinburgh and theology in Cambridge, but became, in the language of his day, a naturalist, a subject not then studied in universities. The point of this is that the Scottish universities being internally governed and poor were more likely to bestir themselves to draw students and their fees. They had greater freedom than Oxford or Cambridge and although Harvard was a Cambridge daughter, she

[6] Ian Weinberg, *The English Public Schools: The Sociology of Elite Education*, New York, Atherton Press, 1967.

did not long follow the mother's teaching or example. Early Presbyterian colleges were likely to be favorable to those of their own faith from the north. Princeton and Dickinson Colleges secured presidents from Scotland, and Princeton's John Witherspoon, who became a signer of the Declaration of Independence, was followed after a long interval by another Scot, James McCosh. These were the most distinguished examples of a class.

Now and then higher education in democratic countries has opened new opportunities for education to working people and others who would not be admitted to any university. It was no accident that the mechanics' institute movement arose in Scotland and spread to England and America. In the latter decades of the eighteenth century, John Anderson, an early professor of science at Glasgow University opened evening classes and invited working men. His money, which amounted to only a thousand pounds, was not enough to support the desired "scientific university" but it supported a chair of physics. The first occupant was George Birkbeck, a Lancashire boy, educated in medicine at Edinburgh.

Needing apparatus and illustrations for his lectures he employed skilled artisans in Glasgow and was surprised to find them interested and enthusiastic. He invited some to his lectures and so many came that he established a separate class for them. His great success was due not only to their interest and intelligence but also to his remarkable skill in explaining technical topics in simple language. He was surprised and pleased to find five hundred men crowding into his lecture hall; but he soon left to practice medicine in London. Anderson's institution, however, continued; and Birkbeck continued to promote the movement, which was spreading in England. From England it was brought to the United States. There are even now a few institutions, museums, and libraries in Rochester, Cincinnati, and elsewhere that had their beginning in the mechanics institutes of England and Scotland. One might suppose that science instruction in schools and colleges destroyed the need for the institutes, but it died of an inner malady —the desire for amusement rather than knowledge.

MODERN ENGLISH UNIVERSITIES

To carry out a topical account along with a chronological one is a simple way to bring on difficulty. The early public schools of England are nearly as old as the earliest colleges of the old English universities; but to avoid a mere listing of historical events the story of each has been carried down to recent times and even to the present day. This procedure tends to make the Scottish universities seem to be more recent than they are. We repeat that they arose in the fifteenth century, and we shall add that Scotland had a complement of parish schools in almost any one of which a bright boy could learn enough Latin, English, and arithmetic to get along comfortably in the first year of a Scottish university. A story, *Beside the Bonnie Briar Bush,* by Ian Maclaren, was popular in the time of the first Roosevelt; it gave a late picture of these schools at the time when the English were trying to develop their own neighborhood preparatory schools. The modern English universities began before there was a good supply of well-prepared students. The demand helped to increase the number.

Influence passed across the border in both directions but the English were largely the gainers. English education was aristocratic because it was strongly influenced by an aristocratic church. This attitude has not completely disappeared. It is reported that some Oxford dons still refuse to recognize a modern university doctor's degree but address the holder as "Mister". The Scottish influence has helped to spread social and civil equality and broad opportunity for progress especially through the new universities. At the same time we must keep in mind the high academic standards in a limited array of special and academic fields that are maintained at Oxford and Cambridge.

The first modern English university, the University of London, was established in 1828 within a year of the accession of Thomas Arnold to the headship of Rugby School. The connection between the two events consists in the support that Arnold for a time gave to the new venture. That support was based on ideas of public interest and had no connection with Rugby; but Arnold, an aristocrat and a conservative, believed himself to be a liberal. He supported the University as he did other good causes; but when he found that the University was to be neutral in religion he called it "that godless institution in Gower Street."

Arnold was positive, rarely neutral. There is a living Arnold cult and his great reputation as a moral reformer of the English public schools, which is based in part on A. P. Stanley's *Life of Arnold* and on *Tom Brown* by Thomas Hughes, may not be entirely deserved.[7]

It is reported that his boys said, "It is a shame to tell Arnold a lie. He always believes us." But in sober fact he once refused to believe a boy who was telling him the truth, and on the contrary believed a tutor who was mistaken. He flogged the boy so severely that the boy became ill. The fate of the tutor is not recorded. The question was merely about the portion of the text that had been covered. Arnold was examining the work of the boys and of the tutor. Every boy in class knew whether the passage in question had been covered; they knew their schoolfellow was telling the truth. Why did they fail to speak up? A headmaster and a school policy that aroused such terror were lacking in the civilization that they were supposed to promote.[8]

[7] See R. L. Archer, *Secondary Education in the Nineteenth Century,* Cambridge University Press, 1921.

[8] T. W. Bamford, *Thomas Arnold,* London, The Cresset Press, 1960, 232 pp. On the flogging, see Chapter Six.

This is not the place to report on the inner history of the English Public Schools. Some of that history known now was hidden in the past. Boys left too much alone became brutal and when found out were brutally punished. The system was bad. It was bad in the classical boarding schools of old Germany. Fichte ran away from one but he went back and finished. Behind high walls, adolescent boys, away from the care of parents, friends, the public, and even of the staff, tend to become a pack rather than a community.

The surprising fact is not Arnold's rejection of the University of London but rather his interest in the first place. He hoped that it would become a modern Oxford. The new university was different not only from the old but also from all the other modern institutions. Flexner doubted that it should be called a university (a view no more surprising than Arnold's rejection). He wrote, "It is not really a university though it does possess central offices and an inclusive court and senate—it is a line drawn about an enormous number of different institutions of heterogeneous quality and purpose." That is granted; but the enclosed space is not empty. The collection of such a variety of schools, hospitals, and other institutions especially offended Flexner. He had a high opinion of some of the units of the University of London—the London School of Economics, for example—and a strong distaste for schools of household arts. He had little to say about the education of women, who were entering most universities including the German. Nearly all universities came under his fire but much of the evidence was concocted of prejudices.[9]

The University of London grew out of University College, which was opened in 1827 by the Duke of Sussex, a son of George III, and an educational liberal. The new college was intended to become a university as the name indicates, but in the next year (1828), King's College, an Anglican institution, was opened. Within a few years an accommodation was reached; and in 1836 a royal charter to embrace both institutions was granted. The charter provided a wide latitude to accommodate any other colleges of university quality. The original idea was that the University of London was to be a teaching institution, but as things turned out it became an examining body granting degrees for work done in both internal and external institutions, over some of which the University had only general regulatory authority. Even now it examines candidates who have prepared in schools not fully recognized as well as some who have prepared themselves by private study. The latter practice will be questioned by those who doubt that examinations alone can give a sufficient report of student achievement. Work done by private study, or with a tutor, or by correspondence will be unequally evaluated by many. Employers, not satisfied with the degree, will ask how the work for the degree was done.

[9] Abraham Flexner, *Universities, American, English, German*, Oxford University Press, 1930, 381 pp., see pp. 231ff.

The University of London has the widest reach of all British universities. The Rhodes scholarships bring many foreign students to Oxford and these often become distinguished at home in politics and higher education. They exemplify abroad the major idea for which Oxford stands at home. The University of London is more cosmopolitan. Its external degrees are conferred on a great many students from all parts of Great Britain and were formerly conferred on applicants from every part of the Empire. But the great city of London itself is a little world from which the great majority of its candidates come by car and train to work as resident students.

The next new university after London was Durham and it was to be like the old in its original aims; but in organization and studies it came to resemble the University of London. Because it was to be a pillar of the church, it is noteworthy that the original idea arose in the mind of Oliver Cromwell. It was founded one hundred and seventy-five years later, in 1832. It is one institution in two places, Durham and Newcastle. The former is the religious center, the latter an urban, scientific, and industrial member. The attempt to change the name to University of Durham and Newcastle has not succeeded.

The main group of the new universities developed in the industrial and commercial north; and if Newcastle were independent she would be a sister institution. The same universities were influenced by the mechanics institutes of Scotland. The first of the group, Owens College, later the University of Manchester, absorbed Frederick D. Maurice's Working Men's College, a kind of mechanics institute. A third factor in the history of the new universities was the adoption, in the early period, of the federal principle adopted directly from London and at one remove from Oxford and Cambridge. Beyond that it is based on the English convention that only a university can confer degrees and a university is composed of colleges, at least two as at Durham. This opinion is not held in America where any tiny denominational school can call itself a university and can confer degrees, both earned and honorary.

Neither London nor Durham is typical of the later institutions that are spread throughout England to educate her middle-class youth. The oldest of these newest foundations was the University of Manchester, which began as Owens College in 1851. Josiah Owens, an industrialist, provided the sum of nearly half a million dollars. He wisely decreed that the money was not to be spent for expensive buildings. The beginning, with only sixty-two students, was unpromising and after six years the number had declined by one half (1857). The school, declared a failure; suddenly began to grow. But it received only local support. Both Disraeli and Gladstone, judging that the public was unfavorable, refused public support. But as the school grew so did public interest. In the latter half of the century, England began to make up for its delay in supporting not only higher but also the lower levels of education. Public elementary education was introduced in 1870, public secondary education after the Bryce Commission of 1895, and the universities gained public support after World War I.

In America the state universities and land-grant colleges, now also universities, began to receive regular financial aid from their states after the Civil War (1861–1865). These are, however, public institutions. They are governed by public boards. In contrast with them, the English universities are private schools; in the United States such institutions as, for example, Yale, Princeton, Chicago, and Stanford Universities receive no public moneys.

With the growth of Manchester, men of wealth and business began to believe that their money could be usefully applied in higher education. And thus Josiah Mason, following Mr. Owen's example, founded Mason College in 1870. The purpose was "to promote thorough, systematic education and instruction adapted to the practical, mechanical, and artistic requirements of the manufacturers and industrial pursuits of the Midland District." Obviously, he had Owens and Manchester in mind; and neither founder was interested in the classics, or the liberal arts, or even English literature. Both colleges hoped to prepare students for the University of London degree, and this would have required concessions favoring the liberal arts. Mason College was opened in 1880 and in the following year the founder permitted the teaching of Greek and Latin and such a course of study as should qualify for a degree in Arts and Science.

The Yorkshire College of Science was opened in 1874 and became the Leeds University after it dropped the "of Science" from its title and added appropriate studies. University College at Bristol was opened in 1876, and University College, Liverpool, in 1881. Others were added at Reading in 1892 and Sheffield in 1897. As a step toward university status, several of the early colleges adopted an existing medical school.

Meanwhile they veered away from the original plan to seek degrees for their graduates from the University of London and secured the incorporation of Victoria University (1880), named for the Queen. Three university colleges, Owens, Liverpool, and Leeds, were admitted and preparation was made to include others; but difficulties soon arose. The meetings of the Victoria Council became frequent, the distances to travel seemed long, and the problems to be solved difficult. The Victoria University was dissolved in 1903–1904; Owens College was chartered as the University of Manchester and each of the others secured the same status under the name of its own city. So much for the founding dates of several of the early new universities; and to these institutions others were added. The University of Wales has four colleges in separate locations; there is a University of Belfast in Northern Ireland. There are twenty-five or more new universities and university colleges in the area reviewed here.

Two new trends in university education began to play important roles in the nineteenth century: First, service to the community, city, or region where the university is located; and, secondly, the higher education of women. One of the reasons, perhaps the chief reason, for the opening of Owens College, or of Mason, was industrial and commercial. Leeds was originally a school of science. The wealthy and practical founders, no doubt, thought science, agriculture, pottery or glassware, trade with India, and economics could be taught with such language, mathematics, and methods of study and investigation as the students brought from the secondary school. As the universities grew from a few hundred to several thousand students, those students came from ever greater distances and more varied social and economic backgrounds. Thus, there was even greater need for varied instruction and services. A noted writer of the past generation, Bruce Truscot, after warning against too much attention to particular local needs, goes on to urge the university to provide adult education, theatre, and general culture to the city, suburbs, and surrounding area of the once too practical institution. (See Chapter 7 in *Red Brick University*.)

Everybody is now in favor of the higher education of women just as everybody was against it in the time of George Washington and George III. Well! It was all right to educate rich and titled girls but the rest were to look after *Kinder, Küche, und Kirche*, the children, kitchen, and church. This view was strongest in Germany and continued into the present century. America and Britain began to open some universities to women at almost the same time.

Two new colleges in Ohio were coeducational from the founding, Oberlin College in 1833 and Antioch under Horace Mann in 1853. Oberlin graduated four young women in 1842. Many academies and the normal schools were coeducational but they were not of college grade. It was the state universities and land-grant colleges on the frontier in Iowa, Wisconsin, and Michigan that early admitted women to degree courses in large numbers and on the same terms as men. The famous women's colleges, Wellesley, Vassar, Smith, Bryn Mawr, and others were established in the latter half of the nineteenth century. After 1900 only a few old-line colleges such as Yale and Princeton refused all participation in the education of women. In both Britain and the United States, university men outnumber university women. One of several reasons for this imbalance is the fact that several branches of study and some vocations do not attract women as much as they do men: for example, physics, mathematics, law, medicine, and ballistics.

The first college for women in the old English universities was Girton at Cambridge (1869), to be followed by Newnham (1871). Oxford began with Lady Margaret (1878) and followed with Somerville (1879), St. Hugh's (1886), and St. Hilda's (1893). A few colleges for women in the University of London were incorporated a little earlier. Bedford was admitted in 1869 and others were Westfield, King's College of Household and

Social Sciences (which offended Flexner), and Royal Halloway. The Scottish universities became entirely coeducational about the same time as the American and so, give and take a few decades, did the new universities of England and Wales. We shall not neglect saying, what should not require it, that the higher education of women is one of the great social and moral advances of modern times.

The number of students in the universities is and has been growing and for this and other reasons, higher education is becoming more expensive. The costs are met by fees, tuition, gifts, endowment income, and state appropriations, plus various other sources. The government grants, or appropriations as they are called in America, have been and are increasing, but so are the costs.

There have been times and places when all schools were private and all the expenses of education had to be met by those who received its benefits. There were cases in early America when each child, each day, brought his teacher two pennies to pay for that day's instruction. In the Middle Ages the church paid for a good share of the cost of education. Later the state took up the burden and gradually the elementary schools, and the board secondary schools were entirely supported by the state. They became free schools. Will higher schools sometime become free schools in the United States and in Britain?

RED BRICK UNIVERSITY

An opinion cited previously and ascribed to Bruce Truscot was taken from his book *Red Brick University*. We shall indicate how this apt but assumed name came to be invented and introduced into educational books and discussions. The name is too apt to be real; it must be an invention. Bruce is a famous name in Scotland, and Truscot lacks only a letter to make it plain English. Bruce Truscot used this name for the presumed author of a book, already mentioned, on the new universities of England, which were partly inspired by the example of, and modeled on, the Scottish. He also called the old universities Oxbridge.

The author's real name seems to have been Allison Peers, Professor of Hispanic Studies at Liverpool. He had taken First-Class Honors in English at one of the old universities, apparently Cambridge. He used a pen name because, as he said, he meant to speak so frankly that he might be accused of prejudice. This seems to be a questionable policy; and it is further complicated by his apparent desire to have his identity discovered. The *Times Educational Supplement*, for January 9, 1953, p. 24, notices his death without identifying him with Bruce Truscot.

We consider the book because it is in itself an event in the history of education. We begin with his complaints and charges. He wrote,

The very heart and root of my criticisms is the deep conviction that in certain respects the modern universities are not pulling their weight and that the responsibility for this lies at more doors than anyone has yet realized. (1) The Treasury has starved Redbrick of money, making its grants so minute that it cannot do a tithe of the things of which it is capable. (2) The (Preparatory) schools have starved it of talent, sending all their brilliant pupils to Oxbridge and encouraging even the average ones to go there if they can. (3) Professors and lecturers, though admittedly underpaid, have been content to spend only a modicum of time on research and to regard themselves as fulfilling their duty by doing a bare eight or ten hours a week of teaching. (4) Laymen with little understanding of academic problems have done untold harm by their activities in university Councils. (5) Undergraduates have pursued a narrow course of study, thought too little of the world beyond Redbrick's unlovely quadrangles, and rejected all kinds of opportunities of widening their vision. And these are only a few items of the diagnosis.

A formidable indictment. Shall we begin on the professors who do only token research, and shall we advise the increase of their class-teaching load to twelve or fifteen hours a week? This will do something, not enough of course, to blunt the edge of Number One; and cautiously applied it might impress the Treasury. We should advise an assigned course of reading, including this and other books dealing intelligently with university needs and problems for council members and of lectures on the subject in the towns where they live. Incited, perhaps, by that "benevolent though astringent critic, Professor [!] Abraham Flexner," the author of Red Brick deals with the puerilities and absurdities of American universities in a way that leads one to think the author may have visited the United States and perhaps taught in a summer term; but this is speculation.[10]

THE ROBBINS REPORT

The report of the Robbins Committee on Higher Education in England was released in October, 1963. It was named after the Chairman, Lord Robbins, a noted economist and university professor. The government at once issued a statement supporting the report and the general principle on which it was founded. This principle was stated as "the basic assumption of the report that courses in higher education should be available for all who are qualified by ability and attainment to pursue them and who wish to do so." The quoted statement is certainly significant, because it will not permit any arbitrary cut-off age or school year to bar further schooling in preparation for admission to a university. Poor as well as rich, low- and highborn, rural or urban, girls and boys may enter upon higher studies. Yet there are

---

[10] Bruce Truscot's *Red Brick University* was first published in 1943; a sequel, *These Vital Days*, was issued in 1945. A Pelican paperback containing the original and the sequel was published in 1951.

qualifications: ability, attainment, and desire; and these will be subject to interpretation.

The Robbins Report is praised by not only the English but also the French, and others; but is the principle in question new? Has it not been practiced in the United States for many years? The youth who is, for any reason or none, rejected by any American college may enter another and after a year or two of good work may enter another more desirable college as a junior and graduate on time. We shall not press the financial considerations, and we admit our admiration of the Robbins ideal; but its basic idea is not new.

Higher education in Britain is carried out by three kinds of institutions: universities; teachers colleges, which have been or are being raised to colleges of education with a three-, instead of a two-year course; and technical colleges of various kinds. These are below the university level and efforts to improve them are in progress. Ten technical schools have been raised to the status of colleges of advanced technology which confer the Diploma of Technology as a first degree. The Robbins Committee attempted to weld these three kinds of higher institutions into a system: universities, colleges of education, and colleges of technology, standard and advanced.

The present general effort to develop a system of education for England began with the lower schools about the time of World War II. A committee was appointed with Richard Archer Butler as Chairman. He was educated at Marlborough and Cambridge and is a member of Parliament. After several years of meetings, investigations, and reports, their activities led to the adoption of the Education Act of 1944. The act provided for the appointment of a Minister of Education, the first in England, and for his powers and administration. Part Two of the act contains the statutory system, the laws that regulate the elementary and secondary schools, religious education in county (public) and voluntary schools, and other matters. A supplementary act was passed in 1945. This legislation and the implementation of the Robbins Report will be the legal framework of the country's educational system.

The raising of the leaving age, or compulsory attendance period, to fifteen years and the provision of free secondary education for all were major results of the act and they at once increased the number of children in the schools. To this a great further contribution was made by the rise in the birth rate. Free secondary education also led many children to stay in school beyond the legal leaving age. In 1938, only 4 per cent of the children aged seventeen years remained in school, but in 1962 this had increased to fifteen per cent. Prosperity raised this number still higher.

This and similar phenomena in other countries have provided a new term for educational use, the word *explosion*. The educational explosion in England has spread to all levels. The present number of university students has about doubled since 1945, and there will need to be an explosion in funds to provide for them. The Robbins Committee considered but rejected the American liberal arts college idea in its suggestions. They took note of the Russian use of part-time and correspondence work for students not in school. This would not please Bruce Truscot, but he would be appeased by the rest of the present paragraph. The committee approved the practice of joining research to teaching as professorial duties; and also the advice that students be given both class and individual (tutorial) instruction. The Report has been called basically English, that is, it is drawn up inductively and pragmatically; it is conservatively progressive in improving on the existing conditions.

THE FRENCH SPIRIT

Contemporary French scholars have been heard to complain that their schools retain too much of the Jesuit spirit and of the abstract deductive method of Descartes; and this in spite of the Revolution and the lesser revolutions both political and academic. "No one," said Albert Duruy, "has claimed that there were no schools or universities in France before the Revolution. People have only said that the teaching is in reverse, going backward, not forward." Long before, in 1763, La Chalotais, in his *Essay on National Education* said, "I should not complain of a good education being given to the high and the low alike. What I regret is that an equally bad one is given to all."

The finest statement of that time, the eighteenth century, or perhaps any time, was written by Condorcet. It introduces his *Report on Public Instruction*, as follows:

To offer to all individuals of the human race the means of providing for their needs, of assuring their welfare, of knowing and exercising their rights, and of understanding and fulfilling their obligations, to assure to each one the opportunity of perfecting his skill, of making himself capable of the social functions to which he has the right to be called, of developing to the fullest extent those talents with which Nature has endowed him; and thereby to establish among all citizens an actual equality, thus making real the political equality recognized by the law, this must be the first goal of national education.

In the year before Condorcet's *Report*, the Constitution of 1791 upheld the ideal of free, public education in the following provision: "There shall be created and organized a system of public instruction, common to all citizens, gratuitous, as regards the parts of education indispensable for all men." The last phrase requires interpretation and it probably meant reading, writing, and arithmetic. The rest of the sentence required the schools to be so placed that they would be accessible, apparently to everyone. Later constitutions had similar provisions, and laws were enacted but could not be carried out. Napoleon in the Imperial University demanded centralized control instead of the local administration that had been proposed.

The principles proposed in the Revolution became effective nearly a century later through the Ferry Laws of 1881 and 1883, under the Third Republic. These laws made primary education free and compulsory and the base on which secondary and higher education rests. Secondary schools became free in 1930. The period since World War II has seen important changes. Roman Catholic and other nonpublic schools are permitted and provide for a large proportion of the primary school children; and except for the teaching of religion they follow the same course of study as the public schools. The public schools are secular but teach morals. The school administration is highly centralized under a minister; and the local community has hardly any control over its local school.

The French system is difficult for Americans to understand, for, although it seems to be like ours, it is really much more intricate. To us it seems sensible to enlist the interest of parents in the schools their children attend; but this would assume that common folks who have recently finished the same course have good ideas about the way the school should be conducted. The parents and the school committee of a commune have little influence on what is taught or how, thanks to the centralizing ideas of a man who won many battles but lost the war, Napoleon.

The French national system, the same in all parts of the nation, also seems simple: elementary (primary), secondary, and higher schools, apparently a straight highway from infancy to maturity. Again, this simplicity is only apparent. Not all young children go to an elementary school. The secondary system has its own junior classes in which children from the age of six are prepared for the language studies of the secondary school by teachers, called professors, especially prepared for this work. Their pupils go to the secondary (grammar) schools on the way to the universities. To a great degree the grammar schools are still classical, but all have admitted some sciences, history, geography, and other modern studies. But many in France still believe that Latin and Greek provide the best preparation not only for literary and scholarly work but also for scientists and executives. The French are, however, divided in their views on the most necessary studies.

The wartime effort to extend the compulsory education age to sixteen became effective in 1967; and elementary education is often continued in complementary courses for several years, and in senior elementary schools. Teachers for the elementary schools are prepared in schools especially designed for them at St. Cloud for men and Fontenay-aux-Roses for women. The inspectors of elementary schools are also a specially prepared class. Those who teach or direct schools for children and those for youth in the secondary system are people of different breeds, as if never "the twain should meet." [11]

FRENCH UNIVERSITIES

To guard the entrances to the universities, institutes, and advanced schools against invasion by the less able and industrious, France has prepared her usual weapons: examinations, chiefly the *baccalauréat*, which has been called "the keystone of the French educational system." The *baccalauréat* is "a diploma awarded after a successful period of seven years of secondary studies and is required for admission to almost all advanced study as well as to many civil service appointments. Its importance is also recognized in the business world." (See Hyslop, p. 7, in the preceding footnote.) In English the title would be Bachelor of Secondary Education and for completion of a modern course would contain the word *scientific*, indicating that no Greek, but possibly Latin, and certainly one modern foreign language had been studied. Until recently, two examinations, one written, the other oral, were given. The oral and individual examination demanded so much time that with the great increase in the number of candidates it is now given only to those who pass the written test.

Is it necessary to guard the gate to advanced study so zealously? An American is apt to reflect that Franklin, once the toast of Paris, his contemporary, Benjamin Thompson, Count Rumford, and Edison could not have passed this examination. More seriously, human excellence has many phases, a range far beyond any that academic examinations can measure and that, on the whole, they measure badly—that is, very inaccurately. It seems, again to an American, that the boy or girl who has survived seven years of secondary school work should be allowed to try the very similar introductory work of the university. Present school conditions must be considered; the population explosion, the lack of employment opportunity for young people, and school overcrowding do indeed pose new questions. But a nation can be overanxious to protect a somewhat mythical academic standard.

The university admissions policy presents a financial as well as a scholarship question. Officials may be expected to consider the number that can be accepted and instructed with the funds available. The population explosion has a two-fold effect on American universities as well. It brings growing

---

[11] F. de la Fontainerie, *French Liberalism and Education in the Eighteenth Century*, New York, McGraw-Hill Book Co., Inc., 1932, 385 pp.; Jean Capelle, *Tomorrow's Education, The French Experience*, Pergamon Press, 1967, 229 pp., translator, W. D. Walls; W. R. Fraser, *Education and Society in Modern France*, London, Routledge and Kegan Paul, 1963, 140 pp.; Beatrice F. Hyslop, *France, A Study of French Education* . . . , 1964, 119 pp., a source booklet of the American Association of University Registrars and Administrative Officers.

numbers of freshmen to all institutions; and the more famous universities receive many upper-class students from the less distinguished smaller colleges and universities. This movement, already noted here, deserves special attention because it is placing a financial burden on the best universities, one that they may not be able to carry indefinitely.

As evidence of this we offer a few paragraphs from a recent report by President Elvis J. Stahr of Indiana University at Bloomington. He had been in office just five years (1962–1967) when he wrote the following:

When higher education managed to accommodate practically all of the great numbers of qualified students seeking admission from 1960 on, it honored the American tradition of keeping educational opportunity open. But the leaders have warned continually of the urgent problems that the public must face if this opportunity is to be sustained. An undeniable financial crisis in higher education, both private and public, is developing of which we have visible proof in recent announcements of the termination of university divisions [i.e., branches] in various parts of the country and even of the shutdown or sale of colleges, and less visible but exceedingly disturbing proof of a general decline of real dollar resources on a per-student basis.

Later in the report he added that, "Altogether we are teaching three students for every two that we taught in the fall semester of 1962–63 (50.9 per cent increase in total enrollment, all campuses). One of the prominent features of this growth has been the increase in the size of the upper classes on the Bloomington Campus."

Even though freshmen ranks are larger by 27.5 per cent and sophomore by 32.7 per cent, there are 62 per cent more juniors and the senior class has more than doubled (101.6 per cent). This is what the diagram shows

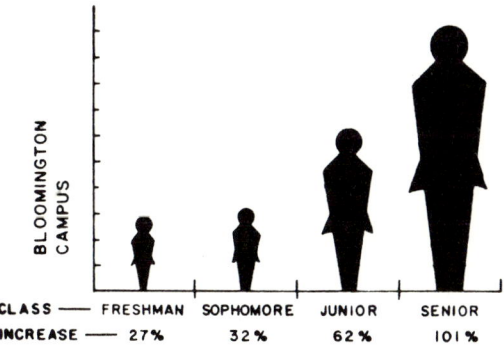

This drawing shows graphically the difference in growth of the classes on the I. U. Bloomington campus between 1962 and 1967.

graphically. And where do these additional students come from? From other, less distinguished colleges. Why do they come? Because they much prefer a degree from Indiana University than one from Whithersee.

There is, however, another source. Many universities have established branches or "feeder" institutions in parts of the state or region where there is no university near. This presents a heaven-sent opportunity to poor youth. After completing a year, or two, or three of a four-year course they may manage to live near the main campus for one or two years and to finish the course. Some of the university branches develop into independent universities. A similar process is taking place in France and to that country we now return.

The higher education provided by the State of France is offered in several kinds of schools including the universities, *Grandes Études,* or "great schools," which began in the Revolution; technical institutes; and other academic and professional institutions. The universities, which will receive most attention here, have four faculties: Letters, Sciences, Medicine, and Law. These divisions, in part with different names and purposes came down from the Middle Ages; but as is reported in Chapter 5, the first two faculties were called Arts and Theology. The Arts were the seven liberal arts, but by the thirteenth century the emphasis was put upon logic, or Aristotle's deductive method of proof. When Canon Law developed, it was included under the Faculty of Law or made into a fifth faculty. In later times a Faculty of Protestant Theology was added and today the University of Strasbourg has two faculties of Theology—one of Catholic, and one of Protestant, complexion.

Similar combinations exist elsewhere. Economics is taught by the Faculty of Law, and degrees in dentistry are given by the Faculty of Medicine, which also trains midwives. The University of Paris has sixteen institutes for specialized medical study and similar provisions are made for other special branches.

The long established universities of France are sixteen in number, as follows:

Aix-Marseilles	Lyon
Besançon	Montpellier
Bordeaux	Nancy
Caen	Paris
Clermont-Ferrand	Poitiers
Dijon	Rennes
Grenoble	Strasbourg
Lille	Toulouse

Three—Nantes, Orléans, and Reims—have in recent times been erected to the level of universities; and there are also university centers that offer one or more years of university work, and have in some cases, a special connection with a complete university. These somewhat resemble American branches but they are called *Collèges universitaires*, or incomplete universities. They may and probably will become universities. There are at present fourteen, as follows: Amiens, Angers, Brest, Chambery, Le Mans, Limoges, Metz, Mulhouse, Orléans, Pau, Perpignan, Rouen, St. Etienne, and Tours. France is meeting present needs and preparing for the rising tide.

The school system of France was instituted by Napoleon and has remained practically unchanged for over a century and a half. As shown in Chapter 14, it is a highly centralized system with power exercised by the Ministry in Paris. Students, teachers, and people have had little to say, but this system is now being challenged.

Student disorders and strikes have recently marred academic life not only in France, but also in the United States, West Germany, Italy, Uruguay, Mexico, and elsewhere. Some of these are certainly led by Communists. In France, the trouble began at the University of Nantes in May, 1968, and spread to the Sorbonne and to other institutions. The students were supported by working men who had reason to demand higher wages. For a time in early summer, civil war was feared. President Charles De Gaulle, however, promised reforms, called a general election, and won an overwhelming victory. De Gaulle and his cabinet approved a measure that was adopted by the National Assembly in October, 1968, which gives the students some choice of studies, the teachers a voice in conduct of schools, and the people a measure of control over schools that should be their own. This is the most sweeping revision of higher education in France since Napoleon established the imperial university system in 1808.

The preceding example from Indiana University may illustrate conditions in numerous large American universities as far as the overcrowding of the senior year is concerned; but the rapidly increasing university enrollments are a much more general fact. Without question American student bodies are growing rapidly; but so are the French. It has been estimated that by 1970, half a million students will be enrolled in the universities of France; and a note in *Education Normale* (March 3, 1966) predicted a gain of fifty per cent in two years. The Robbins Report estimated that the universities of the United Kingdom would attract three hundred and fifty thousand students by 1980, and nobody has proposed a much higher figure. The same expert group believed that by 1980 the technical institutions would teach one hundred and fifty thousand, a realistic figure in comparison with three hundred and fifty thousand in the universities. In Germany and elsewhere the growth of technical and engineering candidates may be less rapid. In the Soviet Union enrollments are set by the government at a predetermined figure and the hopes and desires receive only limited consideration. According to reports there may be cases in which "influence" is successfully applied. In democratic countries, admission to universities is gained by certificate or examination.

In the United States there has been a rapid increase in the number of instructors, the lowest and least experienced grade of teachers in the staff of a university. The increase has been great in actual numbers but also in comparison with the numbers of the more permanent staff members. Many instructors will not be permanent members of the faculty and will have had no professional training. In the total absence of supervision there must be cases of miserable teaching such as merely reading notes in class or even reading the lesson from the textbook; this has actually happened, but such cases are probably not numerous. There should not be any. University teachers, like high school teachers, should be given some first aid by the department head and other able teachers and also be aided in preparing lessons and teaching. When there are two or more inexperienced instructors a class might be formed to study methods of teaching.

Education is an already vast activity or industry, and a rapidly increasing one as well. It engages the interest and effort of the younger third of any cultivated nation and hundreds of thousands of workers, teachers, librarians, caretakers, officials, and medical, dental, and other service persons. When the United States was young its educational forces were a company, now they are an army.

The two chief reason for the change are (1) universal school attendance, and (2) the extraordinary expansion of knowledge and technology. These are two different things and together they have made a vast difference. Knowledge is growing and not merely by accretion—that is, by the addition of more information, new facts of the same kind—but also by a rapid diversification through the invention of new branches and previously unknown sciences. This had unexpected results outside the schools, which in turn reacted on the schools. The first result was the abolition of the old pick-and-shovel industries and of cutting grain with a cradle. A whole array of new technologies, as they developed, had to be taught in schools.

Compulsory schooling became necessary for reasons of safety, health, politics, and industry; and compulsory attendance could be enjoined only by the government. Every new school cost money to build it and then more to maintain it. Only the government, by taxation, could provide the money. How could the government secure the money? A simple answer is that by educating a man you make him twice or twenty times as productive as he was in his ignorant state. Education is the goose; nourish, do not kill her. The golden egg will pay not only for schools but for police, jail, courthouse, and town hall.

To this point governments remain in substantial agreement. In Russia the party recommends and the government honors the party's proposal. In France, the smallest unit, the commune, has little power; but above the smallest unit, power is distributed. However, a great deal is left to the nation. The English speaking nations leave a share of power in the hands of the local units but assign more to the counties and county boroughs. The Minister has several powers and especially that of assigning and disbursing national funds. England treats her large number of private schools with great tenderness; many of the rulers of England have been and are educated in them.

In the United States educational power resides in the townships, counties, and cities. There is little left for the national government to do except to distribute national aid according to the law. This is, however, an important power with special application to desegregation. The states are jealous of the Federal Government's attempts to designate the use to which its moneys are to be applied. They would prefer to receive undesignated appropriations. A great problem of education today is the problem of control: Who shall control, how, and to what end?

IN CONCLUSION

Customs, the arts, and the primary elements of civilization develop earlier than schools. The invention of writing, the appearance of religious books, and the need for business records make formal education necessary. This may be carried on by private instruction, but as the numbers of learners and teachers increase, the school becomes an economical instrument for the maintenance and improvement of education.

Schools teach counting, writing, and other so-called school skills, but they do more. They teach both indirectly, and explicitly. Children and youths in school learn from each other. A school is, or should be, a society where children live and work in cooperation with each other and with the society outside the school. A New Jersey court once held that even the best and best-educated parents are not qualified to educate their children at home. More recently a District of Columbia judge ruled that "Racially and socially homogeneous schools damage the minds and spirit of all children who attend them." Home education and segregated education, the Courts have said, are equally inadequate because all children need to learn the social and democratic qualities and abilities which can be gained only in association with other children with diverse backgrounds. This is a somewhat sophsticated view of the matter. Early schools were for centuries largely knowledge and skill factories. Schools have developed far beyond those early conceptions. They have a history.

History is the record of human experience. Experience that is recorded can be examined at leisure at a later time and compared with new experience. Thus experience is amplified and criticized by later experience. Your experience can be compared with mine, that of America with that of England, and this process may bring wisdom.

The history of education performs a similar function in its proper field. Because formal education is usually carried on in schools, the history of schools is a part of the history of education. Schools were for many centuries carried on by private arrangements or by the Church. Today most schools are maintained by the state, and in the United States most schools are controlled by elected boards. The modern state finds it desirable to have all young people educated and aims to make schools accessible to all and adapted to the capacities of all. School buildings, the organization and administration of school systems, and many other topics become matters of school legislation. The history of education reports on the development of school systems, and comparative education studies these systems in relation to each other. School curricula, management, and teaching methods have all gone through progressive changes and are important topics in the history of education. Method depends upon many conditions, but equipment is an important factor. In 1947 German children were taught to read from lessons written on the blackboard because there were no acceptable books. Long ago there was no blackboard either. Today electronics have been put in the service of the teacher and new equipment, such as television and the computer, is affecting teaching and may revolutionize some phases of it. The history of school equipment is a significant part of the history of education.

Perhaps the most significant event in the whole history of education is the evolution of public school systems including national education. After two thousand years there is a trend toward Plato's proposals in the *Republic*. Is history repeating itself? Many efforts have been made by individuals, societies, business, and especially the Church to establish schools to achieve their own purposes. Today the all-powerful state is more and more directing the school to accomplish national aims. Although the Church and private efforts are still strong, especially in the United States, the state is stronger and is gradually adapting education to its own ends.

In the modern state the school is a national instrument, and public education varies with the nature of the state and its government, as we have stressed in Part IV. Governments have used the schools to select and train able and obedient public servants while providing only limited opportunities for the unselected masses. Governments have seized all means of popular knowledge and intercommunication and have used the schools to indoctrinate whole peoples with a philosophy of aggression and to inflame them with the desire for military conquest. We must not forget the lessons from the past and present dictatorships. The first lesson is that there is something radically wrong with a system that prevents the people from learning the economic and political conditions at home and abroad.

The history of education teaches that there is often a vast difference between theory and practice. It has been said that it is easier to teach twenty what should be done than to be one of the twenty to practice the teaching.

The progressive education movement in the United States may serve as an example. Even to preserve the gains of the past may be difficult. And while inspiration may be gained from the great figures of history, from Pestalozzi or Horace Mann, they are not to be imitated. Their problems are not ours. We must use our historical laboratory to seek and test new solutions of today's problems. However, some old solutions have permanent values: to seek and to teach the truth, to respect the individual person, and to love our neighbor. These deserve to be specially mentioned because they are so often flouted today.

Index

A

Aachen, Council of, 76
Abbotsholme, 365, 417, 423, 513
Abelard, Peter, 82, 104, 106
  Sic et Non, 104, 106
Absolutism, 66
Academies, 170–172, 182, 224
  American, 424, 425, 445–448
  English, 165, 170–171
  free, 519–520
  French, 89, 165
  German "knightly," 89, 165, 349
Accademia dei Lincei, 172
Accademia del Cimento, 172
Accrediting plans, high school, 527–530
Adelhard of Bath, 98
Adler, Felix, 503, 510–511
Adult education, 563–564
  agricultural extension, 564
  correspondence schools, 563
  university extension, 563–564
Aesop, 74
Agassiz, Louis, 272, 481, 495, 498
Agricola, Cneius Julius, 84
Agricola, Rudolphus, 135, 140
Akkad, 7, 10–11
Alberti, Leon Battista, 118, 128–129
  Care of the Family, The, 118
Alcuin, 75–76, 402
Aldhelm, Saint, 85, 402
Aldus, Manutius, 125
  Aldine classics, 125
Alexander the Great, 37, 63
Alfred the Great, 84, 85–86
  translations by, 85–86
Al-Khowarizmi, 98

Alphabet
  Greek, 12, 17–18, 44
  Phoenician, 17
American Adult Education Association, 563
American Education Fellowship, 515
Andreae, John, 169
Andrews, Fannie, 309
Anthropology, social, 115
Antiphon, 28
Apprenticeship, 92–93, 371, 410
  in American colonies, 433, 437–439
Arabic language, 98
Archimedes, 24, 37, 174
Aristophanes, 31
Aristotle, 18, 20–21, 34–37, 70, 74, 99, 103, 114, 122, 129, 133, 144–146
  Ethics, 34–35, 99, 121
  importance in the medieval Renaissance, 99
  Lyceum of, 29
  Politics, 5, 21, 34–36, 99, 121, 227
  recovery of his works, 99
  Topics, Prior and Posterior Analytics, 99
  writings on logic, 99
Arithmetic, *see also* Mathematics
  business, 95
  Hindu-Arabic notation, 24, 92, 96, 98
  study of, 5, 8, 24, 32, 45, 47–48, 70, 96, 127, 132, 181, 262–263, 270, 326, 383, 443
  textbooks, 146
Arnold, Matthew, 413
Arnold, Thomas, 590–591
Ars dictaminis, 74, 95

Art appreciation, 523
Ascham, Roger, 167
Astronomy, study of, 32, 37, 70, 132, 181, 388, 446
Athens, 21–38; *see also* Greece
  gymnastics, 24–25
  higher education, 27–37
  pedagogues, 23
  Periclean Age, 27–29, 38
  schools, 22–37
  Sophists, *see* Sophists
Audio-visual aids to instruction, 564–566
Augustine, Saint, 67–68, 69, 98, 121, 124, 140, 160
  City of God, 68, 142
Australia, English influence in, 423

B

Babylonia, *see* Sumer
Bache, Alexander, 349, 374
Bacon, Francis, 142, 143, 146, 165, 172–173, 176
  Advancement of Learning, 143–144
Bagley, William, 553
Bailey, Liberty, *Nature-Study Idea*, 500
Barnard, Henry, 306, 307, 456, 478, 481, 495, 498, 518
Barop, J. Arnold, 234
Basedow, Johann, 89, 225–231, 236, 350
  Elementarwerk, 226–227
  Memorial, 225–226
  Philanthropinum, 227–231
    criticism of, 229–230
Battersea Training College, 270, 409
Bede, the Venerable, 85, 402
Beecher, Catherine, 479
Bell, Andrew, 270, 405–408, 412
Benedict, Saint, 72, 73
Benedictine rule, 72–73
Bergson, Henri, 312

Bessarion, 122, 125
Bible, the, 13, 146–148; *see also* New Testament
  forbidden by churchmen, 146–147
  translations of, 67, 146–147
  Vulgate, 67, 69, 118, 141
Biology, study of, 388, 391
Birkbeck, George, 424
Bismarck, 356–358
Blair Bill, 472
Boccaccio, Giovanni, 113, 117
Bodet, J. Torres, 312, 313
Boelte, Maria, 502–503
Boethius, 98, 99
  Consolation of Philosophy, 70
Bonnet, Henri, 312
Bookkeeping, 95, 96, 443, 446, 518
  development of, 91
Boston Latin School, 442, 518, 521
Boyle, Robert, 175
Bray, Thomas, 404
Brethren of the Common Life, 135, 139, 140
Brothers of the Christian Schools, 160–161, 325
Brougham, Henry, 349, 408, 410
Brown University, 444, 445
Bruni, Leonardo, 122, 128
Bugenhagen, John, 153
Burgdorf school, 256–258, 263–264
Burton, Warren, 495
Business schools, 95
Butler, Nicholas Murray, 530–531
Butler, Richard, 418, 422

C

Caesar, 63
Calculus, 174, 446
Calvin, John, 154
Cambridge University, 106, 107, 424, 584, 586–588
Campanella, Thomas, 169
Campe, J. H., 229–230, 232, 350
Canada, English influence in, 423

Capella, Martianus, 98
  Marriage of Philology and Mercury, 70
Carnegie Foundation for the Advancement of Teaching, 529
Cassiodorus, Flavius, 71, 98
Castiglione, Baldassare, 89, 133
Catechitical schools, 69
Catechumenal schools, 69
Cathedral schools, 65, 76, 90
  Notre Dame of Paris, 105
Cato, Distichs of, 71, 74, 141
Cato, Marcus, 44, 46
Cellini, Benvenuto, 118
Charlemagne, 75–77
  educational advisors, 75–76
  educational program of, 76
  palace school of, 76
Chemistry, 175, 388
China, People's Republic of, 383
Chivalric education, 88–89
Christian Brothers, schools, 160–161, 325
Christianity and philosophy, 66
Chrysoloras, Manuel, 121, 122, 126, 130
Church, the
  philosophy and, 65–68
Cicero, 41, 49–52, 116, 119, 120, 122, 129, 133
  Brutus, 49, 55, 133
  De Oratore, 49, 50, 55, 121, 133
Classics, 121–125, 140, 141, 336, 443
Clement, 69
Cloistral school, 73
Colburn, Warren, *Intellectual Arithmetic*, 264
Colet, John, 139, 402–403
College Entrance Board, 528, 529
Collège de France, 135
Collège de Guyenne, 135
Collège de Louis le Grand, 323
Colleges, *see also* Universities
  agricultural, 473, 475, 476
  land-grant, 473–478
  technical, 473, 475

Columba, Saint, 65
Columbia University, 424, 444, 445, 474, 482
Comenius, John, 149, 165, 167, 176, 182, 183–189, 263
  on education for peace, 308–309
  Great Diadectic, The, 184, 186, 187–188, 189, 250
  influence of, 189–190
  Janua Linguarum Reserata, 184, 185
  Orbis Sensualium Pictus, 185–186
  School for Little Children, 189
  textbooks, 184–185, 190
  on universal language, 309
Committee of Ten, 422, 528
Common School Journal, 460–462
Compagnons de l'Université Nouvelle, 338
Comparative education, 306–308, 417
  international education and, 308
Comparative Education Society, 308
Compulsory school attendance, 152–153, 189, 348, 358, 390, 413, 419–420, 483–485, 560, 562
Conant, James, 555
Condorcet, Marie, 320–322, 598
  Report on Public Instruction, 321–322
Constance, Council of, 147, 148
Cooperative Study of Secondary School Standards, 539
Copernicus, Nicholas, on scientific method, 173–174
Cornell University, 500
Correspondence schools, 563
Country Day Schools, 514
Cousin, Victor, 326, 349
Crates of Mallos, 44
Criticism lesson, 409
Crusades, 86–88, 150
Culture-epochs theory, 258
Cuneiform writing, 7, 10, 12, 17
Curriculum, 36, 48, 64, 74, 95–96, 115, 123, 127, 132–134, 143,

Cuneiform writing (*continued*)
    153–154, 166–167, 181–183, 213–215, 228, 277–278
  in England, 415–417, 420
  in France, 322, 326–327, 328, 332, 336–337, 341–343
  in Germany, 359–361, 371, 373, 375
  Jesuit, 157–158
  in monastic schools, 73–75
  Renaissance, 132–133
  in Roman schools, 47
  in the United States, 440, 441, 446, 493, 508, 537
    high schools, 521–527, 534
  in the USSR, 384–392, 394, 573–574

D

Daniel of Morley, 99
Dante Alighieri, 113, 116, 117
Dartmouth College, 444, 445, 474
Daudet, Alphonse, *La Dernière Classe*, 330
Decimal fractions, 174
Demosthenes, 28
Descartes, René, 158–159, 165, 172–176, 335
  on scientific method, 173
Dewey, John, 264, 284–285, 306, 386, 511–512, 525, 551–553
Dialectic, 70, 74
Dickens, Charles, 287
Dictamen, 74, 95
Diderot, Denis, 320, 383
  Encyclopédie, 205–206
Diesterweg, F., 352–353, 355
Distichs of Cato, 71, 74, 141
District school system, 456–459
Donatus, Aelius, 98
  Ars major, 70
  Ars minor, 70
Drawing, in American schools, 523
Dubois, Pierre, *Recovery*, 100–101
Dury, John, 169

E

Edgeworth, Maria, *Practical Education*, 270
Education
  comparative, 306–308
  effects of war on children and, 301–304
  influence of revival on, 132–134
  international, 305
    comparative education and, 308
  national, *see* National education
  polytechnical, 386, 576–578
Education, Office of, 311, 478
Educational theories, 126–129
  Addresses to the German Nation (Fichte), 274
  Advancement of Learning (Bacon), 143–144
  of Basedow, 225–231
  Commendation of the Clerk, 102
  Comparative Education (Kandel), 308, 417
  Conduct of Schools (La Salle), 160
  Contemporary Education, A Comparative Study of National Systems (Cramer and Browne), 308
  De Disciplinis (Vives), 142
  of Dewey, *see* Dewey, John
  Education of Man, The (Froebel), 284, 503
  Elementarwerk (Basedow), 226–227
  Emile, see Rousseau
  Ethics (Aristotle), 34–35
  Great Diadectic, The (Comenium), 184, 186, 187–188, 189
  Hadow reports, 414
  of Herbart, 275–280
  How Gertrude Teaches Her Children (Pestalozzi), 256–260
  Institutes of Oratory (Quintilian), 51–54
  of Kant, 235–237
  Leonard and Gertrude (Pestalozzi), 251–252

Lessons on Objects (Mayo), 409
of Luther, 152–153
national education, *see* National education
nature study, *see* Nature study
Nature-Study Idea (Bailey), 500
New Héloise (Rousseau), 207–208
Of Education (Milton), 170
On Character and Liberal Studies (Vergerius), 126–128
On the Education of Girls (Fénelon), 160
On the Recovery of the Holy Land (Dubois), 100–102
Politics (Aristotle), 36
Practical Education (Edgeworth), 270
progressive education, 510–517
Proposals for the Education of Youth in Pennsylvania (Franklin), 224, 448
Quincy methods, 504–507
Ratio Studiorum (Jesuit Society), 156–157
Republic (Plato), 32–34
of Rousseau, 205–220; *see also* Rousseau, Jean
of Salzmann, 233
Some Thoughts Concerning Education (Locke), 177, 178–181, 210, 224, 228, 424
Treatise on the Choice and Method of Studies (Fleury), 178
Treatise on the Education of Girls (Fénelon), 191
Utopian, 168–170
of Vives, 167, 168
Eggleston, Edward, *Hoosier Schoolmaster, The*, 455, 458
Egypt, early, 5–6
Einstein, Albert, 312
Electricity, 175
Elementary and Secondary Education Act, 551
Elyot, Sir Thomas, 89, 258
Engineering graduates
U.S. *vs.* USSR, 396–397

England
academies, 165, 170–171
Butler Education Act, 413, 414, 417, 418–419
provision of, 418
charity schools, 404–405
court case of Bates and Cox, 403
Cowper-Temple clause, 413
early schools of, 401–405
Fisher Act, 413, 414, 419
Forster Act, 412
guild schools, 93
Hadow reports, 414
infant schools, 408
influence of, in foreign countries, 423–425
Lollardry in, 148, 402
Madras system, 405–407
monitorial systems, 405–407, 410
national education in, 299, 409–426
Newcastle Commission, 411–412
Norwood Committee, 420
Pestalozzian movement in, 269–270, 409
Public School Act, 587
public schools, 416, 587–588
pupil self-government schools, 234
Quarterly Journal of Education, 409
Reformation in, 155, 403
reformed grammar schools, 134
Robbins report, 596–598
secondary schools, 413, 415–416
Statute of Artificers, 402
teachers, *see* Teachers; Teachers, training of
tripartite system, 420–421
universities, 106, 107, 424, 584–586
modern, 589–595
vernacular schools, 95
English language, study of, 181, 182–183, 360, 390
Erasmus, 118, 139–143, 147
Adages, 141
Colloquies, 141
Greek text of the New Testament, 141, 144, 146
textbooks of, 141
Ethical Culture Society, 503, 511

Ethics, 30, 31, 181, 447
Eton College, 402, 587
Etruscans, 42, 44
Euclid, 24, 181
  system of geometry, 37
Evans, Luther, 312
Everett, Edward, 460
Exchanges, international
  students and teachers, 310–311
Extracurricular activities, 534–535

F

Federigo, Duke of Urbino, 124
Fellenberg, Emanuel von, 234, 248, 409
Fénelon, François, 160, 190–192
  Treatise on the Education of Girls, 191
Ferrara, 122, 130
  Council of, 122
  court school of, 122, 130
Ferry, Jules, 330–331, 336, 599
Feudalism, 82–83, 88
  effect on learning and the arts, 82
Fibonacci, Leonardo, 98
Fichte, Johann, 273–275
  Addresses to the German Nation, 274
Filefo, 119, 122–123
Fischer, Karl, 364
Fisher Act, 413, 414, 419
Fleury, Abbé Claude, 178, 179, 191, 192, 335
  Treatise on the Choice and Method of Studies, 178
Ford Foundation, 311, 565
Forster Act, 412
France
  academies, 89, 165
  collèges and lycées, 134
  growth of literacy, 342
  higher primary schools, 326–327, 328
  humanism in, 135
  Langevin plan, 338–340
  lycées, 134, 323
  national education in, 299, 319–345, 382
  nationalism and education, 341–344, 598–599
  normal schools, see Teachers, training of
  Primary School Law of 1833, 325–326
  primary schools, 325–327, 328, 330–331, 339, 342
    curriculum of, 332
  schools instituted by Napoleon, 323–324
  secondary schools, 324, 327, 328, 330, 338, 339–340
    curriculum of, 337
    reforms, 335–338
  teachers, see Teachers; Teachers, training of
  teaching reforms, 340
  technical education, 340–341
  universities, 323, 600–603
    student disorders and strikes, 603
  University of, 324, 329
    creation, 324
    description of, 333–334
  vocational education, 338
  vocational guidance, 340
Francis of Assisi, 116
Francke, August, 171, 404
Frankenberg, Caroline, 502
Franklin, Benjamin, 172, 424, 448
  Proposals for the Education of Youth in Pennsylvania, 224, 448
Frederick the Great, 348, 349
French Academy of Sciences, 172
French language, study of, 160, 181, 326, 360, 390, 443, 446
Friends, Society of, 435
Friendship University, 581
Froben, Johannes, 125, 151
Froebel, Friedrich, 189, 234, 263, 269, 280–289, 306, 353, 355, 375, 502, 512
  creation of the kindergarten, 285–286

Education of Man, The, 284, 503
Fulbright Scholars, 311
Fulda, monastery, 65
Fund for the Advancement of Education, 565–566
Füssli, John, 241, 250

G

Galileo, 174, 175
   Two New Sciences, 175
Gallaudet, Thomas, 479
Gaza, Theodore, 122, 140
Geography, study of, 37, 143, 167, 181, 214–215, 261, 262, 388
Geometry
   analytic, 174
   study of, 32, 37, 70, 127, 181, 213–214, 391, 446, 518
   textbooks, 146
George-Deen Vocational Act, 476
Gerard of Cremona, 99
German language, studies of, 183, 390, 443, 446
Germany, 274–287, 348–378, 582–583
   Aufbauschule, 363, 365
   Burschenschaft, 353
   city schools, 94–96
   Deutsche Oberschule, 363, 368
   development of socialism, 357
   education under the Weimar Republic, 361–368
   elementary schools, 352–353
   Grundschule, 362, 365, 370, 387
   guild schools, 93–94
   gymnasiums, 134, 190, 349, 351, 360, 361, 363, 422
   at Strassburg, 135
   Hamburg, school dispute in, 94–95
   influence on American education, 374–378
   kindergartens, 285–286, 355
   "knightly academies," 89, 165, 349
   Kulturkampf, 356
   Lutheran movement, 150–154
   middle schools, 360
   national education in, 299, 348–378, 382
   Oberrealschule, 360, 363; 122
   Oberschulkollegium, 349, 351
   Pestalozzian movement in, 263–264, 269
   Potsdam Agreement, 370
   Realgymnasium, 360, 361, 363
   Realschule, 171–172, 224, 360
   schools
      destruction of, during World War II, 369–370
      reopening of, after World War II, 370
   secondary schools, 360, 361, 363
   teachers, *see* Teachers; Teachers, training of
   universities, 149, 359, 362, 582–583
      American students in, 376
      destruction of, World War II, 369
      lehrfreiheit of, 354
   vernacular schools, 95
   vocational education, 358, 371, 373
   youth movement, 364–365
Gilgamesh, Epic of, 11
Girls, education of, 20, 25, 128, 134, 151, 160, 187, 190–192, 331–360, 446
Gorgias, 28
Göttingen University, 377
Gouge, Thomas, 404
Grading of schools, arguments against, 507–509
Graduate schools, 377
Grammar
   developed by Sophists, 27
   study of, 70, 181
Greco-Roman education, 47–48
Greece, early, 5
   alphabet, 12, 17–18, 44
   geography and astronomy, 37
   geometry, 37
   influence on Romans, 42–44, 47–49
   oratory, 30–31
Greek authors, recovered, 121–123
   manuscript copies of, 123

Greek language, 18, 65–66, 121–122, 132, 153, 154, 157, 181, 182, 277–278, 518
Gregory, Pope, 65, 98
Guarino, Battista, 122, 129, 140
  Upon the Method of Teaching and of Reading the Classical Authors, 129
Guarino da Verona, 121, 122, 130, 131
Guggenheim Fellowships, 311
Guidance
  educational, 338, 340, 372
  vocational, 340, 373
Guilds, 92–94
  Latin schools of, 93
  vocational education, 92–93
Gymnasiums, 375; see also Germany: gymnasiums
Gymnastics, 24–25, 32

H

Hadow reports, 414
Hall, Samuel, 479–480, 493
Hammurabi, Code of, 11
Harnisch, William, 352, 353
Harris, William, 281, 463, 498
Harrow School, 402
Hartlib, Samuel, 169
Harvard University, 377, 424, 444–445
  early curriculum, 44
Hawley, Gideon, 460
Hazelwood School in England, 234, 423
Hebrew language, study of, 149, 153, 157, 182
Hebrew Scriptures, Greek version of, 66
Hebrews
  education, 13–14
  memoriter instruction, 14
Hegius, Alexander, 135
Heidelberg University, 149
Hellenic age, 26–37

Hellenistic age, 37
Helvétius, Claude, 210
Herbart, Johann, 275–280, 365, 375
  on Pestalozzi, 278–279
  psychology of, 279–280
Hieroglyphics, 6
High schools, American, 463
  accrediting of, 527–530
  curriculum expansion, 521–527, 534
  evolution from graded school, 517–521
  standardizing, 527–530
    associations for, 529
    Committee of Ten, 422, 528
Hill, Thomas Wright, 234
Hindu-Arabic notation, 24, 92, 96, 98
Hippias, 27
History, study of, 115, 143, 167, 181, 388, 391, 447, 518
Hoar Bill, 471–472
Hobbes, Thomas, 206–207, 217
Home and Colonial School Society, 409, 497
Home economics, 526
Hopkins Grammar School, 445
Humanism, 114–161
  classical, 114–136
  northern phase, 139–161
Humanists, 116–135
Humphrey, Duke, 134
Huntington, Emily, 511
Huss, John, 148–149, 435
Huxley, Julian, 312

I

Indiana University, 482
Individualism, 22, 508, 510, 513
  Abelard's method, 104
  in the Renaissance, 118
Industrial arts education, 512, 525
Infant schools, 285, 325, 327, 328, 408, 413, 420
Institute of International Education, 306, 310
Integration and states' rights, 556–559

International Bureau of Education, 310, 312
International Committee on Intellectual Cooperation, 311–312
International Conference on Public Education, 420
International education, 305
comparative education and, 308
International Educational Exchange Program, 311
International Institute of Teachers Colleges, 306
International Kindergarten Union, 287, 306
International People's College, 310
Internationalism and education, 304–315
Irnerius, 103, 104
Isidore of Seville, *Etymologies*, 71, 98
Isocrates, 28, 29–31
Against the Sophists, 30–31
Italy, 29, 43
bookkeeping development, 91
court schools, 122, 131, 134
medieval cities, 90–92
renaissance in, 112–134
translations, 98–99; *see also* Translations

J

Jackman, Wilbur, *Nature Study for the Common Schools*, 500
Jahn, Friedrich, 269, 351, 353–354
James, Eric, 422
James, William, 219, 552
Jansenists, 160
Jefferson, Thomas, 442
Jerome, Saint, 67, 98, 121
Jesuit Society, 139, 155–158, 166
schools, 156–158
success of, 156–157
Johns Hopkins University, 377, 573
Johnson, Marietta, 513–514
Jones, Margaret, 497
Judaism, 62

Julian the Apostate, 69
Jullien, Marc-Antoine, 306
Junior college, 531–532
Junior High school, 350–351
Justin Martyr, 66
Justinian, 69
Juvenile delinquency, 303, 548

K

Kalamazoo case, 520
Kandel, Isaac, *Comparative Education*, 308, 417
Kant, Immanuel, 235–237, 276, 574
Katharsis, doctrine of, 36
Kay-Shuttleworth, James, 409, 411, 412
Kellogg Foundation, 556
Kerschensteiner, Georg, 94, 341, 358
Khrushchev, Nikita, 387, 393–394, 577–578
Kindergarten, the, 374
American, 375, 501–504
creation of, 285–286
spread of, 287–289
in the USSR, 385, 390
Koran, 62, 98
Krüsi, Hermann, junior, 409
Krüsi, Hermann, senior, 256, 263

L

La Chalotais, 335
Essay on National Education, 268, 320, 331, 598
Ladder system of education, 485–487
Lancaster, Joseph, 270, 405–408
Lancasterian schools, 408, 452–453, 486
Land-grant colleges, development, 473–478
Langevin, Paul, 338–340

Language and religion, 146–148
Language studies, 181–183, 359, 361
　English, 181, 182–183, 360, 390
　French, 160, 181, 326, 360, 390, 443, 446
　German, 183, 359, 375, 390, 443, 446
　Greek, 121–122, 132, 153, 154, 157, 181, 182, 277–278, 336, 518
　Hebrew, 149, 153, 157, 182
　Latin, *see* Latin language, study of
　modern languages, 140
　Rousseau's theories, 215–218
　Russian, 388, 390
　Spanish, 446
　vernacular, *see* Vernacular speech
La Salle, Jean Baptiste, 160
Lassale, Ferdinand, 357
Latin grammar schools, American, 441–443, 445
Latin language, study of, 74, 84, 94–95, 115–116, 128, 143, 153, 154, 157, 181, 182, 183, 277–278, 336, 360, 518
　Comenius
　　Atrium, 184
　　Janua Linguarum Reserata, 184, 185
　　Palatium, 184
　　Vestibulum, 184, 185
Latin schools, 96
　established by guilds, 93
League of Nations, 304, 309, 311
Lecturing, 104
Leeuwenhoek, Anton, 174
Leibnitz, Gottfried, 175
Leipzig University, 149, 152
Lenin, Vladimir, 385, 386
Leonardo da Vinci, 117
Liber Abaci (Fibonacci), 98
Liberal arts
　Greco-Roman influence, 48–49
　quadrivium, 70
　seven, 70, 74
　trivium, 70
Liberal education, 126–128
Libraries
　classical, organization of, 123–124
　established by UNESCO, 315
　public, start of idea of, 125
Library of Congress, 478
Lietz, Hermann, 365
Life-adjustment education, 559–560
Literacy, growth of, 342, 397
Literature, study of, 115, 127, 132, 157
Livius Andronicus, 44
Locke, John, 89, 165, 173, 175, 176–181, 192, 204, 209, 210, 213, 224, 225, 279, 423, 434
　Essay Concerning Human Understanding, 176–177
　Some Thoughts Concerning Education, 177, 178–181, 210, 224, 228, 424
　theories of, 177–181
Logarithms, 174, 175, 446
Logic, New, 99
Logic, study of, 29, 32, 70, 74, 99, 127, 157, 160, 181, 447, 518
Lollardry, 148, 402
London Infant School Society, 408
Loyola, Saint Ignatius, 155–157
Ludus, 47
Lunacharsky, Anatoli, *The Waif*, 304
Luther, Martin, 140, 149, 150–153
　educational theories, 152–153
　Ninety-five Theses, 150
　translation of New Testament, 151
Lutheran movement, 150–154
Lysias, 28–31

M

Machiavelli, Niccolò, 118, 119
　Prince, The, 118, 119
Maclure, William, 271
Madison, James, 442
Madras system, 405–407
Magna Carta, 91
Mainz leaflet, 96
Mandeville, Bernard, 404
Mann, Horace, 272, 303, 349, 354, 374, 458–461, 494

Common School Journal, 460, 497
common schools, development of, and, 460–461
Manniche, Peter, 310
Mansbridge, Albert, 424
Mantua, court school of, 131–132
Manual training, 512, 523–525
Manuscript copies of recovered authors, 123
Manuscript writers (scrittori), 123
Marcus Aurelius, 64
Marenholtz-Bülow, Bertha von, 287
Marx, Karl, 357, 384, 386
Massachusetts Institute of Technology, 524
Mathematics, *see also* Arithmetic
  inventions, 174, 175, 391
  study of, 98, 99, 132, 157, 359, 361, 388, 391, 447
Maxwell, William, 463
Mayo, Charles, 409
Mayo, Elizabeth, *Lessons on Objects*, 409
Mechanics, 175
Medici, Cosimo de', 91, 124–125
Medici, Lorenzo de', 122
Melanchthon, Philip, 153
Memoriter instruction, 14, 23
Mercers School, 93
Merchant Taylor's School, 93, 182, 587
Mesopotamia, *see* Sumer
Metric system of weights and measures, 323
Milton, John, 216
  Of Education, 170
Mohammed, 62
Monastic schools, 73–75, 76, 82
  closing of, 152, 155
  dictamen, 74
Monasticism, 72–73, 82–83
Monitorial schools, 405–408, 410, 452–453, 455
Montaigne, Michel, 89
Montessori, Maria, 420, 509
Montessori Society in England, 420
Montpellier University, 106, 602
Moravians, 435

More, Sir Thomas, 147, 402
  Utopia, 168
Morrill Act, 473, 475–476
Morton, Charles, 171
Moslems, 62
Motion pictures in education, 564
Mulcaster, Richard, 93, 165, 167, 182, 403, 587
Murray, Gilbert, 312
Music in education, 20, 24, 32, 70, 74, 127, 132, 133
  American schools, 522–523

N

Napier, John, 175
Napoleon I, 323
  system of schools instituted by, 323–324
Napoleon III, education under, 328–329
National Association for the Advancement of Colored People, 558
National Association of Secondary School Principals, 311, 535–536
National Citizens Commission for the Public Schools, 554–556
National Defense Education Act, 550–551, 578
National education
  Condorcet plan, 320–322
  in England, 299, 409–426
  in France, 299, 319–345, 382
  in Germany, 299, 348–378, 382
  La Chalotais on, 320, 598
  systems of, 298–300
  in the United States, 469–488
    evolution of, 430–465
  in the USSR, 299, 384–398
National Education Association, 528
National Home Study Council, 563
National Honor Society, 536
National Science Foundation, 560
Nationalism
  in France, 299, 319–345

Nationalism (*continued*)
  higher education under, 569–605
  rise of, 297–298
  school systems and, 298–300
  Soviet education and, 382–398
  war, education, and, 300–304
Nature study movement, 498–501, 513
Neef, Joseph, 264, 271, 493
Netherlands, humanism in, 135, 139
Neuhof, Pestalozzi at, 246–250, 268–269
New England Association of Colleges and Preparatory Schools, 529
New Haven Gymnasium, 375
New Testament, 64, 65–66, 76
  translations, 141, 144, 146, 151, 154
New York City
  Board of Education, 452
  Lancasterian system introduced into, 408, 452–453, 486
New York State, educational system of, 324, 451, 454
Newton, Isaac, 146, 174, 175
Niccoli, Niccolò de', 122, 124–125
Nicholas V, Pope, 124, 125
Nicolovius, Georg, 263, 269, 352
Normal schools, *see* Teachers, training of
Notebooks, introduction of, 143
Notre Dame cathedral school, 104

O

Oberlin, Jean, 285, 325
Object-teaching, 272, 409, 424, 494, 496–498, 501, 505
Office of Education, 311
  functions of, 478
Old Testament, 37, 62
Oratore, De (Cicero), 49, 50, 55, 121, 133
Oratory, 28, 30–31, 49–54, 133
Oratory, Dialogue on (Tacitus), 30, 54
Oratory of Divine Love, 158
Oratory of France, 158
Oratory, Institutes of (Quintilian), 51–54, 129
Oratory schools, 158–159
Origen, 69
Oswego Method, 272, 409, 497–498, 504
Owen, Robert, 270, 271, 408, 576
Oxford University, 106, 107, 310, 424, 584, 586–588

P

Pagan schools, 68–69
Paganism, 66–67, 118, 146
Page, David, 494
Papyrus, 6
Parker, Francis, 498, 504–506, 508
Pastorious, Francis, 435
Paulsen, Friedrich, 365
Pavlov, Ivan Petrovich, 571–572
Peabody, Elizabeth, 502
Pedagogues, 23, 52
Peers, Allson, *see* Truscot, Bruce
People's Republic of China, 382
Periclean Age, 27–29, 38
Perkiomen School, 435
Pestalozzi, Johann, 175, 189, 223, 240–264, 268, 272, 274–279, 281–283, 306, 352, 409, 424
  Course, Nature, and Development of the Human Race, 255
  How Gertrude Teaches Her Children, 256–260
  influence of, 263–264, 268–290
  Leonard and Gertrude, 241, 251–252
  methods, 256–260
  at Neuhof, 246–250, 268–269
  at Stanz, 255–256, 268
Pestalozzi Children's Village, 272–273
Pestalozzian movement, 375
  in England, 269–270, 409
  in Germany, 263–264, 269, 351
  in Switzerland, 245–263

in the United States, 264, 270–272, 461–463, 493–495
Petrarch, Francesco, 113, 117, 118, 119–121, 123, 130
  De Vita Solitaria, 120
Petty, William, 169–170
Philadelphia Academy, 448
Philanthropinum, 223, 227–233
  criticism of, 229–230
Philo, 66
Philosophy
  church and, 65–68
  study of, 115, 127, 157
Phoenician alphabet, 17
Physical education, 19–20, 24–25, 128
Physical Science Committee, 562
Physics, 146, 215, 388, 391
Pietism, 171–172, 190
Pilger, Karl, 231–232
Place, Francis, 404
Plamann, John, 269
Planta, Martin, 224, 234
Plato, 18, 20, 26–36, 70, 120, 121, 129, 144–145, 146
  Academy of, 29, 30
  dialogues of, 32
  Republic, 32–34, 70, 207, 217
  theory of education, 32–34
Plato of Tivoli, 98
Platter, Thomas, 149
Plethon, Georgius, 122
Plutarch, *Training of Children*, 30
Poetry, study of, 127, 132
Poggio Bracciolini, 119, 121, 122
Politics (Aristotle), 5, 21, 34–36, 99, 121
Polytechnical education, 386, 576–578
Population changes and American schools, 546–548
Port Royalists, 160
Potsdam Agreement, 370
Priestley, Joseph, 171
Princeton University, 424, 444, 445
Printing, 125, 134, 135, 141–142
Printing press, aid to scholarship, 134, 141–142

Priscian's grammar, 70
Progressive education, 510–517
  American Education Fellowship, 515
  Country Day Schools, 514
  Ethical Culture School, 511, 513
  Progressive Education Association, 514–515, 537, 553
  School of Organic Education, 513–514
  Speyer School, 511, 513
  under attack, 515, 551–554
  University Elementary School, 511–513
  university high schools, 537
Progressive Education Association, 514, 537, 553
  Thirty Schools Experiment, 537–538
Propaganda in the Soviet schools, 574–575
Prosser, Charles, 559
Protagoras, 27
Prussia, *see* Germany
Prussian-Pestalozzian system, 264, 352–353
Psychology, study of, 142, 143, 388
Ptolemaic system, 99
Ptolemy, Claudius, 37
  Almagest, 99
Public School Society, 452
Public schools, post-World War II campaign directed against, 554–555

Q

Quadrivium, 70
Quincy methods of teaching, 504–506
Quintilian, Marcus, 30, 47–48, 115, 121, 216
  Institutes of Oratory, 48, 51–54, 129
Quisling government, 301

R

Radios in education, 564
Ramus, Peter, 108, 144–146, 182
Raphael, 117
Ratio Studiorum, 156–157
Ratke, Wolfgang, 183
   influence of, 189–190
Raymond, Archbishop, 97
Readiness principle, 208–209, 215
Realism, 144, 165–193; *see also* Comenius, John; Fénelon, François; Locke, John; Vives, Juan
   curriculum of, 166–167
   meaning of, 166–167
   Utopias of, 168–170
Red Brick University (Truscot), 595–596
Reddie, Cecil, 365, 417, 423
Reformation, 139–161; *see also* Erasmus; Huss, John; Jesuit Society; Martin Luther; Ramus, Peter; Vives, Juan; Wycliffe, John
Regents, New York Board of, 451, 454
Religion and language, 146
Renaissance, 112–136
Rensselaer Polytechnic Institute, 324
Reuchlin, John, 149
Rhetoric, 70, 123, 132, 154, 157, 181, 518
   in antiquity, 28–31, 48–49, 51–54
   deteriorization of, 74
   in early middle ages, 67
Rhodes Scholarships, 310, 592
Ribot Commission, 336
Rienzi, Cola di, 116
Ritter, Karl von, 261–262
Robbins Committee on Higher Education in England
   report of, 596–598
Robert of Chester, 98
Rochow, Eberhard von, 349
Rockefeller Brothers Fund report, 560–561
Rockefeller Foundation, 311
Roman Catholic Church, 64
   school curriculum, 64

Romans, The, 41–55
   early instruction, 45–47
   Greco-Roman education, 47–49
   Greek influence on, 42–44, 47–49
   ludus, 47
   oratory, 49–54
   Twelve Tables of laws, 44–45, 50, 55, 103
Round Hill School, 375
Rousseau, Jean, 175, 186–187, 199–220, 225, 236, 262, 284, 335
   Discourse of 1750, 206, 217
   Discourse of 1754, 206–207
   Emile, 202 ff.
   New Héloise, 207–208
   theories
      intellectual education, 212–215
      language arts, 215–218
      morals and religion, 218–220
      nature and education, 208–210
      newborn child, 210
      readiness principle, 208–209, 215
      social, 205–207
      three kinds of learning, 210–212
Roxbury Latin School, 442
Royal Society of London, 172
Russia, *see* USSR
Rutgers University, 444, 445

S

Sadoleto, Jacopo, 118
St. John's College, Maryland, 443
St. Paul's School, 403, 587
Salzmann, Christian, 230–231, 232–233
   Philanthropinum, 232–233
Sassuolo, 131
Saxe-Gotha School Method, 190
Scandinavian countries, English influence in, 423
Schneider, Friedrich, 305
Scholarships, international, 310
School buildings, and equipment, 134, 547

Schools
  academies, *see* Academies
  Athenian, 22–37
  business, 95
  catechetical, 69
  catechumenal, 69
  cathedral, 65, 76, 90
    Notre Dame, 105
  charity, 404–405
  church, 436
  city, German, 94–96
  classical, 139, 149
  cloistral, 73
  collèges and lycées, 134
  correspondence, 563
  Country Day Schools, 514
  court
    at Ferrara, 122
    at Mantua, 131–132
  "cypher," 383
  dispute in Hamburg, 94–95
  French, 323–344
  German, 358–365, 368, 422
  graduate, 377
  Greco-Roman, 47–48, 49
  guild, 93–94
  gymnasiums, 134, 190, 349, 351, 360, 363
    at Strassburg, 153
  Hebrew, 14
  infant, 285–325, 327, 408, 413, 420
  Jesuit, 156–158
  Junior high schools, 530–531
  kindergartens, 285–289, 374, 375, 385, 390, 501–504
  Lancasterian, 408, 452–453, 486
  Latin, 96
  Ludus, 47
  Latin grammar, American, 441–443, 445
  monastic, 73–75, 76, 82
    closing of, 152, 155
  monitorial, 405–408, 410, 452–453, 455
  normal, *see* Teachers, training of
  Oratory, 158–159
  pagan, 68–69
  parochial, 436
  Philanthropinum, 223–224, 227–234
  Port Royal, 160
  progressive, 510–517; *see also* Progressive schools
  reading and writing, *see* Vernacular schools
  Realschule, 171–172, 224
  Reformation and, 152–155
  Spartan, 20
  State and, 153–154, 155; *see also* National education
  Sumerian, 7–10
  temple, 8
  ten-year school (USSR), 387–392
  trade, 340–341, 358
  in the USSR, 393–398; *see also* USSR
  vernacular, 95–97, 149, 151, 152–153, 182
  vocational, 358, 371, 373
  writing and reckoning; *see* Vernacular schools
Schurz, Mrs. Carl, 303, 502
Schwenkfeld, Kaspar von, 435
Science
  elementary, 496, 498
  influence on education, 175
  modern, development of, 172–175
  natural, study of, 142
  study of, 214–215, 359, 361
Science education
  improved methods of, 560–561
Scientific societies, 172
Scotland, universities, 588–589
Search, Preston, 509
Secularism, 95, 114, 332, 362
Seneca, Lucius Annaeus, 120
  Morals, 118
Septuagint, 66
Sheldon, Edward, 272, 497
Sheperd's Book, 85–86
Shorthand, 181
Shrewsbury School, 402
Smith-Hughes Act, 476, 526
Smith-Mundt Act, 311
Smithsonian Institution, 478
Society for the Promotion of Christian Knowledge, 404, 407, 410

Society for the Propagation of the Gospel in Foreign Parts, 404–405, 424
Socrates, 26–27, 29–32, 36, 144–145
Socratic Irony, 31
Socratic method, 32
Sophists, 27–29, 144
  arguments against, 30–31
South Africa, English influence in, 423
Soviet bloc countries, 424
Spain, translations, 97–98
Sparta, 19–21, 35, 37; *see also* Greece
  discipline, 20, 127–128
  education, 20
  paidonomos, 20
  physical education, 20
Speech, vernacular, *see* Vernacular speech
Speyer School, 511, 513
Stalin, Joseph, 384, 386
Stanz
  Pestalozzi at, 255–256, 268
State, The
  schools and, 153–154, 155, 299–300; *see also* National education
    Basedow's ideas, 226
    Rousseau's proposal, 207
State universities, 473, 474
Stationers School, 93
Stewart, Cora, "Moonlight schools" of, 473
Stoicism, 118, 146
Stow, David, 409
Stowe, Calvin, 349, 374
Straight, Henry, 499–501
Student disorders and strikes, 603
Student exchanges, international, 310
Student self-government, 234
Study, supervised, 508–509
Sturm, John, 135, 139, 153, 360
Sumer, 6–12, 71
  discipline, 10
  Epic of Gilgamesh, 11
  legal code, 11
  libraries, 12
  schools, 7–10
  tablets, 9–12
Süvern, J., 352–353, 354, 362

Sweden, English influence in, 423
Switzerland, 224
  Pestalozzian movement in, 245–263
  Reformation in, 154
Sydenham, Thomas, 174
Symms-Eaton Academy, 442

T

Tacitus, *Dialogue on Oratory*, 30, 54
Tape recorders in education, 564
Tatian, 66–67
Teacher exchanges, international, 310
Teachers
  in England, 424
  in France, 331, 334, 340
    requirements, 326, 339, 340
  in Germany, requirements, 359
  in the United States, 446–447, 453, 458, 493, 494–496, 518
  shortage of, 547
Teachers College, Columbia University, 482, 511
Teachers' guild, 96
Teachers, training of,
  in England, 408–409, 420
  in France, 323, 325, 328, 329, 331, 334, 479
  in Germany, 363, 373, 375
  in the United States, 375, 447, 453, 460, 472–473, 478–483, 493, 494–501, 502–503, 560–561
  in the USSR, 392–393
Technical high schools, 525
Television in education, 565
Ten Commandments, 13
Tertullian, 66–69
Textbooks, 167, 184–185, 190
Theology, study of, 157
Thirty Schools Experiment, 537–538
Thomas Aquinas, Saint, 100, 116
Ticknor, George, 377, 479
Trade schools, 358
Translations, 44, 121, 122, 129, 130
  age of, 97–99
  double, 143

New Testament, *see* Bible, the; New Testament
Trivium, 70
Truscot, Bruce, *Red Brick University*, 595-596
Tübingen University, 149
Turnkunst, 374-375
Twelve Abuses of the Age, 84-85
Twelve Tables of Roman laws, 44-45, 50, 55, 103
Tyndale, William, 147

U

UNESCO, 305, 311-315
  aid to the establishment of free and compulsory public school systems, 315
  fundamental education experiments of, 314-315
  library program of, 315
  membership in, 312
  tasks of, 312
  Universal Declaration of Human Rights, 313-314
United States
  academies, 424, 425, 445-448
  agricultural colleges, 473, 476, 478
  apprenticeship in colonies, 433, 437-439
  Civil War and its aftermath, 470-473
    American Freedmen's Union, 470-471
    American Missionary Association, 470
    Blair Bill, 472
    Hoar Bill, 471-472
    illiteracy, 473
    Morrill Act, 473, 475-476
    Negro education, 470-472
    Peabody Fund, 472
  Colonial period, 431-448
    academies, 445-448
    book-burning, 434
    censorship, 434
    education, 432, 436
    educational institutions, invented, 445 448
    educational institutions, transplanted, 437-445
    Latin grammar schools, 441-445
    leavening influence of Puritanism, 433-434
    old field school, 440
    schools for reading and religious instruction, 439-441
    universities, 444-445
  common schools, 460-461
  compulsory school attendance laws, 483-485
  curriculum in, 440, 441, 446, 493, 508, 537
  district school system, 456-458
    criticism of, 457-459
    discipline in, 457-458
  education
    audio-visual aids to, 564-566
    English influence on, 424-425
    experimental plans, 507-510
    Federal aid for, 549-551
    German influence on, 374-378
    Turnkunst, 374-375
    integration and states rights, 556-559
    ladder system of, 485-487
    national government interest in, 473-478
    problems caused by population increase, 546-548
  engineering graduates, number of, compared with USSR, 396-397
  Federal Office of Education, 478
    Biennial Survey of Education, 478
  George-Deen Vocational Act, 476
  high schools, 463, 517-540; *see also* High schools
  junior high schools, 530-531
  Lancasterian schools, 408, 452-453
  land-grant colleges, 473-478
    for Negroes, 476
  Latin grammar schools, 441-443, 445
  monitorial schools, 424, 452-453, 455

628 INDEX

United States (*continued*)
  national school system of, 299–300
  nature study movement, 498–501
  Ordinance of 1787, 451
  Pestalozzian movement in, 264, 270–272, 493–495
  population changes and the schools, 546–548
  Public School Society, 452
  public school systems, development of, 469–470
  Smith-Hughes Act, 476, 526
  state aid to schools, 456–457
  state systems of education, rise of, 453–463
  state universities, 473
  teachers, *see* Teachers; Teachers, training of
  universities, *see* Universities: American
  vocational education, 473, 476–477, 526, 559
    George Deen Act, 476
United States Air Force Academy, 478
United States Military Academy, 324, 478
United States Naval Academy, 478
Universities, 148
  American
    English influence on, 424
    entrance requirements, 529–530
    foreign students in, 311
    German influence on, 375–378
    junior colleges, 531–532
    loans to college students, 550
    in New England Colonies, 444–445
  decline of, 152
  early, 106
  English, 106, 107, 424, 584–586, 589–595
    modern, 589–595
  French, 323, 600–603
  German, 149, 351, 354, 359, 362, 582–583
    American students in, 376
  destruction of, World War II, 369
  graduate schools, 377
  Italian, 123
  rise of, 103–109
  Scottish, 588–589
  state, 473
  student disorders and strikes, 603
    in the USSR, 396–397, 571–576
    foreign students in, 582
  women's colleges in U.S. and England, 594–595
University of Berlin, 232, 275, 351, 375–376
University of Bologna, 106, 107
University of Chicago, 482, 500
  Division of University Extension, 563
  laboratory school of, 284–285, 511
  University Elementary School, 511–512, 538
University of France, *see* France: University of
University high schools, 537
University of London, 590–592
University of Michigan, 474, 481
University of Moscow, 571–572
University of Paris, 105, 106, 144, 145, 323
University of Pennsylvania, 444, 445, 474
University of the State of New York, 324, 454
University of Virginia, 474
Urban, Pope, 86, 150
Ursulines, Order of, 160
USSR
  curriculum, 573–574
  denial of access to foreign papers, magazines, books, and broadcasts, 575
  education
    politics in, 578–580
    since 1956, 393–398
  educational system, United States interest in, 395

engineering graduates, number of, compared with the United States, 396–397
formative ideas of education, 384–387
Friendship University, 581
intellectual tradition, 384–385
international education and, 581–582
Khrushchev reforms, 387, 393–394
literacy growth, 397
medical institutes, 572
national education in, 299, 384–398
polytechnical education, 386, 576–578
primary and secondary schools, 395
propaganda in the schools, 574–575
Russian Academy of Pedagogical Science, 572, 577
single-track schools, 387–390
Soviet bloc countries, 424
teachers, training of, 392–393
technicums, 390, 395
technological success, 395
ten-year school, 387–392
  effectiveness of, 391
  Khrushchev criticism of, 393–394
  schedule of, 388, 391–392
universities, 396–397, 571–576
  foreign students in, 582

V

Valla, Lorenzo, 119
Vegio, Maffeo, 129
Vergerius, 126–128
  On Character and Liberal Studies, 126–128
Vernacular schools, 149, 151, 152–153, 182
  growth of, 95–97
Vernacular speech, 95, 116, 134, 142, 143, 157, 160, 167, 402
Veronese, Vittorino, 312

Vespasiano da Bisticci, 123–125
  Memoirs, 123, 124
Vinet, Élie, 139
Virgil, 120, 133
Vittorino da Feltre, 119, 122, 126, 128, 130–132, 133
Vivarium, monastery, 71
Vives, Juan Luis, 139, 142–144, 167–168, 175
  De Disciplinis, 142
  Dialogos, 142
Vocational education, 92–94, 338, 358, 371
  United States, 473, 476–477, 526, 559
  George Deen Act, 476
Vocational guidance, 340, 373
Vocational schools, German, 358, 371, 373
Voinov, Nicholas, *see* Lunacharsky, Anatoli
Vulgate Bible, 67, 69, 118, 141

W

Waifs, 304, 385–386
War, effects on children and education, 301–304
Washington, Booker T., 558
Washington, George, 431, 448–449
Webster, Daniel, 460
Wessel, John, 140
Westfield State Normal School, 496
White House Conference on Education, 547, 555
Willard, Emma, 479
William of Champeaux, 104
William and Mary College, 424, 442, 444, 445, 474
William Penn Charter School, 442, 443, 448
Williams, Roger, 434
Winchester School, 402, 587
Wittenberg University, 149, 150, 152

Women's colleges in United States and England, 594–595
Women's Kindergarten Union, 288
Woodward, Calvin, 507, 523–524
Woodhouse, John, 170–171
World Federation of Educational Associations, 306, 310
World War II and education, 301, 304
Writing
 cuneiform, 7, 10, 12, 17
 demotic, 6
 hieroglyphic, 6
 invention of, 6–8
Wycliffe, John, 141, 146, 149, 402, 403
 translation of New Testament, 148
Wyneken, Gustav, 365

Y

Yale University, 376, 377, 424, 444, 445, 474
Young, Robert F., 414
Yverdon, 261–262, 270

Z

Zay, Jean, 338
Zeller, Karl, 352
Zeno, 29
Zook, Georg, 304
Zwingli, Ulrich, 154